TAXATION IN DEVELOPING COUNTRIES

THE JOHNS HOPKINS STUDIES IN DEVELOPMENT

Vernon W. Ruttan and T. Paul Schultz, Consulting Editors

TAXATION IN
DEVELOPING COUNTRIES

Fourth Edition

Edited by

RICHARD M. BIRD

and

OLIVER OLDMAN

The Johns Hopkins University Press
Baltimore and London

© 1964, 1967, 1975, 1990 The Johns Hopkins University Press

The Johns Hopkins University Press, 701 West 40th Street, Baltimore, Maryland 21211
The Johns Hopkins Press Ltd., London

The paper used in this publication meets the minimum requirements of American National Standard for Information Sciences—Permanence of Paper for Printed Library Materials, ANSI Z39.48-1984.

Library of Congress Cataloging-in-Publication Data

Taxation in developing countries / edited by Richard M. Bird and Oliver Oldman. — 4th ed.
  p. cm. — (The Johns Hopkins studies in development)
Rev. ed. of: Readings on taxation in developing countries. 3rd ed. 1975.
  Includes bibliographical references (p.).
  ISBN 0-8018-3943-2. — ISBN 0-8018-3944-0 (pbk.)
  1. Taxation—Developing countries. I. Bird, Richard Miller, 1938- . II. Oldman,
Oliver. III. Readings on taxation in developing countries. IV. Series.
HJ2351.7.T39 1990
336.2'009172'6—dc20
                                                      89-28367
                                                         CIP

Contents

Preface

Twenty-five years ago we edited a book entitled *Readings on Taxation in Developing Countries* (Johns Hopkins, 1964). Our aim in that volume was to bring together in a convenient format a selection of the scattered literature then available on the subject, much of which was hard for students, especially those in developing countries, to find. The fact that the readings book went through two subsequent editions (1967 and 1975) and also was translated into Spanish (Mexico City: UTEHA, 1968) suggests that it met a need at the time.

In recent decades, however, there has been an explosion of literature on this subject: several good introductory books have been issued, as well as a number of specialized monographs, many articles in scholarly journals, and, of course, a continuing flood of documents from such international agencies as the World Bank and the International Monetary Fund. A particularly notable feature has been the growing number of publications by scholars and practitioners from the developing world. Moreover, as in all fields of economics, the content of this literature has on the one hand become more theoretical and mathematical in nature and on the other more empirical and statistical than was the case at the time of the first edition of the readings book. What is needed now is thus not so much to bring together available sparse and scattered materials on taxation in developing countries as to provide both a sampler of the conflicting and diverse literature now available and an integrated guide to the subject that can both stand alone as an introduction and also serve as a supplement to the inevitably cursory treatments of development taxation in most textbooks.

What we have attempted to do in this book, drawing upon both the literature and our combined experience of well over half a century of work on these problems, is to identify a number of critical and recurring themes in development taxation and to assemble a set of readings and commentaries on these themes that will be instructive to students and, we hope, practitioners as well. Students interested in seeing the application of some of the latest trends in public finance analysis to real world problems will find, for example, selections on optimal taxation, on effective tax rates, and on direct expenditure taxes. Practitioners in developing countries will find items dealing with such common problems as taxing the "hard-to-tax" groups, coping with inflation, and computerization. Those interested in economic development policy generally will find material on a broad spectrum of issues ranging from the design of incentives to the alleviation of poverty, as well as a number of illuminating case studies on the design and implementation of policy reform.

To reflect as accurately as possible the current state of the taxation art, a wider variety of material has been included here than in the earlier readings books. Moreover, in order to make these diverse materials fit together and work as a whole, and to improve their comprehensibility to those not familiar with modern economics, we have edited some of the selections heavily and have included substantial integrative commentary. All the items included here (with one exception) were published after 1975: those interested in the earlier literature will find ample references in the earlier readings volumes.

As is always the case with an edited work, our principal debt is of course to the many authors on whom we have drawn, and to whom we are most grateful. Most fundamentally, however, we—and all who labor in these vineyards—owe a great deal to the pioneers from whom we have learned so much, notably Carl Shoup, Richard Musgrave, Richard Goode, and the late Stanley Surrey, as well as to the many other colleagues with whom we have had the pleasure of working in diverse parts of the world over the last twenty-five years. We hope they too will find this volume useful—even if, perchance, their own excellent work did not, in the end, fit into the scheme of this book.

Part One

Approaches to Development Taxation

The relation between taxation and economic growth has long been a matter of concern to policy makers and students of public policy alike. The classical economists devoted substantial efforts to analyzing the effects of taxation on growth and the related question of the distribution of factor incomes, as witnessed by the full title of Ricardo's famous treatise, *Principles of Political Economy and Taxation*. With the rise of Keynesian economics in the postwar era, the effects of taxation on the stability of the economy also became an important subject of analysis. These classical and Keynesian concerns constituted prominent themes in early analyses of taxation in developing countries (Heller, 1954; Kaldor, 1956, 1963, 1965; Higgins, 1959). Subsequently, the range of concerns widened to include the effects of taxation not just on the rate of growth of national income but also on the distribution of that income by income size class (De Wulf, 1975, surveys the many studies on this question), on employment (Bird, 1982, surveys this literature), and on other objectives of policy. Gillis et al. (1987), for example, list the objectives of fiscal policy as the promotion of economic growth, the reduction of income disparities between households and regions, the promotion of economic stability and economic efficiency, and the increasing of host-country returns from natural resource endowments.

As the range of policy concerns widened, the nature of the analysis applied to development taxation altered. Most early postwar studies of taxation in developing countries consisted of the more or less straightforward application of the accepted normative principles of taxation, as passed down from Marshall and Pigou to the textbook writers of the era and as masterfully summed up in Musgrave's (1959) classic treatise. Two decades later, when Atkinson and Stiglitz (1980) produced what soon became the standard advanced text in public finance, both the content and the appearance of normative taxation theory had altered drastically, bringing it more into line with the increased level of mathematical sophistication and theoretical rigor of economics in general (see also Auerbach and Feldstein, 1985, 1987). This new approach has just begun to be applied to taxation in developing countries (as demonstrated in Newbery and Stern, 1987).

There has also been a quantum leap in the volume and sophistication of empirical studies of the effects of taxation. Empirical public finance studies in developing countries once again mirror this trend—although the data are even more recalcitrant than in the developed countries and few, if any, of the basic questions in this field have yet been satisfactorily answered even in the latter (see, for example, Killingsworth, 1983; Bosworth, 1984).

Another important development in public finance in recent years has been the growth of a new approach to the economic analysis of government behavior, often called the "public choice" approach (Mueller, 1989). Although as yet there have been few studies along these lines in developing countries (but see Russell and Nicholson, 1981), there is little question that the skepticism about the purity of governmental motives so prominent in the public choice approach has largely replaced, in the minds of many analysts, the common early postwar view that governments always act in the best interests of their citizens.

The view that, in developing countries as elsewhere, that government is best that governs least may also, of course, be gleaned from the work of Adam Smith and the English classical economists; but the pervasive "policy pessimism" of recent years has undoubtedly been strengthened both by public choice analysis and, to some extent, by some prominent empirical studies in developed countries (e.g., Boskin, 1978; Summers, 1981) which suggested that labor supply, saving, and investment are much more sensitive to tax variables than had earlier been thought. One manifestation of this new attitude has been the much-discussed "supply-side" tax policy, which has figured prominently in the United States in recent years but which has also cast its shadow much more broadly across the world (see Gandhi et al., 1987). Indeed, in many ways the supply-side approach was foreshadowed years ago in development economics by the writings of Peter Bauer (Bauer, 1957; Bauer and Yamey, 1957). Perhaps even more important than either new numbers or old theories in engendering disillusionment with the prospect for sensible and helpful government policy in developing countries, however, has been the apparently disappointing outcome of thirty or more years of "activist" government intervention.

Whether one draws this pessimistic conclusion or not—and in our view the postwar record of development in many countries is by no means as bleak as has sometimes been asserted—the accumulated experience of the last few decades with tax reform in a wide variety of developing countries has undoubtedly played an important role in shaping the way development taxation is now approached. In particular, there is now much more recognition of the vital importance of tax administration in shaping the tax systems of developing countries, as well as of the incredible variety found in these countries and the difficulty of making meaningful policy generalizations in the absence of close and careful attention to local institutional detail. Both of these points had, of course, long been clear to the more astute writers on the subject (see, for example, Surrey, 1958, on tax administration in general; Shoup et al., 1959, for a carefully detailed country study paying close attention both to administration and to local circumstances). It seems, however, to have required the post-OPEC decade of continual fiscal crisis in most of the developing world for the message to be taken sufficiently seriously. The sort of generalized and idealized prescription of what a "perfect" tax system might look like that was once all too characteristic of much writing on tax reform in developing countries has increasingly been replaced by more pragmatic and eclectic attempts to develop better systems than those that now exist, in the face of substantial and continuing political and administrative obstacles to reform.

The best approach to reforming taxes in a developing country—indeed in any country—is one that takes into account taxation theory, empirical evidence, and political and administrative realities and blends them with a good dose of local knowledge and a sound appraisal of the current macroeconomic and international situation to produce a feasible set of proposals sufficiently attractive to be implemented and sufficiently robust to withstand changing times, within reason, and still produce beneficial results. This modest prescription is, alas, still often beyond our reach, owing to deficiencies on all sides, ranging from such theoretical and empirical conundrums as the incidence of the corporate income tax and the effects of income taxes on work effort to such political puzzles as the acceptability of the (usually implicitly) postulated social weights on incomes and the willingness of the powerful to tax themselves (perhaps in the interests of their long-term survival?). Nonetheless, as the literature brought together in this volume demonstrates, much progress has been made since the days when the main question seemed to be "Will the Underdeveloped Countries Learn to Tax?" (Kaldor, 1963), and it was presumed to be simply a matter of time and progress before every country ended up with a global progressive personal income tax as its main source of revenue (as one might perhaps deduce from Hinrichs, 1966; or R. A. Musgrave, 1969—although it should be emphasized that both of these pioneering quantitative studies of tax structure development are much more subtly and carefully written than this reference might imply).

The five chapters in this introductory part illustrate the wide variety of approaches that may legitimately be taken to development taxation. In their different ways and to different degrees, these chapters display the common elements to be found in most of the best of the modern literature: respect for both the theoretical and empirical foundations of the analysis and close attention to the political and administrative aspects of taxation. They also show that in taxation, as in other areas of policy, there remains a great deal of room for divergent analysis and very different policy conclusions. Where one stands with respect to, say, the desirability of a comprehensive income tax inevitably reflects to some extent where one sits with respect to such fundamental questions as the appropriate role of the state and the appropriate trade-off between growth and equity. Philosophers have debated such issues for millenia and wars have been and are still being fought over them, so they are not likely to be resolved in our time, if ever. No definitive conclusion to such big policy debates, or their reflection in the tax arena, can realistically be expected, whether in the developing countries or elsewhere: indeed, it is precisely the never-ending, always changing, but always the same, nature of the tax debate that makes it such a fascinating subject to study.

In another twenty-five years, some of the contents of this book may perhaps look as curiously old-fashioned as do a few of the items included in our first *Readings* volume (1964); others will perhaps turn out to be the harbingers of the future. At the moment, we are no surer than anyone else which is which, but we *can* say with confidence that close study of the material included in this book (perhaps supplemented by such excellent recent treatises as Goode, 1984; Lewis, 1984; Prest, 1985) will provide the reader both with some useful tools and approaches for attacking current problems and with a basic understanding of the major forces and ideas that are shaping the future course of taxation in the developing countries.

1

A Quantitative Overview

As Vito Tanzi notes toward the end of the following chapter, quoting Disraeli, "There are three kinds of lies: lies, damned lies, and statistics"! In no area of economics is the cautionary note sounded by this adage more applicable than with respect to the developing countries, where the deficiencies of statistical coverage are well-known and frequently lamented. Nonetheless, a distinguishing characteristic of economics is its emphasis on the relative magnitudes of the various concepts with which it is concerned, and judicious quantification is an indispensable ingredient of any policy analysis. It is therefore appropriate to begin with a quantitative overview of taxation in developing countries in order to set the stage for the subsequent substantive discussion of the role and nature of taxation and the direction of desirable and feasible tax reform. The recent survey by Tanzi, excerpts from which are included here, fulfills this requirement admirably.

Two distinct quantitative dimensions of tax systems may be distinguished: the *level* of taxation and the *structure* of taxation. Tanzi emphasizes two aspects of the level of taxation in developing countries. The first is the very wide variation from country to country; the second is the general relationship between the level of per capita income—an index of "development"—and the level of taxation. The variation that may be observed in Tanzi's summary tables is of course much greater if one considers the data for individual countries, as indicated in figure 1.1. Every country is different in some critical respects and must be considered individually if anything very useful is to be said about it.

Nonetheless, the relationship between tax levels and economic development is worthy of more comment. As Tanzi stresses, and as an extensive literature (see especially Chelliah, 1971; Bahl, 1971, 1972; Chelliah, Baas, and Kelly, 1975; and Tait, Grätz, and Eichengreen, 1979) has demonstrated, there are of course many factors other than per capita income levels that may be important in explaining the level of taxation in any country: urbanization, monetization, the relative importance of the mining and agricultural sectors, and the importance of foreign trade are only some of the factors that have been emphasized in the past by different authors. In part owing to such factors (see fig. 1.1), much variation may be observed in tax ratios in countries with the same level of per capita income.

Considerable efforts have been devoted to explaining this variation in statistical terms, as a rule entirely in terms of economic structure, with no allowance for more explicitly political factors. The less than complete success achieved by such efforts in part reflects methodological, data, and conceptual problems (see Bird, 1976; Bolnick, 1978; Tabellini, 1985, for criticisms) and in part reflects the important missing "political" variable. An example may help make the point: in the first five years of the Sandinista government in Nicaragua, the tax ratio (taxes as a proportion of gross domestic product [GDP]) rose from 18 to 32 percent (Bird, 1985a). Only political factors can explain this rapid increase, particularly in the face of the adverse changes in Nicaragua's economic structure over this period. On the other hand, a country at a given income level (or with a given economic structure) that has a tax ratio less than the average for similar countries is not necessarily slacking or making an inadequate tax "effort," as was suggested by some of the earlier tax ratio studies. Our knowledge in this field is far too imperfect to allow us to draw conclusions about the "attainable" (let alone desirable) tax ratio in any one country from calculations based on the experience of other countries. Fortunately, as indeed Tanzi's paper indicates, such assessments of tax effort based on cross-sectional regression analyses seem, at last, to have gone out of favor.

A final important point about the level of taxation in many developing countries, not emphasized by Tanzi, is the extent to which the tax ratio (the ratio of total taxation to GDP) has increased in the postwar period (World Bank, *World Development Report*, 1988). Twenty years ago, Sir Arthur Lewis (1966) noted that most developing countries collected less than 10 percent of national income in taxes. He argued that this ratio would have to be raised to at least 17 percent in order to satisfy the minimal requirements of a modern state. Whatever the merits of this calculation (for a skeptical view, see Bird, 1970), on the average, the developing countries long ago exceeded Lewis's standard. There are now few countries at any income level in which the share of national income channeled through government is much below 20 percent (see International Monetary Fund [annual] for current figures). The developing countries have indeed (to paraphrase the Kaldor paper cited earlier) "learned to tax," at least in the sense of securing considerably more revenue than once seemed likely to be feasible. Whether this revenue has been used as efficiently as possible in all cases, however, remains open to question.

Most of Tanzi's paper is devoted not to the level of taxation but rather to the less explored question of tax structure. The apparent substitutability of export taxes and corporate taxes, the similar relation between import taxes and domestic sales taxes, the continuing importance of import and excise taxes, the relatively small importance of personal income taxes—these and other relationships are interestingly, and for the most part convincingly, discussed by Tanzi and need not be repeated here. His conclusion on the "missing links" between the statistical description on which he focuses, the statutory tax law, and the effective tax system deserves special attention, however. Evasion, the widespread use of proxy tax bases, and inflationary distortions are indeed critical elements in understanding how tax systems work in many developing countries: each of these factors is therefore considered more extensively later in this book.

However, even a careful analyst like Tanzi, whose cautious use of necessarily shaky data is generally a model, may slip when moving from description to prescription. A small but telling example occurs toward the end of the following excerpt when, after correctly noting the very minor role played by taxes on wealth, Tanzi remarks in passing that the net wealth tax in particular "has proved to be a costly mistake in developing countries that have attempted to implement it."

Doubtless this statement is true of some, perhaps many, countries; that it is not true of all is conclusively demonstrated with respect to Colombia in an important recent study (McLure et al., 1988; see also chapter 24 below). Indeed, the 1989 abolition of the net wealth tax, defective and imperfectly administered as it is, will undoubtedly make the Colombian personal tax system even less effective, and less progressive, than it was before. The taxation of wealth has clearly had a rough passage in most developing countries, as in developed countries, not least for obvious political reasons; and it will never be easy to implement anywhere. Nonetheless, to the extent that a stated objective of most taxation systems continues to be to levy taxes in accordance with ability to pay, some degree of wealth taxation, however imperfect, seems an indispensable component of a "good" tax system. Even when very poorly administered, as in Bolivia, for example, a death tax may collect as much revenue from the rich as the income tax (Musgrave, 1981). In the case of Colombia, the net wealth tax (and the presumptive income tax based on net wealth) accounted for almost all the nonwage personal income taxes collected (McLure et al., 1988).

The point of these comments is not so much to argue the case for taxing wealth (as is done, for instance, in Bird, 1978) but rather to emphasize that many of the most important aspects of taxation—such as its distributive impact—may be only poorly depicted by revenue data such as those analyzed by Tanzi. Apart from this point, however, the analysis and discussion in the Tanzi paper may be unreservedly recommended as a fitting introduction to taxation in developing countries.

Quantitative Characteristics of the Tax Systems of Developing Countries

Vito Tanzi

THE LEVEL OF TAXATION

The lowest ratios of total tax revenue to GDP are found in Uganda, at 2.6 percent; Ghana, at 5.5 percent; and Bolivia, at 6.3 percent. Ten countries have tax ratios of less than 10 percent. Most of these have very low per capita incomes. At the other extreme, eleven countries have tax ratios exceeding 25 percent. Of these, six have relatively high per capita incomes (Tunisia, Portugal, Yugoslavia, Greece, Israel, and Trinidad and Tobago), whereas the other five (Liberia, Egypt, Swaziland, Botswana, and Congo) are closer to the median income (their incomes range from $500 to $1,100). No country with a really low income appears in this group. [Tables 1.1 and 1.2 summarize the data by per capita income class.]

These results suggest a relationship between per capita income and the tax ratio. Such a relationship would conform with an expectation, supported by various authors, that, as countries develop, tax bases grow more than proportionately to the growth of income. In other words, the capacity to tax grows with the growth of income. (See especially R. A. Musgrave, 1969.) In addition to this supply-side argument, there is also the consideration that, as income grows, countries generally become more urbanized. Urbanization per se brings about a greater demand for public services while at the same time facilitating tax collection. Thus it increases the need for tax revenue and the capacity to tax. It is a fact of life that in the majority of countries a large proportion of total domestic taxes originate in the capital city or in the large urban centers, whereas much of the public expenditure also takes place there.

The correlation of the above tax ratios against the logarithm of per capita GDP supports the above expectation. This correlation is shown below for the eighty-six countries combined [see also the scatter diagram in figure 1.1], for the forty-three countries with per capita incomes of less than $850, and for the forty-three countries with per capita incomes of $850 or more. Figure 1.1 shows the scatter diagram for eighty-six developing countries. The coefficients in parentheses are *t*

Excerpted from Newbery and Stern (1987), pp. 205–41. The data are usually for an average of three years centered around 1981.

Table 1.1 Tax Revenue, by Type of Tax and by Country Group
(percentage of GDP)

Per Capita Income (dollars)		Total taxes	Income Taxes				Domestic Taxes on Goods and Services				Foreign Trade				Social security	Wealth and property	Other
Range	Average		Total	Individual	Corporate	Other	Total	General sales, turnover, VAT	Excises	Other	Total	Import duties	Export duties	Other			
0–349	241	12.90	2.66	1.14	1.50	0.13	-0.11	1.87	1.64	0.60	4.94	3.82	1.05	0.07	0.48	0.24	0.50
350–849	548	12.50	5.50	2.15	2.97	0.23	4.14	1.43	2.24	0.60	6.62	5.92	0.58	0.12	0.49	0.30	0.47
850–1,699	1,195	18.16	5.75	2.15	3.25	0.84	4.73	1.89	1.91	0.92	5.31	4.35	0.81	0.15	1.12	0.53	0.66
1,700 or more	3,392	22.75	8.08	2.35	5.00	0.92	6.30	3.10	2.16	1.40	3.19	2.72	0.42	0.05	3.90	0.64	0.64
All countries	1,330	17.77	5.60	1.94	3.14	0.52	4.81	2.07	1.97	0.88	5.02	4.20	0.72	0.10	1.49	0.43	0.57

Sources: International Monetary Fund, *Government Finance Statistics Yearbook* (1984); World Bank, *World Development Report* (1983).

Table 1.2 Tax Revenue, by Type of Tax and by Country Group
(percentage of total taxes)

Per Capita Income (dollars)		Income Taxes				Domestic Taxes on Goods and Services				Foreign Trade				Social security	Wealth and property	Other
Range	Average	Total	Individual	Corporate	Other	Total	General sales, turnover, VAT	Excises	Other	Total	Import duties	Export duties	Other			
0–349	241	19.68	8.71	10.73	0.97	32.28	14.98	12.86	4.44	39.25	30.14	8.37	0.73	3.23	2.05	3.51
350–849	548	29.55	12.25	15.47	1.22	26.19	8.63	15.73	3.46	38.06	32.87	4.19	0.99	2.02	1.76	2.49
850–1,699	1,195	30.29	11.05	17.50	3.77	25.76	10.11	10.54	5.14	29.47	23.72	4.85	0.89	6.74	3.04	4.66
1,700 or more	3,392	35.63	9.09	23.09	3.89	27.40	12.57	9.95	6.43	15.40	13.01	2.08	0.31	15.64	3.05	2.88
All countries	1,330	28.70	10.25	16.53	2.43	27.93	11.66	12.23	4.88	30.63	24.98	4.91	0.73	6.86	2.48	3.40

Sources: International Monetary Fund, Government Finance Statistics Yearbook (1984); World Bank, World Development Report (1983).

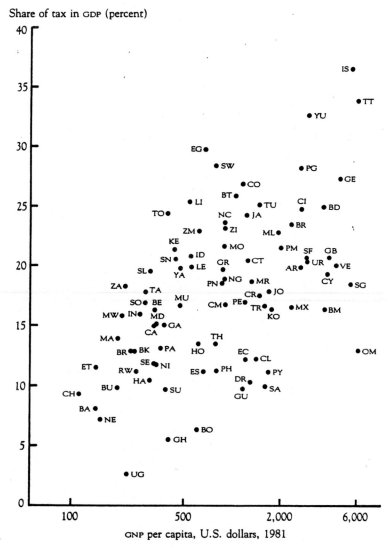

Figure 1.1 Share of Total Tax Revenue, and GNP per Capita

values, two asterisks implying significance at the 1 percent level and one asterisk significance at the 5 percent level. For eighty-six countries:

$$\frac{\text{Total tax revenue}}{\text{GDP}} = -4.8586 + 3.3792 \log (\text{GNP per capita}). \quad (1.1)$$
$$(1.19) \quad (5.61)**$$

$$\bar{R}^2 = 0.264$$

For forty-three countries with per capita income of less than $850:

$$\frac{\text{Total tax revenue}}{\text{GDP}} = -16.0983 + 5.3453 \log (\text{GNP per capita}). \quad (1.2)$$
$$\qquad\qquad (1.69) \quad (3.30)**$$

$$\bar{R}^2 = 0.191$$

For forty-three countries with per capita income equal to or more than $850:

$$\frac{\text{Total tax revenue}}{\text{GDP}} = -3.5262 + 3.1691 \log (\text{GNP per capita}). \quad (1.3)$$
$$\qquad\qquad (0.30) \quad (2.04)*$$

$$\bar{R}^2 = 0.07$$

Some theoretical arguments lend support to a causal relationship between per capita income and tax level (for example, Musgrave's tax-base, or tax-handle, theory), but it would be naive to accept a purely deterministic or mechanical relationship, as many historical, political, or social factors play a role.

For all eighty-six countries combined, the (unweighted) average ratio of tax revenue to GDP was 17.8 percent around 1981. That ratio was 12.9 percent for the twenty-two countries with per capita income of less than $350, however, and 22.8 percent for the twenty-one countries with per capita income of $1,700 or more. For the forty-three countries in between, it was about 18 percent, showing no significant difference between the group of countries with per capita incomes between $350 and $850 and those with per capita incomes between $850 and $1,700. If we ignore Europe (represented by only four countries), then Africa and the Western Hemisphere regions have similar tax ratios (about 17–18 percent), whereas Asia has a considerably lower tax ratio (about 15 percent) and the Middle East a considerably higher tax ratio (about 21 percent), very much the result of oil taxation.

Several studies (Chelliah, Baas, and Kelly, 1975; Tait, Grätz, and Eichengreen, 1979) have shown that the total tax ratio may be influenced by other factors in addition to per capita income. Such factors may include the monetization and openness of the economy, the share of mining in GDP, an export ratio that excludes mineral exports, the literacy rate, and the urbanization rate. Also, of course, the desired level of public expenditure is likely to play a role in determining the extent to which countries take advantage of their "taxable capacity." Rather than duplicating the results of some of these studies in explaining the total tax ratio, I shall consider some of these factors in the analysis of the tax structure.

THE STRUCTURE OF TAXATION

Although many studies have analyzed the level of taxation in developing countries, few have paid particular attention to its structure. Yet it may be fruitful to analyze structure, as there must be specific reasons why, say, one country ends up with a very large share of revenue from taxes on corporate income, whereas another may end up with a tax structure biased toward export duties. Historical or cultural factors clearly play a large role, but more must surely be involved. I shall deal separately with income taxes, domestic taxes on goods and services, taxes on foreign trade, and other taxes.

Income Taxes

For the eighty-six countries combined, the unweighted ratio of income taxes from all sources was 5.5 percent of GDP and 28.7 percent of total tax revenue. Income taxes vary from less than 1 percent of GDP in Nepal, Burma, and Uganda, to 28 percent in Trinidad and Tobago, or from 5 percent to 92 percent of total tax revenue. The wide range results largely from taxes on corporations rather than from taxes on the incomes of individuals.

Individual income taxes account for 1.9 percent of GDP and for 10.3 percent of total tax revenue for the whole eighty-six countries. In only five countries (Liberia, Papua New Guinea, Zimbabwe, Turkey, and Israel) do they exceed 5 percent of GDP. Israel and Turkey have by far the highest ratios at more than 8 percent of GDP. The revenue from taxes on the incomes of individuals exceeds 4 percent of GDP in only eleven countries. Thus it can be concluded that these taxes are much less important (in terms of actual collection) in developing countries than they are in developed countries, where in 1981 the share of individual income taxes to GDP in OECD (Organisation for Economic Co-operation and Development) countries was 12 percent. The share of these taxes in total tax revenue was 32.8 percent. This low level is almost surely due to the combination of high tax avoidance and high levels of exemptions, as the marginal rates are often as high in developing countries as in developed countries. In only six countries (Mauritania, Liberia, Papua New Guinea, Zimbabwe, Turkey, and Israel) do individual income taxes account for more than one-fourth of total tax revenue, and in only seven countries do they exceed one-fifth of total tax revenue. On the other hand, in more than half of the countries considered, these taxes account for less than one-tenth of total taxes.

Economic development, as measured by per capita income, seems to correlate with a growing importance of these taxes; however, the correlation is not strong. The correlation coefficient is 0.26, significant at the 5 percent level. Individual income taxes account for only 1.1 percent of GDP in countries with per capita income of less than $350 but represent 2.4 percent of GDP in countries with per capita income of $1,700 or more. Their share of total tax revenue rises from 8.7 percent in the poorest group of countries to about 12 percent in the next income group. It declines to about 9 percent for the group with the highest income (see table 1.2). If we eliminate Europe and the Middle East, the variation among regions is not very high.

The relative unimportance of taxes on individual incomes is disappointing, as these taxes have traditionally been considered the major instrument for pursuing (through fiscal tools) the objective of income redistribution. Although this result is disappointing, it should not surprise experts who have worked intimately with these countries. The requirements for an effective system of personal income taxation are many and are satisfied, if at all, only when the level of development is high. When the agricultural sector is large, accounting standards are poor, the level of literacy is low, and most economic activity takes place in small establishments, the effective taxation of personal income is difficult (Goode, 1952) even though the greater concentration of income in developing countries as compared with industrial ones reduces the need to impose a mass-based income tax to raise a significant level of revenue (Tanzi, 1966). In developing countries far more than in developed countries, the personal income tax is often a tax on the wages of public sector employees and of the employees of large, and often foreign, corporations.[1] As the proportion of total personal income derived from work in large establishments and in the public sector rises, so does the possibility of taxing personal income.

For fourteen developing countries, it was possible to obtain the proportion of revenue from individual income taxes derived from wages and salaries. These data indicate that for the whole group that proportion was 71 percent, whereas it surpassed 90 percent in four countries.

Corporate income taxes are somewhat more important than the taxes on the incomes of individuals. This is the reverse of the situation in industrial countries. These taxes account for 3.1 percent of GDP and for 16.5 percent of total tax revenue for the eighty-six countries combined. In six countries (Indonesia, Nigeria, Congo, Venezuela, Trinidad and Tobago, and Oman) the share of these taxes as a proportion of GDP exceeds 10 percent; in thirteen countries it exceeds 5 percent. These countries all depend heavily on oil or other mineral exports. These exports are carried out by a few large corporations that make sizable profits and thus provide the government with a source of revenue that is easy to tap. (Mineral production could be taxed through export taxes; but as we shall see below, export taxes are generally applied to *agricultural* exports.) The importance of corporate income taxes can also be assessed by the fact that, in at least twelve countries, they account for more than one-fourth of total tax revenue and in six countries for more than one-half.

The impact of economic development on corporate income tax is greater than on individual income taxes. The correlation coefficient between the share of corporate income taxes in GDP and per capita income is 0.43 (significant at the 1 percent level). Table 1.1 shows that the share of these taxes in GDP rises from 1.5 percent for the group of countries with per capita incomes lower than $350, to 5.0 percent for countries with per capita incomes of $1,700 or more. As a share of total tax revenue, these taxes rise from 11 percent for the lowest income group to 23 percent for the highest income group. These results are somewhat surprising, as corporate income taxes have been falling over time and have become relatively unimportant for OECD countries. For these countries, in 1981, corporate income taxes accounted for only 2.8 percent of GDP and 7.8 percent of total tax revenue. We thus observe an unusual bell-shaped relationship whereby higher per capita income leads first to an increase in corporate income tax revenue and then to a decline. One explanation of this pattern may be that mineral exports raise the per capita incomes of developing countries and at the same time provide them with an important tax handle. By the time countries move into the OECD group, the importance of mineral exports in determining per capita incomes has been somewhat reduced, whereas other tax handles have become available.[2]

Tables 1.1 and 1.2 cast additional light on *total income taxes*. Tables 1.1 and 1.2

show their growing importance in the tax systems of the developing countries as per capita income rises. Whereas the poorest group (with per capita incomes less than $350) collects only 2.7 percent of GDP from total income taxes, and about 20 percent of total tax revenue, countries with per capita incomes of $1,700 or more collect about 8 percent of GDP and about 36 percent of total tax revenue. The relative importance of income taxes on individuals as compared with those on corporations is also shown. The importance of oil (and other mineral exports) and of per capita income is evident. As oil exports become less important and per capita income rises, individual income taxes gain in importance, whereas the corporate income taxes become far less important.

Domestic Taxes on Goods and Services

Domestic taxes on goods and services account for 4.8 percent of GDP and for 28 percent of total tax revenue for the whole group. The importance of these taxes in generating revenue varies considerably among the eighty-six countries. In seven countries (Uganda, the Gambia, Lesotho, Swaziland, Nigeria, Botswana, and Oman) the ratio of domestic taxes on goods and service in GDP is less than 1 percent. It is not obvious what these countries have in common except that they do not have general sales taxes, though most of these countries make heavy use of import duties. (See below for more details.) Nine countries (India, Zambia, Nicaragua, Jamaica, Brazil, Portugal, Chile, Greece, and Israel) collect more than 10 percent of GDP from these taxes, while twenty-two countries collect from them more than 40 percent of total tax revenue. There is no correlation between the share of these taxes in GDP and per capita income. This statement is true for all domestic taxes on goods and services combined and also for general sales taxes and excises considered separately.

There are relatively few countries without some sort of "general" sales tax. Twenty-two countries have value-added taxes, whereas the rest have other forms of general sales taxes. Here the adjective "general" must be read as if it stood between quotation marks, as these taxes are often anything but general. In most countries the value that is added at the retail level, and often even at the wholesale level, is exempt; services are exempt; and so are many categories of goods. Furthermore, in some countries, goods produced under particular conditions (for example, by the cottage industry in Pakistan) are also exempt. These legal exemptions must of course be augmented by the illegal ones owing to tax evasion. The result is that for many countries the tax base consists predominantly of imports subject to these taxes. For several countries for which the information is available, the share of total general sales tax revenue collected from imports often exceeds 50 percent. It is unlikely that in many countries more than 20 percent of *domestic* value added is subject to this form of taxation. (This conclusion is supported by unpublished data for several countries.) The high rate of base erosion explains why in many countries relatively high legal rates generate low tax revenue. Because of these factors, the distinction between a general sales tax (often imposed with multiple rates) and excises is at times more a legal distinction than an economic one.

In twelve countries general sales taxes generate revenue greater than 5 percent of GDP. By far the largest percentage (10.9) is obtained by Chile, where the sales tax accounts for 41 percent of total tax revenue. For all countries combined, general sales taxes account for 2.1 percent of GDP and 11.7 percent of total tax revenue. These taxes are thus slightly more important than the taxes on individual income.

The contribution of *excises* to total revenue is about the same as that of the general sales taxes; 2 percent of GDP and 12 percent of total tax revenue. Only four countries generate more than 5 percent of GDP from excises (India, Zambia, Nicaragua, and Jamaica), with the first place going to Zambia—where excises amount to an extraordinary 7.8 percent of GDP. In nine countries excise taxes account for more than one-fourth of total tax revenue. Bolivia shows the highest percentage with a share of 35 percent.

Excises are imposed on many products and for many reasons. Three products, however—alcohol, tobacco, and petroleum—are known to play a very important role in excise taxation. By and large, petroleum is the most important, followed by alcohol and by tobacco. Forty-three percent of total excise tax revenue [in the fifty countries where information was available] comes from petroleum. Alcohol accounts for another 27 percent, whereas tobacco's share is about 23 percent. Overall, these three products account for the bulk of total excises. In nineteen countries they account for more than 90 percent of total excise tax revenue. In fourteen countries excises on these three products account for more than 2 percent of GDP, and in seventeen countries they account for more than 10 percent of total tax revenue.

Alcohol is a very important tax base in several countries. It accounts for an extraordinary share of total tax revenue, for example, in Burundi and Rwanda (26.5 percent and 19.1 percent, respectively). In Zambia and the Dominican Republic, it accounts for more than 10 percent of total tax revenue. Tobacco is most important in the tax systems of Nepal, India, Sierra Leone, Thailand, Cyprus, and a few other countries, but its highest share is never as high as that of alcohol. Petroleum accounts for more than 25 percent of Bolivia's total tax revenue and for relatively high shares in Mali, India, Zambia, Thailand, the Dominican Republic, Argentina, and a few other countries. (The importance of petroleum is often somewhat higher than these figures indicate, as in many countries it is also taxed with export or import taxes.)

Foreign Trade Taxes

Foreign trade taxes account for a little over 5.0 percent of GDP and for 30.6 percent of the total tax revenue of developing countries. These taxes are thus more important than the taxes on income. The factors that lead a country to rely on export taxes are somewhat different from those that lead it to rely on import taxes. As a consequence, I shall consider these two taxes separately.

Import duties are by far the single most important revenue source: they contribute 4.2 percent of GDP and 25 percent of total tax revenue. Import duties generate more than one-fourth of total tax revenue in almost half of the eighty-six countries. As with other revenue sources, the importance of import duties varies considerably among countries. As a percentage of GDP, import duties are most important in the group of twenty-two countries with per capita incomes below $350. They are least important for the countries with incomes of $1,700 or more (see table 1.1). (This statement does not mean that, in these higher-income countries, imports can come in freely. Quotas and other restrictions may take the place of duties. In such cases the government is transferring the power of taxation to importers.) By region, they are most important in the Middle East and in Africa, where they generate about twice as much revenue as in other regions.

Total tax ratios rise with per capita income, whereas the ratio of import duties to GDP is negatively related to the level of income. There is thus a significant fall in the contribution of import duties to total tax revenue (see table 1.2). That share is 30 percent for countries with incomes less than $350 and 13 percent for countries with incomes of $1,700 or more. The declining importance of import duties cannot be explained in terms of a tax-handle theory; the ratio of imports to GDP (the presumed tax base) is much higher in the countries with per capita incomes of $1,700 or more than in the countries with per capita incomes of less than $350.[3] Explicit policy choices must thus be involved.

We would expect revenue from import duties to be higher in countries that are open and that do not rely much on domestic taxes on goods and services.[4] The striking feature is the degree to which import duties substitute for domestic taxes on goods and services and vice versa. All the great users of taxes on imports make little use of taxes on domestic transactions, and all the great users of domestic taxes on goods and services make little use of import duties.

A more formal test of the above relationship can be made by regressing the share of import duties in GDP (ID/GDP) against (a) per capita income ($\bar{Y}$), (b) the share of imports in GDP (IM/GDP), and (c) the share of domestic taxes on goods and services in GDP (DOM/GDP). The estimated equation is the following:

$$ID/GDP = 4.8482 - 0.0008\bar{Y} + 0.0434\ IM/GDP \qquad (1.4)$$
$$(8.03)** \quad (4.02)** \quad (5.90)**$$
$$-0.2239\ DOM/GDP,$$
$$(2.48)* \qquad\qquad \bar{R}^2 = 0.39$$

where the numbers in parenthesis are t values. Two asterisks indicate significance at the 1 percent level, whereas one asterisk indicates significance at the 5 percent level.

The equation strongly backs our hypothesis. Import duties are positively influenced by the openness of the economy and negatively influenced by the level of per capita income and by the country's reliance on domestic taxes on goods and services. (Incidentally, openness does not play any role in determining a country's total tax ratio. It was not significant in a test that regressed the tax ratio against per capita income and the ratio of imports to GDP).

Table 1.3 summarizes some relevant relationships for these taxes. It shows that, in spite of the fact that imports as a share of GDP rise rather sharply as income rises (see column 3), the share of import duties in total tax revenue falls considerably (column 4). That the importance of imports as a tax base is inversely related to the

Table 1.3   *Basic Relationships for Import Taxation*

Per capita income ($\bar{Y}$) (dollars)	Percentage of GDP			Import duties as percentage of total tax revenue (4)	Import duties as percentage of imports (5)
	Total tax revenue (1)	Import duties (2)	Imports (3)		
0–349	12.90	3.82	20.75	30.57	21.11
350–849	17.50	5.92	38.13	32.87	15.54
850–1,699	18.16	4.35	31.93	23.72	14.05
1,700 or more	22.75	2.72	51.74	13.01	8.50
All countries	17.77	4.20	35.42	25.09	14.87

Sources: Table 8-1 [of Tanzi, 1987] for revenue and data; for import data IMF, *International Financial Statistics.*

level of income can be seen most clearly from column 5: the effective tax rate on imports averages about 21 percent for the low-income countries and about 8.5 percent for the high-income countries.

The behavior of the effective tax rate on import values can result either from a systematic reduction of the statutory levels of import duties as per capita income rises, or from progressively more generous exemptions and exonerations from customs duties without any necessary change in the statutory rates. I am not aware of any study that has assessed whether the level of *statutory* rates falls as income rises. The proportion of exempted imports ranges from 12 percent in the Gambia to 75 percent in Malaysia. The average for the group [of eighteen countries for which information was available] is 45 percent. The reasons for this erosion of the import tax base are several. The most important are (*a*) duty-free imports by the public sector; (*b*) duty-free imports by embassies and by other agents with diplomatic status; (*c*) duty-free imports by private enterprises benefiting from incentive legislation; (*d*) zero rating of imports for social reasons.

Export taxes continue to play a significant role in many countries but have a much more limited importance than import duties. For the whole group they account for 1.1 percent of GDP and 7 percent of total tax revenue. Their importance falls with the rise of per capita income. They generate 11 percent of total tax revenue (1.62 percent of GDP) for the group of countries with per capita income less than $350 but less than 3 percent of total tax revenue (0.44 percent of GDP) for the countries with per capita income of $1,700 or more (see tables 1.1 and 1.2). The ratio of export duties to exports is 11 percent for the lowest income group and falls respectively to 5.1 percent, 4.4 percent, and 3.3 percent for the other three income groups. The ratio is 6.1 percent for the eighty-six countries combined. It is highest in Africa (7.3 percent) and in the Western Hemisphere (5.8 percent), lower in Asia (5.2 percent), and much lower in the Middle East (2.4 percent) and in the few European countries (0.1 percent).

Sri Lanka has by far the highest ratio of revenue from export taxes to GDP (6.2 percent). Export taxes are also very important in Malaysia, Grenada, Rwanda, El Salvador, and a few other countries. In the discussion of corporate income taxes, I argued that those taxes were particularly important in countries that export *mineral* products, as these exports are normally carried out by large enterprises. Following the same line of reasoning, we would expect export taxes to be particularly important in countries that export *agricultural* products, as agricultural production is far less concentrated and the information required to tax agricultural incomes *as incomes* is normally not available. Countries thus often have little alternative but to tax agricultural production through export taxes. If this line of reasoning is correct, the countries that use corporate income taxes extensively should use export taxes very little and vice versa unless of course they are important exporters of both mineral and agricultural products.

Comparing the eight countries with the highest revenue from export taxes (as percentages of GDP) and the eight countries with the highest revenue from corporate income taxes shows that the heavy users of corporate income taxes make almost no use of export taxes, whereas the heavy users of export taxes make little use of corporate income taxes. The major exceptions—Malaysia and Swaziland—export not just agricultural products but also mineral products, so that they can make heavy use of both taxes. It thus appears that the structure of production and exports is a major determinant of the tax structure at least insofar as the choice between corporate income taxes and export taxes is concerned.

Other Taxes

We can be very brief with the remaining taxes. *Social security taxes* generate revenues on the same order of magnitude as the taxes on the incomes of individuals—1.15 percent of GDP and 7 percent of total tax revenue. As their base is wages, and as the share of wages in national income rises with per capita income, it is not surprising to find some relationship between these taxes and per capita income. Tables 1.1 and 1.2 show that these taxes grow in importance as income rises. Per capita income, however, is not the sole determinant of these taxes' importance. Sociopolitical factors are perhaps equally important; many of the countries with the highest share of GDP coming from this source are Latin countries (Costa Rica, Panama, Brazil, Portugal, and Uruguay). In these countries social security taxes account for 5–8 percent of GDP.

Of the three theoretical tax bases—income, consumption, and wealth—wealth is by far the least important. *Wealth taxes* account for only 0.4 percent of GDP and 2.5 percent of total tax revenue for the eighty-six countries taken together. They are very important in Singapore, where they account for 2.6 percent of GDP and for about 14 percent of total tax revenue. Singapore is essentially a city-state, so that a large share of wealth is in the form of buildings. In only six other countries do wealth taxes account for more than 1 percent of GDP. This low yield on the part of these taxes is surprising in view of the fact that they used to be a major revenue source in earlier times (Hinrichs, 1966). In recent times administrative constraints have usually made these taxes both unproductive and inequitable in developing countries. Their most sophisticated version—the net wealth tax—has proved a costly mistake in developing countries that have attempted to implement it. These taxes show some relationship to per capita income (see tables 1.1 and 1.2). The correlation coefficient between the ratio of wealth and property taxes to GDP and per capita income was 0.37, significant at the 1 percent level.

OTHER ASPECTS

This chapter has sought to give the reader a feel for the quantitative aspects of the developing countries' tax systems. If I were now to conclude, however, readers who know little about these tax systems might form the impression that they have learned more from the chapter than they have. The fact is that tax systems differ in more than the statistical aspects described above.[5] Each tax system has its own characteristics and peculiarities, and these cannot be captured by purely statistical summaries. To give a more comprehensive picture of the tax systems of developing countries we would need the *statutory* description in addition to the statistical and what, for lack of better words, we shall call the *real* or *effective* description. The correlation between these three descriptions can be low indeed.

The statutory tax system could be outlined in part by presenting the relevant information about rates, taxable bases, methods of payments, and so on, as described in the laws. This information is generally available for many countries and for most taxes, although absence of codification often makes it difficult to trace. In some countries, locating a given tax law can be a major and frustrating enterprise. Locating the regulations that accompany the law may be even more difficult. If readers were provided with the statutory information, in addition to statistical information, their knowledge would undoubtedly increase but not by as much as they might believe and certainly not by as much as it would increase if we were dealing with advanced countries. The reason is that in developing countries the gap between the statutory tax system and the effective or real tax system may be wide indeed. This gap also affects the quality or the meaning of the statistical description. Two countries could conceivably have similar statistics but totally different statutory systems. They could have similar laws and end up with highly different statistics. How do these differences come about?

First, there is the wedge introduced by explicit and intentional tax evasion. The individual who earns an income equal to x or sells an amount equal to y but declares only half of these amounts has, in an effective sense, reduced the burden of taxation, thus changing the relationship between the statutory system and the statistical description.

Second, a wedge is introduced by poor, or more often nonexistent, accounting. Again, the unwary observer may believe that what shows up in the statistics as an "income" tax was actually imposed on a clear-cut concept of income and that what shows up as a sales tax was imposed on an objectively measured concept of sale. The reality is, however, far different. It is not uncommon for the government to form some idea of income from the volume of the turnover and some idea of sales from, say, the size of the establishment. (Several countries, for example, collect a minimum tax on corporate income. This tax is assessed as a given percentage—often 1 percent—of the turnover. It is generally shown as an income tax, but is it one? See Mutén, 1982.) In these cases, the theoretical distinction between, say, an income tax and a sales tax has no real-life counterpart. It would thus be naive to apply the public finance theories related to specific taxes to these statistical concepts.

Third, the wedge can be introduced by the timing of the payment. Suppose, for example, that a tax on corporate income is paid with a two-year delay, so that this year's collection is determined by the corporate income of two years ago. Suppose, as is frequently the case, that there is a significant and variable rate of inflation. In such a case, this year's revenue from the tax on corporate income might bear no relationship to this year's corporate income. Unfortunately, information about these lags is not readily available and is generally unknown, so that when we compare statistics between countries such information cannot be taken into account.

If tax evasion, accounting standards, lags, and other factors were unchanging, they could, perhaps, be taken into account in an analysis of the tax systems. To complicate matters even more, however, they keep changing, being influenced by factors such as the rate of inflation, the personality of the tax administrators, the political mood, the means available to the tax administration, the rigidity with which the courts are applying the penalties to tax evaders, the degree of corruptibility of the tax inspectors, and the variability in the exchange rate. An intimate knowledge of a tax system is thus necessary before theoretical prescriptions for tax reform are made. In taxation, perhaps more than in any other area, perfection may be the enemy of the good. What looks just right in theory may be quite wrong in practice. The basic truth to remember is that control over the statutory system (over the tax laws) may at times be accompanied by very little control over the effective system. If such is the case, changing the laws may mean far less than we believe.

NOTES

1. The share of wages and salaries in national income is generally much lower in developing countries than in developed. Therefore the need for taxing nonwage incomes is far greater.

2. The statutory rates at which profits are taxed in the developing countries are *grosso modo* of the same order of magnitude as in the OECD countries (Lent, 1977). The use of investment incentives (in the form of tax holidays, allowances, etc.) in the developing countries is at least as widespread as in the OECD countries. The greater importance of these taxes in the former group of countries is therefore probably accounted for by a higher share of profits in GDP.

3. The imports/GDP ratios are, respectively, 23.3 percent for the low-income group and 56.3 percent for the high-income group.

4. The theory of tax structure change argues that, as countries develop, foreign trade taxes are progressively replaced by domestic taxes on goods and services (see Tanzi, 1973, 1978).

5. At this point, Disraeli's well-known observation—that there are three kinds of lies: lies, damned lies, and statistics—appears highly pertinent.

2

Taxes and Growth

The main focus of most analysis of tax policy in developing countries has always been on the relation between taxation and growth. One approach, as mentioned in the previous chapter, focuses on the extent to which the level of economic growth explains the level of taxation. Another approach looks at causality the other way, from taxation to growth. The next two chapters illustrate two quite different versions of this second approach. In chapter 3, Carl Shoup sets out a careful analysis of the theoretical design of a tax system intended primarily to foster economic growth, emphasizing both the appropriate role for different taxes and some of the critical details of tax design viewed from this perspective. In contrast, chapter 2, by Keith Marsden, proceeds from a brief review of some aggregate statistics on tax levels to some rather strong conclusions about the relation between the level of taxation and the rate of economic growth.

In some ways, the following chapter serves to illustrate the treachery of numbers, particularly aggregate numbers (as stressed in chapter 1), as well as the difficulty of deriving plausible generalizations about something as complicated as the relationship between taxation and growth in the extremely varied context of the developing world. Nonetheless, this chapter serves admirably both to introduce many of the central issues of development tax policy and to introduce the "supply-side" tone that has characterized much of the discussion of taxation over the past decade, as developed further in Part 3.

The basic hypothesis—expanded upon in Marsden (1983a)—is simply that countries with lower taxes have experienced higher rates of growth. The evidence adduced is aggregative and to some extent rather casually used: contrast, for instance, the confident assertions about the relation between taxation and distribution with the more careful discussions in Bird and De Wulf, 1973, and De Wulf, 1975. The method employed is simple pairwise comparison and regression analysis. This approach may be illuminating in certain circumstances, but it is of course subject to obvious problems of comparability and interpretation, particularly at this level of aggregation. (See Gandhi, 1987, for an effective critique.) A more recent and more careful discussion of tax trends, for example, shows clearly that tax levels have in general been rising in all countries in recent years, almost irrespective of income levels, economic structures, or growth rates (World Bank, *World Development Report*, 1988). Similarly, a recent detailed study of the role of public finance in one of the countries singled out by Marsden for praise as a "low tax" country, Korea, gives a rather different picture of the role of taxation in the modernization process (Bahl, Kim, and Park, 1986; see also chapter 7 below). Such examples could be multiplied manyfold.

Counterexamples do little, however, to weaken the force of the obvious policy implication of the Marsden study, a conclusion also drawn by others (e.g., Krauss, 1983; Wolf, 1988): if a country wants a high growth rate, its government should restrain its propensity to raise taxes. There is, of course, nothing new about this view. Bauer (1957; Bauer and Yamey, 1957) had said much the same thing long before, and indeed has kept on saying it through the years (Bauer, 1972, 1981). What is new in recent years, however, is the considerable support that this familiar view has received both as a result of its apparent adoption by the Reagan administration in the United States and as a consequence of the increasing empirical evidence in developed countries that taxes may have much more deleterious effects on economic incentives than had previously been thought likely (see Part 3 below).

Other observers than Marsden have drawn similar conclusions as to the desirable nature of the tax system based on the links between taxation and growth suggested by this literature—although by no means all would agree with his strong support for tax incentives to investment (see Part 3) and exports (De Wulf, 1978)—including even the import exemptions singled out for adverse comment in chapter 1. Marsden's argument against the payroll tax (and hence, in effect, against the personal income tax, which in most countries amounts to little more than a payroll tax) as discouraging work effort in the modern sector is, however, more closely in tune with the trend of much modern thought (see Bird, 1982; Prest, 1971). Indeed, although Marsden perhaps emphasizes the effects of taxation on the aggregate supply of factors more than the evidence warrants (Ebrill, 1987; chapter 11 below), his secondary emphasis on the effects of taxation on the efficiency with which factors are used is central to modern tax theory, as further evidenced in chapters 3 and 4 here. Similarly, Marsden's comments with respect to the need for simplicity and for adaption to the inflation characterizing many developing countries also signal important concerns in the design of appropriate tax systems for developing countries, which are further explored later in this book.

A final point raised in the chapter deserves to be singled out for discussion, since the issue raised is in many ways central to the prospects for effective tax reform in developing countries but does not fit easily into the framework of the present volume. It is simply that both the "revenue requirement" (Ahmad and Stern, 1986; Musgrave, 1965)—that is, the needed level of taxation in a particular country at a particular time—and the feasibility of attaining it are inextricably related to the efficiency with which the revenues are spent. Stanley Please (1967, 1970) long ago made the obvious point that if the idea in increasing taxes was to increase public saving, as seemed evident to such early authors in the field as Heller (1954) and Lewis (1966), then it was important to ensure that the additional revenues were not simply eaten up by increased expenditure unrelated to development. Please went on to suggest—as was to some extent supported by later statistical studies (Singh, 1975; Heller, 1975), though not by all (Bahl, Kim, and Park, 1986)—that since, in practice, increases in taxes tended to be matched, or exceeded, by increases in nondevelopment expenditures, increased taxation might prove to be a weak reed upon which to build a development program.

As with all aggregate conclusions, this view is of course subject to many variant interpretations when examined in detail. Even such blatant current consumption expenditures as food subsidies, for example, may be conducive, even essential, to the productive utilization of the labor force, and hence be growth-oriented (Shoup, 1965). On the other hand, even if increased taxes do result in increased public saving, such saving may be less likely to be used productively than if the resources had been left in private hands (Lindbeck, 1987; chapter 5 below).

Although it is perhaps not appropriate to delve further into the details of public expenditure in a book devoted to taxation, two additional basic points should be made here about the relation between taxation and expenditure. First, how much taxation is needed (from a development point of view) depends upon what is done with the money. Just as the need to invest in expensive new energy sources may be reduced by curtailing the inefficient use of existing energy supplies, so the apparently inexhaustible need for more taxes in most countries may be reduced by curtailing inefficient expenditure activities. There are in most countries both ample opportunities to do so and some well-established procedures available to help in the task (Bird, 1984; Premchand, 1983): it will not, of course, be easy to do so anywhere!

Secondly, public attitudes to taxes, and hence the feasibility of collecting direct taxes in particular, are clearly influenced to some extent not only by perceptions of how fair the tax system is—as is commonly emphasized by tax experts—but also, and perhaps more importantly, by perceptions of how sensibly the government is likely to use the money. As stressed in Parts 4 and 7 of this book, effective tax systems in developing countries rest more on the success governments have in taking money away from people before they know they have it than on their goodwill. Nonetheless, in any society the boundaries of what is considered to be "reasonable" tax evasion are quite elastic and, in part at least, depend upon how government is perceived by citizens. The acceptable level and form of taxation is thus constrained to some extent by the acceptability of expenditures. Moreover, it can be argued with considerable force that both taxation and expenditure are likely to be more efficient when they are explicitly linked (Bird, 1976a)—a point long ago recognized by Wicksell and Lindahl (reprinted in Musgrave and Peacock, 1958).

For these reasons, particularly in the case of developing countries, where inefficiencies are likely to be both more prevalent and relatively more costly and where the apparent need for more taxes is usually greater, there is good reason to link taxes and expenditures as explicitly as possible, whenever doing so is technically feasible and politically acceptable. As recent authors have recognized, the standard textbook condemnation of "earmarking" as a pernicious practice thus needs to be reconsidered in the context of development (Musgrave, 1981; Bird, 1984). In some circumstances, and much more widely than is true in some developing countries (e.g., Africa)—though less, or at least rather differently, than in others (e.g., Latin America)—linking additional taxes explicitly to the expenditures they are to finance may be a good idea. These good words apply equally to the much-discussed (but as yet seldom practiced) virtues of proper price/tax policy for public utilities (World Bank, *World Development Report*, 1988; Ahmad and Stern, 1986) and to the strong case for mobilizing local resources for local purposes (Bahl,

Miner, and Schroeder, 1984; chapter 32 below). Of course, even the best-designed "benefit-based" tax system can produce only a fraction of the revenues needed to run a state these days: but the failure of a device to solve all the world's problems is hardly a reason to reject it. In the end, there are few stronger cases in development tax policy than the case for adopting properly-designed benefit tax policies wherever possible.

Taxes and Growth

Keith Marsden

The arguments in the great tax debate are well known. Lower taxes should stimulate higher output by increasing incentives to save, to invest, to work hard, and to innovate. But, say the skeptics, will increased economic growth really occur? Moreover, since taxes are progressive, will not lower taxes mean that the rich benefit at the expense of the poor, who are more dependent upon the social services financed out of tax revenues? A review of the experience with growth and taxation in twenty countries, representing almost the entire spectrum of world incomes, does not pretend to answer these questions, but it sheds some light on their empirical foundation. The countries in question were Brazil, Cameroon, Chile, Jamaica, Japan, the Republic of Korea, Liberia, Malawi, Mauritius, New Zealand, Paraguay, Peru, Singapore, Spain, Sweden, Thailand, United Kingdom, Uruguay, Zaïre, and Zambia.

Half of the countries selected had tax revenues relative to gross domestic product below the average for their income groups during the 1970s, while the other half had tax/GDP ratios above the average (see table 2.1; the income groupings were fairly narrowly defined). The choice of countries was constrained by data availability and by the exclusion of Organization of Petroleum Exporting Countries members and other countries which have extensively used nontax instruments for revenue purposes. The selected countries were grouped into ten pairs with similar per capita incomes but contrasting tax levels, and their growth rates over the past decade were then compared.

The economic structures of the countries covered were not identical of course. It may be administratively easier to extract higher levels of tax from certain sectors and activities. But this does not mean that it is desirable to do so from the point of view of long-term economic development. This depends, first, on the impact of higher taxes on incentives and output in the sectors subject to tax and, second, on whether government uses its additional revenues efficiently. This article focuses primarily on the first issue.

In all cases, the countries that imposed a lower effective average tax burden on their populations achieved substantially higher real rates of GDP growth than did their more highly taxed counterparts. The average (unweighted) annual rate of growth of GDP was 7.3 percent in the low-tax group, and 1.1 percent in the high-tax group. Every member of the low-tax category, including three from Africa (Mal-

Excerpted from Marsden (1983).

Table 2.1 Comparative Performance of Selected Countries

Country	Total tax revenue[a] as a percentage of GDP	Real Average Annual Growth Rates, 1970–79						Gross Domestic Investment as a percentage of GDP	
		GDP	Consumption		Gross domestic investment	Exports	Labor force	1960	1979
			Public	Private					
Malawi (low tax)	11.8	6.3	6.1	5.7	2.3	4.6	2.2	10	29
Zaire (high tax)	21.5	-0.7	-2.2	-1.8	-5.0	-1.1	2.1	12	9
Cameroon (low tax)	15.1	5.4	5.4	5.3	7.9	0.5	1.3	—	25
Liberia (high tax)	21.2	1.8	2.3	4.3	5.2	2.3	2.6	28	27
Thailand (low tax)	11.7	7.7	9.1	6.9	7.7	12.0	2.7	16	28
Zambia (high tax)	22.7	1.5	1.8	-2.2	-5.6	-0.7	2.4	25	21
Paraguay (low tax)	10.3	8.3	4.8	7.4	18.7	8.4	3.1	17	29
Peru (high tax)	14.4	3.1	6.5	2.9	2.7	1.7	3.0	25	14
Mauritius (low tax)	18.6	8.2	13.5	9.8	16.1	—	—	30	38
Jamaica (high tax)	23.8	-0.9	8.0	-0.6	-9.6	-6.8	2.2	30	18
Korea (low tax)	14.2	10.3	8.7	8.0	14.9	25.7	2.8	11	35
Chile (high tax)	22.4	1.9	-0.5	1.9	-2.0	10.7	1.9	17	16
Brazil (low tax)	17.1	8.7	8.6	9.1	10.1	7.0	2.2	22	23
Uruguay (high tax)	20.0	2.5	1.5	(.)c	7.5	4.3	0.1	18	17
Singapore (low tax)	16.2	8.4	6.4	7.2	6.0	11.0	2.7	11	39
New Zealand (high tax)	27.5	2.4	—	—	—	3.4	2.1	24	22
Spain (low tax)	19.1	4.4	5.6	4.4	2.5	10.8	1.1	19	20
United Kingdom (high tax)	30.4	2.1	2.8	1.7	0.8	8.2	0.3	19	19*
Japan (low tax)	10.6b	5.2	5.0	5.3	3.2	9.1	1.3	34	33
Sweden (high tax)	30.9	2.0	3.2	2.0	-1.1	2.6	0.3	25	20

Sources: World Bank, 1981 World Bank Atlas; World Development Report, 1981; and Accelerated Development in Sub-Saharan Africa (Washington, D.C., 1981). IMF, International Financial Statistics Yearbook 1981 and Government Finance Statistics Yearbook, Volume V (Washington, D.C., 1981). International Labor Office, ILO Yearbook of Labour Statistics, 1980.
Note: — Indicates data are not available.
[a]Central government tax revenues only.
[b]Includes nontax revenue but excludes social security contributions.
[c](.) Indicates that figure is less than 0.05.

awi, Mauritius, and Cameroon), exceeded the economic growth of the most rapidly expanding economy (Peru) in the high-tax category. Yet in most of sub-Saharan Africa (except Nigeria), GDP grew by only 1.6 percent per annum during the decade compared with 6.2 percent for Latin America and the Caribbean.

Although—with three exceptions (Jamaica, Zaïre, and the United Kingdom)—tax/GDP ratios rose during the period under review, the year-to-year variations were small and the relative tax positions of the low-tax and high-tax countries remained unchanged. The rise seems mainly to reflect a broadening of the tax base rather than an increase in tax rates in the low-tax group, although it did coincide with a general slackening of economic growth during the second half of the decade. The average tax/GDP ratio in the low-tax group increased from 13.3 percent at the beginning of the decade to 15.2 percent at the end, while it rose from 21.0 percent to 23.9 percent in the high-tax group.

Higher rates of economic growth allowed a substantial rise in real living standards in the low-tax countries, shown by their higher levels of private consumption. At the same time, an expansion of the tax base was associated with growth and generated increased revenues, which financed more rapid expansion of expenditure on government services such as defense, health, and education in all the low-tax countries except in the Paraguay/Peru pairing. In Peru, faster growth of public services was achieved at the expense of both private consumption and investment.

Direct information on changes in the incomes of different social groups is scarce and not very reliable. However, available data on income distribution seem to refute the argument that distribution in countries with high taxes is more equitable than in those with low ones. The share of the poorest 40 percent of households in total income remained relatively high in five fast-growing low-tax countries: Japan, Korea, Malawi, Spain, and Thailand, ranging between 16.9 percent and 21.9 percent.

Life expectancy is also an important indicator of progress in reducing poverty, because it is the poor who are most afflicted by deficient diets, polluted water supplies, and inadequate health services, which cut short their lives and bring the average down. Life expectancy rose in all the selected countries over 1960–79 and the improvement was greatest in low-income societies. The increases averaged 8.0 years in low-tax countries and 6.2 years in high-tax countries. By 1979, the overall levels in the two groups were about the same (63.1 years and 63.9 years respectively).

TAX/GROWTH LINKS

What accounts for the superior economic performance of the low-tax countries? The level of taxation is clearly not the only factor, and perhaps not even the most significant one. Development is complex. Its pattern can be influenced by many variables, endogenous and exogenous. Growth was retarded in some countries in the sample by political instability and by a deterioration in their terms of trade. Inflation, high interest rates, the oil price hikes, and trade barriers have made progress difficult for most countries. Nations' responses to fiscal measures are influenced by the faculties, motivations, and mores of their peoples.

The "quality" of the tax system is also important. A country with a higher tax/GDP ratio but a favorable tax structure may outperform a country with a lower overall tax level that discourages growth-promoting activities or imposes an excessive burden on the most productive or innovative segments of the population. Other important considerations include the complexity of the tax system, the efficiency and integrity of its administration, and the degree of horizontal and vertical equity (within as well as between income groups).

But the links between the level of taxation and economic growth are there, if mostly indirect—operating through the capital, labor, and product markets. Tax levels affect the amount of capital available by encouraging or discouraging domestic savings and foreign investment, and may also affect the allocation of investment. They affect the level, productivity, and distribution of employment by influencing individual choices between work and leisure (or housework), the intensity of effort on the job, and employers' decisions on technology. Taxes affect a firm's ability to diversify and expand through their impact on input costs and managerial behavior. They may also have a bearing on less tangible factors such as entrepreneurship and technical progress.

Some empirical evidence suggests causal relationships between the level and types of taxes and key growth determinants for investment, exports, employment, productivity, and innovation. This evidence is partly qualitative, based upon field surveys and observation of economic behavior by analysts and development institutions. Some findings can be cited from an analysis of the sample data and other published studies.

EVIDENCE OF LINKS

The impact of taxes, taken as policy variables, on economic growth was investigated by the use of regression analysis, based upon average tax/GDP ratios in the selected countries during the 1970s and, among other information, the data included in the table. The overall results suggested significant negative effects. An increase of 1 percent in the tax/GDP ratio was associated with a decrease in the rate of economic growth of 0.36 percent. Forty-five percent of the intercountry variance in GDP growth was explained by differences in the overall tax burden. When gross domestic investment and the labor force growth were taken into account, 78 percent of the growth variance was explained. But since labor and capital include the effects of taxes on the supply of these factors, the residual tax variable, measuring their effects on productivity, dropped to −0.12 percent.

The results of the comparison of the effects of taxes on lower and higher income countries suggested that taxes had a significantly greater effect in the former. A 1 percent increase in the tax/GDP ratio was estimated to reduce GDP growth by 0.57 percent when tax was the only independent variable considered and by 0.30 percent when it was combined with investment and labor force growth.

The results suggest that taxes may affect growth in two ways: first, by influencing the aggregate supply of the main factors of production by raising or lowering their net (after tax) returns and, second, by influencing the efficiency of resource utilization (total factor productivity). A possible explanation for the larger and more significant effects of taxes on growth in the lower-income countries is that these offer greater scope for productivity gains from the spread of modern technology, improvement in skills, and the transfer of capital and labor to more productive sectors and activities. They may also benefit to a greater extent from "externality effects." The application of more efficient management and production techniques in leading sectors (such as exports) eventually results in higher productivity in the backward sectors through emulation and dissemination of know-how. In higher-income countries, productivity differences between sectors tend to be narrower and the existing levels of efficiency higher. Structural and institutional rigidities that limit the mobility of resources or retard the acceptance of new techniques may restrict their potential for tax-induced gains.

INVESTMENT

Gross domestic investment grew at substantially higher rates in the low-tax countries, averaging 8.9 percent annually, compared with an annual decline of 0.8 percent in high-tax countries. The regression analysis relating investment growth to variations in tax/GDP ratios indicated that an increase in the total tax ratio of 1 percentage point was associated with a reduction of the rate of growth of investment of 0.66. Among the different types of tax, corporate income tax seemed to be the strongest deterrent to investment.

These findings generally correspond with the results of other research based upon U.S. experience, which estimates that progressive reductions in corporate profit taxes would increase both business investment and the capital stock substantially. Other estimates (also based on U.S. data) show that social security taxes reduce total saving and labor supply (through induced early retirement) and have marked negative effects on the long-run levels of owned capital and income. Corporate taxes and social security contributions combined were generally lower in the low-tax countries in the sample.

There is evidence, too, that tax policy in the sample countries influenced the pattern of investment, with consequent effects on overall efficiency. Generous corporate tax holidays and import duty concessions were offered by low-tax countries to investors in priority areas, particularly exports where economic returns have been shown to be high. The ratio of total indirect taxes and duties to GDP was lower in low-tax countries in all the pairs in the sample, and, except for Cameroon, their exports rose more rapidly, expanding at an average annual rate of 9.9 percent compared with 2.5 percent in the high-tax group. Most countries experienced a deterioration in their terms of trade but the extent of the decline was about the same in the two groups of countries on the average and did not explain the disparity in their performances.

The regression analysis of the growth of exports found that taxes on foreign trade had a significantly negative effect on the growth of that sector, while tax alleviation offered to exporters increased domestic and foreign sources of capital. Net direct foreign investment was important in all low-tax developing countries. It quadrupled in Brazil, for instance, and tripled in Singapore between 1970 and 1977.

In contrast, most high-tax countries experienced a secular decline in their investment ratios, which fell to an average of 18 percent of GDP in 1979. In some cases, taxes on major export commodities deterred foreign investors and diverted domestic capital into unproductive activities, such as real estate speculation. World Bank data for 1970 and 1977 show negative direct foreign investment in some high-tax countries. Research has shown that the efforts of several governments in the late 1960s and early 1970s to abandon liberal tax incentives and introduce ad valorem export taxes were often successful in maximizing revenues in the short run but were disappointing in their long-term effects. Formal systems for providing tax exemptions or rebates to exporters exist in some high-tax countries but are often ineffective because of weak administration or overcomplicated procedures. Trade specialists also stress the role of overvalued exchange rates, which act as a hidden tax on exporters, in hampering growth.

Inflation rates were higher in high-tax countries in seven out of the ten pairs during the decade and seem to have exacerbated the negative effects of taxation on growth. There is econometric evidence that a shift in investment from plant and machinery to owner-occupied housing, which is more favored by tax rules, is accentuated by inflation, because nominal interest payments are tax deductible. In contrast, inflation tends to increase the tax burden on business capital. First, because deductions for fixed investment are calculated according to historic costs, a higher rate of inflation reduces their real value and understates the costs of replacement. Second, the owners of the equity of business firms often pay capital gains tax on the rise in the nominal value of the capital stock.

It has also been suggested that interest rates have been driven up in countries that allow interest rate deductions for tax purposes, while taxing interest and dividend income, and that economic growth has been negatively affected by the high interest rates in recent years. High rates have been maintained or pushed higher by inflation, which has been shown to have a substantial negative effect on investment in plant and equipment.

EMPLOYMENT AND PRODUCTIVITY

Nonagricultural employment rose more rapidly in low-tax countries, as did productivity (GDP per member of the labor force)—by 5 percent a year on average, compared with a decline of 0.1 percent in high-tax countries. This latter figure probably also reflected growing unemployment and underemployment but data are lacking for most countries.

Policies providing exporters with duty-free imported inputs and other tax incentives facilitated the growth of exports in low-tax countries, particularly in labor-intensive manufactures where competitive material costs are critical for successful penetration of international markets. This accelerated the transfer of surplus labor out of agriculture into more productive jobs in industry and related services. Productivity was also raised by higher levels of investment, already discussed, which allowed wider adoption of modern technology. The regression analysis found that a reduction in the total tax/GDP ratio of 1 percentage point was associated with an increase in labor productivity of 0.28 percent. Corporate taxation had the greatest impact among the individual taxes.

In high-tax countries, on the other hand, high tariff protection, mostly on finished goods, often removed the competitive stimulus for efficiency in the production of domestic substitutes and frequently led to failure to achieve economies of scale in areas of potential comparative advantage—an effect long recognized by trade and fiscal experts. (Paradoxically, the efficiency in some import-substitution industries was also undermined by smuggling.) Manufacturing output grew more slowly in high-tax countries in all but one of the pairs (Cameroon/Liberia), averaging only 1.5 percent annually compared with 9.1 percent in low-tax countries. Agricultural output growth averaged 3.1 percent in low-tax countries compared with 1.5 percent in the high-tax group—although there were obviously factors other than distorted tariff structures involved, including pricing policy and climatic conditions.

Employment growth was retarded in some high-tax countries by payroll and sales taxes, which pushed up the cost of labor. The regression results indicated significant relationships between labor force growth and tax levels. In the poorer countries, relatively small differences in the income tax/GDP ratio can have a substantial impact on individual tax burdens and work incentives because its incidence is generally confined to a relatively small group engaged in the modern sector. Withholding income tax at source, for example, tends to create a de facto tax bias against employees, particularly government workers. If wage and salary earners feel that they are being discriminated against, both productivity and the availability of national technical manpower may be adversely affected.

There is some evidence from more affluent societies that people will work more if income taxes fall, but may prefer leisure if taxes rise, and this may also be a factor reducing labor supply and productivity in the study's sample. Ratios of personal income tax to GDP were higher in all the high-tax countries except Uruguay. (Personal incentives are, of course, particularly affected by high marginal rates, but the only macroeconomic indicator available on the effective burden of this tax is the average ratio. This is still a useful measure of the magnitude of this particular tax "wedge.")

INNOVATION

Several studies have shown that a substantial proportion of economic growth can be attributed to technical change, in addition to the contributions of capital and labor. Technical change encompasses improvements in technology and managerial techniques and product innovations. Lower corporate and personal income taxes provide entrepreneurs with the resources and stimulus to launch new firms and new products and to introduce or develop new technology. In Korea, a low-tax country, exemptions from indirect taxes and tariffs for exporters and other fiscal incentives, including some fostering technical development specifically, were accompanied by a substantial broadening and deepening of the industrial structure.

Of course, if a rapid growth momentum is established in response to these incentives, incomes rise and new opportunities are created in the domestic market, thus stimulating further growth of output. This, in turn, brings in higher tax revenues and allows government to expand its public services and investment while maintaining tax rates and ratios at relatively low levels.

CONCLUSIONS

The evidence suggests that tax policy in the countries under study affected economic performance via two basic mechanisms. First, lower taxes resulted in higher real (after tax) returns to savings, investment, work, and innovation, stimulating a larger aggregate supply of these factors of production and raising total output. Second, the focus and types of fiscal incentives provided by low-tax countries appear to have shifted resources from less productive to more productive sectors and activities, thus increasing the overall efficiency of resource utilization. The reverse seems to be true for some high-tax countries.

The findings do not imply that tax changes bring immediate results. The timing and context of tax reform are probably critical. Recent experience in the industrial countries indicates that tax cuts may not stimulate output sufficiently while deflationary monetary policies and overvalued exchange rates are pulling strongly in the opposite direction; or when extensive government borrowing to meet large budgetary deficits crowds out private sector investment by raising real interest rates. Nor does a global recession provide the most propitious occasion for tax policy initiatives. Even in more favorable circumstances, the responses of investors, workers, entrepreneurs, and consumers may take years to take full effect.

The gestation period for investment is long but the evidence cited projects that long-term benefits will accrue. No inferences can be drawn about the short-term effects of tax changes in any particular country. It is doubtful if tax cuts could ever serve as a "quick fix" for a sick economy. A more pragmatic approach for high-tax, low growth countries might be to seek progressive improvements in the "quality" of the tax structure. Fiscal incentives may generate faster growth and increased revenues in the long run if they are focused on areas with high incremental income yields (such as exports). Further study of many aspects of tax/growth relationships should be rewarding. But, at least, these preliminary findings indicate that lower taxes are compatible with a pattern of development that raises output and reduces poverty significantly.

3

A Growth-oriented Tax System

What would a tax system designed primarily to foster the growth of per capita income look like? This is the question Carl Shoup, one of the pioneer analysts of tax systems in developing countries (Shoup, 1965a; Shoup et al. 1949, 1959, 1970), sets out to answer in the paper excerpted in this chapter. Shoup systematically and carefully reviews the key elements of such a growth-oriented tax system. First, and quite unusually, he emphasizes the need, on growth grounds, to exempt the very poorest people in most developing countries from taxation (see also Shoup, 1965).

More conventionally, Shoup goes on to note that taxes on profits in such a system should be low or nonexistent—a goal which he suggests can be achieved through exempting investment. Subsequent analysis has shown both that the "expensing" Shoup discusses is equivalent to economically neutral taxation of new investment (Harberger, 1981) and that it can be achieved by the explicit exemption of capital income, that is, by moving from an income to a consumption tax base (Meade et al., 1978; U.S. Treasury, 1977; Bradford, 1986). The latter analysis has recently been applied to the case of developing countries (Zodrow and McLure, 1988; McLure et al., 1988; see also chapters 18 and 22 below)—although it is of interest to note historically that Kaldor's (1955) earlier recommendation of personal consumption taxation had its only adoptions, albeit short-lived, in India and (as it then was) Ceylon (see Kaldor, 1956, 1960; Goode, 1961).

There are few more contentious issues in development taxation than the appropriate taxation of income from investment, and the discussion in this selection provides an appropriate introduction to some of the central aspects of this problem. Shoup's analysis of the effects of taxation on risk taking is especially worth noting. Although to a limited extent the theoretical literature on this subject has since advanced (Atkinson and Stiglitz, 1980), there has as yet, as Ahmad and Stern (1986) note, been almost no application of this analysis to the case of developing countries—in many ways a curious omission, given the centrality of risk taking to development success that has been alleged since at least Schumpeter (1961; originally published in English in 1934).

Two other points raised by Shoup's discussion of the effects of taxation on saving and investment deserve emphasis. In the first place, although he views the taxation of wealth in the context of a growth-oriented tax system with some ambivalence, he argues that even from this point of view, there remains some case for such taxes, perhaps particularly to encourage the efficient use of land. This point is taken up again in Part 6. Secondly, Shoup mentions in passing that most developing economies are at least partially "open" economies, with the result that tax policy designers in such countries must be alert both to the effects of their policies on capital inflows and outflows and (although he does not mention this) to the effects of policies in other countries. As a recent example, it may be argued that an important consequence of recent U.S. tax reforms has been to encourage still more capital flight from Latin America (McLure, 1988). More importantly, there are few more critical issues in development tax policy than the extent to which a country can be considered to be open to the world capital market (McLure et al., 1988)—and few on which the evidence is more murky (Harberger, 1980; Feldstein and Horioka, 1980). At one extreme, if a country is isolated from outside influences, tax policies to encourage savings may result in expanded investment and consequently faster growth. At the other extreme of a small open economy, such policies may change the ownership structure of the existing capital stock but not alter the level of that stock at all (Hartle et al., 1983). Unfortunately, few analyses of the effects of tax policies on saving, investment, and growth seem to take adequate account of this problem: see Part 3 for further discussion.

As the brief conclusion to the following excerpt indicates, the author is well aware of the very important, often dominating, role played by both administrative and political factors in shaping real-world tax systems. As he correctly notes, in reality the outcome of these factors in many countries has been less the "growth-constraining" tax system assumed by some to prevail (e.g., McKinnon, 1973; Krauss, 1983) than a system that in many respects—with the very important exception of its arbitrariness and uncertainty—seems about as "growth-facilitating" as one might wish.

In the euphoria of the postwar period, when colonial regimes were thrown off and all things seemed possible to the governments of many developing countries, ridiculously high nominal rates of tax were sometimes imposed on income and profits. As a rule, however, both evasion and "incentive" policy ensured that these rates were seldom, if ever, effectively applied. Indeed, if low or zero taxes on profits and little if any effective taxation of high personal incomes were the magic path to economic growth, many developing countries should already be well on their way: supply-side taxation has long been in vogue in practice if not in law.

This conclusion is obviously overly facile in the sense that although the tax systems applied in many countries may not have imposed very high rates on average, they may have done so on some critical margins, particularly in the presence of inflation. Moreover, even in the absence of inflation, the resulting variation of effective tax rates on different types of investment (King and Fullerton, 1984) was probably seldom, if ever, conducive to sound patterns of economic development: see chapter 14 for further discussion. Nonetheless, as Shoup notes in his concluding paragraph, a strong case can be made that what has been most sacrificed in the tax systems of many developing countries has been not so much efficiency and growth as equity and other social objectives.

Taxes and Economic Development

Carl S. Shoup

The characteristics of a tax system designed primarily to promote growth may be conveniently divided into the economic and non-economic.

ECONOMIC CHARACTERISTICS

1. To avoid decreasing gainful consumption [defined as consumption that pays for itself in part or in whole through increased production], there would be no taxation, direct or indirect, impinging on families at very low income levels.

2. To stimulate entrepreneurship, and especially risk taking, profits would be taxed at a low rate, if not exempted. Moreover, government would share appreciably in risk-taking by allowing full deductibility of business losses, either against other income of the current year, or by carry-back or carry-forward against income of past or future years respectively.

The low tax rate, or the exemption from tax, may be limited to profits from investment spending undertaken after the new tax regime is introduced. But it is difficult to isolate such income from the remainder of a firm's profits. The simpler way to restrict the tax advantage to investment made after a certain date is (a) through accelerated and excess depreciation of facilities constructed after that date, or (b) by granting the low tax rate or exemption to business firms, or to establishments within a firm, set up after that date.

The extreme form of accelerated depreciation is full deductibility of the capital outlay in the year of expenditure. This instantaneous depreciation amounts to full tax exemption of the return on the investment. In other words, completely accelerated depreciation gives the same result as reducing the tax rate to zero (apart from risk premium), assuming, of course, full loss offset for any book loss that may occur under this deduction. The treasury gets no net revenue from such a tax.[1] If, in addition, the profits tax allows more than 100 percent depreciation, the treasury's net revenue from the tax is negative; we are dealing then with a subsidy. A further subsidy for investment through the corporate form can be given by allowing an individual taxpayer to deduct the amount he devotes to the purchase of corporate securities.

Method (b) above, a low tax rate or exemption, must of course contain a promise that the low rate or exemption will continue for a period of years. The state must bind itself by a tax covenant with the enterprise. Such a commitment is sometimes

Excerpted from Shoup (1966).

opposed on the grounds that the state should retain more freedom of action, since fiscal and economic conditions may change unexpectedly before the exemption term is up. But what alternative is there? Accelerated or excess depreciation commits the state just as completely, and indeed more firmly; the state cannot go back on its bargain unless it repeals the depreciation provision retroactively. No doubt this is one reason why business firms plead so forcefully for special depreciation provisions.

A tax based on capital value might prove less repressive to entrepreneurship than an income tax, but only under certain circumstances, and to a limited degree. An illustration is a tax on the capital value of land that is being held idle. This capital value, its market value, might not rise much if the land were put to use. Hence the owner's tax bill might not rise much (but his income tax bill would rise). The capital value tax would thus be only a mild check to entrepreneurial exploitation of the land, in its marginal effect; and by taking money from the land owner, it might make him search for income.

As to risky enterprises compared with safer ones, the capital tax is by no means wholly favorable to risk-taking. The capital tax works both for and against risk-taking.

On the financial level, consider first the market value of the ownership interest in the enterprise. The capital value of an ownership interest in a risky enterprise is a low multiple of its anticipated (actuarial value) income stream, because of risk-aversion. The tax liability of an owner in a risky venture is thus less under a capital tax than under an income tax yielding the same total revenue from all business, risky and non-risky.

If, however, the anticipated income stream is low in the early years and higher later, the current capital value of the enterprise may be very high relative to current income. If the income stream is expected to fall, capital value will on the contrary be relatively low. In this sense, the capital value tax, compared with the income tax, places a greater immediate financial burden on growing firms, or on their owners, than on declining firms.

In the event of failure of a risky venture, the income tax law can provide for a refund, or reduction, of earlier, current, or future income tax, through deduction of the operating loss or capital loss against the taxpayer's income from other sources. No such refund or reduction is provided by a tax based on capital. In this respect the capital tax is less favorable to risky enterprises than an income tax.

Also, the rate of a capital tax can be raised to a level where it is equal to more than 100 percent of the income, unless the capital value is adjusted downward promptly to reflect the effect of the tax itself (i.e., in theory, if the capital tax took more than 100 percent of the income, the business would have no capital value—or a negative value!—hence would pay no capital tax). Entrepreneurs, and savers and investors generally, may fear that a capital-value tax will be raised to such a rate, or near to it, whereas they are sure that no income tax will be imposed at more than 100 percent.

A capital tax is sometimes said to provide more incentive than an income tax because as one adds to his wealth by additional income that he saves, he pays only, say, 1 percent (wealth tax) on the increment as against, say 20 percent (income tax) on the increment of income (implying for equal-yield taxes, a profit rate of 5 percent). But the income tax is levied once-for-all on this increment; the wealth tax on it is repeated every year, as long as the increment is not consumed. Both taxes are therefore equal deterrents to extra work for income to be saved. On the other hand, the taxpayer who contemplates working overtime in order to increase his consumption may indeed be deterred by the income tax and not by the wealth tax (unless—an unlikely case—the wealth tax is levied almost continuously through time, so that it catches every increment of income, even those increments held but briefly before being spent).

A capital tax does not, in practice, reach human capital, like that built up by educational expenditures. The capital tax thus gives more incentive to additional effort for the purpose of financing one's education than does the income tax.

On balance, we should not expect to see a general tax on capital as a feature of a growth-oriented tax system. But the capital-tax idea would still be useful if it were limited in its application to certain physical factors of production, especially land, where it could play a stimulating role as a tax on potential rather than actual income. A tax on capital value is also applicable to durable consumer goods, especially houses; the effects of such a tax are covered in the discussion under numbers 4 and 5 below.

Agricultural enterprise generally contributes little to an income tax, anyway, because of administrative and political considerations. In theory, a tax on pure land rent, either as a rental value tax or as a capital value tax, would not restrict application of capital to agriculture and would not discourage rapid adoption of technological improvements. It would share with the income tax the disadvantage of coming, in part, out of savings (see number 5 below). Moreover, because of the difficult task of segregating the pure rent component from the total value of the farm real estate, a more practical approach would be a land tax based on a cadastre reflecting only potential or presumptive yield. Although the average rate of tax for any one agricultural enterprise might be high, the marginal rate would be close to zero, at least over the short term. However, if the cadastre were not revised for decades, it would lose its function of measuring potential yield, especially in money terms if inflation ensued. If the cadastre could be revised frequently enough, its measure of potential yield would capture for the government the increment of agricultural income arising from development; but to the same degree it might discourage development. This dilemma is inherent in any tax based on a potential that extends beyond a pure rent concept.

A sales tax, too, restrains entrepreneurship and risk-taking. If the venture turns out to be profitless, the entrepreneur is still responsible for payment of the tax. More generally: whether the tax is legally payable by the business firm or the consumer (spendings tax), any new venture must trim its estimates of demand for its product to allow for the sales tax load. A heavy excise tax on a particular product enhances these risks and financing problems, and tends to restrict entry of firms into the taxed industry. We do not know much about this aspect of sales taxation; a theory of risk-taking under sales taxation has not yet been fully developed. For the time being, we may perhaps assume that sales taxation is less inimical to risk-taking than an income tax without complete loss offset, but our view may change as this subject is explored further.

3. Where capital markets are so imperfect that commercial and industrial firms must expand chiefly from their undistributed profits, if at all, a growth-oriented tax system would impose little or no income tax on undistributed corporate profits, whatever its treatment of distributed profits, and it would attempt similar treatment for sole proprietorships and partnerships under the personal income tax.

4. To release resources for investment, the tax system would attempt to reduce what I here term non-gainful consumption. To reduce consumption in general by taxation is not difficult: almost any tax on the household will come partly out of consumption. But to reduce only non-gainful consumption is very difficult indeed.

5. If private generation and direct control of savings are considered important, the two-fold task of releasing resources from non-gainful consumption without also impairing the rate of private saving is even more difficult. This objective cannot readily be reached by changing the after-tax rate of return to the saver, because some households need an increase in reward to stimulate saving, while others will only increase their saving if the rate of return decreases. Thus there is no easy choice between the ordinary type of income tax, which lowers the rate at which future consumption can be substituted for present consumption, and the Irving Fisher-type of income tax, which would exempt saved income (an expenditure tax). Note that even a progressive-rate expenditure tax does not increase the rate of reward for postponing consumption if the tax rate is increased. Suppose, for example, that the interest rate is 6 percent, and that the expenditure tax is levied at a rate of 400 percent. Consider a taxpayer who has $500 to spend now: $400 in tax, $100 on goods. If he waits a year he will have $530 to spend then, of which $424 will go in tax, $106 in goods. His reward for waiting a year is just 6 percent, no more, no less, despite the high rate of the expenditure tax.

But if the taxpayer's choice is between spending now and saving indefinitely for the prestige and power that wealth gives him, a high-rate spendings tax may induce an appreciable restriction in his consumption. The extent to which the well-to-do members of the society make their choice in these terms must be gauged before a rational decision can be reached on whether a progressive-rate spendings tax will contribute significantly to economic growth.

Under a progressive-rate spendings tax, another factor enters: the individual's lifetime pattern of planned spending. If, before the spendings tax was introduced, his plan had been one for level spending throughout the remainder of his life, the progressivity of the rate scale results in the following comparison: a decrement in consumption now gives rise to a smaller increment in consumption in a later year (ex the interest factor, which, as just noted, is unaffected by the spendings tax). Only if the plan had been one for substantially declining spending in the future would the progressive feature of the spendings tax enable the taxpayer to get more consumption later by restricting consumption now.

Whether a permanent spendings tax encourages growth or discourages it, compared with an income tax, is thus very much an open question, to be answered only by consideration of the facts in each case.

A temporary spendings tax, on the other hand, can almost surely induce a substantial amount of saving. Such a tax would exercise so strong a substitution effect in favor of future consumption that on balance it would increase saving appreciably in the early periods, provided that the taxpayers believed in the time schedule. A low-income developing country may therefore gain a breathing spell for itself by imposing a high-rate spendings tax now, with the promise that the rate will be reduced beginning with, say, the fifth year from now, still more in the sixth year, and so on. The time schedule for the reductions in rate might be made roughly consistent with the expected increases in consumer goods from the capital investments to be made in the intervening years.

In part, the objective of having taxation come little if at all out of saving may be attained by taxing only those who save little or nothing. But even some of these households might dissave, to pay the tax. And the dangers of taxing gainful consumption have already been noted, not to mention the equity problem.

On balance, then, up to this point, a priori reasoning does not supply us with a neat blueprint for a tax system that will promote private saving (as distinct from private investment), at least any more than any other tax system of equal yield. A word must be added, however, on the estate and gift taxes, and on compulsory loans.

Death duties probably reduce private saving more than almost any other type of tax. The decedent-to-be probably does not try to save more, as death tax rates rise, in order that his heirs may receive a certain set sum; he is not usually a target saver on behalf of his heirs. The heirs, in turn, probably do not try to make good, by further saving (either before or after the death of their benefactor), the decrease in their net inheritances caused by a rise in death tax rates. In other words, an increase in the rates of a death duty probably does not check anyone's consumption appreciably. Thus a purely growth-oriented tax system would contain no death taxes, however necessary they might be on grounds of social justice, the disadvantages of concentration of wealth, and so on.

Compulsory loans, as through an income tax increase that will be refunded to the taxpayers in later years, are of little use for most underdeveloped countries. Since mass income taxation is not administratively practicable in most of those countries, a mass program of compulsory lending is likewise impracticable, or even more so. Compulsory lending from the higher-income groups in the economy is peculiarly likely to come largely "out of" saving, much more so than a straight nonrefundable income tax. The label "compulsory saving," sometimes attached to this device, is obviously a misnomer.

We must recall that not all the saving absorbed by the tax would have been available for investment within the taxing country. To the extent that the tax comes out of saving that would have been used to purchase, for instance, consols in London, it has little direct effect on the growth of the low-income country. Low-income countries probably differ widely in the degree to which the savings of their residents flow abroad for investment.

6. In some low-income countries certain natural resources can be sold on the world market, steadily, or at least in favorable years, at prices that are well above operating costs for the bulk of the output. The low-income country may be ex-

pected to share in that excess of receipts above cost, if it does not itself own the resources outright. The sharing may occur through a production tax, an export tax, or a profits tax. Or it may be realized through the profits of a marketing board, or indirectly by means of multiple exchange rates.

If these resources are owned by large foreign corporations, the tax or other revenue will probably not come out of saving, if by saving we mean saving available for investment within the country in question, not for investment abroad. A large oil company will probably not decrease its world-wide investment program because of the income effect of a special tax in one country. To the extent that it does so, the cutback may well occur in some other country. (The corporation's investment plans will of course be sensitive to the substitution effect of the tax.) If, on the other hand, the natural resource is owned by residents of the taxing country, the government's share will no doubt come in large part out of saving that would have sought investment within the country.

Outright government ownership makes it feasible to devote the entire profit to investment.

7. Shaping the tax system to encourage the supply of labor, as through marginal rates of tax little higher than, or even lower than, average rates, is designed to increase the total product, but says nothing with respect to the use of that product, hence nothing as to growth. Moreover, the practical possibilities of mass income taxation of wage earners or the self-employed in low-income countries are so limited that disincentive effects on labor are not likely to be important. Mass taxation through general sales taxes or heavy excises may pose rather more of a problem than is generally realized; in effect, part of the extra hour's wage is taken by tax.

8. What taxes remain in this hypothetical system designed solely to promote growth? Chiefly, taxes on wages above a low level, on salaries, and on professional earnings, and on land ownership, or taxes on personal expenditures by the recipients of these incomes. This is not a very attractive tax system from other points of view: equity, social justice, deconcentration of wealth and income, and so on. Perhaps no one would be willing to sacrifice these other objectives completely for the sake of growth. Yet it is instructive to see just where we may be led if we seek to "maximize" growth, a phrase that has no meaning unless we are willing to discard all other values.

Moreover, growth itself may be imperiled in the long run if these other social values are not kept in view. An economy growing rapidly but with an ever increasing concentration of wealth may generate social strains that one day will lead to a destruction of much of that wealth. Thus even from the narrow viewpoint of growth alone, the prescriptions given above must be qualified by these broader and longer-run considerations.

NON-ECONOMIC CHARACTERISTICS

We now turn to what may be called the non-economic features of the hypothetical tax system that is to be expected a priori in a low-income developing country, if the tax system is in fact oriented to development. These non-economic features have economic consequences, but they are themselves non-economic in the sense that they have to do with aspects of administration, legislative procedure, and similar matters.

Here, Adam Smith's maxims come again into prominence, especially those dealing with certainty and convenience.

1. The certainty factor is quite likely the most important non-economic aspect of a tax system for a developing country, and it may well exceed in importance any directly economic feature of the system. Private capital investment and private saving are strongly encouraged by a stable governmental fiscal system in which the tax consequences of any private action are fairly well known in advance. In addition to a stable price level (or conceivably an assured rate of inflation, which in practice seems most unlikely), the certainty criterion implies stability in tax legislation. This aspect of the certainty factor takes time to impress itself on the savers and the entrepreneurs. We might therefore expect to find in our hypothetical low-income developing country, if its tax system had for some time been oriented to growth, a record of absence of capricious change in tax legislation.

As Pigou (1949, p. 6) puts it, "unequal treatment of different people, where no good cause can be shown for it, leaves a sense of insecurity all around; for everyone feels that he may be the next victim," and this "indirectly strikes a blow at accumulation of capital." To this we may add that even if a good cause is shown for a particular instance of unequal treatment, insecurity may be bred if one good cause continually replaces another, with accompanying shifts in tax legislation.

2. The low-income developing country faces the question, how much resources in manpower, mechanization, materials, and so on should be poured into tax administration, to assure the climate of certainty, that is, to assure freedom from arbitrary discrimination or favoritism or foot-dragging that is necessary if long-term investment by private enterprise is to flourish. On these grounds a good argument can be made for alloting to tax administration in such a country a much larger proportion of the national income, or at least a much larger proportion of the tax revenues, than is found in more advanced economies. Usually there is a heritage of instability and discrimination that must be renounced by change to a carefully thought-out and precisely drafted body of tax law and regulations and by strict but fair enforcement. The task is the more difficult, in that a low-income developing country often has a large proportion of its money national income accounted for by the self-employed, and in every country the self-employed pose a most troublesome problem of tax enforcement.

In any event we have here something more than a comparison of the incremental yield of revenue with the incremental dollar of tax administration expense that produces that yield. Even if the immediate incremental yield is smaller than the incremental expenditure, the expense may be justified, if it makes the taxpayer feel protected from arbitrary taxing authority and from tax-favored or illicit competition, and thereby encourages him to the saving and investment that the country desires. In effect, part of the cost of tax administration in this instance should be termed a cost of obtaining a given volume of investment. By this reasoning, we might expect to see in our hypothetical country a tax administration staffed by some of most able and most devoted individuals, working with an administrative budget that would compare favorably with that of any of the developed countries.

3. The urgency of the administrative problem in the low-income developing economy is emphasized by the fact that the economy will normally include a substantial non-monetized sector, operating by barter or self-subsistence. If only the immediate revenue yield is to be considered, the monetized sector is the part to which administrative efforts must be directed; it is also the part that the law should tax most heavily. But if the country is to develop, the monetized sector must grow, relatively; the non-monetized sector must be monetized. Such a transformation will be impeded if legislation or administration causes the tax system to weigh more heavily on the monetized than on the non-monetized sector. For development, there can be but one answer: tax effectively (or even discriminate against) the non-monetized sector, even at an extremely high cost of tax administration.

4. Taxpayer compliance is perhaps but one aspect of tax administration but it can be cultivated, and no tax system can be effective without a considerable degree of it. Where compliance ends, and avoidance begins, through the sophisticated network of legal counsel, accounting advice, and the mechanics of litigation, is still an unsettled issue.

5. In principle, the tax system can be designed so that evasion of one tax tends to leave the taxpayer open to higher assessment under other taxes, or so that taxpayer M's endeavors to make sure that he is not overassessed lead to information that taxpayer N might attempt to hide (Higgins, 1959; Kaldor, 1956). If the tax system in question is desirable on other grounds, this feature is to be reckoned as somewhat of an advantage, but it is not worth purchasing at the cost of foregoing other features of merit. Usually the same results can be obtained by simply requiring the information (e.g., on inventories) in the administration of tax A that would be supplied, or on the basis of which the taxpayer would regulate his action, under tax B. The administrators of an income tax are justified in demanding from taxpayers, at least those of high income, detailed data on change of net worth from one year-end to the next, simply to check on the statements of taxable incomes.

6. The economy's structure of financial institutions and procedures will need to be reshaped somewhat, to aid in tax enforcement. Bearer securities must be prohibited; an independent and skilled accounting profession must be fostered; specialized law tribunals must be set up to handle tax cases.

SUMMARY

In practice, in most of the low-income developing countries the primary task of getting some revenue in, somehow or other, is so difficult that the choice among different types of tax system is very limited indeed, even when the revenue is no more than seven or eight percent of the national income. Legislative drafting skill, administrative talent, and taxpayer compliance are so lacking that there is little point to considering sophisticated tax systems. Fortunately for growth, the unsophisticated systems, relying largely on special excises, export duties, and shares in natural resources, are probably as growth-facilitating as are most of the other systems.

Indeed, it is the other values—equal treatment of equals, avoidance of socially dangerous concentration of wealth, promotion of a rational tax consciousness, and so on—that are being sacrificed by the existing tax systems of many of the underdeveloped countries, rather than the goal of growth. The sacrifice is being made, not so much from a desire for growth, as from the self-centered views of those who shape policy in those countries, from administrative limitations, and, no doubt, from indifference to the issues, growth or other.

NOTE

1. For example: let the tax rate be 40 percent and the investment $1,000. This investment is financed $400 by the state (the $1,000 expenditure is deducted from taxable income) and $600 by the enterprise. The state claims, in tax, 40 percent of the future income from the $1,000 investment. The value of this claim is presumably 40 percent of the $1,000 (since the present discounted value of the income stream is presumably $1,000), or $400.

4

Optimal Tax Reform

In effect, two traditions shaping development tax policy have been distinguished in the preceding discussion: the interventionist and the reductionist. As noted earlier, the interventionist tradition was represented in the early postwar period by such prominent analysts as Heller (1954), Kaldor (1965), and Lewis (1966): government not only *could* influence the achievement of a variety of policy objectives through the tax system, but it *should* do so. The reductionist tradition, harking back to classical economists, was long represented by the lone voice of Bauer (1957) but has recently secured a wider constituency, for reasons noted above: government not only *cannot* achieve many of the policy goals earlier postulated but it *should not*—or, as the "public choice" school would have it, will not—try to do so. This position is articulately argued by Lindbeck (1987): see chapter 5 below.

Interventionism is by no means a dead issue in public finance analysis, however. On the contrary, much of the most interesting theoretical work of recent decades has consisted precisely in setting out more clearly than ever before just what a well-intentioned government must know and do if it is to achieve its goals. Much of this literature has been subsumed under the generic title "optimal taxation."

The implications of the optimal tax approach for taxation in developing countries, as well as some applications, have recently been developed at length in a study published under the auspices of the World Bank (Newbery and Stern, 1987). The brief introduction contained in this chapter is excerpted from a paper by two of the leading practitioners in the field (Ahmad and Stern, 1986a). Although some of the terminology in this paper may perhaps turn off some readers, there is nothing here that should discourage anyone who has survived an introductory microeconomics course.

We think it is important to include this material both for its own sake and to give a flavor of how well-trained modern economists are likely, for better or worse, to approach the analysis of tax issues in developing countries. On the whole, while it is clear that the tools sketched here are as subject to misuse and misinterpretation as is economic analysis in general, and while we share the healthy skepticism expressed by Lindbeck in the next chapter with respect to some of the policy recommendations emerging from this analysis, we think that the increased formalization and rigor introduced in this analysis is all to the good.

The principal reason for this positive conclusion is the critical role of theory both in sorting out what has been called elsewhere "the grammar of the argument" (Atkinson and Stiglitz, 1980) and in providing the essential foundation for sound empirical work. Improvement in both respects is clearly needed in this as in most fields of applied economics.

It is, for example, simply not possible to talk intelligently about a multi-instrument, multi-objective policy like taxation without some formal analytical apparatus to enable us to keep straight what we are talking about. Some of the assumptions needed to make such analysis tractable may appear to render it too unrealistic to be directly applicable to policy. But what is the alternative: policy without theory? or theory that mirrors the complexity of the real world so closely that it becomes completely intractable and yields no answers at all, not even bad ones? In particular, as contentious as the use of a social welfare function in this literature may appear, we have at present no better way of attempting to depict and understand the nature of the efficiency-equity trade-off that lies at the heart of so many tax policy conundrums. At the very least, those who disagree with the policy implications emerging from this literature should, as a result of considering the kind of analysis set out here, be forced to think through their own assumptions more carefully and clearly than before.

Similarly, the kind of "empirical" analysis without theory which has characterized so much of the quantitative work on taxation and development (see Bird, 1976; Bird and De Wulf, 1973, for critiques of two such bodies of literature) is simply not possible in this framework. While the models set out in the optimal tax literature can seldom be estimated in any meaningful sense, nonetheless the careful empirical work done by practitioners such as Ahmad and Stern (1983, 1984, 1986b, 1987) on such questions as the design and reform of indirect taxation in India and Pakistan has no equal in the literature. Such analysis serves as a model—doubtless an imperfect one, but nevertheless a model—of the sort of empirical study that is needed to advance our knowledge of such critical issues as the distributional effects of the adoption of a value-added tax beyond the stage of guesswork (see also Bird and Miller, 1989a).

Despite its difficulty for some readers and its undoubted dangers and defects—as vividly set out by Lindbeck in the following chapter—we therefore commend close study of the Ahmad and Stern piece, and the associated literature set out most extensively in Newbery and Stern (1987), to all those interested in development tax issues. This approach is clearly particularly deficient in a number of ways: from a public choice perspective (Lindbeck, 1987); in the heavy demands it makes on the available data (Deaton, 1987); and in the very limited recognition it gives to the administrative dimension of tax reform (Bird, 1989a; Slemrod, forthcoming). In particular, the stress on the desirable nonuniformity of commodity taxation—one of the central theoretical results at the present stage of development of this analysis—is obviously subject to severe question on all these grounds (see Bird, 1985; Cnossen, 1982). Nonetheless, the merits of the optimal tax approach, judiciously employed, in our opinion on the whole substantially outweigh its demerits; so we unreservedly recommend that all students of development taxation become familiar with at least the rudiments of this approach, as set out in brief in the following extract.

The "optimal" approach to tax reform applied in the following excerpt requires, in addition to the unquestionably useful calculation of effective tax rates, the more controversial explicit quantification of welfare judgments. In principle, as noted earlier, this procedure, despite its obvious artificiality, is hard to criticize. Moreover, in practice all those engaged in reform exercises must in effect carry out such an analysis implicitly. The apparent reluctance of many to admit that such direct welfare comparisons are inherent in proposing tax changes probably reflects two facts of life. On the one hand is the continuing influence on today's economists of the 1930s revolt (Robbins, 1935) against the "old" welfare economics of Pigou (1932). On the other hand is the same squeamishness (not to mention inconsistency) that repels people when an economist asserts, for example, that by not abolishing level railway crossings a human life lost as a result is being implicitly valued at, say, $100,000, while saving an additional life through a heart transplant implies that a life is valued at, say, $1 million. The facts may be correct as stated, but people do not want to think about such issues in such a cold-blooded way. For the same reason, they may not want to hear that, say, adopting a uniform value-added tax implies that, as Ahmad and Stern would say, their "inequality aversion" coefficient is some unfashionably low value.

In our experience, however, the main problems in practice with the procedures advocated in this chapter have nothing to do with the questions of judgment and taste involved in the choice and use of social welfare functions. In the first place, the data requirements are very difficult to satisfy (Deaton, 1987). Ahmad and Stern, perhaps because they have worked primarily in two of the largest and statistically most sophisticated developing countries, appear to overestimate the availability and adequacy of data in most countries. Few developing countries have a good household survey or a good input-output table, and almost none have adequately estimated demand systems—all of which are required for calculating effective rates and estimating demand responses. Secondly, even if the data are available, one may well doubt in most countries whether the scarce talent available for tax analysis is really best employed in work of this nature rather than in the sorts of more eclectic analysis and fire-fighting sketched in chapter 6.

Nonetheless, in the long run, there is little doubt that the increasing sophistication of data bases, computational facilities, and academic training will combine to facilitate and produce more rigorous analysis along these lines in an increasing number of at least the larger developing countries (Newbery and Stern, 1987). Even at the present time, those interested in tax reform in developing countries can only gain by careful consideration of the interesting set of general policy principles and suggestions that emerges from even the bare outline in the following excerpt of the complex empirical and theoretical analysis of "optimal" tax reform in India and Pakistan. The case for a separate corporation income tax, the role of "presumptive" taxes, and the appropriate role and design of public sector prices and user charges, for example, are all touched on in this discussion, in addition to the central focus on the appropriate design of the indirect tax system.

The Analysis of Tax Reform for Developing Countries: Lessons from Research on Pakistan and India

Etisham Ahmad and Nicholas Stern

The central question we have sought to address is the one faced by governments of most developing countries: how best to raise additional revenue. In answering we should consider the consequences of extra taxation for different groups and households, the effects of possible changes on incentives and behavior, effects on the productive system and how the changes are to be enforced and at what cost. These issues are closely intertwined and the job of treating them together in a coherent way can be formidable. However, it is possible to combine many of the elements in one analysis, and one of our objectives was to develop systematic methods for doing this whilst taking proper account of those aspects which are less amenable to quantitative treatment.

Throughout the research the problems of administration, collection, and feasibility have been prominent. These considerations have been central to our treatment of data, our assumptions concerning how policies have been chosen, and in the agenda for reform. In the data, evasion and difficulties of collection are taken into account by using actual revenue collections rather than announced or legal rates. These are difficult to apply, even if there were no evasion, given the multiplicity of rates and exemptions. We also show how costs of collection can be explicitly incorporated into the theory and discussion of reform, in a way that could be easily adopted by policy makers.

Our overall recommendations flow from a combination of the basic principles, application of the techniques, examination and discussion of the practical matters of administration and collections, lessons from the experience and literature of public finance, and the politics of the country. Thus the techniques and principles presented here must not be considered in isolation. On the other hand, it would be misleading to ignore the contribution of economic analysis simply because other matters are relevant.

DESCRIPTION OF THE TAX SYSTEM

In discussing reform, one has to describe the existing tax system in a manner that permits proper understanding of the point of departure. Where the taxation of

Excerpted from Ahmad and Stern (1986a).

domestic and imported inputs—both intermediate goods and raw materials—is important, the description of the effects of taxation can be quite complicated. This is done with the help of an input-output framework with which we describe the direct and indirect effects of the taxation of interindustry transactions.

The analysis requires assumptions concerning shifting and a number are possible, ranging from 100 percent forward shifting to the case where the price of a good is exogenously determined and changes in input prices merely affect factor payments and not output prices. Thus, in a competitive model, crucial elements are the rebating or otherwise of taxes on inputs, the openness of the economy, and the relations between domestic and foreign products (e.g., the patterns of substitutes and complements in production and consumption), and the general equilibrium effects operating through factor prices. For this last aspect computable general equilibrium models may be useful. In the noncompetitive model a very broad range of outcomes is possible. The empirical evidence from Pakistan suggests that 100 percent shifting may not be an unreasonable assumption.

In both the India (Ahmad and Stern, 1983) and the Pakistan cases, a reliance on input taxation has meant that the tax element in the price of final goods, or effective tax, often appears quite different in comparison with nominal taxes. This may indicate, in some cases, the unintentional effects of government policy, which in both India and Pakistan succeeded in heavily taxing goods which they had apparently intended to subsidize, not to tax, or to tax lightly. Examples are provided in Ahmad and Stern (1986b) for Pakistan.

THE THEORY OF REFORM

In the theory of reform we try to characterize improvements relative to a given status quo, and for the India project we developed some simple methods for describing desirable directions of reform (see Ahmad and Stern, 1983 and 1984). This essentially involves the marginal cost in terms of welfare, λ_i, of raising an additional rupee of government revenue from taxation of the ith good. Thus, for constant revenue, one would increase the taxation of the ith good relative to the jth if $\lambda_i < \lambda_j$. The welfare cost of a unit tax change is determined by the money cost to households (equal to $x_1{}^h$), weighted by welfare weights (β^h) and aggregated across households. The revenue response to the price change involves aggregate demands (x_i), the effective taxes (t^e), and aggregate demand responses. We then have

$$\lambda_i = \frac{\sum_h \beta^h x_i^h}{x_i + t^e \cdot \dfrac{\mathbf{x}}{q_i}}, \qquad (4.1)$$

where β^h are the welfare weights, x_i^h the demand for commodity i by household h, x_i the aggregate demand for commodity i, t^e the vector of effective taxes, and $\mathbf{x}/q_i$ the vector of demand derivatives with respect to the ith price (for a derivation and further details see Ahmad and Stern, 1984).

The data requirements are the welfare weights β^h, the consumptions by household x^h, the tax rates t^e, and the aggregate demand responses. The β^h are value judgments which can be discussed directly and can be varied to allow for more or less egalitarian viewpoints. The x^h come from household surveys, the demand responses from estimates of consumer demand systems, and t^e is the vector of taxes on final goods (effective taxes).

We discuss briefly some of the problems of applying and extending the method of focusing on demand responses and tax rates. Usually it will be very difficult to estimate cross-price elasticities in any detail in demand analysis. The number of cross-price terms goes up as the square of the number of goods and the number of observations on each price is often small (for example, one per year or quarter). Thus many of the cross-price effects may be imposed by the demand structure selected for estimation. This may have important consequences for "optimal tax" calculations. For example, Atkinson (1977) showed that if everyone is identical except for the wage, preferences are described by the linear expenditure system, and there is an optimum uniform poll-subsidy or tax, then optimal commodity taxes are uniform. In the case of reform, however, sensitivity to the demand system is qualitatively less, since we do not predict individual demands away from the status quo but use actual or observed demands. The demand structure appears only in the aggregate terms in the denominator. We found that, for higher levels of inequality aversion (or when the poorer are accorded a higher welfare weight) the distributional characteristic dominates demand responses and determines the direction of reform.

The theoretical result is nevertheless very useful here since it (1) points to a practical advantage of the reform approach over optimality in using less information, (2) alerts us to the requirement to check on sensitivity to demand estimates, (3) emphasizes the importance of using actual rather than fitted values, and (4) leads us to ask about the role of poll-subsidies or taxes. This last point is an example of a very important and general principle concerning the interrelationship between different policies and the danger of looking at a single set of taxes in isolation. And in our applied work it led us to ask whether the combination of rations and subsidies could be construed as embodying an optimal poll-subsidy; we found that it could not.

REFORM AND SHADOW PRICES

The reform analysis discussed in the previous subsection forms part of the more general theory of shadow prices. The shadow price of a good is defined as the increase in social welfare when an extra unit of public supplies becomes available. This is the standard opportunity cost notion and is the only definition of shadow prices which permits their use as a test for identifying whether or not a project improves welfare. The welfare impact of a reform such as a price change is simply given by the direct effect on social welfare, through household welfare, less the cost of the extra net demands at shadow prices.

There are many economies where shadow prices have been calculated. We have seen that their use is not confined to project appraisal but applies also to the analysis of reform. Care should be taken, however, to ensure consistency of the models used in the reform discussion and those used to calculate shadow prices.

The shadow prices capture a great deal of information, essentially the full general equilibrium effects on welfare of a policy change. In principle they should be derived from a fully articulated general equilibrium model, and one could argue that if such a model is available then welfare effects of policy changes can be calculated directly. However, in many cases the set of shadow prices will be a tool which is more flexible, reliable, less demanding, and more easily understood than the full model. They provide sufficient statistics for policy from the full model and can be discussed directly. And one supposes that corresponding to any plausible set of shadow prices one could construct a general equilibrium model and welfare judgments which would be consistent with the shadow prices. Hence, for example, if one argued that population growth and better labor market policies were likely to bring about a substantial reduction in the shadow wage, one could then examine fairly rapidly the consequences for tax policy. On the other hand it may involve a great deal of effort to redesign a large model (if such already exists) to take account of the changed assumptions.

In our calculation of shadow prices for India and Pakistan we have used a standard Little/Mirrlees (1969) procedure. We thereby take account of the role of trade restrictions in distorting the prices producers face, imperfections in factor markets, and any premium on saving. Their calculation is based in large part on input-output data but this requires considerable extension. Different sets of shadow prices were calculated corresponding to different assumptions concerning the classification of tradeables and nontradeables and different valuations of factors.

DATA AND ESTIMATION

The methods we have described examine reform in terms of its effects on households, revenue, and production. The analysis of the consequences for households involves certain basic data requirements, including (1) revenue collections, by commodity group for indirect taxes and by income group for income taxes; (2) household income and expenditure information; and (3) interindustry transactions data or an input-output table. Some estimates of aggregate demand responses are also necessary if one is to make a judgment concerning the effects of reforms of indirect taxes on revenue. And a system of shadow prices is necessary to analyze the effects of reform on the production side. These sets of information are also useful for other analyses, and accumulating a systematic set has had several externalities.

TEN BASIC PRINCIPLES

We now take a step back from the detail and ask what kinds of tax policy the general application of these methods might bring. Thus we ask about the principles of tax design which emerge from the methods of modern public economics. We shall try to present in simple terms the conclusions and underlying arguments of relevance for tax policy in the countries under study. Given their main sources of revenue our focus is on indirect taxes and tariffs, although we shall comment briefly on the role of personal income and corporation taxes.

1. *It can be very misleading to look at one set of policies in isolation from others.* We have already seen one example of this in our discussion of the theory of reform, where we noted that theorems describing circumstances under which uniform indirect taxes are optimal include the assumption of an optimal poll-subsidy. Thus the status of the argument for uniformity depends critically on other policies (we discuss this further below). A second example, also discussed below, concerns public sector pricing and indirect taxes where inconsistency, misallocation, and substantial revenue loss can arise from treating them as separate topics subject to different principles.

2. *It can be costly to restrict the set of options.* An example here is land taxation. Inadequate or incompetent land taxation can lead to revenue being raised in ways which lead to substantial misallocations, for example agricultural prices being held too low. Or constitutional allocation of certain taxes to states (e.g., many sales taxes in India) may lead to the center using other tools with unfortunate consequences (e.g., excessive reliance on tariffs or domestic excises, which have important distorting effects).

3. *Indirect taxes should be levied on final consumption irrespective of origin.* This means that we should avoid the taxation of domestic or foreign intermediate goods through domestic excises or tariffs. The argument is essentially that different producers should face the same relative prices for goods if production is not to be inefficient. This cannot be true if the sale of a good between producers is taxed. The argument applies also to trade, since this may be seen as simply the production process of transforming one good into another through the world market. The application of the principle would involve rebating taxes on inputs and a VAT which applies also to imports is one way of doing this. Notice this could effectively dismantle protection. The argument may be justified formally in terms of the standard efficiency theorems (see, e.g., Dreze and Stern, 1987). The assumptions involved in the theorems point to the major exceptions to the principle. These are (a) where a final good cannot be taxed, certain forms of input taxation may be a surrogate, (b) where there are profits which cannot be taxed in other ways then again input taxation may be surrogate, and (c) where there are compelling reasons to help domestic industries through a process of adjustment, and there are no other ways of providing support, then protective tariffs may be justifiable.

4. *Public sector prices should be set according to the same principles as indirect taxes: this involves price equal to marginal social cost (MSC) for intermediate goods and MSC plus an element for taxation for final goods.* This is an application of the preceding principles where one simply notes that the difference between price and MSC plays the same role as a tax in that an increase impinges on the consumer or producer and the difference goes to the government. The amount for taxation in the case of final taxation should be based on the usual considerations of equity and efficiency summarized below. The MSC rule applies only for intermediate goods where we suppose revenue can be raised from taxation of the final good. The commonly advocated price equal to marginal cost rule applies for the usual

reasons, only in an economy where sufficient revenue can be raised by nondistorting taxes, and we take it that this is not a realistic possibility.

5. *Industries should be expanded where incremental output is profitable at shadow prices. Other indicators such as effective protection rates (EPRs) or domestic resource costs (DRCs) are only reliable if they coincide with shadow prices. There are many tools to encourage expansion: taxes, subsidies, infrastructure, and so on.* The first sentence is almost tautological if shadow prices are correctly defined, since they are designed and defined to measure improvements in welfare. The second sentence also follows automatically and is worth stating only because some appear to think that EPRs and DRCs are themselves reliable. The EPRs fail in general to take proper account of the opportunity cost of nontradeables and distortions in factors or markets since both are effectively valued at market prices and DRCs fail to take proper account of distortions in factor markets. These failures of EPRs and DRCs are explained clearly in Krueger (1972) and modifications can be made to bring them closer to shadow prices; and when equal to shadow prices, of course, they would become (theoretically) reliable measures.

6. *A reform rule which adjusts tariffs to move towards uniform effective protection is incorrect.* This follows immediately from principle 5. Two steps in the argument would be required and both are unreliable. The first step says that a decrease in the EPR for an industry with above average EPR will contract it and similarly an increase in the EPR for a below average industry would expand it. These movements cannot be taken for granted (see, e.g., Dixit and Norman, 1980). Second, we have just seen that the EPR rule for expansion and contraction is incorrect unless it coincides with the results using shadow prices.

7. *Indirect taxes should be guided by a trade-off between efficiency and equity.* Crudely speaking we want to raise revenue whilst distorting the overall pattern of consumption as little as possible and taking account of the distribution of consumption. Thus, and now very crudely, one taxes more heavily goods in inelastic demand and those consumed by the rich. This last version requires great care because one cannot consider goods in isolation and must both pay careful attention to the way substitution amongst goods affects revenue and consumption patterns and look at the way price and income elasticities interact (e.g., goods with low price elasticities may also have low income elasticities). Further the degree of concern with distribution will depend on how far other tools for income support have been utilized.

8. *In the absence of well-functioning schemes for income support there is no prescription for uniformity of indirect taxation.* Under certain special circumstances one can show that it is optimal to have uniform proportional indirect taxes. This involves close similarity of the income tax. One of the results was described above and there are different variants (see, e.g., Atkinson and Stiglitz, 1980). They all have in common the optimality of some form of income taxation. The weakest assumption concerning the income tax amongst these results (and it has to be married with the strongest assumption on preferences, i.e., identical linear Engel curves) is that there is an optimal poll-subsidy. It is relatively straightforward to check these assumptions and we suggest that the poll-subsidy would

usually in practice be substantially lower than the optimum would require (there are good administrative reasons for this), given any reasonable concern about distribution. It would therefore be desirable to take distribution into account in setting indirect taxes and this would mitigate in favor of lower taxes on goods consumed by the poor. The results are useful not only in clarifying the restrictive conditions under which such taxation is optimal but also in pointing to the interrelation between different forms of taxation and highlighting the distributional potential of taxes other than indirect. And one can argue that a system of family income support (e.g., child benefits or grants subsidized rations linked to family structure) greatly strengthens the case for uniformity in indirect taxation. Abandoning uniformity does not, however, mean that we need a plethora of rates. It is likely to be possible to go a long way towards accommodating distributional considerations using a few rates. We have found that three or four may be adequate.

It should be noted that this discussion of uniformity is in terms of taxes on *final* goods. There is nothing in the theory that supports uniform tariffs other than at the zero level. Tariffs would come in only insofar as they were levied on final goods or rebated on intermediate goods.

It is important to set these theoretical considerations side-by-side with those concerning administration and political pressures or interest groups. For administration uniformity has substantial advantages but nevertheless most countries would be capable of allowing certain exemptions, for example for food, and having one or two luxury rates together with, say excises on tobacco and alcohol. Such a system could probably be organized to accord quite well with the basic principles we have been describing. And it could be fairly robust against special pleading for low tax rates on particular goods from special interest groups.

9. *A central role of the corporation tax is as a means of taxing personal incomes.* Incomes and wealth accrue eventually to households, so there are difficulties in arguing for the taxation of the corporation as a separate entity. A primary reason for levying corporation tax is, we suggest, as a means for collecting personal income taxes. This would suggest a focus on dividends as the basis of taxation, and this lay behind our recommendations for Pakistan. Further reasons for corporation tax include the taxation of foreign capital and monopoly rents. There may also be a role for the tax in raising the overall level of saving should this be a goal of policy. A withholding of tax from dividends is an efficient means of collection.

10. *The same principles of equity and efficiency which underlie indirect taxation apply to the personal income tax.* The two forms of taxation impinge on the distribution of welfare and on incentives and they should be analyzed together. In most circumstances revenue requirements would be such that both were needed. The balance between the two would be determined using the principles already described (e.g., in 5 and 6 above) and considerations of administration and collection which are not the subject of this section.

SUMMARY

We have tried to distill some of the important results of the modern theory of public finance in a simple way. Some of the results, understandably, have long been important elements of the literature, but others, such as those concerning efficiency and input taxes, public sector pricing and uniformity are relatively new and often poorly understood. In the formation of policy these principles have to be combined with explicit calculations of the effects of reform and careful consideration of costs of collection and administration. This is what we attempted in Pakistan and India.

We have focused here on efficiency and distribution. It should be clear however that the analysis also concerns growth. To a large extent concern for growth is a concern for efficiency and distribution over time. Minimizing distortions in savings and investment markets is a key element in this and forms part of the approach. And any premium on savings and considerations of distribution over time should enter directly into the shadow prices and weights on different disposals of personal and corporate income. Similarly our analysis includes concern with the balance of payments. The efficient treatment of trade has been a central element. Thus a coherent approach embodies savings and foreign exchange directly in one analysis and it is misleading to think of savings, foreign exchange, and internal productivity/efficiency as separate compartments.

Our methods apply most directly to indirect taxes and public sector prices. These present for many developing countries the central revenue questions and the methods would therefore be well focused for analyses of tax reform elsewhere. The main data requirements: household expenditure surveys, tax collections by commodity, estimates of demand systems, and shadow prices are also quite widely available, or can be constructed.

On the overall structure of indirect taxes, our methods and principles would be likely to lead to a system of taxation based much more strongly on final goods than is presently the case. This would involve a move away from domestic excises and tariffs where these impinge on intermediate goods and raw materials, and towards a VAT or wholesale or retail sales taxation.

The rate structure of the indirect taxes should not in general be uniform. It could, however, be made fairly progressive with one or two luxury rates and certain exemptions. There could also be specific excises on certain goods such as tobacco, alcohol, and fuel.

One can therefore design a system of indirect taxes which accords well with the basic principles of policy in a constrained economy, with concern for efficient administration and with a desire for firmness against interest groups. It is therefore a mistake to direct our energies into a bogus horserace between good economic theory and good administration/politics. And the right way to do this is to understand theory properly and not, as some commentators appear to do, claim for it results concerning, for example, uniformity, which it does not provide.

The application of this approach to public-sector pricing would be likely to lead to substantially higher prices in many countries, particularly for final goods such as electricity. It may also raise prices for certain agricultural inputs where these are below marginal cost or where outputs cannot be taxed.

Important elements in the public-sector pricing and system involve fuel, power, and transport. These have not been a central part of our research because they have been studied intensively elsewhere, although not always with a clear understanding of the basic principles of public policy. However, the principles we have described can and should be applied in these sectors—for example, social marginal cost for intermediates and this plus an element for tax for final goods (or where the final good cannot be taxed). The usual public economics dictum of taxation for external diseconomies is important here, too, particularly for damage of roads and congestion in road transport.

In general there is nothing in the analysis here which would deviate from the old adage that land is the appropriate basis of taxation for agriculture.

With the personal and corporate income taxes the central issues are likely to be coverage, collection, and administration rather than those arising from detailed empirical or theoretical economic analysis. The analytical and administrative considerations, do, however, combine in pointing both to presumptive methods for calculating income and to dividends as the basis of corporate taxation. Presumptive methods are based on simple indicators of income or sales, or potential income as, for example, with land, and thus both disincentive and administrative problems may be eased.

Overall we would argue that there is now sufficient experience with the methods and understanding of the principles behind them for the approach to be usefully applied elsewhere. This may take the form of a substantial research project which could provide much useful data and detailed recommendations. On the other hand the basic principles and experience could also be very helpful to a more speedy mission which was seeking a package of recommendations to improve equity, efficiency, and revenue.

5

Market-oriented Taxation

The case for the "optimal" approach to tax reform in developing countries has been clearly made in the previous selection; the case against it is eloquently stated by Lindbeck in the following chapter. In addition, Lindbeck's paper serves to illustrate the wide variety of approaches more supply-oriented economists may take to tax issues: in contrast to Marsden in chapter 2, for instance, his emphasis is more on the structure rather than the level of taxation as the critical factor. Finally, and perhaps most importantly in the present context, this chapter provides a brief analysis and discussion of the important "political economy" dimension of taxation in developing countries.

The excerpt included here is taken from a broader paper (Lindbeck, 1987) concerned with all aspects of the public finances in developing countries adopting the sort of "liberalization" policies that are now not only commonly urged on them by agencies such as the World Bank but also represent more or less the conventional wisdom of the economics profession. The central aim of liberalization in this sense is, so to speak, to "get the prices right"—to allow the market to play the major role in the allocation of resources—and the principal means to be employed for this purpose is the reversal of existing policies—for example, reducing protectionism and related distortions, discouraging exports, freeing interest rates to find their market levels, and removing tax disincentives to save, invest, and work. In contrast to Marsden, for example, this orientation leads Lindbeck to urge the reduction and complete removal of investment incentives (see also Gillis, 1985; chapter 6 below). In contrast to Ahmad and Stern (chapter 4), it leads him to recommend uniform commodity taxes (but see Cnossen, 1978—chapter 29 below—for a compelling argument in support of continued reliance on selective taxes in many instances). In common with everybody, it leads him to stress the importance of administration (Bird, 1989a), though, again in common with almost everyone, no specific guidance is given as to what should be done to cope with administrative problems.

There is clearly much to be said for policies such as those proposed by Lindbeck; and, indeed, many authors have said much. With respect to trade policy, for example, Krueger (1978) and Bhagwati (1978) and with respect to monetary policy McKinnon (1973) and Shaw (1973) have provided book-length analyses of the virtues of market-oriented as opposed to *dirigiste* policies (see also Fry, 1988). As Lindbeck argues, similar assumptions about the fallibility of governments relative to markets (Wolf, 1988), and the relative unimportance of market imperfections, lead to similarly sweeping arguments in support of simplified and uniform taxes—and, some (but not Lindbeck) would add, lower taxes in general (Marsden, 1983; Krauss, 1983). In addition to the case Lindbeck makes with respect to uniform commodity taxes—levied uniformly, for reasons long known (Johnson, 1965; Gillis and McLure, 1971), on both imported and domestically-produced goods—similar arguments have led many to favor uniform marginal tax rates on investment (a point developed further in Parts 3 and 4) and low, if not single, rates on personal income (e.g., Collins, 1985).

The case for reducing marginal personal income tax rates has sometimes been linked, as Lindbeck suggests, to the widespread evasion of such taxes in developing countries. Plausible though it may appear, however, it is well-established in principle that there is no reason to expect lower tax rates in themselves to reduce evasion (Yitzhaki, 1986). Although the technical argument leading to this general conclusion is quite different, at a plebian level this perhaps surprising assertion may be explained as follows: if evasion is costless, that is, the probability of detection and penalization is infinitely small, as is the case in all too many countries, then the mere reduction of the nominal tax rate will have no effect at all on evasion.

Finally, in some respects perhaps the most important point Lindbeck makes, and one which should be taken seriously to heart by all would-be tax advisers, is his last objection to the optimal tax approach, namely, that there is no reason to assume that any relevant policy maker will follow such advice. What he does not say, but what is surely obvious, is that the same can be said of any approach to giving policy advice, including his own. Why should a politician who thinks markets are seriously distorted—perhaps simply because he does not like their outcome, perhaps because he is distressed by the misery of some of his fellow citizens, perhaps because he is more concerned to secure his country's sovereignty than to obtain higher incomes for his countrymen—pay any attention to advice premised on the assumption that markets function perfectly and that the outcome of market economics is the best of all possible worlds?

As Head (1968) cogently noted some years ago, in the end the persuasiveness of welfare norms in theory—whether explicitly stated, as in the optimal tax approach, or implicitly assumed, as is generally the case in the market-oriented approach—rests entirely on the extent to which people are persuaded by them in practice. Given the enormous difficulty of knowing what the real beliefs of policy makers are in one's own country, let alone in someone else's, most good tax advisers fall back on a pragmatic and eclectic approach, which may perhaps be summed up as a combination of an ethical approach, an acceptable approach, and a positivistic approach (Bird, 1970). The approach is ethical in the sense that the desirability of certain policy objectives (e.g., the growth of per capita income) is assumed. It is, it is hoped, acceptable in the sense that there is believed to be considerable congruence between these objectives and those of the ruling groups. And it is positivistic in the sense that, with respect to issues (e.g., the distributional effects of taxes) about which there is clearly concern but where the real interests of those in power are far from clear, it confines itself to presenting information that makes the alternatives clear. Advisers would, of course, be less than human if they did not occasionally overstep these bounds and try to slip in some of their own beliefs in the guise of implicit assumptions and sometimes even biased presentations of facts. Nonetheless, the relatively modest mandate suggested above seems more likely to produce advice that is perceived as useful, and perhaps even acceptable, than more grandiose attempts to short-cut the political process by tricking those in power into acting like benevolent dictators (or the "invisible hand"). Whether the advice thus proffered, even if accepted, can be successfully implemented, however, is another and quite different matter, as discussed further in Part 7.

Taxation in Market-oriented Developing Countries

Assar Lindbeck

The level and structure of taxes, subsidies, and tariffs differ so much between various developing countries that generalizations about their taxation problems are difficult. However, the general level of taxation in this group of countries is still usually much lower than that in developed countries—typically 10–25 percent of GDP, as compared to about 30–55 percent in Western Europe, 33 percent in the U.S. and 25 percent in Japan. Among developing countries for which information is available, the average tax share of GNP seems to have been about 18 percent in the early 1980s (Tanzi, 1987), with taxes on goods and services and foreign trade playing a much more important part than in developed countries. Thus, disincentive problems for private agents, due to a *generally* high level of tax rates, cannot possibly be a serious problem in most developing countries. However, these figures underestimate the "tax bite" for those sectors that actually pay the bulk of the taxes. (For instance, if we assume, as an extreme case, that agriculture pays no taxes at all, the average tax rate for the rest of the economy would be about 24 percent as compared to 18 for the entire economy.)

One dilemma, though, is that a given level of taxes (as a percent of GDP) may "hurt" people more in a poor than in a rich country by depressing an already very low level of private consumption. However, this is not really a problem of economic disincentives for private agents, but rather an issue concerning the ability, or disability, of the political process to generate a reasonable allocation and distribution of resources between private consumption, public consumption, and investment. It is also an issue of the efficiency of the allocation of investment, as in a country where this allocation is more efficient than in other countries, it is not necessary to squeeze private consumption so much by way of taxes.

It is not clear whether a liberalization of the economic system requires, or can be expected to result in, a higher or lower total level of taxation. Reductions in the level of tariffs no doubt raise the need for new tax sources. Moreover, if increased reliance on markets results in a more uneven distribution of income, and indeed if it is already *believed* that this is the case, the political process may generate strong pressure for more redistribution via public budgets and hence a need for tax increases.

However, there are also factors that *reduce* the need for taxes in connection with

Excerpted from Lindbeck (1987).

economic liberalization, since some expenditure items would tend to disappear, or at least fall. In particular, a reduction in the need for subsidies to enterprises—private as well as governmental—would be an important part of a shift to a more market-oriented economic system, provided profitability is kept up sufficiently, which requires that the real exchange rate is not overvalued. The need for taxes would also recede to some extent if public authorities shifted to a greater reliance on users' fees for various types of public services, a reform for which there are well-known allocative and efficiency arguments. A reduction of the public bureaucracy, and increased competition for public service agencies from private agents would further reduce the need for taxes—partly because competition would most likely increase efficiency in the public sector, and partly because the size of the public service sector would be smaller due to the existence of private alternatives.

Another feature of economic liberalization is that increased incentive for private saving would reduce the need for public saving, though the recent fall in public saving in some developing countries is a reason for not advising the authorities to make substantial tax reductions on this ground.

However, even though the level of taxes in most developing countries cannot be regarded as excessive, or "harmful," the *structure* of taxes, subsidies, and tariffs is certainly already a serious problem. It is hardly necessary to say that high and strongly selective tariffs and taxes on foreign trade—export discrimination policies—often result in a suboptimal size of foreign trade, and hence in an underutilization of the gains from the international division of labor. Indeed, it is today quite well established that such policies, often designed to promote "import substitution," when pursued for long periods (such as several decades), have been highly detrimental to most developing countries which have pursued them.

It is also quite clear that highly selective commodity taxes, as in fact implemented, have often created inefficiencies in the allocation of resources in the private sector, on both the consumption and the production side, without always providing advantages in terms of the distribution of income. And in cases where selective taxes and subsidies actually have improved the distribution of income (on the basis of certain values), the same improvements could perhaps in many cases have been achieved by a structure of taxes and subsidies with smaller efficiency costs.

Severe distortions may also come out of some other taxes. The provision of accelerated depreciation for investment and subsidies to some investment, in combination with payroll taxes on labor, may contribute to raising the wage/rental ratio—though recent increases in interest rates may have reversed this feature in several countries. Moreover, some developing countries do have quite high statutory *marginal* income tax rates for high-income groups, and sometimes also for middle-high income earners—such as households with two or three times the national average. For instance, according to a study by Sicat and Virmani (1987) referring to the situation in the early eighties for married couples with one earner and a "standard" number of children (three), about half out of fifty developing countries studied have marginal income tax rates above 30 percent for incomes three times the average, and about a third of the countries have marginal income tax rates of at least 40 percent for that (relative) income bracket. (The mean marginal rate was 34 percent for that income bracket, as compared to 19 percent for the middle-income bracket.) If separate statistics had been available for the former sector in urban areas we would certainly have found much higher figures. Of course, legal avoidance and illegal evasion mean that many taxpayers do not in fact pay those rates, even remotely. However, the statutory marginal rates are an indicator of the incentives to avoid and evade, which is part of the process by which marginal tax rates distort the allocation of resources and human effort.

Of course, an overhaul of the tax system makes perfectly good sense even without a shift to a more market-oriented system. However, a reform of the price and incentive system is clearly more crucial for a pronounced market-oriented system than for a highly regulated and centrally planned system, as the gains of shifting to a more market-oriented system cannot be fully achieved without reforming the price and incentive system in conformity with efficiency criteria. Indeed, this truth has been well illustrated in recent decades by the attempts of socialist countries in Eastern Europe to rely more heavily on markets and economic incentives. Moreover, if capital movements, too, are liberalized, it is important to adjust capital taxation to levels that make domestic and foreign wealth owners and firms willing to invest enough in the country in question, rather than abroad—and to allow remittances of earnings, as well as providing guarantees of property rights in general. Stability of the domestic currency is, of course, also crucial in this context. Indeed, the problem of "capital flight" in developing countries is to a large extent a "confidence problem" concerning property rights and the value of the domestic money.

What then are the most important specific changes to be considered in the tax system when an economy shifts over from regulations and central command to increased reliance on markets? Some economists may want to base their policy advice on sophisticated calculations of *optimal* tariffs, taxes, and subsidies. There is no doubt that the literature on optimum taxation has helped us understand the general problems of taxes and subsidies in cases where compromises have to be made between the requirements of tax revenues, on one hand, and the losses of economic efficiency due to the "excess burden" of positive marginal tax rates on the other. The literature on optimum income taxation has, for example, given precision to the old idea that marginal tax rates should be higher the smaller the elasticity of effort with respect to rewards is, *ceteris paribus*. And the literature on optimum commodity taxation has formalized old views among economists about how to make a compromise between the allocative efficiency of consumption and concern for the distribution of income. While in the interest of economic efficiency tax rates should be relatively high on goods and services for which the demand and supply elasticities are small, the rates should, for distributional reasons, be high also on goods and services that play a relatively important part in the consumption pattern of groups of households that are supposed to be discriminated against in redistribution policy; these groups are often, of course, high income earners. Taxes should, *ceteris paribus*, also be high on goods and services which are close complements, for the consumers, of untaxed or indeed untaxable goods and services, like leisure. Quite complex formulas have in fact been derived to strike a balance between these different, often conflicting aspects, using a social welfare function as the criterion for the trade-off (Atkinson and Stiglitz, 1980; Stern, 1984).

However, there are strong objections to the strategy of using such calculations *as a basis for actual policy advice*—in developing as well as developed countries. Firstly, formulas of optimum taxation catch only one, or possibly a few, types of mechanisms for adjustment by the individual agents, such as a shift between leisure and work, and/or between the consumption of different commodities. In reality there are, of course, myriads of other adjustment mechanisms for taxes, such as variations in the amount of do-it-yourself work and the intensity of work; adjustment of the level of saving and the composition of portfolios; changes in the level and type of investment in physical and human capital; changes of profession, workplace, or location of residence; emigration across national borders; the use of more time to search for tax loopholes, or even for cheating with taxes; etc. Formulas that would simultaneously reflect all such major adjustment mechanisms, or most of them, are quite simply beyond the range of useful analysis.

Secondly, even to derive an optimum tax formula that takes into account just *one single* type of adjustment mechanism, such as the choice between leisure and income, or between different consumer goods on the demand side, it is in fact necessary to rely on extremely special assumptions, such as identical preferences of all individuals, and special forms of the production function, such as Cobb-Douglas functions.

Thirdly, all optimum tax formulas, even rather modest ones, require statistical information that is not very reliable. Not only do we need an "arbitrarily" chosen social welfare function, but also information about individual capabilities and preferences, specific enough to quantify the sensitivity of the response to contemplated tax rate changes of the various types of adjustments that are supposed to be covered in the study. On most of this we will never get sufficiently reliable information. This is serious, as the tax rates that are derived from optimum tax formulas are very sensitive to alternative specifications of the various functions and the statistical parametrization.

Indeed, if all the necessary information on individual capabilities and preferences that is required for empirical application of the theory of optimum taxation were available, we would not be too far from the type of knowledge that is necessary to design lump-sum taxes and transfers, and hence *avoid* the economic distortions, which is the reason for choosing an optimum tax approach in the first place! More specifically, in order to design optimum tax systems we would need information about both individual abilities and preferences at the same time as it is the difficulty in obtaining information about matters like these which is the basic reason why we are not able to use lump-sum taxes, and hence why there is a case for a second-best solution by way of "optimum taxation."

Applications of the theory of optimum taxation are also confronted with a severe aggregation problem. More specifically, the tax rate that is assigned to a specific product in the context of an optimum tax formula depends crucially on the degree and type of aggregation of commodities. For instance, if furniture is put into the group of durable consumer goods, it gets one tax rate, but if it is put into some other group of goods it would get a different rate—or even a zero rate or a subsidy. In other words, the tax rate of an individual good will be highly arbitrary depending on which other goods and services it is lumped together with. This means that optimum taxation will to a large extent be "arbitrary taxation." It is in reality also difficult to group the goods in such a way that only consumers' goods are included in the tax base. Many inputs in the production process will in fact also be taxed, which means that distortions of the allocation of resources will arise from the production side as well, without these distortions being considered in the calculation of the optimum tax structure. Attempts to differentiate the tax rate of one and the same type of good when used for direct consumption and when used as an input in the production process are bound to raise severe problems of administration and evasion.

Several of these difficulties with optimum taxation are, of course, well known by the adherents of optimum taxation. But it seems to me that they have not taken these problems seriously enough when ruling out "traditional" principles of uniformity of commodity taxes and tariffs, as well as "comprehensive" income taxation with similar tax rates for all sources of income (for instance the so-called Haig-Simons principle). However, there is an even more fundamental objection to using optimum taxation as a basis for policy advice:

There is no reason to assume that politicians and public administrators would follow advice that is based on calculations of optimum taxation by the help of some (assumed) social welfare function. Politicians have their own targets and ambitions, which may not bear much relation to the ideas which lie behind calculations by economists of optimum tax or tariff structures. Indeed this is exactly the background for various attempts in recent years to endogenize the behavior of politicians and public administrators, as well as for suggestions tying the behavior of politicians to various types of "rules." More generally, there is no reason to assume that tax rates that are the outcome of political processes—with conflicts and compromises between various political parties and interest group organizations—would be much correlated to the tax structure that some economists may derive from optimization calculations.

This point about political behavior is important regardless of whether the main ambition of politicians is to satisfy some strong interest group, to increase the probability of being elected, or to adhere to some personal or ideological idiosyncrasy. Politicians and public administrators, with the help of their economic advisers, can always present some reasonable-sounding argument for their particular choice of a differentiated structure of taxes and subsidies—for instance by referring to aspects that have not been considered in the calculations of the optimum tax specialist, or by exploiting the wide choice of "reasonable" elasticities of the demand and supply responses to taxes. The fact that calculated "optimum rates" for individual goods depend crucially on how goods are aggregated also opens the possibility for various interest groups to argue about the "proper" way of aggregating goods in official statistics.

If optimum tax theory then is not the most appropriate basis for tax policy advice in developing countries (or developed ones for that matter), what types of considerations should be used instead? The general answer, in my judgment, is that it is better to rely on approaches that are less ambitious and less demanding concerning knowledge about private behavior patterns, statistical information, and administrative competence, but instead more ambitious with respect to basic insights about the functioning of the political process. In other words, it is important to focus on more "pedestrian," practical, and common sense-oriented aspects than those emphasized in the optimum tax literature. For instance, the following types of tax reforms are worth considering in a great number of developing countries:

1. As several developing countries, in particular those in Latin America, often have high and highly variable rates of inflation, an adjustment of tax assessment and tax collection to inflation is often crucial. Though inflation functions as an implicit "inflation tax" on the stock of money and government bonds (with less than fully adjusted interest to inflation), inflation often also implies that the government loses "explicit" tax revenues in real terms due to the time lags in tax collection. Inflation often also erodes the tax base, because of the deductibility of *nominal* interest rates, which in an inflationary situation means that part of the amortization of the debt, in real terms, can be deducted from the tax base. If the latter two effects dominate the former, inflation will generate (or accentuate) higher budget deficits (in real terms), which then often feed back into even higher inflation rates. Obvious reforms to solve these problems are to shorten the time lags in tax collection, make inflation adjustments to the tax rates (or tax brackets), and redefine the tax base in order to make a distinction in real terms between (deductible) interest payments and (nondeductible) amortization.

2. As the tax base is often very narrow in developing countries, the tax rates are often relatively high for certain sectors and groups of taxpayers. For instance, in many developing countries today income taxation is, in fact, mainly a tax on public servants and employees of large corporations, rather than on capital owners, or on employers and employees in agriculture or in the "informal" urban sectors. The tax system is also plagued with other types of "asymmetries" with respect to the effective tax rates for different agents and sources of income, and these asymmetries are often accentuated by inflation. These asymmetries could, of course, be mitigated by moving in the direction of a Haig-Simons type "comprehensive" income tax, with uniformity between different sources of incomes, different assets, and different types of income earners. Basically that would mean a broadening of the base and a lowering of the rates—as has recently been tried in some developed countries. The tax system would then, most likely, be improved both in terms of efficiency and equity (and perhaps even equality), while attempts to make differentiations based on optimum tax formulas are likely to be exploited by various interest groups in their own self-interest. In other words, uniformity, as the basic rule of taxation, is probably less vulnerable to manipulation by powerful interest groups than is the principle of "differentiation" according to optimum tax principles.

3. As the small degree of household saving that exists in most developing countries largely takes place among the very top income earners, attempts to

redistribute income from these groups *on a large scale* are likely to conflict with ambitions to stimulate private saving and to increase the supply of risk-capital. This is a reason for being careful about heavy increases in income and wealth taxes for upper-middle and high income groups. Moreover, as corporate saving plays an important part in aggregate saving in some developing countries, and could play an even more important part in the future, there is a strong case also against raising taxes drastically on corporations.

Superficially, it may be argued that tax increases that reduce private saving are not really a problem, as it does not matter if saving is done by private agents or public authorities. However, this argument is seriously flawed for two reasons. First, it neglects imperfections in the political process in the sense that tax increases that are originally designed to increase public saving often, in fact, will release increased public consumption or subsidies of private consumption. Second, public saving is *not* a perfect substitute for private saving in market-oriented economies, as private saving contributes to a decentralization of decisions regarding investment, the entry of new firms, and innovation. To keep down private consumption is not the only purpose of saving; another important role which it plays in market-oriented economies is to allow and stimulate the emergence of a system of decentralized decision making, and hence to help channel resources to alternative types of assets in an efficient way.

Indeed, it may be argued that one of the most important prerequisites for a successful shift to a more market-oriented economic system is just this, namely the stimulation of private saving—a conclusion that follows from informal (Hayek- and Schumpeter-type) common sense views on the functioning of markets, rather than from formalized general equilibrium theories.

In fact the history of economic development in the Western world during the last one or two hundred years illustrates vividly the importance of private saving and private supply of capital for the entry and growth of new firms, for entrepreneurship, and hence also for innovation. In other words, it is difficult to keep an important role for the entrepreneur if the private capitalist is destroyed—partly because these are often the same persons. Thus, while both centrally regulated economies and market-oriented economies have to be careful not to destroy incentives to work, it is in market-oriented economies also important to watch out for disincentive effects on private saving and entrepreneurship. This means, of course, that certain sacrifices have to be made in the ambition to redistribute incomes from high to low income groups—though less so in the case of redistribution from economically "passive" groups, such as traditional wealth holders keeping their assets in idle land and various types of collectors' items.

What then are the conclusions for indirect (commodity) taxation? My basic assertion is that if we opt for a reasonably nondistorting structure of taxes, tariffs, and subsidies, it is advisable to choose, at least as a starting point, a uniform structure (same tax rate on every commodity and the same tariff rate on every importable)—rather than attempting to find some optimum tax structure. The rationale simply being to avoid a situation where something even further away from an optimum structure will *in fact* be implemented by way of party competition and the influence of strong interest groups. It is difficult for voters to judge if a highly differentiated tax structure reflects an attempt to implement "optimum tax rates" or if it is simply designed to assist some politically strong pressure groups. It is probably easier for voters to judge on this matter if the norm is a proportional structure of indirect taxes, rather than some asserted optimum structure.

Moreover, it is likely that highly selective taxes and subsidies, like direct regulations, breed both "rent seeking," via political lobbying, and corruption (Myrdal, 1968). This means that while a liberalization of the economic system in developing countries is most likely a necessary requirement for a drastic removal of rent seeking and corruption, this outcome could partly be jeopardized if a system of highly selective taxes and subsidies is introduced, as suggested by proponents of optimum tax theory.

An obvious objection to this reasoning is that it may, in fact, be difficult to induce politicians to follow a norm about uniform indirect taxes and tariffs. However, it is well known that politicians sometimes may find it in their own interest to "strait-jacket" themselves by accepting various types of norms— obvious examples being international GATT (General Agreement on Tariffs and Trade) rules on tariffs. Indeed, commitment by way of binding rules has been discussed frequently in game theory in recent years, emphasizing that this may be a method of preventing various groups in society from exploiting the difficulties of the government, without such rules, to commit itself in advance to a policy which it would like to pursue.

A braver strategy would be to use a uniform tax structure as the *basis* for the tax system, but to allow some additional, selective taxes on goods for which there are really strong and uncontroversial reasons to believe (1) that the supply and demand elasticities are very low, and (2) that the goods are consumed proportionally much less among groups of citizens with low incomes than among high-income groups (assuming that an improvement in incomes of low-income groups relative to high-income groups is desired). Of course, there is then an equivalent case for deviating from the basically proportional tax structure by low tax rates (or even selective indirect subsidies) on goods and services for which there is overwhelming reason to assume have the opposite characteristics.

Such a modification of a strategy of uniform indirect taxes would be a modest attempt to accommodate some of the basic ideas of the optimum tax theory, without using that theory as the basic foundation for tax policy recommendations. It would differ from the idea of optimum taxation in the sense that (1) attempts to adjust tax rates to differences in demand and supply elasticities would be the exception rather than the rule, and (2) consideration to the functioning of the political process would be paramount.

However, in a short- and medium-term perspective, the most important aspect of tax reform in developing countries is probably to improve tax collection and tax compliance. Not only is the administrative capacity of the tax authorities often weak, but in addition, firms are often small and difficult to control, and the loyalty to the national state is rather limited in some developing countries—often due to historical experience. Greater uniformity and less differentiation in the treatment of different taxpayers, products, and sources of incomes may often facilitate both tax administration and tax compliance. Moreover, it may be advisable to use a sales tax on wholesale trade rather than a comprehensive value-added tax or a sales tax in retailing. Reductions in the element of "arbitrary discretion" by local tax collectors may also help to increase voluntary tax compliance, as would the earlier suggestion about a broader base and lower rates.

To summarize my general points on tax policies: policy advice that relies on (1) sophisticated analytical techniques, combined with (2) extreme oversimplifications of the functioning of the economic system, (3) enormous requirements of sophisticated statistical information, and (4) total neglect of the functioning of the political end administrative system, is likely to create more distortions than would recommendation of simple rules of thumb, using uniform and broadly based taxes and tariffs—possibly modified by some selective taxes or subsidies where the case for such a modification is particularly strong. Thus, there is a strong case for the "traditional" recommendation in public finance of a "comprehensive" income tax a la Haig-Simons, with uniform rates between different sources of income assets and types of income earners, and a similar case for uniformity of the tax rates for commodity taxation as the basic starting point, though exceptions may be made where strong cases can be put forward.

Part Two

Lessons from Experience

One way to approach the fiscal problems of a developing country is to draw upon the literature to construct a model fiscal system, to examine the actual situation in order to determine precisely how it diverges from that model, and then to suggest how the existing system may be transformed into something more closely approximating the ideal. This approach, in the hands of a skilled practitioner, may sometimes be of great value. It suffers, however, from the important shortcoming that it does not generally require close enough examination of the country in question to ensure that the assumptions postulated in the model are consistent with reality, that the changes proposed can in fact be successfully implemented, or that, if implemented, they will produce the desired results.

An alternative approach is first to study in detail the existing system to determine precisely how it works and why it works that way in order to provide a firmer basis for understanding what changes may be both desirable and feasible. Of course, the relevant literature is again drawn on for guidance and ideas, but the emphasis in this approach is more on what *can* be done in the country in question than on what *should*, in some abstract sense, be done in the name of development, redistribution, or whatever. Analysts taking this approach are therefore likely to make more conservative, incremental recommendations for change than those taking the first approach sketched above.

Examples of both approaches to development taxation may readily be found in the literature. The more far-reaching and ambitious proposals made in some developing countries, generally by foreign-led missions, have sometimes proved to be invaluable in introducing new ideas and in widening the agenda of tax reform. Sometimes, as in the case of the Shoup mission in Japan (Shoup et al., 1949) and the Musgrave mission in Colombia (Musgrave and Gillis, 1971), such proposals have both influenced later tax reforms and to a considerable extent served as a reference point for subsequent fiscal discussion. In other cases, such as the Shoup mission in Liberia (Shoup et al., 1970) and the Musgrave mission in Bolivia (Musgrave, 1981), comprehensive reports have had little obvious effect on either policy or subsequent discussion.

Most tax policy most of the time in most countries is in any case concerned with small changes over short time horizons. Less ambitious studies, which in effect accept more administrative and political constraints as immutable for the immediate future, may thus in the long run play a more important role in influencing policy, although by their very nature such studies are less likely to appear in published form.

Whichever approach to reform is taken, there is much to be learned through a close study of experience. Indeed, one of the attractions of development finance as a field, apart from its intrinsic importance—there are few good ideas in development policy that do not have budgetary implications—is the extent and variety of experience available to be studied. Almost every developing country faces, or at least thinks it faces, the same tax problem: not enough money! Nonetheless, study of the problems of development taxation seen in different contexts yields new understanding. In our own experience, for example, we have never yet looked at an old tax problem in a new setting without learning something new about technique or impact or why differences exist. One important reason for including some case studies in this book is simply to convey to the reader something of the contrasts of experience.

Most of this book inevitably focuses on particular aspects of taxation in developing countries: the effect of taxes and tax incentives on investment, the effect of inflation on taxes, the structure of income taxes, how to levy a sales tax, and so on. Such questions are of course important and worth close consideration. In reality, however, none of them arises in isolation. Each feature of a tax system must be understood as part of a *system*—and, as some of the selections included here emphasize, not simply a tax system but a political-economic-administrative system as a whole. A second salutary purpose of these case studies is therefore to provide the reader with a broader overview of the problems of development taxation in different contexts.

Finally, a third purpose served by the inclusion of these case studies is to illustrate, so to speak, method in action. Each of the four chapters included here in a sense represents a different approach to the analysis of development taxation: Chapter 6, on Indonesia, for example, illustrates what may be called the comprehensive, eclectic approach to tax reform. This paper describes both what was recommended and why. The next two items, though quite different in nature, similarly present retrospective views of particular tax reform experiences. Chapter 7, on Korea, summarizes what may perhaps be labeled an "aggregative" economic analysis of the role of taxation in the impressive economic development of that country. In contrast, chapter 8, on Israel, presents an administrative and political critique of a tax reform inspired and shaped by economists. Finally, chapter 9 contains a useful overview of tax reform in developing countries. The full diversity of experience and the richness of the subject cannot really be conveyed in only four excerpts from a vast literature, but at the very least this part should provide an excellent starting point for further explorations.

6

Comprehensive Tax Reform

One of the most far-reaching tax reforms in any developing country in recent years took place in Indonesia in the early 1980s. Chapter 6, excerpted from a paper by Malcolm Gillis (1985), who led the large team of expatriate experts involved in this reform, both outlines the content of this reform and sets out clearly just how the reform package was designed. This paper also serves to introduce and supplement Parts 3 and 4 by touching on many aspects of incentives and direct taxation.

To begin with, Gillis briefly sketches the organization and nature of some of the earlier tax reform studies carried out largely by foreign experts, such as those led by Carl Shoup in Japan, Venezuela, and Liberia (Shoup et al., 1949, 1959, 1970) and by Richard Musgrave in Colombia and Bolivia (1981, Musgrave and Gillis, 1971). Since similar missions continue to be mounted—for example, in Jamaica (Bahl, forthcoming), Zimbabwe (Chelliah, 1986) and, again, Colombia (McLure et al., 1988)—Gillis's observations both on the earlier experience and on what he sees as the unique features of Indonesia are well worth reading.

One interesting question that may be raised about such large-scale missions concerns the relevant role of foreign and domestic participants. Gillis, for example, stresses that the desire on the part of policy makers both to get implementable policies out of the reform effort and to maintain a low profile for foreigners was behind the critical organizational decisions not to have a large resident group of foreign experts, to develop policies carefully and in detail over a substantial period of time, and to envisage the product of the effort as a series of tax changes rather than a major published report. What he perhaps does not emphasize sufficiently is the dependence of each of these decisions on two crucial factors: first, the relatively stable position of the governing group in Indonesia and, second, the close relation of trust he himself had built up over the years with the major Indonesian decision makers in this field.

In the absence of such stability and such trust, the situation in other countries may often be very different. Sometimes, for example, tax reform has been, so to speak, thrust upon the country, as was the case in Japan under the American occupation and as is often the case with respect to studies carried out under the auspices of international lending agencies. Sometimes, foreign advice is sought by one group in a relatively unstable political situation, and by the time the work is finished another group is in power, as happened in Bolivia, Venezuela, and Colombia. In these circumstances, it may be essential to work much more quickly than in the Indonesian case and to publish a report that will be ready on the shelf when tax reform again seems possible. This strategy worked quite well in Colombia, for example (see Gillis and McLure, 1977), and to some extent also in Venezuela (Gittes, 1968)—though not at all in Liberia.

In still other circumstances, domestic expertise may be sufficiently developed to permit the role of foreign advisers to be reduced to that of catalyst rather than prime source of reform ideas. Perhaps the best example of this process is again Colombia where, by the 1980s, it was possible in some fields for major reform initiatives to be largely shaped (Bird, 1984) and subsequently implemented (Bird, forthcoming) by Colombians—although in other cases the role of foreign experts was still dominant (McLure et al., 1988).

The main lesson to be learned from the Indonesian experience may be simply the obvious one that the best way to organize and carry out a major tax reform effort depends more on the circumstances of the country in question than on any general lessons that may be derived from experience elsewhere. Some of the other lessons drawn by Gillis from the Indonesian experience seem of more general value, however. In particular, his stress on the importance of the non-economic component of successful tax reform experiences—for example, the need to involve lawyers from the beginning and to view legislative drafting as part of the reform process, as well as his repeated stress on the administrative aspects of reform—is surely universally applicable. Unfortunately, as Gillis makes clear and as experience in all too many other countries supports, it generally turns out to be much more difficult to reform tax administration than tax policy, a point which is further emphasized in chapter 8. Some (e.g., Bird, 1989a) have concluded from this fact that it may be desirable, even necessary, to take this critical administrative constraint on tax reform more into account than seems to have been the case in Indonesia.

Another interesting question raised by Gillis concerns the appropriate scope of tax reform. As he notes, the Indonesian reformers were in effect given a clean slate—and indeed used the leeway thus afforded by going so far as to abolish all tax incentives for investment! Most comprehensive tax reform reports have similarly assumed that the task at hand was to design a new tax system from scratch and made similarly far-reaching recommendations, if not usually with such apparent success.

As a rule, however, and certainly in the absence of a relatively strong government such as that in Indonesia, the prospects for comprehensive tax reform in most developing countries do not seem great. Indeed, it may even be argued that attempting to do too much may sometimes hamper rather than facilitate tax reform—for example, by stirring up too much opposition from powerful groups. Perhaps the best that may be hoped for in such circumstances is to shape the inevitable responses to recurring fiscal crises in a way that creates an improved tax structure over time, a task which would seem to require the establishment of an ongoing tax analysis division rather than reliance on a flying group of foreign experts (Bird, 1970a; McIntyre and Oldman, 1975). Even in this case, however, periodic review and appraisal by outsiders may occasionally prove useful in setting out the long-term goals for tax improvement, particularly if the results are published and may thus enter into public discussion.

Two additional contributions in Gillis's stimulating paper deserve brief note. The first is the very useful characterization of different reform issues in terms of their complexity, importance, and, especially, their conflict potential. This approach, while reminiscent of Carl Shoup's (1969) division of policy issues into consensus and conflict issues, goes considerably beyond it. Anyone contemplating undertaking a major tax reform in any country would seem well-advised to undertake a similar classification exercise and to concentrate always scarce analytical resources on the main critical issues rather than dissipating them across the endless list of topics that might conceivably be studied.

The second point is the strong emphasis placed in Indonesia on the revenue requirements of the tax reform. In contrast to some earlier writings on tax reform in developing countries (e.g., Heller, 1954), it is perhaps fair to say that there has in recent years been an increasing tendency to emphasize that the main function of tax systems in developing countries is simply to raise revenues. For most such countries most of the time, what this usually means is *more* revenues. Following a path of analysis apparently first set out clearly by Musgrave (1965) for Korea, the Indonesian tax reform was largely motivated by the apparent need to enhance both the size and the elasticity of non-oil revenues.

Two comments may be made about this approach. First, it is probably correct to say that the major motivation for tax "reform" in developing countries generally has been, and will likely continue to be, the felt need (by someone with influence) for increased tax revenues. If so, however, it would seem to follow that the analytically correct way to consider such matters as the distributive effects of tax reform would be to take into account the effects of the expenditures thus financed rather than to follow the "differential" tax incidence approach generally used to analyze distributional outcomes, whether in Indonesia or, to cite another recent major reform, Jamaica (Wasylenko, 1986, 1987). Depending upon whether it is assumed that, in the absence of additional taxes, expenditures would be lower or, more likely, reliance on inflationary finance greater, either an absolute or a balanced budget approach to incidence analysis would seem required (Musgrave, 1959; Break, 1974). Of course, many other questions might be raised concerning the meaningfulness of the distributional analysis of comprehensive tax reforms, but this point cannot be pursued here: see Bird, 1980; De Wulf, 1975; McLure, 1987, for critiques of conventional incidence analysis.

An even more important point in the context of this book concerns the exclusive concentration, in Indonesia, on the tax side of the budget. In reality, neither the "need" for additional tax revenues nor the ease of obtaining those revenues can be severed from questions of the structure and efficiency of expenditures. One cannot discuss everything, and even the most comprehensive analysis must draw the line somewhere. It is unfortunate, however, that so often the line is drawn so as to exclude all discussion of such alternatives to comprehensive tax reform as improved expenditure control (but see, for exceptions, Musgrave, 1981; Bird, 1984), more use of "user charges" and benefit finance (Bird, 1976a; Jimenez, 1987), or alternative methods of providing public services (Roth, 1987). The inevitable concentration of most of the tax literature—and of course the present book—on tax issues should not blind the reader to the great, and possibly overriding, importance of such nontax aspects of public finance in shaping what sort of tax system is desirable, or feasible, in a particular country at a particular time.

Micro- and Macroeconomics
of Tax Reform: Indonesia

Malcolm Gillis

The government of Indonesia adopted a major tax reform in late 1983. The new legislation replaces income tax laws enacted decades earlier by the former Dutch colonial administration and a sales tax enacted in 1951. Complete overhaul was necessary. Use of higher tax rates for revenue purposes or other forms of tinkering with the old system were never seriously considered. The reformed system contrasts sharply with tax regimes reflecting decades of traditions of fine-tuning tax instruments to achieve multiple objectives; the impact of the reform upon income distribution should nevertheless be positive.

The reform legislation as enacted was to a significant extent based on the view that, in the Indonesian context if not elsewhere, the principal function of a tax system is that of raising revenues. The reform represents an attempt to secure revenue, income distribution, and efficiency goals by reliance upon a vastly simplified tax system imposed on a very broad base, at rates appreciably lower than in most LDCs and North America,[1] but not very dissimilar from rates used in Pacific Asia. The income tax contains several innovations and applies both to individuals and to businesses. The new value-added tax (VAT) does not yet extend to the retail level, for administrative reasons, but is one of the few examples of a VAT imposed at a uniform rate on all taxable transactions with no exemption by product category.

APPROACHES TO TAX REFORM

Antecedents

More has been written, to perhaps less effect, on the topic of tax reform than perhaps any other set of economic policy issues in LDCs. Still, there have been several comprehensive proposals that are especially salient, not so much for having been successfully incorporated in actual reform legislation by governments, but because of the residue of theoretical and applied insights they left. The prototypical study was that led by Carl Shoup for the war-torn (then less-developed) Japanese economy in 1949 (Shoup et al., 1949). Over the next three

Excerpted from Gillis (1985). Gillis was organizer and director of a twenty-eight–member technical expatriate team on Indonesian tax reform. The team consisted of economists, lawyers, tax administrators, accountants, and computer scientists from eight nations.

decades, Shoup, together with another internationally known fiscal theorist, Richard Musgrave, organized and crafted innovative reform packages in countries as diverse as Japan, Liberia, and Venezuela (Shoup), Colombia, Korea, Taiwan, and Bolivia (Musgrave). Quite apart from the fact that parts of many proposals were enacted into law, particularly in Colombia and Japan, each of these comprehensive tax reform proposals generated important lessons for later undertakings of this genre. The Shoup mission to Japan was perhaps the first example wherein a group of distinguished analysts had the opportunity to apply their formal skills to the revamping of an entire tax structure. The Shoup report also contained the first detailed concrete proposal for value-added taxation in the English language. The Shoup study of Venezuelan taxation was one of the first to provide a modern, systematic treatment of natural resource tax issues in the context of tax reform. The Shoup volume for Liberia brought to the tax reform literature applications of innovations in economic analysis outside of public finance, including topics in effective protection and national income accounting. The 1968 Musgrave Colombia Commission unhesitatingly incorporated a number of earlier tax reform proposals by Taylor (Taylor et al., 1965) and Bird (1970a), but went well beyond both studies. This undertaking was distinctive for several reasons, not least of which was that six years later most of the Musgrave Commission proposals were adopted in a comprehensive tax reform. This was also perhaps the first reform package conditioned to specific revenue targets derived from forecasts of the expenditure side of the budget. And, while earlier Shoup missions had utilized lawyers, the Musgrave Colombia study was the first to make integral use of an international team of expatriate and local lawyers to draft actual tax reform legislation. Finally, the Musgrave Bolivia report went much further than previous efforts in stressing the interplay between tax policy and other policy instruments including exchange rate, monetary, and agricultural as well as expenditure policies.

There were four basic similarities between the comprehensive tax reform studies cited above. First, each of the efforts was undertaken under tight time constraints. The 1968 Musgrave Commission report had to be completed in nine months from the day it was first requested by President Carlos Lleras; the 1975–76 Musgrave Bolivia report was completed in about one year's time. General MacArthur received the Shoup mission proposals for Japanese taxation within six months after the study was begun, while the Shoup-led efforts in Venezuela and Liberia were both completed within six months. Second, in all cases extensive reliance had to be placed upon use of expatriate fiscal (and in some cases, legal) specialists, not so much because of a shortage of domestic economists and tax lawyers, but because of a dearth of trained fiscal economists and tax lawyers in academia and in government. Third, in no case did the impetus for tax reform come from those responsible for assessing and collecting tax (tax administration). Rather, the request for the studies came either from a donor government (the United States in the case of Japan and Liberia), or from the president (Colombia) or the finance minister (Bolivia, Venezuela). Finally, in all instances cited above, the final report of the various missions or commissions was viewed as the principal product of the undertakings. Decisions concerning the implementation of tax reform were, when adopted, in each case deferred until appearance of a final report.

The Indonesian Approach

Indonesian economic policy makers in 1980–81 were broadly familiar with both the content and the results of the several Shoup- and Musgrave-led tax reform missions in other countries. Early in 1981, a series of eight ministerial-level decisions regarding tax reform strategy and tactics were made; in many instances, the decisions reflected to one degree or another lessons learned from similar undertakings elsewhere.

The first decision related to timing of completion of technical studies. The ministers of finance and other members of the economic cabinet considered that, in planning tax reform in the Indonesian context, the appropriate time horizon was best expressed not in terms of months (as in Colombia, Japan, Bolivia, and Liberia) but in terms of years. The Indonesian fiscal system had not been studied as intensively as that of Colombia before 1968, and the Indonesian tax administration in early 1981 was not as well-prepared for fiscal innovations as that of, say, Japan in 1950. Substantial time would be required to convey the rationale and specifics of tax reform to those who would ultimately collect the revenues. Finally, decision makers did not expect any major revenue shortfall until sometime late in 1983, or even as late as the initiation of the fourth five-year plan in 1984. Accordingly, two and a half years was allotted to technical studies on reform.

The second decision was undertaken after consideration of the experience of the 1968 Musgrave Commission in Colombia. There, a team of domestic and expatriate lawyers was given the responsibility of converting tax policy decisions into tightly crafted draft legislation. In the process of drafting, inconsistencies in policy decisions were detected and sent back to decision makers for resolution before final drafting. This model proved immensely effective in Colombia, particularly as it reduced the technical difficulties of implementing tax reform when much of the package was adopted six years later. This model was chosen for Indonesia; beginning after the second year of technical studies, a team of expatriate and Indonesian lawyers was to begin the process of drafting new legislation based on decisions taken to that point. Inasmuch as all technical studies and basic decisions were to be settled after two and a half years, another three months was allocated for the process of final drafting. Thus, the overall time horizon from initiation of technical studies to final drafts of legislation was thirty-three months.

The experience of the Musgrave Commission in Colombia suggested that, at least where international tax missions or commissions were concerned, ultimate adoption of reform programs is critically and directly dependent on the degree of involvement by domestic officials and academics in fashioning reform options.[2] Mindful of hundreds of dust-gathering reports on a variety of policy options done exclusively by expatriate consultants, Indonesian policy makers adapted this aspect of the Colombian model to Indonesian conditions. A steering committee of senior government officials was designated. Drawn from all parts of the Finance Ministry, including several from the tax department, the committee was to oversee, monitor, and participate in the work of the technical expatriate team, ideally responding to specific options presented by the technical team.[3]

A fourth decision was that, at least in the first two years of preparation for tax reform, the effort would be low-key, in contrast to the high-profile, publicity-intensive effort prescribed for the Musgrave Commission by the Colombian government. This involved both advantages and disadvantages. On the one hand, the high-profile approach employed in, say, Colombia, allowed for substantial commentary and feedback on tax reform from the private sector, whereas the low-key approach adopted in Indonesia precluded any substantial discussions with the private sector.[4]

Fifth, the much tighter time constraints faced by earlier comprehensive tax reform studies meant that design of reform was constrained by existing levels of training and education of tax officials. The longer time horizon for the Indonesian reform meant that explicit provision could be made both for formal and informal training. The government sought to establish a cadre of well-trained officials to operate the new tax system over the coming decades. Accordingly, resources allocated for the reform initially included a substantial sum for overseas training of several younger tax officials. Within six months, the Ministry of Finance expanded the training target to include finance of overseas degree and non-degree training for upwards of fifty such officials, several of whom returned with advanced degrees in 1984.

Sixth, the decision was made that reform efforts could begin with a clean sheet of paper, meaning that nothing in the old system *had* to be retained. At the same time, no effort was to be expended in repairing elements in the old system that were not broken. For example, sumptuary excise taxes on cigarettes were, by and large, administered well (bringing in more revenues than the sales tax on all other goods), involved very little welfare costs, and were not particularly regressive in the Indonesian context.

A seventh decision was to broaden the tax reform program to include matters not ordinarily covered in such undertakings. From the author's own experience in Chile, Colombia, Ghana, and Bolivia, it was clear that tax reform confined to changes in tax structure was likely to end in no reform, or abortive reform. Earlier comprehensive studies in Japan, Colombia, Liberia, and Bolivia did not by any means avoid consideration of such nonstructural issues as tax administration, taxpayer identification numbers, the tax information system, and tax procedures. Indeed, the special blue return administrative innovation of the Shoup mission to Japan survives to this day. But under the tight time constraints facing these efforts the prime focus was necessarily on structural reform. The longer time horizon for the Indonesian study meant that the reform effort could go well beyond consideration of structural reform of taxes, to include procedural, administrative, and implementation issues. Further, shortly after initiation of technical studies, a decision was made to invest in a new computerized tax information system to be on stream by 1984 as part of the new tax regime. This set of decisions dictated that the complement of talents on the technical team would ultimately have to include tax administrators, accountants, and data communications specialists as well as the usual mix of economists and lawyers. As it turned out, the work on the taxpayer I.D. system and the computerized information system progressed more rapidly than expected; that on preparing for implementation of reform and on tax administration fell short of success.

Eighth, in contrast to earlier comprehensive tax reform undertakings, and in keeping with Ministry of Finance decision-making traditions, the end product sought was not a formal final report drawing together all recommendations into one volume, nor was consideration of reform options to await completion of all technical studies. Rather, technical studies on particular tax issues were to be made available to decision makers as they were completed. In the process, several egregious features of the old tax system were abolished well before all reform options were finalized.

In the end, the approach toward tax reform incorporated a faintly syncretic blend of lessons derived both from experience elsewhere and from previous experience in Indonesia. Moreover, decision makers were wedded to no particular aspects of this approach; as conditions changed (for example, a new director general of taxation in mid-1981 and a new minister of finance in early 1983), accommodating modifications were made in strategy for pursuing reform.

OBJECTIVES

From the beginning, ultimate objectives of Indonesian tax reform were fourfold: (1) increase in non-oil revenues, (2) more effective income redistribution, (3) removal of tax-induced incentives for waste and inefficiency, and (4) reduction in the transactions costs of transferring resources to the public sector.

The tax reform package seeks to offset most, but not all, of the projected decline in the share of oil taxes in GDP, at 1983 oil export prices. If oil prices decline further below levels prevalent in mid-1984, cuts in government spending and/or increases in foreign commercial loans will have to make up for the shortfall: no conceivable tax reform could forestall those exigences.

The reform package was geared to two other proximate objectives thought essential for obtaining several important ultimate objectives. The two proximate objectives were drastic simplification of the tax structure and the depersonalization of tax administration. The ultimate objectives were first, more effective income redistribution; second, removal of tax-induced incentives for waste and inefficiency in private sector decision making; and third, reduction in the transactions costs of transferring resources to the public sector. Reduction in transaction costs represents a polite euphemism for reducing the scope for corruption in tax compliance and collection—one of the reasons for low non-oil tax revenues.[5] Depersonalization implies a shift toward less, not more, frequent contact between tax officials and taxpayers. In turn, this means greater reliance on withholding methods, electronic data processing of tax information, and a shift from official assessment of liabilities to taxpayer assessment of same. It also means imposing clearer and more uniform criteria for exemptions for small firms, and a general reduction in discretionary authority in the hands of tax officials.

Simplification, however, was by far the most important of the proximate objectives. Over decades, hundreds of amendments intended to serve nonrevenue objectives were imbedded in the system. The tax system was employed to promote investment in favored industries, to promote exports, to encourage development of backward regions, to promote transfer of technology, to encourage construction of bowling alleys, to encourage chess players, etc. These efforts to fine-tune the system to serve nonrevenue goals resulted, in the end, in an excessively complicated tax system unable to perform its revenue function, replete with anomalies and vulnerable to corruption.

To devotees of some versions of supply-side economics, simplification means little more than lower, more unified tax rates, with emphasis on the lower. The Indonesian reform, however, was guided by a rather different notion of simplification. Simplification was taken to mean, first, base-broadening and, only secondarily, lower and more uniform tax rates. A simple income tax is not one under which many income items are not taxable. A simple sales tax is not one under which close substitutes are taxed at widely differing rates. Implicit in the consensus view of tax reform was the futility, certainly in the Indonesian context, of efforts to fine-tune the tax system to achieve nonrevenue objectives. Virtually every item of excluded income or lightly taxed income, from housing and auto allowances to physicians' fees, civil servants' income, and interest income and most others is received by the top 20 percent of the income distribution. All of these will, for the first time, be included in the tax base.

Simplification also required the dismantling of all tax incentives of all kinds, from income tax holidays for priority industries to tax incentives to use public accountants, hold domestic equities, and invest in particular regions. In the end, all such incentives were abolished, but only after decision makers had vetted both empirical and theoretical evidence of their ineffectiveness in achieving purposes intended.

Income distribution considerations played a significant role in shaping many of the final decisions on reform, in ways that some might find surprising. It became clear, upon examination of the evidence, that Indonesia's income distribution objectives were poorly served by the pre-1984 system of high progressive rates of income tax and a set of sharply differentiated rates of sales tax (low on "necessities," high on "luxuries"). The effective rate of income tax on the top 5 percent of the income distribution was but 4 percent, in spite of 50 percent tax rates. Indeed, the share of personal income taxes in GDP had hovered at just under one half of one percent for fifteen years. Rather, the combination of base-broadening and higher tax revenues from tax reform in general appeared to be far more effective tools for meeting income distribution goals.

Base-broadening clearly contributes to redistribution because excluded income is largely received by high income families. But the role of higher tax revenues in income redistribution merits special comment. Studies of the impact of the budget on income distribution, whether in the United States, Colombia, Malaysia, or Chile,[6] strongly indicate that if the budget is to serve redistributive purposes effectively, the primary emphasis must be placed upon the expenditure, not the tax, side of the budget.

The relative efficacy of the expenditure side of the budget in securing goals of income redistribution was examined in a series of studies of the incidence of the Indonesian fiscal system for 1980. This exercise was undertaken in spite of recognition of the inherent limitations of such studies. The results, however, stand up well to sensitivity analysis, and are consistent with findings of other research on the impact of rural development programs in the late seventies (see Collier et al., 1982, pp. 84–100). In brief, the incidence studies suggest that the expenditure side of the Indonesian budget has been a much more effective means of shifting income and services to the poor than the tax side.

The implications of these studies were clear. As long as the expenditure side of the budget remained no less heavily targeted on rural works, primary education, food subsidies, and supply of potable water as in 1980, the most significant contribution to income redistribution from the tax side of the budget would be that of raising large amounts of tax revenues from the type of base-broadening measures contained in the reform, thereby compensating for much of the anticipated revenue shortfalls from declining oil revenues.

THE REFORMED TAX SYSTEM

Little would be gained by a detailed depiction of the old system, one of the most complex and surely among the least productive employed anywhere in recent years. The centerpieces of the reformed system are as follows.

Income Taxation

Tax Base

The new income tax law applies to both individuals and businesses. It replaces a complex maze of four separate taxes on individuals, businesses, interest, dividends, royalties, and withholding tax. Income is now very broadly defined to include any increase in economic well-being. All income is, for any given income level, taxed at the same rate, thereby eliminating the former practice of taxing different types of income at different rates, when not exempt altogether.

Rates and Exemptions

Tax rates have been lowered to a maximum marginal rate of 35 percent, instead of 50 percent (for individuals) and 45 percent (for firms) under the old law. The exemption structure allows incomes below rupiah 4.88 million (US $4,800) to escape tax entirely, for a one-earner family of four. This structure was intended to free the poorest 90 percent of Indonesians from income tax obligations. To avoid discouraging female entry in the labor force, an extra exemption of Rp. 960,000 is allowed for a working wife.

Income Tax Incentives

Numerous tax incentives were allowed under the previous income tax regime. The new law replaces these differential tax incentives with a generally available incentive that is much simpler to administer: lower income tax rates for all firms. For any investment made after the effective date of the new income tax law, no income tax incentives of any kind will be allowed.

Business Expenses and Certain Fringe Benefits

(a) *Fringe benefits.* The tax treatment of fringe benefits has been an immensely controversial and complicated issue in all countries. Where many such benefits are not generally subject to taxation (e.g., the United States) or where they are nominally subject to tax but effectively exempt owing to administrative problems in taxing them (e.g., Indonesia), there are strong incentives to switch compensation from cash income to fringe benefits. Inability to effectively tax fringe benefits meant, in Indonesia, that a substantial share of employee compensation in the modern sector had come to be in the form of housing allowances, transport allowances, vacation cottages, and the like. Consequences include both foregone tax revenue and deterioration in both horizontal and vertical equity (the latter since fringe benefits accrue primarily to higher income employees).

Many nations, however, do attempt to subject many cash and in-kind fringe benefits to taxation; few countries have enjoyed much success. When serious efforts are made, as in Sweden, to enforce taxation of in-kind fringe benefits in the hands of millions of employees, intractable problems of tax administration can also arise. Taxation of in-kind fringe benefits at the level of the employee was the approach prescribed in the old Indonesian income tax; at the same time expenditures for such benefits were deductible at the level of the firm. Under the new law, this sequence will be reversed. In-kind fringe benefits will generally no longer be allowed as a deduction for firms, *but* such benefits will no longer be taxed at the individual level.[7] Fringe benefits, in the form of cash, however, will be fully taxable to individuals and fully deductible to firms. This treatment represents a vast simplification over the former provisions, particularly in that the number of firms is a small fraction of the number of individual taxpayers.

(b) *Depreciation, indexation, loss carry-forwards, and interest deductions.* Under the old system, depreciation was generally computed under the vintage accounting method using historical costs as the basis. Assets were classified into a large number of groups and depreciation was computed in a variety of ways (e.g., straight line or declining balance). The new depreciation method is much simpler. First, vintage accounting is no longer allowed for income tax purposes. Instead, open-ended accounting (as in Canada) is now required. Assets are classified into four major groups depending on useful life with the shortest useful life at four years, the next shortest at eight years. Purchases of assets increases the balance of an asset group, while ordinary retirements and sales reduce the balance of a particular asset classification. Depreciation is then computed based on the product of the balance in any asset account (less prior year's depreciation) and the appropriate depreciation rate.

The method used to compute depreciation is the *double declining* method, with the exception of the building classification. For instance, the applicable rate for the four-year asset classification will be 50 percent, and the rate of the eight-year classification 25 percent. For firms outside the oil sector, the new method provides generally more rapid depreciation allowances.

Indexation of depreciation allowances for inflation had been ardently requested by large firms since 1970. The technical team and the Ministry of Finance accepted the view that the use of historical cost methods (failure to index depreciation) overstates income of firms. However, unanticipated inflation also has other effects on a tax system that tends to *understate* income, primarily because of the deductibility of nominal interest. To correct for one inflation-induced distortion in the income tax—use of historical costs for depreciation—without correcting for an equally major distortion that understates income at the level of the firm, would result in heightened advantages for debt finance and major reserve losses, particularly inasmuch as firms in Indonesia habitually report high debt-equity ratios, and most interest was nontaxable.

The technical team took the position that *partial* indexation of the type strongly desired by companies (indexation of depreciation) was inadvisable, not only on grounds of tax revenues but for efficiency reasons. Rather, it was argued that only *full* indexation was advisable, or at a minimum "double-barreled" indexation, where only depreciation *and* nominal interest are indexed. However, implementation of full indexation has proven to be a formidable task even in countries with sophisticated tax administration. Although the technical team devised a fairly simple system for full indexation of the income tax and although simulation of the system on actual books of accounts of several firms indicated that the system would increase tax revenues relative to no indexation, the ministry decided in the end not to incorporate full indexation into the draft law. The ground for the decision was the likely administrative complexity involved; so much of the tax system was to be changed in one fell swoop that further complications were not wanted. For individuals, however, rates and exemptions are indexed to inflation.

Although full indexation was not ultimately accepted, deliberations over this issue did have the effect of focusing official attention on a serious related issue. Many firms, both foreign and domestic, consistently report debt-equity ratios well in excess of those generally accepted under an arms-length standard. This practice overstates interest deductions quite independently of inflation, shielding substantial income from Indonesian taxes.[8] The reform will curb this practice by denying interest deductions beyond specified debt-equity ratios established by the Ministry of Finance.

(c) Tax treatment of pensions and insurance. In order to simplify tax administration and to secure neutral treatment between savings in the form of pensions and life insurance, the tax treatment of both items has been rationalized so that both items will now be taxed only once. Life insurance premiums will not be deductible from income; however, proceeds of life insurance are not taxable. Contributions to approved pension funds are fully deductible, while pension benefits are taxable to the extent that they exceed the personal exemption under the income tax.

Withholding Mechanisms

The new income tax relies heavily on withholding mechanisms intended to enhance simplification and enforcement. Employers must withhold tax from employees at the applicable rates; employees will not need to file tax returns if they earn no other outside income. Organizations are required to withhold tax from domestic payments of dividends, interest, rents, and royalties at a rate of 15 percent. Enumerated payments made abroad (whether by individuals or by corporations), are subject to withholding tax of 20 percent (reducible to 15 percent by tax treaties). Interest on time deposits is taxable under the law, but by decree was temporarily exempted from tax, at least through 1984.

Other Features of Income Tax Structure

Several other features of the new income tax structure are indicative of the stress placed on base-broadening and on simplification. Examples include: the ending of deductibility for charitable contributions, the taxation (for the first time) of income of civil servants and of certain income items of foundations and cooperatives, and the use of special norms to calculate income for small businesses with inadequate records.

Indirect Taxation

The Value-added Tax

By 1983, seventeen LDCs employed one or another form of value-added tax, collecting an average of 4.5 percent of GDP from this source. Indonesia was one of the last nations in the world still using the highly defective turnover tax, with difficulties in administration compounded by use of several rates and a complicated exemption structure. As a result, sales tax revenues were only about 1 percent of GDP. This tax has been replaced by a variant of the VAT, which is expected to provide at least 60 percent of additional revenue expected from tax reform. The VAT has other distinct advantages. The VAT, unlike the turnover tax, does not promote vertical integration, does not have undesirable "cascading" effects, is easy to rebate on exports, and, in principle (and usually in practice) is easier to administer. The variant chosen by Indonesia is a tax-credit VAT of the consumption type extending through the manufacturer-importer level (although some wholesalers must necessarily be included).

Under a tax credit type of VAT, a taxable firm merely applies the VAT tax rate on all its sales to obtain tentative taxes due the government. Then the firm subtracts all VAT paid on purchases from other firms. The difference is the firm's tax liability for the period. The result is that the firm pays a tax on its value-added, not its sales. Further, this type of VAT creates a potential conflict of interest between seller and buyer, a conflict that can be exploited by the tax administration to improve compliance. If a seller undercharges VAT on sales to a buyer, the buyer has less VAT to credit against his sales tax liability.

The tax is a consumption-type VAT because firms are allowed to credit taxes paid on all inputs including capital goods. The consumption variant of VAT is almost universally used in both developed and developing countries both to simplify tax administration and to minimize undesirable effect of the VAT on growth and efficiency.

(a) Rates. The new VAT is levied at a flat rate of 10 percent on all taxable goods and services whether imported or of domestic origin. This is in marked contrast to the old turnover tax, which imposed seven different rates and under which imports

were subject to generally higher rates. Because the new VAT is based on the destination principle, a special rate of 0 percent is applied to exports, and VAT paid by the exporter is to be refunded, removing all VAT burden on export activity.

(b) Taxable firms: goods and services. The tax is a manufacturers' tax; liability for tax generally does not extend beyond sales made by a manufacturer. The VAT law, however, contains a provision for eventual extension of the base to the wholesale and retail level when maturation in VAT administration allows effective enforcement.

Taxable goods include all manufactured goods; the tax is assessed on imports in the customs house. Taxable services are confined to construction. Manufacturing is defined as any activity, including mining, that changes the form or nature of a good from its original form. Several activities are specifically defined as non-manufacturing: growing crops, raising livestock, fishing, and drying or salting of fish. Commodities produced in these activities are not taxable. The effect will be to exempt from VAT all unprocessed food items, items that account for over half of the consumption of lower income groups.

(c) Exemptions. Because the presence of exemptions is, in virtually all countries, a major reason for difficulties in administering sales taxation, the law provides for no exemptions of any manufactured products consumed domestically. Given the uniform 10 percent rate and the absence of exemptions, VAT liability for all manufacturing or importing firms (except very small firms or those engaged in exporting) can be clearly determined merely by applying a 10 percent rate to all sales, then subtracting taxes paid on purchases. There is, however, an exemption for small firms, designed primarily to simplify tax administration by reducing the number of taxpayers. Firms with an annual turnover of less than Rp. 60 million (US $6,000) or total capital of less than Rp. 10 million are exempt from VAT.

Luxury Sales Tax

As long as a single flat rate is employed for the tax, and as long as exemptions remain limited, the VAT should become the most important tax in the non-oil revenue structure. To protect the principle of the flat rate VAT, and to contribute to the overall progressivity of the tax system, a separate new indirect sales tax to apply to goods that are highly income elastic in Indonesia was adopted. This tax is to be levied on a limited number of "luxury" goods (such as autos, motorcycles, beer, and carbonated drinks) only at one point in the chain of production and distribution, at rates of between 10 or 20 percent. Revenues from this tax are expected to be no more than 8 percent of VAT revenues.

PRIME ISSUES IN TAX REFORM

A Taxonomy of Issues

The foregoing sketch of the nature of the new tax system conveys little of the flavor of the debate over Indonesian tax reform issues, nor of the theoretical and empirical analyses affecting many of the pivotal decisions that determined the thrust of the reform.

Experience elsewhere suggested that in reforming an entire tax structure, one may expect to encounter four sets of issues. Identification of these issues in advance is essential to determine where efforts should be concentrated and resources focused. Grouped according to their most dominant characteristics these four sets are: (1) non-issues, (2) complex issues, (3) difficult issues, and (4) politically controversial issues.

Examples of non-issues include the tax treatment of manufactured exports, the desirability of withholding on payrolls, and the abolition of most stamp taxes. No country wants to tax exports of manufactures; the need for income tax withholding is rarely questioned, and stamp taxes are widely and correctly viewed as unproductive nuisance levies. This, then, is the null set, the set that does not contain any issues. It is small.

Complex tax issues are those that are not easily understood except by specialized practitioners in law or economics. Such topics include the tax treatment of banks, insurance companies, and other financial institutions, most international tax issues (creditability of local taxes against foreign taxes), and most issues in natural resource taxation. While often intricate, complex issues are not necessarily "difficult." Once objectives are specified, widely acceptable solutions can often be readily devised and explained by competent analysts.

While the set of complex issues often intersects the set of difficult issues, there is no union of the two sets. Difficult issues are those for which there is not only a wide divergence in *objectives* among decision makers, but also in the *premises* upon which views are founded. In Indonesia, for example, difficult fiscal issues included the question of the efficacy of tax incentives and fine-tuning of taxes in general, almost every issue in taxation of capital income (especially the tax treatment of interest), and the question of inflation-proofing the tax system.

Finally, there are issues that are controversial in a political sense. Virtually all issues involving taxation are politically sensitive for someone, but some are particularly so. In Indonesia, examples include taxation of income of civil servants (exempt before 1984), taxation of fringe benefits, tax treaty issues, and the efficacy of steeply progressive rates of tax for income redistribution.

Aside from the null set (non-issues), we then have three sets of issues:

Set A - the complex set,

Set B - the difficult set,

Set C - the politically controversial set.

Unfortunately, the sets intersect, as in figure 6.1. Several essentially complex tax issues are also "difficult," in the sense I have used that word (area II in the figure). Many difficult issues are also politically controversial (area V), as are a few complex issues (area IV). Finally, there are "impasse" type issues, where all three sets intersect (area VII). Examples of each type of issue are provided in table 6.1.

Type I, or merely complex, issues can often be resolved relatively easily by application of capable specialized talent. Accordingly, most empirical and other work on such questions was postponed until the last stages of work on the reform, to avoid distracting effort and attention from tougher issues. For example, studies on the tax treatment of financial institutions and on most international tax issues

Table 6.1   *Fiscal Issues: Subsets and Intersections, Some Illustrations*

I.	(*Set A alone*) complex	*Income taxes:* taxation of banks, insurance companies, and financial institutions; taxation of capital gains; taxation of foreign source income; treatment of affiliated firms, definition of permanent establishment
		Sales tax: exemptions versus zero rating, tax treatment of wholesalers and retailers
II.	(*Set A, set B*) complex, difficult	*Income taxes:* depreciation reform, indexation of tax system for inflation, relative tax treatment of pensions and insurance proceeds
III.	(*Set B alone*) difficult	*Income taxes:* loss carry-forwards, computerization of information system treatment of small taxpayers (presumptive income taxes), tax treatment of two-earner families, global versus schedular taxes
		Sales tax: tax credits for capital goods, exemptions for small firms, structure of refund system
IV.	(*Set A, set C*) complex, politically controversial	*Income taxes:* net impact of reform on oil companies' liabilities and excess credits, treatment of inheritances, tax treaty issues
		Sales tax: tax treatment of fertilizer and agricultural inputs
V.	(*Set B, set C*) difficult, politically controversial	*Income taxes:* taxation of civil servants, tax treatment of fringe benefits, tax treatment of partnerships, taxation of state-owned firms, deductibility of charitable contributions
		Sales tax: relative tax treatment of imports and domestic goods, use of uniform rate in value-added tax, number of exemptions for products
VI.	(*Set C alone*) politically controversial	*Income taxes:* limits on exemptions for dependents, taxation of cooperatives, taxation of foundations, income tax amnesty; integration of wealth taxes with income tax
		Sales tax: use of special luxury taxes, nature of exemptions
VII.	(*Set A, set B, set C*) complex, difficult, and politically controversial	*Income taxes:* tax incentives, taxation of interest, efficacy of steeply progressive tax rates
		Sales tax: no examples

were finalized only in July 1983, two years after studies were initiated.

It is particularly important to identify in advance issues of type II (horizontal shading), V (vertical shading), and above all VII (crosshatched area). Education and research must necessarily be concentrated on issues in those intersections. In area VII there lurked three central issues, the resolution of which would determine not only the tenor of tax reform but also its chances for success. Accordingly, a disproportionate share of available talents and energies was deployed on them. The remainder of this section focuses on three such questions: (1) tax incentives, (2) the utility or futility of steeply progressive tax rates in generating revenue and income redistribution, and (3) tax treatment of interest income.

Prime Issues

The first two issues are inextricably related, and are best discussed together: tax incentives and income tax rate structures.

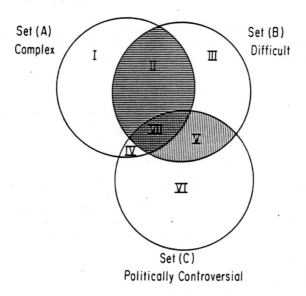

Figure 6.1 Heuristic Illustration of Interlocking Issues in Tax Reform

Tax Incentives and Income Tax Rate Structure

The Indonesian fiscal system prior to 1984 was replete with tax incentives of very dubious value. Like most other LDCs, Indonesia offered five and six year income tax exemptions (tax holidays) for foreign and domestic investors. A by no means exhaustive list of other incentives, excluding the more bizarre examples, would include incentives to induce firms to sell shares to the public, incentives for using public accountants to audit returns, special investment allowances for "priority" projects, investment tax credits, and incentives to promote development of cooperatives.

Tax incentives were major policy tools in Indonesia from 1967–83; the government generally viewed them as successful. Nevertheless, it was clear from the beginning that a strong case could be made, in the Indonesian context at least, against reliance upon tax incentives. Five general reasons and several specific reasons supported this point of view.

1. After twelve years of intermittent studies of Indonesian tax incentives by various analysts, there was abundant evidence indicating that few if any of the incentives in the system had yielded the desired results. Rather, the principal impact of incentives was massive hemorrhages from the treasury. And to the extent they have been effective, they have tended to result in bias toward capital intensity (large investments received longer tax holidays).

2. While there is evidence that tax incentives offered by a particular country can increase foreign investment in that country (Bond and Guisinger, 1983), this represents no assurance that the net social benefits of such investments will be positive. In general, the desired result of incentive programs is not that of maximizing investment in a particular country but that of attracting *beneficial*

investments to that country, where benefits are usually defined to include employment, foreign exchange, and taxes, net of all environmental costs. The list of tax incentives that have achieved the desired results anywhere in the world is a very short one.[9]

3. Tax incentives, in Indonesia as elsewhere, often create intractable problems in tax administration. Tax holidays in particular often involve hidden costs well beyond the transparent costs of taxes foregone during the tax holiday period. Such hidden costs include *negative* tax rates for firms that receive holidays, through use of transfer price manipulations and abuse of tax holiday privileges. As an example of the latter, there have been cases where firms have managed to stretch five-year tax holidays to a twelve-year tax free period.

4. Presence of tax incentives requires higher tax rates on taxpayers not benefiting from them. Although recent research (Frisch and Hartman, 1984) on the determinants of location of foreign investment suggests that higher after-tax returns on investment do draw more investment money,[10] such findings do not necessarily support granting of tax incentives, including tax holidays. Rather, such evidence is more sensibly deployed as an argument for replacing tax incentives with generally lower rates of corporate tax. The Frisch-Hartman (1984) results together with the evidence cited below suggest that lower and more enforceable tax rates in place of tax incentives might actually attract *more* investment than tax incentives, without the "reverse foreign aid" effect often present in the incentive structures of many LDCs with lower revenue losses and without discriminating against small firms.

5. In Indonesia, if not elsewhere, tax incentives discriminate against small firms who lack the resources and the influence to file for and receive incentives. Such producers have been an important source of employment growth in Indonesia: in 1971–80, the largest job gains by far occurred in the cottage and small-scale industry sector.

The positive case for tax incentives, and particularly income tax holidays for foreign investment, is in any case not a convincing one. There is scant empirical evidence conclusively demonstrating that tax incentives are more important to potential investors than such factors as political stability, potential market size, economic growth, or availability of transport infrastructure. And for a large country such as Indonesia, investors in import-substituting industries may be particularly unresponsive to tax incentives. Such firms tend to seek the benefits of Indonesia's potentially large market. The economic case for tax incentives to attract investment in natural resources is ridiculous at best (see Gillis and Beals, 1980, chap. 5). Further, one of the principal lessons of the modern theory of corporate finance is that of the effects of risk on investment decisions. If the risk of making losses is an important factor in the reluctance of firms to invest abroad, tax holidays are of little consequence, since they offer no protection against losses. Finally, tax holidays are weak tools for attracting investment from countries such as the U.S. which tax foreign source income but refuse to allow tax sparing (credits for income taxes *not* paid).[11]

These arguments for discontinuing tax incentives had been advanced in Indonesia for over a decade before 1983, to little avail. Dealing with the issue of tax incentives in isolation is generally hopeless; too many decision makers believe incentives are necessary, even if only for symbolic reasons. But in the context of a general tax reform many things are possible. There was now one more argument for repeal of *all* tax incentives: the possibility of replacing differential tax incentives with a much superior incentive: lower tax rates on *all* firms. Indeed, the possibility that lower nominal rates might allow tax incentives to be abolished became itself a strong argument for lowering rates.

One does not have to be a follower of extreme versions of supply-side economics to recognize the case for realistically lower, enforceable rates in Indonesia. First, the very low ratio of income taxes to GDP was ample testament of the low revenue productivity of high tax rates. In one sample of nine hundred firms, it was found that less than 13 percent of all *foreign* MNCs (multinational corporations) paid the maximum 45 percent corporate rate. Nor did high marginal rates of personal income tax contribute much to income redistribution. Recorded instances of persons paying the top, 50 percent, rate could not be found, even though that rate should have been assessed at taxable income levels of US $12,000. Indeed, other than employees subject to wage withholding, only one in every thousand citizens paid personal income tax in 1982. Lowering of maximum corporate and personal tax rates to a more enforceable 35 percent involves few risks in such circumstances.

The debate was settled by stages. First, it was shown how expensive and ineffective were rather bizarre tax incentives *other* than tax holidays. The first to be abolished were tax incentives to "go public." These were incentives to induce firms to "Indonesianize equity" and to promote the embryonic stock market in general. Theoretical analysis indicated that the economic benefits to Indonesia in inducing firms to "go public" were nil. Empirical analysis showed that, in some cases, the value of foregone tax revenues caused by the incentive exceeded, by three to four times, the value of the stocks issued. Similar evidence on other incentives, except tax holidays, had similar results: abolition.

Finally, using raw data submitted by investors themselves, it was shown conclusively that a uniform, lower 35 percent tax rate would have almost exactly the same impact on investors' net present value as the tax holidays they requested (given a 45 percent rate after the holiday). As a result of this evidence, the new income tax law contains no incentives. It does contain lower tax rates for all firms and individuals large and small. In turn, the lower tax rates were critical for all efforts to broaden the base of the income tax. Without lower rates, it is doubtful that a plausible case could have been made for taxing fringe benefits and pensions, to end interest deductions for individuals, abolish deductions of life insurance premiums for individuals, to tax income of civil servants, or to fully tax interest. Also lower tax rates would likely not have been possible had the tax incentives continued, given the combined cost of lower rates and tax incentives.

Interest and Depreciation

Indonesia's old income tax functioned very poorly. One reason is that most interest income was effectively exempt, but interest expenses were fully deductible, both by individuals and firms. In formulation of proposals for the tax treatment of interest income *and* expenses, several complex *and* difficult questions were involved. Resolution of this set of questions is particularly important because decisions about the tax treatment of interest are also decisions about other key elements of a tax structure (including how depreciation is to be handled), and because important income distribution and macro issues are involved as well.

First, consider the macro implications. Indonesia is an open economy with no foreign exchange controls at all. Both economic theory and empirical evidence indicate high mobility of capital. Therefore, it would perhaps appear quixotic to attempt to impose tax on interest. Unless before-tax rates of interest adjust (now more likely since Indonesia deregulated interest rates in June of 1983), surely capital would tend to flow out of Indonesia to Singapore and points beyond. This possibility was clearly recognized, but nevertheless it was strongly recommended that all interest income be made taxable. The rationale was as follows. First, it was the obvious remedy when interest income being exempt from tax was simply not feasible, for non-economic reasons. This remedy is to end deductibility of interest expenses. This was an attractive option. Relative to the old system, it would have, on balance, increased tax revenues. It would also have simplified tax administration, improved income distribution and ended gross overstatements of firms' debt-equity ratios for tax purposes. Also, ending interest deductibility would have made it possible to consider full expensing of assets (100 percent depreciation the first year), which would have further simplified tax administration *and* would have made indexation of depreciation unnecessary. But with deductibility of interest in the presence of full expensing, the tax rate on income from expensed assets can easily be negative (as in Britain in recent years), particularly when firms are as highly levered as in Indonesia.

Gradually the options narrowed. But even in light of macro considerations, a strong case could be made for including interest income in the tax base, given that it was going to continue to be deductible as an expense. Basically, full taxation of interest was proposed in order to ensure some future for income taxation. Otherwise, as long as interest is deductible, "tax pumps" involving various easily fabricated "sham" loans could be expected to proliferate, resulting in large tax revenue losses. But if interest was to be deductible, we saw earlier why one must also recommend indexing of both nominal interest and depreciation, particularly in a country where typical reported debt-equity ratios lie between 3 : 1 and 8 : 1.

In the end, the quandary was resolved by the inclusion of the following set of measures in the draft law:

1. No indexation of depreciation *or* of nominal interest, solely on grounds that the tax administration was not at present prepared to handle the attendant complications.

2. Adoption of limits on debt-equity ratios (for tax purposes only). For example, a firm could report a D/E of 15 : 1, but deductions of interest would be

restricted to those consistent with the limits established by government.

3. Ending the deductibility of interest on consumer debt, but not business debt.

4. Full taxation of interest, through withholding. This was a complex issue, in the sense that full understanding of all the elements involved brings one near the frontiers of applied fiscal economics. It was a difficult issue in that it was necessary to deal initially with strongly-held preconceptions against disallowance of interest deductions and full taxation of interest *and* indexation of depreciation and nominal interest expenses. And it was politically controversial in several respects.

In the end, full taxation of interest was incorporated in the reform legislation passed by Parliament. However, the beneficial effects of this provision were eroded by a subsequent decree providing for temporary exemption of interest on time deposits and savings bonds.

CONCLUDING OBSERVATIONS

There is no way of determining which, if any, of the lessons from the Indonesian experience may be transferable, in whole or in part, to other national circumstances. However, among the lessons of greatest possible relevance elsewhere is the importance of identifying, at the outset, those problems which lie at the intersection of the sets of complex, and difficult, and politically sensitive issues. These are impasse type issues; decisions about them significantly constrain other decisions and shape the overall scope and tenor of policy reform. Although presentation of prime issues in this fashion did not ensure that all these issues were ultimately resolved in a fully consistent manner, it did have the result that decision makers were acutely conscious of the nature and details of policy trade-offs involved in tax reform.

Prospects for successful implementation of reform are as yet unknowable. At a minimum, complexity of tax laws and regulations can no longer be a reason for Indonesia having among the lowest income and sales tax ratios in the world. Much will depend on the readiness of middle-level tax officials to break with well-imbedded traditions, particularly those involving official rather than taxpayer assessment of liabilities and the wide latitude allowed for exercise of official discretion in tax administration.

One factor auguring for some success in the tax reform is that it was introduced as the last of a wider series of belt-tightening measures intended to gear the economy to an era of lower oil export prices, all of which gained a substantial measure of public acceptance.[12] These measures, all adopted in 1983, included (1) drastic reductions in subsidies to domestic consumption of oil products, (2) adoption of an austere program of noncapital spending for the 1983–84 budget, (3) a major devaluation of the rupiah, from 700 to 970 rupiah per dollar, (4) sizable cutbacks and postponements in large-scale, capital-intensive public sector projects, including refineries, and (5) major reform in financial policies toward money and credit, including virtual deregulation of interest rates. With the exception of the financial reform, all six measures, including the tax reform, were designed to reduce budget deficits anticipated because of weakness in world oil markets. In addition, four of the 1983 reforms altered significantly the structure of incentives facing private and public sector decision makers.

Although assessment of the effects of the tax reform would be decidedly premature in 1984, the results of the other components of the 1983 set of belt-tightening policy measures did exceed original expectations. Consumer demand for energy products (and budgetary subsidies for them) responded sharply to higher prices; official international reserves almost doubled within nine months after the devaluation; real GDP growth rose from almost zero in 1982 to nearly 5 percent in 1983; domestic inflation in 1983 was only 7 percentage points higher than world inflation, in spite of large increases in the prices of energy and imported goods, and time deposits in the organized financial system rose by 80 percent within nine months of the financial reform.

Most of the other 1983 policy adjustments required little in the way of administrative effort for their implementation, operating as they do primarily through the price system. This was clearly true for reform of domestic energy subsidies, the devaluation and deregulation of interest rates. The impact of these adjustments is difficult to evade. Tax reform is, however, another matter. While incentives for tax evasion may be lower and the risks of discovery higher under the reformed tax system, lcng-standing traditions of noncompliance, dating from the Dutch Colonial period, may be altered only slowly, and only then if the machinery of tax administration responds as required.

NOTES

1. Inspiration for the Indonesian income tax reform arose not from any worldwide movement toward flat-rate income taxes, but recognition of the futility, in the Indonesian context, of unenforceably high progressive rates of tax.

2. See Gillis and McLure (1978). Several high-level Colombian officials and not a few middle-level ones participated closely in the technical studies prepared for the Musgrave Commission in 1968. Not only was this group intimately familiar with all aspects of the reform package when they rose to prominence in a later government that adopted the reform, they justly viewed much of it as their own handiwork.

3. As the effort proceeded, the role of the steering committee alternatively waxed and waned, but in the end the committee was an active participant in all basic policy discussions, with final decisions left to the minister of finance.

4. In addition, the low-profile approach dictated that a large resident group of specialists over a thirty-three-month period was out of the question. Accordingly, there was only one resident expatriate, who arrived a year after the effort began. The other twenty-seven expatriates made periodic visits to Jakarta at intervals over the period 1981–84.

5. The government began to employ stronger legal and administrative measures against taxpayer–tax collector corruption in 1981, a campaign that through 1984 enjoyed mixed results. Virtually all evidence on corruption in tax collection is still anecdotal in Indonesia. In other countries, such as Colombia in the mid-seventies, it has been estimated that for every peso of bribes paid to tax officials, the government lost 20 pesos in revenue (Vasquez and Palomeque, 1976, p. 29). This figure squares roughly with anecdotal evidence in Indonesia.

6. For the United States, see Musgrave and Musgrave (1984, ch. 12). For evidence on the relative roles of the tax and expenditure sides of the budget in income redistribution in LDCs, see, for Chile, Foxley, Aninat, and Arrellano (1979, ch. 6), for Colombia, Selowsky (1979, ch. 1), and for Malaysia, Snodgrass (1974).

7. Since the prohibition of deductions for in-kind fringe benefits paid to government officials would be meaningless, in-kind benefits provided by the government will be included in the income of civil servants.

8. Large numbers of firms in Indonesia, including foreign firms, report debt-equity ratios in excess of 3 : 1 and even 4 : 1. While Japanese and Korean firms may in fact have debt-equity ratios as high as 2 : 1 (given the close involvement of financial institutions in their operation), debt-equity ratios much above 1 : 1 elsewhere in the world are not credible for manufacturing firms. For Canada in the period 1977–80, manufacturing firms reported debt-equity ratios of 1 : 2; for U.S. manufacturing firms in 1982, the average D/E ratio was 1 : 22 (*Fortune* magazine, January 27, 1984).

9. For many years, the Puerto Rican tax incentive program was cited as an exception to this rule. Recent work by Bond has called even this case into question (Bond, 1981).

10. Recent work on the experience of sixteen countries indicates that an increase of 1 percent point in the net rate of return caused by a decline in the effective local corporate tax. rate boosts investment in that country by more than 30 percent over a four-year period (Frisch and Hartman, 1984).

11. U.S. multinationals take a credit against their U.S. tax liability for income taxes paid to foreign countries. For *branches* of U.S. firms, a tax holiday therefore results in immediate "reverse foreign aid," since with the holiday there are no Indonesian taxes to credit against U.S. taxes. For *subsidiaries* of U.S. firms, U.S. income tax is not due until income is repatriated to the U.S. parent. This deferral of U.S. taxes means that tax holidays can benefit U.S. firms to some extent. The benefit is greater the longer repatriation is postponed.

12. It is significant to note that none of these measures were undertaken at the behest of international aid donors; Indonesia has not had a stand-by agreement with the IMF since 1974.

7

Taxation and Success

Much has been heard in recent years of the economic prowess of the so-called four dragons of East Asia: Korea, Taiwan, Hong Kong, and Singapore. The development of these and a few other "newly industrializing" countries over the past three decades undoubtedly represents one of the principal economic success stories of the postwar era. In the context of a book on taxation and development, an obvious question is: What, if anything, did the tax policy followed by these countries have to do with their success? Perhaps the most obvious answer, as noted earlier, in chapter 2, is that none of these four countries is a "high tax" country. Indeed, some have seen this as the major, even only, lesson to be drawn from their experience by other developing countries. In particular, Hong Kong's especially low and flat income tax has often been put forward as a policy that should be emulated elsewhere (Krauss, 1983).

As always, however, life, and the key to development success, is considerably more complicated than such simplistic remedies admit. On the one hand, the development of these four countries reflects such common factors as cultural heritage (respect for education, traditional social discipline, and so on), the initial impact of the Korean War, and then the subsequent rise of Japan in influencing both the scale and the export orientation of their growth. On the other hand, each country's experience was in many ways unique. Singapore and Hong Kong are city-states, Korea and Taiwan are medium-sized countries. Hong Kong and to a lesser extent Taiwan are mainly "free enterprise" economies, with countless small and medium-sized firms actively striving for success through exporting. In Singapore and especially Korea, however, the pattern of growth has been much more government-directed, with Korea in particular coming close to emulating the Japanese pattern of large industrial groups working closely with government to achieve planned targets, again primarily in terms of exporting.

The future also looks very different for each of these countries. Singapore, for instance, appears to see its future lying in its development as a technological and financial center for the Southeast Asian region. In a few years, Hong Kong is scheduled to be reincorporated into China, a huge country with a totally different economic and political system. Taiwan's political system is currently in the throes of its first major changes in forty years, and it is impossible to say how its relations with China (and the United States) will develop in the future or what might be the economic implications of such developments. Korea too suffers from continuing political uncertainty, both internally and externally, and of course its economic future too is unclear and largely dependent on developments in Japan and the United States.

In the future, as in the past, the role of the fiscal system in development will doubtless continue to be secondary, although it may be none the less critical for that. A good tax system in itself is clearly not enough to foster development; but a bad one may be enough to hamper it. One feature that all four Asian success stories have in common, for example, is the export-led nature of their growth. A major factor in this growth was obviously their avoidance of the trap of overvalued exchange rates, a policy adopted in many developing countries in the name of protecting domestic industrialization and one which usually ensures that the industries thus fostered are thoroughly uncompetitive (Krueger, 1978). A secondary factor was that none of these countries unnecessarily hampered their exporters through heavy regulation or taxation. Both Korea (see chapter 31) and Taiwan, for example, have recently adopted value-added taxes, partly to free exports from "cascading" indirect taxes and partly, perhaps, to permit some modest expansion of government expenditures without the necessity of relying more heavily upon income taxes.

Somewhat contrary to the "Hong Kong myth," however, the other three countries have tax systems very similar to those in many other developing countries, with fairly conventional income taxes, as well as varying degrees of reliance on tax incentives to direct investment—perhaps most in Korea and least in Taiwan. That the precise role of the tax system in each country in influencing its rate and pattern of development is a complex subject is underlined by the following brief excerpt from the conclusion of a recent book-length study of the role of public finance in Korea's development. Similar tales, though quite different in detail, may be told for both Singapore (Asher and Osborne, 1980; Asher, 1988) and Taiwan (e.g., Riew, 1988).

In the case of Korea, as Bahl, Kim, and Park (1986) make clear, tax policy played a secondary, supporting role in development. In particular, they stress that the relatively "hard" nature of the Korean state (see Myrdal, 1968, on the crucial distinction between "hard" and "soft" states) enabled it largely to neglect equity issues, to rely heavily on indirect taxes, to keep tax (and expenditure) levels relatively low, and to make plentiful use of tax incentives to foster "supply-oriented" policies. The sorts of tax reform that this success story suggests thus seem much closer to those sketched by Marsden (1983) in chapter 2 than the "incentive-free" environment aimed at in the Indonesian reform (chapter 6) or the equity dimension emphasized in the optimal tax approach (chapter 4). Whether countries with different cultural and political environments than Korea could, should, or would want to emulate this path is quite another, and much more complex, question.

Tax Policy and the Modernization Process in Korea

Roy Bahl, Chuk Kyo Kim, and Chong Kee Park

The primary objective of Korean tax policy during the modernization period was to mobilize resources for capital formation in the public sector, while not discouraging investment in the private sector. Even though there were many structural changes in the 1950s, policy was not very effective. Compliance problems were severe, in part because counterpart funds were a readily available substitute for increased tax effort. Moreover, a continuing high rate of inflation limited what could be done through structural reform. It is true enough that the tax ratio increased during this period, but these increases were more due to temporary measures (for example, a foreign exchange tax) than to permanent improvements.

The foundations for a more permanent contribution of tax policy to the development process were laid in the disruptive 1961–64 period. The tax share of GNP fell from 12 percent in 1960 to 7.2 percent in 1964. Beginning from such a low level of taxation and having given itself the mandate to substantially increase the tax share of GNP over the next five years, the government would have ample opportunity to reshape the tax structure in a short period of time. This it did in two ways. First the creation of the Office of National Tax Administration (ONTA) resulted in a fairly quick and marked improvement in tax administration. Second, there was a successful and productive reform in the structure of income taxes. These two reforms, together with a rapidly growing economy and controlled government consumption expenditures, resulted in a doubling of the tax ratio between 1964 and 1970, a shift in revenue emphasis toward modern income taxation, and very large increases in the savings ratio.

Tax policy from 1971 to 1975 considerably reversed the direction and initiatives of the late 1960s. There was a move back toward indirect taxes, and taxable capacity was used less fully. The emphasis had shifted quite decidedly from the need to mobilize more resources for government capital formation to the need to use tax policy to increase the rate of return to capital and thereby stimulate private sector investment.

By the end of the modernization period, the levels of Korean economic development and price stability were such that the focus of tax policy could shift toward structural matters. By 1975, the Korean tax structure had begun to take on the characteristics of tax systems found in the industrialized countries. The personal

Excerpted from Bahl, Kim, and Park (1986).

income tax had been converted to a global system and indirect taxes would soon be combined into a value-added tax.

If the entire modernization period, 1950–75, is considered, the direction of tax policy might be summarized as follows:

1. tax policy played a supporting rather than a leading role in the modernization process, the exception perhaps being the 1966–71 period;
2. the primary objective of reform was the stimulation of economic growth;
3. the income elasticity of the tax system was kept above unity with a series of discretionary changes; and
4. the reliance on indirect taxes was maintained.

The modernization of the Korean fiscal system between 1953 and 1975 was almost as dramatic as the rate of economic growth during that period. In the early 1950s, the share of the government sector in GNP was quite small, there was little reliance on modern direct and indirect taxes, tax collection rates were poor, fiscal policy was preoccupied with stopgap stabilization measures, there was heavy dependence on foreign assistance, and the government savings rate was nil. By 1975, the government share in GNP had tripled, a global income tax system was adopted, a value-added tax was in the immediate offing, the concern of fiscal policy was with stimulating savings and investment, foreign aid had become a relatively unimportant source of financing, and the government savings rate was impressive. Is this modernization of Korean public finances a transferable experience? Will the policies that led to these improvements work elsewhere? In order to answer these questions, one needs to consider not only the different fiscal choices made in Korea but the setting in which they were made.

The conclusion one reaches is that, while the Korean case shows one interesting path to fiscal modernization, the necessary setting is not likely to be duplicated in many countries. This point needs to be emphasized to those who would look to the Korean experience for fiscal policy guidance. The formidable accomplishments make it tempting to argue that government budgetary policy was the major force in the modernization process. In truth, however, many of these changes came about because of the growing economy, an observation that leads us to conclude that government finances played more of a supporting than a leading role.

THE SUPPORTING ROLE OF BUDGETARY POLICY

It would be difficult to argue that government tax and expenditure policies were as instrumental in stimulating economic growth as were government actions with respect to liberalization of the trade sector, interest rate policy, inducements for foreign and domestic private-sector investments, credit availability through the private sector, and export incentives. Throughout the period, fiscal policies were adjusted to support government objectives—reconstruction finance and controlling inflation in the 1950s and encouraging export-oriented industrialization in the 1960s and 1970s.

Budgetary policy did not lead the process for several reasons. First, the size of the public sector is relatively small and has been kept that way ostensibly to keep from slowing the rate of private investment. Second is the range of tax incentives, reductions, and structural changes adopted after 1965 to encourage investment— the policy was one of providing the inducements but leaving the action to private firms. Third, there was much use of temporary fiscal measures in the late 1950s, and even in the late 1960s, in lieu of more permanent changes in fiscal structure that may have altered economic behavior. Examples here are the foreign exchange tax, the land income tax, and the postponement of creation of a global income tax until the mid-1970s. On the expenditure side, budgetary policy also supported the industrialization strategy with relatively heavy investment in economic services at a cost of relatively little government investment in social services. Throughout the period, the issue seemed to be how to adjust the tax-expenditure system to accommodate the goal of stimulating industrial exports.

The one period of exception to this general rule was 1965–70. During these years, there was vigorous use of tax and expenditure policy to increase the government savings rate—with the result that the government savings rate exceeded that in the corporate sector. Current expenditure growth was controlled, ONTA was created, and the personal income tax was reformed and its effective rates were increased. These policies had the effect of pushing Korean tax effort to a peak level and raising the government savings rate to 7 percent by 1970. After the growth process had begun, in 1971, budgetary policy reverted again to a more supporting role and the size of the government sector, relative to GNP, began to shrink.

None of this is to say that government per se was not the moving force behind Korea's modernization, for it surely was. However, the government budget, particularly the expenditure side, was not the major policy instrument used in generating economic growth.

KOREAN FISCAL CHOICES

Because budgetary policy played this kind of supporting role, and because Korean economic growth strategies have been atypical, Korea's pattern of tax and expenditure structure development has also been different. The most striking difference is the choice of a small government sector—for a country with its characteristics, Korea taxes and spends at well below expected levels. While this strategy has left more funds in the hands of private-sector investors and consumers, it also has placed more of the onus for supporting social services (particularly education and health) on the private sector.

There have also been differences in the development of the tax structure. Typically, the reliance on direct taxes increases during the development process. This was not the case during the Korean development period, though a modern direct-tax system did emerge. Direct taxes in the late 1950s and early 1960s were temporary measures—a land income tax, a foreign exchange tax—whereas, in the 1970s, the direct taxes were the more modern personal and corporate income levies. Still, direct taxes were of little more importance in the 1970s than in the 1950s, and indeed there was a decided shift back toward indirect taxation beginning in 1972. Again, this reflects the development strategy: encourage export production, selectively discourage domestic consumption, and provide incentives for savings and investment in export activities. What seems to have been most different about Korean tax policy (versus other countries) was the holding to a heavy reliance on indirect taxes. In order to keep the income elasticity high and the tax rate on exports low, commodity tax rates have been steadily increased on luxury goods and the base has been continuously expanded. These policies have kept the revenue raising pressures off the income taxes.

Korean expenditure structure choices were also different from those made in other countries. Most notable are the relatively low share of GNP devoted to public expenditures for health, education, and welfare-related services. Spending for these services was well below international norms, while spending for defense and economic services was well above. The emphasis on capital investments for economic services was in keeping with the needs of a growing industrial sector.

The financing pattern in Korea after 1964 reflected yet another fiscal choice that was nontraditional. There was very little borrowing or foreign aid, which implies that relatively little of the financing burden was shifted to the future or abroad, that is, most services were provided through reductions to current income. The benefits of public investment, however, were being shifted to the future as budgets were heavily oriented toward capital projects. The size of this intergenerational transfer, roughly measured as the savings rate, was extraordinarily high in Korea during this period.

It seems safe to conclude that Korean fiscal choices were not traditional, largely because they were supporting a very nontraditional economic growth program. Every indication is that this strategy was successful, at least insofar as promoting an increased savings rate and promoting an export growth strategy. Such choices may have cost some measure of improved income distribution, but this loss was at least partly offset by the favorable distributional effects of growing employment.

THE SETTING FOR KOREAN FISCAL CHOICES

Why did Korean budgetary policies "work," and would they be feasible and bring the same results elsewhere? That Korean fiscal choices were so atypical, and apparently successful, suggests that the setting for public finance development was different in Korea and that the differences may be due to more than the economic growth strategy. Indeed, the special setting in which these tax and expenditure policy decisions took place may make Korean fiscal patterns not replicable in other developing countries.

Five main factors enabled this development. First, income distribution objectives could be given secondary importance, because income and wealth were quite evenly distributed at the beginning of the modernization period. The expulsion of the Japanese after World War II, the Korean War, the education system, and land reform all led to an equal distribution of income by developing-country standards. This meant that equity would not have to play a major role in tax and expenditure policy formulation. As our results, and those of others, have shown, even substantial changes in budgetary policy do not have large and lasting effects on the income distribution.

Second, there is a high income elasticity of demand for education in Korea. This means that the government sector could afford to underspend for human capital development knowing that the private sector would pick up the difference through tuitions and so forth. In fact, households financed about two-thirds of all education expenditures during the modernization period.

Third, inflation was brought under control in the early 1960s, thereby giving the government the flexibility to pursue economic goals with structural tax and expenditure changes. One lesson of the 1950s is that a government that goes from one stabilization program to another cannot afford the luxury to tune tax rates to achieve particular goals or to initiate the kinds of public investment programs that might yield significant future returns.

Fourth, there was a phasing out of counterpart assistance by the mid-1960s, putting the government in a position of having to mobilize substantial domestic resources in a relatively short period of time. For this reason, the withdrawal of counterpart assistance was probably the major American contribution to Korean modernization.

Fifth, there was the centralization of power after 1963, which made Korea a "hard" state, capable of putting even unpopular policies into effect. Without this capability, it would not have been able to sustain such important fiscal initiatives as high tax rates to discourage consumption, ONTA, and the movement to a global income tax system.

Finally, the possibilities for fiscal development were greatly enhanced by the 1961–64 disruption period. A combination of inflation and the military takeover reduced the expenditure share of GNP from 24 to 16 percent and the tax share from 12 to 7 percent. Beginning from such a low level of government activity in 1964, the government would have ample opportunity to reshape the tax and expenditure structures in a very short period of time. Such an opportunity to start over rarely comes along, and the Koreans made the most of it.

8

Implementation Problems

The importance of administration has already been mentioned several times. Those concerned with tax policy in developing countries are well aware of the importance of tax administration in general, of its obvious deficiencies, and of the critical importance of improving administration in order to secure better results. Careful readers of Gillis's generally upbeat paper on Indonesia (chapter 6) may, for example, detect a slight current of uneasiness with respect to the last of these points. A similar sense of uneasiness should, indeed, afflict all tax policy analysts in developing countries, for the fact is that almost never has the administrative aspect of tax reform been studied sufficiently carefully (but see Shoup et al., 1959, for an exception).

In particular, far too little attention has been paid to the difficulty of changing such fundamental aspects of a country's culture as, for example, the "personalization" of the tax process that Gillis deplores in the case of Indonesia. A major turning point in the development of modern society in the Western world was the change from a "status" (personal) to a "contract" (impersonal) society. Such major turning points cannot casually be assumed to occur at the convenience of would-be "reform-mongers" (to use an evocative word of Hirschman's [1963]).

The only full-length study of the administrative dimension of taxation in developing countries is by Radian (1980), a provocative book which should be on the reading list of all would-be tax reformers. Some of the flavor of this work is conveyed in the following selection by Radian and Sharkansky (1979) on the problems of implementing a tax reform in Israel, a country which is often thought of as being considerably more advanced in such matters than many developing countries. While this reputation is somewhat exaggerated (see Wilkenfeld, 1973), it is quite true that Israel has a highly educated population and a well-trained and generally efficient administration. All the more striking then is this tale of the relative failure of all but the easiest parts of a modestly ambitious income tax reform.

Parenthetically, it is interesting to note that two of the principal authors of this reform entitled their own paper on it "The Political Economy of Tax Reform" and emphasized the pragmatic and compromised nature (from the point of view of pure theory) of what they had been able to accomplish (Ben-Porath and Bruno, 1977). Their outraged reaction (Ben-Porath and Bruno, 1979) to a subsequent critical comment by Radian (1979) along the lines of the excerpt included here is thus perhaps understandable: here they had gone along with all kinds of politically necessary compromises only to be attacked for administrative unrealism! It is impossible to read this exchange, however, without feeling that such a response completely misses Radian's central point—that reforms that do not take administrative limits adequately into account are likely to turn out in practice to be quite different in their effects than they look on paper. Since experience shows that even in countries as sophisticated as the United Kingdom tax policy designers can easily outreach the grasp of tax administrators (Hood, 1976), this lesson should surely be taken to heart by would-be reformers in all countries (see also Pressman and Wildavsky, 1973). It is simply not good enough to assume that all administrative problems will resolve themselves—whether in ten years (Papua New Guinea, 1971) or twenty-five years (Taylor, 1967, on Nigeria), to mention only two of the many such prophecies that have been proven wrong by time. Tax administrations reflect the society in which they operate and cannot realistically be expected to evolve much in advance of that society. This may not be good news, but it does seem to be accurate counsel.

Some question might therefore be raised about the stress placed by Radian and Sharkansky on the relatively short time period allowed for the Israeli reform. Indonesia had three years to prepare its reform (see chapter 6). Colombia has been actively engaged in a series of administrative and structural reforms for twenty years (Perry and Cardenas, 1986). India has had numerous studies of tax structure and administration (e.g., India, 1955, 1960, 1972, 1978). Nevertheless, it would be stretching the truth to say that there have been substantial changes for the better in tax administration yet in any of these countries, despite these efforts. Of course, there have been improvements, occasionally major ones, here and there, as in the Korean case mentioned in chapter 7—a better taxpayer register in one country, improved withholding in another—but what has not changed significantly for the better as a rule has been the basic nature of either the tax administration or the country in which it must operate.

Apart from illustrating this general lesson, the following brief account of the Israeli experience brings out at least two other interesting points. First, as mentioned earlier, tax reform in a developing country usually means tax increases— and tax increases engender opposition which often dims the prospects of successful reform.

Secondly, partly because of such opposition, partly because of the usually pressing need for revenues, and partly because of the simple ease of doing so, the major impact of "comprehensive" income tax reform is often on wage earners in the modern sector. Since such wage earners are often among the better-off groups in the country, this outcome may in the circumstances of many developing countries be less inequitable than might at first be thought, as was suggested might be the case in Bolivia (Musgrave, 1981). Indeed, it might even turn out to improve the vertical equity of the tax system, as appears to have been true in Jamaica (Wasylenko, 1987). Nonetheless, higher taxes on wages are not usually what people have in mind when they urge income tax reform in the name of social justice or the need to tap ability to pay. Moreover, it is by no means clear that raising the cost of employing workers in the modern sector is the best way to achieve the presumably desired goal of development, one important element of which is precisely the expansion of such employment (Bird, 1982).

Tax Reform in Israel

Alex Radian and Ira Sharkansky

Implementation is now a key word in the vocabulary of public policy. It has come to imply that simple translation of goals into performance is not likely. In our study of an income tax reform in Israel we have sought to find out how organizations respond to policies they can neither fully implement nor ignore.

The study of policy implementation is, to some extent, specific to each field of service, and innovations in tax policy encounter special problems. Central to taxation is voluntary compliance—the need to elicit from a large mass of taxpayers both accurate reports of income and timely payments of tax. Without voluntary compliance, the scale and scope of problems that need to be solved may overwhelm the ability of any tax agency (Radian, 1980). Citizens may suspect that reforms in tax policy are likely to cost them more, even if the propaganda emphasizes greater equity or administrative simplicity. Tax reforms require administrators to accept changes in their own procedures and to cope with taxpayers who, out of either ignorance or intention, exhibit an increased rate of noncompliance in the face of new procedures. Experts in the tax field believe that they can induce greater cooperation on the part of taxpayers by making returns more simple and by some redistributions of the tax burden to reduce the appearance of inequities. To the extent that the government's need for *more* revenue is at least part of the explanation of the reform, however, there is an obvious limit to the capacity of the reformers to give their creation a positive appearance.

A tough reform—such as one that taxes certain kinds of income for the first time, removes well-established kinds of exemptions or deductions, or changes requirements for record keeping in ways that make evading taxation more difficult—can have serious consequences for the tax agency as well as for taxpayers. The tasks of tax administrators become more unpleasant at the same time that the public's need for tax expertise increases. The result may be a drain of expertise from the tax agency—with former employees selling their skills as private tax advisers—just when the agency must have a high level of expertise to absorb the new procedures. This problem is especially acute in a country, such as Israel, that is poor and has a limited supply of skilled accountants and of those with expertise in both taxation and administration. Changes in the leadership of a tax agency, for whatever reason, can have adverse effects; the departure of a key manager may deprive a reform of its driving force.

The successful implementation of tax reform depends partly on personnel out-

Excerpted from Radian and Sharkansky (1979).

side the tax unit. Prosecutors and the courts must also accept the reform and work to impose sanctions on taxpayers who do not comply. Several problems may trigger a lack of cooperation from judicial agents. New demands on taxpayers may fail to comply with procedural requirements or with guarantees of citizen rights contained in the constitution or basic laws. The new demands may so increase problems of compliance that prosecutors or the courts cannot cope with the increased workload. The prosecutor or courts may make their own decisions to go slow in dealing with the new cases, perhaps out of a feeling of pique at being left out of the reformers' consultations, or because they were denied an extra dose of resources as an integral part of the reform package, or because they feel that enforcement problems outside the tax field are more urgent. The penalties imposed on those who refuse to comply with the tax reform may not be severe enough to induce the mass of taxpayers to adopt new practices.

Along with all these problems, unforeseen changes in the larger environment may frustrate a tax reform. Changes in the economy, perhaps originating outside the country, may upset the macroeconomic predictions that underlie the reform. Natural disasters, changes in international affairs, or pedestrian events in national politics may divert the attention of the legislative or executive personnel who must provide the resources that a reform must have in order to succeed.

A common consequence of all these problems is the dilution of a reform's original goals. Dilution may be decided unilaterally by a tax agency's leadership in recognition of such problems, may occur in a process of bargaining between adversaries, or may simply result as officials variously give in to harsh conditions. A dilution of goals may bring the level of enforcement into line with administrative resources, with the inclinations of prosecutors or courts, or with the level of compliance tolerable to a large majority of taxpayers. Certain provisions of the reform may be enforced while others are ignored. Certain kinds of noncompliance may be pursued administratively, but not to the point of asking the prosecutor to begin indictment procedures against recalcitrant citizens. Requirements may be enforced against "easy" classes of taxpayers, but not against "difficult" groups. Some features of the reform may be left to sleep for a while, perhaps until the tax agency can receive appropriate increases in its budget or can recruit additional personnel.

In studying the implementation of a major reform in Israel's income tax, we focus on issues of organization and politics, rather than of economics. In part, this emphasis reflects our expertise in political science and public administration. In part, too, it reflects the conclusion that the economists primarily responsible for the reform heavily discounted the organizational and political issues relevant to its success.

THE CONTEXT AND DEFINITION OF REFORM

Difficulties occur in every field of government, but only a few become problems for which solutions are sought. The definition of a problem partially determines its solution, just as the phrasing of a question determines the range of possible answers. Even before implementation is attempted, a process of policy choices shapes the results of implementation. We therefore start our analysis with an examination of the context of reform and the process by which the reform proposals were reached.

Factors Leading to the Reform

In the wake of the 1973 war, Israel faced an inflationary economy with a tax structure that did not invite use as a policy tool. High tax rates defied further increase. The marginal rate climbed steeply to 53 percent at average income and went higher to 87 percent. A complex system for defining taxable income kept substantial income out of the tax network, and tax evasion was a serious problem. Tax administration was cumbersome. Each file was examined by an inspector, who determined the final assessment. The Department of Income and Property Tax (hereafter, Income Tax Department) took nearly six years to complete assessments for one tax year. Collection was chronically slow. With low penalties for late payment, a cumbersome system of enforcement, and the value of money declining rapidly while the overdue tax bill stayed fixed, it was a wonder that any self-employed taxpayer paid on time.[1] (Indeed, few did.)

The Reform Commission and Its Recommendations

On 15 December 1974 the minister of finance appointed a commission of experts to solve major problems in the tax field. He asked the commission to (1) broaden the tax base, (2) simplify the tax system, and (3) increase the effectiveness of collection.

Trouble started there. Such goals are not precise. They emphasize broad subjects of policy rather than details of enforcement. The composition of the commission and the time limit placed on the commission's activities helped shape its work further. Three commission members were professors of economics, one was a lawyer, and the other was an accountant. None was an expert in administration. The minister asked the commission to submit a final report within three months of its appointment. Due to this time pressure and to the professional interests of the members, as well as to the minister's instructions, the commission was inclined to focus on major goals of policy and techniques of administration. It did not consider systematically how these reforms could be implemented.

The commission focused on the steep rate structure, where marginal rates became very high at the low level of income. These high tax rates had put great pressures on employers to disguise wage increases as payments for nontaxable categories of fringe benefits, such as allowances for professional books, telephone service, and cars. The commission saw a reduction of rates and the inclusion of all benefits within the tax structure as the key to a successful tax system. If taxpayers could pay lower rates they would pay more willingly. The question was how much to reduce rates. The commission's choice was largely intuitive. With a top rate of 60 percent, the commission felt it would be possible to launch a public campaign against tax evasion, to induce social pressures on behalf of new reporting practices, and thus to create a new tax ethic.

The commission recommended these changes in administrative procedures:
1. Universal compulsory filing
2. Compulsory bookkeeping for every business with more than three employees or with a turnover above I£250,000 per year (the Income Tax Department would issue detailed regulations concerning the types of records to be kept)
3. An end to existing methods of agency assessment, linked to new procedures of self-assessment and selective audits (this would be implemented at the same time as the Tax Department cleared its backlog of existing assessments)

Issues of implementation, or how to accomplish these goals, received little attention from the commission.

The Effects of Haste

The first task of reformers is to convince policy makers and to generate public support. After the 1973 war, Israelis were inclined toward simple, radical changes in order to eliminate problems of the past. To meet this demand Israeli tax reformers decided to work fast and produce a sweeping new system. They perceived that a small change would be seen as a continuation of old vices. This is a common approach to tax reform. Richard Bird (1977) describes how economists in poor countries often fall "into the trap of assuming, on the basis of some usually quite simple ideas, that they have all the answers to the manifold problems of implementing an adequate revenue system." They propose holistic, across-the-board reforms and treat piecemeal reformers "as mealy-mouthed compromisers rather than pragmatic realists."

Two of the reform commission's economists have written (Ben-Porath and Bruno, 1977) that "the fear that this atmosphere [conducive to radical reform] would change, that objective economic difficulties would eventually supersede the demand for reform, was a major reason for the urgency and haste with which the commission prepared its report." The commission avoided time-consuming research. It left out important topics because there was no time or because no information was readily available. Although it did indicate that extensive administrative reform would be necessary if its goals were to be reached, it did little to describe specific reforms or plans for their accomplishment. It gave little or no attention to the administrative feasibility of those specific reforms it did recommend. It did not take into account constraints on implementation, such as the supply of technically trained personnel, taxpayers' responses to new demands, or new problems of enforcement.

IMPLEMENTING THE REFORM

The commission's report sped through the Knesset with virtually no changes. As of March 1978, the third year of implementation, however, accomplishments have been thin. Although the reform was ambitious, actual practice has changed only marginally (see table 8.1).

Table 8.1   *Failures of the Israeli Tax Reform Exceed Its Accomplishments*

Accomplishments
  Majority of nontaxable fringe benefits eliminated
  Rate structure and system of deductions at source, or pay as you earn (PAYE), greatly simplified

Partial Accomplishments
  Increase in use of cash registers and formal bookkeeping
  Greater and increasing demand for accountants, bookkeepers, and tax advisers
  Sharp rise in number of students applying for admittance to accounting programs
(These signs suggest that the economy is undergoing changes towards more formal and rational procedures.)

Failures
  Requirements for universal filing not implemented
  Returns prepared according to self-assessment viewed by the Income Tax Department as inade-
    quate; reported changes in gross incomes not keeping pace with inflation
  Presumptive assessments not entirely discontinued
  Backlogs in assessment not eliminated (backlog of uncompleted files greater in 1977 than in 1974)
  Continued long delays in collections from companies and the self-employed

Doing What is Easy

Things worked well at the beginning. The Income Tax Department concentrated on implementing the new rate structure and the inclusion of all income within the pay-as-you-earn (PAYE) system. Most employers cooperated with the changes required in their withholding practices. Wage earners were assuaged by the promise that take-home pay would not be reduced as a result of the changes. There were contrary pressures only from certain groups of workers, such as airline crews and seamen. (Part of their salaries was paid in foreign currency, but taxed as if one U.S. dollar were equivalent to one Israeli pound—the exchange rate in 1974–75 being about six pounds to the dollar. These groups demanded that they continue to enjoy this privilege, or that their after-tax incomes be raised to their preform level.)

Changes in the rate structure and the definition of taxable income were relatively easy. The basic structure was already in place. PAYE had wide coverage and worked generally well. The concessions that wage earners had enjoyed as nontaxable benefits were a matter of record. Once there was political agreement about new rates and a new procedure for defining taxable income, there were few obstacles to implementation. It was a case of a relatively small number of employers having to cooperate in supplying information and payments about their large number of employees.

Special Problems with the Private Sector

The comfort and certainty of familiar routines hindered the Tax Department when it sought to introduce the reform to self-employed and professional people in the private sector. Here the department confronted problems that exceeded its knowledge and power. Compliance was a serious problem. For the self-employed in the private sector, a reform in legal procedures would be meaningless unless they were convinced that the Income Tax Department had a new capacity to enforce the law and to make evasion a risky practice.

The components of accurate bookkeeping, self-assessment, and selective audit are mutually dependent. The Income Tax Department cannot move from universal to selective auditing unless most taxpayers are actually keeping books and making self-assessments of reasonable accuracy. In order to stimulate compliance, the department might have completed the first batch of selective audits faster and more thoroughly than anything done before. The audited taxpayers—and, perhaps more so, their relatives and acquaintances—could have learned that the department was alert to the various schemes designed to hide taxable income. By applying stiff penalties against those who ignored their warnings, collectors could have behaved as if they had the support of law enforcement agencies.

In fact, the department's actions were not clear and determined. Deadlines for implementing procedures were announced and then postponed, or were officially held but without efforts to enforce them. Occasionally the department would flex its muscles by well-publicized raids to inspect bookkeeping procedures for compliance with the new rules, but such actions were rare and unproductive. The momentum of the reform that had been felt with the implementation of the new rate structure for wage earners was not maintained with regard to the self-employed.

The Income Tax Department was under great pressure to change several procedures and routines quickly. The Knesset adopted the reform commission's recommended timetable for implementation, which required the department to complete all the required changes that would enable it to operate in 1977 on the basis of self-assessment and selective audit. Comprehensive filing had to be instituted by July 1977, and the enforcement of bookkeeping practices completed in 1976. The reform was a salient issue drawing intense public attention. Hardly a day went by during the first year of implementation without some report in the newspapers about progress and shortfalls. The reporters' work was facilitated by the existence of binding deadlines. Reporters could make headlines by informing the public that this or that change had or had not been carried out within the reform's timetable. The state comptroller conducted a thorough overview and reported on the smallest deviation and shortfall from original goals. To maintain credibility and induce compliance, the department had to act fast and effectively. Previous attempts to strengthen tax administration, starting as early as 1952, had not succeeded in removing problems the same as those that were targets in 1975. For this attempt to succeed, the public as well as the bureaucrats had to be convinced that the reform was serious.

Self-assessment and Selective Auditing

The Income Tax Department could not move toward self-assessment and selective auditing. It lacked the essential skills to uncover sophisticated evasion. It was equipped to assess independent taxpayers with the help of the presumptive method. Its inspectors, in fact, refused to accept self-assessed returns on the grounds that they knew income was not being reported. A backlog of nearly half a million files awaiting assessment hindered the department from moving full-force toward selective auditing. The old files could not be ignored (too much money being at stake) in order to move faster in the implementation of the reform.

The department tried a procedure that mixed old and new methods. Taxpayers were offered the option of correcting earlier returns and thereby winning the department's approval of their self-assessment. Such an approach risked the department's credibility. If it was not capable of getting to the bottom of things then, why should taxpayers assume that selective audits would be serious once they began? Few taxpayers accepted the Income Tax Department's offer; only 17 percent of self-employed individuals and 5 percent of the companies amended their returns. The voluntary changes showed increases in income reported ranging from 26 percent to 63 percent, depending on the category of taxpayer. These levels of evasion bring into question the wisdom of relying on selective audits. Although taxpayers are required to prepare and file their own returns, the department still accepts only a few at face value. The backlog remains considerable. After a small reduction in 1975, it grew again in 1976 and 1977.

Comprehensive Filing

Given the inability to introduce actual self-assessment and selective audit, it is no surprise that the government has taken hardly any steps towards implementing comprehensive filing. The state comptroller points out that in March 1976 the agency had 68,000 files of salaried taxpayers, while there should have been 854,000. In other words, 92 percent of employed taxpayers did not file returns for tax year 1975. In its plans for 1976 the department did not go beyond the modest goal of mailing returns to 100,000 taxpayers. Yet lack of implementation here may do more good than harm. The department cannot handle the new mountain of paper that would result from the formal requirement to receive returns from all salaried taxpayers, many of whom owe no tax beyond that already deducted at source. Other problems also deter the implementation of comprehensive filing. Many employers (even large ones such as universities and municipal authorities) do not make the necessary wage and tax statements available to their employees on time. In September 1977 the Income Tax Department announced that it would seek an amendment of the law to limit the filing requirement to a selected category of highly paid wage earners.

Bookkeeping

Reforms in the record keeping demanded of taxpayers have been especially troublesome. About a year after legislation, compulsory bookkeeping practices were to be enforced on some 140,000 taxpayers. The law required taxpayers to adopt costly and difficult procedures to make it easier for the Income Tax Department to extract more taxes. Such reforms require changes in the attitudes and behavior of many taxpayers. Israel's economy is not as formal as those of other Western countries. Many concerns operate without any meaningful books. Closed companies and family businesses lack formal internal controls.

The announcement that the department would enforce the new bookkeeping regulations aroused a commotion in the diamond industry. Its members threatened to leave the country in mass unless they were given special privileges with respect to bookkeeping. Petty merchants in Jerusalem shut down their stores. Their colleagues in the bazaars followed suit. Diamond traders and the sellers of fruits and vegetables gained concessions. At the end of 1976 the Jerusalem organization of merchants appealed to the Supreme Court of Justice against the new requirement to use cash registers to support books of account. The court ruled that cash registers are superior to hand-kept records and decided not to interfere with the commissioner's decision. Nevertheless, little progress was made in inducing petty merchants to adopt cash registers. It was decided to waive the obligation for them entirely.

The Income Tax Department has inadequate sanctions for enforcing compliance with its bookkeeping regulations. Taxpayers who do not keep books are not permitted to deduct depreciation, interest, and bad debts from their taxable incomes. Furthermore, such taxpayers must pay a higher tax rate than if they kept proper books. Taxpayers without records, however, can make up for such penalties by deflating their claimed income. Even by the most optimistic counts there are 100,000 taxpayers who do not adhere to required bookkeeping practices. And no one has yet surveyed the *quality*—that is, reliability—of the records kept by those taxpayers who seem to comply.

The Income Tax Department has tried to identify taxpayers who do not comply with the bookkeeping requirements. Yet the department cannot use experienced auditors for the survey; such personnel are needed to assess the considerable backlog of returns. At one point the department hired temporary personnel for the surveys of compliance with bookkeeping requirements. Because they were not trained extensively, the surveyors could not determine the quality of the records they were shown. Although the department received substantial quantities of data, it took no systematic action against noncompliers.

Reform and Technical Personnel

Reform is expensive. It requires resources over and above what is needed to continue existing routines. The Income Tax Department's supply of personnel was inadequate even before the reform. The reform made things worse. While imposing new demands and leaving old problems (unresolved assessments and overdue accounts) the reform did not bring with it the resources needed for implementation. The department actually became poorer instead of richer.

A drain of skilled personnel began with the start of implementation. Within a little more than a year the department lost a third of its force of inspectors. Three factors contributed to the drain of personnel. First, another reform commission recommended that all special salary payments be abolished in the public services. Revenue officials were heading the list, with their special benefits among the highest. As the government implemented the recommendations to do away with special payments, revenue personnel needed to implement the tax reform were facing *reduced* salaries. Second, at the same time government salaries were reduced, the demand for people skilled in accounting shot upward in the private sector. The reform in income taxation that had boosted the department's need for accountants also boosted the need in the private sector. The department lost skilled personnel just when it needed them most. All levels of experienced officials left the department—from low-grade inspectors to legal counsels and a deputy commissioner. Third, the government was operating an austerity program that included a freeze on civil service jobs. Every increase in personnel had to be authorized by a special cabinet committee. When the commissioner of income tax requested budget and personnel increases to implement his reform, he added one more urgent need to a long list of requests from all corners of government. Any massive help to the Income Tax Department would have encouraged others to press for relief, and would have endangered the entire policy of restraint.

Strikes and slowdowns in the department brought some increases in salary, but not enough to stop the continued loss of personnel. The department faced difficulties in finding replacements for those officials who left. Israel lacks sufficient numbers of skilled accountants. Supply problems range back to the universities. In response to the demand for accountants the universities have projected new or expanded programs, but neither teaching staff nor funds are handy.

Personnel problems wreaked havoc with the plans to implement income tax reforms. Instead of finishing the first year with a reduced backlog, the Income Tax Department ended up with an even larger one. There were plans to launch a selective audit program covering 10,000 files, but no more than a few hundred were completed. Even routine work suffered. The department lost the public support it had gained with the successful implementation of the withholding. Many news items and editorials in all major newspapers proclaimed that the reform was dead or dying.

SIGNS OF THINGS TO COME

The implementation of ambitious reforms evolves through encounters with various conditions. Instead of the simple enactment of plans, there is an adaptation of original goals to constraints and opportunities. The original proposal of reform becomes only one of several inputs to the process of change. At the end of three years of implementation, signs of the reform's impact were mixed. The reformers encountered some disappointments. Other accomplishments are apparent, both in the Income Tax Department and in auxiliary institutions.

Because of shortfalls in the goals of self-assessment and selective auditing, the department developed fallback procedures to cope with its growing workload. One fallback is an estimated assessment based upon certain income indicators. The department hopes that this will replace the careful examination of each self-employed taxpayer's file. A second measure increases steeply the monthly advances on taxes that the self-employed are required to pay. The idea is to move towards a full PAYE system of assessment and collection, cutting down on the need to examine individual files at the end of each year. The trouble with this tactic is its dependence on the willingness of taxpayers to comply. It is one thing to calculate the tax of a wage earner and then require an employer to withhold it; it is a different matter to demand, without individual calculation, an increased rate from a self-employed taxpayer. The Income Tax Department risks noncompliance if it persists in demands of this kind, especially as they are made by officials who are not able to carry out assessments or other tasks according to a predetermined schedule.

The work plan of the department is increasing in its targets. The cases of noncompliance with the bookkeeping regulations sent to criminal investigation increased from 600 to 10,000 in one year. Plans are being made for carrying out selective audits, backed up by a central information-processing unit for handling returns and selecting the sample for audit.

It is still too early to tell for certain how the courts will treat taxpayers who commit offences under the new law. Without severe penalties it may not be possible to improve voluntary compliance. The courts have been getting tougher. In one judgment after another the judges have accepted the principle that tax evasion deserves a serious penalty. Justices of the Supreme Court usually uphold lower court decisions, even against appeals to reduce prison sentences on grounds of ill health. The reform may strengthen this trend. It is also too early to assess bookkeeping practices. Although more taxpayers are now keeping books according to the Income Tax Department's requirements, it is not possible to determine the reliability of their books. Unreliable accounts might be worse than no accounts at all; when a taxpayer keeps books the onus of proving evasion falls more heavily on the department.

CONCLUSION

An attractive policy is not sufficient to assume implementation. Unless policy is designed with an eye to the constraints and opportunities of administration there will be serious gaps between goals and outcomes. The income tax reform in Israel illustrates the problems that reformers encounter when they concentrate on goals at the expense of implementation.

Our goal is not only to provide another confirmation of the Pressman-Wildavsky (1973) thesis of incomplete implementation, but to see how an organization adapts to policies that it can neither fully implement nor ignore. Our main finding can be put in one word: *dilution*. The only components of the reform implemented completely were those focused on the easiest group of taxpayers—wage earners. All their benefits are now taxed as income, with a new, and reduced, rate structure applied to incomes. For the components of the reform meant to deal with independent business and professional people—that is, comprehensive filing, record keeping, self-assessment, and reliance on selective audits—the record is one of compromised and abandoned goals. What started as a rational and systematic process of policy formulation ended in an implementation process where events were determined by the push and pull of available skills and resources, pressures to do this while paying less attention to that, capacity to do what comes closest to existing routines, and the judgment of department personnel.

We should not expect that a complex and ambitious reform will be implemented exactly as planned. In engineering physical projects it is taken for granted that reality will look different from what is portrayed on the drawing board. But the first commandment of reform is to make things work better, not worse. When a reform is designed without ample consideration of the mechanisms of implementation there is a danger—which materialized in the case we have studied—that more harm than good may be done in certain aspects of a program. In this case, backlogs have worsened. Recently, senior Income Tax Department officials stated that the brain drain triggered by the reform has reached proportions of total collapse. The department may not be able to question returns and may have to accept taxpayers' reports as filed.

More than implementing the reform, the principal concern now is to get the department back to its previous strength. Long-term achievements may outweigh failures. Reformers may be able to argue that their own ambitious goals contributed to the results actually achieved. We may need, as Laurence E. Lynn has written (1977), "new ideas and . . . active efforts to inject them into public debate"; too much emphasis on "the technocracy of implementation" may stifle innovation. Convincing as this argument may be, however, it is not much help to those who must collect revenue for the coming year.

NOTE

1. A pay-as-you-earn system is used to collect tax from salaried taxpayers, while companies and the self-employed pay advances and must file a return at the end of the year. For a detailed description of these procedures see Wilkenfeld (1973), pp. 76–79.

9

An Overview of Experience

Some tax reforms introduced (if not always effectively implemented) in developing countries have in part reflected large-scale research activities staffed mainly by foreigners. In other instances, similar proposals have fallen on stony ground and led to little or no perceptible reform, owing to such factors as adverse political conditions, intervening economic disaster, or the simple lack of a sufficiently large corpus of trained and motivated people to oversee and implement tax reform. Sometimes, tax reforms have originated from more indigenous sources—though seldom if ever in isolation from solicited or unsolicited advice from abroad—but have equally been more or less successful depending on their nature, the circumstances under which they were proposed and implemented, and the criteria by which success or failure is to be judged.

Large-scale, "once-and-for-all" reform proposals continue to be generated, of course, and will doubtless continue to flourish or fail, as the case may be. Most tax changes in most countries, however—whether they are best characterized as reforms or "deforms" (Musgrave, 1982)—will likely continue to occur in a piecemeal, incremental fashion and to reflect more the response of hard-pressed revenue authorities to the exigencies of the day than a principled approach towards comprehensive tax reform. Nonetheless, such responses are often shaped to some extent by the general trend of thinking about tax policy in the world at large, whether it be the interventionist optimism of the immediate postwar period or the supply-side pessimism of more recent years. In particular, given the financial dependence of many developing countries on bilateral and international aid, such bodies as the U.S. Agency for International Development, the World Bank, and the International Monetary Fund have over the years served as a particularly important channel of outside influence on tax policy in many developing countries.

No single body has been more important in this respect than the Fiscal Affairs Department of the International Monetary Fund. The magnitude of this group's contribution to the literature on taxation in developing countries will quickly become obvious if one scrutinizes the reference list for this book. Many of the items included come directly from the extensive output of the Fiscal Affairs Department or from people (including one of the editors) whose work has been influenced by their former association with the department. In addition to its research, the Fiscal Affairs Department has, since its creation in 1964, played an important role in training hundreds of officials from developing countries and in providing short- and long-term technical assistance to a wide range of countries. Unfortunately from the view of improving knowledge, IMF rules require all such technical assistance reports to be held strictly confidential. Nonetheless, this vast experience exists and has obviously been drawn upon, albeit only in general terms, by Richard Goode, director of the Fiscal Affairs Department for some sixteen years, in formulating the following account of the principal obstacles to tax reform in developing countries.

Perhaps the first point to note about Goode's paper is that, as earlier emphasized, the starting point in the discussion of tax reform in developing countries is assumed to be the need for additional revenue. Major tax changes occur as a rule when taxes increase. Conceivably, circumstances, such as a mineral bonanza, may at times permit a reduction in taxes so that potential losers from reforms may be compensated. The latter seldom occurs in developing countries, however; and even when it does the reaction to reduced pressure on the revenue system is often more likely to be no reform than more reform (Bird, 1970a). Almost never does one encounter in practice the textbook exercise of an equal-revenue "tax substitution."

Secondly, as pointed out in chapter 4, the data problems in determining what needs to be done and how best to do it cannot be overemphasized, particularly when it comes to the critical connections between fiscal means and economic ends. The behavior of households as suppliers of labor and consumers and the behavior of firms as investors are hard enough to pin down in countries overwhelmed with data, such as the United States (see the on-going controversy on the effect of taxes on saving: Sandmo, 1985). One may readily imagine how much more difficult the task must be, in, say, Botswana, Thailand, or Ecuador. Indeed, in some countries it may be exceedingly difficult to put together even the sketchiest picture of the actual tax base, let alone to simulate the effects of proposed changes on revenues. As a rule, however, our combined experience in several dozen countries suggests that, with some effort, it is usually feasible to pull together sufficient data to say something useful about how the existing system really works and even to some extent what the effects of certain changes might be. For examples of this patchwork approach, see Shoup (Shoup et al., 1959) on Venezuela, and Bahl (forthcoming) on Jamaica.

A third point which emerges clearly from Goode's discussion is the danger of bad advice. Examples, unfortunately, abound, ranging from the apocryphal tale of an early adviser who traveled the world urging, in effect, the adoption of the U.S. internal revenue code, to the all too many examples of flying visits by experts who have no idea of the real nature of the institutional setting in which they are so confidently recommending changes—and who too often seem to believe that their advice is equally valid in all conceivable settings.

Indeed, probably the greatest problem with outside experts is their inevitable ignorance of many of the critical factors that have not only shaped the existing system but will also influence what can and will be done in the future. On the other hand, this invincible ignorance may at times prove to be the greatest strength of outsiders relative to more knowledgeable locals, since the latter may be so paralyzed by their knowledge of the many reasons why nothing can be done that they do nothing—even in circumstances where something really must be done. Still, as a rule, advice from outsiders is likely to prove more palatable and more likely to succeed if it is, as Goode suggests, incremental, pragmatic, and closely adapted to the changing conditions of the specific country concerned.

Obstacles to Tax Reform in Developing Countries

Richard Goode

Although progress has been made in improving many tax systems, it is easy to find fault with existing systems. Most of them fall far short of the ideals promoted by the authors of treatises and textbooks and official reports. There is a large stock of reform proposals that have neither been put into effect nor definitively rejected. Why is tax reform so difficult? In considering obstacles to reform, I shall concentrate on developing countries, though industrial countries face similar difficulties.

SHORTCOMINGS OF EXISTING TAX SYSTEMS

The most obvious shortcoming of the tax systems of the great majority of developing countries is their inadequate yield. They do not produce enough revenue to pay for the ambitious expenditure programs that governments have undertaken. The resulting budget deficits have been financed to an excessive extent by money creation and borrowing abroad with consequent inflation and foreign debt problems. In principle, the deficit problem could be resolved by cutting expenditures and raising charges for services. But, with realistic allowances for expenditure economies and nontax revenue, it seems clear that many countries will need to increase tax revenue.

Tax reform for these countries should provide both for improvements in the tax structure and for additional revenue. Structural improvements would make it possible to raise more revenue with smaller undesirable effects than would occur if rates of existing taxes were simply increased or another tax were added to those in effect. Admittedly, there is a risk that controversies about structural revisions will unduly delay revenue increases and also a risk that the attempt to raise more revenue will solidify opposition to the whole program, including revisions that otherwise would be acceptable.

Recognition of these risks has stimulated interest in the possibility of revenue-neutral tax reform. In my opinion, however, that approach would rarely be advisable for a country that needs more revenue. Significant changes in tax structures usually are connected with revenue increases or decreases. One reason is that, with

Goode (1987). The author is Guest Scholar, the Brookings Institution, Washington, D.C. Opinions and interpretations are the author's and should not be ascribed to the trustees, officers, or staff members of the Brookings Institution or to the International Monetary Fund, where the author served as director of the Fiscal Affairs Department from 1965 to 1981.

many subjects competing for attention, decision makers in government are unlikely to take up taxation repeatedly in any short period of time. Another reason may be that in a revenue-neutral reform the redistribution of taxes between groups and individuals is obvious and is especially likely to arouse the hostility of losers, who cannot be mollified by arguments about the dangers of the budget deficit or the harm in cutting expenditures.

Over time, revenue adequacy would be enhanced by revisions that would make tax yields more responsive to economic growth and less vulnerable to inflation. Sometimes it is argued that revenue elasticity is objectionable because it allows a tax increase without explicit legislation. I find that position unrealistic. In the great majority of countries government expenditure tends to grow faster than national income (Goode, 1984, 53–59). Political leaders are reluctant to propose frequent increases in tax rates or the introduction of new taxes, probably because they believe that by doing so they would use up political capital needed for other purposes. Hence, the absence of revenue elasticity is likely to be more conducive to large budget deficits than to expenditure restraint or frequent discretionary tax increases. Of course, the share of government expenditures and tax revenue in national income cannot grow without limit; at some point, high income elasticity will cease to be a virtue.

A second set of criticisms concerns inequities in taxation in the developing countries. If judged by strict standards, horizontal inequities occur because the excises and import duties that are prominent in the revenue systems of these countries discriminate among persons on the basis of their taste for the taxed items rather than more appropriate indices of ability to pay or benefit. By less exacting standards, horizontal inequities result from unequal and incomplete application of both indirect and direct taxes. Because of the predominance of indirect taxes, the revenue systems of developing countries are often believed to be regressive. That opinion, however, was not confirmed by the incidence studies examined by De Wulf (1975). The studies, it should be recognized, are inconclusive because of statistical and theoretical weaknesses.

Taxation is charged with creating or aggravating economic inefficiencies in developing countries. The unequal incidence of taxes—due partly to legal provisions and partly to incomplete enforcement—tends to direct activities to lightly taxed sectors, which may not be those that are most productive. Tax systems, combined with other forms of government intervention, frequently handicap exports, provide unintended and excessive protection from imports, discriminate against the employment of labor compared with capital, and distort business organizations. The interaction of taxes with inflation tends to discourage saving through financial intermediaries and to encourage borrowing and speculation.

Tax systems are unnecessarily complex. Some of them include scores or even hundreds of taxes adopted over time with little consideration of how they relate to each other or to economic objectives. A series of taxes and surcharges may be levied on the same base or, worse, on slightly dissimilar bases. Many of the measures may yield only trivial amounts of revenue.

Tax administration in many developing countries is weak and taxpayer compliance poor owing to a variety of causes. Technical divisions tend to be under-staffed while more routine positions are often overstaffed. Training is generally inadequate and compensation too low. Revenue organizations, influenced by countries' colonial heritages, may disperse responsibility for different taxes among agencies, while within each agency excessive centralization of authority exists. The spirit of voluntary compliance with tax laws is weak, and modern accounting and other information sources are little developed.

INTELLECTUAL OR ANALYTICAL DIFFICULTIES THAT HINDER REFORM

The shortcomings of the tax systems of developing countries have been described in detail in numerous reports and journal articles. Proposals for their correction have been repeatedly presented. Why then has not greater progress been made in tax reform? One obstacle may be intellectual complexities and analytical problems that, though not peculiar to taxation, limit our ability to assess the consequences of existing tax systems and possible changes.

Analytical difficulties occur at both the microeconomic and macroeconomic levels. Since reliable estimates of elasticities and cross-elasticities of demand and supply of taxed and untaxed goods are seldom available for developing countries, the revenue effect and economic impact of changes in commodity taxes are problematical. Revenue estimates often appear to imply the assumption of zero elasticity of demand and either perfectly elastic supply or a special kind of oligopolistic pricing. More serious is the absence of consensus, even of a qualitative nature, about questions such as the effect of a tax on interest income on the amount saved, of a tax on wages on work done, of a corporate profits tax on prices. Hard as it is to answer such questions on the simplifying assumptions (often made but seldom emphasized) that the market is unified nationally but closed internationally, the difficulties multiply when these assumptions are relaxed. A realistic analysis has to relax the assumptions and to allow for movements of factors of production and goods between the modern sector and the traditional sector of the taxing country and between that country and other countries—movements that often are sluggish but sometimes are surprisingly quick.

Another kind of difficulty is the lack of sufficient statistical data on the yield of detailed tax provisions, consumer budgets, and the distribution of household incomes to serve as a basis for quantitative estimates of the incidence of existing and alternative taxes.

Persons who are acutely aware of the theoretical uncertainties and the statistical gaps could well be immobilized. That would be especially likely if they considered it necessary to have a planning-model of the economy in order to identify even a limited set of improvements in the tax system (as has been maintained by critics of the customary pragmatic approach of tax specialists [Andic and Peacock, 1966]). Indeed, tax revisions that appear to rectify inefficiencies and inequities may make them worse. The now widely accepted "general theory of second best" (Lipsey and Lancaster, 1956) leads to the conclusion that, where many separate tax provisions causing economic inefficiencies exist, the elimination of some of them can move the economy farther away from an optimum allocation of resources. Many apparent inequities have been mitigated, or eliminated, by adjustments of prices and factor rewards and particularly by tax capitalization.

The intellectual and analytical difficulties have hindered tax reform, but I do not think that they have been the main obstacle. They have not prevented tax specialists and general economists, including some of those who have elaborated on the difficulties, from confidently advancing many recommendations for tax revision. My impression is that the theoretical uncertainties are most often adduced to cast doubt on the efficacy of measures disliked for other reasons. The uncertainties do figure to some extent in the deliberations of government policy makers. The possibility of finding respectable experts on both sides of questions greatly helps those who wish to defeat a proposal or to delay action.

POLITICAL OBSTACLES

Political obstacles are important barriers to tax reform. Loosely defined, they include the clash of values or objectives, the influence of the desire of government leaders to remain in power, the activities of interest groups, and the efforts of bureaucratic elites to retain and enhance their power and perquisites.

Tax reform seldom has a strong and active constituency outside government. To be sure, demands for changes are common, but usually they call for specific tax reductions or tinkering rather than principled reform. In the suggestive terminology of Albert Hirschman (1981), systematic tax reform may generally be classified as a "chosen" problem selected by policy makers for attention rather than a "pressing" problem forced on the policy makers by the pressure of interested or injured groups. The pressing problems are likely to be given priority.

The best way for advocates of reform to induce action on a chosen problem may be to link it to a pressing problem by asserting that the former is the root cause of the latter, or that the solution of the chosen problem must precede the solution of the pressing problem. Only rarely is such a link successfully forged for tax reform. Although government expenditures usually are required to attack pressing problems, expenditures for particular purposes are not perceived as depending on tax reform, even when the reform would raise additional revenue. Fiscal conservatives can argue that other, less essential expenditures should be cut to make room for the new or enlarged program. Or, following an easier course, the government may finance the expenditures by money creation or borrowing abroad. If, as seems to be so, tolerance of inflation and opportunities for borrowing abroad have diminished, the connection between a strong tax system and the possibility of responding to expenditure demands may become clearer to political leaders and others.

In regard to taxation, real or apparent conflicts exist among economic objectives. Individual political leaders often may find it hard to choose their preferred tax package. For example, shall liberal investment incentives be offered to stimulate growth, or shall progressive taxes be applied to profits to prevent increased concentration of wealth? Shall variable export duties be used to mitigate cyclical instability, or shall exports be tax-free to promote growth? Shall import duties be applied selectively to encourage the substitution of home production for imports, thereby emphasizing self-reliance at the cost of slower growth and greater income concentration? These choices may pose intellectual or moral dilemmas for anyone. They become political issues because of the different weighting that participants in the decision-making process place upon the objectives.

Even in a government regarded as a dictatorship, a considerable number of persons usually are able to influence decisions on taxation, either in their official capacities or as informal advisers. Although differences in economic priorities and consequent disagreements about taxation are better publicized in open, democratic systems than in dictatorial or authoritarian regimes, they usually exist also in the latter and may inhibit tax reform. Issues may continue unresolved for a long time because the head of government finds other questions more interesting, more important, and easier to understand or because his power is less absolute than it may appear.

Closer to the popular understanding of politics are the efforts of government leaders to prolong their tenure by favoring their actual and potential supporters, or at least not alienating them. The concerns of interest groups or pressure groups in regard to taxation are acute and are particularly significant in blocking tax reform. In less developed countries, institutions for the articulation and aggregation of interests are less numerous and weaker than in politically more mature societies, but this does not mean that either idealistic leaders or technocrats can dominate the formulation of tax policy. As examples of interest groups, large landowners and representatives of multinational enterprises may come first to mind, but also influential are the military—an especially strong interest group in many developing countries—and the political and bureaucratic elites.

The emergence of a strong middle class has been considered favorable to vigorous growth and development, and that seems to be correct. But the consumption demands of the urban middle class often inhibit the taxation of nonessential goods, particularly durables, which if properly applied could direct resources into development and constitute a progressive element in the revenue system.

The bureaucratic elite may identify more with the interests of client groups than with broad objectives as visualized by other policy makers. The close community of interests between highway departments and road and bridge builders and highway users is an example. This community of interests tends to hold down gasoline taxes and other taxes on road users and to perpetuate earmarking of the gasoline taxes that are imposed. Officials in financial agencies such as central banks, development banks, and security market commissions tend to oppose strict taxation of investment income and to support tax exemptions for interest and dividend income. The staffs of development agencies frequently advocate generous tax holidays and other tax benefits for foreign investors and oppose the curtailment of any existing privileges. In official circles, proposals for tax reform are met with statements of fear of capital flight or loss of additional investment, which are not always based on objective evidence and careful analysis.

But are the pressures of interest groups always antagonistic to tax reform? Is there no political counterpart of the invisible hand that Adam Smith believed would guide participants in the market to serve the public interest? Becker (1983) suggests that there is such a counterpart. He argues that competitive pressure groups, comprising taxpayers and recipients of government subsidies, will favor and lobby for economically efficient taxes, that is, for taxes with lower deadweight costs, because not only will taxpayers benefit but beneficiaries of government expenditures will gain because of lessened opposition to taxation. I find this proposition unconvincing. Tax revisions are almost never Pareto improvements in the strict sense. They almost invariably increase taxes on some and frequently decrease taxes on others; the losers are never compensated.

A reform that eliminates tax provisions causing economic inefficiencies may result in a widely shared gain in real national income. But, unless total revenue is reduced, it will increase taxes for some. If those whose taxes would be increased by a proposed reform compose a relatively narrow group but not a petty one—for example, investors and workers in an industry—they may successfully oppose it. Narrow interest groups are easily made aware of their particular benefits or losses from legislation and can be mobilized to support or oppose changes, whereas individual members of the general public, having less at stake and being more numerous, usually are less informed, less motivated, and harder to organize and hence are less influential even in democratic countries (Olson, 1965).

The disparity between the influence of narrow interest groups and the broad public need not always be unfavorable to tax reform. It could facilitate adoption of a proposal to eliminate a provision that causes a misallocation of resources by applying a high tax to a narrow sector and to make up the revenue loss by a widely shared tax increase. If the general analysis is correct, this situation will be less common than the opposite one, because the efforts of influential interest groups will tend to prevent the introduction of provisions unfavorable to them or to cause the early elimination of such provisions.

UNSUITABLE ADVICE

Another reason for slow progress in tax reform in developing countries is the character of much of the advice received by policy makers. In the majority of developing countries—but by no means all of them—there is a shortage of local fiscal experts. Governments have not established official tax research and planning units. There are few if any independent research organizations concerned with public affairs, and university studies usually are not oriented toward immediate issues in taxation. Advice on tax policy has often come from national officials who lack specialized knowledge or experience of the field or busy tax administrators who may take a parochial view or from visiting foreigners acting under various auspices and with different degrees of experience and expertise. My remarks are directed particularly to the work of the visiting foreigners.

However well conceived and presented, advice may fail to be accepted. Sometimes governments request advice, not because of serious interest in it, but to please an international organization or bilateral aid donor or to be quiet domestic critics. But the advisers often are partly to blame for the failures. They frequently advance proposals that seem unrealistic to political leaders and impracticable to administrators. Concepts of allocational efficiency and excess burden—not to mention the more esoteric doctrines of optimal taxation—that economists may employ without adequate explanation and justification are puzzling or repugnant to most politicians and officials. Economists often fail to recognize the shortness of the time horizons of most politicians. Economists tend to emphasize long-run benefits of tax changes and to neglect intervening transitional costs; politicians tend to do the contrary. Foreign experts may fail because they are unfamiliar with the country's history and institutions and are insensitive to the constraints that political leaders consider binding.

Of course, all advisers are the products of their culture and personal experience, and the advice they give inevitably will be shaped by that background, sometimes obviously, often in more subtle ways. Persons who are knowledgeable and experienced in regard to the tax systems of their own countries frequently suffer from ignorance of other systems and from lack of recognition of the connection between tax provisions that they take for granted and conditions existing in their own country but absent in the developing country they are advising.

Advisers may present their findings and recommendations in a form that decision makers find either too general or too detailed or obscure. They may address their reports more to fellow experts or to the world at large than to the readers who must be convinced if tax reforms are to be undertaken. This obstacle is less easily surmounted than may be supposed. Many good tax experts are poor writers. A clear and jargon-free prose style is not always highly valued in either the bureaucracy or the academy. Experts have their professional standards and are understandably reluctant to omit qualifications and refinements that seem significant to them though esoteric to ministers of finance. Furthermore, it is prudent to recognize that ministers often seek second and third opinions and to try to present a report in a way that will guard against damaging criticism by other experts without overcomplicating it for the original readers. Not an easy task.

Another weakness often found in tax reports is the advocacy of a comprehensive set of proposals for the complete reconstruction of the tax system rather than selected urgent revisions. Only rarely is the time ripe for a sweeping reform. Those who elaborate proposals for the full reconstruction of a tax system tend to underestimate the extent to which the existing system has influenced relative prices and property values and to pay too little attention to the economic costs and impairment of legitimate or quasi-legitimate vested interests when sudden, drastic changes in taxation occur. Moreover, a set of interrelated proposals that depend for their success on the enactment of the entire set is almost certain to fail because some components will be rejected or, if accepted in form, will not be effectively applied.

ADMINISTRATIVE AND COMPLIANCE WEAKNESSES

Many tax administrators are skeptical of innovations. They will oppose changes at the discussion stage and sometimes will withhold their best efforts to apply them if they are enacted. Policy makers may hesitate to accept recommendations because of the opposition of administrators or because of well-founded doubts about the administrative capacity of the revenue department.

Weak administration and poor compliance have made some tax legislation that seemed attractive in principle ineffective or inequitable in practice. For example, provisions for the taxation of capital gains, income from foreign sources, or personal wealth may be so sporadically applied that they become a trap for the unwary or the unlucky rather than a contribution to equity and revenue. India and Sri Lanka were unable to apply the direct taxes on personal consumption expenditures that they adopted on the recommendation of a distinguished foreign economist, Nicholas Kaldor, who put in concrete form an idea which had appealed to John Stuart Mill, Alfred Marshall, Irving Fisher, and Luigi Einaudi—and which Kaldor had unsuccessfully advocated for his own country.

CONCLUDING REMARKS

The obstacles to tax reform are formidable. But I do not wish to leave too dark a picture. Progress has been made. In most developing countries, tax revenue has grown faster than national income, as the result of the introduction of new taxes and rate increases, though revenue has lagged behind government expenditures in many cases. An important innovation has been the wide adoption and reasonably successful application of broad sales taxes. Global income taxes have replaced schedular taxes in several countries, and global complementary taxes usually supplement the schedular taxes in countries that have not adopted a unitary tax. Revenue departments have become more competent. The pressing need for revenue and the gravity of economic adjustment problems may concentrate the minds of government leaders and make them more receptive to new measures and to the elimination of unproductive and harmful provisions.

I believe that ordinarily fairer, more productive, and economically less harmful tax systems can better be achieved by a series of incremental improvements than by attempting one-time, comprehensive reforms. Because of the complexity of tax problems, competition among objectives, conflicting interests, and weak administration, ideal solutions may be difficult to state, except perhaps in highly abstract terms, and impossible to put into effect. There is no one model tax system suitable for all countries or even a few models for large groups of countries. Conditions differ too much to allow such a model or models to be acceptable. For any country, tax reform should be seen as a process of adaptation to changing conditions and priorities, informed by experience and innovations elsewhere, rather than a quick or slow movement to a fixed goal.

In most countries, desirable directions of immediate change on many points are fairly clear. While it may not be possible to demonstrate that the particular measures are optimal in any strict sense, it is possible to establish a rebuttable presumption that they are improvements. Opportunities for reform may arise when a new minister of finance or a new government takes office. Policy decisions often have to be taken to meet a specific problem or to respond to an emergency. It is important that these opportunities not be wasted by either inadequately considered ad hoc actions or in debate about stylish but impracticable ideas.

Part Three

Taxation and Incentives

The countries with which this book is concerned may be defined in many ways: "poor," "backward," "nonindustrialized," "less developed," "developing," and "Third World" are only some of the labels found in the literature at different times and with different shades of meaning. Whatever these countries may be called, however, one thing they presumably have in common is a desire to increase their rate of economic growth. A central concern of tax policy makers in developing countries, therefore, is how best to produce adequate revenues to finance public sector activities without unduly discouraging the private sector's essential contribution to growth.

In recent years the classical stress both on the desirability of keeping government as lean as possible, thus reducing the total need for taxes, and on the damaging economic effects of improperly designed taxes has undergone a revival. One manifestation of this revival is what has been called "supply-side economics," a major policy tenet of which is to reduce the deleterious effects of taxes on growth. In particular, the progressive personal income tax has often been singled out as misconceived, by those who take this approach.

Two quite different approaches are sometimes subsumed under the label of supply-side taxation. One concentrates on designing the basic tax structure so as to extract the needed revenues with the least damage to economic growth. This approach, earlier explored by Carl Shoup (1966) in chapter 3, has recently been developed further in such studies as Wanniski (1978) and Canto, Joines, and Laffer (1983) and is reviewed by Ved Gandhi (1987) in chapter 10. This review is supplemented by Liam Ebrill (1987) in chapter 11 with a review of the scanty evidence available on the actual effects of taxes on savings and investment in developing countries. (For a similarly inconclusive review of the third part of the supply-side trinity, labor supply, see Ebrill, 1987.) In general, as Gandhi emphasizes and as is pointed out by Assar Lindbeck (1987) in chapter 5, supply-siders who take this structural approach tend to be against selective tax incentives—the alternative supply-side approach mentioned above.

One reason for this view is the underlying supply-side view that "the market knows best" how to allocate investment resources, so that there is little need for government to influence investment through selective incentives. Another is the perception that such incentives have little beneficial effect in any case. This conclusion emerges strongly from the survey of fiscal incentives for investment by S. K. Shah and John Toye (1978) included as chapter 12. In addition, Shah and

Toye stress that the incentives currently in place in many developing countries both complicate administration and reduce the equity of the tax system. In chapter 13 Dan Usher (1977) makes the point that it is extremely difficult, even in principle, to design effective investment incentives, let alone to operate them efficiently in practice.

Despite these difficulties, many countries will undoubtedly continue in the future, as in the past, to attempt to influence both the level of private investment and its structure. The second of these objectives seems more likely to be achieved than the first. Most studies suggest that the level of investment is not particularly sensitive to tax incentives (Bird, 1980a). In an open economy, however, depending in part on the international interaction of tax systems (see Part 4), it is not impossible in principle for a country to be able to increase total investment marginally by attracting more net foreign investment (Hartman, 1984). In any case, the structure of investment is clearly more responsive to tax-induced changes in profitability, whether they be directed (as Keith Marsden, 1983, suggested in chapter 2) to fostering higher-productivity exporting sectors, to influencing the regional direction of investment, or perhaps simply to encouraging those sectors and activities that are favored for some reason, good or bad, by those in a position to influence policy.

The case has been strongly made for export incentives as one component of the move towards a more "outward looking" development policy (Balassa, 1975), although most of those who discuss this matter give more emphasis to "getting the prices right" in the sense of exchange rates and tariff levels than to the more selective export incentives surveyed in De Wulf (1978). As for regional incentives—for which, incidentally, it is possible to construct an efficiency rationale in some instances (Sanchez-Ugarte, 1987)—most of them are poorly designed (McLure, 1971), difficult to administer (McLure, 1980), and not very effective (Modi, 1982). Nonetheless, there is no question that such incentives may to some extent influence the location of activities (Hirschman, 1968), although, as with all incentives, it is open to question whether the resulting allocation will be better or worse than that which would have prevailed in the absence of the incentive.

Special fiscal incentives may also be given for saving. The evidence is that such incentives more clearly affect the structure of financial saving than its level (Byrne, 1976). Moreover, in an open economy savings incentives are likely to affect more who owns a country's capital stock than the size of that stock. If a country induces its citizens to hold more of their savings in the form of domestic financial assets through tax incentives (on the Japanese, Canadian, or French models, for instance), the effect will be more to displace foreign savings than to raise the level of savings (or investment). The reason, of course, is simply that in a completely open (small) economy, the rate of return on savings, being set in world capital markets, is not affected by such measures. If locals save more locally, foreigners must contribute less to savings in the country in question: total savings do not change. In open economies, investment incentives are thus more likely to be efficacious than savings incentives—which is not to say that investment incentives are necessarily a good idea!

In any case, however efficient and effective they may or may not be, fiscal incentives for investment are likely to continue to exist in many countries for some years to come. Chapters 14 and 15 illustrate some techniques for designing such incentives as efficiently as possible and for analyzing how well they work. The concept of the marginal effective tax rate, introduced by Anthony Pellechio, Gerardo Sicat, and David Dunn (1987) in chapter 14, has, for example, come into wide use in empirical work in recent years (King and Fullerton, 1984; Boadway, 1987). Although the policy implications of divergent effective rates are open to dispute (Mintz and Purvis, 1987), there is no question that such calculations are of considerable use in understanding and comparing different tax incentives. The "cost-benefit" approach to incentives set out by Wayne Thirsk (1984) in chapter 15 has, in addition to its obvious intrinsic merits, the considerable virtue of showing how importantly other policy parameters—in this case trade policy—can affect the outcome of particular tax incentive packages.

Despite the widespread use of tax incentives in developing—and developed—countries, their efficacy has in fact seldom been evaluated. The data required are almost never collected by the investment promotion agencies or planning authorities that are generally responsible for initiating and administering incentives. Nor do the tax authorities track the benefits received by the favored firms. Indeed, in most countries, even those which have made most use of incentives, such as Puerto Rico (Taylor, 1957, 1960), as a rule no one has a good idea of either the revenue cost of the incentives or the size of any net economic benefits that may be attributable to them. The latter notion is, as Usher (1977) shows in chapter 13, conceptually difficult to pin down—although, as Thirsk (1984) shows in chapter 15, at least in some cases it may be approximated roughly. In most countries, however, no good records are kept with respect to the revenue cost of incentives. Nevertheless, as Lotfi Maktouf and Stanley Surrey (1983) argue in chapter 16, while there are both conceptual and practical problems in recording such "tax expenditures," the problems are much less than those of a full cost-benefit analysis. Such cost information is an obvious and essential first step in the analysis of fiscal incentives.

The conflicting advice and information on tax incentives for investment set out in this part (and elsewhere in this volume) is hard to summarize. One way to do so may be to postulate three rules for incentive-oriented tax designers. The first rule—one of much wider applicability with respect to taxation in developing countries—is to keep it simple. Complex provisions and attempts to "fine tune" the economy are generally not suitable in the circumstances of developing countries, most of which, by definition, have neither the information nor the administrative capability required to implement such incentives. Tax incentives in such countries should therefore be few, simple, and preferably limited in duration, both to increase their impact on investment timing and to comply with the third rule stated below.

A second rule, equally obvious and equally often ignored in practice, is to keep good records on who gets incentives, for how long, and at what estimated cost in revenue forgone (under the usual assumptions as set out in chapter 16). In the absence of such information, there is no chance at all that incentives will play any useful role in development policy. They will more likely prove to be little more than an advertising gimmick to attract foreign capital or a means of rewarding worthy political supporters.

Thirdly, combining certain aspects of the first and second rules, incentives should always be subject to a "sunset" provision, requiring them periodically to be explicitly evaluated in quantitative terms and, if not found worthwhile, terminated. If a country is unwilling or unable to do this, it should not be in the incentive business at all.

To a country adhering to these rules, it will be of little importance whether incentives are granted in the tax law itself (like accelerated depreciation) and given to all those who qualify, or are dispensed under a separate investment code by a special agency to those firms which accord with a set of priorities. On the whole, however, experience suggests that it is probably best to keep any (simple) incentives in the tax law and to charge the tax administration explicitly with the task of maintaining the required records. The common "two-track" system of a special investment incentive regime for favored firms too often results in what are in effect totally different tax systems being applied to investments of equal national importance. The path of wisdom for most developing countries is to avoid extensive and detailed attempts to deflect private investment into preselected channels—all too often with no follow-up to see what really happens and with no set procedures for ensuring that the infants thus expensively fostered grow up to be full taxpaying citizens.

10

Supply-Side Taxation

The careful review in the following chapter of the set of ideas known as "supply-side taxation" shows clearly that, although some of the ideas put forward under this heading are unlikely to work well, if at all, in the context of developing countries, the general direction and strategy of this approach is both widely acceptable and basically workable. Since one major conclusion of this discussion is that the basic supply-side prescription, realistically interpreted, amounts to broadening tax bases and lowering tax rates—precisely what has been traditionally recommended by "mainstream" tax reformers—this is not too surprising. The attention sometimes paid by supply-siders to such minor matters as the top marginal rate of the personal income tax is undoubtedly excessive, and in many ways the entire "supply-side revolution" may prove to be little more than a flash in the pan. Nonetheless, the recent supply-side discussion has usefully served to call attention to the potentially important implications of some details of tax design for the achievement of the growth objective.

A number of features of the following review of this discussion by Ved Gandhi deserve particular attention. In the first place, in line with most of the supply-side literature Gandhi focuses mainly on direct personal taxes (including the income versus consumption debate taken up again in chapter 18). Although he notes in passing the possible role of taxes in internalizing externalities, he does not discuss the many ways the detailed design of indirect taxes may affect desired policy outcomes (McLure, 1975). One reason for this relative neglect may be because Gandhi sees no place in an ideal supply-side system for a general sales tax. Although this conclusion is superficially similar to the optimal-tax position (see chapter 4), it is arrived at for quite different reasons, since concern for tax equity is conspicuously absent from supply-side considerations.

Secondly, like Lindbeck (chapter 5) and Gillis (chapter 6) but unlike Marsden (chapter 2) and the case of Korea (chapter 7), Gandhi interprets supply-side analysis as being clearly against the use of selective incentives. That is, he sees it as strongly market-oriented rather than pointing the way to increased fiscal interventionism in the name of economic growth.

Thirdly, he sees little role in an ideal supply-side tax system for wealth taxes other than on land (but see chapter 24), corporate taxes (see chapters 19 and 22), or export and import taxes (see chapters 27 and 28). Most of these positions, as Gandhi himself notes, fly in the face of reality and are in any case, as the references to other selections in this volume show, arguable. In the end, supply-side taxation, like optimal taxation (see chapter 4) or the growth-oriented system sketched by Shoup (1966) in chapter 3, is more an ideal than a feasible objective. Countries may wish to take some or all of the characteristics of such ideal systems into account in designing or reforming their taxes; but they are most unlikely, given the multi-objective nature of taxation as a policy instrument, to follow such prescriptions blindly.

Tax Structure for Efficiency and Supply-Side Economics in Developing Countries

Ved P. Gandhi

A review of selected traditional and modern literature on taxation shows that there is agreement as to the bases that should be taxed if allocative efficiency were the only consideration of policy makers (see table 10.1). Those taxes that either have no effect on relative prices or have no substitution effects would be considered most desirable. The next in line would be those taxes that have least distortionary effects on relative prices.

APPROPRIATE TAXES FOR EFFICIENCY OBJECTIVE

A tax system geared toward efficiency or supply-side objectives alone would consist of the following taxes:
1. taxes for internalizing negative externalities
2. poll tax
3. taxes on land area
4. taxes on windfall or monopoly profits
5. taxes on items with inelastic demand (such as basic necessities)
6. taxes on the ability of individuals to earn income, or on potential income (The second-best alternatives to this proposal would be either a tax on accrued income of an individual coupled with taxes on the consumption of complements to leisure, or a tax on life-time personal expenditures.)

The rationale for taxes for internalizing the externalities and the poll tax is clear although the poll tax is justified only when the assumption of no migration is made. Taxes on land area are defensible on the assumption that land is in inelastic supply, so that the ground rent of land is a sort of economic rent. Taxes on windfall or monopoly profits are justified on the ground that they will not affect price and production decisions made by producers before the imposition of such taxes. Taxes on basic necessities are defended on the ground that these commodities tend to have inelastic demand.

A tax on ability to earn income or on potential income is also acceptable but this requires further explanation. Whereas a tax on actual earnings allows a person to favor leisure over work, a tax on potential income as determined by ability (which is inelastic in supply) is said to be nondistortionary (Tanzi, 1980; Millward et al.,

Excerpted from Gandhi (1987).

Table 10.1   *Characteristics of a Tax System Consistent with Efficiency and Supply-Side Economics*

Objective(s)	Tax Base(s)	Tax Rate(s)
No effect on relative prices	User prices for most public services and a lump-sum tax and/or a tax on completely inelastic base to finance pure public goods	User prices as determined by the equilibrium of demand and supply for public services and any rate of lump-sum tax as well as tax on completely inelastic base
Affect relative market prices but only to correct market failures and externalities	Taxes on negative production and consumption externalities	A rate of tax which will capture the degree of externality
Least distortion of choices of economic agents	Taxes on items of relatively inelastic (or less elastic) demand and relatively inelastic (or less elastic) supply of both commodities and factors of production	Tax rate inversely related to elasticity of demand and positively related to elasticity of supply

1983). However, ability is difficult to measure, so that a tax on potential income will be difficult to administer. Hence a tax on accrued income (including own consumption, transfers by gifts and bequests, and unrealized capital gains), though a poor second best, is considered a vast improvement over existing income tax systems, which are based on realized money incomes and which contain many tax shelters and loopholes. But a tax on accrued income, besides entailing the well-known problem of how to measure the unrealized gains, would still suffer from intratemporal and intertemporal inefficiencies: the leisure component of welfare or economic capacity would still remain tax free, resulting in intratemporal welfare loss from distortions in work-leisure choices, and savings would continue to be penalized by double taxation causing intertemporal inefficiency. (The latter would be exacerbated by inflation.)

To avoid the distorting effect of income taxes on intratemporal choices, and recognizing the difficulties of taxing leisure, taxes on consumption goods that are complements to leisure are generally recommended. To avoid the distorting effect of income taxes on intertemporal choices, the exemption of savings from the tax base is favored and the levy of a flat-rate tax on the lifetime consumption of an individual (with a personal exemption or an exemption that recognizes differences in family circumstances) is considered theoretically attractive. Leisure will, nonetheless, remain untaxed even under a personal consumption or expenditure tax, producing a disincentive to work; consequently, even the proposal to replace an income tax by a personal consumption tax will not be completely satisfactory on efficiency grounds. However, the efficiency losses of an expenditure tax are stated to be much smaller than those of the present income tax, which is frequently based on realized incomes and a nonindexed tax base, and which arbitrarily discriminates among various forms of savings (e.g., in favor of owner-occupied housing and against equity investment).

Efficiency or supply-side considerations would thus demand that many taxes existing in the tax systems of developing and developed countries should be eliminated. There is no place, for example, in such a system for the following:

1. A separate corporation income tax—for without imputation (adequate credit to the shareholder), it is an additional tax on the form of business organization, and all incomes and taxes must, in the final analysis, be imputed to individuals. In addition, a corporation income tax also tends to be nonneutral whenever (a) tax depreciation differs from economic depreciation; (b) inventory valuation in inflationary times is different from that on replacement basis (last in, first out rather than first in, first out); and (c) dividends are treated differently from interest payments. The tax can become neutral provided these differences are eliminated or the tax allows "free depreciation" and is based on cash flow rather than on profits.
2. Tax loopholes, special tax preferences, or tax incentives—for they affect relative taxes and prices. (Although some of these may be defended on the grounds that they accommodate market failures, an expenditure subsidy rather than a tax expenditure is the proper vehicle for meeting this objective.)
3. A wealth tax—for in the final analysis this is only an additional tax on savings and capital accumulation.
4. Gifts and transfer taxes—for a tax on accrued incomes would theoretically cover all receipts from gifts and transfers.
5. A general sales tax—for this tends to affect consumer choices, especially as all goods and services with very different elasticities of demand and supply tend to be taxed relatively uniformly.
6. A payroll tax—for it is an arbitrary additional tax on wage incomes.
7. A separate capital gains tax—for capital gains are theoretically included in accrued income.

In the specific circumstances of developing countries, an efficiency-based tax system would require, in addition, the elimination of both export duties (unless they are seen as taxes on windfalls only, not affecting incentives) and import duties (unless they are seen as protecting domestic industry only temporarily during which the externalities resulting therefrom can be internalized).

There will also be no case for other narrowly based taxes, such as an urban property tax or a rural land tax, which affect relative sectoral prices.

HOW REALISTIC IS SUCH A TAX SYSTEM?

How realistic is it to institute in developing countries a tax system solely for the efficiency objective, as described above?

First, the normative theorizing implicit in the strictly efficiency-oriented tax structure is based on certain assumptions that may not be valid in the special circumstances of developing countries. It assumes that government is not, and in fact should not, be a major producer in its own right, beyond being a supplier of a few essential public goods. Moreover, it assumes that all private individuals are rational and optimizing agents responding to price signals alone (where the market

prices reflect true social costs) and that there are no social and institutional determinants of, and constraints on, either market prices or their behavior (which can be
removed by government actions). Other assumptions are that there is perfect
mobility of factors of production and that income distribution is reasonably appropriate without redistributive taxation and expenditure policies of the government.

Second, an efficiency-oriented tax system (especially one that consists of taxes
on basic necessities while luxuries could be exempt) will be politically unacceptable.

Third, there is little resemblance between the efficient tax bases consistent with
supply-side considerations and the existing tax systems of developing countries,
which would suggest the introduction of a completely new tax system. But experience shows that the barriers to changing existing tax systems even modestly tend to
be fundamental because of the view that old taxes are good taxes. Moreover, major
tax changes profoundly affect capital values and imply sizable income and wealth
redistribution (capital-based taxes may already have been capitalized and reflected
in asset prices). Therefore, in a real sense, fundamental tax reform to institute a
completely new tax system, however desirable that may be from the efficiency
point of view, may well be just about impossible in reality (Feldstein, 1976).

Finally, the efficiency-dictated tax system, described above, may not provide
enough revenue to run a modern government, especially if a tax on potential
income is found to be administratively infeasible.

To conclude: The ingredients of a tax system for efficiency or supply-side
objectives are well known, as are the limitations of adopting such a system in the
real world. Therefore, in making their recommendations, tax reformers of developing countries not only must take all these factors into account, they must also be
aware that attempts at moving existing tax systems in the direction of meeting
efficiency and supply-side objectives are likely to be gradual at best.

A TAX SYSTEM DICTATED BY POPULAR SUPPLY-SIDE ECONOMICS: SOME IMPLICATIONS

Taxation is in practice an instrument with multiple objectives and will continue
to be so despite what economists profess. The conflict between the objectives of
equity and efficiency is fundamental. A tax system based solely on efficiency
grounds is unrealistic, while that designed solely for equity purposes cannot be
justified on allocative grounds. The degree of progressivity will, in practice,
continue to be dictated by political and social consensus rather than by the optimizing formulas of tax economists. One solid contribution of supply-side economics
has been to remind us that the way out of the conflict between the equity and
efficiency objectives of taxation is not to have high and progressive nominal tax
rates and generous tax incentives and preferences, as most developing countries do
(they achieve neither income redistribution nor desired resource reallocation), but
to have as wide a tax base as possible, as well as lower nominal tax rates. Tax
reforms along these lines will be consistent with supply-side economics as well as
with the same or even a greater degree of income redistribution.

Whether or not rates of taxes on incomes and profits in developing countries should be lowered significantly all at once or simply be restructured to reduce the degree of progression would depend very much upon the height of the present tax rates, government revenue from the existing high tax rates, the validity of the elasticity optimism of the popular supply-side approach in the context of developing countries (i.e., whether lowering tax rates will have much effect on production), and the relevance in the particular circumstances of a developing country of the assumptions on which supply-side theory is based. Should a developing country be serious about adopting the popular supply-side tax policy and lowering its income tax rates significantly, it must take into account the following five considerations.

First, the lowering of income tax rates must be accompanied by reforms in the income tax base, viz., the removal of tax preferences and tax concessions. The removal of narrowly based foreign trade taxes (e.g., export duties) and certain other taxes important to their tax systems (e.g., payroll and other selective taxes) may be equally, if not more, important on efficiency grounds. High tax rates and narrow and selective tax bases can create distortions, encourage unproductive activities, erode the revenue base, and lower the effective tax rates below the intended nominal tax rates. Tax cuts without reforms in the tax base can introduce more distortions of efficiency and equity than they correct, especially if they result in inflationary finance.

Second, tax rate reductions must be permanent or, at least, be perceived by taxpayers to be so if they are to have significant effects on savings and investment behavior. The theory of rational expectations suggests that investors change their behavior according to their expectations of the costs of capital, including their expectations of future tax rates over the lifetime of an investment. The same holds true for the behavior of savers. Besides, tax rate reductions would have to be substantial if they are to have a marked "net" effect on behavior, especially because selective tax exemptions and concessions, which may have been enjoyed by savers and investors and which may have had some positive economic effect on their behavior, may now be withdrawn from the tax structure.

Third, short-run elasticities frequently tend to be lower than long-run elasticities for a given change in prices; consequently, it would be advisable to expect the full supply-side effects of a reduction of tax rates to become evident only in the longer run.

Fourth, reducing tax rates for supply-side effects (including to improve tax compliance and to further other objectives) must go hand-in-hand with government expenditure cuts and reforms of public enterprise pricing, at least in the short run, or until elasticity optimism materializes. Otherwise there will be a growing budget deficit and a likely rise in inflation (depending upon the sources of financing) with its own distortions and unintended economic consequences. For example, if people expect inflation to continue, and interest rates do not adjust with inflation, they will spend rather than save in the current period, thereby negating the effect of tax cuts on savings and investment.

Fifth, the use to which tax revenues are put in developing countries is also relevant. If a large proportion of government expenditure is directed at financing desirable human capital and social and economic infrastructure in an efficient manner, it removes supply bottlenecks, aids the development process, and provides the justification for higher tax rates. On the other hand, if government revenues go toward financing a large and unproductive civil service or nonpriority capital expenditure, they support wasteful consumption rather than capital formation.

In the final analysis, a tax structure for efficiency and supply-side economics calls for fundamental reforms in the existing tax systems of developing countries. The reforms will have to be directed at reducing the distortionary effects of their existing taxes, which would require removing most exclusions and exemptions and widening the tax base, while reducing rates of taxation. In the context of the tax structures prevalent in developing countries, this strategy would apply not only to personal income tax, which is often an unimportant source of revenue in low-income countries, but to all other direct and indirect taxes as well.

11

Taxes, Saving, and Investment

The recent interest in supply-side taxation has to a considerable extent been fueled by increasing evidence that the adverse economic effects of taxes are much more serious than was once thought to be the case. Twenty-five years ago, for example, public finance students were commonly taught that savings were virtually insensitive to taxes. Over the last decade, however, there has been an enormous outpouring of empirical studies, many of which suggest both that savings and investment (as well as labor supply) are quite sensitive to tax-induced changes in the expected rate of return and that taxes also impose substantial deadweight losses (Sandmo, 1985). Most of this work, of course, has focused on the developed countries, and most notably on the United States. As chapter 11 by Liam Ebrill (1987) shows, however, there is also a surprisingly large body of empirical evidence bearing on these questions in developing countries. Unfortunately, as is the case in the United States as well (see Summers, 1981; Bosworth, 1984, for example), despite all these studies no clear conclusions have emerged on the key issues.

With respect to the effects of taxes on saving, for instance, the main conclusion appears to be that the aggregate level of saving is not particularly sensitive to tax-induced changes in the rate of return, although tax factors may well alter the composition of financial savings. Of course, domestic private saving is only one component of total national saving in any country: the other two components are public saving (the excess of taxes over current expenditures) and foreign saving. It has sometimes been argued that any discouraging effect taxes may have on private savings can readily be offset by the resulting increase in public savings (Musgrave, 1963). As was mentioned earlier in connection with chapter 2, this position may be countered by the argument of Stanley Please (1967) to the effect that increased taxes are more likely to be matched by increased government expenditure than by increased public saving. Please's argument receives little support from Ebrill, however.

Although Ebrill notes in passing at the end of the section on savings that matters are different in open economies, he does not perhaps sufficiently emphasize that savings incentives in completely open economies cannot affect the stock of capital at all and are therefore not particularly useful policy instruments. Of course, few if any economies are completely open in this sense, but the evidence is that at least to some extent the modern sectors of most economies today must be considered partially open. (For two opposing reviews of the conflicting evidence on openness, see Feldstein and Horioka, 1980; Harberger, 1980.)

Nonetheless, while increasing private savings as such may not be a particularly appropriate goal for tax policy in an open developing country, such a country may well wish to increase the share of those savings that flows through organized financial markets. An important aspect of taxation in developing countries is thus its effect on the size and structure of the financial sector. In some circumstances, taxation may well form one component of the system of "financial repression" (McKinnon, 1973; Shaw, 1973) that holds down financial savings and hence acts as a barrier to the separation between saver and investor that is a hallmark of developed economies.

For this reason, those concerned with the development of capital markets have frequently recommended the use of tax incentives to equity markets or other tax changes as one part of the needed package of financial liberalization (Wall, 1981). Although, as Ebrill notes, there is some evidence that investment in certain forms of financial assets may indeed be responsive to such inducements, with the size and direction of the response depending in part on the degree of financial repression, it is far from clear that any benefits thus purchased are worth the costs incurred in terms of fiscal losses, economic distortions, and diminished equity. Too often (as Gillis, 1985, noted in passing in chapter 6) tax devices intended to foster the development of capital markets are among the most complex, ineffective, and the most subject to abuse of all the many incentives found in developing countries. On the whole, those who wish to foster capital markets would seem better advised to consider the role of taxation in damping down inflation—the primary destroyer of financial stability—rather than its marginal role as an incentive mechanism.

The literature on taxation and investment is both more substantial and, for open economies, perhaps more policy-relevant than that on taxation and savings. Nonetheless, since so many of the empirical studies in developed countries are based on the neoclassical framework which, as Ebrill notes, is less widely accepted in developing countries (see chapters 13 and 14 for contrasting views), the applicability of results based on this analysis is similarly obscure. Indeed, it should perhaps be emphasized that this framework's wide use is more for its pedagogical convenience than because it affords a better description than competing theories of business investment behavior even in developed countries. See, for example, the recent review in Mintz and Purvis, 1987. Nonetheless, as chapters 14 and 15 below illustrate, there is no good substitute for the conventional approach when it comes to undertaking quantitative analysis of tax incentives.

All in all, it is difficult to read the following selection without concluding that the case for specific tax incentives to encourage either savings or investment seems at best weak. This impression is further reinforced by the next two chapters.

Taxation, Savings, and Investment in Developing Countries

Liam P. Ebrill

SAVINGS BEHAVIOR

Theoretical Background

The theoretical microeconomic literature on how savings behavior is affected by tax policy has tended to concentrate on the issue of how various tax instruments affect the net rate of interest. The presumption of much of that literature is that, once the incidence of a tax has been determined, all that remains is to calculate the interest elasticity of savings. In this, the relevant literature parallels that in which the effects of taxes on labor supply are discussed. It is easy to show, within the context of a two-period life-cycle framework, that the impact of a change in interest rates is ambiguous, since it depends on a balancing of substitution and wealth effects (Atkinson and Stiglitz, 1980). Some of the ambiguity is removed when it is recognized that the balanced-budget incidence analysis used in the optimal tax framework allows one to concentrate on the compensated rather than on the total price elasticity. Ambiguity remains, however, in that, within the two-period life-cycle framework, the elasticities are defined in terms of consumption, whereas the compensated elasticity of savings to interest rate changes is of greater concern to the analysis here. The conclusion is that that interest elasticity can take on any sign.

The supply-side perspective as it applies to developing countries should also be concerned with the question of savings behavior in countries experiencing growth, that is, how does aggregate savings respond to increases in income? A substantial theoretical literature exists on this subject. This literature was the outcome of an attempt to reconcile early empirical work undertaken in developed countries in which it emerged that cross-section data indicated the existence of a nonproportional relationship between consumption and income, while time-series data suggested that the relationship is proportional. The best known reconciliation (the permanent-income hypothesis) of these two observations can be reduced to the argument that the cross-section regressions tend to estimate short-run consumption functions, while the time-series regressions estimate the analogous long-run function (Ando and Modigliani, 1963). From a development perspective, the long-

Excerpted from Ebrill (1987).

run function is most relevant. Should the proportional relation hold for developing countries, it implies that the income elasticity of savings would be unity—with economic growth, the share of output devoted to savings would remain constant, everything else being held equal.

The above macroeconomic debate took place in the absence of tax considerations. When taxes are accommodated in this framework, as they are, for example, in Feldstein (1974), the crucial link is viewed as being how the redistribution of income from the private sector to the government affects aggregate savings. If the government's marginal propensity to save exceeds that of the private sector, the net effect of an increase in taxation with a concomitant increase in government expenditures is an increase in capital formation.

Just as in the case of labor-market behavior, there are difficulties in uncritically applying the results of the above literature to developing countries. Indeed, the situation in many developing countries is such that the efficacy of tax-based savings incentives programs may be questioned. Issues associated with the mobilization and deployment of domestic savings are often viewed as being central. Financial institutions may not be well developed. Further, the exchange rate and domestic climate may be such as to encourage capital flight.

Finally, it has often been pointed out (e.g., Galbis, 1979), that, in many developing countries, interest rates are often set at artificially low rates. This has resulted in a large literature in which it is argued that such an institutional constraint will result in financial repression. Thus, with the incentive for financial savings being greatly weakened, it is argued that the reduced supply of such savings requires the introduction of rationing mechanisms as far as investment is concerned. The work of Shaw (1973) and McKinnon (1973) is perhaps the best known.

Empirical Evidence

Much of the empirical development economics literature on savings behavior has not addressed the issue of the interest elasticity of savings. Data availability is a major reason for this. As Mikesell and Zinser (1973) point out in their survey, data on savings are inaccurate by the very nature of their method of calculation, that is, savings figures are frequently obtained residually. As a result, it is quite conceivable, for example, that the result obtained by Krishna and Raychaudhuri (1982) for India of a marginal propensity to save out of permanent income exceeding that out of transitory income—an unexpected outcome—is the product of inaccurate data. Further, given the widespread use of interest rate ceilings, it is not clear what should be the appropriate choice of a rate of return variable. As a result of all of these difficulties, many of the empirical results should be approached with great caution. So as to emphasize that the difficulties are genuine, it should be noted that Williamson (1968) found interest rates to have an insignificant impact on savings in India, while Gupta (1970), using a different data set, found that, for some specifications, they had a significant positive effect.

Instead, a large proportion of the available empirical research has been concerned more with the macroeconomic issues raised above. Thus, a major effort has been made to estimate consumption functions for developing countries. Various hypotheses are tested. In particular, the life-cycle model is frequently tested, as is the hypothesis that savings rates increase with income levels. Many of the early contributions have been exhaustively surveyed elsewhere (Mikesell and Zinser, 1973; Snyder, 1974). The consensus of this literature is that some relationship between savings and income does exist and, further, that some versions of the life cycle/permanent income hypotheses are appropriate. More specifically, McDonald (1983), in his study of savings behavior in Latin America, found that the income elasticities of consumption were, with a few exceptions, in the range of 0.7 to 1.1. This lends some support to the hypothesis that the proportionality result of the permanent-income framework applies to developing countries. Of course, it also implies that, as countries develop, there is no particular tendency for the savings rate to increase.

The empirical work also shows that there are other important determinants of savings, where these include demographic factors (e.g., dependency rates and age distribution, occupation, income distribution, life span, and the urban-rural distinction). Note that to the extent that growth affects these variables, savings rates will change. Further, insofar as income distributions can be altered by tax policy (Goode, 1961), that provides a potential lever for government intervention. The policy might prove to be unpalatable, however, to the extent that the government tries to increase aggregate savings by distributing income from the poor (low propensity to save) to the rich (high propensity to save).

A large number of papers examine the impact of the growth in the government sector on aggregate savings. These papers constitute the empirical analogue of Feldstein's (1974) theoretical contribution, although it must be emphasized that the concept of government savings is particularly difficult to pin down. The relevant papers have concentrated on evaluating the "Please effect," where this can take either a strong or a weak form (Please, 1967, 1970). The strong form maintains that aggregate savings will decline with the growth of the share of tax revenues in gross domestic product (GDP), whereas the weak form contends that under such circumstances aggregate savings may increase but not by much. The consensus of the literature seems to be that the Please effect is not valid. Bhatia (1967) concludes that aggregate savings increase quite sharply on the basis of a cross-sectional study of twenty African countries—for every 1 percent increase in the tax-GDP ratio, private consumption declined by 0.21 percent of GDP, while public consumption increased by 0.05 percent of GDP. Morss (1968), using data drawn from a cross-section of forty-six developing countries, felt confident in rejecting the Please effect. Tahari (1979) reached a similar conclusion. Thimmaiah (1977), using time-series data from India, could not reject the weak form of the Please effect. On the other hand, Landau (1971) did find evidence to support the Please effect in the case of Latin American countries.

There is also an important body of literature that attempts to evaluate the empirical significance of the financial repression which is presumed to be an inevitable outcome of institutionally setting interest rates at artificially low rates. The consensus is that financial repression does exist and can be a severe drag on economic development. For example, in a paper by the Research Department of the Fund (International Monetary Fund, 1983), the authors concluded that there is good prima facie evidence to support the assertion that countries with positive real rates of interest experience a higher rate of growth than that enjoyed by countries in which the real rate of interest is negative. Fry (1980) finds that savings are affected positively by the real deposit rate of interest. He argues that his estimates of savings and growth functions are such as to allow him to conclude that the cost of financial repression is around one half of a percentage point in growth forgone for every percentage point by which the real rate falls below the equilibrium rate. In another paper, Fry (1978) finds further evidence of the importance of financial repression. He concludes that the specific transmission mechanism proposed by Shaw (1973) appears to fit the facts better than that proposed by McKinnon (1973). In particular, McKinnon's twin assumptions to the effect that investments are lumpy and entirely self-financed, which, taken together, imply that potential investors must accumulate money balances prior to investing, lead to the testable hypothesis that money and physical capital are complements. This hypothesis is not sustained by the data. Shaw's alternative approach, which assumes that investors are not constrained to self-finance because of the emergence of noninstitutional markets in response to financial repression, does receive support.

All of the above suggests that, even though aggregate savings may not be very interest-sensitive, the allocation of that aggregate between conventional financial assets and alternatives such as curb market funds and works of art is indeed responsive to economic incentives.[1] Presumably, this responsiveness extends to the behavior of asset holders as they determine their portfolio allocations within the category of conventional financial assets. There is, unfortunately, little empirical work addressing this issue. An exception is a paper by Bürkner (1982), in which he concludes on the basis of financial data collected for the Philippines, that investors in the Philippines react to relative changes in rates of return just as their counterparts do in developed countries.

Assessment

To the extent that the empirical literature on savings behavior addresses the concerns of supply-side economists, it does it best in its evaluation of the financial repression hypotheses of Shaw and McKinnon. While the empirical work in this area demonstrates that savings may be sensitive to changes in interest rates and, therefore, are also sensitive to changes in tax policy, it also raises the issue of whether savings-based tax incentives represent the most effective reform route for countries to pursue. Specifically, the distortion to savings decisions implied by the existence of financial repression may be far larger than that associated with the fact that interest income is subject to income tax. To place the relative magnitudes of these distortions in some context, consider that, for Ghana during the late 1970s, official market interest rates on savings deposits rarely exceeded 10 percent, while the rate of inflation was frequently in the neighborhood of 100 percent.

As for the remainder of the empirical literature, most of it is concerned with macroeconomic aggregates rather than supply-side issues. In particular, inadequate attention has been devoted to the question of whether aggregate savings, as opposed to its components, is affected by the type of tax structure. Is a consumption-based tax preferable to an income-based tax, for example, as argued by Due (1976)? This is an important issue since it raises the possibility that the substantial reliance of developing countries on broad-based consumption taxes may have been conducive to savings. As an aside on this, it is interesting to note that Tahari (1979) has found on the basis of his cross-section work that (private) savings behavior appears to be stimulated more by direct than indirect taxation! While theoretically possible, too much store should not be placed on this somewhat surprising conclusion given the heterogeneous nature of the countries in his sample and the aggregative nature of his regression results. Besides, the net effect of government's actions on aggregate savings depends on the manner of disposition of the tax revenues.

As is well known, aggregate savings do not necessarily equal gross investment for any single country. Thus, for a given country, investments can be made by domestic or foreign investors. Further, since this survey is concerned with results that have implications for supply-side policies, the term "investment" is interpreted here in a restricted sense as referring to those increments in the stock of a nation's capital which result in increases in market output. Investment in works of art and so on are accordingly excluded. Given this potential difference between savings and investment and given that there exists a wide range of specifically targeted tax instruments, for example, those aimed at manufacturing and tourism investment, we turn now to consider investment behavior as a separate topic.

INVESTMENT BEHAVIOR

Theoretical Background

The theory of how investment behavior responds to changes in tax policy has been heavily influenced by the neoclassical framework established by Jorgenson (1963). The most important conclusions of the literature can be found in Atkinson and Stiglitz (1980) and King and Fullerton (1984). For our purposes, it is important to note the observation that attempting to gauge the impact of tax policy on the cost of capital (and, therefore, on the rate of investment) by concentrating on the corporate tax rate is misleading. In many countries, the corporate tax structure interacts with the personal tax system (for example, through the tax treatment of dividends and capital gains) and, further, the specific provisions of the corporate tax are of critical importance. On the latter point, the corporate tax will not affect the cost of capital if companies are allowed to make deductions against their tax liabilities that accurately reflect the contribution of capital to the production process. For example, in the context of the U.S. tax system, there are two approaches to ensuring that the tax system would be neutral with respect to the cost of capital. First, if the corporation uses debt finance on the margin and if debt interest is deductible and depreciation allowances accurately measure the value of the capital used up (a difficult quantity to measure in an inflationary environment), then increases in the corporate tax rate will leave the cost of capital unaffected. The alternative approach, easier to implement administratively, would disallow interest deductions and replace depreciation allowances with expensing. The two approaches are equivalent in present value terms.[2]

The above literature refers to the effects of taxes in a world without risk. There is, however, an additional body of work that relaxes this constraint and allows for the existence of risk. The emphasis has been on the role of the government as a risk-sharer through its tax instruments. The question of interest has been whether taxation encourages more or less risk taking. The answer depends on factors such as the degree of investor risk aversion and the extent of loss-offset provisions (cf. Atkinson and Stiglitz, 1980). It should be noted, with respect to the latter, that the present value of loss-offset provisions are of greatest relevance—the fact that many countries permit full loss-offset for an indefinite period in nominal terms does not take account of the cost associated with the postponement of the tax benefits.

When one turns to consider that part of the theoretical literature concerned with developing country issues, one finds that it differs from the papers cited above in a number of important respects. First, given the variety of developing country experiences, it is more concerned with the multitude of direct tax structures in existence (cf. Lent, 1967; Usher, 1977). Many of these tax structures employ devices not commonly used in developed countries. For example, Agell (1986) shows how tax holidays can be accommodated with the neoclassical cost of capital model.

Second, there is a belief that the neoclassical model may not apply readily to developing countries. Capital markets are imperfect. Therefore, financial policy and, in particular, policies concerning dividend/retained earnings behavior, are no longer irrelevant to aggregate investment behavior. More important, the structure of a country's system of financial intermediation can be significant. Thus, as pointed out in the previous section, the fact that interest rates are maintained at an artificially low level in some countries could well lead to financial disintermediation with the result that the demand for investment funds must be met by rationing. This manifestation of financial repression raises the possibility that investment may increase with interest rates as a result of an increase in available savings.

Third, and related to the possibility that financial repression may imply that investment behavior is quantity-constrained rather than price-constrained, is the argument that the growth performance of some countries (where this is influenced by their investment efforts) may be limited by the availability of foreign exchange. This possibility, commonly referred to as the two-gap hypothesis, is discussed by McKinnon (1964), among others.

Fourth, recognition of the fact that aggregate investment consists of a number of components in addition to private domestic investment has stimulated research. Attention has been devoted to the determinants of foreign direct investment and foreign aid. To what do these capital flows respond? It is clear, for example, that if a complete explanation of how taxes affect private foreign investment flows is to be determined, the interactions of differing national tax systems must be taken into

account. For example, Hartman (1981) considers how U.S. foreign direct investment might be influenced by U.S. tax policies. An important element of the
current U.S. tax structure is that income from foreign sources is liable to taxation
only on repatriation, which implies that firms should finance foreign investment
out of foreign earnings to the greatest extent possible. Work in this area is still at an
early stage.

Fifth, at this macroeconomic level, there has been concern over the degree of
complementarity or substitutability between the components of aggregate investment. In particular, are capital inflows a substitute for domestic saving and investment? Thus, Chenery and Strout (1966) viewed all capital inflows as a net addition
to a developing country's capital stock, whereas Weisskopf (1972) viewed such
inflows as being a substitute for domestic savings. Papanek (1972) argued for an
intermediate position. There has also been concern over the impact of public
investment on private investment.

Finally, investment behavior can be influenced by taxes and distortions other
than direct income-based taxes. Notable among these other instruments are trade
taxes or marketing boards and agricultural price support systems. While these
devices may be introduced for a number of reasons (e.g., with a view to levying an
optimum export tax whereby a country exploits its market power in world markets
[Corden, 1974; Sanchez-Ugarte and Modi, 1987]), they can frequently have unintended effects, particularly at the level of individual industries.

Empirical Evidence

The available empirical work reflects the bias mentioned above against the
neoclassical framework. For example, Bilsborrow (1977) tests an eclectic theory
of investment behavior that allows for variables representing the internal financial
structure of the firm. He finds, using data drawn from Colombia, that accelerator
effects, cash flow effects, balance sheet risk variables, and, most notably, the
availability of foreign exchange were important determinants of investment flows.
However, the rate of return to investors can still be an important determinant of
investment behavior. In her study of the inflationary process in India, Ahluwalia
(1979) found that the interest elasticity of private investment exceeded 2, which
would suggest that a tax policy aimed at altering the rate of return could be
stimulative. In contrast to this result, the papers cited earlier, in which the financial
repression hypotheses are evaluated, find—almost as a corollary to the existence
of artificially low interest rates—that investment is quantity-constrained by rationing. For example, Fry (1978) finds for his sample of countries that an increase in
the real rate of interest has a positive effect on growth. Related to this is the work of
Thirlwall (1974), who discovered, for his global sample of countries, that inflation
exercises a positive influence on investment, but on further examination found
that, if the sample is limited to developing countries, this influence is negative. If
the role of the inflation variable for the case of developing countries is interpreted
as its being a proxy for the degree of financial repression, then the sign of the effect
is understandable. It should be noted that, to the extent that these effects are
important, they reduce the effectiveness of tax incentive programs for investment.

More neoclassical in nature is the example of Lim (1983). He concentrates on the specifics of the investment incentive programs in peninsula Malaysia, calling attention, in particular, to the role of generous tax holidays that tend to be awarded on an indiscriminate basis. He finds that there is some evidence of investor reactions to these incentives—there is some tendency for both capital intensity and utilization rates to increase.

There is little empirical work on the determinants of foreign investment flows. Hartman (1981a) finds that U.S. aggregate foreign direct investment does, in fact, respond to changes in tax policy. In particular, it is influenced negatively and quite strongly by the after-tax rate of return to domestic investment. As further evidence of the sensitivity of foreign investment flows to economic variables, Hartman (1984) shows that foreign investment flows into the United States respond to changes in U.S. tax policy. However, when one considers the experience of developing countries, there are fewer grounds for optimism over the ability of tax policies to attract investment flows. Lim (1983) finds in his work on a cross-section of twenty-seven developing countries that the presence of natural resources and a proven record of economic performance were far more important than fiscal incentives in attracting such flows. Although they do not consider the impact of tax incentives per se, Root and Ahmed (1979) corroborate Lim's results for nonextractive industries in that they find that those countries that have attracted the most foreign investment have substantial urbanization, relatively advanced infrastructures, and so on.

Assessment

All of the above implies that investors do react to economic incentives and that, therefore, a tax-based policy of incentives could have some role to play. However, the empirical results above also suggest that investment is influenced by a number of factors. These run the range from the existence of capital market imperfections due to financial repression as evidenced by the role of liquidity effects to the existence of other distortions such as those associated with price support systems and marketing boards.

NOTES

1. Note that, in this context, the alternatives include placing savings overseas. This alternative emphasizes the important role of confidence in the determination of savings allocation decisions.

2. It must be recognized that, in practice, the two systems may not be equivalent. Thus, for example, start-up companies will not in general have the profits against which they can deduct their investment expenditures. While it is true that these companies can be compensated by allowing them to carry their expensing allowances forward, for equivalence to be maintained, these carry-forward provisions would have to be indexed for inflation and the real rate of return.

12

A Survey of Tax Incentives

The basic classification of fiscal subsidies to investment set out in the following excerpt from a paper by Shah and Toye (1978) gives a good picture of the range and type of incentives commonly employed, although the details of the particular tax schemes in different developing countries have been omitted as partly obsolete. (For other useful surveys, see Heller and Kauffman, 1963; Lent, 1967.) This paper also provides a useful review of some of the surprisingly few attempts to evaluate the effectiveness of such incentives. Although there have subsequently been a few more "neoclassical" evaluations than those cited by Shah and Toye (e.g., Agell, 1986; Ebrill, 1987a), their survey basically confirms the conclusion in the preceding chapter on the lesser use of such methods in developing countries. On the whole, Shah and Toye are quite scathing both on the conceptual difficulties in evaluating incentives (see also chapter 13) and on the inadequate data available even in those countries that have made most use of fiscal incentives.

While the authors speak eloquently for themselves, a few points deserve to be singled out. In the first place, their long footnote on tax incentives for employment is almost the only mention of this potentially important subject in this book, apart from a brief critical discussion in chapter 13 (see also Prest, 1971; Lent, 1971). As Bird (1982) shows in detail, however, the more important implications of taxation for employment have less to do with generally picayune specific incentives than with such questions as the internal terms of trade between industry and agriculture and the relative attractiveness of exporting and import substitution.

Secondly, it is interesting that the authors, writing in 1978, specifically cite Indonesia as a country where tax incentives do not make much sense. It will be recalled from chapter 6 that in fact Indonesia is one of the few developing countries which has since (or ever) completely abolished such incentives.

Finally, while Shah and Toye's rather cynical conclusion that the governments of most developing countries are simply tools of capitalist interests is undoubtedly both simplistic and overdone, they are quite right in pointing up sharply the importance of the "political economy" aspect of incentive policy. Indeed, it is always a good idea in analyzing the persistence of a public policy which does not seem to achieve its stated objectives to ask who gains from its continuance, since inevitably the gaining group will be the strongest supporters of the policy in question, generally clothing it in "national interest" garments, of course. It was not simple Marxism that led Best (1976), for example, to analyze the tax systems of Central America in terms of which economic groups were most hurt and most helped by the prevailing structures; it was rather the correct perception that a country's tax structure inevitably reflects not only its economic structure (see chapter 1) but also its political structure. To some extent, it follows that radical changes in taxation may require as a precondition radical political (and/or economic) changes, although it would be going too far to argue that revolution must precede reform! A more balanced appraisal is that the tax system in any country at any point of time, like other institutional structures, reflects both the prevailing balance of political forces and the opportunities afforded by the structure of the economy and the level of administrative sophistication. The nature, importance, and persistence of tax incentives, like all other parts of the tax system, reflect such factors as much as, or more than, they do the results of careful, objective cost-benefit evaluations, of the sort set out here in chapter 15.

Fiscal Incentives for Firms in Some Developing Countries: Survey and Critique

S. M. S. Shah and J. F. J. Toye

Among governments of developing countries, it is a widespread practice to operate schemes which give tax concessions (or, more rarely, subsidies from public expenditure) to newly established firms or old firms starting new activities. The rationale for such schemes seems straightforward enough, and is conveyed by the description "fiscal incentives." It is that governments which want to promote economic growth in a mixed economy should use appropriate fiscal means to induce private sector firms to make their contribution to the desired expansion of national output.

FISCAL INCENTIVES IN DEVELOPING COUNTRIES

The first task in presenting a summary of fiscal incentives in developing countries is to choose the categories by which to order the available information. It seems to make sense to adopt a two-way classification capable of distinguishing four different types of scheme from each other, as in table 12.1.

The four types of fiscal incentive scheme shown in table 12.1 are as follows:

(A1) Subsidy is independent of scale of investment, but conditional on a maximum level of profits. The main scheme of this type is the tax holiday, defined as total (or partial) exemption of new or expanding firms from direct taxation for a specified period.

(A2) Subsidy is dependent on the scale of investment and conditional on a minimum level of profits. There are a variety of schemes of this type, including "special first year" and subsequent annual percentages of an asset's cost that are deductible from taxable income. The allowances are also known as accelerated depreciation, because they allow the asset to be written down for tax purposes faster than would be possible under normal accountancy depreciation rules. Also in this category fall tax credits, investment allowances and development rebates, which allow a further percentage of the asset's costs to be deducted from taxable income, over and above the depreciation provisions for writing down the asset's historic cost.

(B1) Subsidy is independent of the scale of investment and not conditional on a minimum level of profit. The main scheme of this type is the waiver or rebate

Excerpted from Toye (1978).

Table 12.1   *A Classification of Types of Fiscal Incentive Scheme*

	(A) $J^0 > J^*$	(B) $J^0 \leq J^*$
(1) $S \neq f(K^0)$	Tax holiday Tax deductible loan interest	Import duty exemption

(2) $S = f(K^0)$	Tax credit
	Investment
	  allowance
	Accelerated
	  depreciation
		Investment grant

Notes: S is the amount of public subsidy; K^0 is the cost of acquiring investment goods; J^* is the level of corporate profits at which tax becomes payable; J^0 is pre-tax profits.

of duty paid on imported capital goods (and sometimes also raw materials) by new or expanding firms.

(B2) Subsidy is dependent on the scale of investment but not conditional on a minimum level of profit. The example here is the investment grant whereby a given share of a firm's investment cost is paid for by the government.

Other distinctions can be made than those used in this classification of types of incentive scheme. One is the different phasing of benefits in different types of scheme. Investment grants confer all their benefits right at the start of any new economic activity. Import duty exemption confers initial benefits in respect of capital good imports and continuing benefits in respect of raw materials imports. Tax holidays and tax credits spread their benefits over quite a number of years while a project is establishing itself. The exact pattern of benefits depends on the timing of profit accrual and the detailed provisions of the scheme.

But, although the exact timing of benefits (in conjunction with the appropriate discount rate) is crucial to firms, and governments, who wish to know the present value of alternative forms of subsidy, it does not provide a clear-cut criterion for categorizing incentive schemes.

From the existing literature on fiscal incentive schemes in developing countries, a summary analysis can be prepared of the form which such schemes take in twenty-eight developing countries. Of the twenty-eight developing countries for which information is readily available, no less than eighteen are former British colonial territories. Because of this obvious bias in the sample, it may be that the conclusions to be drawn from this sample cannot be extended to cover developing countries as a whole.

Inspection of this sample immediately suggests a number of points. The first concerns the relative popularity with developing country governments of the different types of fiscal incentive scheme. The most popular type of scheme with developing country governments was type (A1)—the tax holiday. Out of our twenty-eight countries, twenty-six offered some form of tax holiday.[1] Only Tanzania and Zambia did not do so. The second most popular type of scheme is (A2), provision for the accelerated depreciation of investment in determining tax liability, and associated investment tax credits. Sixteen of our twenty-eight countries offered one or more of the following concessions: an especially high deprecation allowance in the first year of operation; an especially high annual depreciation allowance; an investment allowance, investment tax credit or development rebate over and above the normal or the concessionally high depreciation allowances; a special allowance for the regular working of more than one shift. The third most frequently observed type of scheme is the exemption of imported plant and machinery (and sometimes also parts and raw materials) from customs duty or other import taxation. This exemption operated in ten of the twenty-eight countries. Type (B2), the investment grant was the least popular of all the incentives. Among the twenty-eight countries, only Fiji offered investment grants, and then only in the hotel construction sector. It would be interesting to speculate on the reasons for this particular popularity ranking.

But before we do so, there is a second point that emerges. It is that, in practice as opposed to theory, tax holidays and tax credits, subsidies to earnings and subsidies to investment are not alternatives. Almost half of the countries in the sample were operating both tax holidays *and* accelerated depreciation or other tax credit schemes. It is not clear merely from reading the tax legislation how these two different types of scheme are operated in a complementary fashion. There seem to be three possibilities. It could be that tax holidays are enjoyed by new firms, while tax credits are given to all new investment that is not undertaken by new firms. Firms could be allowed to opt, to benefit under one scheme or the other, according to which would provide the greater subsidy. More likely, however, is that firms first of all enjoy their tax holidays, and, when these are exhausted, enjoy the different kinds of depreciation allowance and tax credit that are also available to them (cf. Heller and Kauffman, 1963, 108–9).[2] Again, while in theory there is a clear distinction between subsidies proportional to investment and subsidies not proportional to investment, in practice this distinction is often blurred. This happens when tax holidays, normally considered a form of subsidy not proportional to investment, are offered on a sliding scale, with the length of the holiday linked to the amount of capital expenditure involved. This kind of link has been made in Indonesia, Malaysia, Nigeria, Singapore, Sudan, and Surinam.

The third point that arises is that the most popular type of scheme, the tax holiday, usually has a number of additional features which make it more attractive than an initial period of x years during which no business taxes are payable. As well as the tax-free period, which in the sample typically lasted between five and ten years, about half of the countries allowed a further period, after the tax holiday, during which losses made in the tax holiday period could be used to offset later, otherwise taxable, profits. The period during which losses could be carried forward in determining tax liability was normally between four and six years. Almost all the countries which offered tax holidays also exempted dividends paid out to shareholders from the levy of personal income taxes,[3] so that there is no special reward for firms that retain profits in order to reinvest. Only six of the countries surveyed set an upper limit to profits that could go untaxed, and the maximum varied between 7 and 50 percent of initial capital expenditure allowable as tax-free profits in any one year.

The final proposition is that the use of fiscal incentive schemes has a certain geographical pattern. As already noted, some countries offered both tax holidays and accelerated depreciation and other tax credits. These thirteen "hypergenerous" countries can be divided into two geographical categories. Nine are islands, or have such small island-like economies that they could be called quasi-islands. They are Barbados, Fiji, Jamaica, Singapore, Trinidad and Tobago, Ecuador, Guyana, Malaysia, and Surinam. The remaining four are the South Asian neighbors India, Pakistan, Bangladesh, and Sri Lanka, which falls also into the category of islands, of course.

THE ECONOMIC IMPACT OF FISCAL INCENTIVE SCHEMES

It has been shown that fiscal incentive schemes are a much used tool of fiscal policy in developing countries. One is bound to go on to ask whether they are an effective tool of fiscal policy. By the effectiveness or impact of a scheme is understood its power to change behavior from what it would otherwise have been, in a direction which the relevant policy makers prefer.

The first and crudest method which has been used to measure the impact of fiscal incentive schemes is to investigate whether, in the period after they are introduced, the share of investment in gross national product rises. This test has been applied in studies of these schemes in, for example, Mexico (Katz, 1972) and Ecuador (Tanzi, 1969). The obvious objection to it is that investment's share in GNP may change for many different reasons. Thus any recorded change that is observed after introducing a fiscal incentive scheme cannot be assumed to be a consequence of its introduction. The results from this method would be valid only if it could be shown independently that non-scheme influences on the investment/GNP share were constant over the period of measurement. Since no attempt was made to control for non-scheme variables in the studies mentioned above, their results do not require further discussion.

A second method applied to measure the impact of these schemes is to interview a representative sample of businessmen who have benefited from the schemes. The aim is to ascertain by direct questioning how many of them were influenced in making their investment decisions by the availability of the scheme's benefits. This approach was used in case studies of schemes in Mexico (Ross and Christensen, 1959), Jamaica (Chen-Young, 1967), Pakistan (Azhar and Sharif, 1974), Brazil (Goodman, 1972), and Nigeria (Olaloku, 1976). There are many ways in which questionnaire/survey results can be invalidated. Sample size can be too small, the sample can be inadequately stratified, the response rate can be inadequate or nonrandom, questions can be ambiguous or otherwise inadequate, the respondent may not have the requisite information and so on. In addition, the researcher may classify and/or interpret the responses subjectively.

It is not possible to scrutinize fully the exact methods used in the five case studies cited. One merely has to keep the sources of potential bias in mind when considering their results. In the Mexican study, of twenty-four firms enjoying tax exemptions, fourteen reported that they would "definitely" have invested exactly as they had done, even without the tax exemptions. A further nine firms said that they "probably" would have invested as they had without the tax exemptions. Only one firm said that it would not have invested as it did, but for the fiscal inducement. Of fifty-five Jamaican firms asked to state the influences on their investment decision, only two volunteered a mention of tax exemptions. Of forty Pakistani firms studied, only eight were reported to have had their investment decision swayed by tax exemptions. On the other hand, in Goodman's study of northeast Brazil, the regionally differentiated tax incentives were reported as a decisive influence on the choice of plant location.[4]

In common with the first method, the survey/questionnaire approach assumes that the impact of incentive schemes is to be looked for solely in the area of investment behavior, focusing either on the decision whether to invest at all, or on where to locate an investment. But the effect on investment does not emerge from these studies very clearly. Results are reported for numbers of firms, not for the net value of investment that has been induced or relocated. There is no systematic attempt to distinguish large investors from small investors, or capital-intensive enterprises from labor-intensive enterprises.

Nevertheless, the evidence of these studies does seem to point towards the ineffectiveness of these schemes in inducing new investment. It could be argued that the method is biased in favor of this conclusion, because businessmen will understate the impact of tax incentives in the hope of encouraging the government to make them even more generous. But one could just as well suppose an opposite bias in favor of overstating the impact of tax incentives: if the government became convinced that these incentives were having very little impact, it might decide to withdraw them to boost tax revenue. One might reasonably suppose that these two sources of bias offset each other; if so, the original conclusion of apparent ineffectiveness still stands.

When interpreting the results of these survey/questionnaire studies a further limitation of the method needs to be borne in mind. They draw their evidence only from those businessmen who did decide to invest in the country concerned. Therefore they do no necessarily capture the full net impact on investment of fiscal incentive schemes. This is because the investments which are actually subsidized by the scheme may crowd out the investments which other firms might otherwise have been willing to make without the subsidy. The subsidized firms might even compete existing firms out of the market. The possible losses of investment caused by the fiscal incentive scheme have to be accounted for to assess its full net impact, and these are excluded by assumption when the survey/questionnaire method is used. One is led to conclude that the impact of incentive schemes on investment is small even on the optimistic assumption that they are causing no loss of investment.

The third method of assessing the effectiveness of tax incentives relies on inferences made from the published profit levels of tax exempt firms. The net present value of a firm's profits is calculated first with tax exemptions (NPV_e) and then assuming no tax exemptions were enjoyed (NPV_n). Both figures are then compared with Q, the critical minimum rate of profit which firms require, and without which they will not invest. Inferences are then drawn about the impact of the tax incentives as follows:

    a. If $NPV_n < Q$ and $NPV_e < Q$, the incentive was not sufficient to make the venture attractive as an investment, and thus was ineffective.

    b. If $NPV_n > Q$ and $NPV_e > Q$, the venture was profitable and would have been undertaken regardless of the incentive, which, hence, was ineffective.

    c. If $NPV_n < Q$ and $NPV_e > Q$, the incentive has been effective because it alone has made the investment sufficiently attractive to the firm to ensure that it was in fact undertaken.

This procedure is valid only on certain assumptions, which need to be spelled out carefully. They are, in part,

    1. that the firm's objective is the maximization of profits;

    2. that the firm does not face any capital constraint;

    3. that the firm enjoys perfect foresight, so that realized profits are a correct reflection of the *ex ante* profit possibilities which faced the firm when it took its economic decisions;

    4. that the value of Q can be quantified. (If Q is set equal to $r/l - e^{-rb}$ (where r is the private discount rate and b is the life of the project), each firm is assumed to have only one project);

    5. that the tax burden of the firm is not shifted.

In addition, it must be noted that this method, in common with the survey/questionnaire approach, excludes by assumption any loss of investment arising from the competition of subsidized firms or investments with other existing or potential unsubsidized firms or investments (Usher, 1977, 140).

This method has been employed to analyze the impact of tax incentives in Pakistan (Azhar and Sharif, 1974; Kemal, 1975) and Colombia (Bilsborrow and Porter, 1972). The first Pakistan study uses the formula $Q = r/l - e^{-rb}$ and concludes that 20 percent of tax exempt firms had been stimulated to invest by the tax holiday. The second Pakistan study uses the same formula for Q, but increases the value of b to lengthen the time horizon. It concludes that the proportion of tax exempt firms stimulated by the tax holiday to invest was 30 percent. The Colombia study does not attempt to calculate the value of Q for each firm. Instead, the NPV_n and the NPV_e are compared with the average profit rate for the industry in which the firm operates. On this basis only four out of forty Colombian firms were found to have been stimulated to invest by the tax exemptions.

In order to meet the objection that to assume profit-maximizing firms is unrealistic, the third method can be varied to fit the assumption that investment results from the firm's liquidity, rather than its expectations of profit. There is considerable support in the literature for a liquidity motive for investment in relation to developed economies. One could argue that the scarcity of capital and the weakness of capital markets in developing countries indicate an even greater reliance there on internal sources for investment funds. However, a study of Colombia using a method similar to that outlined above found that only a small number of firms satisfied the effectiveness criterion that had been set (Bilsborrow and Porter, 1972).

A fourth method of measuring the impact of fiscal incentive schemes has been tried using data for developed economies (Helliwell, 1976, 157–255). Its foundation is the neoclassical theory of capital investment, on which is built a variety of closely related computable investment models. From such models, the effect on aggregate investment of changes in tax variables can be estimated. To our knowledge, this method has not yet been applied to data for tax incentives in developing countries. No doubt it will be before long; but the effort will be wasted because of the often discussed flaws in the production function approach to capital theory (cf. Usher, 1977, 141–44).

Thus, at the moment, empirical evidence on the impact of fiscal incentive schemes derives from only two methods, the survey/questionnaire approach and *ex post* analysis of profit levels. The results from both seem to show that those schemes have very little impact on the level of aggregate investment, but might be somewhat more influential in steering investment, once it has been decided, to the location which policy makers prefer. At the same time we have seen that both the methods used to arrive at these conclusions have important defects which make their results unreliable, but unreliable to an unknown degree.

Logically, then, it is not possible to arrive at a single definite conclusion about the economic effect of these schemes. It would be reasonable to come to either of two conclusions. The first is that, if two independent procedures discover the same result, i.e. that fiscal incentive schemes have little impact on investments, that result becomes probable, even though each method taken separately is rather crude. The second is that the agreement of the results of the two procedures is no more than a coincidence of errors, and that one is obliged to remain entirely agnostic on the issue of whether these schemes affect investment or not. The most that can be said is that their impact is either slight or unknown.[5]

A PUZZLE AND SOME EXPLANATIONS

The puzzle which now has to be posed to the reader is a simple one. It was shown that fiscal incentive schemes are widespread and popular in developing countries and that their impact on their major policy target, the level of investment, is either slight or unknown. Why should schemes whose impact is either slight or unknown be so widespread and popular in developing countries? What is the explanation of this apparent paradox?

Let us begin by indicating, in a rough and ready way, four possible types of explanation. One could argue that because in developing countries normal tax rates are so low, the importance of fiscal incentives has been greatly exaggerated, and that the size of the subsidy which they create is very small. The absence of any firm evidence of impact can then be explained in terms of the weakness of the incentive effect which the schemes generate (cf. Heller and Kauffman, 1963, 67). A second, closely related argument is that, even where tax rates are high, the evasion of taxes is endemic, particularly in the unorganized sector. Fiscal incentive schemes are not really intended as incentives, but are either a formal recognition that the government would not be able to collect substantial revenues from the favored firms if it tried, or an admission that, although the revenues could be collected, it would be unfair to do so given the general poorness of tax compliance. This explanation says that the slight or unknown impact of these schemes is irrelevant, because they are really a means of legitimizing noncollection of revenues or of getting large firms domestic and foreign to register their activities for government monitoring.

Another quite different line of explanation relies on the notion of fierce competition between countries with poor resource endowments and little in the way of technology and labor skills for footloose foreign manufacturing investment. In the vain attempt to out-bid each other for the available scarce foreign manufacturing investment, these countries compete away their potential revenues from corporate taxation. As this happens, the foreign firms decide where and how much to invest in accordance with nontax criteria, knowing that they will pay precious little to the exchequer wherever they go. Thus the competition hypothesis simultaneously explains the ubiquity of the schemes and their slight or unknown effects.

The final explanation is a variant of the competitive hypothesis. It suggests that governments are indeed forced to forgo corporate revenue which they might otherwise collect, but not because their neighboring country is offering a more attractive package of tax exemptions. The compulsion arises, in this explanation, directly from the power of large domestic and foreign firms to pressure the government of the country they have invested in, or want to invest in, to take measures favorable to their economic well-being.

The first of these explanations, that the weakness of the incentive results from the lowness of the normal corporation tax rates, is not very satisfactory as it stands. The reason is that most developing countries prefer to have high nominal rates of corporation tax (to impress the ignorant with the seriousness of the government's attempts to mobilize resources) and then to grant exemptions selectively. This is certainly so for the South Asian countries which operate incentive schemes. This explanation might be still relevant for the large international firms, however. As long as only one or two developing countries impose low rates of corporation tax, large international firms can, by manipulating intrafirm transfer prices, ensure that profits are brought to taxation in countries where corporation tax rates are lowest. Then all the other developing countries will find it very difficult to influence the size and/or the location of the investment of such firms by selective dispensation from their high nominal tax rates. But where a firm does not have the size and sophistication to decide the tax jurisdiction in which its profits are declared, and when nevertheless it is making a substantial profit in relation to its investment, the offer of tax exemption or tax allowances cannot be described as insignificant or inconsequential. It is usually a very important windfall gain, even if there are other powerful influences on its decisions, of when, where, and how much to invest. One is still left with the task of explaining why such an important windfall gain is handed by governments to private firms.

The claim that the nominal tax liabilities of these firms could not be collected by the governments of developing countries if they wished to collect them is not very persuasive. Much is always made of the technical obstacles to tax collection from farmers and petty traders in developing countries. But to try and extend the argument to the large, organized industrial firms operating in urban areas with extensive direct or indirect involvement in foreign trade is to stretch an already thin argument to the point of destruction. This is particularly so for countries which have set up fiscal incentive schemes of which the benefits are discretionary and not automatic. It is absurd to claim that a developing country possesses the administrative skills to operate a selective incentive scheme efficiently but does not have the administrative skills to collect a corporation tax. The alternative claim, that in equity foreign investors should be granted parity with tax-evading domestic investors, also loses its force. If there are no immovable technical obstacles to collecting corporation tax from domestic firms, equity is served just as well by refusing tax exemption to foreign and domestic firms alike.

To explain the ubiquity and inefficacy of incentive schemes as the results of a competition in tax liberality has the unpleasant ring of truth. This explanation is most convincing with respect to developing countries which are very small and/or very poor. Among the ultragenerous of the twenty-eight developing countries surveyed was a group of island or quasi-island economies. This group, consisting of five Caribbean economies plus Malaysia, Singapore, Fiji, and Ecuador, is, with possible addition of Senegal and Sierra Leone, Bangladesh, and Sri Lanka, that to which the competitive hypothesis is most likely to apply.

But the competitive hypothesis is not prima facie appropriate to economies like those of Indonesia and Nigeria or, in South Asia, India, and Pakistan, which have substantial natural resource endowment and a large internal market. Here the potential for industrialization based on home resources, skills, and market is substantial, and indeed already partly realized. If such countries compete for foreign investment by forgoing tax revenues to no purpose, they do not do so as a result of external pressures. For them, such policies must result either from gullibility or from internal political pressure. It is rather hard to maintain that developing countries have been insufficiently warned of the disadvantages of fiscal incentive schemes. Even supporters of private sector development have come forward to warn of the doubtfulness of most alleged advantages of these schemes and of the likelihood of most of the drawbacks.

Furthermore, if one looks at the strategy of economic development adopted for these large and relatively well-endowed economies, it is clearly inconsistent with fiscal incentive schemes. In most, the main instrument used by the government to promote indigenous industrialization has been administrative control of foreign trade and payments in a manner that stimulates domestic production of import substitutes. Often this stimulus is so powerful that the government in addition has to start licensing the installation of extra industrial capacity in order to try to prevent scarce investment resources being diverted to non-priority uses. The combination of foreign trade control and industrial licensing actually creates spare industrial capacity in approved industries, partly by allowing bottlenecks in the supply of imported spare parts and raw materials, and partly by making it profitable to keep factories idle and sell import entitlements on the black market. It cannot be economically desirable for the government to operate both an industrial licensing system (which implies that certain investments have to be prevented) and an automatic fiscal incentive scheme (which implies that investment in general has to be encouraged). The latter makes even less sense when the economy has already developed a sizable margin of spare industrial capacity. To introduce an additional tax incentive for firms which work their capital equipment in double or triple shifts (as has been done in India, Pakistan, Sudan, and Jamaica) is a backhanded admission that investment stimulants are redundant.

If a developing country adopts and persists with a policy about which even private enterprise pundits are lukewarm and which is inconsistent with the economic strategy being pursued, and does so without the compulsions of distress which make the policy unavoidable for small islands, it does not seem unreasonable to suggest that its government is doing the bidding of those who make windfall gains from these schemes—large-scale monopoly capitalists. This supposition is buttressed by the pattern of incentive schemes. The most popular type of scheme is the tax holiday, which of all types, provides the largest element of subsidy to firms which earn profits (Heller and Kauffman, 1963, 85; Usher, 1977, 131–32). The basic tax holiday is in most countries added to, extended, and elaborated by other types of tax concession. The almost complete avoidance by developing country governments of investment grants, which is the only type of scheme that would ensure that the cost of the subsidy would appear in the government's budget and accounts, seems to be an attempt to exploit the public's "expenditure blindness," just as revenue-raising often exploits the public's "tax blindness" (cf. Prest, 1978, 28–29).

It is no surprise, therefore, that when fiscal incentive schemes are thought up by the developing country's government and its capitalist paymasters, "little or no opposition to their enactment is likely in most countries." As the same point is rather delightfully put elsewhere, "while arguments that the country would be better off in the balance with tax incentives than without . . . may be oversimplifications, they appeal to important segments of the politically articulate public" (Heller and Kauffman, 1963, 7). The power of capitalism is the power to weep at academic criticism all the way to the bank.

NOTES

1. In some countries, like Costa Rica, Ecuador, and Sierra Leone, only part of corporate earnings was exempt from tax; while in Israel corporate earnings were exempt from one type of tax, income tax, but not exempt from another type, profits tax. Normally the period of exemption begins on the "production day," i.e., the day when normal quantities of output start to be produced. There were some departures from this norm: for example, in Antigua exemption for hotels began when construction work was complete; in Dominica, Grenada, and St. Vincent exemption began from the date of granting of import licences (Smith, 1975).

2. Some countries explicitly provide for the postponement of all depreciation allowances so that they can be claimed once the tax holiday is over.

3. Dividend exemption applied during the tax holiday itself and, quite commonly, for a

further period up to two years after the end of the holiday (e.g., in Guyana). Most developing countries exempted distributed dividends up to the total amount of tax-free profits, but India, Pakistan, Sri Lanka, and Sudan limited dividend distribution to between 5 and 10 percent per year of capital expenditure (e.g., Singhal, 1973). Some developing countries had special provisions designed to prevent individuals liable to pay income tax at the highest rates using the income to buy assets for "close companies" which they control and which do not pay dividends. Such "close company" provisions existed in India, Barbados, and Trinidad and Tobago.

4. Regionally differentiated tax incentives are fiscal incentive schemes which give greater benefits to firms or investments which locate themselves in regions or areas designated by the government as less developed than the remainder of the country. Regionally-differentiated schemes can be classified in the categories already adopted in the text.

5. If one had been led to the conclusion that fiscal incentive schemes have no effect on investment, one would have no interest in examining the different kinds of economic effects produced by the different types of fiscal incentive scheme. Since our conclusion leaves some room for agnosticism on the impact of these schemes on investment, it is necessary to look at this point. It is often said that tax incentives for investment are one of the governmental measures which encourage the use of excessively capital-intensive technology, which is inappropriate to labor-surplus developing economies (e.g., Morawetz, 1974, 142, 158). There are several ways in which this could happen. Most obviously, schemes of types (A2) and (B2) confer benefits in accordance with capital expenditure and thereby encourage the producer to choose a more capital-intensive method of production than he would otherwise have done. Secondly, a selective tax incentive scheme which is more accessible to large-scale operators will have the effect of making industry more capital-intensive than it would otherwise be if the large-scale operators already tend to use the more capital-intensive techniques. Thirdly, one could argue that tax incentives whatever their form are a subsidy raising the real rate of return in the industrial sector. If they succeed in inducing capital to move from other sectors where the marginal capital/labor ratio is lower, one could say that the economy as a whole becomes more capital-intensive. A debate has taken place on the policy measures needed to eliminate these types of procapital bias arising from fiscal incentive schemes. One suggestion is to graduate the benefits from these schemes in accordance with the volume or intensity of labor employment of the project (Lent, 1971; Gupta, 1976; Olaloku, 1976). Another suggestion is to subsidize the use of labor directly (Prest, 1971; Ahluwalia, 1973). A third is to tax capital rather than subsidize labor (Peacock and Shaw, 1971). Using a Cobb-Douglas production function and assuming that for either policy a balanced budget must be maintained, Peacock and Shaw argue that a capital tax will be more effective in increasing employment and easier to administer. After various criticisms, their model in a modified version shows that, when the level of output is constrained, the government incurs the same level of budget deficit whether it uses a labor subsidy or a capital tax, a result confirmed by a CES production function analysis (Peacock and Shaw, 1972, 1973). Thus, as it is administratively easier, the capital tax would be the superior policy. The importance of these results in practice depends, of course, on the existence of significant scope for factor substitution in the real world. Apart from that, if the government's trade and monetary policies are the major pressures towards excessive capital intensity of production, one may be pardoned for wondering whether the government will have the slightest interest in finding fiscal means to nullify them.

13

The Economics of Tax Incentives

The analysis in the following chapter of the conceptual impossibility of allowing for "redundancy" and the critique of the neoclassical approach is an analytical counterpart to the critical survey by Shah and Toye (1978) included in the preceding chapter. In addition, this excerpt from Usher (1977) discusses how such subsidy programs might best be administered, and it analyzes different types of tax incentives.

An important point raised by Usher, although not discussed in detail in any of the papers included in the present chapter, concerns the interaction of tax systems in host and home countries. Usher asserts that the incentives granted by host countries to foreign investors will be ineffective unless the home country of the investor allows what is called "tax sparing," that is, allows the investor to claim a credit against taxes owed to the residence country for the taxes he would have paid to the host country in the absence of the tax incentive (see also chapter 20). Unless such "sparing" is permitted, it is alleged, the only effect of a tax incentive will be to transfer funds from the treasury of the host (developing) country to that of the home (developed) country. Since the investor will in these circumstances receive no benefit from the incentive, it cannot be expected to have any stimulating effect on foreign investment.

This argument is indeed correct in certain circumstances, but those circumstances are much more limited than is generally realized. In fact, only investments financed from new equity capital by investors resident in countries with a foreign tax credit system (and without tax sparing) and who repatriate their profits and have no current or accumulated excess credits from earnings in high-tax countries would be affected this way. Such investors are few and far between, especially among significant multinational enterprises. Some foreign investors are in countries with an exemption rather than credit system (e.g., France or the Netherlands): such investors are not subject to tax in their home country on foreign profits. Other investors are in countries which generally grant tax sparing (e.g., Sweden and Germany): they too will receive the full benefit of incentives. Still other investors, indeed most of them, finance new investments primarily out of the profits of mature subsidiaries already abroad and hence face no tax on repatriation in any case: Hartman (1981a), for example, shows that such reinvestment of nonrepatriated foreign earnings accounts for almost 90 percent of U.S. foreign investment. Moreover, like those in other countries, American foreign investors can avail themselves of a wide range of legitimate means of minimizing taxes, in large part because no residence tax is assessable until funds are repatriated, and there is often no need to repatriate funds at all. In this case too, the benefits of tax incentives in host countries will be reaped entirely by the investor and not by their home treasury. Finally, even if the investor does repatriate funds from a country in which his taxes were lowered by tax incentives, he will lose the full benefit of the incentives only if he cannot average these profits with those from countries with taxes higher than the United States: admittedly, the probability of being able to so average was reduced by the 1986 U.S. tax reform, but it was by no means eliminated. After allowing for all these possibilities, it does not seem at all exaggerated to say that, if incentives for investment have any effect at all, that effect is unlikely to be much dampened by the interaction of different national income tax systems.

The Economics of Tax Incentives to Encourage Investment in Less Developed Countries

Dan Usher

INTRODUCTION

Many of the less developed countries have instituted programs of tax incentives to encourage investment, but we typically do not know and have not the means to discover the effects of these programs upon the economies where they are adopted. Nor can we say with any degree of assurance how incentive programs might best be designed to maximize the amount of investment induced for any given expenditure on the subsidy program, to slant investment toward labor intensive techniques, to foster technological change, and so on, whatever the list of ultimate objectives might be.

THE DESIGN OF AN INCENTIVES PROGRAM

Criteria for the Disbursement of Subsidies

There would seem to be four main strategies a country might adopt: (1) it might refuse to discriminate among firms and decide instead to subsidize all new firms or all new investments (the choice between firms and investments as objects of subsidization will be discussed below) to the same extent; (2) it might limit subsidies to all firms within a well-defined set of industries; (3) it might award subsidies as prizes to firms that score well on certain tests, that have particularly high labor-capital ratios, that export a significantly high proportion of their output, and so on; or (4) it might entrust the selection of firms to a committee that would try to restrict subsidies to firms that would not invest without a subsidy and for which the required subsidy does not exceed the value of the firm to the country. These alternatives—indiscriminate subsidization, indiscriminate subsidization for a limited class of industries, subsidization of firms according to their characteristics, and subsidization of firms that "need" subsidies—will now be discussed in turn.

1. Indiscriminate subsidization of investment. An incentive program could be designed to increase the rate of return to all investment in the host country. There might be a uniform tax credit for investment or a permanent reduction of the

Excerpted from Usher (1977).

corporate income tax. The principal advantage of indiscriminate subsidization is that, alone among the strategies we are considering, it is reasonably certain to increase total investment to some extent. By increasing the present value of every potential investment, it raises the rate of return on some investment above the minimum required by the investing firm, inducing those firms to invest without at the same time discouraging others.

There is, however, some question as to whether an indiscriminate investment incentive would be feasible within the existing international tax arrangements which entitle the home country of an investing firm to levy corporate income tax at the difference between the tax rates in the home country and the host country. These arrangements are modified by tax-sparing agreements according to which firms granted incentives to encourage investment are treated by their home countries as though they had paid the full rate of corporation tax in the host country, but it is unlikely that tax-sparing would extend to the case where the incentive takes the form of a uniform tax reduction. In the absence of tax-sparing, the incentive boils down to a transfer of income from the government of the host country to the government of the home country of the investing firm, leaving the firm no better off than it would be in the absence of the incentive program and negating any effect the program might otherwise have upon investment in the host country. It is perhaps unfortunate that international tax arrangements have prevented the less developed countries from using what may be, all things considered, the best way of encouraging investment through tax policy, namely to, arrange to have a rate of corporation income tax below that in developed countries.

Leaving aside the possibility that it will run foul of international tax arrangements, the indiscriminate incentive may be a very expensive way of promoting investment, because the incentive has to be provided to all investment, including the greater part which would have taken place even in the absence of the incentive program. The host country may consider indiscriminate subsidization to be unacceptable because of the high cost of tax collection or the high alternative cost of public funds, or because it is reluctant to permit what is in effect a transfer of income from the population as whole to local or foreign owners of capital. But, one cannot rule out the possibility that tax revenue would actually increase because the gain in revenue from tax levied on investment induced by the incentive exceeds the loss on all other investment. We shall return to this issue.

2. Restriction of subsidies to a selection of industries. Though there are instances of incentive programs in which advantages are granted indiscriminately to all investment—accelerated depreciation can be looked upon as an incentive of that sort—most programs in the less developed countries restrict incentives to a limited range of industries believed to be especially useful to the economy. The phrase "new and necessary industries" often finds its way into the legislation of incentives programs, though the distribution of privileges is rarely as restricted as that self-contradictory phrase would suggest.

The advantage of restricting privileges in this way is, of course, that they can be concentrated upon those industries in which extra investment (over and above that which would take place without special encouragement) is considered to be especially desirable or especially likely to be forthcoming. It is difficult to say a priori how such industries might be identified but not altogether unreasonable to suppose that they can be identified in a particular time and place.

3. *The prize principle.* Regardless of how broadly or how narrowly the class of admissible industries is defined, subsidies granted under an incentive program can be restricted to firms that are particularly desirable as measured by one or more criteria such as the capital-labor ratio, the propensity to export, the demand for local intermediate products, or the likelihood of fostering technical change in the economy as a whole.

Though superficially attractive, the prize principle is likely to be an inefficient and expensive way of selecting pioneer firms, because firms that are especially desirable to the host country are likely to be profitable as well. This is obviously so for firms that are desirable as a source of tax revenue, but not only in that case. The profitable firm is often the one that makes the best use of local resources and the comparative advantages of the host country; it is the labor-intensive firm in a country where capital is scarce, or it is the firm that can make use of local raw materials. Thus the prize principle is especially subject to redundancy. A subsidy program which seems to be a glowing success because subsidized firms are in the forefront of economic progress of the host country may in reality be having no impact upon the country at all.

4. *The disbursement of subsidies by a committee.* A committee might be instructed to allocate subsidies by whatever criteria it thinks best. This is in fact the procedure adopted in many countries, though, of course, the enabling legislation would refer to the "good of the nation" or "economic development" or some such criterion. There is something to be said for a procedure of this kind. The main problem in disbursing subsidies is to restrict them to firms that would not come otherwise, and no set of criteria I can imagine would serve as a means of identification. Perhaps the best one can hope for is that the right firms will get chosen by a committee of men who are very knowledgeable about the specifics of each potential investment.

The difficulties are obvious: the information and skill required may be beyond the reach of any committee of experts, however devoted they may be and however much they may seek to inform themselves about the market. Without intending to do so, the committee may, in fact, grant privileges to a group of firms that would have invested without them, in which case, the incentive program turns out in the end to be nothing more than a transfer of income to local or foreign businessmen. This outcome is particularly likely if the committee, having no other basis for choice among firms, decides to play it safe by subsidizing firms that are especially beneficial to the economy and, therefore, in all probability, especially profitable and especially likely to invest in any case. There is also some danger of dishonesty in these circumstances because there is not and cannot be a precise and accurate way for an outsider to determine whether the appropriate firms were chosen or not.

Alternative Ways of Providing Subsidies

Incentive programs can differ in form and in magnitude. Among the possible forms of incentives are tax holidays, accelerated depreciation, tax credits per dollar of investment, subsidization of labor, and direct grants of money in proportion to the amount of investment that takes place. We wish to compare the economic consequences of the different forms of incentives, but to do so we must first devise a standard for comparing their magnitudes, because we will not get at the characteristics of the different forms if we try to compare a big subsidy of one kind with a small subsidy of another.

To compare magnitudes among alternative forms of incentives, we make use of a scale which we call the "capital subsidy equivalent" (CSE), defined as

$$CSE = \left(\frac{1}{K}\right)\left(\sum_{n=1}^{\infty} \frac{S_n}{(1+i)^n}\right), \tag{13.1}$$

where K is the quantity of investment, i is the rate of interest, and S_n is the value of the subsidy in year n. In principle, the capital subsidy equivalent of an incentive program might be different for the donor than for the recipient; this might occur, for instance, if the donor and recipient discounted at different rates of interest. But we shall suppose that their perceptions of capital subsidy equivalents are the same. It is usually possible to work out the value of S_n for each year n from the detail of the subsidy program. For instance, in a five year tax holiday, the value of S_n for $n = 1, 2, 3, 4$, and 5 is the earnings of the firm in the year n multiplied by the rate of corporation income tax to which the firm would be liable if it were not enjoying a tax holiday; and the value of S_n is zero when n exceeds 5 because the tax holiday is no longer in force. Typically, some care must be exercised in computing capital subsidy equivalent to be sure that the fine print in the subsidy program is represented in the values attached to the S_n, but that problem need not concern us here. The name "capital subsidy equivalent" is chosen because the measure connects all possible forms of incentive to one particularly simple form, namely a direct cash grant as a percentage of capital invested. The capital subsidy equivalent of any incentive program is the proportion of investment that would be covered by a direct grant with the same present value as the incentive.

Table 13.1 is intended to give the reader an idea of the magnitudes involved. The numbers in the body of the tables are capital subsidy equivalents for several actual and fictitious forms of subsidy in Malaysia for the year 1972. The table is a comparison between tax holidays (complete exemption from corporation income tax for a certain number of years) and tax credits (exemption from tax of all earnings up to a certain percentage of capital investment). The reference at the top of the left-hand column to the long-run rate of return signifies that the calculation of capital subsidy equivalents is based on the assumption—a reasonable assumption to make about firms entering a new country or a new line of business—that a new firm earns no profit at all in the first two years of operation, that it earns half its long-run rate of profit in the third year, and only reaches its full profitability in the

Table 13.1   *Capital Subsidy Equivalents of Alternative Forms of Subsidy*

Long-run rate of return before tax	Five-year tax holiday	Ten-year tax holiday	25% tax credit	40% tax credit	100% tax credit limited to 40% per year
0	0	0	0	0	0
5	3.78	9.07	6.9	9.2	13.93
10	7.56	18.15	7.6	11.3	18.71
20	15.12	36.30	8.0	12.3	26.92
30	22.67	54.45	8.1	12.7	29.02
40	30.23	72.63	8.3	12.9	30.09
50	37.79	90.75	8.4	13.0	30.89
60	45.35	108.89	8.4	13.2	31.54
70	52.91	127.05	8.4	13.4	32.19
80	60.47	145.19	8.4	13.5	32.85
90	68.02	163.35	8.4	13.5	32.85
100	75.58	181.49	8.4	13.5	32.85

Note: The value of i in equation 13.1 is set at 10 percent.

fourth. The interesting point of comparison between tax holidays and tax credits is that the capital subsidy equivalent of tax holidays is much larger than the capital subsidy equivalent of tax credits at the rates shown as soon as the long-run rate of return becomes at all high. The median long-run rate of return for firms which I have observed in Malaysia is about 20 percent. The Malaysian system of incentives sometimes provides firms with a choice between a tax holiday (from five to ten years depending upon the characteristics of the firm) and tax credits at 25 percent. As one would expect, the former is normally preferred.

1. Subsidization of the firms versus subsidization of investment. An incentive program may be designed to subsidize the creation of firms (all new firms or a selection of them) or to subsidize investment (all investment or certain types of investment) regardless of whether the firms undertaking the investment are old or new. Each of these policies has its own instruments. The tax holiday is the instrument for subsidizing the firm, because the exemption is based upon the earnings in all of the firm's activities. The tax credit on the other hand has to be extended in some proportion to investment. It may, of course, be restricted to new firms, but there is no technical requirement for such a restriction. Similar investments, one by a new firm and one by an established firm, could be treated alike.

A case can be made for subsidizing firms rather than investments. Some firms might desist from entering a country, despite the fact that they could make profits there in excess of the world rate of interests, because the return would be even higher elsewhere. That argument applies particularly to firms rather than to investment as a whole. A firm already established in the country might be willing to reinvest as long as the overall rate of return exceeds the world rate of interest. There is unlikely to be as close a comparison among opportunities in different countries as there was with the original investment that established the firm in one country rather than another. The argument for subsidizing firms rather than investments is that the establishment of a firm is a barrier that need be crossed by a special effort. Once the barrier is crossed, commercial principles can be relied upon to assure that the right amount of investment is forthcoming. Of course, an established firm wishing to undertake a major and innovative project can, as a rule, make it eligible for subsidy by establishing a new subsidiary firm for that purpose.

On the other hand, the subsidization of firms rather than investment can give rise to business practices that have no purpose other than tax avoidance and are disadvantageous to the economy of the host country. The owner of several firms, some with tax holidays and some without, has an incentive to arrange his affairs so that profits appear in the firms with tax holidays. Fly-by-night firms might be established with no expectation of continuing business beyond the end of the tax holiday. To prevent this, some governments insist that firms granted incentives be provided with new capital equipment—a policy which could be wasteful of capital, for it may be preferable to use cheaper second-hand equipment in many cases. There is also a bias against the modernization of established firms because that kind of investment would automatically be ineligible for subsidization. By contrast, subsidization of approved investment through the use of tax credits need not distort choices between new and second-hand equipment or between modernization of existing plants and the establishment of new ones, for all investment can be treated alike.

2. Subsidization of capital versus subsidization of capitalized earnings. Tax holidays and tax credits differ in another, equally important respect. The subsidy conveyed by a tax holiday is proportional to profits regardless of whether they result from a large investment with a low rate of return or from a small investment with a high rate of return. The subsidy conveyed by a tax credit is proportional to investment regardless of the rate of profit. As may be seen in a glance at table 13.1, the tax credit is a better subsidy than the tax holiday when the rate of return is low, but the capital subsidy equivalent of the tax credit soon stabilizes while the capital subsidy equivalent of the tax holiday continues to grow more or less in proportion to the rate of return until, at high rates of return, the capital subsidy equivalent of the tax holiday becomes the larger by quite a wide margin. By the same token, the tax credit concentrates the subsidy upon the relatively unprofitable firms while the tax holiday concentrates the subsidy upon the relatively profitable ones.

The tax credit can therefore be thought of as containing an element of insurance. Whether that is advantageous to the host country depends in large measure on the characteristics of the market for investment. If competition for investment among countries is relatively unimportant, so that firms would be content to invest if they could be confident of earning rates of return in excess of the world rate of interest, the very high rates of subsidy provided to the very profitable firms by the tax holiday would be superfluous for the most part, and the tax credit would be superior in so far as it concentrates subsidies where they are most likely to recruit new investment. If, however, the market for investment is such that many potential investments with high rates of return will not materialize because rates of return are even higher elsewhere, and if some of these might be recruited by incentives, then there is something to be said for an incentive program based on gross profits, for there is a presumption that profitable investments are the ones most appropriate to the special conditions of the country.

3. Subsidization of the employment of labor. In a one-sector model, the effect of incentives upon the demand for labor depends exclusively on the amount of capital recruited by the program. The larger the capital stock, the greater the demand for labor, and that is all there is to it. The situation changes when we make allowance for some of the complexities of the market for investment. There is each year a great collection of potential investments differing one from another in many respects. It is therefore open to the host country to try to select investments that are particularly labor intensive or to count labor intensity as one of the desirable characteristics in the selection process. This object can be achieved automatically in an incentive program by, for instance, granting subsidies in dollars per man employed over the first five years of operation rather than as a tax exemption.

An incentive program in which all or part of the subsidy is granted per man employed would tend to pick up more labor-intensive investments, would make it somewhat less likely—though still not impossible—for subsidized capital-intensive investments to displace relatively more labor-intensive firms already established in the country, and would provide an inducement for new firms to adopt relatively labor-intensive techniques.

On the other hand, a subsidy per man employed could raise several problems of its own. There is, first of all, the distinction between direct and indirect labor. A new firm creates a demand for labor by hiring men itself and through the employment associated with its purchases of raw materials and intermediate products. The subsidization of the firm's own labor force exclusively leaves out of account what for many firms is their main influence on demand for labor in the host country. But the attempt to subsidize direct and indirect labor combined would probably give rise to so many administrative problems that it may not be worth the red tape involved. The quantity of indirect labor must be computed. There should be some attempt to deduct or disregard indirect labor used in making products that could be sold on the world market if they were not purchased by the new firm; a manufacturer of rubber tires in Malaysia does not create employment on rubber estates. There would have to be some attempt to consider whether or not the new firm displaces firms already established in the economy. Second, too much emphasis on employment can divert an incentive program away from firms that are valuable to the economy for other reasons, for instance, because they are conveyors of technical change or good sources of tax revenue. Third, subsidization of employment could induce firms to increase employment temporarily, just for the duration of the tax holiday, or in ways that do not affect the demand for labor in the economy as a whole; firms could expand vertically to incorporate processes not otherwise eligible for subsidization. Fourth, subsidies per man employed may have more of an impact upon relative wages between the traditional and modern sectors of the economy than upon employment in the economy as a whole. Typically, wages in the modern sector exceed wages in the traditional sector because the modern sector is organized, because of skill differentials, or because of friction impeding the movement of workers from one sector to the other. Regardless of the reason for the existence of the differential, subsidization of employment might serve to widen it; the effect of the incentives would then be to transfer income to relatively prosperous workers in the modern sector leaving workers in the traditional sector worse off than they would be in the absence of the incentive program. Admittedly, any subsidization of investment may have this effect, but subsidization of employment is particularly likely to do so. There is, finally, the queer possibility that subsidization of employment in new industries might be self-justifying—subsidization of labor raises the relative wage of labor in the industrial sector of the economy, the high relative wage is taken as an indicator of high labor productivity, and the high output per man in these industries is taken as sufficient reason for their promotion.

There is considerable doubt in my mind about the alleged advantages of subsidization of employment, for the wage of labor in less developed countries is already very much lower than the wage of labor in developed countries, lower by a factor of ten or fifteen. It is hard to imagine that the relatively small additional wage differential, which is all that an incentive program is likely to provide, could make much of a difference to a firm for which the existing wage differential is an insufficient inducement to invest.

4. Bias toward large firms. Incentive programs are probably slanted in favor of large firms if only because the administrative cost, both to the firm and to the civil service, of deciding whether or not a firm is entitled to an incentive is smaller per dollar of investment for large firms than for small ones. There may in addition be regulations that limit incentives to firms of a certain size or that make the size of the incentive (as a percentage of profit on investment) dependent upon the size of the firm.

5. Bias against long-term investments. A tax holiday is not neutral between short- and long-term investments. The longer the term of the investment, the greater the proportion of the total return accruing after the end of the tax holiday, and the smaller the impact of the tax holiday upon the present value of the firm. A tax holiday is best for a firm that invests all at once before commencing production, and is less beneficial to a firm that extends its investment over a considerable period of time encompassing all or part of the tax holiday. Subsidization of labor over a given period of time would run into the same problem. Tax credits on investment would avoid the problem because the credit would be valid regardless of when the investment occurs or when the returns accrue.

THE PROBLEM OF REDUNDANCY

No matter how incentives are provided—by tax holidays, tax credits, or supplements to the wage bill, selectively among firms or indiscriminately to all new firms, to new firms exclusively or to investment of new and old firms alike—the central consideration in assessing the impact of incentives on the economy and in deciding whether they are on balance beneficial or otherwise is the efficiency of the incentive program in generating new investment. This can be measured (negatively) as a rate of redundancy defined as the difference between the dollar value of the subsidized investment and the net increase in the total investment of the country attributable to the incentive program, all expressed as a proportion of the dollar value of the subsidized investment: if two million dollars worth of investment has to be subsidized to increase net investment by one million dollars, then the rate of redundancy is 50 percent. Incentives can be redundant because the subsidy is larger than is necessary to attract the investment, because subsidies have been granted for establishment of firms that did not require them, because subsidized investments displace other investments of potential new firms or of established firms, or because subsidized firms drive other firms out of business.

A subsidy program can, of course, be so generous as to be harmful to the host country even if it is not redundant to any significant extent. But a five-year tax holiday, which is typical of what is provided in many incentive programs, would have to be counted as an unqualified success if the rate of redundancy were close to zero and as an unqualified failure if it were 100 percent. Suppose (contrary to fact) the only consideration in the assessment of benefits of investment were jobs created and the tax revenue gained or lost. At a rate of redundancy of zero, that is if all of the subsidized investment represented a net increase in the investment in the host country, then the incentive program must be credited with both jobs created by the subsidized investment and with tax revenue accruing after the end of the tax holiday. The tax forgone during the tax holiday cannot be counted as a loss to the host country because that tax could not have been collected in the absence of the investment that gave rise to it. At a rate of redundancy of 100 percent, that is if no net investment were generated by the incentive program, the tax forgone during the tax holiday is a loss to the host country because it could have been collected in the absence of the incentive program, and there is no corresponding gain either in jobs created or in tax revenue after the end of the tax holiday. At a rate of redundancy between zero and 100 percent the increase in jobs created and the gain of tax revenue after the end of the tax holiday on that part of subsidized investment which is not redundant must be balanced off against the loss of tax revenue from the redundant investment during the tax holiday.

The relation between tax loss or gain and jobs created is illustrated in figure 13.1. The rate of redundancy is shown on the vertical axis, and the present value of tax forgone per job created is shown on the horizontal axis, tax loss to the right and tax gain to the left. The curve representing tax loss or gain per job created is of course upward sloping, indicating that loss per job increases with the rate of redundancy. The tax loss per job is infinitely large when the rate of redundancy approaches 100 percent, it diminishes steadily as the rate of redundancy decreases; the loss per job is transformed into a gain when the rate of redundancy is small, and the gain per job is greatest when the rate of redundancy is zero.

The exact shape of the curve depends on the nature of the incentive program and on assumptions about the rate of return to investment, the capital-labor ratio and so on. It is a simple matter to produce such a curve numerically. For Malaysia, where the average wage of unskilled labor is about 1,000 Malaysian dollars a year, I estimated that the tax loss per job created would be about $40,000 if the rate of redundancy were 95 percent, that the breakeven point between tax loss and tax

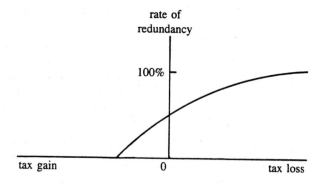

Figure 13.1 Present Value of Tax per Job Created

gain would come at a rate of redundancy of about 60 percent, and that the tax gain per job would be about $4,000 if the rate of redundancy were zero.[1]

The great stumbling block to the assessment of incentive programs to encourage investment in less developed countries is that we do not know the rate of redundancy in these programs and have no means of discovering what it is. A country embarking on such a program subjects its industrial development to a gamble where the odds are unknown.

The most commonly used method of determining the impact of tax cuts or subsidies upon investment is that based on the work of Hall and Jorgenson (1967), which in turn is based on Jorgenson's neoclassical theory of investment (1963).

Reduced to bare essentials, the theory is as follows: We assume that the economy can be represented by a production function $Q = f(K,L)$, where Q is total output, K is capital stock, and L is labor employed. The optimal quantity of capital K^* is what is required to equate the marginal product of capital with an externally given rate of interest r at the existing rate of the corporation income tax t,

$$K^* = g(r, Q, t), \qquad (13.2)$$

where g is the inverse function of the relation $r = [\partial f / \partial K][1 - t]$. In this derivation, it is assumed that capital and output are the same stuff so that one rate of return can serve at once as the own rate of interest on output and capital alike. The investment each year is a distributed lag function of the difference between desired capital and actual capital,

$$I_t = d(K_{t-1*} - K_{t-1}, K_{t-2*} - K_{t-2}, \dots). \qquad (13.3)$$

A reduced form of equations 13.2 and 13.3 can then be estimated to express investment each year as a function of other variables in the system, the important ones being r, Q, and t,

$$I_t = f(r, Q_t, K_t, Q_{t-1}, K_{t-1}, \dots , t). \qquad (13.4)$$

In the full development of the model (of which the statement here is a gross simplification) any incentive system or change in the tax law can be interpreted as a change in t. Thus, the answer to our question about the effect of incentives upon investment can be expressed as a derivative of I with respect to t in the system as a whole.

The neoclassical model, in its original form or as subsequently revised and extended, does appear as though it might provide us with a way of assessing the impact of incentives in less developed countries. Certainly, the functions that have been fitted to British or American data could be refitted to the data of a less developed country, and estimates of the impact of incentives could be obtained.

There are, however, reasons for doubting whether such estimates would be of much help to us, for there are analytical problems with the model and discrepancies between the assumptions of the model and the significant facts about the market for investment in less developed countries. I shall briefly review several objections that might be raised against the neoclassical model. It should be kept in mind in assessing the significance of these objections that the method was originally designed and is now used almost exclusively as a means of predicting the impact of incentives as an instrument of countercyclical policy in developed countries. By contrast, the policies we are concerned with have to do with the long-term impact of incentives in a very different set of circumstances. It could be that the neoclassical method is appropriate to the problem for which it was developed but inappropriate for our purposes.

The neoclassical model treats the post-tax rate of interest as exogenous and as invariant with respect to changes in the tax laws. As Harberger (in Fromm, 1971) has pointed out, this implies that the supply curve of saving to finance investment is perfectly elastic.[2] If this were not so—if the supply curve of saving were less than perfectly elastic with respect to the rate of interest—then part of the effect of the incentive would be shifted away from the intended recipient, to the suppliers rather than the users of funds. The effect of neglecting the flexibility of the rate of interest is to overstate the impact of incentives on investment.

Curiously, this criticism of the neoclassical method would seem to have greater relevance to the developed economies where the method has been applied than to the less developed countries, for it is not unreasonable to suppose that investors in a less developed country can borrow, one way or another, at a rate of interest independent of the quantity of investment in the country concerned.

A second line of criticism has to do with the concept of desired capital stock. This concept seems inconsistent with the production function from which equation 13.2 is supposed to be derived. A production function tells what amount of labor and capital would be sufficient to produce a given amount of output. To turn the equation around—reinterpreting K as desired capital, allowing desired capital K^* to differ from the actual capital stock in existence, and then connecting desired capital and actual output in accordance with the original production function—is in effect to admit that output Q could be produced with less capital than is required by the production function. If output Q is already being produced without the desired capital stock K^*, then why is K^* desired at all? Either K^* is necessary, in which case Q could not have been produced without it, or K^* is not necessary, in which case we have no explanation of why K^* is desired.

There are ways around this dilemma. One might argue, for instance, that the production function portrays the normal relation between output, capital, and labor, and that it is possible for output to exceed what is consistent with the production function if resources are used with an intensity that would not be economic to maintain in the long run. The trouble with this defense is that it brings into play forces which are explicitly ruled out in the formal model. It is not clear whether or in what way the predictions of the model would be affected by the introduction of a mechanism connecting Q in a production function to a capital stock larger than the one with which Q was produced.

The final objection, and the one I would like to emphasize is that the process of investment cannot be adequately described as a movement along a production function. The first and most important assumption in the model is that there is a production function which is sufficiently invariant over time that the estimate of the interest elasticity of investment is valid beyond the period over which the time series of Q, K, and other variables are observed.

The crux of the problem is that one cannot estimate the effects of incentives upon investment because there is no persistent technical or behavioral relationship that can be presumed to generate the observed data. We can estimate demand curves because, and only in so far as, there is a constancy of taste reflected in the detail of prices and quantities consumed. We can estimate supply curves because and in so far as there is a constancy of technology. We might be able to estimate the effects of incentives on investment if a marginal product of capital schedule were either stable or shifting in some consistent and predictable way as postulated in the one sector model. We cannot estimate the effects of incentives on investment if and in so far as the market is correctly represented by the array-of-opportunities model, for the appearance of new opportunities every year creates a situation where each year is different from all preceding years and time series data cannot convey the information we require about the options as they are today.

NOTES

1. It should be borne in mind that a subsidy can generate investment but not jobs. Consider this example in which the rate of redundancy is 80 percent: Suppose that subsidies are granted to $1,000 of investment, that of this $1,000 of investment $600 would have been forthcoming without the subsidy program, that an additional $400 of investment is displaced by competition with the subsidized firms, that the subsidized investment employs two men per $100 while the displaced investment employs four men per $100. Total employment of the subsidized firms is twenty men. The $400 of investment that would have been undertaken without the subsidy accounts for eight men. The $400 of investment displaced accounts for sixteen men. The overall effect on employment is a reduction of four men. It should also be noted that "jobs created" is shorthand for shifting the demand curve of labor to the right; the net effect of creating jobs could be either to mop up unemployment or to raise wages.

2. The supply of saving is likely to be somewhat more elastic to the corporate sector than to the economy as a whole, but by the same token, the increase in investment in the corporate sector as a result of reduction in the corporate income tax is to some extent at the expense of investment in the noncorporate sector of the economy.

14

Comparing Tax Incentives

Judging from the previous two chapters in this part, tax incentives for invest-ment are either no good at all (chapter 12), or it is almost impossible to evaluate their effectiveness (chapter 13). In these circumstances, it may seem paradox-ical—or, in Usher's (1977) words, "redundant"—to include the next two selec-tions, which suggest methods of evaluating fiscal incentives. The reality, however, as noted in the introduction to this part, is both that many developing countries already have specific tax incentives of various sorts and that they are likely to continue to do so. Few seem likely to emulate Indonesia's sweeping rejection of all such schemes (see chapter 6). More seem likely to follow the more interventionist Korean model sketched in chapter 7, if not always with similar results. Indeed, the use of tax incentives for business is so widespread and apparently enduring a feature of the fiscal landscape that it might be said that if the corporate income tax did not already exist, it would have to be invented, so that governments would have something to give away to their favorite region, sector, or type of investment.

Over the last few years, one of the most intensively employed tools of empirical tax analysis has been the effective rate approach used by King and Fullerton (1984) and since elaborated, modified, and applied in a wide variety of countries, includ-ing some developing countries (see, e.g., Agell, 1986; Ebrill, 1987a). As those who have encountered examples of this burgeoning literature may already know, in this approach—based firmly on the neoclassical theory of investment so castigated by Usher in chapter 13—the relevant rate for determining the effects of taxation on investment is the "marginal effective tax rate," which indicates the difference between the gross and net returns on alternative investments and hence the relative tax burden. (For a useful recent survey of alternative methods of calculation, see Boadway, 1987.)

The following paper by three World Bank staff members applies this concept, utilizing a number of specific assumptions considered to be not unrepresentative of many developing countries, to a comparison of different forms of tax incentives. Implicit in this analysis, which interprets differences in marginal effective tax rates as indications of the extent to which the tax system deviates from investment neutrality, is the assumption that the best system is one in which marginal effective tax rates are identical for all investments. Of course, since there are as a rule important nontax distortions in the economies of developing countries, it cannot be simply presumed that a tax system that is neutral towards investment will necessarily yield the best of all possible allocative worlds. Nonetheless, even those who want to direct investment consciously, rather than let the market do it, should find calculations like those set out in this paper of considerable use in helping to understand what they are really doing.

An important aspect of the incentive debate in many countries, which is highlighted in the following discussion, is the effect of inflation on business income taxation (see also chapter 21). As Pellechio, Sicat, and Dunn (1987) show, inflation has a substantial impact on effective tax rates and hence on the relative impact of different tax incentives. Also, some forms of incentive, notably accelerated depreciation, are often introduced and supported more or less explicitly to counter the enervating effects of inflation on investment. In the case of Colombia, for example, a recent analysis (McLure et al., 1988) found that the existing depreciation schedules and other investment incentives, when combined with the prevailing average inflation rate of around 25 percent, produced uniform marginal effective rates. Such results are simply coincidental, however. Moreover, if the purpose of a tax incentive is to provide a special inducement to particular types of investment, it hardly achieves this purpose if it only offsets the discouraging effects of the interaction of the tax system and inflation.

Effective Tax Rates
under Varying Tax Incentives

A. J. Pellechio, G. P. Sicat, and D. G. Dunn

Tax incentives are designed specifically for investments in high priority areas. Often, tax incentives are authorized as part of the investment promotion legislation of a country. The most preferred areas of investment are accorded the highest incentives. Ordinary investments are taxed in accordance with the provisions of the regular tax code, which sets the overall level of taxation from which effective rates are reduced by incentives.

Below we analyze the effects of different types of tax incentives, starting from a common base of a given tax rate, depreciation schedule, capital gains treatment, interest deduction, and other regular tax provisions. We evaluate the different forms of tax incentives by incrementally calculating their effect on the marginal effective tax rate of the firm. Some of these incentives are additive in their effects. In other cases, the incentives have a competitive effect, canceling one benefit over another. This is partly due to the tendency of governments to introduce features in which there is a choice of one incentive over another. Sometimes this is done simply by providing offsets of some benefits against other incentives.

A useful outcome of this exercise is the comparison of various tax incentive regimes with ordinary enterprises, the so-called base case. Quantifying these differences can be useful to country policy makers. Any large disparities in the effective taxation of tax-incentive–induced investment and ordinary investment are likely to signal resource transfers that may not necessarily conform with longer run objectives or efficient resource allocation.

The justification for incentives, of course, is to reduce the risks for particular investments and to improve their profitability. Tax incentives can be powerful in differentiating the incentives to invest in particular activities. Whether tax incentives promote productive activity or not is a separate issue.

BASIC ASSUMPTIONS

In order to undertake the comparisons needed to evaluate various types of incentives, we follow the strategy of using a single representative investment, with a certain mix of assets, and utilizing a common corporate tax rate and tariff rate for imported machinery and equipment. Several assumptions are made in order to

Excerpted from Pellechio, Sicat, and Dunn (1987).

carry out the calculations. The representative investment is taken to consist of 40 percent building, 40 percent machinery and equipment, 10 percent vehicles, and 10 percent land. Replacement investment is undertaken at the rate of economic depreciation for each asset. Such replacement investment holds the real value of each depreciable asset constant. At the end of the tenth year the assets are sold at a nominal value that reflects their real value plus inflation over the ten years. Sale of the assets is included in the analysis to capture the effect of capital gains treatment (see Pellechio, 1987).

The standard corporate marginal tax rate is 35 percent of taxable income. Statutory rates in many developing countries predominantly lie in the 30 to 40 percent range. The use of a single tax rate is convenient but also quite realistic. Depreciation follows the standard straight-line depreciation method with lifetimes (rates) of twenty years (5 percent) for buildings, ten years (10 percent) for machinery and equipment, and five years (20 percent) for vehicles. The double-declining method based on the same lifetime is examined also. Following standard treatment, land is not a depreciable asset. Carry-over of losses is such a common feature of ordinary taxation that it hardly merits discussion as a tax incentive and, as mentioned, is included as part of ordinary taxation. It is assumed to be available for an unlimited number of years into the future for ordinary investment.

A tariff duty of 10 percent is used for imports of machinery and equipment. The rate of duty on machinery varies across countries. The tariff for machinery and equipment tends to be low in contrast to the rates for other manufactures, which are often high. Machinery and equipment are considered essential imports and therefore qualify for lower tariffs. Thus, a 10 percent duty is taken as a realistic rate.

The final assumption concerns the breakdown of imported and domestic components for the investment. For buildings, it is assumed that there is an (indirect and direct) import component of 20 percent with the rest being domestically procured. Investment in machinery and equipment and in vehicles is 75 percent imported and 25 percent domestically procured.

The quantitative effect of tax incentives is examined by calculating their effect on the marginal effective tax rate for the representative investment. The ordinary investment or base case (case 1) does not benefit from any tax incentives. The tax incentives that will be taken into account are as follows:

1. Corporate income tax holidays: for five years (case 2) or for eight years (case 3). These periods are the common ones found in many countries.
2. An investment deduction equivalent to 20 percent of the investment is available immediately (case 4); an investment deduction is very similar to generous tax depreciation treatment.
3. An investment credit equivalent to 20 percent of the investment (case 5).
4. An exemption on tariffs on machinery and equipment (case 6). In many countries, the exemption from import duty extends to raw materials used in production. However, this was not included in the analysis.
5. A tax credit on wages for unskilled labor (case 7); specifically, the tax credit is 10 percent of one-half of the wage bill. This is a type of tax credit favored by economists who want to direct tax incentives in favor of employment.
6. A tax credit based on net value added (case 8); specifically, this is equivalent

to 10 percent of the value added. If a country has a value-added tax (VAT) at 10 percent, this essentially creates a tax holiday from the VAT.

To compute the effects of these incentives on the marginal effective tax rate, incentives are applied one at a time. These calculations are made for two sets of depreciation deduction methods: straight-line and double-declining balance depreciation methods.

INDIVIDUAL EFFECTS OF INVESTMENT INCENTIVES

There are two ways to calculate the effect of investment incentives. One way is to consider the individual effect of one incentive on the representative investment. In other words, no other incentive is present in the calculation. The second way is to calculate the incremental effect of an incentive when it is added to preexisting incentives.

Table 14.1 shows the individual effects of tax incentives on the marginal effective tax rate (METR) for the representative investment. The METR for the representative investment is 45.6 percent for straight-line depreciation and 42.5 percent for declining balance depreciation. The import duties cause the effective tax rates to exceed the statutory rate. World prices of imports are assumed to be fixed, which is standard for small countries. Thus, the incidence of import duties falls entirely on the firm.

The most powerful incentive is the 20 percent investment tax credit (case 5). The investment credit is immediately available to reduce tax liability. The METR falls from 45.6 to 11.1 percent for straight-line depreciation and from 42.5 to 11.6 percent for double-declining balance. The reason the METR with the credit is higher for double-declining balance is that higher depreciation allowances reduce tax liability more and, as a result, reduce the effect of the credit. More of the credit is carried forward and the higher capital gains under double-declining balance outweigh the effect of the credit.

Table 14.1 *Individual Effects of Tax Incentives*

	(1)	(2)	(3)	(4)
	METR under		METR as Ratio of Statutory Rate	
	SLD	DDB	(1)/35%	(2)/35%
Statutory rate, 35%	—	—	1.00	1.00
Case 1: Ordinary investment	45.6%	42.5%	1.30	1.21
Case 2: Five-year tax holiday	29.3	34.8	0.83	0.99
Case 3: Eight-year tax holiday	23.2	28.0	0.66	0.80
Case 4: 20% investment deduction	33.1	31.2	0.94	0.89
Case 5: 20% investment credit	11.1	11.6	0.31	0.33
Case 6: Exemption from import duty	37.0	33.4	1.05	0.95
Case 7: 10% credit for wages	40.1	36.7	1.14	1.04
Case 8: 10% credit for value added	29.7	29.1	0.84	0.83

Notes: METR = marginal effective tax rate; SLD = straight-line declining method; DDB = double-declining balance method.

The corporate tax holidays come next in magnitude of effect. Of course, the longer the tax holiday the greater the effect. The effective tax reduction implied by an additional three years of tax holiday from the five-year is about six percentage points.

Turning to the incentives that are related to value added, the net value-added incentive (case 8) creates a larger reduction in the METR than the incentive for low-wage workers (case 7). The reason for this is simply the coverage of the incentive. Net value added, aside from including all wages paid (which is higher than the value for the low-income wage bill), also has the other components of value added: interest payments, rents, and profits. The low-wage incentive (case 7) covers only half of the wage bill (by assumption).

Straight-line versus Double-declining Balance Methods of Depreciation Deduction

The schedule of depreciation allowances is an important determinant of the METR for an investment. As a general rule, accelerated depreciation lowers the METR. However, as in the case of the 20 percent investment tax credit, this general rule does not apply in the presence of certain investment incentives.

Table 14.1 shows that the double-declining balance method of depreciation generally reduces the METR. However, the reduction is not significant in some cases. For the 20 percent investment tax credit (as mentioned) and tax holidays, the double-declining balance method produces a higher METR than straight-line depreciation. The presence of strong incentives at the beginning of the investment reduces the effect of large depreciation allowances in early years. Simply put, accelerated depreciation produces large deductions when they are not needed. As a result, depreciation allowances are carried forward and their present value is reduced. This enhances the effect of the taxation of the higher capital gains that result from accelerated depreciation.

Thus, accelerated depreciation can be beneficial for investment when it is compatible with the other tax incentives in force. However, a corporate tax holiday or investment tax credit can nullify the benefit from accelerated depreciation because larger deductions in early years are of little value.

INCREMENTAL EFFECTS OF INVESTMENT INCENTIVES

Incremental effects of incentives are examined by adding one incentive on top of another. More specifically, the effect of incentives is calculated with the five-year tax holiday and the import tax exemption for machinery and equipment already in effect.

Table 14.2 presents incremental effects of incentives. These computations are again undertaken for straight-line and double-declining balance depreciation. The percentage point decreases in the marginal effective tax rate are given in the last two columns of the table.

Case 9, the five-year income tax holiday and import tax exemption for machinery and equipment, is used as the reference point for all calculations shown in Table 14.2. The effect of the tax holiday and import tax exemption for machinery and

Table 14.2 *Incremental Effects of Tax Incentives*

Tax incentive combinations	(1) METR under SLD	(2) METR under DDB	(3) METR as Ratio of Statutory Rate (1)/35%	(4) METR as Ratio of Statutory Rate (2)/35%	(5) Decrease in METR SLD	(6) Decrease in METR DDB
Statutory rate, 35%	—	—	1.00	1.00	—	—
Case 2: Five-year tax holiday (base)	29.3%	34.8%	0.83	0.99	—	—
Case 9: Case 2 + Exemption from import duty	19.9	25.3	0.56	0.72	9.4%	9.5%
Case 10: Case 2 + 20% investment deduction	19.9	21.7	0.56	0.62	9.4	13.1
Case 11: Case 2 + 20% investment credit	9.4	14.4	0.26	0.41	19.9	20.4
Case 12: Case 2 + 10% credit for wages	15.2	20.4	0.43	0.58	14.1	14.4
Case 13: Case 2 + 10% credit for value added	8.4	14.7	0.24	0.42	20.9	20.1

Notes: METR = marginal effective tax rate; SLD = straight-line declining method; DDB = double-declining balance method.

equipment is enough to wipe out the effect of some incentives. For example, the 20 percent investment deduction does not reduce the marginal effective tax rate. The investment deduction does not have an incremental effect because corporate taxes are already zero in the first five years due to the tax holiday.

The 20 percent investment tax credit produces a large drop in the marginal effective tax rate (case 11). This follows from the fact that tax credits can be carried forward for five years. Also, the credit applies to replacement investment, which, of course, contributes to its effect. Unless benefits are carried over, as is the case with tax credits, they are lost.

The reduction in the marginal effective tax rates is roughly the same for the two methods of depreciation deduction. For reasons already discussed, the straight-line depreciation can produce lower METRs than double-declining balance. The acceleration of depreciation only leads to a loss of depreciation allowances because a tax holiday reduces the value of deductions.

ROLE OF INFLATION

The computations so far assume that there is no inflation. Tax incentives are often made partly to provide a hedge against inflation. Acceleration of depreciation deductions, the grant of initial investment allowances, and the favorable tax treatment of capital gains are examples of this.

In conformity with provisions in most countries, depreciation allowances are not indexed to the inflation rate, either fully or partially. Also, capital gains are taxed as ordinary income, when assets are sold (in year ten for our representative investment). These features of taxation will raise the METR in the presence of inflation. In order to examine the effect of inflation, a 10 percent inflation rate is included in the METR calculation.

Table 14.3 Effect of Inflation on Tax Incentives

	(1) SLD t = 35% infl. = 0%	(2) SLD t = 35% infl. = 10%	(3) (2)/(1)	(4) DDB t = 35% infl. = 0%	(5) DDB t = 35% infl. = 10%	(6) (5)/(4)	(7) (4)/(1) DDB/SLD infl. = 0%	(8) (5)/(2) DDB/SLD infl. = 10%
Case 1: Ordinary investment	45.6%	65.6%	1.44	42.5%	60.3%	1.42	0.93	0.92
Case 2: Five-year tax holiday	29.3	44.3	1.51	34.8	46.7	1.34	1.19	1.05
Case 3: Eight-year tax holiday	23.2	33.2	1.43	28.0	35.9	1.28	1.21	1.08
Case 4: 20% investment deduction	33.1	54.2	1.64	31.2	49.9	1.60	0.94	0.92
Case 5: 20% investment credit	11.1	33.3	3.00	11.6	30.9	2.66	1.05	0.93
Case 6: Exemption from import duty	37.0	57.2	1.55	33.4	51.4	1.54	0.90	0.90
Case 7: 10% credit for wages	40.1	60.0	1.50	36.7	54.4	1.48	0.92	0.91
Case 8: 10% credit for value added	29.7	48.1	1.62	29.1	44.7	1.54	0.98	0.93
Case 9: Case 2 + exemption from import duty	19.9	34.8	1.75	25.3	37.2	1.47	1.27	1.07
Case 10: Case 2 + 20% investment deduction	19.9	34.8	1.75	21.7	37.2	1.71	1.09	1.07
Case 11: Case 2 + 20% investment credit	9.4	25.8	2.74	14.4	28.1	1.95	1.53	1.09
Case 12: Case 2 + 10% credit for wages	15.2	30.8	2.03	20.4	33.2	1.63	1.34	1.08
Case 13: Case 2 + 10% credit for value added	8.4	24.2	2.88	14.7	27.5	1.87	1.75	1.14

Notes: METR = marginal effective tax rate; SLD = straight-line declining method; DDB = double-declining balance method.

Table 14.3 shows the effect of a 10 percent inflation on the METRs computed for the two methods of depreciation deduction. For the sake of comparison, the METRs at zero inflation rate are included in the table. Column 2 shows the METR at 10 percent inflation for all cases with straight-line depreciation. These rates are substantially higher than those in column 1. Column 3 shows the METR for 10 percent inflation as a proportion of the zero inflation METR for straight-line depreciation. As can be seen, the METR rises by 51 percent for the five-year tax holiday and 43 percent for the eight-year tax holiday due to 10 percent inflation.

Inflation can cause a substantial increase in the taxation of investment, even with substantial incentives, due to the structure of the corporate tax system assumed in these calculations. This structure reflects the main features of tax systems found in many developing countries.

Inflation and the Depreciation Deduction Method: Accelerated versus Straight-line

Columns 7 and 8 compare METRs based on the straight-line method and the double-declining balance method. Both columns present ratios of METRs based on the double-declining balance method to the straight-line depreciation method computed for zero inflation (column 7) and for 10 percent inflation (column 8). The main result presented by these ratios is that accelerated depreciation, in the form of double-declining balance method, helps to reduce effective taxation in the presence of inflation—except in the case of the tax holiday. Columns 7 and 8 present this result from another angle by showing that METRs for accelerated depreciation increase proportionally less with inflation over straight-line depreciation.

In the incremental analysis in which a tax holiday is supplemented by other incentives, the METR under double-declining balance is still higher than that under straight-line depreciation. However, there is a reduction in the gap between the two methods. This result is consistent with the fall in the relative value of the depreciation deductions as the nominal value of income rises with (in this case, 10 percent) inflation.

SUMMARY AND CONCLUDING REMARKS

Some important general observations can be drawn from the results presented in this study. Certain incentives, like corporate tax holidays and investment tax credits, lower effective taxation of investment substantially more than other incentives. This happens because the tax benefits of these incentives occur at the beginning of the investment where they have the highest present value to the investor.

The presence of other incentives can significantly reduce or reverse the effect of accelerated depreciation, which is widely regarded as being favorable for investment. If tax incentives have their effect at the beginning of an investment when accelerated depreciation is also supposed to have its effect, the benefits of the latter are reduced. The benefits can be so reduced that the higher capital gains resulting from accelerated depreciation outweigh them, and effective taxation is actually greater than under straight-line depreciation.

The interaction of incentives is important. Some incentives can render others ineffective. The examination of incremental effects of incentives showed that the five-year tax holiday and import tax exemption eliminated the beneficial effect of an investment deduction. When the benefits of tax incentives occur at the same time they become redundant. Policy makers have to be careful about offering tax incentives that have no value.

Indiscriminate granting of tax incentives may only erode the tax base and may not even promote the desired mix of investments. Lack of knowledge about the exact impact of tax incentives on the effective tax rates faced by investors, on the composition of overall investment, and on the substitution of factors of production can create an excessive number of incentive instruments.

It is important to recognize that investors may examine the tax regime after considering nontax factors. Investors may examine the regulatory environment and the stability of the political and economic situation before deciding to invest in a country. If this is the sequence of decision making, tax incentives play a secondary, albeit potentially significant, role.

An important objective in the design of tax incentives is that they not distort the use of factors of production, especially capital and labor. In other words, incentives should be as neutral as possible in their effect on the allocation of resources. Incentives that are tied closely to depreciable assets, like additional depreciation allowances or investment tax credits for machinery, can induce a substitution of capital for labor. Employment credits, of course, act in the opposite direction. A more desirable incentive with respect to neutrality might be a deduction or credit based on the value added of the investment activity.

The corporate tax holiday has the desirable feature that it does not discriminate between capital and labor. However, its rationale is questionable. If an investment is able to produce positive taxable income during a corporate tax holiday then the exemption appears to be merely a "tax windfall." This seems especially unjustified if the investment is profitable due to other tax incentives. It is simply not possible to assert that the exemption is valuable to investors and deny that revenue is being forgone from profitable investments.

15

A Cost-Benefit Analysis of Tax Incentives

The methodology set out in the preceding selection is designed to analyze and compare different tax incentives, whether within one country or across a number of countries. In contrast, in the following selection, Wayne Thirsk (1984) develops a careful analysis of the costs and benefits of a particular incentive program in a particular country, Jamaica. Analyses of this type are not uncommon in the literature (e.g., Heller and Kauffman, 1963; Chen-Young, 1967), but this example is unusually complete and careful.

Apart from the general method, a point of major interest in this paper is the sharp contrast between the generally deleterious effects of incentives in the context of the "import-substituting industrialization" policies traditionally followed in Jamaica, as in many other countries, and their conceivably beneficial effects in the context of more export-oriented policies (recall the somewhat similar argument in chapter 2). In addition to adding a little further impetus to the already strong tide in the economic literature in favor of the latter policies, this paper provides an excellent example of the importance of the setting—in this case, the interaction of trade and tax policies—in determining the effects and worth of particular incentive policies.

Indeed, this point may well be extended to say that it is not really possible to appraise any economic policy in the absence of a considerable series of assumptions (unfortunately, all too often implicit) as to the initial conditions of the country in question and the settings of other policies. The incidence of a particular tax change at a particular time in a particular country will depend in part upon the prevailing market and macroeconomic conditions; the effects of a tax-induced change in rate of return on new investment will depend on the same factors, as well as monetary and exchange rate policy; and the effectiveness or otherwise of a particular tax incentive program will depend on all the foregoing and more besides. Only a rash analyst would draw general conclusions about the efficacy and suitability of particular policies in the absence of close examination of the country in question.

It is therefore unfortunate that economists—even development economists, who really should know better since their daily work exposes them to the enormously wide range of reality—seem so prone to make one of two equally extreme assumptions: either that the competitive model is a good approximation to reality (as "market-oriented" economists are prone to think) or that planners have sufficient knowledge to replace markets completely (the assumption of "dirigiste" economists, a group out of fashion in the academic West these days but still important in the real world). In fact, the competitive model is only dubiously a long-run approximation to the fragmented reality of developing countries and is almost invariably a poor short-run depiction of that reality. On the other hand, the notion that a few planners possess more information about all the relevant facets of the problem than market participants whose very livelihood depends upon such knowledge is even more ludicrous. No general solution to the resultant dilemma is obvious; if it were, there would be more success stories in the world! On the whole, however, restraint in intervention, albeit not to the point of doing nothing, seems advisable.

Three other points of interest are suggested by Thirsk's paper. The first reverts to a theme sounded earlier in this book, namely, the pervasive data problem in developing countries. As Jamaica is no better and no worse than many countries in this respect, it is interesting to note the extent to which Thirsk was able to cobble together bits and pieces of information with a few critical assumptions into a coherent argument. This paper is an excellent example of the development economist at work: starting with an important policy question, thinking through the theoretical framework required to answer it, and then, to the extent possible, covering that framework with quantitative clothing. Note, however, that Thirsk was not able to overcome the critical problem of "redundancy": perhaps, as Usher suggests in chapter 13, no one ever will.

A second point of interest is the explicit allowance made in this analysis for the excess burden of taxes, that is, the loss in welfare resulting from the distortion in relative prices consequent upon almost all feasible taxes. There have in recent years been many attempts to measure the size of this deadweight loss, particularly in the United States. While the estimates made range widely (Whalley and St. Hilaire, 1982) and invariably simplify considerably the complex theoretical issues at stake, especially in economies that are obviously far from a competitive optimum, Thirsk's assumption that the excess burden of taxes amounted to at least 20 percent of the revenue collected would probably be a minimal consensus estimate these days. The cost of taxation is clearly greater than the simple cost of tax administration: there are, for example, compliance costs (borne by taxpayers) as well as deadweight costs (borne by society as a whole, and shared in no very clear way). Although the size and mixture of these and other costs varies considerably from tax to tax and country to country (Bird, 1982a), tax analysts should always keep their existence in mind when designing or reforming tax systems.

Finally, Thirsk, like many other analysts of tax incentives (see also chapter 16) appears in the end to favor direct subsidy programs to tax incentives. Matters are not quite so one-sided in this respect as is sometimes alleged, however. It is true, of course, that the budgetary costs of subsidies are—at least in the absence of the "tax expenditure" approach advocated in chapter 16—more obvious than those of tax incentives. Although this is no small matter, as experience with agricultural subsidies in all countries shows, it is by no means obvious that it is easier to design rational subsidy programs than tax incentives, let alone to eliminate them. Moreover, as just noted, subsidies must be financed—and taxes carry costs additional to those shown in the administrative budget.

Nor is the lesser discretion generally available to administrators with tax incentives necessarily all bad. It is unlikely that even the best informed planners can or should do much more than indicate in broad terms a favored sector and then stand back to let the market do the detailed work of allocation within the policy parameters provided.

In particular, it deserves to be emphasized that perhaps the chief distinction between a tax incentive program and a direct subsidy program is that the former is of benefit only to those who would otherwise have made profits and consequently paid taxes. As Wolfgang Stolper (1966) long ago argued, even in the face of the characteristically distorted prices in developing countries, much can be said for relying on real profitability rather than calculated shadow prices as a guide to what is worthwhile. Subsidies suffer at least as much as tax incentives from misdirection, redundancy, and poor administration. In addition, as experience shows in all too many countries, subsidies to business are all too likely to be paid out to economic losers. Tax incentives are certainly not ideal policy instruments; indeed, many developing countries would perhaps do well to follow the Indonesian example (chapter 6) and get rid of the lot of them; but if, for whatever reason, a country wishes to influence the direction of investment, tax incentives may indeed have a minor role to play.

A Benefit-Cost Evaluation of Tax Incentives in Jamaica

Wayne Thirsk

An attempt is made here to obtain a quantitative feeling for the performance of the tax incentive program in Jamaica and to determine to what extent the country's welfare has been either enhanced or harmed by it. At the outset, it should be recognized that there is enough uncertainty concerning the appropriate size of some effects to make the results of this exercise suggestive rather than definitive. Only some rough orders of magnitude are offered here, not precise estimates. Despite this lack of precision, it is unlikely that any reasonable revision of the values of key parameters would overturn the basic conclusions which emerge from this exercise. Only if some neglected benefits were to turn out to be important, and to be more important than some neglected costs, would it become necessary to withdraw or temper the conclusion that, during the import substitution phase of Jamaica's economic development, the tax incentive program was detrimental to Jamaica's economic welfare. Only with the recent emphasis on export promotion does the program promise to contribute to economic welfare.

Below, net social benefits arising from the tax incentive program are evaluated under both import substitution and export promotion regimes by choosing parameter values that are appropriate to each policy. The value of new technologies and additional manpower training are ignored in what follows along with the costs of preemption. These effects, unfortunately, do not lend themselves to easy quantification. Instead we weigh the labor market benefits against the revenue depletion and consumption cost attributes of the tax incentive program.

In equation 15.1, LY denotes labor income generated by incentive projects; KY represents gross national capital income; β is a parameter measuring one minus the social opportunity cost of a dollar of labor income;[1] t_c is the effective tax rate on gross capital income; γ is a parameter measuring the fraction of incentive project investment I that is *not* induced by the provision of incentives; P_d and P_w, respectively, are domestic and world prices for output; Q' is the amount of output produced by incentive projects; ξ is the induced loss of noncorporate tax revenue; A represents administration costs of the program; and η is the fraction of induced investment, $(1 - \gamma)I$, that is of foreign origin. Therefore, net social benefits (NSB) of the incentive program can be expressed as

$$NSB = \beta(LY)(1 - \gamma) - t_c\,(KY)\gamma - \xi\gamma - (P_d - P_w)Q'(1 - \gamma)\eta - A. \qquad (15.1)$$

Excerpted from Thirsk (1984).

Taking account of the effectiveness of the incentive program and the social opportunity cost of labor, through the parameters $(1 - \gamma)$ and β respectively, the first term in equation 15.1 captures the tangible benefits of the program. Succeeding terms measure the various costs of the program. The second and third terms refer to the loss of corporate and noncorporate tax revenues respectively. The fourth term measures the consumption cost of the program or the extent to which it redistributes income to the rest of the world, while the final term incorporates the costs of operating the incentive program.

While the expression in equation 15.1 is the basic instrument for evaluating the performance of the incentive program, it is easier to implement empirically if it is rewritten in the following form:

$$NSB = \beta \, \frac{LY}{VA} \, \frac{VA}{PQ'} \, \frac{PQ'}{I} \, (1 - \gamma)I - t_c \frac{KY}{VA} \, \frac{VA}{PQ'} \, \frac{PQ'\gamma I}{I} - \gamma\xi$$

$$- \frac{(P_d - P_w)}{P_d} \frac{P_d Q'}{I} (1 - \gamma)In - A, \tag{15.2}$$

where VA represents value added, while PQ' indicates the value of total output produced by tax incentive projects. The ratio LY/VA is an indicator of the labor intensity of a project, or series of projects, while the ratio VA/PQ' is a measure of the reliance on intermediate inputs, which in the Jamaican context invariably means imported intermediate inputs. Although it conveys a proper sense of the information that is required to evaluate the incentive program, equation 15.2 is notationally inconvenient. To simplify it, the following substitutions are made:

$$\alpha = \frac{LY}{VA} \, , \quad \Phi = \frac{VA}{PQ'} \, , \quad \omega = \frac{PQ'}{I} \, , \quad \text{and } \Delta = \frac{P_d - P_w}{P_d} \, .$$

Moreover, it is necessary to modify equation 15.2 to take into account the recoupment of the revenue loss from other sources of taxation. To do this, let σ measure the differential excess burden of a dollar of additional taxation. Making these substitutions and expressing the previous equation on the basis of a dollar of investment spending, we have:

$$\frac{NSB}{I} = \beta\alpha\Phi\omega(1 - \gamma) - t_c(1 - \alpha)\Phi\omega\gamma(1 + \sigma)$$

$$- \Delta\omega(1 - \gamma)\eta - \frac{\xi(1 + \sigma)\gamma}{I} - \frac{A}{I} \, . \tag{15.3}$$

Each of these terms has the same interpretation as before, except that they are now on a per unit of investment basis. As in equation 15.1, the first term measures benefits of the program while the various costs that are incurred appear in subsequent terms.

Equation 15.3 is designed to assess the interaction of trade and tax incentive policies. As such it can be adapted to a wide range of different situations. If the tax incentives have had no effect whatsoever on the volume of investment, the parameter γ is defined to be one, and the equation simplifies to the sum of the second, fourth, and fifth terms above. There are no benefits in this case, only costs in the form of forgone revenue and administration costs. Although there would still be a consumption cost associated with investment in trade protected activities, it would be a mistake to attribute this cost to the tax incentive policy since the investment would have occurred in any event, and thus the third term in the equation becomes zero in this case.[2] Similarly, if the tax incentives are completely effective, γ becomes zero, and the second and fourth terms in the equation disappear. In this case there may be sizable employment benefits and, although there are no revenue costs, these must be weighed against consumption and administration costs.

Moreover, if the trade policy is switched, the parameters of equation 15.3 must be appropriately modified. For example, if only investment in labor-intensive export activities is promoted by tax incentives, there is a zero consumption cost and the third term in equation 15.3 vanishes. In addition, the value of the parameter α will be higher than it otherwise would be and the term for noncorporate revenue containing ξ may safely be ignored.

The values of the various parameters used for evaluative purposes, along with their exact definition, are given in Table 15.1. Some discussion of this choice of values is necessary as some of these parameters are much harder to pin down than others. The richest source of published data on industrial structure is the 1971 JIDC [Jamaica Industrial Development Corporation] Statistical Report of Manufacturing Enterprises Approved and Operating under Industrial Incentive Laws. For 192 predominantly IIL [Industrial Incentive Law] firms, total domestic sales were about J\$115 million, capital investment was nearly J\$100 million, payroll was J\$18 million, and imports of raw materials and other inputs were about J\$58 million. From these data, it can be established that, approximately, $\alpha = 0.35$, $\Phi = 0.50$ and $\omega = 1$. The same report indicates that η, the degree of foreign ownership,

Table 15.1 *Benefit-Cost Parameters*

Parameter	Definition	Plausible value
β	One minus the social opportunity cost of a dollar of labor income, $0 \leq \beta \leq 1$	$\beta = ?$
Φ	Ratio of value added to output value	$\Phi = 0.5$
ω	Output/capital ratio	$\omega = 1$
η	Share of foreign investment in total investment	$\eta = 0.5$
t_c	Effective tax rate on gross corporate income (prior to depreciation)	$t_c = 0.3$
α	Share of labor income in value-added $\alpha \leq 1$	$\alpha = 0.35\text{--}0.65$
Δ	Excess of domestic over world price as a fraction of domestic price	$\Delta = 0.26$
$(1 - \gamma)$	Fraction of total incentive investment actually attracted by tax incentives; $0 \leq \gamma \leq 1$	$\gamma = ?$
ξ	Induced loss of noncorporate revenue	see text
A/I	Administrative costs of tax incentives per unit of investment	0.35
σ	Excess burden of an extra dollar of taxation.	$\sigma = 0.20$

was also about one-half.[3] The corporate tax rate has been, and is currently, 45 percent with some reduction occurring on account of the additional corporate profits tax (ACPT). For companies distributing at least 27 percent of taxable income the rate is 35 percent.[4] We assume that the effective tax rate on *total* corporate capital income, including depreciation, is 30 percent. An adjunct of Ayub's (1981) study is the calculation of effective protection coefficients measuring the excess of domestic over world prices for different activities. For all manufacturing it is estimated that the ratio $(P_d - P_w)/P_w$ is 0.35. This implies that the value of Δ is 0.26.[5]

The correct empirical values of the parameters γ, σ, and β are much more problematic. One view is that an investment promotion agency is doing well if one-half of the investment which it sponsors would not have been realized without that sponsorship. A key item on any future research agenda would involve an effort to pin down this parameter more precisely. All that can be said with much assurance now is that the value of the parameter is greater than zero and less than one.[6]

The excess burden parameter σ depends on the type of tax being raised, is generally higher the larger are marginal tax rates, and has been estimated in developed countries to have a range of between 0.1 and 0.5. A value of 0.2 may be a conservative estimate in the Jamaican context.[7]

A value for the parameter β is no easier to determine. Generally speaking, its value will vary from project to project and will depend on the type of labor required on a project, especially if labor markets are segmented or compartmentalized, as they may very well be in Jamaica. If the labor market is highly segmented, the increase in labor demand due to a new project is likely to increase wages rather than employment, and higher wages will diminish either profits or the demand for labor in other parts of the economy. In either case, the social opportunity cost approaches the wage paid and the value of β will be closer to zero than to one. If markets are not segmented, the impact of an increase in labor demand will be felt more on the employment side as the increase in demand percolates through the economy's labor markets and leads eventually to the use of unemployed labor, whose social opportunity cost may be very low. In this case β will approach the value of one.

In a previous section [of Thirsk, 1984] it is estimated that forgone commodity tax revenue would likely be twice as large as the amount of corporate tax revenue sacrificed under the import substitution regime. Thus, corporate revenue losses per unit of investment are evaluated as $0.3\,(0.65)(0.5)(0.1)\,(1.2)\gamma = 0.117\gamma$, and noncorporate revenue losses, $\xi(1 + \alpha)\gamma/I$, are assumed to be twice as large, or 0.234γ.

The remaining term requiring empirical evaluation is A/I. In 1982 annual expenditures of JNIP (Jamaica National Investment Promotion Ltd) were J\$7.325 million but it is difficult to know how to amortize this expenditure flow properly since it is a mixture of current and capital expenses. If no amortization is made and if one believes that, as JNIP claims, 6,032 jobs were to be created on new projects at an average investment cost of J\$19,148 per job, A/I has a maximum value of

Table 15.2   *Value of Net Social Benefits per Dollar of Investment*
(in Jamaican dollars)

γ/β	0	.25	.50	.75	1
		A. Import Substitution Model			
0	−.17	−.12	−.08	−.03	.01
.25	−.22	−.19	−.15	−.12	−.09
.5	−.27	−.25	−.23	−.21	−.19
.75	−.30	−.28	−.27	−.26	−.25
1	−.39	−.39	−.39	−.39	−.39
		B. Export Promotion Model			
0	−.03	.05	.13	.21	.29
.25	−.05	.01	.07	.13	.19
.5	−.07	−.02	.01	.05	.10
.75	−.08	−.06	−.04	−.02	0
1	−.10	−.10	−.10	−.10	−.10

J$.06. A similar kind of calculation using the data in Chen-Young's (1967) study yields a value of 0.035, and it is taken to be a more suitable measure of per unit administration costs in the benefit-cost exercise below. Substituting into equation 15.3 the estimated values of the various parameters generates the result that

$$NSB/I = 0.175\beta(1 - \gamma) - 0.117\gamma - 0.13(1 - \gamma)$$
$$- 0.234\gamma - 0.035. \tag{15.4}$$

In part A of table 15.2 this expression is evaluated for alternative values of β and γ ranging from zero to one. Out of twenty-five possible cases only one suggests that net social benefits may be positive. Losses are a more likely prospect under the ISI (import-substituting industrialization) strategy and could vary from as little as 3 cents to as much as 38 cents for each dollar of investment associated with the incentive program.[8]

As expected, the sign, but not the size, of the net benefits of the incentive is largely independent of the proportion of projects induced by the incentives. When the incentives are ineffective, revenue losses are important. On the other hand, when they are effective, although revenue losses are inconsequential the consumption cost becomes important and offsets the employment benefits that occur.

Under the new regime, which attempts to promote labor intensive exports and agriculture, this welfare loss could be transformed into a welfare gain. If the new investment projects have characteristics such that $\alpha = 0.65$, a value that is consistent with EIEL (Export Industry Encouragement Law) data, and all of the other parameters remain unchanged, then, recalling from earlier discussion that $\Delta = \xi = 0$ under an export promotion scheme, the equation for net social benefits per unit of investment becomes $NSB/I = 0.325\beta(1 - \gamma) - 0.063\gamma - 0.035$.

Part B of table 15.2 shows the different values for this equation when it is evaluated for alternative measurements of β and γ ranging from zero to one. Thirteen out of twenty-five possible cases indicate that a loss of anywhere from 2 cents to about 10 cents per dollar of investment may be sustained under the export promotion strategy. However, welfare gains of from 1 cent to 29 cents per dollar of investment are nearly as likely as welfare losses. Clearly, as the parameter β increases in size and as the parameter γ diminishes in size (toward maximum incentive effectiveness), the benefits of the tax incentive program become greater.

That the results of this benefit-cost exercise should be treated with a great deal of caution can hardly be overemphasized. For one thing, some benefits—for example, training and technology transfer—have been overlooked as have some costs—for example, preemption costs—because of the absence of data. With an incomplete accounting of all of the effects of the incentive program, the best that one can hope for is that the neglected benefits roughly match the size of the neglected costs.

For another thing, there may be different interpretations of the Jamaican experience than the one expressed here. For example, a plausible view of Jamaica's economic situation is that it is a small price-taking economy functioning in the middle of an efficient international capital market which injects capital into the Jamaican economy only if there are investment opportunities generating an after-tax yield in excess of after-tax returns in the rest of the world. An implication of this view is that all taxes levied on foreigners, corporate as well as noncorporate levies, are borne by Jamaicans either in the form of higher consumer prices or lower wages and land rents. If one accepts this view, one concludes that the provision of tax incentives will contribute to lower consumer prices so that any revenue loss will always be counterbalanced by a consumer gain. If, however, the loss of tax benefits on foreign investment always finances an equal value consumption subsidy, there can never be any revenue sacrifice for a tax incentive program.

In terms of the ISI model presented above, this perspective implies that, while there are never any real tax benefits from taxing foreign investment, neither are there any revenue losses associated with a reduction in tax burdens on foreign investment. The revenue loss terms could be ignored in equation 15.3, for, unless these losses were incurred, the consumption cost would be greater by a like amount. In part A of table 15.2 the equation for estimating net social benefits per dollar of investment would become

$$NSB/I = (1 - \gamma)(0.175\beta - 0.13) - 0.035. \qquad (15.5)$$

A little experimentation with this modified formula indicates that, while the size of the losses reported in part A of table 15.2 will be reduced, there is not a single instance in which a loss is transformed into a gain. The analysis differs little if this alternative view of foreign capital supply conditions is adopted, but this, of course, does not rule out the possibility of other views that could make a difference to the analysis.

Nearly twenty years ago, Chen-Young (1967) offered an extremely optimistic assessment of Jamaica's tax incentive program, concluding that its benefits far exceeded its costs. More recently, this conclusion has been challenged by both the World Bank and the International Monetary Fund. These institutions have accused the incentive program of being overly generous and distorting in its economic impact and have recommended in one case (the World Bank) its elimination and in the other (the IMF) its retrenchment.

This paper has taken issue with all of these positions. Chen-Young's optimism is unwarranted because his analysis rests on assumptions that are either inconsistent or implausible. On the other hand, the pessimism voiced by the international institutions cannot be taken too seriously, since it is based only on informal analysis and impressionistic judgments.

On the basis of the benefit-cost exercise carried out in this paper there is scope for cautious optimism concerning the desirability of the incentive program. An important characteristic of the program is its interaction with different foreign trade policies. Not only the amount but also the type of investment that is attracted will determine whether or not the tax incentive schemes have been worthwhile. Prior to 1981, tax incentives were tied to the creation and support of import substituting activates and likely resulted in damage to Jamaican welfare. Welfare biases ranging between 3 and 38 cents per dollar of investment may have occurred. Since 1981, however, the tax incentive program has been given an outward-looking orientation and been geared to the promotion of exports. Although welfare losses may still occur in these new circumstances, welfare gains are at least as likely and depend on the ability to attract investments that would not otherwise have come to Jamaica and which have large labor market benefits. A welfare gain of between one and twenty-nine cents per dollar of investment may be experienced under these favorable conditions.

Tax holidays and a waiver of consumption, stamp, and customs duties have been the major instruments employed by the incentive program. Compared to other instruments that are available, tax holidays are relatively neutral in their impact on the economy and fairly easy to administer. The waiver of duty, on the other hand, acts as implicit investment tax credit which encourages the adoption of capital intensive techniques of production. Both instruments, but especially the waiver of duty, favor shorter-lived investments and are both non-neutral in this respect. The active employment of both instruments has in the past led to an annual revenue loss of between 1 and 3 percent of total revenues.

NOTES

1. There is no unique formulation for the measurement of the social opportunity cost of labor. A frequently used approach is to assume that labor migrates from rural to urban areas until the expected urban wage equals the rural wage, where the former is estimated as the product of the urban wage and one minus the urban unemployment rate. If the rural wage approximates the social opportunity cost of labor, an urban unemployment rate of 25 percent implies that net social benefits from hiring more urban workers are 25 percent of the urban worker wage bill. For a formal analysis of this matter see Stiglitz, 1974.

2. Only foreign induced investment, working through the parameter η, involves a consumption cost because it is only in this instance that there is a redistribution of income between Jamaica and the rest of the world. For domestic investment there is a similar redistribution of income, but it is only between Jamaicans, from consumer to producer interests.

3. This report, and others, indicate that about one-half of all investment is locally owned. However, among the other half there are some joint ventures with an unknown proportion of mixed ownership. Setting the value of η at 0.5 implicitly assumes that Jamaicans have a minority interest in any joint venture.

The 1981 *Statistical Yearbook* for Jamaica contains similar data for the year 1973. Those data indicate that the labor shares (α) were .28 and .54 for IIL and EIEL (Export Industry Encouragement Law) firms respectively. A weighted average of these shares, assuming IIL firms were twice as prominent, is .36.

4. An amount equal to 37.5 percent of corporate distributions is withheld and can be credited against ACPT up to 10 percentage points of corporate taxable income. Thus, ACPT liability is extinguished when corporate distributions are 10/37.5 (= 26.7 percent) of taxable income. This provision makes the effective corporate tax rate a function of the firm's dividend distribution policy.

5. For all of manufacturing, Ayub (1981) estimates $(P_d - P_w)/P_w = 0.35$. Thus,

$$P_d = 1.35 P_w \text{ and } \frac{(P_d - P_w)}{P_d} = 1 - \frac{1}{1.35} = .26.$$

6. In the case of the cement industry in Jamaica, Williams (1977) found that the favorable liquidity effects of tax incentives could explain as much as one-quarter of the investment in that industry. In general, the value of γ may be expected to vary with the type of tax incentive offered. Because tax holidays are particularly attractive to highly profitable firms, the value of γ may be relatively low for this form of tax incentive.

7. The narrowness of the Jamaican tax base for both personal income and commodity taxes argues for a relatively higher value for σ. On the other hand, σ is a measure of differential excess burden so it could conceivably be zero or even negative. If its value is set to zero for later simulation purposes, some experimentation indicates that all of the simulation results should be increased by about 15–16 percent. That is, losses will be smaller by about this order of magnitude.

8. That more investment may make a country worse off because it encourages the growth of the "wrong" industries, in the sense that these activities are ones in which the country has a comparative disadvantage, is not a new finding. For an earlier demonstration, but one that emphasizes excessive production rather than consumption costs, see Johnson (1967).

16

Tax Incentives and Tax Expenditures

The introduction to the preceding chapter stressed the importance of, at the very least, keeping good records on the revenue cost of tax incentives. This approach has been most fully developed by Stanley Surrey (Surrey, 1973; Surrey and McDaniel, 1985) under the name of "tax expenditure analysis," and to some extent has become a regular feature of budgeting in a number of developed countries (OECD, 1984; McDaniel and Surrey, 1985). The final selection in Part 3 applies Surrey's concepts to developing countries and provides an appropriate bridge to the discussion of direct taxes in Part 4.

When applied to tax incentives, tax expenditure analysis basically means measuring the revenue costs of incentives, in contrast to the more ambitious measurement of both costs and benefits set out in chapter 15. As Surrey and Lotfi Maktouf emphasize in the following selection, at the very least it seems obvious that governments should have a clear idea of the revenue cost of their incentive programs.

Unfortunately, there are at least two important problems with the tax expenditure approach that have on the whole made it more useful as a persuasive tool for would-be tax reformers than as an analytical approach. In the first place, most active proponents of tax expenditure analysis have tended to define its scope so broadly as to divert discussion to the pros and cons of different normative definitions of the appropriate tax base rather than the merits or otherwise of particular tax provisions. Maktouf and Surrey, for example, clearly overstate the ease of reaching agreement on such normative concepts. One way to obviate many of the resulting problems, however, may simply be to focus solely on costing those tax provisions—e.g., accelerated depreciation, investment credits, tax holidays, etc.—that are specifically presented and justified as incentives. In these cases, unlike such more controversial matters as the appropriate treatment of capital gains or the appropriate integration of corporate and personal taxes, there should be no dispute as to the suitability of measuring the revenue cost of such deviations from the "norm."

The second problem with tax expenditure analysis cannot be so easily resolved, however, since it is in effect the "redundancy" problem (see chapter 13) reappearing under the guise of the assumption that there is no behavioral response to tax incentives. Maktouf and Surrey correctly note that similar problems arise in all budget estimating exercises, but they are perhaps consciously naive in neglecting the obvious truth that costing an incentive on the assumption that it does not "incent" anything is loading the dice against it. In the end, while sensible quantitative analysis of tax incentives must certainly start with "tax expenditure" estimates, it cannot stop there, any more than sensible analysis of a particular expenditure item in the budget consists solely of looking at its magnitude without considering what the purpose of the expenditure is and whether its objectives may be more efficiently accomplished in some other way.

Tax Expenditure Analysis in Less Developed Countries

Lotfi Maktouf and Stanley S. Surrey

Despite multiple warnings against the systematic use of tax incentives in less developed countries (LDCs), governments of these countries continue to enact tax holidays and other devices for the purpose of attracting foreign multinational investment. Tax administrators in LDCs do not always realize that the enactment of such tax incentives involves high revenue costs. Even when they do, administrators do not place enough emphasis on the issue, probably because they lack appropriate instruments to measure the extent of these costs.

In many developed countries, the use of tax expenditure analysis enables the government to measure the costs of tax incentives and other tax benefits. The purpose of this article is to suggest the application of the tax expenditure analysis to the tax and budgetary systems of LDCs. Rather than developing a particular tax expenditure budget for a specific tax system, this article raises the general issues that governments of developing countries would face should they apply the tax expenditure concept to their tax and budgetary systems. Although generalizations are often arbitrary, it is believed that the tax expenditure concept represents an analytical tool that could be applied to a broad variety of developing countries' tax and budgetary systems.

TAX EXPENDITURE ANALYSIS

The Emergence of the Tax Expenditure Concept

Tax expenditure analysis represents a new approach to the tax system and budget process in a given country. Tax expenditures can essentially be defined as those measures that depart from the normative structure of the tax with the intent to encourage private behavior in line with government objectives or to relieve hardships. Essentially, by reducing normative tax liabilities, tax expenditures represent government assistance delivered through the tax system rather than through the direct budget.

The United States was the first country to publish a detailed tax expenditure budget—a list of tax expenditures. The 1968 Annual Report of the Secretary of the U.S. Treasury contained the first U.S. tax expenditure budget, and the 1974 Congressional Budget Act formally made the concept an integral part of the congressional budget process. Each year, a special analysis listing tax expendi-

Excerpted from Maktouf and Surrey (1983).

tures and estimating their cost is attached to the general budget.

Following the United States, other developed countries are steadily adopting tax expenditure budgets. Thus, Canada, France, the United Kingdom, and Spain have developed their own lists, and Sweden, Belgium, Australia, and the Netherlands are among countries considering the adoption of such a budget. West Germany presently has a limited form of tax expenditure budget.

While the tax expenditure concept has gained wide recognition in the developed world, it has not been applied to LDCs. The contradiction between the LDCs' extensive use of tax incentives as a major instrument for achieving government objectives and the absence of any tax expenditure analysis in these countries is striking. To focus consideration by LDCs on the desirability of adopting tax expenditure analysis, this article first will present a brief introductory description of the essential components of that analysis: the definitional and measurement aspects.

The Definitional Aspect of the Tax Expenditure Concept

The basic assumption underlying the tax expenditure concept is that any given tax of wide application is typically made up of two components. The first component consists of the provisions that constitute the normative structure of the particular tax. These provisions are indispensable to the implementation of the tax itself. They include the definition of the normative tax base, the determination of a taxable unit, the determination of taxable periods, the specification of rate schedules and exemption levels, the determination of the geographical scope of the taxing jurisdiction, and the administration of the tax. The second component consists of the special provisions that deviate from the normative structure for the purpose of implementing certain government nontax goals. These deviations, or special provisions,[1] exist in every tax system and, through the government assistance represented by the special provisions, are aimed at encouraging certain economic behavior, such as investment, savings, manufacture, or export, or providing relief to certain social groups, such as the needy, families, or retired persons.[2] The essence of tax expenditure analysis is to view these special provisions as a method of government spending that is an alternative to direct budget expenditures. The taxing jurisdiction's waiver of its tax claim to produce a special reduction in tax payment is, in effect, a means of providing government assistance that should be taken into account in determining the overall degree of government spending. Thus, tax expenditure assistance can be viewed as if the normative tax were first collected and the government then provided direct grants to the beneficiaries under the tax expenditure provisions.

McDaniel and Surrey (1985) identified a normative tax structure through six questions:

1. Is the provision necessary to determine the base of the tax, normatively defined, in accordance with the fundamental nature of the tax?
2. Is the provision part of the generally applicable rate structure?
3. Is the provision necessary to define the taxable units liable for the tax?
4. Is the provision necessary to assure that the tax is determined within the time period selected for the imposition of the tax?

5. Is the provision necessary to implement the tax in international transactions?

6. Is the provision necessary to administer the tax?

Answers to these questions may be considered by some as controversial because of differences among various tax systems. Tax experts, however, not swayed by a desire to inject tax incentives or hardship relief into the tax system, can readily reach general agreement on the normative structure of a tax.

The first step in tax expenditure analysis is thus to develop the normative structure of a tax system. The second step is to identify the tax provisions that are departures from that normal structure. These departures are present in the provisions designed to provide incentives for desired conduct or activities and relief from certain hardships. The whole array of such departures constitutes the list of tax expenditures that will serve as a tax expenditure budget.

The Estimates of Tax Expenditures

Once a tax expenditure list is drawn up, estimates of the revenue loss involved in each item should be determined. This is not an easy task, but it is not an impossible one either. Technicians working on national tax expenditure budgets have been able to prepare estimates for most tax expenditures listed. The technical problems encountered in setting up such estimates are the same as those technicians encounter in preparing estimates of changes in the tax system or in budget programs. Thus, direct outlays—namely, standard spending programs through budget expenditures—also involve estimates of the scope and amount of the entitlements under the programs.

Also, in most countries, as with the direct budget, each time a change in the tax law is proposed a revenue figure is attached to the change, even if, in certain cases, the lack of data makes the task particularly difficult. Tax expenditure estimates involve the same techniques that are utilized in making these other estimates. Hence, criticisms directed at the method of estimating tax expenditures can, in fact, be aimed at the estimating processes government officials use for both direct outlays and tax changes.

Both tax expenditure and direct program estimates are based on a static view of the economic situation. These estimates do not take into account economic conditions changing in response to the tax expenditure. There is, indeed, a two-level approach employed in estimating tax expenditures and direct programs. The first level is generally called first-order estimates, where only the present revenue picture is given and the direct effect of a change in that picture is then estimated. For example, if a special exclusion from taxable income permits a 40 percent reduction in taxable income, with a prior taxable income of 100 and a 50 percent tax rate, the taxpayer saves 20 percent in tax liability. The revenue loss attributed to the tax expenditure for the government's point of view is 20 percent. A second level of estimates relates to the effect in the economy of the change resulting from the special exclusion. An attempt at such an estimate generally leads to highly intricate speculation as to the possible effects of the change in the economy. Therefore, revenue estimators have generally considered only first-order effects, realizing that the estimates merely represent the initial effect of the change in the tax system, in the same way that estimates of a change in direct outlays reflect the initial consequences of the change.

THE APPLICABILITY OF TAX EXPENDITURE ANALYSIS TO LESS DEVELOPED COUNTRIES

Once tax expenditures are recognized to represent a form of government assistance, a government may decide to develop a tax expenditure budget. The purpose of such an exercise is to ensure publicity on government spending and develop control over the spending involved in tax expenditures. Three steps are required, the first of which is to determine the taxes subject to the tax expenditure analysis. The second step is to classify the provisions identified as tax expenditures, and the final step is to present an estimation of those provisions.

In many LDCs, as a result of the codification process, a groundwork for developing a list of departures from the normative structure presently exists. Tax incentives in LDCs are often grouped together in special laws or regulations. It may be even easier to develop a list of tax expenditures for those LDCs than it is for an industrialized country, where tax expenditures are spread throughout complex tax laws and regulations. Some LDCs, however, do not have a separate code for tax incentives, but rather, a diverse set of rules accumulated over the years.

While LDCs admittedly lack some data, drawing up a tax expenditure budget with estimates does not appear to be an impossible task if certain factors are taken into consideration. Technicians from finance departments who are already accustomed to preparing entitlements for direct budget purposes are competent to handle tax expenditure estimates. It is of crucial importance that the elaboration of a tax expenditure budget be made at the level of the finance department because it creates an opportunity for a comparison between direct outlays and tax expenditures. It also places the debate and reflection on tax expenditures at a high government level so that conflict between agencies, where the trees hide the forest, are avoided. Also, the technicians working on direct entitlements possess special skills in setting approximations, which are useful in preparing a tax expenditure budget.[3]

The Integration of the Tax Expenditure Budget into the Budget Process

Once the classification and estimation processes have been completed, the government should consider integrating the tax expenditure concept into the budget-making process. Integration will require that tax expenditures be submitted to the legislative authority's scrutiny in the same way as direct budget programs. Tax expenditures will thereby be subject to regular reconsideration and control.

The budgetary procedure applied in some LDCs, however, calls for certain observations. The political structure is heavily weighted in favor of the executive power, with little or no room left for a legislature to play an important part in the budgetary decision-making process. Despite the legislature's minor role in the budget adoption process, however, establishing a tax expenditure budget still remains useful from both a budgetary and tax policy point of view. Regardless of the legislative aspect, the government itself needs to know more about its assistance programs and the way funds are allocated.

The Usefulness of the Tax Expenditure Concept

One finding that emerges from the reading of a tax expenditure budget is the comparison between tax spending and budgetary spending, each being a means of achieving government goals. The governments in LDCs are usually highly interventionist. Their functions in such roles as economic regulator, employer, and investor are quite extensive as compared to the governments of developed countries. In pursuing their interventionist role, governments in LDCs use both direct expenditures and tax expenditures, alternatively or cumulatively. Through an examination of the respective roles of tax subsidies and direct outlays, government authorities may determine the relative efficiency of government assistance measures. Indeed, one of the functions of the tax expenditure budget is to permit such a comparative examination of the two methods of assistance. As tax expenditures are a way of spending money, the expenditure should be confronted by an alternative direct expenditure program.

For example, suppose there are two tax incentives, A and B. Incentive A represents a special 20 percent exclusion from income tax for farmers or farming corporations engaged in greenhouse cultivation. Measure B represents a total exclusion from corporate income tax of profits derived from engaging in the textile industry. The question that should be asked is whether the goals sought by measures A and B could be attained through direct outlays instead of tax expenditures. Measure A could be replaced by a direct monetary grant. Thus, the government could decide to allow a certain amount of money to any farmer or farming corporation willing to conduct greenhouse cultivation. Among the motivations that may lead the legislature or the department of finance to enact the tax expenditure, rather than to utilize a direct grant, may be apparent simplicity or political invisibility. In comparing these two instruments of government assistance, however, a tax expenditure may be inadequate because of the existence in the tax system of permission to calculate agricultural income under a lump sum approximation of actual income and expenses. The tax expenditure does not have the same incentive impact on taxpayers subject to the approximation regime as it does on taxpayers using actual data to determine their income.

In the preceding example, measure B is intended to foster investment in the textile industry. The host country, by waiving its tax claim, hopes, among other things, to create additional jobs, obtain a transfer of modern technology, and reduce the balance of trade deficits for its textile industry. These goals could theoretically be achieved through direct subsidies. Investors in the textile industry may simply be granted special funds for creating new jobs or operating a plant in a remote area. Suppose, however, it is obvious that the tax incentive is in fact offered to worldwide fashion manufacturers. In this situation, one reason why measure B might not be replaced by a direct assistance grant is that the principal beneficiaries would be foreign investors, and it is unlikely that a developing country would directly give away considerable amounts of money for the benefit of a multina tional group from an industrialized country. Many LDCs have developed complex control systems over direct spending. Therefore, before a grant is given to any enterprise, a series of controls must be satisfied. This procedure could make it highly unlikely—if not impossible—for a government to assist foreign corporations through direct outlays. The subsequent resort to tax expenditure assistance should not hide the fact that moneys are in reality being spent on the foreign investor. The recognition of this fact could result in a reconsideration of the tax expenditure, leading to its repeal as costly and in contradiction to the country's policy of budget allocation.

The tax expenditure is often seen as an instrument that fits into the image of government neutrality and reliance upon private sector initiative, whereas a direct grant is by definition evidence of an interference into private, social, and economic life. The difference in perspective is really illusory, however, for the tax expenditure is neither neutral nor relies on private sector initiative, since it entails government assistance to the private sector, just as in the case of a grant. Theoretically, the more a government is interventionist, which is the case in some LDCs, the more it would seem inclined to use direct assistance. Industrialized countries, where the business community is particularly sensitive to government intervention, may prefer the use of the tax expenditure as a "soft instrument" to guide private behavior. The interesting question is whether these assumptions are borne out in actual experience.

Improving Tax and Budget Policies in LDCs

As one approach to reviewing the tax system of a country and its budgetary process, tax expenditure analysis permits a new look at government action. As described above, a tax expenditure is a form of government assistance and represents an alternative to direct programs. Generally speaking, governments know very little about their spending through the tax system. When presenting their spending programs, governments usually stress only the direct budgetary aspects of their action. Conversely, if cuts in government spending are considered, these usually lead only to reductions in budget outlays, namely direct expenditures. This results in a misallocation of resources and a waste of government funds.

Once a government becomes knowledgeable about both facets of its assistance—tax expenditure and direct outlay—the knowledge may lead to reform of its tax spending programs. This reform could mean the repeal of certain tax expenditures, or at least their reconsideration, and possibly the substitution of more effective and less costly direct programs. The application of tax expenditure analysis permits a thorough scrutiny of tax expenditures to eliminate those that do not accomplish any significant social or economic purpose or whose function could be more efficiently carried out by other fiscal instruments, such as direct grants.

To be realistic, any reform of government spending must deal with the tax expenditure issue. The first question that should be addressed in the process of scrutinizing a tax expenditure list is whether the government wants to commit government funds to the objective of the expenditure. The second question is the extent to which tax expenditures represent an efficient instrument in implementing government policy, keeping in mind the extent to which tax expenditures prevent the achievement of tax equity and less complexity in the tax system. The final question is the extent to which tax expenditures are preferable to other forms of government assistance, such as the direct spending form, in achieving that policy objective. Answers to these questions should have the effect of improving the structure of the tax system and the budgetary process.

NOTES

1. This terminology is adopted in M. McIntyre and O. Oldman (1975).

2. The identification of tax expenditures entails a definition of tax penalty. A tax penalty is a tax measure contrary to the normative structure and thereby creating an additional tax burden for the purpose of achieving certain social or other public order-related purposes. An example of this is the denial of deduction for bribery expenses.

3. Although tax expenditure analysis has not been applied at the official level in developing countries, certain countries have already felt the need for an estimation of what is spent by way of tax incentives. Gabon organized a system whereby a computer automatically memorized paid or waived customs duties, giving the customs department a total of the exact amount of customs receipts collected and also the amount of revenues waived because of customs incentives. Prior to this procedure, a World Bank study revealed that the then-existing customs regime in place for major corporations had reduced revenues by 30 to 40 percent.

Tunisia also developed a computerized system to record all imports. Regulations impose a compulsory statement for imports that the importer must present. In order to enforce this rule, Tunisia imposes a general tax, called *taxe sur les formalités douannières* (tax on customs formalities) on all importers. The amount of the tax is symbolic, but its virtue is to place all imports into the computer. Thus, the computation of the actual loss to the government becomes a simple mechanical operation. Although limited to the customs area, these two experiences provide signs for the possibility of developing estimates for tax expenditure budget purposes.

Part Four

Problems in Direct Taxation

Most tax revenue in developing countries comes from indirect taxes levied on foreign trade and on the sale of goods and services. Most of the literature on taxation in developing countries, however, focuses on the design and effects of direct taxes on income and wealth. (To some extent, the optimal tax literature, represented by chapter 4, which tends to have more to say about indirect taxes, where the relevant theoretical framework is more highly developed, is an exception.) This emphasis on direct taxes may simply reflect the bias in the public finance literature, or perhaps the predominant role of such taxes in developed countries. Or it may simply be that people are more aware of taxes which directly reduce the income they have to spend than they are of taxes that achieve the same result by increasing the prices of the goods and services they purchase.

Rather than attempting to review all the issues that come up with respect to the design of income taxes in developing countries—a list that would be at least as long as the similar list reviewed in standard public finance texts—this part takes two different tacks. First, it reviews a number of particularly troublesome areas with respect to personal and business taxation in developing countries. Secondly, it introduces some interesting recent work on the design of an alternative approach to direct taxation in developing countries.

An obvious problem in the design and implementation of income taxes in developing countries is the appropriate scope and structure of the personal income tax (chapter 17). Another is the companion question of the appropriate structure of the business income tax, and its relation to the personal income tax (chapter 19). An important subdivision of this second question that comes up in many countries concerns the appropriate way of taxing the extraction of mineral resources—a matter that in many ways takes us well beyond the conventional income tax model (chapter 23). Another pervasive problem is the effects of inflation on the income tax (chapter 21).

An area of increasing importance and technical complexity in developing countries is the taxation of income from international activity, primarily the taxation of income going to foreigners and foreign corporations. Chapter 20 provides a brief introduction to this complex area. As noted there, tax treaties between particular developed and developing countries have been the subject of much discussion in recent years (Surrey, 1978; United Nations, 1979, 1980). In practice, a principal function of tax treaties between developed countries is to reduce the taxes paid on income remittances to foreign investors, whose country of residence is given the primary right to tax such income. If the flow of income is reciprocal, this division of tax priority may seem reasonable, but this condition will seldom obtain where developing countries are concerned. For this and other reasons, detailed in chapter 20, the case for developing countries to enter into tax treaties is not very strong.

The final problem area touched on here is in many ways the most important: it is simply how to implement whatever tax system is designed. Basically, there are three main ways in which attempts may be made to improve the effectiveness of direct taxation in any country. The first is to rely on the voluntary compliance of taxpayers and to depend on such standard administrative techniques as selective auditing (Surrey, 1958) and the application of sanctions (Gordon, 1988; see chapter 36) to keep them up to the mark. This approach is as essential in developing countries as anywhere else, but it is likely to be much less effective. Few taxpayers in developing countries keep consistent records, or are willing to show them to the tax authorities if they do. Even should they do so, the authorities are seldom in a position to do much with them anyway; and sanctions are seldom applied, as taxpayers are well aware. As a result, even with respect to business income taxes, it is seldom sufficient to rely on taxpayers to produce meaningful records to be subjected to scrutiny by knowledgeable tax officials. Only for the largest—often foreign firms—does this approach offer much chance of success. Unfortunately, all too often these are the very firms that are subject to special "incentive" regimes (see Part 3) rather than the regular income tax.

The second approach is through withholding, the main way in which personal income taxes are collected in all countries. Withholding simply means taking the money before taxpayers actually get their hands on it. The major difference between developed and developing countries in this respect is that the scope of the modern organized sector in which withholding, particularly of wages, can be applied is relatively much smaller in developing countries. Withholding (and its companion, current payment systems) should obviously be applied wherever possible—to wages in the modern sector, to incomes paid by firms (and governments) to individuals in the form of dividends, interest, consulting and contracting fees, and so on. But there still remains a major problem in attempting to enforce any direct tax in the important "cash" or informal urban economy (Bird, 1983), let alone the largely nonmarket rural sector (Bird, 1974). No country has been very successful in reaching such "hard-to-tax" groups as small businessmen, farmers, and professionals—most of whom in developing countries operate in the cash economy and maintain few if any visible records that could serve as a basis for enforcing taxes. It is the misfortune of the developing countries that so much more of their potential tax base is to be found in these difficult categories.

In these circumstances, more reliance must inevitably be placed on the third approach, namely, some form of "presumption" or method of estimation for the determination of the tax base (e.g., income) on the basis of some more readily observable factor such as wealth (chapter 24) or turnover (chapter 25). The equity, vertical or horizontal, of such crude approaches is obviously open to question. In their absence, however, many of those thus taxed might otherwise escape entirely.

Similarly, the efficiency effects of presumptive methods may be quite different from those conventionally associated with income taxes (Morag, 1957), but again the outcome is likely to be more efficient than letting the income tax become solely a tax on wages in the organized large-scale modern sector.

Incidentally, it is important to distinguish a "presumptive" system along these lines from the superficially similar "forfait" system (Tanzi and Casanegra, 1987). The latter can become the worst of all possible systems for a developing country in that, while apparently based on similar objective factors, in reality it usually amounts to no more than a deal resulting from face-to-face negotiations between taxpayer and tax official. Without at least a limited range of standard assessments tied to objective factors, the temptation to bribery on one side and extortion on the other may prove too great to be resisted in the conditions of many developing countries.

As these brief comments, and some of the chapters included in this part, demonstrate, there are indeed many problems in implementing income taxes in developing countries—including many not mentioned here, such as determining the appropriate tax unit (a culturally relativistic concept, as shown by experience in both Hindu and Moslem countries). Much of the material in the present book is based on the extensive experience that has been accumulated in recent decades with respect to these problems in a wide range of income taxes in a broad spectrum of developing countries. It is this experience which has led us to stress above, and in Part 7 below, the overwhelming importance of the administrative factor in determining what can and should be done (see also Bird, 1989a).

In contrast, the discussion of "direct" consumption taxes in chapters 18 and 22 is inevitably more speculative. This discussion arises both from much sad experience with attempting to implement income taxes in developing countries and from an important trend in modern tax policy analysis demonstrating that the distorting effects of inflation on the taxation of business income (as well as some other problems of income tax design and implementation) may be most neatly solved by changing the basis of taxation from income to consumption (Bradford, 1986). While recommendations along these lines were made some years ago for developing countries (Kaldor, 1956)—and were even to a small extent implemented, although not very successfully (Goode, 1961)—recent analysis has, as chapters 18 and 22 show, considerably advanced our understanding of what is involved in moving to expenditure-based taxation and how best to do it. Indeed, many of the points made in these selections have substantial merit even if, in the end, no one turns out to be bold enough to lead the way in terms of adopting the consumption tax solution.

17

Schedular or Global Income Taxes?

The appropriate design of an income tax has long been the main focus of attention for tax analysts and tax reformers in developing countries. Almost without exception, the result of their cogitation has been to propose a move away from the once-dominant "schedular" income taxes—with different rates and often exemptions and deductions for different types of income—to a "global" income tax, the comprehensive tax base familiar from such sources as Henry Simons (1938) and Canada's Royal Commission on Taxation (1966), and earlier represented here by chapter 16.

One of the first, and best, reports on taxation in a developing country, for example, that on Venezuela by a distinguished team headed by Carl Shoup (Shoup et al., 1959) explicitly dealt with this problem and came to the usual conclusion. Attempts such as Forte (1964) to raise questions about this analysis have been almost universally ignored. Nonetheless, the question continues to be topical in many countries. Recently, for instance, the editors of this book have been involved in an attempt to replace the so-called "mixed" system of Senegal—a set of schedular taxes capped by a complementary global tax—by a unified global levy.

As this last point suggests, we too think that such a change generally makes sense from the point of view of both tax policy and economic development. Nonetheless, as the following selection makes clear, we also think it is important to realize that whatever the form of an income tax in a developing country may legally be, in reality such a tax will always be administered on a schedular basis (Rezende, 1976). The following chapter is our attempt to reconcile this schedular reality with the global ideal. Although some of the references to practices in particular countries may now be outmoded, the arguments remain valid.

An important point mentioned in passing in this selection, but not otherwise discussed in this book, is the determination of the rate structure of the personal income tax. In practice, this problem often turns out to be surprisingly complicated owing both to the usual data problems and to the need to reconcile a number of conflicting objectives in the context of a highly visible rate structure. These problems may of course be worked out to some extent in particular countries: see Musgrave (1981) and Alm and Bahl (1986) for two instances of differing sophistication. Nevertheless, when it comes down to choosing a rate structure, matters in most countries seem similar to what a senior Canadian tax official said about his own country some years ago: "The writer has made up dozens of rate schedules for successive Ministers of Finance. After much humming and hawing and staring at the ceiling this citizen will finally put his finger on one schedule and simply say 'that one looks about right'—and that is it." (Eaton, 1966, p. 27)

In recent years, a good deal of attention has been paid to one particular solution to the rate problem, namely, the adoption of a single-rate "flat" tax (Hall and Rabushka, 1983). This solution is attractive both because it is obviously coming into vogue in some developed countries (as evidenced to some extent by the U.S. reform of 1986) and, more relevantly, because it can result in substantial administrative simplification. With a flat-rate tax, for example, no longer does the tax designer have to worry about such complex problems as the choice of an appropriate tax unit or tax period—except to the minor extent that personal exemptions may still give rise to problems. Hong Kong (Jao, 1984) has long had a flat-rate income tax, and Bolivia (American Chamber of Commerce, 1986) has recently adopted one. Other flat-tax policies are no doubt on their way in a wide variety of developing countries.

One example where such a tax was recently proposed is Papua New Guinea (Collins, 1985). In this case, however, closer analysis suggests that moving to a single tax rate makes little sense (Bird, 1989). Since many developing countries, like Papua New Guinea, originally adopted the income tax largely to tap the income of expatriate employees, and it is still used largely for this purpose in some countries, the reason for this conclusion is worth mentioning. The taxpaying population is distributed bimodally, with expatriates (and the nationals who have stepped into their jobs and salaries) being clustered in the higher range of the tax schedule and nationals at the lower range. The result of moving to a uniform rate, keeping revenue constant, would thus be to lower taxes on expatriates and raise them on national workers in the modern sector. Neither of these results makes sense. Once a level of taxation on expatriates has been established, lowering those taxes will not achieve any equity or efficiency gain—although raising them (as Saudi Arabia recently found) may be impossible too. Raising wage taxes in the modern sector is also questionable in development terms (Bird, 1982), given the desire to expand rather than contract such employment, traditionally considered the main engine of both employment and income distribution in developing countries (Kuznets, 1966). The moral of this story is, of course, not that there is no role for flat taxes in developing countries; rather it is simply that, as always, the particular circumstances of the country in question must be carefully considered before recommending the application of any currently fashionable solution to the problems invariably besetting its tax system.

The Transition to a Global Income Tax

Oliver Oldman and Richard Bird

INTRODUCTION

Only a few years ago it was customary in considering the design of income taxes to contrast the schedular and the global approaches to taxing income. Today the latter approach has triumphed, at least in principle, throughout the world. The income tax in virtually every high-income developed country is now global in concept, although there are still important gaps in most countries and the move is recent in others (e.g., 1974 in Italy). Among the developing countries, those influenced by British colonial administrations have long had global-type income taxes, and almost no country in the world now has a pure schedular system, with completely separate taxes on income derived from different sources. The prevalent form of income tax in much of Latin America, as in Francophone Africa, is probably still the "mixed" system (schedular taxes capped by a complementary global tax), but present indications are that any changes in this situation will likely be in the direction of increased globalization. As Plasschaert (1976) notes, "To our knowledge no reverse sequence, from a global to a schedular or mixed frame, can be mentioned."

This worldwide move towards a "global" income tax has both an economic and an equity rationale. Although equity rationales are of course always matters of social judgment (and hence disputable), it is widely accepted in principle that income, broadly defined to include all accretions to economic power (potential spending power), provides a particularly suitable measure of ability to pay and hence the best basis for personal taxation. From an equity point of view, then, the tax implications of an additional dollar of net income (thus defined) should be the same, regardless of the source of that income.

Exactly the same rule is advisable from an economic point of view to avoid distorting unduly the pattern of economic activity by diverting resources into relatively lightly-taxed activities. This assumes, of course, that such neutrality is an appropriate characteristic of the tax system, which may not always be the case, especially in developing countries where a main aim of policy is often precisely to change the prevalent pattern of resource allocation.

Arguments such as this are one reason why no country, even the most highly-developed, has actually gone all the way to a truly comprehensive or global income tax—although detailed proposals along these lines have been made both in Canada and in the United States.

Excerpted from Oldman and Bird (1977).

Three reasons for the common retention of (often significant) schedular elements even in the most globalized income tax systems may be distinguished: principle, policy, and administration. Perhaps the major question of principle concerns the appropriate tax treatment of "earned" and "unearned" income. A secondary issue that may also be decided on grounds of principle concerns the treatment of gifts and bequests. In practice, such receipts are rarely (a partial exception exists in Colombia) taxed as income to the recipient, although both Henry Simons (1938), one of the intellectual parents of global income taxes, and the Canadian Royal Commission (1966) have argued that they should be so taxed.

In addition to the possible "incentive" motivation for desiring differential tax treatment of, say, income from certain sectors (or, more usually, of certain uses of income, e.g., investment), other "policy" issues also arise with respect to the treatment of international income (income going to foreigners and foreign income going to residents) and such matters as personal deductions, the treatment of pension income, and so on. A few of these issues are discussed briefly later.

Finally, and in practice perhaps most importantly, administrative realities have forced considerable modification of the ideal of a truly global income tax even in the most highly-developed countries. As a rule, the easiest income to tax effectively is wage and salary income; everything else gives rise to problems of varying difficulty. In the past, many countries apparently concluded that the resulting lower probability of catching a dollar of capital (or self-employment) income in the tax net should be recognized by imposing a higher tax rate on such dollars than on wage income. The trouble with this approach is twofold: (1) it leads to neglect of the need to improve the administration of the tax on nonwage income (precisely because of the belief that the differential rates take care of the problem); and (2) the belief that the differential rates take care of the problem is almost certainly wrong (precisely because the neglect of administration means that evasion will tend to escalate to offset the differential).

The argument in the preceding paragraph is, of course, by now widely accepted. What seems to be less widely understood, however, is that simply abolishing the various schedular taxes resolves no problems.[1] Indeed, unless the move to globalization is accompanied by significant administrative tightening on nonwage income, its immediate effect may even be to increase the taxes on wage and salary earners relative to those receiving other forms of income (as appears to have happened in Bolivia in early 1976). Much of the present paper is concerned with pointing out the sorts of steps which are needed to reach income from property effectively under an income tax.

The focus of this paper is thus on certain problems of principle, policy, and administration likely to be encountered in the course of transition from a schedular or mixed system to a more global income tax. Globalization in this sense is essentially a question of the *base* of the income tax. Sometimes the requisite base-broadening has been made more politically palatable by reducing tax *rates* (as in Canada) or raising personal *exemptions* (as also in Canada, and as proposed in Musgrave [1981] for Bolivia), but the determination of the appropriate structure of rates and exemptions for personal income tax is really a quite different matter that cannot be discussed here.

THE TREATMENT OF EARNED INCOME

There appear to be two principal rationales for differentiating in favor of earned income (apart from the administration argument noted above). The first is the argument that a dollar of income received from investment carries with it a greater inherent "capacity to pay" than a dollar received from work—for example, because he who receives the former dollar (the "man of property") receives two substantial additional benefits: the income flows without taking much, if any, of his time or effort; and his source of income, his wealth, provides a sense of security and power over and above that of the job of the man who works.

Without developing this line of thought further, it may simply be noted here that (1) it flatly contradicts the underlying rationale of a global income tax ("a dollar is a dollar is a dollar"), and (2) if true, it points more to the desirability of an additional tax on wealth as such rather than lighter income taxes on earned income. Nevertheless, arguments such as this help explain such income tax differentiations as the important earned income credit in Britain, the former surtax on investment income in Canada, and perhaps also the large exclusions from earned income found in such countries as Bolivia.

Sometimes such arguments for special treatment of one *source* of income are confused with arguments for favoritism to lower *levels* of income, for example, when the earnings of those receiving the minimum wage are exempted. It should be clear, however, that these two questions are quite distinct in principle. If there is a case for exempting low-income earners—and there is—that case does not depend on the *source* of their low earnings.

More consistent with the general framework of a global income tax is the view that income from labor is, so to speak, less "pure" (or net) than income from capital (e.g., because of the lack of explicit tax provision for the costs of acquiring and maintaining "human capital"). What this argument seems to reduce to is the view that inadequate allowance is made for expenses of earning labor income compared to capital income. Presumably the income of the self-employed— usually "mixed" income—would come in between on this scale.

Within the framework of the personal income tax, two broad approaches to differentiating earned and unearned income may be distinguished in different countries, with the dividing line to some extent perhaps reflecting the two rationales noted above (as witness the treatment of the self-employed).

In the United States, for example, earned income from personal services was at one time entitled to a credit of 10 percent up to $4,000 of earned income, with the credit being reduced for higher incomes until it vanished completely at $8,000 of earned income. A quite different approach towards rate differentials was employed at one time in Canada, where before 1961 all investment income was subject to a *surtax* of 4 percent. In contrast, Bolivian recipients of labor income were entitled to a *deduction* from gross income of 25 percent of such income up to a quite high maximum in Bolivian terms, not to mention exemptions for vacation and severance pay. All of these provisions applied whether the income was earned through employment or self-employment.

There are also in most countries, even in those which do not have special tax treatment for all labor income, special provisions for employees only. These provisions are of two types: exclusion of various fringe benefits paid by the employer (such as in the Bolivian case mentioned above), and, more closely related to the basic issue of differentiation by source of income, some allowance for employment expenses.

There is indeed a case in most tax systems for providing some recognition of the "costs" of earning labor income. Different countries have done this in various ways. In principle, optional deduction of itemized employment expenses (excluding such basic costs of living as food, shelter, and commuting expense) is probably the best system. In practice, some countries provide a small "standard" deduction of a certain percentage of employment income (often up to some maximum, e.g., 3 percent up to $250 in Canada at one time), for administrative convenience. The United States and Canada also recognize, within limits, moving expenses incurred by employees who change their place of residence and work. To some extent, a case can also be made along these lines for tax recognition of certain educational expenditures.[2]

Since self-employed taxpayers can usually deduct all costs of earning income anyway, they are not usually extended any special deduction for "employment" expenses: indeed, in their case the problem is often the opposite, to limit the deduction of what are really "personal" expenses (e.g., for the use of an automobile). Many countries have therefore imposed arbitrary limits on the deductibility of expenses by the self-employed; for example, Canada has complex rules on personal use of automobiles and the United States has severely restricted deductions for offices located at home.[3] Furthermore, since withholding is, by definition, not readily applicable to the incomes of this group, they should in principle be required to pay on a "current payment" basis, as is now required in Colombia, for example. In addition, the self-employed are often subject to special review and "estimated income" procedures. Small businesses, professionals, and farmers (especially the last) are subject to such procedures in many countries.

THE TREATMENT OF INCOME FROM CAPITAL

The rationale for special treatment of income from capital rests not on principle but on considerations of policy and administration. Perhaps the most important policy rationale for taxing income from capital lightly arises from the desire to increase savings and investment. In addition to exempting (or otherwise favoring) income that is saved or invested, many countries provide favorable tax treatment for some or all income from capital (e.g., interest or capital gains) either in order to raise the rate of return on such activity and hence make it more attractive or else on the presumption that such income is more likely to be used in a socially useful way (i.e., saved). The fact that the efficiency of such incentive measures has been severely questioned in most empirical studies has not, apparently, weakened their attractiveness to policy makers. A closely related set of issues concerns the appropriate treatment of investment income accruing to foreigners.

Many varieties of exclusions, exemptions, deductions, and credits for income that is saved or invested (or for income *from* savings or investment) may be found in different countries (e.g., Canada, Venezuela). It is not possible to summarize these measures here: instead, we shall simply note that this area of income tax design is particularly difficult to generalize about because what is best for any country depends so heavily on factors specific to that country, such as its degree of openness (linkage to the international capital market), its preference for financial versus fiscal means of mobilizing and channelling savings, the efficiency of tax-induced changes in the rate of return, and other difficult (and often largely unknown) matters.

One might well think that the administrative problem in taxing income from capital would be much less severe than in the case of the self-employed, at least to the extent that such income is received from such organized modern-sector institutions as corporations and banks. One complication in this regard occurs when bearer securities are important, as they are in Canada and most Latin American countries. Even in this case, however, it would appear in principle easy to avoid income tax collection problems by requiring the paying institution to withhold tax at a high rate—ideally, at the highest rate in the income tax rate scale (which, it should be noted, would therefore probably have to be lower than that which is often levied, in effect, only on high-salaried groups). The withheld tax would then be fully creditable against income tax otherwise due. This system would be equally suitable for bearer and nominative securities were it not for the fact that the former also provide a means of avoiding capital gains and wealth taxes (whether levied annually or at the time of gift or death): for this reason, a higher rate on bearer shares may be advisable, as in Bolivia and Mexico. Another possible approach would be to levy a higher tax on the retained earnings of corporations whose shares are not registered, in order to obtain at least some compensation for the revenue thus forgone on capital gains, gifts, and inheritances.

Despite these problems, interest, dividends, and royalties should all be fairly easy to tax. The fact that they are not in most countries very effectively taxed thus, in a sense, reflects as much policy as administrative factors.

The administrative problem is much more severe with regard to property incomes paid by other than large enterprises, for example, most rents, interest to moneylenders, etc. Administrative problems are particularly severe with regard to the imputed income on owner-occupied houses: the partial attempt to tax such income in the United Kingdom was abandoned some years ago, and even the ambitious Royal Commission Report did not recommend that such income be taxed in Canada. Indeed, it may well be that the most effective, albeit crude, way to reach such income is through a simple annual tax on real property.

There seems no easy way to collect tax on such generally unorganized sources of capital income except by techniques similar to those alluded to above for self-employed taxpayers. As in the case of the self-employed, there is no short-cut to an alert and well-informed tax administration.

Even such an administration will have a great many problems in taxing one particular type of capital income, namely, capital gains. Where such a tax exists, it cannot be enforced effectively even on shares (usually the easiest case) if bearer shares exist. Nor can it be enforced effectively on real property in the absence of an up-to-date and accurate cadaster. Furthermore, gains on closely-held businesses, objets d'art, and similar items tax the taxman in the most advanced countries— witness the cases of France and Canada—so severely that it seems hopeless to expect less developed fiscal administrations to be able to deal with them very effectively.

Finally, even where large corporations are concerned, there is always a serious problem in controlling the conversion of ordinary income of corporations into nontaxable (or partly taxable) capital gains. *Any* differential between the rate of personal income tax levied on, say, dividends and interest and that imposed on capital gains gives rise to many avoidance possibilities which have to be anticipated and blocked in one way or another if the global character of the income tax is not to remain in large part a mere illusion.

The only way to avoid serious administrative problems in this respect is by approximating as closely as possible to a position in which *all* payments from corporations to shareholders are taxed similarly, no matter how they are labeled. This aim can, of course, be achieved by lowering all taxes on income from capital to the rate levied on capital gains (which is more or less what Canada did in 1977, only five years after introducing a tax on gains in the first place). In effect, of course, this policy then introduces a substantial degree of discrimination against labor income.

A more desirable approach, and one more consistent with the concept of a global income tax, would be to treat all such payments (including those arising through liquidation, "thin capitalization," full and partial redemptions, and so on) as ordinary income of shareholders. Obviously, a fairly harsh and arbitrary set of administrative rules would be needed to achieve this aim, but there is no other way even to approach the goal of an equitable global income tax. Some further thoughts bearing on this point are sketched in the concluding section.

SOME SPECIAL PROBLEMS

Many other particular problems have been encountered in different countries in the process of "globalizing" the base of the personal income tax. As in the case of the more basic issue of the relative treatment of income from labor and income from capital, the solutions found to these problems in different systems illustrate a changing and varied mixture of rationales derived from principle, policy, and administrative need.

In the case of pensions, for example, the U.S. treatment (non-deduction of individual social security contributions and exemption of benefits) may be contrasted to the Canadian and Bolivian treatments (deductibility of contributions, taxation of benefits). An additional important question on the treatment of pensions in general is the extent to which analogous treatment is extended to private pension schemes—from which the more highly-paid generally receive most benefit. In Canada, for example, pressure from the self-employed has led to the allowance of considerable deductions from income for contributions to such private schemes.

In the case of international income, the U.S. (and to a lesser extent Canadian) treatment (taxation of foreign income of residents—citizens in the United States—and flat-rate taxation of most payments to non-residents) may be contrasted to the Bolivian and Venezuelan applications of the territorial principle (exempting foreign income of residents, though still taxing payments to non-residents). This whole area, of course, poses some of the most difficult questions in income tax design.

All countries make considerable use of a wide variety of tax incentives, the usual effect of which is to lighten the weight of taxes on income from capital. Most countries also have significant sectoral differentiation, with special regimes (at least with respect to the determination of net income) for industries such as agriculture, mining, and the financial sector (banking and insurance).

Some countries, such as Canada and the Netherlands, have introduced automatic indexation schemes for personal exemptions and rates; others, such as the United States, have preferred to rely on discretionary adjustments in personal tax structure to offset undesired tax increases as a result of inflation. Still others—including perhaps many of the developing countries—may even welcome such inflationary increases as a relatively painless way of increasing tax revenues. Still more difficult questions are posed with regard to adjusting the *base* of the income tax for the effects of inflation. The principal areas of difficulty here are depreciation, inventory valuation, and—an often-neglected but important offset to the other two—financial items on the balance sheet. (The important point here is that those who owe money in fixed nominal currency amounts, as do many business firms, gain in inflation.) While some countries (e.g., Brazil and Argentina) have gone much further than others in dealing with these problems, it seems fair to say that there is as yet no real consensus in either theory or practice as to how best to recognize inflation in income tax structure. A partial solution, such as the inflation-adjusted depreciation commonly advocated by business, may be worse from a social point of view than no action, while a comprehensive solution seems beyond the reach of even the most advanced country at this time.

In all these cases, there are no simple answers to the question of the appropriate tax treatment of many items, whether one is operating within the framework of a global system or not. Perhaps the major contribution of the notion of globality in this context is to serve as a standard (or principle) requiring all deviations in treatment from the treatment applied to the "standard case" of wage income to be specially justified in terms of the social benefits to be achieved from such deviation (policy) or the social costs of not so deviating (administration). This is no small contribution, but it does bring out again the important point that the adoption of a global framework alone does little to resolve the hard problems of designing an effective personal income tax in an evolving society.

CONCLUSION

Although in principle globalization means treating all income alike, regardless of source, in practice "policy" rationales, different degrees of "netness," and the various administrative problems alluded to above mean that no tax system anywhere really treats all forms of income alike. Nor does it seem reasonable to posit this as a short-run goal in any developing country.[4] Instead, attention should be focused on (1) strengthening administration in those areas in which it is inherently weakest—the self-employed, rental incomes, etc.—and (2) considering carefully the extent to which policy objectives (or simply politics?) require more favorable treatment of certain types of income than seems warranted in the name of the principle of globalization. To the extent that such schedular elements remain, it must also be carefully considered whether it is best to mark them out explicitly (e.g., by special tax rates on interest income) or to allow them to exist in practice but not in form (as with agricultural income in many countries).[5] The former would seem better in principle, but the latter is clearly the more common practice.

One important function of law in any country is to state or announce social ideals or goals, even if they cannot, for the moment, be fully or adequately implemented. In this sense, the imposition of a global framework for the income tax may serve an important role as a statement of goals which may provide administrators and judges alike with some basis for deciding difficult cases of interpretation.

One way to achieve this purpose is by providing, for example in a preamble to the taxing statute, that any tax avoidance scheme intended to circumvent the statute will fail to do so if it is determined to violate the broad intent of the statute (i.e., to tax equally all forms of income received by persons). The Canadian income tax law, for instance, contains more or less just such a provision permitting the Treasury Board (a committee of cabinet ministers and hence a political body) to so rule. The fact that this provision has seldom been used, and not at all for several decades, is in the present context perhaps less important than the mere fact of its existence—as it were, as a kind of ultimate deterrent.

In addition to a general "anti-avoidance" provision, the administrative structure of the Canadian income tax contains several related provisions of more specialized scope but operating below cabinet level. There is, for example, a provision that, at the discretion of the revenue minister, transactions involving the "stripping" of dividends from a corporation (and their conversion into capital gains) can be disregarded and the proceeds taxed as ordinary income. Such broadly-worded statements in effect confer substantial power on the tax administration. The very vagueness of the language employed, while it invariably annoys and disturbs taxpayers—and especially their lawyers—increases the effectiveness of the law (and hence presumably its compliance with the goal of globalization) at the expense of reducing its certainty and perhaps increasing its arbitrariness.

In turn, these broad provisions in the Canadian law are supported by dozens of detailed provisions intended to prevent and block off particular modes of tax avoidance. To use a military metaphor, these detailed provisions are like snipers aiming at well-identified targets, supported by the machine guns of the broader provisions against avoidance in such contentious fields as capital gains, dividend-stripping, associated corporations, and pensions, and backed up ultimately by the big gun of a general anti-avoidance provision.

Obviously, the legal, and political, situation varies in every country. The point of including this brief account here is in no way to put forth Canada as a model but simply to bring out clearly the need, even in developed countries with a very global tax structure and generally high levels of administrative competence and taxpayer compliance, to support the legal transition of the personal income tax to a more global concept with an effective legal structure for tax administration (and, of course, an effective administration). Global income taxes make sense in both equity and economic terms; they also may make sense, as at least an aspiration, even when they cannot be effectively enforced; but there is no getting around the fact that the key to moving towards an effectively global income tax lies in improved tax administration at many levels. For this reason, the present brief account of some of the issues encountered in different countries in the course of making such a transition has heavily stressed the administrative aspect.

Questions of principle and policy are of course important and even decisive in many instances, and much more could be said about them than has been done here. But what can be said without fear of contradiction is that in the end the administrative constraint will very likely be a decisive constraint on what can actually be done in any country about globalizing its income tax. Moreover, for this and other reasons, a strong case can, we believe, be made for avoiding large, sudden changes, especially in the taxation of income from capital: too often such changes lead to over-reaction, especially in periods of economic distress. "Nature," said Alfred Marshall, the well-known English economist, "does not proceed by jumps"—and neither should tax reforms in such delicate economic and administrative areas as this. Small, regular changes (e.g., gradual increases in withholding rates) may be absorbed more easily, and hence seem in general a better way to go, providing both less occasion for extreme adverse reaction and more time for the necessary accompanying administrative improvement.

NOTES

1. For a rare exception, see Rezende (1976).
2. For a careful discussion of this question, see Goode (1976), pp. 80–92. Canada, in fact, permitted the deduction of tuition expenses by students (not their parents), as Goode recommends.
3. The complex issues involved in devising such rules are discussed in Popkin (1973).
4. Indeed, Rezende (1976) has gone so far as to argue that a revised form of schedular taxation would be more suitable for most developing countries than further moves towards ineffective globalization.
5. For a careful discussion of agricultural income taxes, see G. E. Lent (1973).

18

Taxes on Income or Consumption?

The manifold problems of implementing income taxes in developing countries and the distortions attributable to even well-implemented income taxes in inflationary conditions have led an increasing number of tax economists in recent years to favor a shift in the basis of personal taxation from income to consumption. While advocacy of such direct consumption taxation, as opposed to impersonal taxes on transactions, has a long history (Kaldor, 1955), its modern revival is largely attributable to two influential reports published in the late 1970s, one in the United States (U.S. Treasury, 1977) and one in Britain (Meade, 1978).

Over the last decade, the ideas in these reports have been substantially refined and elaborated (see especially Bradford, 1986). As yet, however, no developed country has actually implemented such a consumption tax, and none seems likely to do so in the near future (OECD, 1987). It may therefore seem premature to devote much space to the topic in this book, given our emphasis on the difficulty of designing and especially implementing tax policy in developing countries. Nevertheless, neglect of these important ideas would be a serious mistake. In an earlier incarnation (Kaldor, 1955), the direct consumption tax received its only real world trials in two developing countries, India (Kaldor, 1956) and Ceylon (Kaldor, 1960) as it then was. The experience was hardly a success (Goode, 1961; Kelley, 1970), but it would not be at all surprising to see a developing country—perhaps Colombia (McLure et al., 1988)?—be first off the mark once again in turning this latest revival of expenditure taxation into reality.

Even more importantly in the present context, consumption tax advocates have come increasingly to stress its administrative rather than its equity or efficiency advantages. The equity case for taxing consumption rather than income is largely a matter of taste, despite the superficial attractiveness to some of Thomas Hobbes's famous dictum on the greater equity of taxing people on what they take out of the common pot (consumption) than on what they put into it (income). The efficiency case, in terms of removing the income tax disincentive to save, is hardly convincing either, given the possibly counterbalancing deterrent effect on labor supply and the obscurity of the critical empirical parameters (see chapter 11). In contrast, not only does the consumption basis avoid the very serious difficulties income taxes encounter in inflation (see chapter 21), but it also permits tax designers and administrators to bypass many other important timing problems that would otherwise arise—for instance, in connection with capital gains. In view of the stress throughout this book on the importance of administrative considerations in shaping what can and should be done in developing countries, ideas such as those expressed in the following selection therefore deserve close attention.

Two points raised in this chapter require a brief prior explanation. First, the equity aspects of a consumption tax may be viewed from two quite different perspectives—annual or lifetime. Taxing consumption solely on an annual basis means that gifts and bequests received are included in the tax base but deductions are allowed for gifts and bequests made. This result could be roughly approximated simply by not bringing gifts and bequests into the tax base in the first place. This approach amounts to the adoption of what the following chapter calls a "dynastic" view of taxation: tax is paid only when resources are finally consumed by some generation of a family; and under such a consumption tax, families could of course accumulate substantial wealth over the generations.

In contrast, the consumption tax discussed in this selection takes a "lifetime endowment" view of taxation, which means that gifts and inheritances received are included in the tax base and gifts and inheritances made are not deducted (Aaron and Galper, 1985). In effect, each generation thus stands on its own tax feet, in the sense that its tax base includes all resources at its command (that is, wages and salaries as well as gifts and inheritances received). Those who find this prospect attractive should remember, however, that it is notoriously difficult in practice to tax bequests and gifts in any country, developed or developing (Bird, 1978).

Secondly, a direct consumption tax may be implemented in two quite different ways, called here "cash flow" and "tax prepayment." Under the cash flow approach, a deduction is allowed for saving channelled into "qualified" accounts— loosely, any legitimate investment—and withdrawals (including earnings) from such accounts are included in the tax base. The proceeds of loans are similarly included, while the repayment of interest and principal, or the use of such proceeds to finance investment, is deductible. In other words, the tax base is cash receipts less cash saving, or net cash flow, which equals consumption. In present value terms, this tax base is equivalent to a tax which exempts the yield from capital income (Zodrow and McLure, 1987), so a simpler way of achieving the same results would be to simply ignore the receipt of capital income. Interest, dividends, and capital gains would thus be omitted from the tax base; at the same time, interest payments would not be deductible, so that loans would have no tax consequences. Deductions for savings are also no longer allowed. In effect, the tax base then consists only of wages plus such other labor-related receipts as pensions. This approach may be called tax prepayment because the tax that would be paid under the cash flow approach on the withdrawal from savings of principal and interest is, so to speak, prepaid by the disallowance of the savings deduction. In present value terms, the cost of the lost deduction is equal to the benefit of the exemption of the future capital earnings. In the following chapter, Zodrow and McLure favor this approach largely on administrative grounds and make a good case for developing countries taking this route, should they decide the benefits of adopting a consumption tax outweigh the costs.

Quite apart from the merits of the case for taxing consumption directly, this selection also serves the useful purpose of reviewing carefully many basic tax design issues that come up with respect to income taxes also: timing issues, inflation adjustment, and so on. Although Zodrow and McLure, like most expositors of new devices, perhaps tend to underrate the complexities of the consumption tax alternative, their points on the problems of income taxes are well taken. Incidentally, given the worldwide tendency to downgrade wealth as a tax base (see chapter 1), their stress on the equity of taxing wealth as well as consumption seems especially noteworthy.

Replacing the Income Tax with a Direct Consumption Tax

George R. Zodrow and Charles E. McLure, Jr.

Paralleling the rise of the use of the value-added tax (VAT) has been increased interest in a different form of consumption tax, a direct tax that can be tailored to the economic circumstances of the taxpayer. Direct consumption taxes have been given such names as an expenditure tax, a personal tax on consumption, a tax on consumed income, a cash flow income tax, a personal exemption VAT, and simply "Plan X."[1] Academic economists have been interested in taxes of this type primarily because they generally do not alter the terms on which present consumption can be exchanged for future consumption; under certain highly restrictive assumptions, a consumption tax that exhibits such intertemporal neutrality is an "optimal tax" in the sense that it minimizes tax-induced distortions in individual decision making. Opponents of the double taxation of capital income inherent in the traditional income tax favor a switch to a tax based on consumption for a somewhat different though related reason: it is believed that such a switch would stimulate saving and capital formation. To others, the attraction of a tax based on consumption is quite different. They see the possibility of avoiding the two most difficult income measurement problems that are inherent in the implementation of an income tax; specifically, under a consumption-based direct tax, timing issues do not exist, and there is no necessity for inflation adjustment in the measurement of income.[2]

The primary focus of this report is the possibility of using a direct tax on consumption as a replacement for existing income taxes, a topic on which little has been written in the developing country context.[3] The relative merits of income and consumption as the basis for a system of direct taxation have been debated at length in the literature. Our exposition of the consumption versus income tax debate is limited to discussing those major points which are particularly relevant in a developing country context.[4] The discussion considers in turn issues of simplicity, equity, economic neutrality, and economic development.

Simplicity

The goal of simplicity is frequently invoked in tax reform debates in both industrialized nations and developing countries, but it is seldom attained in either. Simplicity is even more important in developing countries than in developed ones,

Excerpted from Zodrow and McLure (1988).

for at least three reasons. First, administrative skills are generally extremely scarce in developing countries, and the use of such resources to administer or comply with an unnecessarily complex tax code is a highly unproductive use of a very scarce and thus valuable asset. Second, on average, the ability of individuals and firms to comply with a complex tax structure is low; thus, complexity increases the likelihood of filing errors and, by increasing the cost of compliance and administration, increases the attraction of evasion. Third, since evasion is frequently endemic, a simple tax structure implies that more governmental resources can be devoted to finding tax evaders rather than regulating and monitoring honest taxpayers. For these reasons, the relative simplicity properties of taxation on the basis of consumption and income are of particular importance in developing countries. Generally, taxation on the basis of consumption rather than income is superior on simplicity grounds, as can be seen from a discussion of the following areas.

Timing

Issues of timing give rise to some of the thorniest problems in the construction and implementation of an income tax. The most obvious problem lies in the measurement of depreciation for depreciable assets. Although allowances for economic depreciation are obviously required for accurate measurement of economic income, the determination of economic depreciation is exceedingly difficult. The data required to obtain estimates of economic depreciation are seldom available even in highly developed countries, and the few existing estimates of economic depreciation are highly controversial. Such data are virtually nonexistent in developing countries. As a result, rules for tax depreciation are inevitably arbitrary and generally result in taxes on the income from various types of depreciable assets that are either too high or too low from a theoretical standpoint. This leads to investment distortions (and perhaps inequities), as well as attempts to influence depreciation schedules through the exercise of political power. In contrast, under a consumption tax, the need for determining economic depreciation is eliminated, since purchases of depreciable assets are simply expensed.

The same point applies to a wide variety of other costs which must properly be capitalized or amortized under an income tax, such as advertising, research, and the costs of developing natural resources, for which depletion allowances are commonly provided; under a consumption tax all these costs are simply expensed in the year an asset is purchased or an expenditure is made. The simplicity of expensing under the consumption-based tax is clearly in marked contrast to the complexity of an income tax, where precisely accurate allocation of costs is virtually impossible, where even rough approximations introduce considerable complexity, and where inaccuracies induce economic distortions.

Similarly, under a consumption tax there is no problem with investments which generate income over many years and, under an income tax, raise issues of when to deem such income to be realized. For example, taxing income from multiyear production processes only upon completion of a contract allows deferral of tax liability, and therefore creates inequities and distorts economic decisions. By comparison, special "percentage of completion" rules for the realization of income for tax purposes may be preferable from the point of view of income measurement, but they add considerable complexity to the tax code. As receipts are simply included in the tax base when received under the proposed consumption-tax treatment of business receipts and expenses, there is no need to choose between these unsatisfactory alternatives.

In addition, accounting rules are much simpler under a consumption tax. Since all receipts and expenditures are dealt with on a cash flow basis, no attempt need be made to devise accrual accounting rules, and avoidance problems related to the manipulation of cash and accrual accounting systems are eliminated. Other issues which disappear under a consumption tax are special tax rules for original issue discount obligations, installment sales, expenditures on goods placed in inventory, indirect costs of self-constructed assets, and bad debt reserves of financial institutions and other firms.[5]

Capital Gains

Under an income tax, (real) capital gains should theoretically be taxed on an accrual basis. Since accrual taxation is administratively impossible in many instances, virtually all income tax systems that tax capital gains do so on a realization basis, and frequently at preferential rates. However, the taxation of gains only upon realization creates a wide variety of tax avoidance opportunities via deferral of tax obligations and, together with the application of preferential tax rates to capital gains, creates obvious incentives to recharacterize ordinary income as capital gain; both situations lead to considerable administrative complexity as tax authorities attempt to limit these avoidance techniques.

In contrast, under a consumption tax, the treatment of capital gains of individuals is very straightforward: under the tax prepayment approach, gains are simply excluded from the tax base, while under the cash flow approach, the taxpayer has no basis in assets, so all of the proceeds of sales of capital assets are fully included in the tax base without preferential treatment. In both cases, administration and compliance is greatly simplified. In particular, there is never a need to maintain records regarding the basis of capital assets for purposes of calculating gain upon sale, since the proceeds of the sale are either excluded or fully included in the base. In addition, the cross-checking of deductions for purchases of capital assets against proceeds reported as income is relatively straightforward, since both are reported in the same year. By comparison, if only capital gains on assets are subject to tax, it is necessary to compare the basis reported by the seller against the proceeds reported by the previous owner in some previous tax period; this is clearly an administratively difficult task, especially in developing countries. Finally, there is no need to create a set of complex rules which distinguish between capital gains and ordinary income for tax purposes, and a wide variety of tax avoidance techniques based on the distinction between capital gains and ordinary income are simply eliminated.

Inflation Adjustment

The accurate measurement of real economic income requires an integrated approach in which balance sheet items are adjusted for inflation and these adjustments are reflected in income for tax purposes (see Casanegra, 1985; McLure et al., 1988). Alternatively, a less precise approach involving ad hoc adjustments to depreciation, capital gains, inventories, and interest payments and receipts can be employed. The integrated approach involves complexities and nontax issues that most countries have been unwilling to accept. Correct (or even approximately correct) ad hoc inflation adjustments, especially for interest payments and receipts, are difficult to design and also inevitably add complexity for both taxpayers and tax administrators. The degree of difficulty can be gauged from the problems experienced by the U.S. Treasury Department (1984) in designing even a partially indexed system, as well the fact that all of the Treasury Department proposals were rejected in the final version of tax reform enacted in the United States. In contrast, under a consumption tax, the complexity of inflation adjustment is unnecessary, since all quantities included in the tax base are simply measured in monetary values of the current year.

Tax Arbitrage

The income tax systems in most countries, including developing countries, have many features which are appropriate only in a consumption tax context. These include exemptions for various forms of income from capital, deductions for certain forms of saving, and extremely generous provisions for capital-cost recovery, including accelerated depreciation and first-year write-offs. Such features create opportunities for various forms of tax arbitrage, such as borrowing with fully deductible interest to invest in tax-preferred assets. This arbitrage, in turn, undermines the equity and neutrality of the tax system. For political reasons, tax authorities generally are unable to eliminate the inappropriate provisions that lie at the heart of the problem, and so respond (at best) with rules designed to eliminate or limit such arbitrage, greatly increasing the complexity of the tax system. In contrast, under a consumption tax, all investments are equally tax-preferred as long as particular investments are not actually subsidized through the tax system. Thus, the tax arbitrage problems characteristic of hybrid income/consumption tax systems are eliminated.[6]

Saving and Investment Decisions

The type of special provisions that create opportunities for arbitrage also distort investment decisions under an income tax. To the extent that all investments are equally preferred under a consumption tax, investment decisions can be made solely on the economic merits of projects rather than on the basis of differential tax treatment. Moreover, uniform treatment of all types of saving decisions removes the tax treatment of alternative saving instruments as a further complicating factor in saving and investment decisions and as an area requiring administrative scrutiny.

In most developing countries, a consumption tax would greatly simplify and rationalize saving and investment decisions. Of course, the same could be said of a comprehensive tax on real economic income. However, experience with income tax reform in both developed and developing countries suggests that prospects for "levelling down"—or providing equally preferential treatment of all investment under a consumption tax—are probably greater than the prospects of "levelling up"—eliminating all preferential treatment of certain investments under an income tax.

Corporate Tax Integration

One of the most difficult questions under most income taxes is the integration of the corporate and individual income taxes (McLure, 1979). It is generally accepted that complete integration, which requires treating corporations like partnerships for tax purposes, is infeasible. But various means of reducing double taxation of dividends have been implemented in many countries and proposed in others; these include imputation of corporate taxes on income underlying dividends to individual shareholders, application of lower rates to distributed earnings than to retained earnings, and full and partial deductions for dividends paid. All of these add to complexity, and none has proved entirely satisfactory. Under a consumption tax, integration problems virtually disappear, since the marginal effective tax rate on capital income is zero at the business level, and capital income is either ignored at the individual level (the tax payment approach) or is subject to a zero marginal effective tax rate (the cash flow approach). It is true that inframarginal returns are taxed at the rate applied to business income, rather than at the marginal tax rates of the various owners of businesses, but that is generally thought not to be a major reason for concern. Most owners of corporate shares in developing countries are likely to have income that would (or should) subject them to the top marginal rate in any case, and owners of small businesses can generally achieve de facto integration by paying themselves deductible wages and salaries.

Extent of Coverage

One potentially troublesome feature of consumption taxes is that universal coverage of businesses—very broadly defined—is generally desirable to eliminate possibilities for tax avoidance. Attempting such broad coverage is unrealistic in many instances, because it is likely to impose large administrative costs for relatively low revenue gains, especially in developing countries, where a large number of very small businesses exist. Moreover, it is generally not feasible to require that every individual who engages in business transactions, no matter how infrequently or how casually, should file a business tax return. But if this is not done there may be opportunities for avoidance, for example, on real estate transactions. However, such problems also exist under an income tax, and it is difficult to draw a distinction between the two taxes on this basis.

Equity

Perhaps the most contentious issue in the consumption versus income tax debate concerns the relative merits of the two tax bases with respect to the criterion of equity or fairness. There are several aspects to both the horizontal equity (equal treatment of equally situated individuals) and the vertical equity (progressivity) aspects of the debate.

The most fundamental question is whether income or consumption represents the better measure of ability to pay, for tax purposes. Income tax advocates stress that the potential to consume in any given period (say, a year) is a better measure of ability to pay than the exercise of that potential in the form of actual consumption. Consumption tax proponents frequently rely on the assertion by Hobbes that fairness requires taxation on the basis of what an individual takes out of the common pool of society's resources (consumption) rather than what the individual contributes to the pool (as measured by his income). Strictly speaking, the latter view argues for the type of consumption tax associated with the dynastic view of taxation. Although we have precluded such a dynastic consumption tax from consideration, it seems clear that those who find the Hobbes argument compelling will favor consumption taxes—even if of the lifetime endowment variety—over an income tax, while those who do not will favor income taxation.

More critical to our evaluation is the question of the extent to which the lifetime endowment view of taxation is relevant for equity purposes. Suppose that tax rates and discount rates are constant over time and that income and consumption tax bases are defined in terms consistent with the lifetime endowment view (i.e., gifts and inheritances received included in the tax base with no deduction for gifts and bequests given). If the individual's lifetime is indeed the appropriate time period for evaluating the equity of a tax system, a consumption-based tax of the type favored here—that is, a lifetime income tax—will be superior to an annual income tax; this is true because, with constant tax rates, the present value of the lifetime tax burden is independent of the time path of earnings or of gifts and inheritances received. In contrast, an annual income tax will assess a larger tax burden on those who save more during the life cycle, because they either earn relatively early or consume relatively late during their lifetimes. Consumption tax advocates argue that the present value of the lifetime endowment is the appropriate basis for evaluating the equity of a tax system, and that the invariant burden of the consumption tax is one of its major advantages, while the fact that income tax burdens vary as described above implies that annual income taxation is inequitable.

From a theoretical perspective, the lifetime endowment perspective has considerable appeal. Income tax proponents frequently argue that individuals do not plan their lifetime consumption decisions in the meticulous manner consistent with a lifetime endowment calculation and that capital markets are not perfect, as is assumed in such calculations. However, it is unclear that such conditions would necessarily imply a preference for income over consumption taxation. Income tax proponents also argue that a relatively short time period is more appropriate for evaluating the fairness of a tax system than is an individual's lifetime. However, the use of a relatively short accounting period coupled with a progressive rate structure implies that tax burdens will be larger for individuals with uneven earnings streams than for those with smooth earnings streams. Such a pattern of tax burdens would be desirable only if the marginal utility of income is lower during high-earning years than during low-earning years; this line of reasoning does not seem compelling. Moreover, the view that a short time period is the more appropriate for judging equity is inconsistent with the widely accepted view that income averaging is desirable, where feasible, in order to offset the effects of bunching of income.

We have argued that developing countries should consider only consumption taxes consistent with the lifetime endowment view of tax equity. This decision has major implications for the vertical equity of a consumption tax system, since it implies that the measurement of individual ability to pay will include gifts and bequests received, a component that is highly concentrated among the wealthy. As a result, to the extent such a policy could be implemented effectively, it would be easier to obtain any particular vertical equity goals with respect to the distribution of lifetime income than if the dynastic view were adopted. (Vertical equity goals can also be furthered by coupling a progressive consumption tax with a wealth tax which would affect only the wealthiest individuals in the economy.)

Several more minor points bear on the equity question. First, income taxes in practice are commonly replete with tax preferences for capital income that are of little benefit to the average taxpayer but enable the wealthy to lower their tax burdens dramatically. As a result, high-income individuals may actually bear a smaller share of the tax burden than they would under a progressive consumption tax with a comprehensive base. The enactment of a comprehensive income tax would eliminate such tax avoidance opportunities, but experience suggests that such reform is often politically infeasible. A comprehensive consumption tax with progressive rates may be more effective in achieving the vertical equity goals of a developing country than a preference-riddled income tax, and the political prospects for its enactment may be more favorable.

Second, it is possible that conspicuous consumption is accorded little weight or is even seen to be contrary to the goals of a developing country, while the accumulation of wealth is desirable to the extent it results in more domestic investment, employment, and growth. Such a set of priorities implies that progressive taxation based on consumption, rather than on income, is desirable from a social standpoint.

Third, to the extent that the greater incentives for saving inherent in a consumption tax result in a larger domestic capital stock, wages should be higher and the inequality of income distribution should be less. Fourth, political barriers to fairly progressive marginal tax rates should be reduced if, as under a consumption tax, such rates no longer reduced marginal incentives to save and invest; the end result might be a more progressive rate structure than under an income tax.

Economic Neutrality and Economic Efficiency

In one sense, economic neutrality provides the same prescription for income and consumption taxes—tax all elements of the base equally.[7] Nevertheless, several important additional questions remain. The basic point is that a consumption tax eliminates the distortion between current consumption and saving inherent in an income tax, but probably at the cost of increasing the distortion between current leisure and work effort. It is theoretically unclear which approach involves less costly tax-induced distortions of economic decisions. For example, in a static two-period model with individual utility defined over current and future consumption and leisure, the consumption tax approach corresponds to the "optimal" way of taxing wage and capital income if present and future consumption are equally responsive to changes in the net wage. In contrast, if leisure is more (less) substitutable with current consumption than with future consumption, some taxation (subsidization) of capital income is optimal (see Atkinson and Stiglitz, 1980; King, 1980). Although one could argue that a consumption tax is optimal—or approximately optimal—under a "plausible" set of assumptions, such a conclusion would obviously be a tenuous one.

A related point is that accurate income taxation of many activities is exceedingly difficult, as demonstrated in the discussion of simplicity issues above. In addition, different types of saving are typically treated very differently under existing income taxes in developing countries. Accordingly, non-uniform taxation of various business activities and various forms of saving is likely to result, even under the best of circumstances. This in turn implies distortion of saving and investment decisions and efficiency costs. To the extent a consumption tax avoids subsidies to various industries (by taxing all marginal capital investments at a zero marginal rate in present-value terms) and treats all forms of saving identically, this source of economic inefficiency would be eliminated.

It is likely that any income tax reform in a developing country would leave some sectors, including owner-occupied housing and certain other industries, and perhaps nonprofit entities with business activities, with preferential tax treatment. The result is that capital investment in such industries is not fully taxed and is perhaps even subsidized. In this case, the desirability of full taxation of capital investment in other areas becomes questionable, since it may result in relatively large investment distortions in favor of the lightly taxed or subsidized activities. The consumption tax solution is to eliminate such investment distortions by offering "preferential" or zero marginal tax treatment to all capital investment. This may be viewed as a reasonable solution to the problems caused by existing and immutable tax preferences (provided that currently tax-preferred activities do not subsequently become tax-subsidized under the consumption tax).

Consistency with Economic Growth

Although the question is far from decided, many consumption tax proponents argue that eliminating the taxation of capital income would result in significantly greater economic growth. In the developing country context, this may occur for a variety of reasons. First, domestic saving may increase in response to higher after-tax returns to saving. The response of saving to changes in the net return is theoretically ambiguous (Feldstein, 1978). Moreover, it would clearly vary across developing countries. Nevertheless, recent empirical research for the United States suggests that a positive response is certainly possible, and arguably the likely outcome (Boskin, 1978). To the extent that increased domestic saving led to increased domestic investment (rather than simply replacing foreign-financed investment), a higher level of investment would be achieved.

Second, the amount of domestic savings invested domestically may increase. For example, suppose that domestic savings invested at home bear some income tax burden in the developing country. Investors generally have the option to invest abroad, even when they are subject to exchange controls. The return to such investment is likely to be free of domestic tax, either because such returns are legally exempt from income taxation or because any domestic income tax is easily avoided. Moreover, the foreign tax burden is likely to be light; for example, the United States does not tax the capital gains (other than those on real estate) or most interest receipts of foreigners, European bearer bonds provide tax-free interest, and investment channelled through the tax haven countries is largely free of tax. Such a situation implies that domestic investors face a strong tax incentive to invest abroad. Implementation of a consumption tax would mean that the tax treatment of funds invested at home would be as generous as that available for investment abroad. The elimination of the tax incentive to investing abroad should naturally increase the fraction of domestic saving invested in the developing country. Again, total investment in the developing country might increase as well, although any increase in domestically-financed investment would be partially (and perhaps fully) offset by a reduction in foreign-financed investment.

The effect on foreign investment in the developing country is also obviously critical. Decisions by the United States and other capital-exporting countries regarding the availability of tax credits for consumption-based business taxes paid by their multinationals would be important in many cases; no developing country can afford to levy heavy taxes that cannot be credited. Of course, taxes on business income are likely to be reduced under a consumption-based business tax that allows expensing for foreign-owned as well as domestic investment. In this case, revenue loss to the developing country may be as important a problem as the potential loss of creditability. Also, to the extent that taxes on foreign investment are reduced, some additional foreign investment may be expected, as long as the tax reduction is not absorbed by reduced foreign tax credits in capital-exporting countries.

NOTES

1. Among standard references are Andrews (1974), Bradford (1986), Meade (1978), Aaron and Galper (1985), and U.S. Department of the Treasury (1977).

2. For such an argument, see King (1980).

3. Experience with direct consumption taxes in developing (and developed) countries has been very limited. India and Sri Lanka (then Ceylon) both twice tried and then abandoned a personal expenditure tax more than twenty years ago. In these cases, the direct expenditure taxes were abolished on the grounds that administrative costs were high while revenue yields were low (see Cutt, 1969; Goode, 1984). These experiences appear to have limited current relevance. The direct consumption taxes in India and Sri Lanka were quite limited in scope, as they were applied at relatively low rates to only high income individuals. Moreover, they were structured following a "cash flow" approach, rather than a "tax prepayment" approach; these terms are explained in the introductory notes to this chapter. Administrative considerations suggest that the tax prepayment approach is clearly the more appropriate method of direct taxation of consumption in a developing country context. Thus the negative experiences of India and Sri Lanka are of quite limited relevance for the type of direct consumption tax that is the primary focus of this paper—a broad-based tax that follows the tax prepayment approach.

4. Extensive discussions of the general consumption versus income debate are provided in Pechman (1980).

5. See Bradford (1986) for an extensive discussion of the simplicity advantages of taxation on the basis of consumption rather than of income.

6. It is easy to be overly sanguine about this advantage, however. For example, deductions may be allowed for mortgage interest on owner-occupied housing, even though no other interest expense is deductible and interest income is exempt.

7. Although the prescriptions of optimal taxation do not equate economic efficiency with the uniform taxation implied by economic neutrality, achieving efficiency in practice is much more likely under a uniform tax system.

19

Taxing Corporate Profits

The last two chapters focused on the appropriate design of direct personal taxes in developing countries. Some of the most difficult conceptual and practical problems, however, arise with respect to the taxation of business income, which is therefore the concern of most of the balance of this part.

The following chapter first sets out the basic variations in corporate tax structure found around the world and then focuses on a problem of universal interest and concern: the relation of corporate and personal taxes. Although some of the references in this paper to particular countries and many of the details may be a little out of date (for a more current account, see Modi, 1987), the basic picture remains as varied as that painted here. Corporate income is taxed in many different ways throughout the world, but such taxes continue to fulfill at least two critical roles in all countries; first, as a backstop to personal income taxes, and secondly, as a means of taxing foreign investors.

One aspect of corporate taxes touched on in this selection concerns their incidence. Over the last few years, opinion has changed substantially with respect to the relevance of the uncertain incidence of the corporate income tax to the desirability of integrating it with the personal income tax (McLure, 1979). Lent basically argues against such integration on equity grounds. In contrast, others have favored integration both on equity (Musgrave and Musgrave, 1984) and especially efficiency (McLure et al., 1988) grounds. This matter too, however, is substantially complicated when the international dimension of corporate taxes is taken into account (Bird, 1987), and in fact a good case can still be made for Lent's position. Further discussion of this complex issue, however, would require much more extended treatment than is possible here. As with the international aspects of corporate taxation (see also chapter 20), all we can do is alert readers concerned with these issues to the need to pursue much more detailed analysis and discussion than may be found in this book.

Corporation Income Taxes in Developing Countries

George E. Lent

The basic problems of taxing the corporation stem from its recognition as a juridical person, separate from its shareholders. Corporation tax structures vary basically according to their treatment of distributions to shareholders—that is, according to whether, and by what method, the tax on dividends is integrated with that on corporate income.

Separate Entity Systems

As in the case of other taxes, the corporation tax structure originally adopted by most developing countries replicated that of the colonial power under whose influence they came. Perhaps the most commonly accepted form employed in continental Europe had its origins in the schedular system of taxing different classes of income at different proportional rates.[1] This is the prototype of the so-called classical system of treating the corporation as a separate entity according to the business income schedule; shareholders are taxed independently on their income from "movable property," that is, from shares. This system was introduced early, not only in the French colonies of West Africa, Equatorial Africa, North Africa, and Indochina but also in Belgian and Dutch colonies throughout the world (for example, the Congo—now Zaïre—and Indonesia). With few exceptions, this system has been preserved in Francophone countries, notwithstanding France's income tax reforms of 1948 and 1966, which substantially modified the traditional form of the corporation tax. In addition, a number of countries in South America (for example, Argentina, Brazil, Chile, Colombia, Peru, and Venezuela) apparently have followed the Continental precedent.

Through a succession of reforms, the United States has departed from its original concept of the corporation tax, adopted in 1913, that provided for coordination with the personal income tax. Its basically "classical" system has served as a model for several developing countries (for example, Bolivia and the Philippines). More recently, other developing countries, such as Kenya, Tanzania, Uganda, and Zambia, have converted from integrated tax systems that originally followed the British colonial model to systems that treat the corporation as a separate taxable entity.[2]

In the classical model, shareholders are taxed separately on dividends received,

Excerpted from Lent (1977).

and usually no provision is made to reduce the individual income tax on earnings distributed. Many countries, however, treat the juridical person (that is, the corporation) as they do the natural person, and do not levy a separate tax on dividends. The graduated tax scales of Central American and Middle Eastern countries are the best-known examples of this practice. A few countries, including Colombia and Thailand, provide for partial exemption of dividends, while others, such as Oman and Saudi Arabia, do not have a conventional personal income tax. Uruguay has abolished the personal income tax, but it does withhold tax on distributions of earnings to residents and nonresidents.

Integrated Systems

As distinguished from the classical system that follows the original Continental model, there are two accepted systems that integrate the corporation tax with the personal income tax on dividends. Integration may be accomplished at either the corporate or the shareholder level. The former, known as a split-rate system, taxes distributed earnings at a lower rate than retained earnings.[3] Integration at the shareholder level is accomplished by what is known as the imputation method. An undistributed profits tax is the ultimate form of the split-rate system; it provides a deduction from corporate earnings for dividends paid, leaving only retained earnings chargeable to tax. Shareholders are taxed on dividends received, with distributions abroad subject to a withholding tax; nonresident corporations, including foreign branches, usually are subject to the standard corporation tax rate on their declared earnings. This system is now in effect in only a few countries: Afghanistan, Ecuador, Egypt, Greece, and Mauritius. Iraq also has an undistributed profits tax, although resident shareholders are not subject to tax on dividends. Other countries (for example, Rhodesia [now Zimbabwe] and Uruguay) that once employed undistributed profits taxes have converted to other forms.

The imputation system, similar to the traditional form employed by the United Kingdom prior to 1965,[4] provides for a basic tax rate on corporate income that is credited, in whole or in part, to shareholders on dividends received; resident shareholders are required to include in their taxable income cash dividends received, grossed up by the amount of corporation tax applicable, and are entitled to deduct the tax withheld from their income tax liability. This system, known as the withholding method, was incorporated in the British colonial Model Income Tax Ordinance of 1922 and was introduced in many colonies, several of which have retained it with little or no modification after gaining independence (for example, Cyprus, Ghana, Malaysia, Nigeria, Sierra Leone, and Singapore). Other countries have either replaced this form with a separate corporation tax (for example, India, Kenya, Zambia, Tanzania, and Uganda) or have supplemented it by a separate profits tax (for example, Barbados, Guyana, Jamaica, Malaysia, and Trinidad and Tobago). Such a hybrid corporation tax structure is referred to as a partial imputation system.[5]

Table 19.1 *Combined Effective Tax Rates on Companies and Individuals under Separate Entity, Full Imputation, and Undistributed Profits Tax Systems, with Different Distribution and Marginal Personal Tax Rates (percentage of taxable earnings)*

Personal tax rate	No Distribution			50% Distribution			100% Distribution		
	Tax Payable			Tax Payable			Tax Payable		
	Company	Individual	Total	Company	Individual	Total	Company	Individual	Total
Separate Entity System									
15.0	40.0	—	40.0	40.0	4.5	44.5	40.0	9.0	49.0
25.0	40.0	—	40.0	40.0	7.5	47.5	40.0	15.0	55.0
40.0	40.0	—	40.0	40.0	12.0	52.0	40.0	24.0	64.0
50.0	40.0	—	40.0	40.0	15.0	55.0	40.0	30.0	70.0
65.0	40.0	—	40.0	40.0	19.5	59.5	40.0	39.0	79.0
Full Imputation (Withholding) System									
15.0	40.0	—	40.0	40.0	−12.5	27.5	40.0	−25.0	15.0
25.0	40.0	—	40.0	40.0	−7.5	32.5	40.0	−15.0	25.0
40.0	40.0	—	40.0	40.0	—	40.0	40.0	—	40.0
50.0	40.0	—	40.0	40.0	5.0	45.0	40.0	10.0	50.0
65.0	40.0	—	40.0	40.0	12.5	52.5	40.0	25.0	65.0
Undistributed Profits Tax System									
15.0	40.0	—	40.0	20.0	7.5	27.5	—	15.0	15.0
25.0	40.0	—	40.0	20.0	12.5	32.5	—	25.0	25.0
40.0	40.0	—	40.0	20.0	20.0	40.0	—	40.0	40.0
50.0	40.0	—	40.0	20.0	25.0	45.0	—	50.0	50.0
65.0	40.0	—	40.0	20.0	32.5	52.5	—	65.0	65.0

DISCRIMINATION BETWEEN DISTRIBUTED
AND UNDISTRIBUTED EARNINGS

The central issue in the taxation of corporations arises over the tax treatment of corporate distributions. If the corporation is taxed as a separate (juridical) person, it is held that further taxation of dividends results in double taxation, unless this is avoided by providing for integration of the two separate taxes. Because such double taxation of dividends discriminates against this source of income and is claimed to have undesirable effects, on the grounds of both equity and economic efficiency, it is necessary to assess the alternative corporation tax structures from these points of view in formulating tax policy.

Equity Considerations

Both the full imputation and the undistributed profits (split-rate) tax are intended to improve the horizontal and vertical equity of the tax system. By avoiding so-called economic double taxation of distributed earnings, the tax on dividends is brought into alignment with the tax on other returns to capital such as interest, and the tax is distributed progressively, in accordance with ability to pay. These systems make it possible, by full distribution of earnings, to attain complete neutrality in the taxation of corporate earnings.

Table 19.1 illustrates the comparative marginal tax burden on companies and shareholders under the three different systems, assuming a corporation tax rate of 40 percent and marginal personal income tax rates ranging from 15 percent to 65 percent. It is clear that the combined marginal tax rate on companies and share-holders in different tax brackets varies with the proportion of earnings distributed: with no distribution, the rate remains the same on shareholders in all three systems; with 50 percent distribution, the combined marginal rate ranges from 44.5 percent to 59.5 percent under the separate entity system, as against 27.5 percent to 52.5 percent under both the imputation and the undistributed profits tax systems. With full distribution, it can be seen that the marginal tax rates under the integrated systems correspond to the personal income tax rate schedule, as against a much higher double tax on the company and its shareholders under a separate entity system. The differential is greatest—34 percentage points—in the lower tax brackets; it declines—to a minimum of 14 percentage points—as the size of personal taxable income increases. Because of the 40 percent corporate rate, the effective tax burden of the separate entity system, assuming full distribution of earnings, ranges from more than 200 percent higher for a shareholder in the low-income brackets to only 21 percent higher in the highest income bracket, than it would be under integrated systems.

It may be neither feasible nor advantageous to distribute corporate earnings so as to realize the neutrality objective. If the corporation tax rate is below the marginal tax rate of the controlling shareholders, they would be subject to additional tax on distributed income. This situation might inhibit dividend payments, and the corporation tax burden would approach that existing under a separate system of corporation tax. However, because integrated systems eliminate so-called economic double taxation of dividends, the corporation tax rate would have to be somewhat higher than the rate prevailing under a separate entity system if the same total revenue is to be realized. The opportunity for avoiding the personal income tax would thereby be reduced under either the full imputation system or the undistributed profits tax, and equity would be improved.

On the other hand, the economic double taxation of dividends is rationalized by some who believe that "unearned" income is properly more heavily taxable than "earned" income, such as wages and salaries. This view, traditionally held in Colombia, was one consideration that militated against reform of its separate corporation tax (Musgrave and Gillis, 1971). Some support for heavier taxation on returns to capital can also be found in the inducement that may thereby be given to more labor-intensive methods of production in order to promote employment (Lent, 1974). However, such policy runs the risk of deterring new investment.

Implications of Incidence of Corporation Tax

The above observations must be qualified by the assumptions that the incidence of the corporation tax rests on the shareholders—that is, on capital—and that it is shifted neither backward to labor through lower wages nor forward to consumers through higher prices. The opportunities for short-run shifting in developing countries are somewhat circumscribed. In most developing countries there is a limited market, with manufacturers usually protected by tariff rates that tend to set a ceiling on prices; moreover, government price controls are frequently operative. Firms producing for export markets are constrained in their pricing by world prices. Still other local industries—banks, service companies, marketing companies, hotels, etc.—may operate under competitive conditions. Therefore, if a corporation tax were introduced, the tax would tend to rest on the corporation in the short run. But the diversity of economic conditions and institutional factors in developing countries makes it impossible to generalize about the final resting place of the corporation tax.

In promoting new enterprises and planning for expansion, the corporation tax is taken into account as a factor of cost, so that the target rate of return on capital, after tax, equals at least the opportunity cost of capital. This would be true especially of open economies, where foreign investors seek a return on investment comparable with that available in alternative situations. In the long run, therefore, the corporation tax tends to be shifted either to labor through lower wages or to consumers through higher prices of goods, or to both. If this, indeed, is the case, there is no economic double taxation of dividends, and provision for shareholder relief from the tax on dividends is not warranted on equity grounds. Because of the lack of empirical evidence, and because of likely variations in the experience of different industries in different countries, this hypothesis provides a rather uncertain basis for corporation tax policy.

As in industrial countries, the weight of expert opinion on the incidence of the corporation tax in developing countries is inconclusive. Bird (1970a) believes that oligopolistic conditions favor the shifting of corporation taxes in Colombia. The Colombian Commission on Tax Reform (Musgrave and Gillis, 1971), in rejecting integration of corporation and personal taxes, concluded that there was too much uncertainty about the incidence of the corporation tax to justify this step. Several statistical analyses of the corporation tax in India have yielded conflicting results. Lall concluded that the corporation tax was shifted back to labor; Ambirajan's study indicated that it may not have been shifted at all since 1951; Laumas's analysis showed that the tax was more than fully shifted to consumers between 1951 and 1962; and Gandhi concluded that the corporation tax was not shifted during the same period, but fell essentially on capital, reducing either dividends or retained earnings.[6]

If the corporation tax in developing countries does not rest on capital in the long run, equity purposes are not served by its integration with the individual income tax. If it is shifted forward to consumers through higher prices—the most likely outcome—the tax is equivalent to an indirect tax on consumption, and there is equity justification for separate taxation of dividends. A serious question of tax equity might therefore be raised about the exclusion of dividends from the individual income tax, as practiced by many countries. Discrimination is not so evident in countries with no personal income taxes; however, some of these countries have a corporation income tax (for example, Oman and Saudi Arabia) but do not tax the income of unincorporated businesses.

Allocative Considerations

Corporation tax policy plays an important role in the savings and investment decisions of shareholders. Not only does the rate of corporation tax (and the conceptual basis of taxable earnings) determine the availability of earnings for new investment, but the tax treatment of dividends may also influence the amount of earnings retained for investment. In this respect the separate (double) taxation of dividends is generally believed to encourage the retention of earnings and thereby to enhance savings and investment, while an integrated tax system—whether of the imputation or the split-rate form—tends to encourage distribution.

Separate taxation of dividends places a premium on retention of earnings that varies directly with the (marginal) rate of personal income tax that is applicable to shareholders. Under integrated systems, however, there is a tax advantage in retaining earnings only if the corporation tax rate is lower than the marginal personal income tax rate. To minimize the taxes of a closely held corporation, distributions would be made only to the level at which these two rates are equivalent for then major shareholders.

Needless to say, the minimization of income taxes is only one of many factors influencing dividend policy, and it is substantially limited to companies whose ownership is closely identified with control. Cash distributions also depend on corporate liquidity and access to alternative sources of financing working capital and new investment. On the other hand, especially for publicly held companies, it may be necessary to satisfy shareholders' expectations of a reasonable yield on their investment, and thereby attract capital for expansion by means of new stock issues. In order to maximize shareholders' after-tax income, management has a greater obligation under integrated systems to distribute, rather than to retain, earnings.

There is virtually no empirical evidence on the effects of different corporation tax regimes on dividend policy in developing countries.[7] These effects would be extremely difficult to establish on an aggregate basis because of the different tax treatment of dividends paid to nonresident and domestic shareholders, especially when there is substantial foreign ownership. Imputation does not normally apply to nonresidents, and special withholding taxes are usually levied on distributions abroad under both separate entity systems and undistributed profits taxes. Mauritius, for example, taxes only the undistributed income of resident companies, while it taxes the entire income of foreign companies (that is, companies whose control and management is exercised outside Mauritius), both at a standard 45 percent rate.

Neither the imputation system of Malaysia nor that of Singapore appears to have discouraged the retention of profits. In 1964, dividends *and* interest payments amounted to only about 17 percent of corporate profits assessed in the former, and about 25 percent in the latter (Edwards, 1970). If accurate, this rate of distribution is comparable to the 17 percent of earnings distributed in cash by 658 nonfinancial corporations in 1959 under Argentina's (then) separate entity system and is even less than the 26–28 percent payout ratio estimated under Kenya's former imputation system.[8] These data are in sharp contrast to Colombia's experience with its separate corporate tax over the period 1956–59, when between 45 percent and 50 percent of all corporate after-tax profits was distributed. The distribution rate of 54 nonfinancial corporations listed on the stock exchange was even higher, averaging over 70 percent (Taylor et al., 1965). Although the above data are fragmentary, they raise doubts about claims that separate taxation of corporations and shareholders encourages the retention of earnings. One possible explanation is the comparative importance of foreign ownership: because of political uncertainties and the lack of viable domestic investment opportunities, earnings may be repatriated rather than reinvested.

It should be observed that retention of earnings by no means assures their optimum investment. Expansion of an existing business may, in fact, divert resources from other more urgent investment requirements for new industries promising higher rates of return. If there is an efficient capital market, shareholders may seek out investment opportunities (for distributed earnings) that are more profitable than those provided by the corporation. However, relatively few developing countries have organized stock markets to facilitate the mobilization of capital. Many, indeed, have few local investors; corporations, including subsidiaries of multinational corporations, are owned and controlled predominantly by foreign residents.[9]

On the other hand, it may be argued that corporate retention of earnings maximizes the total savings of the country. Dividends to resident investors are spent partly on consumption and, if they are saved, may be invested abroad. Distributions to nonresident investors are a net loss to the economy. Since investment in an open economy is influenced principally by the comparative profitability of economic opportunities in that country and abroad, differences in corporate tax structure would appear to have only a marginal effect on domestic savings. The effects would be somewhat greater in a closed economy. If the capital market is sufficiently well developed and the economy is expanding, much can be said for a tax policy that encourages distribution, rather than reinvestment, of earnings.

Incentive Effects

The rate of income tax paid by the corporation probably is more important to the investment decision than the combined tax burden of the corporation and its shareholders. Whether or not the corporation tax is creditable, in whole or in part, to shareholders, the prospective return on capital after the payment of corporation income taxes is a decisive factor in evaluating investment in a new venture or expansion of an existing enterprise; the lower the tax rate is, the shorter the capital recovery period will be, and the lower will be the risk of undertaking the investment. From the standpoint of the foreign investor—other factors being the same— a country with a low corporate tax rate offers a more attractive long-range prospect for investment than a country with a high rate.

In this respect, a separate corporation tax structure normally has an advantage over an integrated tax structure that yields an equivalent amount of revenue. Since the tax collected from its shareholders is additional to that charged the corporation, a lower corporate rate is indicated. The corporation tax rate for a separate entity system that will yield the same amount of revenue as an imputation system in a particular country depends on the proportion of earnings distributed under each system and the comparative tax rates on earnings distributed abroad. Assuming that the same amount of earnings is retained under each system, it can be seen that the separate entity system tax rate would be substantially below that called for by an amputation system. If, for example, a typical 40 percent rate applied by developing countries under an imputation system were replaced by a separate corporation tax, and the same amount of earnings was retained under both systems, the rate could be reduced to, say, 24 percent.[10] If greater earnings were retained as a result of separate taxation, the corporate tax rate would have to be higher to compensate for the loss of personal income tax revenue. These rates assume that all shareholders are resident individuals. If corporations were owned by nonresidents who were not entitled to a tax credit, withholding rates would have to be 40 percent to yield the same revenues as an imputation system with a 40 percent rate.[11]

Notwithstanding these revenue implications, Barbados and Zambia retained the same corporation tax rate—40 percent—when they eliminated the credit for corporation tax; the 45 percent corporation tax rates in Kenya and Uganda and the 50 percent rate in Tanzania are now higher than the rate (40 percent) under their previous imputation systems. These shifts in corporation tax policy appear to have been decided principally on revenue grounds.

NOTES

1. The basic schedules (*cédules*) in France covered income from (1) real property, (2) dividends and interest, (3) business, (4) farming, (5) wages and salaries, and (6) noncom-

mercial activity. Each schedule had its own rate and special rules for determining income. Some developing countries have elaborated the schedules; Venezuela, for example, has employed as many as nine different schedules.

2. Barbados, in 1975, and Trinidad and Tobago, in 1966, also abandoned similar integrated systems in favor of the separate entity approach; but, after a brief experience with it, they both adopted partial integration (imputation) systems.

3. Prior to 1977, for example, the Federal Republic of Germany taxed undistributed income at 52.23 percent and distributed income at 15.45 percent. If a German company distributed its entire income, the effective tax rate was 24.55 percent because the income retained to pay tax was taxed at the retention rate. Germany has combined a split-rate system with a partial imputation system. Undistributed profits are taxed at 56 percent and dividends at 36 percent, the latter tax being allowed as a credit to domestic shareholders.

4. It remained in a pure form until 1937, when it was supplemented by a separate corporation tax; imputation was repealed in 1965 and reintroduced in 1972. In its original concept, the corporation tax was equivalent to the standard rate charged individuals; accordingly, dividends were subject only to surtax.

5. Guyana, for example, has company tax rates of 45 percent to 55 percent, of which 20 percentage points are creditable against tax paid on dividends. Malaysia has a corporation tax rate of 40 percent which is fully creditable, plus a noncreditable corporation rate of 5 percent.

6. For a summary of these analyses, see Gandhi (1970), pp. 68–89.

7. Nor has econometric analysis reached any firm conclusions in the industrial countries. See Byrne and Sato (1976), p. 267.

8. Data supplied by East African Statistical Department, plus data contained in East African Community, East African Income Tax Department, *Report*, 1967/68, 1970/71 and in Banco Central de la República Argentina, *Inversiones y Fuentes de Recursos Balances Agregados y Resultados de un Conjunto de Sociedades Anónimas Nacionales, años 1955–59* (Buenos Aires, 1961).

9. Over 95 percent of Papua New Guinea's corporate equity is owned abroad, mostly by Australian investors.

10. This assumes the following: (1) retained earnings, and therefore taxable dividends (including the grossed-up dividends under the imputation system) are the same under each system; and (2) all shareholders are residents in the country. Assuming an average marginal personal income tax rate of 50 percent and a dividend of 40 cents per share, the separate tax system with a 24 percent rate would yield 44 cents on a dollar of corporate income, equivalent to that yielded under imputation: 40 cents plus 20 cents tax on dividends ($0.40 × 0.50) less 16 cents tax credit ($0.40 × 0.40). In other terms, the rate of a separate corporation tax yielding the same total income tax revenue as an imputation system is equal to the tax rate of the latter multiplied by the percentage of earnings retained.

11. Forty cents in dividends at a rate of 40 percent equals 16 cents personal income tax on the dollar, *plus* 24 cents corporation tax equals 40 cents—the same amount yielded by a 40 percent imputation tax with no separate dividend withholding.

20

Taxing International Income

The international aspect of corporate taxes raises particularly complicated questions of tax policy for many developing countries, not least because of the substantial administrative problems they face in determining their appropriate share of the tax base. Any flow of income across national borders is affected by the interaction of two different income tax systems, one at each end of the flow, as well as by treaties which attempt to govern the impact of both systems on such flows. Most of the legal literature on this subject emphasizes the dangers of "international double taxation" and the need to avoid this presumably undesirable outcome. In fact, however, as the economic literature has long stressed (e.g., P. B. Musgrave, 1969), it is far from clear from the point of view of any one country that it is advantageous to adopt the usual methods of avoiding such double taxation through exempting foreign-source income or crediting foreign taxes on such income against domestic taxes.

Why should developing countries be concerned with ensuring the efficient international allocation of capital?—if that is what these methods actually achieve, which is open to doubt (Bird, 1987a). Their best interests, from a narrow point of view, may instead lie in extracting, primarily through taxation (see Hartman, 1985), the maximum *national* benefits from foreign investors and especially in discouraging their own residents from investing abroad. (For a recent review of this issue from the point of view of a small developed country, see Bird, 1987a.) On the other hand, considerations of international political economy (Frey and Schneider, 1984) may induce them to play the international tax game under the rules set out by the major capital-exporting countries. Even then, however, there is little question that the failure of most major developed countries (including, since 1984, the United States) to levy any significant taxes on investment income paid to foreigners has contributed undesirably to capital flight from many developing countries (McLure, 1988).

In any case, the task of taxing international income flows effectively is probably well beyond the capability of the undertrained and overworked tax administrators found in most developing countries. In recent years, it has been suggested that the only way to deal with this problem may be to alter completely the present system of dividing the tax take between home and investor countries—the so-called "separate entity, arm's length" method (OECD, 1977; United Nations, 1979)—in favor of some form of formula apportionment similar to that used within federal countries, like the United States (Oldman and Brooks, 1987). Although further exploration of this subject would take us far beyond the scope of this book, it is perhaps worth noting that, as has been shown by the experience of U.S. states with the similar problems that arise within a federal state (McLure, 1984; Bird and Brean,

1986), no one country alone is likely to be able to proceed with such schemes. Instead, what seems required for progress in this direction is a prolonged international negotiating process at least as arduous and complex as a GATT "round" or the Law of the Sea negotiation (Bird, 1988).

Taxation of International Income

Oliver Oldman

This paper discusses some aspects of how less developed countries *do,* and how they *should,* tax foreign income and the income of foreigners. The point of view taken is that of the less developed countries, not that of government or business in the developed countries.

TAXATION OF FOREIGN INCOME

Before dealing with LDC taxation of income of foreigners, a brief discussion is in order of three points relating to LDC taxation of foreign income. First, the trend in LDCs is toward taxing the income of their nationals on a worldwide basis, at least so far as personal income taxes are concerned. The trend is less clear in respect to taxation of corporations. The difficulties of taxing worldwide income of domestic corporations or those owned or controlled by nationals led at least one country, El Salvador, to retain the principle of territorial jurisdiction for corporations, while adopting the worldwide principle for personal income taxes (Oldman, 1964). The Salvadoran approach seems workable, pending the development of suitable arrangements for operating a worldwide principle for corporations. The most promising way to do this is probably through some variant of the unitary method. This approach begins by combining the worldwide income of the components of a multinational enterprise (MNE) and then assigns portions of that income to each country in accord with the MNE's activities and contacts with each, as measured, for example, by the MNE's use of property and labor and its sales in each country.[1]

Secondly, LDC taxation of foreign income need not be the same as LDC taxation of domestic income. For example, LDC policy on the use of a foreign tax credit may be established in accordance with its foreign economic policies. Thus, a country may decide to allow its nationals a deduction for foreign income tax, as Chile does, rather than a credit. Such an approach is desirable in terms of maximizing national welfare since it leads investors at the margin to equalize net-of-tax returns from investment abroad with gross returns from domestic investment. The rationale, of course, is that the country receives the benefit of both the tax revenue and the net-of-tax profit from domestic investment but only the latter from investment abroad (P. B. Musgrave, 1969). Alternatively, a country might allow a credit up to the full amount of domestic tax with respect to foreign income tax paid on income derived from neighboring countries with which arrangements for tax harmonization or

This paper is a substantially revised and updated version of Oldman (1966).

regional economic integration have been made or are being made, and at the same time permit only a lesser credit with respect to taxes on income derived from other LDCs, with perhaps no credit at all for taxes on income from developed countries. Such an approach is intended to minimize the loss of revenue through the credit and to affect the geographical direction of trade and investment (Goldfarb, 1965).

Thirdly, it is important that LDCs improve the means by which they obtain international tax information with which to compute and collect tax on foreign income. This is also important in the taxation of income derived by foreigners from sources in the LDCs. These countries are not doing all they might do to obtain information useful in international tax enforcement. Much useful information could be obtained about particular taxpayers, for example, if LDCs hired private international accounting firms to audit information furnished by taxpayers with foreign income or by foreign taxpayers with LDC income. Information might be obtained with the aid of foreign governments through the operation of tax treaties; but long experience with tax treaties among developed countries has, so far, apparently produced little of the tax administration cooperation that one might have expected. It is to be hoped that this aspect will work out differently for the treaties which have been and will be entered into with the LDCs. However, entering into treaties has made it difficult for LDCs even to consider the important formula approach to the geographical division of business income of modern MNEs. The existing bilateral treaty network ties signatory countries to the separate accounting, arm's-length transfer-pricing approach and virtually prohibits the use of the unitary method.

The rapid increase in the number of tax treaties concluded between LDCs and DCs in the past twenty-five years calls for further comment. The United States has participated in few of these, because of its steady refusal to give tax sparing, that is, credits against U.S. tax otherwise due for tax waived by LDC tax incentives. Nevertheless, the flow of U.S. investment to LDCs was large, absolutely and compared to that of other DCs, until the most recent years, because of international economic forces and the practical and complex interaction of foreign taxes and the U.S. income tax system. Other than making potential investors aware of a "climate" sympathetic to international business and providing educational benefits to tax officials of both LDCs and DCs, few observable significant benefits have accrued to the LDCs from having entered into this network of bilateral treaties. The large staff costs of negotiating and operating them have yielded too little additional administrative cooperation.

The most valuable part of the tax treaty literature has been the information developed under the aegis of the United Nations in the meetings and documentation leading to the adoption of a model bilateral treaty for use between the LDCs and DCs. The model gave some LDCs the courage to resist disadvantageous provisions; but more importantly, a careful reading of the model together with its substantial prior documentation establishes the model's limited usefulness.[2]

Perhaps what is needed to develop international tax information is organized pressure by LDCs, brought to bear through the United Nations, for the creation of what might be called "Intertax" (Surr, 1966), an institution analogous to Interpol to facilitate the international flow of information needed in tax compliance. Consideration of the role of Intertax would explore the ways in which developed and less developed countries might exchange general information about tax enforcement techniques, as well as specific information about particular types of income or particular taxpayers.

TAXATION OF FOREIGNERS

Now, let us turn to taxation of foreigners who have income from less developed countries. What principles can be identified as guides to LDCs in the taxation of income going to foreigners? Not much thought has been given to identifying such principles, either for developed countries or for less developed ones.[3]

Principles

First, one might latch on to the principle of equality: tax the foreigner and the national equally, to the extent that technical means of doing so can be designed and operated. From this starting point, certain income going to foreigners might be taxed either more heavily or less heavily than income going to nationals. These departures from equal treatment would be made only when compelling reasons of policy so dictated and when it appeared likely that the objectives of such a policy would be achieved by the departure from equality.

A second starting point might be the principle of charging whatever the traffic will bear: tax the foreigner as much as he will pay without his ceasing to engage in activities the LDC wants. If the LDC knows what it wants of the foreigner, the LDC, under this principle, will design its system as both a protective device and a revenue device, always subject to modification in the light of changing needs or demands of the LDC and changing supplies of foreigners. This principle finds its support in the following lines of reasoning: A less developed country's power or jurisdiction to tax is not significantly limited by general international rules of law. Less developed countries need tax revenues for social and economic development in amounts greatly in excess of those available from their own resources, from international economic aid programs, and from their share of international trade. Therefore, it is argued, a less developed country should tax income going to foreigners with primary regard only to the effects of the system.

Categories of Income

Now let us look at different categories of income going to foreigners and how such income should be taxed under either the equality principle or the "traffic" principle, as these principles might be applied in actual circumstances. The categories to be examined are: (1) income derived by foreigners from raw materials produced in and exported from LDCs, including agricultural and mineral products; and (2) profits derived from direct foreign private investment. Of course, the categories themselves are not crystal clear in the scope of their coverage; and also, many other categories of income are excluded from the present discussion, such as income from interest paid to foreigners on sums lent by them for use in LDCs, passive investment income, and payments made for technical services.

Income from Production and Export of Raw Materials

Less developed countries have for a long time regarded raw materials income as fair game for application of the "traffic" principle. Higher taxes have been levied, in one form or another, on agricultural and mineral exports. Source rules have been broad, income tax rates have been raised, and special export or production taxes have been used. One justification for applying the traffic principle here is that payment must be made for depletable national resources. Another is that the extra tax burden would be levied, even if the income were to go to nationals rather than to foreigners. The chief restraining influence on the use of the traffic principle is the nature and extent of competition in world markets for the raw materials exports of particular LDCs. In the absence of, for example, international price agreements or restrictive trade channels, heavier taxes levied by one country than by another on foreign receivers of income might lead the foreigner to move his production, if it were economically and technologically feasible to do so. Thus, LDCs find themselves less able to impose heavy tax burdens on income for agricultural exports than on income from mineral exports. Of course, to the extent that the LDCs are able to organize themselves and keep world prices for their products higher than without organization, the LDCs may also seek to tax the resultant increase in private incomes more heavily than other income.

I cannot, and will not try to, unravel the complex economic forces at work in world trade in raw materials—not to mention the political forces. It may be expected, however, that each LDC, acting alone or in concert with others, is going to try to get the most it can out of its raw materials production and that it will use tax measures to do so where feasible. Horse trading will take place among governments and between governments and private business. Less developed countries will accommodate foreign tax systems where that is technically easy and not costly in revenue. Moreover, it should come as no surprise that for some materials under certain market conditions the LDC tax will turn out to be in excess of the foreigner's home country tax and, equally important, that a developed home country may not allow the resultant excess credit to be used to offset any other tax liability, current or future. In short, it should neither create shock nor raise a storm of protest if sometimes the less developed country's effective rate of tax is higher than the rate in the developed country.

Profits from Direct Private Investment

The second category of income going to foreigners is profits arising from direct private investment in plant and operations, let us say manufacturing business. Perhaps in this category, more than any other, most countries state that their policy is to tax foreign business in the same way as domestic business. Tax incentives are given to both or neither. Two strong and opposing forces operate in many LDCs to keep the equality principle in existence. One is that national or domestic business in the LDCs is often anything but enchanted by the prospect of competition from foreigners from the developed countries. The other is the desire of the LDC governments to raise efficiency and promote growth by bringing in the latest techniques of production, by producing new products, and by introducing or increasing competition. In some LDCs, the government's desire for these benefits is limited by the fear that foreign political pressure will follow in the wake of a large number of foreigners or large-sized foreign firms. While the equality principle may be the most generally announced one for this category of income, at least two questions about its implementation may be asked. First, is it applied at the administrative level? It is often said that domestic businessmen avoid or evade more tax than foreigners do. To the extent that this is true (and with the increasing number of joint ventures, it is said to be less true), foreigners can press for equal treatment by seeking compensatory reductions negotiated through the treaty process, or foreigners can lend support to thorough-going tax reform programs for LDCs.

Second, what does equal treatment mean with respect to such a broad issue as the tax burden on the far-away shareholder in a complex network of international corporations? And what does it mean with respect to such narrow, difficult, and important issues as head office expenses, intercompany pricing, and other transfer-pricing problems—not to mention allocation, apportionment formulas, and other source-rule problems and problems of establishing jurisdictional rules as broad as source rules? On the broad issue, the impracticality of reaching the far-away shareholder leads at least some LDCs to tax LDC income going to foreign-owned corporations at a supplementary flat rate imposed to make up for lack of LDC tax on the ultimate shareholders. Indeed, this well-established practice was adopted by the United States in the Tax Reform Act of 1986, which imposed the so-called branch tax, a supplementary tax on U.S. source income of branches of foreign corporations. The amount of such a tax is the issue, and pragmatic considerations govern. On the narrower issues, the pressures of the developed countries might be brought to bear, not on getting LDCs to conform to developed country rules, but on getting LDCs to announce their rules with more clarity and precision than heretofore. Where the LDC rules clash with rules of developed countries, in attempts of less developed countries to maximize revenue, the result will be equivalent to an increase in rates.

With most LDCs taxing at rates lower than the U.S. rate until 1988, the effect was mainly to move some tax revenue from the U.S. Treasury (or from tax-haven depositories) to LDC treasuries. Where, because of the clash of source rules or because of generally high rates, the LDC tax is greater than the U.S. tax, the LDC policy is perhaps the sound one; and the United States ought not to exert pressure for the LDC to modify its rules or rates so as to reduce the tax rate to the U.S. level. If the LDC wants U.S. business to come in, but U.S. business is not coming in because of the high tax, the LDC will have to consider whether or not its policy is sound and how it might be modified. Incidentally, one effect of LDC rules and rates which result in high rather than low taxes on foreign business is that such businesses are in a poorer position to argue for tax concessions from their home countries; for no longer can such businesses argue effectively that lower rates in other developed countries put their businesses in a better competitive position in the less developed countries.

CONCLUSION

To sum up: First, administrative factors significantly influence the design and operation of LDC international tax rules. These factors limit the ability to provide equal treatment of foreigners among themselves and with nationals. Also, these factors require that more attention be given to international methods of enforcement. Second, in designing a system for taxing income going to foreigners, despite its problems, equality is probably the soundest principle with which to start. Modifications may be needed for administrative reasons, but should be reexamined from time to time as tax collection techniques change. In particular, concessions have to be questioned in terms of their effectiveness and also have to be reexamined regularly. Modifications by way of extra burdens or charges on foreigners may not be objectionable when justified on grounds of special benefits conferred on them or as partial payment for using up national resources. Such charges may sometimes, as with oil royalties, be labeled as income taxes in order to qualify for the foreign tax credit in the foreigner's home country. When the extra charges take the form of export taxes, the less developed countries might even seek, under tax treaties, to get the developed countries to allow all or part of these taxes to qualify for the developed countries' foreign tax credits.

In the end, although the less developed countries can learn a good deal about the technical implementation of policies which have been used by the developed countries in order to formulate their own policies, they will have to examine closely the economic conditions under which their policies are to operate and whether or not these conditions bear any resemblance to those under which the developed countries formulated their policies.

NOTES

1. For more detail, see Oldman and Brooks, 1987.

2. The total documentation, not yet compiled anywhere, remains a treasure of knowledge about taxing foreigners. See: United Nations, 1979 and 1980.

3. See, however, the pioneering paper by Richard and Peggy Musgrave (1972). This paper discusses several possible bases for dividing between nations the tax base created by international income flows: the benefit principle, the source and residence principles, a national "rental" approach under which the capital-importing country levies a special tax on foreign investment to secure its "fair share" of the total gains from (factor) trade, and an explicitly redistributive international tax system. The "traffic" principle discussed below is obviously close to the national rental principle while the equality principle is in effect a modified version of the traditional source-residence approach.

21

Coping with Inflation

Many developing countries are plagued by inflation, sometimes at quite high rates and often for long periods. As chapter 18 pointed out, inflation has substantially distorting effects on taxation in at least three important ways. In the first place, contrary to the "inflation bonus" of additional revenues developed countries usually expect to receive as rising nominal incomes move taxpayers up the progressive income tax rate schedule, the effect of inflation in developing countries is usually to lower income tax revenues, owing to the effects of delayed payment systems and poor collection and enforcement (Tanzi, 1977). The effects of inflation, indeed, are a principal factor explaining the otherwise paradoxical finding that in many developing countries the elasticity of direct taxes in response to changes in nominal income is not only less than that of indirect taxes but also less than unity. The only solution to this problem is to move the income tax as far as possible onto a current payment and withholding basis and to improve tax administration—never an easy task and not one that can be accomplished quickly.

Secondly, even if taxpayers pay their taxes, inflation distorts the intended distributional effects of the income tax. This distortion can of course be offset by adjusting rate brackets (and amounts such as exemptions fixed in nominal currency terms) by an appropriate index (Petrei, 1975; Aaron, 1976), as has been done at various times in different countries. On the other hand, it may be argued that any resulting small distortions within the taxpaying population of an unindexed tax may be more than offset by the advantages of expanding that population—and hence the scope of the income tax—more rapidly as a result of inflation (Musgrave, 1981). As usual, the correct answer for any country cannot be determined in abstract, but it does seem likely that rate and bracket indexation makes sense only when inflation is either high or, especially, prolonged.

Finally, and most importantly, inflation has similarly distorting effects on the taxation of business and capital income that are much more difficult to take into account. No country has suffered more from such distortions than Chile, and, as the following selection outlines, few have done as much to adjust their tax systems to inflation in all three of the respects mentioned above. As Casanegra de Jantscher shows, Chile's move to a full-fledged adjustment system was incremental and gradual. Other countries that may contemplate similar moves would seem well-advised to follow a similarly cautious path. A particularly interesting aspect of the Chilean experience is the reliance of the inflation adjustment system on net wealth information (a point picked up in a different context in chapter 24 below).

A common argument against any form of inflation adjustment is that adjusting to inflation may weaken the will to resist it. Given the large and undesirable costs of not adjusting, this argument carries little weight so far as the tax system is concerned. Of course, no (or little) inflation is better than a lot, but any country which, for whatever reason, has high and persistent inflation will almost certainly eventually have to take this unpleasant fact into account in its tax system. Whether the result will be full adjustment (as in Chile), partial adjustment, as in Colombia (McLure et al., 1988), or perhaps even a move to a completely different tax system, as suggested in chapters 18 and 22, remains to be seen.

Inflation Adjustment in Chile

Milka Casanegra de Jantscher

The mechanisms currently used to index Chile's tax system were not established overnight. They are the product of a gradual evolution extending over more than four decades, during which different indexation schemes were tried out in an effort to adapt Chile's tax system to the inflationary conditions prevailing since the early 1940s. Chile's yearly inflation rates were highly variable between 1940 and 1983 (roughly the period covered by this study), with annual rates ranging from 5.5 to 508.1 percent. In general, however, annual price rises have usually been sizable, though seldom large enough to warrant the description "hyperinflation."

Recurrent periods of substantial inflation have forced Chile's tax experts to exercise their ingenuity in order to devise mechanisms to reduce the inequities and revenue losses resulting from the impact of inflation on the tax system. The taxpaying public and tax administrators have adapted to the complexities of these mechanisms, so much so that in spite of such complexities Chile's ratio of taxes to GDP has been for several years one of the highest in Latin America.

PROFITS ADJUSTMENT SCHEMES

Nonrecurrent Mechanisms

The earliest attempt to introduce an indexation mechanism in Chile's tax system was made in 1942 in connection with the establishment of an excess profits tax. Years of inflation had greatly distorted the profits-capital ratio, and the imposition of a progressive tax on annual profits in excess of 15 percent of capital made it necessary to update capital values. Taxpayers were allowed to revalue only upon paying the normal income tax on the increase in book value, but many willingly revalued to reduce their excess profits tax.

In 1948 and in 1952 further one-time authorizations were granted to business taxpayers to revalue their fixed assets. Taxpayers were required to pay a tax on the revaluation amounts, but the rate of this tax was considerably lower than the income tax rate on business income.

Initial Experience with Permanent Systems

By 1954, in view of the high inflation rates prevailing at that time, authorities decided that a more permanent adjustment scheme was called for. The adoption

Excerpted from Casanegra de Jantscher (1985).

that year of a permanent system for revaluing fixed assets constitutes the first step toward a systematic approach to profits adjustment. Like its nonrecurrent predecessors, this scheme was voluntary and required payment of tax on the revaluation amounts. It was obviously a crude way of adjusting profits because it dealt with only one aspect of the problem—the valuation of fixed assets.

Due to the limited nature of this adjustment scheme, a number of provisions enacted between 1954 and 1959 authorized sporadic revaluations of inventories, up to replacement costs. These provisions were severely criticized at the time by the tax service because their ad hoc nature made them difficult to control. Because in some instances these revaluation provisions were included in tax packages that also granted tax amnesties, they gained a somewhat unsavory reputation. On the other hand, taxpayers claimed that these revaluations were sorely needed to prevent taxation of nominal profits that greatly exaggerated their real income. The debate on this subject led to the enactment in 1959 of a statute that established an optional system of net worth revaluation for taxpayers subject to business income taxation. As part of the income tax reform of 1964 some features of the system were changed and revaluation became mandatory. This system was retained until the end of 1974, when the entire revaluation mechanism was overhauled.

Net Worth Revaluation System Applied from 1959

The system introduced in 1959, which was to remain basically unchanged until the end of 1974, was based on the concept of net worth. The fundamental principle of this system is that only the net worth of an enterprise—defined as the difference between the firm's assets (less all accounts that do not represent actual investments) and liabilities—ought to be protected against erosion by inflation, that is, that firms with a large ratio of liabilities to total assets require less protection than firms with a smaller ratio. The revaluation system in force until 1974 operated indirectly. Only fixed assets were directly revalued. All other adjustments were made through an aggregate adjustment process that took place each year and was based on the values appearing in the beginning-of-year balance sheet. The total amount of readjustment available to a firm was determined at the end of the year by multiplying its net worth at the beginning of the year by the relative change in the consumer price index during the year. The readjustment amount had to be allocated by the taxpayer in the following manner:

1. Fixed assets were revalued by multiplying their net book value at the beginning of the year by the same relative change in the consumer price index.
2. The increase in fixed asset values was subtracted from the readjustment amount and the difference was allowed as a deduction from profits. This deduction could not exceed 20 percent of profits, a limit imposed to protect government revenues.[1]

This system was attractive by reason of its simplicity, particularly because it left book values of most assets and liabilities unchanged. This same characteristic, however, meant that the system did little to correct financial statements, which became increasingly unrealistic as time passed. Another major defect of the system was its lack of symmetry: it attempted to tax firms only on their real income (thus preventing tax-induced decreases in net worth) but did not tax real increases in net worth attributable to inflation. The 20 percent limitation on deductions from profits discriminated against enterprises with few fixed assets but large holdings of other assets, such as inventory. Firms whose fixed assets constituted a large fraction of their capital could use much of the revaluation amount to revalue their fixed assets, and therefore were not affected by the 20 percent ceiling.

To obtain relief from this provision, taxpayers pressed once again for extraordinary revaluations of assets. They were joined by other taxpayers who obtained little benefit from the permanent system because of its net worth approach, primarily taxpayers with large ratios of liabilities to total assets, who accordingly were eligible only for small revaluations. As a result, one of the main purposes that led to the enactment of this scheme—to prevent periodic ad hoc revaluations—was not fulfilled. Between 1959 and 1974 the authorities were constantly authorizing one-time revaluations of fixed assets and inventories up to replacement costs (frequently combined with tax amnesty provisions). This dual system of revaluations—a permanent system and a succession of ad hoc revaluations—was not integrated and was difficult to administer.

Current System

The new revaluation scheme, enacted in late 1974 (in force starting from 1975) is also based on the net worth concept but is much more comprehensive than the previous system. This can be attributed partly to the fact that the current scheme was enacted during a period of hyperinflation, when only a fully comprehensive adjustment system could be expected to correct grossly unrealistic income statements. Moreover, the lengthy previous experience with less comprehensive systems had shown that they gave rise to a host of administrative problems and inequities.

The main differences between the current profits adjustment system and the pre-1975 mechanism are the following:
1. All of a firm's assets and liabilities are now carried in its books at current value.
2. There are no limits on the deductions from or additions to profits that may result from the adjustment mechanism.
3. The current system treats taxpayers symmetrically, restricting the tax base to their real income (thus preventing erosion of their net worth) but also taxing them on real increases in net worth attributable to inflation.
4. The capitalization requirement included in the pre-1975 system was rescinded, and firms may capitalize their revaluation amounts or not, as they like.
5. The prohibition upon using revaluation amounts to undertake investments unrelated to the business of the enterprise was repealed because it was impossible to enforce.

The main objective of the current profits adjustment system is the determination of the real income of business enterprises when the price level is changing. In principle, real income can be measured by comparing the beginning-of-year net worth of a firm with its end-of-year net worth, both expressed in end-of-year values. To make a correct comparison, however, it is necessary to recognize that inflation affects costs of each kind of asset and liability differently according to the nature of each. In order to update end-of-year book values, one must discriminate between those assets and liabilities whose historic costs reflect their current costs and those whose historic costs do not reflect current costs. The present profits adjustment scheme is based on the idea of comparing beginning-of-year net worth with end-of-year net worth, although in practice it operates through direct adjustments to net income. The concept of initial net worth is crucial to the system, as will be seen below. Initial net worth is defined as the difference between a firm's assets (less all accounts that do not represent actual investments) and liabilities.

The current profits adjustment system has been changed very little during the past ten years and has functioned adequately in periods of widely different inflation rates. It is doubtful, however, whether the private sector and the tax administration would have been able to cope with this sophisticated mechanism if they had not previously had lengthy experience with simpler profit adjustment schemes. Because the current system is highly comprehensive, there has been no need for ad hoc revaluation authorizations such as the ones enacted in earlier periods. This has simplified administration and prevented inequities arising from the abuse of ad hoc revaluations.

In spite of the advantages of the current system, it is by no means perfect. Its main problems arise from the fact that adjustment indices, whether general or special, can at best result in adjusted costs that approximate true current costs but, in many instances, give rise to book values that differ widely from current costs. In the case of fixed assets, for example, the index used to adjust net book values is the consumer price index, which is also used to adjust beginning-of-year net worth and most other adjustable assets with the exception of inventories, which are valued at replacement cost. In practice, it has been found that the cost of fixed assets fluctuates according to factors that have little relation to consumer price changes. Thus, during periods of economic recession the value of some fixed assets has fallen in real terms but consumer price levels have continued to rise. In such circumstances, the adjustment of all fixed asset costs by the change in the consumer price index has resulted in unrealistic costs that have distorted financial statements. The effect of these unrealistic adjustments on the level of tax burdens is somewhat unclear. In the short run, such adjustments result in higher taxable incomes than if the adjustments had been more realistic (adjustments to fixed asset values are added to net income). This effect is partially offset, however, by the fact that beginning-of-year net worth is also adjusted according to the change in the consumer price index and this adjustment is deductible from net income. In the longer run, of course, firms can take advantage of higher fixed assets costs by taking larger depreciation deductions. In the case of imported inventory items, the rules for establishing replacement costs rely heavily on exchange rate variations. When major devaluations have coincided with a period of economic recession, imported merchandise has been adjusted to replacement cost values that are considerably higher than current domestic prices. In such instances, taxpayers have suffered a sizable upward adjustment of taxable profits (because inventory adjustments are added to net income) while holding stocks of imported merchandise that is worth much less in the domestic market than its adjusted book value. It is argued, however, that when taxpayers dispose of these goods, the loss that arises will be reflected in future income statements, offsetting the earlier profits.

Much thought has been given in Chile to ways of minimizing the anomalies described above. Consideration has been given to the idea of using special indices for adjusting fixed assets—based on prices of industrialized products, for example. Unfortunately each possible solution adds to complexity or may create new inequities. The general consensus seems to be that the current system, as it now stands, is a reasonable solution to the problem of profits adjustment, and has the great advantage of having proved administratively feasible.

INDEXATION OF TAX BRACKETS, ALLOWANCES, CREDITS, AND MINIMUM TAXABLE AMOUNTS

The statute that introduced the first permanent profits adjustment scheme in 1954 also introduced several other far-reaching tax indexing mechanisms. Among these was the indexation of the progressive income tax (Impuesto Global Complementario). This was accomplished initially by expressing tax brackets and basic personal allowances in terms of the minimum wage. When basic allowances were transformed into tax credits in the tax reform of 1964, these were also expressed in fractions or multiples of the minimum wage. Later, in 1975, the minimum wage was replaced throughout the tax system by the tax unit as the major indexing tool.[2]

Indexed brackets and personal allowances are no longer a novelty in countries that have experienced high rates of inflation for considerable periods of time. In 1954, however, their enactment in Chile was a move into uncharted territory. Equity considerations were paramount in the initial decision to index the brackets and personal allowances of the progressive income tax. It was argued that the introduction of a permanent profits adjustment scheme addressed only some of the distortions in income tax burdens created by inflation. The phenomenon known as bracket creep (moving to higher rate brackets because of increases in nominal income) was thought to deserve as much attention as the problem of adjusting business profits, particularly because wage and salary earners were paying a large share of all the receipts from the global complementary tax.

Over time, indexing has been extended to all the deductions allowed under the global complementary tax. Thus, for example, property tax payments during the tax year are deductible in determining the net taxable income subject to the global complementary tax. Taxpayers may adjust such payments by the change in the consumer price index before deducting them from their global net income.

It is not only tax brackets, allowances, and credits of the income tax that are indexed in Chile. In the tax reform of 1964, the brackets and the personal exemptions of the inheritance and gift taxes were converted into multiples of the minimum wage and are currently expressed in tax units. An important application of the principle that tax credits should be indexed was made to the value-added tax

(VAT). Like taxpayers in a number of other Latin American countries that impose a VAT, taxpayers in Chile whose tax credits for taxes paid on purchases exceed the VAT due on sales during the same month when the input taxes were paid are usually required to offset the excess credit against future VAT payments instead of being entitled to a refund. In recognition of the fact that inflation would erode the value of such credits if they were not adjusted, taxpayers are entitled to convert the balance of the credit into monthly "tax units" and thus the credit is automatically adjusted until it is used up as an offset against future VAT payments. This mechanism is of particular importance in the case of credits arising from investment in plant and equipment, which normally are too large to be used up in a short time.

The indexation of brackets, allowances, tax credits, and minimum exempt amounts has prevented major distortions in tax burdens during periods of high inflation and particularly during the hyperinflation that took place between 1972 and 1976. The fact that the indexation system is fully automatic and thus requires no exercise of discretionary powers by authorities has ensured smooth application and equitable results. As regards personal income taxation, in particular, indexing has prevented bracket creep and kept the number of taxpayers within manageable limits.

COLLECTION LAGS AND ARREARS

In most countries, initial attempts to adjust tax systems for price level changes have focused on ways to minimize hardships to taxpayers. Chile is no exception to this rule. As explained above, for several years the only form of tax indexation consisted of partial profits adjustment schemes. Because these schemes attempted to tax firms only on their real income but did not recognize the fact that inflation can cause real increases in net worth, they could only reduce tax burdens, never increase them. The indexation of the personal income tax in 1954 through the automatic adjustment of brackets and allowances also reduced tax burdens below the levels they would otherwise have reached in the absence of legislative relief.

Concurrently with the indexation of personal income taxation in 1954, however, the first measure was enacted to protect government revenues from erosion caused by inflation. For some years property tax revenues had been steadily declining because their base—the assessed values of real property—had become increasingly outdated owing to inflation. The 1954 statute provided for a general reassessment of real property, to be followed by annual automatic adjustments according to indices specified in the law.

It was several years before other measures were enacted to correct features of the tax system that, interacting with inflation, depressed the system's elasticity. The delay was due, however, to the political difficulty of enacting such measures rather than to any lack of awareness of the problem. A major study of Chile's tax system that was commissioned by the government in 1956 and conducted by a group of Chilean tax experts had clearly identified, among the major reasons for the lack of elasticity of the tax system, the problem of collection lags, unindexed arrears, and the multiplicity of specific rates.

During the early 1960s the problem of specific rates was attacked systematically and by the end of the decade most had been replaced by ad valorem rates. The issue of collection lags and arrears was, however, more politically sensitive. During the 1962–64 tax reform, Congress rejected a proposal to index income tax payments other than those collected through withholding as a way to compensate for the fact that such payments were made the year following the year in which the income was earned. The measure was finally enacted in 1965, but indexation was limited to 50 percent of the change in the consumer price index; in 1966 the limit was removed.

The enactment of this measure was an important step, because until 1973 there was no system of provisional income tax payments in Chile. The establishment of estimated income tax payments on current year income had been suggested on several occasions but had been rejected by the government because the tax department felt it did not have the resources to administer such a mechanism. Only in 1973 was a system of provisional income tax payments implemented, thus considerably reducing income tax collection lags. The adjustment of income tax payments remains in force, however, with respect to the balance (if any) that taxpayers pay when they file their yearly return.

In 1973, at the peak of the hyperinflation that lasted from 1972 to 1976, the indexation of tax arrears was finally addressed. As in the case of collection lags, the problem had been identified much earlier, but political obstacles prevented the enactment of the necessary measures. Starting from 1973, delinquent taxes have been adjusted by the change in the consumer price index and interest for late payment is calculated on the indexed amount.

It was only in 1975, however, that refunds due to taxpayers were also indexed. Full and painful awareness of the effects of hyperinflation on the value of assets and liabilities had finally led to an indexing system that attempted a comprehensive correction of the distortions caused by delays in collecting or refunding tax monies. In order to minimize the number of indexation measures required, efforts were made between 1972 and 1976 to reduce collection lags as much as possible. For example, larger taxpayers were required to make value-added tax payments twice a month, thereby almost eliminating the delay from the time of a sale until the tax was paid.

LESSONS FROM THE CHILEAN EXPERIENCE

The Chilean experience with indexation raises a number of highly interesting questions. Some of the more important ones concerning the effects of indexation on the distribution of tax burdens, incentives to invest, price stability, and the elasticity of the tax system, require more information than is now readily available before they can be answered. It is noteworthy that despite dramatic year-to-year changes in GDP growth rates and in price levels, both the ratio of total taxes to GDP and the ratio of income taxes to GDP have not fluctuated wildly. During this same period, Chile's experience with indexation developed. At the same time, important changes in the tax structure and in the tax administration took place. For example, the general turnover tax was replaced by a value-added tax, the level of the schedular income taxes was greatly reduced, the base of the personal income tax was broadened, a net wealth tax on individuals was introduced and then repealed several years later, specific rates were converted into ad valorem, etc. As regards tax administration, major efforts succeeded in modernizing the structure and the operational systems of the tax department. Within this context, how much of the relative stability of tax revenues as a fraction of GDP is attributable to the indexation of the tax system? Would the importance of income taxation in the tax structure have increased without indexation? Or, as is generally believed, has indexation decreased resistance to income taxation and thus helped to preserve the relative importance of income taxes?

Leaving aside these broader issues, there are other questions about indexation that the Chilean experience can help to answer. Many doubts have been expressed about the administrative feasibility of indexing certain aspects of tax systems, particularly in the case of profits adjustment schemes. The Chilean experience shows that comprehensive profits adjustment schemes can be administered, provided the tax service and the private sector have had previous experience with such schemes and they are based on the indexation of assets and liabilities rather than on the indexation of income and expense flows. In the case of nonbusiness taxpayers, indexation of monthly incomes, provisional payments, and even of interest income received, has also proved feasible.

Another important lesson from the Chilean experience is that political constraints make it very difficult to enact indexation schemes that take into account both the hardships that inflation inflicts on taxpayers and the gains that some of them derive from inflation. Thus, while it is relatively easy to enact profits adjustment schemes that remove illusory gains from the tax base, it is difficult to tax the real gains derived from inflation. Measures designed to correct the negative revenue impact of collection lags and arrears during inflationary periods are politically difficult to implement. Yet, if such measures are not adopted, particularly in periods of high inflation, tax revenues will decrease markedly in real terms. Such a decrease will tend to increase fiscal gaps, thus further contributing to price instability.

NOTES

1. This description refers to the system in force during 1974.
2. The "tax unit" consists of an amount adjusted periodically for changes in the consumer price index.

22

A New Design for Business Taxation

As mentioned in the introduction to the previous chapter, one way of coping with the distorting effects of inflation on the taxation of business income would be to shift the basis of such taxation from income to, in effect, consumption. Such a tax would obviously be similar in many ways to the direct tax on personal consumption discussed in chapter 18.

The following excerpt from a recent report first sets out the salient effects of such a "consumption-based" business tax and then considers the case for such a tax in the context of a tax system based on consumption rather than income. The ideas set out here are presented both for their intrinsic interest and because they raise many interesting questions about the purpose and design of conventional business taxes. Although no scheme along these lines has yet been implemented in any country, developed or developing, in many respects the so-called "resource rent" taxes (Garnaut and Clunies-Ross, 1983) applied in some countries (e.g., Papua New Guinea) to certain natural resource industries come close (see chapter 23).

A Consumption-based Business Tax

Charles E. McLure, Jr., and others

A "consumption-based" business tax is distinguished from an "income-based" business tax in primarily two ways. The first is the tax treatment of business-related receipts and expenditures. Business expenses incurred in a given year are deductible under an income tax in that year only to the extent that they result in business receipts in the same year. Expenses that give rise to receipts in later years must be capitalized and deducted in those years; that is, the deduction of expenses must be "matched" with the inclusion of the related receipts on a year-by-year basis. Thus, under an income tax, expenses that give rise to receipts in later years are capitalized and recovered through subsequent deductions such as those for depreciation, depletion, amortization, and cost of goods sold from inventory. In marked contrast, under a consumption tax, all business-related expenditures are fully deductible in the year they are made.

The second major difference between a consumption-based and an income-based business tax is in the tax treatment of debt and interest. In both cases, the proceeds of a loan are not included in the tax base, and repayment of the principal is not deductible. However, under an income tax, both the real and the inflationary components of business-related interest payments are generally fully deductible. In contrast, under a consumption tax, both the real and the inflationary components of interest expense are not deductible.[1]

CASH FLOW ACCOUNTING FOR RECEIPTS AND EXPENDITURES

Under a consumption-based business tax, all gross sales receipts (including those from exports and sales of fixed assets) and all business-related expenditures are treated on a cash flow basis; that is, receipts are included in the tax base in the year the firm receives cash payment, and deductions for expenditures are allowed from the tax base in the year cash outlays are made. For this reason, such a tax is also commonly referred to as a business "cash flow" tax. Equity contributions are not included in the tax base, and dividends are not deductible. Symmetrically, business purchases of the stock of another firm are not deductible and dividends received are not included in the tax base of the firm owning the stock.

Cash flow treatment of sales receipts and business-related expenditures contrasts sharply with the treatment of these transactions under an income tax, where accrual accounting is required.[2] Indeed, the use of cash flow rather than accrual

Excerpted from McLure et al. (1988).

accounting gives rise to many of the simplicity advantages of a consumption-based tax, relative to an income-based tax. In particular, all of the multitude of troublesome timing problems under an income tax disappear because all receipts and expenditures simply enter the tax base on a cash flow basis. Moreover, the problems of inflation adjustment under an income tax also disappear under a consumption-based tax; all receipts and expenditures are simply measured in monetary values of the current year.

Included among the expenditures treated on a cash flow basis under a consumption-based business tax are all purchases of inventories and of depreciable assets, as well as all other expenditures which, under an income tax, should be capitalized and amortized over several years or give rise to depletion deductions. (To simplify exposition, the term *depreciable asset* will hereafter refer to all such assets and the term *depreciation allowances* will refer to all the associated methods of cost recovery.) Again, cash flow treatment or "expensing" of expenditures on inventories and depreciable assets is much simpler than the inventory accounting and depreciation allowances required under an accrual-based income tax.

The most striking difference between an income-based and a consumption-based business tax is in the differing treatments of depreciable assets. The traditional Haig-Simons definition of the individual tax base under an income tax is annual consumption plus the change in net wealth. Ideally, changes in the net wealth of businesses would be attributed to individuals and taxed at the individual level. In practice, most countries that tax income at the individual level also tax business income, commonly with a corporate income tax; the extent to which the business and individual income taxes are integrated varies widely. If a business tax is used to supplement an individual income tax, the Haig-Simons definition of income suggests that the business tax base should equal the change in the net wealth of the business. (In addition, any individual consumption expenditures that are disguised as business expenses should be included in the tax base of either the business or the individual.)

Consider the application of this definition to a firm making an investment in a depreciable asset which costs $1,000. The purchase of the asset, in and of itself, has no effect on the tax base of the firm; the cash outlay of $1,000 (a reduction in cash assets) is exactly offset by the firm's claim on an asset worth $1,000 (an increase in fixed assets). A deduction for income tax purposes should theoretically be allowed only to the extent of the physical or "economic" depreciation of the asset during the year. For example, if the asset depreciates 10 percent per year, a deduction of $100 would be allowed in the first year of ownership, with subsequent deductions similarly based on actual economic depreciation.

In contrast, under the consumption-based business tax, deductions are allowed for all cash outlays, and changes in net wealth by definition have no effect on the tax base. Thus, the firm would receive a deduction of $1,000 in the year of investment, and no further deductions would be allowed.

The effects of the alternative treatments are summarized as follows. With deductions for economic depreciation under the income tax, the entire return to the capital investment—the economic income resulting from the investment—is subject to taxation at the statutory rate. With expensing under the consumption tax, the effect depends on the nature of the investment. Define a "marginal" investment as one with a return equal to the firm's discount rate or opportunity cost of funds, and an inframarginal investment as one with a higher rate of return.[3] Under a consumption tax, the returns to a marginal investment bear a zero rate of tax in present value terms. If the investment is inframarginal, the inframarginal or above-normal returns to the investment are subject to taxation at the statutory tax rate, while the marginal or normal returns are untaxed.

A more instructive way of thinking about these results is to note that allowing expensing rather than deductions for economic depreciation implies that the government is a silent partner in the investment, sharing in both the risk and the return. Under this interpretation, the government gets a rate of return on its investment (the tax revenue deferred by allowing expensing rather than deductions for economic depreciation) equal to the difference between the actual return and the normal rate of return. That is, the government gets no revenue in present value terms on a marginal investment but earns a share of any inframarginal returns on the investment in the form of an increase in the present value of future tax revenues. This interpretation implies that both marginal and inframarginal returns to the business share of the investment are untaxed, while the government share of the investment results in higher revenues in present value terms only to the extent that inframarginal returns are earned.

Since these results are not intuitively obvious, they are illustrated with some simple two-period examples of the treatment of investment under income-based and consumption-based business taxes. The examples are highly stylized; nevertheless, they illustrate all of the essential differences between the two alternative tax treatments. This analysis considers only the tax burden at the business level.

In the model, a firm purchases an asset on the last day of Year 1 for $1,000. The asset lasts exactly one year and has no salvage value. The internal rate of return on the asset is assumed to be 10 percent; thus, the asset generates gross receipts of $1,100 in Year 2.[4] The internal rate of return is also the discount rate used by the firm to calculate present values of future cash flows; thus, the investment is a marginal one (as defined above).

This two-period model obviously includes monetary values in both years. Accordingly, in order to compare these monetary values, they must be converted into present values of one of the years. The standard approach is to convert all monetary values into present values in Year 1. However, in the examples to be analyzed, all returns and deductions except the deduction for expensing occur in Year 2. As a result, it is much more convenient to measure all monetary quantities in present values of Year 2; this approach is followed throughout the analysis. Of course, an analysis in Year 1 present values would yield identical qualitative results; all Year 2 present values would simply be divided by one plus the interest rate.

The marginal tax rate faced by the firm is assumed to be 30 percent. The firm is assumed to have other sources of income that may be offset by the deductions generated by the investment; alternatively, it could be assumed that losses may be carried forward indefinitely with interest. Expensing under the consumption tax alternative results in a Year 1 deduction of $1,000, which has a Year 2 value of $1,100. Economic depreciation allowances under the income tax alternative result in a Year 2 deduction of $1,000.

The results for the income-based and consumption-based taxes are as follows. For the income tax, gross receipts in Year 2 of $1,100 less a deduction of $1,000 for economic depreciation result in taxable income of $100. Taxable income thus equals economic income, which is equal to the internal rate of return of 10 percent times the investment of $1,000. The tax paid in Year 2 is $30. Thus, the effective tax rate, defined as the tax paid divided by economic income, is equal to the statutory income tax rate of 30 percent (0.30 = 30/100).

The results are quite different in the consumption tax case where expensing is allowed. The Year 2 value of expensing ($1,100) equals the value of gross receipts. Thus, the present value of the business tax base under the consumption tax is zero, which in turn implies a zero marginal effective tax rate.

This simple example also illustrates another significant difference between an income-based and a consumption-based business tax. In the year of the investment, expensing unambiguously reduces the firm's tax burden by an amount equal to the product of the tax rate and the amount of purchase. However, the firm's tax burden in subsequent years is uncertain at the time of the investment, since it depends on the gross receipts generated by the investment. As a result, the government shares in the risk and in the return of the investment. As noted above, the government effectively becomes a silent partner in the investment.

To see this, note that expensing has a revenue cost to the government of $300 in Year 1 since the firm's taxes are reduced by that amount; this is the amount of the government's share of the investment. In Year 2, the government receives $330 in tax revenue. This tax revenue is in fact simply a return on the government's share of the investment purchased through the reduction in the firm's taxes in Year 1. On a marginal investment such as the one analyzed, the present value of taxes on gross receipts generated by the investment exactly equals the present value of the forgone revenue; that is, the government's share of the investment earns the same 10 percent return earned by the investor. Thus, it is easy to reconcile the paradox between a zero effective tax rate on the income from a marginal investment and the fact that the government collects tax revenue from the returns to the investment; the tax revenue received in Year 2 is exactly equal in present value terms to the tax revenue forgone in Year 1.

Of course, this interpretation of the effects of expensing implies that the investor's share in the investment is reduced by the amount of the government's share. That is, the tax reduction in Year 1 implies that the taxpayer effectively invests only $700 rather than the full $1,000. Since the after-tax return in Year 2 is $770, the investor realizes the full 10 percent rate of return on his original investment.

Note that the government does not play such a risk-sharing role under the income tax approach. In each year, a deduction is allowed only for the actual economic depreciation of the asset. Thus, although the government shares in the return to the investment, it provides none of the finance; this is in contrast to the expensing case, where the government effectively finances a share of the investment equal to the product of the tax rate and the "excess deduction," or the difference between expensing and economic depreciation.

Thus far, the analysis has considered the differences between income-based and consumption-based taxation only for a marginal investment. Suppose instead that the gross return on the investment is 20 percent rather than 10 percent, while the opportunity cost of funds remains at 10 percent. That is, the investment is an inframarginal one, where the return consists of a 10 percent normal rate of return and an additional 10 percent above-normal return. In the above example, this implies gross receipts of $1200. Under the income tax, gross receipts less economic depreciation yield taxable and economic income of $200 in Year 2, implying taxes of $60. The effective tax rate is again equal to the statutory rate of 30 percent (0.30 = 60/200).

Under the consumption-based approach with expensing, gross receipts of $1,200 result in taxes of $360 in Year 2. The present value in Year 2 of the $300 tax reduction due to expensing of the investment in Year 1 is $330. Thus, the government collects $30 (360 − 330) of net revenue in present value terms. The effective tax rate on the investment can be viewed in three ways. First, the average effective tax rate, again defined as the net tax paid divided by total economic income, is 15 percent (0.15 = 30/200). Alternatively, a second interpretation is that the business tax can be viewed as assessing no tax in present value terms on marginal returns and assessing tax at the statutory rate on the inframarginal or above-normal returns; that is, the tax rate on the inframarginal return of $100 is 30 percent (0.30 = 30/100). Under this interpretation, the marginal effective tax rate on the normal returns to the investment is still zero, as in the case of the marginal investment with the 10 percent return.

However, a third interpretation, which uses the government risk-sharing analogy described above, provides the most instructive way to view the results when inframarginal returns are earned. Recall that under this interpretation the investor's share of the $1,000 investment is $700, with the government providing the remaining $300 in the form of a tax reduction in Year 1. The investor receives $840 in Year 2 ($1200 in gross receipts less $360 in taxes). This implies that the investor gets the full 20 percent return on his $700 investment (840 = 700 × 1.2). At the same time, the government, which receives $30 of net revenue in present value terms, earns only the inframarginal returns on its investment of $300 (30 = 300 × 0.1). Alternatively, the government does not merely receive the value of its original investment which is worth $330 in Year 2; it earns an additional $30 so that its net revenue increases by the amount of the inframarginal return.

Thus, under the government risk-sharing interpretation of the effects of a consumption-based business tax, private returns to investment are exempt from tax on inframarginal as well as marginal investments. The government receives positive net revenue in present value terms only if inframarginal returns are earned; the net revenue obtained equals the amount of the inframarginal returns on the government's share of the investment.

These simple examples demonstrate the sense in which a business tax that allows expensing of depreciable assets is a consumption-based tax. Specifically, such a tax imposes no tax burden in present value terms on either marginal or inframarginal returns on the individual's share of an investment. Thus, capital income is effectively exempt from tax. This is in marked contrast to an income tax which allows deductions only for economic depreciation and thus taxes the return to capital investment at the statutory rate. Government revenue generated by the consumption-based business tax consists of two components. The first is the revenue earned from the taxation of normal returns to investment. This component does not contribute to net revenue in present value terms, such it is equal in present value to the revenue forgone due to the deduction for expensing rather than economic depreciation; this forgone revenue can be viewed as the government's share of the investment. The second component is the revenue earned from the taxation of above-normal or inframarginal returns to the investment. This does represent net positive revenue in present value terms, and is best viewed as the government simply receiving its share of the inframarginal returns generated by the investment which it partially financed.

Finally, note that the present value of government revenue will be positive only if positive inframarginal returns are earned on average. This will normally be the case if private investors are risk averse, as is assumed here. However, note that with sufficiently poor private investments, the government could lose revenue in present value terms under a consumption-based business tax.

THE TREATMENT OF DEBT AND INTEREST

The second major difference between an income-based and a consumption-based business tax is in the treatment of debt and interest. Under an income tax, interest payments are treated as a cost of obtaining income and are therefore deductible. Symmetrically, interest receipts are a form of income and are included in the tax base.

Consistent application of these income tax rules to a partially debt-financed investment yields results which are analogous to those in the case in which the investment is fully equity financed. Consider the first example above (with gross receipts of $1,100) when the investment is 80 percent debt-financed and the interest rate is 10 percent. Gross receipts are still $1,100 in Year 2. However, the firm receives deductions in Year 2 for both economic depreciation ($1,000) and interest expense ($80). The taxable income of the firm ($20) is again equal to economic income, and the resulting tax burden is $6.

The result is that, under the income tax, the effective tax rate on the equity investment of the firm is again equal to the statutory rate of 30 percent. To see this, recall that the project is 80 percent debt-financed; thus, the firm's equity in the project is only $200. Accordingly, the after-tax return to the equity investment is 7 percent ($0.07 = 14/200$), and the effective tax rate on the equity investment is 30 percent ($0.30 = 6/20$). Recall, however, that this analysis considers only taxes at the firm level in calculating the effective tax rates in this section; the analysis thus neglects any additional individual taxes paid on interest income, dividends received, and capital gains.

Consider next the treatment of debt under a consumption-based business tax.

Two alternative methods of treating principal and interest on loans are consistent with the consumption approach. Under both methods, results analogous to those in the case of a fully equity-financed investment are obtained.

The simplest method of treating debt under a consumption-based business tax is to ignore altogether interest payments and receipts, as well as loan proceeds and repayments. Thus interest expense is not deductible, interest income is not taxed, and borrowing and lending (and repayment of debt) have no tax consequences. This method obviously has no effect on the calculations of effective tax rates presented above.

Such treatment of debt is consistent with the consumption tax treatment of investment in depreciable assets in the following sense. Recall that the effective tax rate on the income attributable to the share of an investment financed by a business is zero on both marginal and inframarginal investments under the consumption-based business tax. As noted above, this government risk sharing interpretation of expensing implies that such treatment is equivalent in present value terms to exempting capital income from tax. Accordingly, simply exempting interest income from tax is consistent with allowing expensing of depreciable assets. In addition, tax exemption of interest income implies that no deduction should be allowed for interest expense. Without such treatment, negative marginal effective tax rates at the firm level would result.

Note that under such treatment of debt, financial institutions (and other businesses to the extent they lend money) are obviously untaxed since borrowing and lending transactions have no tax consequences. The above analysis indicates that such treatment effectively is also accorded to nonfinancial businesses on a present value basis, since they are allowed to expense their investments in depreciable assets. In both cases, marginal and inframarginal returns to investment are effectively exempt from tax; thus, exempting interest income from taxation and disallowing all interest deductions does not result in a tax distortion favoring financial institutions. Whether perception problems are worse than for nonfinancial sectors depends on the degree that firms in the nonfinancial sector are able to avoid paying any tax or "zero out." This, in turn, depends on the rate of growth of investment, compared to the rate of return, and the prevalence of inframarginal returns in the nonfinancial sector.

The alternative treatment of debt under a consumption-based business tax is to include the proceeds of loans in the tax base, but to allow a deduction for both interest and the repayment of principal. Such treatment clearly has a zero net effect in present value terms on the business tax base; it is thus equivalent to the first consumption-based approach described above. In terms of the two-period example, $800 would be included in the business tax base in Year 1, but a deduction of $880 (principal plus interest) would be allowed in Year 2. These quantities are equal in present value terms, and thus have no net effect on the present value of tax burdens.

To summarize, the treatment of debt differs dramatically under the income-based and consumption-based business taxes. However, allowing debt finance has no effect on the results presented in the previous subsection, provided that debt is treated correctly. Under the income tax, capital income is still fully taxed. Under a consumption tax, the effective tax rate on the income attributable to the share of an investment financed by a business is zero on both marginal and inframarginal investments under the consumption-based business tax. The latter result holds for both of the two alternative methods of treating debt available under the consumption-based business tax.

THE CASE FOR TAXING BUSINESSES

The first and most obvious business tax issue is whether such a tax should even be included in a tax system which is based on the taxation of consumption. Some consumption tax proponents argue that a business tax is unnecessary and inappropriate in a consumption tax framework, since only individuals consume. According to this view, tax burdens should be solely a function of personal consumption levels; the only role for a business tax would be that of a withholding device.

This position has some theoretical merit. Nevertheless, a business tax that includes receipts and allows deductions on a cash flow basis, including expensing of purchases of depreciable assets, is generally consistent with consumption tax principles. Such a consumption-based business tax provides an important and desirable complement to a consumption-based individual tax, for five reasons.

One important justification for including a business tax within a consumption tax framework is that any reform which provided for complete elimination of business taxation would very likely be viewed as grossly unfair Complete elimination of the taxation of businesses would be seen as an unjustifiable give-away to the rich and powerful and would probably encounter determined political opposition. Of course, similar concerns are likely to be expressed regarding a consumption-based business tax, since the effective tax rate on the income attributable to the private share of business investment is zero under such a tax. Nevertheless, even if such a tax would represent a reduction in the effective tax burden on business, it would appear to be potentially much less controversial than complete elimination of a business-level tax. Due to the elimination of deductions for interest expense, the business tax base may actually be larger than it is under the current income tax.

Second, the business tax provides a potentially important means of preventing tax avoidance involving the purchase of personal consumption items disguised as tax deductible business expenditures. Such tax avoidance techniques are common under both income and consumption taxes; however, they would be more troublesome or offensive under the latter tax, since personal consumption expenditures are a larger share of the tax base under a consumption tax than under an income tax. Such abuses would be eliminated under the consumption tax to the extent deductions for personal expenditures were denied under the business tax. Of course, it is exceedingly difficult to devise workable rules that distinguish between business and personal use in an economically appropriate and administratively enforceable manner under either income- or consumption-based taxes. Nevertheless, the business tax provides an important vehicle for reducing opportunities for this form of abuse. In addition, employer-provided fringe benefits that are not taxable to the employee can be viewed as another form of the same sort of abuse. Full or partial denial of deductions for such fringe benefits under the business tax is a way to limit this form of tax avoidance.

Third, under a consumption-based business tax, the government will collect revenue that is positive in present value terms on inframarginal investments. This revenue source is potentially important, since it would not be surprising to observe above-normal returns in the petroleum and other natural resource industries as well as other industries which are characterized by some degree of monopoly power. Also, note that a consumption-based business tax is likely to be a fairly efficient source of revenue. This is true both because revenues represent only the government's share of inframarginal and not marginal returns, and because it reduces distortions by allowing lower rates on personal consumption.

Fourth, a consumption-based business tax provides a means of taxing foreign investors—an objective that presumably is generally accepted.

Finally, a business tax is desirable at least as a transitional device during the switch from income to consumption taxation. Individuals making investments prior to the enactment of a consumption tax would have expected the returns to those investments to be subject to tax. If the business tax were simply eliminated, such investors would receive an arbitrary windfall gain. Thus, the business tax provides a means of assessing tax on the returns to capital existing at the time of enactment; the magnitude of this tax, relative to that expected under the income tax regime, would depend on the transition rules applied to capital extant at the time of enactment of reform.

The above discussion represents a compelling argument for including a business tax in any consumption tax framework.

NOTES

1. An alternative treatment of debt and interest under a consumption tax provides for inclusion of the proceeds of the loan in the tax base coupled with full deductibility of principal repayments and interest expense; as will be shown below, such treatment is roughly equivalent in present value terms to the treatment described in the text.

2. The treatment of equity contributions is identical under the consumption-based and income-based taxes. The treatment of dividends at the firm level is similar to that in most countries, as firms do not receive a deduction for dividends paid.

3. This terminology follows from the notion that firms undertake investment projects in decreasing order of expected returns, and continue investing until the expected return to an investment is equal to the opportunity cost of funds. The final investment that is just profitable is the marginal one.

4. Note that all returns are assumed to be real. Inflation is a separate issue, which is ignored in the analysis below.

23

How to Tax Mineral Extraction

Many developing countries face a special and important tax problem: how can they get the most tax revenue out of the large multinational enterprises involved in the natural resource industries without, so to speak, killing the goose that lays the golden eggs? This problem is important simply because of the importance of such revenues in many developing countries (see chapter 1). It is complex both because of the special characteristics of nonrenewable resources (Gaffney, 1967; Scott, 1973) and the international nature and size of the firms engaged in their exploitation. In view of these special factors, many countries prefer to deal with such matters outside the framework of the regular tax code via special "mining codes" or special concession agreements. Whether mineral extraction is brought within the general tax code or treated separately, however, similar questions arise.

It is not possible here to do more than introduce a few of the salient aspects of taxing mineral extraction; for fuller discussions, see Gillis and Beals (1980), Due (1970), Gillis et al. (1978), and Gillis (1982). In recent years there has been an especially large explosion of literature on the "resource rent tax," essentially a variant of the cash flow business tax described in chapter 22: see Garnaut and Clunies-Ross (1983), Palmer (1980), and Nellor (1984). The following selection compares this approach to mineral taxation with four other ways in which government can collect revenue from mineral companies.

Two points in Jenkins's generally critical appraisal of an early version of the resource rent tax deserve to be singled out. In the first place, note again the importance of the interaction of tax systems in different countries in determining the effects (and effectiveness) of a particular tax regime in a particular country (see also chapter 20). Jenkins lays special stress on the great difficulty administrators would have enforcing such a tax in the international setting. It is precisely problems such as these that have led some in recent years to explore alternative means of apportioning between countries the taxes levied on international businesses (Oldman and Brooks, 1987).

Secondly, as Jenkins notes, the fact that the resource rent scheme in essence allows the full recapture of any initial investment by the investor before any taxes are collected makes such proposals politically vulnerable. Nellor has developed this idea more systematically and shown that, when the political dimension is taken into account, both companies and countries may in the long run find that a royalty scheme is more beneficial, despite its well-recognized distortionary effects (Nellor, 1984). To paraphrase Hamlet, there are more things in heaven and earth than are dreamt of in the technical efficiency analysis of economics!

Alternative Systems of Taxing Mineral Industries

Glenn P. Jenkins

In their pursuit of revenue from mineral enterprises, governments have resorted to a wide variety of taxes and levies. They can be organized into four broad categories: fixed charges such as rents, fees, and license charges; royalties and other payments levied on the amount or value of the mineral extracted; taxes levied on the income earned by the enterprise, personal or corporate income taxes, withholding tax, or any other type of income tax such as an excess profits tax; direct equity participation by the government in the mineral corporation.

Before discussing the specific proposal of the resource rent tax (RRT), I wish to point out the advantages and disadvantages inherent in the four broad procedures of revenue collection outlined above. In this way, we will have a better understanding of the attractions and pitfalls inherent in the specific scheme for mineral taxation that has been outlined by Garnaut and Clunies-Ross (1977).

RENTS, FEES, AND LICENSE CHARGES

These charges are usually levied as part of the payment to obtain the right to the use of mineral lands, to carry out exploration, or to operate an enterprise within a jurisdiction. The obvious advantage of these forms of raising government revenue is the administrative ease of their collection. As they are usually a fixed charge per period, then, if they are not so large as to prevent the opening of a mineral body for production, they will not alter the marginal variable costs of production and thus not distort the production decision of the mineral enterprise. When combined with a royalty on production to generate a target amount of government revenue, the existence of the fixed fees or rentals per period will enable a lower royalty rate to be set, hence lowering the distorting influence of the royalty on operating decisions.

The disadvantage of such fixed charges is that they are seldom related to the quality of the mineral deposit; therefore, they may distort the decision to begin or not to begin production. Also, since they do not vary with the annual profitability of the project, they will increase the risk of the project, where risk is measured by the variance of the annual returns. Because of these features, fixed charges generally will not be effective instruments for the collection of a large proportion of the economic rents that may exist in the mineral sector. Nevertheless, rental and

Excerpted from Jenkins (1977).

license fees have constituted approximately 25 percent of the total government revenues from oil production in the province of Alberta, Canada. In this case, these fixed charges have been combined with a scheme of bonus bidding for the sale of mineral rights and a royalty that has been approximately 16 percent of production.

ROYALTIES

Royalties are usually levied as a fixed percentage of the gross value or physical amount of mineral production. In certain situations, such as in the Middle East oil producing countries, while de facto royalties are collected, they are called income taxes because they are applied to a previously fixed amount of profits per barrel. In this discussion, any tax levied or negotiated as a fixed amount per unit of output prior to production is treated as a royalty. The principal advantage of a royalty as a form of taxation is the ease with which it can be collected. When a government is attempting to levy an income tax on the profits of a corporation, it may have great difficulty determining the true amount of profits from the investment. The widespread use of transfer prices between affiliates of integrated multinational corporations, along with the absence of reliable auditing procedures of financial statements in many countries, prohibits the use of genuine corporation income or excess profits taxes. On the other hand, the amount of output from the operation can ordinarily be easily identified; thus the government can readily measure the base on which the royalty is to be levied.

The principal drawback of a flat-rate royalty on the production of a mineral is that it is levied on costs as well as economic profits. Such a tax will often lead to bypassing high-cost ores in the production from a mineral body that would have been utilized in the absence of the tax. Thus an economic loss is inflicted.

The high-grading effect of a fixed-rate royalty can be somewhat overcome by using a variable royalty rate which will move inversely with the costs of production from a mineral body. This is especially important in the case of a mining operation where the quality of the ore may vary greatly within a given mine. While a substantial royalty may be appropriate for the high-grade ores, it would cause production from some lower-grade deposits to be unprofitable, consequently these lower-grade ores would be wasted. In this case, multiple royalties would be required in order to have economic efficiency even for the production from a single mineral body.

A system of variable royalties requires much of the same information as that needed for an effective business income tax. As in the case of the business income tax, estimates are needed for the costs and revenues for each property before a calculation can be made of the available economic rent to be captured by the royalty.

INCOME TAXATION

When the accounts of a mineral enterprise accurately reflect the private costs and revenues of its operation, then a tax levied on the firm's net income has a number of advantages over other forms of taxation. A tax based on income or profits will avoid the problem of having to estimate the costs of extraction and the price of the output before the period of production, as would be necessary if a variable royalty were levied. The income tax also eliminates the problem of high grading, since there will always be an incentive (when the firm is operating competitively) to use the poorer grades of ore up to the point where the marginal cost of production equals the price of output.

When a mineral body is being developed by a corporation which is a foreign affiliate of a multinational corporation, the tax policies of the country of the parent corporation will be an important factor in determining the attractiveness of the income tax on mineral production in the foreign country. For example, affiliates of U.S. parent corporations are allowed to use income taxes paid to foreign countries as tax credits against the U.S. tax liabilities due on this foreign-earned income (Jenkins, 1975).

By being able to credit foreign taxes against the home country's income taxes, a multinational corporation can pay income taxes to foreign countries up to the level of home country income taxes due on this income without increasing the total worldwide tax burden of the multinational corporation.

The home countries of most multinational mineral corporations have allowed a wide range of taxes to be used as creditable foreign income taxes. In the case of U.S. oil companies operating in the Middle East, the taxes paid to these countries are allowed as foreign tax credits to offset the U.S. income tax liability on the foreign income, even though the foreign taxes are calculated on artificially constructed "incomes" having little or no relationship to the true profitability of the foreign affiliates. For the international petroleum industry, it can be shown that in most foreign producing countries, while the average tax rate on income from crude oil production is substantial, the marginal tax rate is zero. This occurs because the income taxes in these countries are calculated as an amount per barrel of crude oil produced, not on the amount of true economic profits generated by the production. Therefore, these petroleum companies have had an incentive—one which they have acted upon—to transfer taxable income from their downstream activities located in the consuming countries to the producing countries. In this way they can decrease income taxes paid to consuming countries such as Canada, Europe, and Japan, where the income tax varies with recorded profits, and yet not increase taxes paid to the producing countries (Jenkins and Wright, 1975).

This transfer of income between affiliates is facilitated by the integrated nature of mining and petroleum corporations. The vertical integration of activities often extends from primary production through the transportation sector to the final sale of the product. This leads to a situation where there is an absence of market prices for many of the products traded between affiliates; hence, shifting taxable income between countries by transfer pricing is easy to execute.

For a country to stop these transfers of taxable income, it must estimate the correct values of the costs and revenues for each firm. The problems that tax authorities would have in constantly monitoring and correcting the accounting data for a set of mining and petroleum corporations are difficult to exaggerate. Before a government embarks on a policy of taxing the mineral industries by a tightly controlled income tax system, it should compare the economic loss that is created by the administrative costs of enforcing such a scheme with the economic ineffi-ciency of other methods of mineral taxation.

EQUITY PARTICIPATION BY GOVERNMENTS IN MINERAL ENTERPRISES

In recent years, governments of mineral producing areas have tended to insist upon owning a part of the equity of the mining or petroleum enterprises operating within their jurisdiction. In some cases, governments have obtained a share of the equity of firms for amounts less than the normal market prices of the stocks. We can view the profits which accrue to the government's shares obtained in this manner partly as a profits tax on the income generated by the private sector's investments.

Some governments see equity participation as a way, on the one hand, to monitor the activities of the mineral enterprise to ensure that citizens receive training in the operation of the firm and, on the other, to collect revenue from the mineral production. While this approach may be very advantageous for a country planning to take over the operations of the firm eventually, there are some serious drawbacks inherent in minority equity participation agreements.

Unless there is a very close surveillance of the prices used in the accounting of interaffiliate transactions, the minority shareholder (here the government) may find itself receiving less than its share of the total income generated by the enter-prise. The Middle East countries with participation agreements for petroleum production reduced the incentive for the international petroleum companies to transfer income out of their ventures by contracting for their portion of the "prof-its" of the activity in terms of a fraction of the barrels of oil produced, rather than a percentage of accounting profits.

Although equity participation has sometimes been considered a way in which a government can effectively control foreign-operated enterprises, it can easily become just another expensive way to collect an income tax.

RESOURCE RENT TAX

The tax system proposed by Garnaut and Clunies-Ross is essentially an income tax (applied to the mineral extraction sector) with a zero rate up to the point where a threshold rate of return is being earned on the investment and a very high marginal tax rate on income in excess of this threshold rate. As a tax based on accounting profits, it has all the advantages as well as the drawbacks of the income tax discussed previously. However, this tax would provide a much larger incentive for corporations to shift income into tax haven countries or engage in wasteful practices than would an ordinary corporation income tax designed to collect the same amount of revenue.

To illustrate, assume that a mining corporation with 100 percent equity is earning a gross of tax rate of return on its investment of 20 percent and is paying a corporation income tax of 40 percent. In this situation, the corporation earns a net of tax rate of return of 12 percent and pays corporation income taxes each year equal to 8 percent of the value of the investment. Now let us assume that the threshold rate of return allowed by the RRT (resource rent tax) is 10 percent and the government again wishes to collect an amount of revenue equal to 8 percent of the value of the investment. To do this, it will have to set a marginal income tax rate equal to 80 percent on the RRT base in order to collect the same amount of tax revenue as with the ordinary corporation income tax of 40 percent. In this example, the incentive to avoid taxation by transferring taxable income out of the country has doubled. Alternatively, the management of the corporation may find it worthwhile to decrease profits by superfluous business expenses which they enjoy as a substitute for earning profits, since now the government will bear 80 percent of these additional expenses through reduced tax revenues.

While this tax system attempts to allow for a normal rate of return on investment and then to tax only the excess profits, there are serious difficulties in determining what is the relevant investment base on which to apply the threshold rate of return. To enable a mineral enterprise to survive through time, it must either engage in exploration and development expenditures or purchase proven ore bodies or reserves. If it does its own exploration and development work, then for every successful mine there will also be many failures. Garnaut and Clunies-Ross would not allow these expenses to be included in the investment base of an operating mine, but instead, suggest raising the threshold rate of return of all successful mines. Increasing the threshold rate of return for the mineral extraction sector does not change the basic problem: if mining companies engage in unsuccessful exploration activities the government does not share in these expenses, while at the same time it may be taxing the existing operating mines on their "excess" profits.

The reaction of a mining industry to this set of tax incentives will likely be to divide its operations into two parts: an exploration and development sector and a mineral extraction sector. If the exploration and development sector is taxed under a normal corporation income taxation system, it will expense or depreciate its costs and sell its proven properties to the mineral extraction branch. The fair market price of these properties will already have capitalized into them any of the economic rents that exist. Thus, the exploration and development sector will be taxed on its profits including the economic rents by a corporate income or capital gains tax system, while the mineral extraction sector will be taxed by the RRT. The government's problem of taxing economic rents in the mineral extraction industry will now be solved, because no economic rents will exist there to be taxed under the RRT system.

The difficulty of determining what is the relevant investment base on which to calculate the threshold rate of return is aggravated by the existence of working capital. While Garnaut and Clunies-Ross say that they would not allow "idle funds" as part of the investment base, nevertheless any mine operating as a going concern must have a significant amount of working capital which may, at various times, include securities as well as cash and inventories. Depending on the invest-ment plans and payments structure of the firm, these different kinds of working capital are unlikely to remain in a constant proportion to the fixed capital stock.

A novel feature of the RRT, as designed by Garnaut and Clunies-Ross, is that it would allow for a complete recapture of the present value of the invested capital of the firm before the government would begin receiving any tax revenues. In most cases, this would entail a wait of five years or longer before any tax revenues are collected. Few governments could politically afford to give what would appear to be a tax holiday for such a period of time.

Any tax system applied to the mineral industries will only be as efficient in its capture of economic rents and in avoiding the creation of economic distortions as the quality of information available to the tax authorities allows it to be. The same type of information is required to successfully implement the RRT as is needed for most income tax or variable royalty systems. While the RRT is an interesting attempt to construct a tax system which has a minimum influence on the risk of a mineral extraction project, the economic distortions that it would create with its very high marginal income tax rates and administrative complexity make it an undesirable way of taxing the mineral industries in most situations.

24

Putting a Floor under Direct Taxes

No matter how well designed the tax system in a developing country, direct taxes will always be difficult to administer fairly and effectively, especially with respect to taxpayers other than large, well-organized enterprises and their employees. The next two chapters explore two methods by which direct taxation might be made more effective in developing countries.

Chapter 24 draws upon Colombia's extensive experience with a "presumptive" minimum tax system to argue that information on net wealth, difficult although it may be to obtain, may play a vital role in enforcing an income (or consumption) tax—just as chapter 21 showed to be the case when it comes to adjusting income taxes to inflation. Moreover, as Colombian experience also suggests, a good case can be made for imposing a tax on net wealth in developing countries in any case (Tanabe, 1967). Even when such taxes are poorly enforced, their contribution to the equity of the tax system as a whole may be substantial (see, for one instance, Musgrave, 1981, on Bolivia). In addition, as the literature on land taxes discussed in Part 6 suggests, to some extent wealth taxes may also have some beneficial efficiency effects—certainly if compared to income taxes paid by the same people.

For these reasons, although at the present time proposals for increased or strengthened wealth taxes seem as unlikely to receive a favorable hearing in developing countries as they are in most developed countries (OECD, 1988), we think that the merits of taxes on net wealth (as well as gifts and bequests) as part of a tax system have been substantially underrated (for further discussion, see Tait, 1967). Moreover, while we are hardly the ones to downplay administrative problems—indeed, a central theme of this book is precisely the importance of the administrative dimension of taxation in developing countries—the difficulty of doing something useful along these lines appears to have been substantially overrated. No doubt it is impossible to apply a full-fledged tax on net wealth in any developing country: but even a partial tax confined largely to real property (as in Colombia) seems, from most relevant points of view, to be a lot better than nothing.

Net Wealth and Presumptive Taxation in Colombia

Charles E. McLure, Jr., and others

The major problem in the administration of direct taxes in developing countries is the underreporting of income. Although Colombia has as many difficulties in this respect as most developing countries, over the years it has nonetheless managed to maintain the relative importance and to some extent the progressivity of its system of income and complementary taxes largely through the net wealth tax and the concept of presumptive income.

PRESUMPTIVE INCOME TAX

Quite apart from the inherent merits of net wealth as a tax base (discussed below), net wealth plays an important role in the Colombian tax system as the principal basis for the calculation of the minimum income tax base known as presumptive income. The taxable income of all taxpayers, individuals and companies alike, is the greater of 8 percent of net wealth at the end of the previous year, 2 percent of gross receipts (excluding occasional gains) for the current taxable year, or the amount of taxable income reported.[1] The inclusion of limited liability companies in the scope of these provisions in 1983, rectifying a change made a few years earlier, substantially strengthened the importance of the presumptive income tax.

The importance of these "minimum tax" provisions is suggested by the fact that in 1984 one-third of all companies were taxed on a presumptive basis, with the proportion being as high as 43 percent in the financial sector and 39 percent in the agricultural sector. Slightly less than 13 percent of company taxes were assessed on this basis in that year. Two-thirds of those assessed on the presumptive basis were taxed on the basis of net wealth and the remainder on gross receipts, with the former basis being most important in the agricultural and financial sectors and the latter in the manufacturing and commerce sectors. The presumption based on gross receipts was introduced in 1983 largely in the belief that firms in these latter sectors were substantially underreporting inventories and hence net wealth.[2] Although comparable figures are not available for individual taxpayers, studies for earlier years suggest that perhaps as much as 30 percent of all income taxes are based on presumptive assessments, particularly those based on net wealth (Perry and

Excerpted from McLure et al. (1988).

Cardenas, 1986). Even these figures may substantially understate the importance of the presumptive provisions if, as has been suggested, many taxpayers deliberately report ordinary income a little larger than that which would otherwise be presumed in order to reduce the likelihood of being investigated.

The current presumptive income tax originated in 1974, following several earlier, and not particularly successful, attempts to apply such minimum taxes in the agricultural sector, where it was felt that the underreporting of taxable income was particularly chronic and widespread. It is thus rather ironic that a number of specific provisions favoring agriculture, and in particular the cattle industry, have crept back into the law in recent years, notably the outright exclusion from the net wealth basis for calculating presumptive income of 40 percent of the net value of property used for cattle raising and the inclusion of only 75 percent of the value of rural land. Other important exclusions include the value of urban property subject to rent control and (since 1986) stocks and partnership interests in Colombian corporations. Similarly, receipts affected by price controls are excluded for purposes of the presumption based on gross receipts.[3]

Viewed as part of the Colombian income tax system, the presumptive income tax has undoubtedly been a major success in the sense of maintaining a certain minimal degree of integrity in the system and in particular in ensuring that most of the better-off sectors of society contribute to the cost of government at least roughly in proportion to their ability to pay.

Wealth-based Presumptive Income

The rule (hereinafter referred to as the "wealth-based" rule) that the taxpayer's taxable income is presumed to be no less than a specified percentage (currently 8 percent) of the taxpayer's net wealth as of the beginning of the year serves two principal functions. First, the rule makes it more difficult to avoid tax on income from capital. For example, if a taxpayer owns an apartment building and includes the value of the building in net wealth, the taxpayer will obtain benefit from failing to declare rental income, only to the extent that net income from the building exceeds 8 percent of the net declared value of the building. Second, in cases where the rules relating to the timing of the taxation of income from capital fail to tax such income currently, the wealth-based rule effectively imputes such income, thereby making it currently taxable. For example, if the taxpayer holds property that is appreciating in value, but does not sell the property, the realization requirement defers the taxable income until the time of realization, but the wealth-based rule in effect taxes the appreciation currently (to the extent of 8 percent of the net declared value of the property). Both of these functions are of great importance as a back stop to the income tax. The wealth-based rule should be rationalized and strengthened so as to better fulfill these objectives.

As currently applied, the wealth-based rule does not distinguish between the taxpayer's earned and unearned income. This is a serious flaw. There is no reason to expect a close relationship between a taxpayer's *earned* income and his or her prior wealth. The wealth-based rule should rather presume that the taxpayer's *unearned* income is at least equal to a given percentage of the taxpayer's net wealth. Such an assumption is reasonable on an ex ante basis. A given amount of wealth, no matter what form it takes, can be presumed to earn, on average, a given rate of return (assuming that the taxpayer invests the wealth in a rational manner). Accordingly, the taxpayer's earned income should be segregated from unearned income in applying the wealth-based rule.

Thus, in comparing the taxpayer's presumptive income with the taxpayer's income as determined through ordinary methods, earned income should be subtracted from ordinarily determined income. If the presumptive income exceeds the amount of unearned income calculated in this fashion, then the taxpayer's taxable income would be the presumptive income plus the taxpayer's earned income. For example, if the taxpayer's net wealth is $10,000,000, earned income is $1,000,000, and the taxpayer reports no unearned income, then under current law the wealth-based rule would not increase the taxable income beyond the $1,000,000 that is reported; but under the proposal the presumptive income of $800,000 would be compared with the taxpayer's unearned income (0), and so total taxable income would be $1,800,000.

The exclusions for property used in cattle raising and for property in a non-productive period should be eliminated. The exclusions are not justified as a matter of principle, and also serve to complicate administration and perhaps furnish an opportunity for evasion. Cattle raising should not be accorded preferential treatment. Plants and animals that are not currently income-producing are precisely the type of asset that should be included in the taxpayer's wealth in determining presumptive income, in order to deal with the issue of the proper timing of income for tax purposes. Even though such assets do not yet yield a crop, they can be presumed to earn an economic return, in the form of an increase in their value. Thus, a two-year-old coffee tree is worth more than a one-year-old tree, even though it has not yet borne a crop. The same reasoning applies to the exclusion for nonagricultural assets in an nonproductive period, such as real property under construction. Inclusion of assets in a nonproductive period in the calculation of presumptive income can result in taxation of this increase in value, depending on the general relation between the taxpayer's ordinarily determined and presumptive income. Where this increase in value is effectively taxed, because presumptive income exceeds ordinarily determined income, this imputed increase in value could be added to the basis of the property and recovered after the property becomes productive.

Similarly, exclusions for property subject to rent control or development restrictions and real property affected by volcanic activity should be repealed. There is no reason not to expect such properties to yield the same rate of return over the long run as other properties. An event such as the imposition of rent control or a volcanic eruption may diminish the fair market value of property. If the fair market value consequently falls below the value used for net wealth tax purposes, the taxpayer should be allowed to petition for revaluation of the property to its fair market value. Because most property is substantially undervalued, such a petition procedure is not likely to be used frequently and accordingly should be administrable.

If the suggested reforms relating to the taxation of net wealth (see below) and excluded assets (see above) are adopted, the net wealth base will be much closer to fair market value than under current law. On the assumption that presumptive income is only unearned income and that the base for calculating presumptive income is roughly equal to net wealth at current market values, an 8 percent real presumed yield is excessive. Four or 5 percent is more realistic. However, given that transition to the new system will likely not be immediate and that there may be a considerable understatement of net wealth due to fraud and other reasons, a reduction of the presumed rate of return should be made with care, so as not to lose revenue, worsen equity, and unintentionally reduce the role of presumptive income. One possible approach would be to reduce the presumed rate from 8 percent to 5 percent by one percentage point per year, starting in the year in which changes in the presumptive income tax base first become effective.

Receipts-based Presumptive Income

In contrast to the wealth-based rule, which is based on a reasonable assumption of a minimum rate of return on net wealth, the presumption that net income is at least equal to 2 percent of gross receipts does not correspond to economic reality. The receipts-based rule is based on net receipts, which are defined as gross receipts less returns and discounts. Accordingly, the cost of goods sold is included in net receipts. Different firms will have different profit margins on their receipts, even within the same industry, depending on their level of integration. For example, if Firm A manufactures a product at a cost of 90, sells it to Firm B for 100, which further manufactures it at a cost of 90 and sells the finished product for 200, Firm A's profit would be 10 percent of gross receipts, while Firm B's profit would be only 5 percent of gross receipts. If instead Firm B were to complete the entire manufacturing process itself, it would have a profit of 10 percent of gross receipts. Moreover, the amount of profit margin on gross receipts will vary from industry to industry.

One undesirable effect of the receipts-based rule may be to encourage mergers, thereby increasing economic concentration. A taxpayer that is unfairly treated by the rule has an effective avenue of self-help: it can merge with a company with a high ratio of profits to sales (or enter such a line of business without merging with an existing company). By reason of such self-help measures, the revenues from the receipts-based rule are likely to erode over time.

Moreover, the receipts-based rule is difficult to justify as a means of controlling evasion, since by hypothesis it only operates if the taxpayer includes a substantial level of receipts in income. By contrast, the wealth-based rule can catch a taxpayer who reports its wealth but underreports its receipts.

The receipts-based rule may be justified under the current scheme of things to deal with taxpayers who can avoid the wealth-based rule because their net wealth is understated. Such understatement can result from a number of factors, including the failure to adjust asset values for inflation, the use of LIFO (last in, first out), failure to fully capitalize production costs, and the use of accelerated depreciation. The proposed reforms to the net wealth tax (see below), should ameliorate this problem. The receipts-based rule could be retained for a transitional period for this purpose, as the net-wealth base of companies approaches more closely to fair market value.

For the above reasons, it is recommended that the receipts-based rule for determining presumptive income be repealed, but retained for a transition period as the changes to the net wealth base come into effect.

THE CASE FOR A NET WEALTH TAX

A tax on net wealth in essentially its present form has existed in Colombia since 1935, although both its rates and its base have been altered several times since then. The original purpose of this tax was explicitly to impose a heavier tax on income from capital than on income from labor, apparently on the ground that capital income had a greater "ability to pay" than labor income because it constituted a "purer" form of net income (perhaps on the theory that the provision of capital services involves less disutility than working). A net wealth tax, rather than a higher tax rate on capital income, was chosen to accomplish this goal in recognition of the fact that it is generally easier to identify taxable assets than to locate the income to which they give rise.

Additional arguments for the net wealth tax have frequently been made in Colombia. First, in view of the obvious difficulty in any developing country in taxing capital income effectively, it may be argued that a tax on wealth is needed not so much to tax such income more heavily than labor income but in many cases just to tax it at all. Secondly, the possession of wealth, whether it produces taxable income or not, may be thought to imply an ability to pay over and above that shown by any measurable income flow. Wealth can confer power, social acclaim, or peace of mind, quite apart from any income it may generate or any consumption it may finance. By expanding the options for consumption available on the taxpayer, wealth can bestow a further benefit. If wealth gives rise to such extra benefits, a tax on net wealth is needed simply in order to achieve horizontally equitable treatment of taxpayers who are in essentially the same position in terms of their ability to pay. Thirdly, since the concentration of wealth is greater than the concentration of income in every country, even a proportional tax on wealth will increase or at least preserve the progressivity of the fiscal system, a goal generally considered desirable. Fourthly, achieving any given degree of progressivity with the combination of a moderately progressive income tax and a tax on net wealth may create fewer disincentives to saving and investment than would a more steeply progressive income tax. Fifthly, as has often been noted in Colombia with respect to rural land in particular, a tax on wealth may provide a useful stimulus to employ capital more productively in order to generate a flow of funds with which to pay the tax.

Finally, in light of the difficulty of taxing intergenerational wealth transfers as they occur, a net wealth tax may play the role of reducing the inequality of wealth distribution that could otherwise be played by a smoothly functioning transfer tax. Under current law, there are no wealth transfer taxes, but gifts and bequests are taxed as occasional gains of their recipients. The value used for this purpose is not fair market value, but is the value as reported on the donor's previous wealth tax return. The net wealth tax performs a complementary function to the taxation of gifts and bequests as income, since it too reduces the inequality in the distribution of wealth. Some gifts and bequests escape the net of the income tax, as such transfers may simply not be reported or may be undervalued. By contrast, a net wealth tax may be more difficult to avoid or evade, since it needs to be avoided or evaded every year, not only in the year of the transfer.[4] Moreover, since there is no special tax on generation-skipping transfers, the income tax burden on gifts and bequests can also be reduced by making transfers that skip generations. The net wealth tax does not suffer from this problem, since the wealth would be subject to tax regardless of which generation owned it.

On its own, each of the arguments noted above may be vulnerable to attack on various grounds. In combination, however, these arguments provide a compelling case for taxing net wealth in any country, particularly in developing countries such as Colombia in which it is always difficult to bring the full weight of the income tax to bear on some of the most affluent sectors of society. The fact that the net wealth tax accounts for almost one-third of the total income and complementary tax paid by individuals, with most of this revenue almost certainly coming from higher-income individuals, suggests the importance of the tax in the present Colombian fiscal system. Moreover, the continued endurance of the net wealth tax through more than a half-century of huge social, economic, and fiscal changes in Colombia suggests that the rationale for this tax is well accepted.

When coupled with the importance of net wealth as a basis for determining presumptive income, the case for the continued existence and indeed the strengthening of the net wealth tax as a key component of the Colombian tax system thus seems overwhelming.

STRENGTHENING THE NET WEALTH TAX

If all assets were valued at fair market value and there were no taxpayer fraud, debts would not be a cause for concern under the net wealth tax. Net wealth would be properly measured by subtracting debts from assets. The actual net wealth tax is, however, plagued by problems of valuation and fraud. As a result, debts can become an avenue of tax avoidance or evasion. Such avoidance or evasion can occur in two ways: borrowing against appreciated property, and concealment of the proceeds of borrowing.

Consider first the taxpayer who reports all of his or her assets and debts. All of the debts will of course be stated in current pesos. But many of the assets may be valued (either legally or illegally) at less than fair market value. By borrowing against the appreciated value of property, the taxpayer could substantially reduce and in some cases eliminate his or her net wealth for tax purposes. In the case of debt denominated in pesos, accomplishment of this result may require periodic borrowing as the taxpayer's assets appreciate in value. In the case of debts denominated in foreign currency, the taxpayer need not even take out additional debt, since the peso amount of such debts for net wealth tax purposes is adjusted upward each year according to the exchange rate, while the value of the corresponding asset is generally not adjusted to reflect the rise in its fair market value.

The taxpayer who is willing to conceal assets has an even easier time. If there are certain assets that the taxpayer cannot conceal (for example, the taxpayer's residence or a business operated by the taxpayer in Colombia), the taxpayer can simply borrow up to the value of those assets, and conceal assets purchased with the loan proceeds, thereby totally eliminating reported taxable net wealth. (Of course, if total elimination would be regarded as suspicious, the taxpayer may exercise restraint, and refrain from entirely offsetting his or her reported wealth with debt.)

Both types of abuse can be addressed by limiting the debts that are deductible in computing net wealth to those debts the proceeds of which were used to acquire an asset that is listed in the taxpayer's net wealth, and by limiting the deductible amount of such a debt to the taxable value of such asset for net wealth tax purposes.

Restricting deductible debts to those used to acquire an asset would have the effect in some cases of including in the tax base amounts that represent prior purchases of nondurable goods, thereby causing the tax base to exceed the net wealth of some taxpayers. Nevertheless, the advantages of the rule outweigh the potential inequity of any such overtaxation. There would be no such inequity in two types of cases where debt proceeds are used for personal purposes. First, there would be no overtaxation to the extent that loan proceeds are used to purchase consumer durables that are still in existence but are not reported on the taxpayer's return. Second, in the case of debt that was used to purchase nondurable consumption items, to the extent that the debt takes the form of borrowing against appreciation in value of the property that is not included in the net wealth base, the taxpayer has no cause for complaint.

Under a 1986 law, only 60 percent of the assessed value of real property is included in the tax base for purposes of all national taxes, namely the net wealth tax and the presumptive income tax. This provision is especially important because in practice real property is undoubtedly the single most important component of the net wealth tax base. The history of the last few decades in this respect consists of a largely unsuccessful struggle to keep these assessed values from falling too far behind the pace of inflation. Indeed, it was only with the introduction of an automatic inflation adjustment system in 1983 that the real value of assessed property ceased to decline, for the first time in over a decade. This improvement in the local property tax base was, however, achieved at the price of allowing the property tax to be credited against the net wealth tax. The 1986 reduction of this important component of the net wealth tax base marked a considerable step backward in terms of strengthening the scope and effectiveness of both the net wealth and presumptive income taxes.

The value assigned for real property is particularly important in this context because it is almost the only value that can be readily checked by the tax administration. Other elements of the net wealth tax base—both assets and the liabilities set against them—are for the most part in effect self-assessed and difficult to audit. Even with respect to publicly quoted shares, it has been claimed that the market is so thin and closely controlled that prices are commonly depressed at the end of the year in order to keep the net wealth tax base low. The strong suspicion that commercial firms substantially underreported the value of their inventories was the reason for the introduction of the receipts-based presumptive income rule in 1983. The decline in bank balances and other visible evidence of wealth at the end of the year, when their value is supposed to be taken into account for purposes of calculating net wealth, is a well-known phenomenon. Fictitious debts are reportedly widespread, despite the existence of provisions intended to check this practice. All in all, it is difficult to think of any measure that would do more to improve the effectiveness and equity of the net wealth tax than the inclusion of the full assessed value of real property in the base, and the continued adjustment of that value in accordance with inflation. The concession already given in 1983 with respect to the crediting of property taxes against the net wealth tax seems more than adequate to deal with any legitimate concerns with respect to the overtaxation of real property, especially given the very low levels of even adjusted assessed values.

Full inclusion of real property in net wealth is necessary to achieve a rational net wealth tax. This tax can never be satisfactory if some elements of the base are included at fair market value and others are substantially discounted. Moreover, the integrity of wealth-based presumptive income depends on full inclusion of all assets in the base for calculating the presumed rate of return.

NOTES

1. In addition, the tax administration may, if it wishes, treat any increase in net wealth over the course of the year (less any exempt income) as taxable income. Unlike the measure discussed in the text, however, this provision is not applied automatically and, more importantly, is rebuttable by the taxpayer. It appears that in practice this provision is hardly ever used.

2. Such underreporting can be due either to a misstatement as to the quantity of inventory or to undervaluation due to incomplete cost capitalization rules or the use of LIFO (last in, first out).

3. For 1984, the fiscal cost of this last exclusion alone was estimated at 5.2 billion pesos (about 8 percent of total assessed company taxes).

4. Evasion of tax on a transfer takes the form of one-time concealment of the asset transferred, while evasion of the net wealth tax requires concealment not only of the assets, but also of future income from the asset. It is often easier to conceal the existence of the asset for one year than to conceal it and the income it produces indefinitely. Moreover, avoidance of tax on a donative transfer often takes the form of understating the fair market value of the asset. There is often a colorable basis for such understatement, such as reasonable uncertainty as to valuation, minority discounts, blockage discounts, splitting of interests via "estate freezing" transactions, and the like. While peculiar circumstances may facilitate undervaluation at the time of the transfer, these circumstances may not continue forever, and may therefore preclude subsequent undervaluation for net wealth tax purposes. Thus, for example, if the heir subsequently sells the asset, its fair market value will be less subject to dispute.

25

Reaching the Hard-to-Tax

Few tax experts have spent more than a day in a developing country without hearing sad tales of the great difficulty encountered in taxing professionals (doctors, lawyers, etc.), small businessmen, and—of course—the better-off farmers who fall within the (legal) scope of the income tax (Taylor, 1967). As a rule, these people operate largely in a cash economy. They are most unwilling to supply any information about their operations to the tax authorities, and the latter have a hard time in extracting such information—sometimes for political reasons, but sometimes simply because taxpayers in fact do not have records. Moreover, the authorities usually have equally great difficulty in constructing any alternative basis upon which to bring the incomes of such notoriously "hard-to-tax" groups within the ambit of the income tax. The result is that wage earners in developing countries generally feel, and very often are, overtaxed in relation to their self-employed equals.

One reaction to this situation is to develop the sort of "schedular" income tax described, and criticized, in chapter 17. Another is to attempt to balance the undesired generosity to the self-employed by a compensating generosity to the employed, for example, through the creation of a battery of special tax-free allowances such as prevailed in Jamaica before its recent tax reform (Alm and Bahl, 1985). A third approach, which was described in the preceding chapter, is to redress the balance not by lowering taxes on the employed but by raising them on the self-employed (and recipients of capital income) through the imposition of general "minimum taxes." Such taxes have come to play an important role even in such developed countries as the United States and Canada in recent years, and the arguments in their favor seem clearly stronger in most developing countries.

A related but in principle quite different approach to the same end is described in the following excerpt from a report on Bolivia. Basically, this approach consists in developing special "presumptive" techniques for estimating income in different industries. This approach, which has perhaps been most extensively developed in Israel (Lapidoth, 1977) has also been employed to varying extents and with different degrees of success in a wide range of other countries (Bird, 1983; Tanzi and Casanegra, 1987). The following selection sets out the advantages—indeed, almost the necessity—of such an approach in a developing country, and describes in some detail how to go about implementing it. Although the details obviously need to be varied to fit the circumstances, the general method set out here seems worthy of close attention in many countries.

Two additional general comments on the presumptive method espoused here seem essential. First, as mentioned in the introduction to this part it is important to distinguish it clearly from the superficially similar "forfait" system. In both, income is estimated on the basis of more "objective" factors such as wealth or turnover. In the forfait system, however, as it operates in most former French colonies for example, the final determination of tax liability is negotiated between taxpayer and tax official. In contrast, in the presumptive system the task of the tax official—like the property tax assessor in a mass appraisal system—is simply to record the facts on turnover or whatever. The final tax liability is then determined on the basis of industry norms worked out by a completely different (and, supposedly, technically more competent as well as less personally involved) official, or group of officials. In other words, the presumptive method is the direct tax equivalent of the separation of functions between classification and valuation which has been considered by some (e.g., Carson, 1972) to be the foundation of modern customs administration. The system may of course still be beaten by corrupt officials and determined taxpayers; but the scope for maladministration has clearly been reduced.

The second point about presumptive systems is that the resulting tax may be called an "income tax" only as a matter of legal convenience. It is true that the income thus determined (estimated) may be combined with income from other sources and subjected to the usual income tax rates, but the effective incidence of a presumptive tax is nonetheless clearly on the objects on which income is estimated (Morag, 1957). This has both its bad and its good sides. On the one hand, taxes on, say, turnover or number of employees may clearly have undesirable effects—encouraging cascading and discouraging employment, for example. On the other hand, since the rate at which income is estimated with respect to such factors is determined by some industry norm, the marginal rate of taxation on above-average returns is zero. In other words, such taxes, like the taxes on agricultural land long advocated by some (Gandhi, 1966), exert pressure on taxpayers to perform at least up to average standards and provide an incentive for them to do even better. This equivalent of the progressive lump-sum tax of theory (see Tanzi and Casanegra, 1987) is of course subject to the same sorts of problems in practice as its agricultural counterpart (see Bird, 1974, and chapter 35 below). Nonetheless, it is striking to see how—as, indeed, was suggested by Shoup in chapter 3 above—an administrative compromise forced by dire necessity may in some ways come close to what might be considered the ideal form of taxation for developing countries.

Income Taxation of the Hard-to-Tax Groups

Richard A. Musgrave

Tax administrators all over the world have found it difficult to tax small- and medium-sized firms, professionals, and farmers. The need to deal with a large number of individual taxpayers results in heavy administrative costs, which may ultimately be larger than the amounts of revenue actually collected. Moreover, administration is difficult because many of these taxpayers, especially the farmers and the small businesses, find it too burdensome to maintain books of account. Even if such books are kept, the tax officials have little evidence by which to judge their accuracy.

Faced with these problems and constrained by limited resources, tax administrators tend to neglect the hard-to-tax groups and to find it more profitable to devote themselves to a smaller number of large taxpayers. Although this attitude may be justified in practice, equity and potential revenue gains require that a serious attempt be made to tax these groups.

We propose that all taxpayers be divided into the following groups:

1. Very small taxpayers, who should be exempt.
2. Small taxpayers, who should be subject to a *presumptive* tax in lieu of all other income and sales taxes.
3. All other taxpayers, who should be subject to the regular system of filing income tax declarations. Within this category, however, a distinction should be drawn between
   a. the hard-to-tax groups, for which we propose a system of review based on *estimated* income; and
   b. all others, who should be required to prepare proper returns based on adequate bookkeeping and records.

The *presumptive* approach (for group 2 above) is the simplest one and should therefore be applied to a large number of small taxpayers. This approach imputes an income to each of the different categories into which the population of small taxpayers has been divided and then presumes that the income imputed to a particular category applies to all members of the category. The imputed incomes are set at conservative levels so that they will be lower, on the average, than the real incomes.[1] The simplicity of this system is aimed at minimizing administrative costs and simultaneously providing a reasonable minimum amount of revenue. The eventual target, however, is to transfer this group of taxpayers to the estimated income system and then to regular income tax system.

Excerpted from Musgrave (1981).

Under the *estimated* approach, taxpayers (in group 3 above) are required to file returns and to declare their incomes. If, upon review of a taxpayer's declaration and tax payment, the tax official finds that the taxpayer's declared income falls short of the estimated level, then the tax is imposed on an estimated-income basis. Taxpayers are again divided into categories, but not all taxpayers in a particular category pay the same tax. Certain characteristics of each category are applicable to all taxpayers in the category, but in other respects, the particular circumstances of each taxpayer are allowed for in estimating his income. The information generated by this process is highly useful even in the case of enterprises that maintain books, because the tax officers often have very little evidence by which to judge the accuracy of these books.

THE PRESUMPTIVE-INCOME APPROACH TO SMALL TAXPAYERS

The presumptive-income regime is to apply only to those taxpayers who have no more than two employees. The lower limit for the presumptive-income group (that is, the level separating those who are exempt from those who must pay a presumptive tax) is expressed in terms of gross sales. The level at which the tax begins to apply will differ from one category to another, however. This level should be set so that it matches the level at which the individual income tax begins but also so that it assures that the revenue gains will cover the administrative costs. Similar considerations should be taken into account in setting the upper limit, the level of sales at which the presumptive-income approach will cease to apply and the regular income tax system takes effect.

The new tax table should be prepared by dividing the population of small taxpayers according to two criteria, as illustrated in table 25.1. The first division is by type of activity and reflects the fact that the ratio of profits to sales (the margin) varies substantially from one activity to another. The taxpayers in each activity are further classified by their level of sales. Each taxpayer is then required to pay a flat amount of tax (determined by applying the appropriate margin to the average sales in the bracket), which is shown in the table. This tax amount is set so as to approximate the liability that would result if the regular personal income tax, enterprise tax, and sales tax rates were applied. The taxpayer should also be required to keep minimal books of account; this requirement will facilitate his subsequent transition to a superior form of assessment. A short return should be filed because it is essential to obtaining the information required for a proper classification of the taxpayer.

Although the classification of taxpayers by type of activity presents no great difficulty and the typical profit margins can be estimated, the major difficulty with this approach lies in the classification of taxpayers by sales level. A declaration of sales should be required in the short return, but the reported level will hardly be reliable; thus, further procedures for classification by sales level must be developed. For this purpose, rough physical indicators that are more or less similar to those used in the preparation of estimated income levels (see below) should be

Table 25.1 Amounts of Presumptive Tax Payable by Small Taxpayers

Type of Business	Gross Sales										
	Below 75,000	75,000–100,000	100,000–120,000	120,000–160,000	160,000–200,000	200,000–250,000	250,000–300,000	300,000–350,000	350,000–400,000	400,000–500,000	500,000 and over
Commerce in foods and beverages	0	0	0	0	0	0	0	0	1,200	1,600	R.S.
Commerce in clothing, shoes, and textiles	0	0	1,200	1,800	2,400	3,600	R.S.	R.S.	R.S.	R.S.	R.S.
Commerce in electrical appliances, furniture, and other durables	0	0	0	0	0	1,200	1,800	2,800	3,000	3,600	R.S.
Jewelers; souvenir, watch, and optical stores	0	1,200	2,400	3,600	R.S.	R.S.	R.S.	R.S.	R.S.	R.S.	R.S.
Pharmacies, commerce in cosmetics, and the like	0	0	1,200	2,400	3,600	R.S.	R.S.	R.S.	R.S.	R.S.	R.S.
Restaurants and confectioneries	0	1,200	1,500	1,800	2,400	3,000	3,600	R.S.	R.S.	R.S.	R.S.
Barbershops, beauty shops, and repairmen	0	2,500	3,600	R.S.	R.S.	R.S.	R.S.	R.S.	R.S.	R.S.	R.S.
Artisans and construction subcontractors	0	0	1,200	2,400	3,600	R.S.	R.S.	R.S.	R.S.	R.S.	R.S.

Note: R.S. = Regular system.

used. The procedure in this case, will be less detailed and exacting, however. As the sales information is developed, the basis of the presumptive-income approach will move closer than that of the estimated-income approach.

THE ESTIMATED-INCOME
APPROACH TO SOMEWHAT LARGER TAXPAYERS

We now turn to our third category of taxpayers, namely, taxpayers who are subject to the regular system of income taxation, personal and enterprise, but to whom the normal procedure of review (which is based on duly verified books and declarations) cannot be effectively applied. This group, which includes those taxpayers who cannot keep adequate books as well as those who fail to do so or who have a record of low compliance, is an important one. In dealing with a taxpayer in this group, the tax official must decide whether the taxpayer's declared income is a fair approximation of his actual income. Unless the official is given a definite basis upon which to reach this judgment, "bargaining" results, which is highly detrimental to the integrity of the tax system. To permit subjective factors to enter into this judgment invites collusion between taxpayers and tax officials. In order to avoid these difficulties, we propose that a set of specific *guidelines for estimating income* (GEIs) be developed for each of the major branches of business. On the basis of these GEIs, a taxpayer's estimated income can be determined in a more or less objective fashion.[2] Such an approach has been developed successfully in Israel, where it is referred to as the *Takshiv* (imputed income) method. We recommend that this approach be adapted to the Bolivian setting.

If the Israeli pattern is followed, the GEIs should be published so that they can be used by taxpayers as well as tax officials. Because the amount of income declared by the taxpayer would, in most cases, have to be as great as the amount derived by applying the GEIs, the latter may also become an instrument of self-assessment. In any event, the GEI approach should be temporary and should be conceived of only as a step toward the keeping of complete and adequate books of account by the entire taxpayer population. The ultimate target should be to tax all groups only on the basis of their books of account and to thereby render obsolete the use of GEIs as bases for determining minimum tax liabilities in the review process.

In the meantime, the GEIs will provide tax officials with an invaluable aid in calculating estimated incomes according to the size and type of business and the characteristics of specific economic activities. The availability of the GEIs will also enable a tax official to become thoroughly acquainted with a particular economic activity in a short time. The expertise thus acquired will greatly improve the official's efficiency in reviewing the declarations of taxpayers within that activity because he will gain an understanding of the principal characteristics and operational aspects of that activity. In the process, the GEIs can also be helpful in securing improved compliance with the sales and service taxes.

The taxpayer population to which this approach applies must have a level of sales above the level given in table 25.1 as the ceiling for the group to which the presumptive-income approach applies. At the same time, not all of the taxpayers whose sales are above that level need be subject to the estimated-income approach. These taxpayers should be given every opportunity to file declarations of actual income which are based on correct and complete records.

Estimating Procedure

The estimating procedure, which is at the core of the GEI approach, for any economic activity involves three steps:

1. The estimation of gross sales by indicators
2. The estimation of gross income by deducting all nonaccountable expenses from gross sales
3. The estimation of net income by deducting all accountable expenses from gross income

Gross sales. The estimation of gross sales should be based on several indicators. In this way, the accuracy of the estimate is improved, and the taxpayer is prevented from responding by altering the regular conduct of his business—that is, from reducing his tax liability by making less use of a specific indicator. Among the major indicators of gross sales are the following:

1. The number of employees
2. The skill level of employees
3. Installed machinery and equipment
4. The level of inventory
5. Materials purchased
6. Information obtained from other taxes

On the basis of these and other indicators, the average relationships between the indicators and the gross sales typical for the groups of taxpayers included in a particular category and broad branch of business must be determined. These average relationships may then be used to estimate the gross sales of firms falling in that particular category. No direct determination of such outlays for the particular taxpayer in question is to be made. Specific allowances may be made for products proven to be damaged or for obsolete inventory.

Net income and the enterprise tax. In order to move from gross income to net income, "accountable" expenses are to be deducted. These expenses include payroll and overhead expenses such as rent, tax payments, and so forth, as well as major purchases of materials. The taxpayer will be allowed to deduct only those expenses which are properly documented. Losses should not be allowed for under the GEI procedure. Taxpayers claiming losses during the period in question should be required to provide acceptable accounting evidence to support their claims. Once the net income of a business has been established, the enterprise tax may be computed.

Personal income tax. The income that remains after payment of the enterprise tax should then be added to the owner's other income in order to determine his global income subject to the personal income tax. In principle, only personal compensation and distributed profits should be thus included. The administrative difficulties of allowing for retained profits would, however, be excessive under the estimated-income approach. If the taxpayer wishes to exclude retained profits, he should be required to file adequately supported documentation.

Rebuttal and "Blue Returns"

As we noted earlier, the taxpayer's estimated income and the tax based thereon will set the minimum liability, even though the liability stated on the taxpayer's declaration may be less. A rebuttal of the estimated tax should be permitted only if the taxpayer can meet the exacting accounting standards set by the Ministry of Finance. Care must be taken, however, that the estimated base does not come to serve as an upper limit. To avoid this situation, the use of "blue returns," similar to those used in Japan [Tanabe, 1973] should be introduced. The taxpayer should be given inducements to follow this procedure. For this purpose, certain privileges, such as an allowance for losses and the use of investment incentives, may be made contingent on the rendering of such a return.

Illustration

To illustrate the GEI method, we now provide an example, shown in tables 25.2 and 25.3, for restaurants in La Paz. This sample GEI is sufficient to indicate the procedure that must be followed, but it has not been designed with enough care to permit it to be applied in its present form. Table 25.2 presents the relevant indicators. Lines 1–6 of table 25.2 show the various characteristics that are considered in classifying restaurants into the eight groups that are presented in the successive columns. Next, gross sales are computed for a sampling of the restaurants in each group. This computation is based on the following formula:

$$\text{Gross sales} = [(\text{Clients per lunch} \times \text{Price of average meal})$$
$$+ (\text{Clients per dinner} \times \text{Price of average meal})$$
$$+ (\text{Snack clients} \times \text{Price of average snacks})]$$
$$\times \text{Days open per year} \times 1.23^3$$

We then find that within each group, fairly stable relationships appear to exist between gross sales and certain indicators. In the present illustration, the level of gross sales for service personnel is used for this purpose, although several relationships should be used in a real GEI. This indicator, shown in line 7 of the table, may be used as a shortcut to estimate the gross receipts for a particular restaurant, after it has been classified into one of the eight categories. A similar procedure is used to estimate the average ratio of nonaccountable expenses to sales for each of the eight groups. This percentage, which is given in line 8, may then be used as a shortcut in estimating such expenses for particular firms. On this basis, the tax liability for Restaurant XX is computed in table 25.3. The characteristics of this particular restaurant place it in the fifth category; and its sales and nonaccountable expenses are estimated on the basis of the corresponding indicators given in lines 7 and 8 of table 25.2.

Administrative Aspects

A number of further considerations enter into the implementation of the GEI approach. We will elaborate them here.

Potential taxpayer population subject to the GEI approach. The GEI approach will be very useful for medium-sized enterprises, including unincorporated businesses and unipersonal enterprises, as well as small corporations. The ideal goal is

Table 25.2 · Sketch of GEI Information for Restaurants in La Paz

	Exclusive Restaurants				Popular Restaurants			
			Other					
Category characteristics	Chinese-style (1)	European-style (2)	(3)	(4)	(5)	(6)	(7)	(8)
(1) Price of average meal								
(a) Fixed menu	—	—	—	—	$b15	$b14.50	*	*
(b) A la carte	$b70	$b120	$b75	$b65	$b45	$b45.00	*	*
(2) Days open per year	300	300	300	300	300	300	300	300
(3) Number of waiters	1–2	2–3	2–3	1–2	4–5	2–4	*	*
(4) Seating capacity	40–50	60–80	60–100	30–60	150–200	80–100	*	*
(5) Type of clients	Tourists, middle and upper class	Tourists, professionals, upper class	Tourists, middle and upper class	Tourists, middle and upper class	Middle class, employees, small businessmen	Low- and medium-income, pensioners		
(6) Location	Main streets, downtown	Main streets, downtown, exclusive suburbs	Downtown, exclusive suburbs	Downtown, middle-class suburbs	Commercial areas	Commercial areas	*	
Key indicators								
(7) Gross sales per waiter	$b700,000–900,000	$b850,000–1,300,000	$b1,000,000–1,500,000	*	$b420,000–450,000	$b300,000–400,000	*	*
(8) Nonaccountable expenses as percentage of sales	33–35%	25–28%	26–30%	30–35%	45–50%	45–50%	*	*

*Not determined.

Table 25.3   *Restaurant XX (A Real Case)*

Description	
Location:	Active commercial area
Type of food:	Local
Number of waiters:	Five
Other personnel:	Seventeen
Prices:	Fixed menu lunch, $b15; a la carte, $b45
Main hours:	11 a.m. to 9 p.m.
Services:	Snack stand (salteñas, hamburgers, hot dogs) with three employees
	Stand for pastries, pizzas, and so forth
	Premises rented for parties
	Bread and pastries baked on the premises

Assessment	
Description fits that of a popular, fifth-class restaurant (because of prices, location, customers, and style)	
Gross sales from restaurant XX	
(five waiters × $b420,000)	$b2,100,000
Gross sales from other services	
Pastries	200,000
Parties	200,000
Total gross sales	2,500,000
Nonaccountable expenses (45%)	1,125,000
Gross income	1,375,000
Accountable expenses	
Salaries	264,000
13% tax	113,000
Rent	42,000
Utilities	48,000
Depreciation	50,000
Other	100,000
	617,000
Net income	758,000
(If waiters actually received a 10% service charge in addition to their salaries, allow a deduction of:)	94,000

Taxes	
Estimated (GEI) taxable income	$b664,000
Tax	199,200
1974 declared taxable income	45,244
Tax paid	13,573

to prepare between five and ten GEIs each year. In choosing the economic activities (trades or businesses) for which to prepare GEIs, the administration should give priority to those activities (*a*) which encompass a large number of businesses; (*b*) in which more than one indicator is required in order to calculate income; (*c*) which offer a reasonable number of sources of information; (*d*) whose indicators involve measures of quantity, rather than quality, for which there is no sharp variance from one firm to the next larger one; (*e*) whose revenue potential should be substantial; and (*f*) which are noticeably prosperous.

In formulating a GEI, the close cooperation of the relevant trade organizations should be secured, especially at the beginning. In order to obtain such cooperation, these organizations should be shown that it is to their advantage to have all of their members pay taxes; otherwise, if some of their members pay and others do not, distortions will occur and unfair competition will result.

Sources of information. In order to prepare the GEI for a particular activity, a representative sampling of business firms should be examined by using both direct and indirect information-gathering techniques. Information about purchases and prices should be compared with information supplied by wholesalers and other external sources. In addition, relevant data should be obtained from the books of firms that are known for keeping reliable records and for declaring a reasonable income. The information thus obtained should be cross-checked and appraised by experienced tax officials who are known for the quality of their reviews of declarations.

Publication. The GEI for each economic activity should be published in the form of a pamphlet. This document should contain the general characteristics of the activity and the relevant tables for estimating the income of taxpayers engaged in the activity. These pamphlets should be distributed to tax officials, taxpayers, and the interested public.

Training tax officials. Short courses that would explain the nature and objectives of the GEI approach and its implementation in diverse situations should be offered to assessing officials. If difficulties arise in applying a particular GEI, the tax official should be able to consult with the individuals who designed it.

Unit for preparing the GEIS. In order to develop the GEIs required for the major economic activities, a unit should be created in the Ministry of Finance. Composed primarily of economists, this unit should be separate from the regular staff of tax assessors so that it will not be confused with the tax officials in charge of assessments. This distinction would be especially important in the use of indirect survey techniques, because it is easier to obtain the necessary information in a less official manner. At the same time, the members of this unit should have legal authorization, particularly if they are conducting direct interviews, to visit and audit various businesses. The economists in charge of developing the GEIS should work in close and constant association with the tax officials in order to inspect firms, audit cash balances, and undertake other necessary investigations. A system for reimbursing the expenses incurred in the process of developing the GEIS should be established. The GEIS should be updated periodically—if possible, every year—in accordance with changes in prices and production techniques.

PROFESSIONALS

The hard-to-tax groups include not only owner-operated small enterprises, but also the professions. The income tax coverage of this group is highly imperfect, partly because a lack of adequate records makes it difficult to check tax returns adequately and partly because of extremely poor compliance. Moreover, political pressures render the application of adequate enforcement measures especially difficult for the tax administration. Yet, professionals are fully capable of filing adequate returns, and their income levels fall well within the middle or even upper ranges of the taxable income scale. A determined and effective attack on this weakness in the coverage of the income tax system is called for and should be given high priority in the move toward improved tax administration.

Proposed Approach

In our judgment, the problem of taxing professionals cannot be solved by offering them a separate and preferential tax regime. We suggest that professionals be made subject to the regular income tax rates and that measures be taken to apply this tax with the use of GEIs similar in nature to those used in dealing with small business firms. For this purpose, it is again necessary to develop indicators and guidelines for each profession, on the basis of which taxable income can be reviewed with a minimum of subjective judgment and negotiation. Again, the taxpayer should file a regular return, and then the GEIs should be used to review the accuracy of the declared income level and the tax paid.

Procedure for Estimating Income

As in the case of the income of business firms, GEIs must be developed in order to estimate the income of professionals. Again, these GEIs should be designed in conjunction with the representatives of relevant professional associations, and they should be reviewed periodically. The first step in their design is the estimation of gross income. For this purpose, gross income equals the total yearly income before wages, rent, taxes, utility charges, and general expenditures have been deducted. In order to estimate gross income for a particular profession, we begin by estimating a basic minimum gross income. Next, the various factors influencing this basic income should be identified, and values should be assigned to them. In order to estimate the gross income of individual professionals, these factors should then be allowed for. For instance, a certain percentage should be added to the basic minimum for every year of an individual's experience in the profession.

Once the taxpayer's gross income has been estimated, his net income must be determined. For this purpose, we begin with an allowance for nonaccountable expenses; this allowance is to be made through the deduction of stipulated percentages of gross income. However, a deduction for accountable expenses should be permitted only if it can be supported by proper documentation. The basic items to be deducted as accountable expenses include the following: wages (provided the income tax has been withheld and paid), office rent (if both the name of the owner and receipts are supplied), depreciation (according to law), utility charges (if receipts are presented), and the costs of professional books and magazines, seminars, conferences, and so on (if receipts are furnished). As in the case of small enterprises, the net income thus estimated will serve as the basis for determining a minimum tax. Rebuttal will be permitted only on the basis of declarations supported by adequate accounting records.

After the net income from the professional activity is determined, the professional's net income from other sources should be added in order to determine his total net global income. Next, the general deductions allowed should be applied, and his taxable income should be determined. The tax should then be calculated on the professional's global income, including his professional income as well as his income from other sources. To calculate the tax separately on professional income would be to take a step backward toward a schedular system and would discriminate against nonprofessional taxpayers.

Implementation

The implementation of this system of review for professional income must be preceded by the preparation of the necessary GEIs; again, this function is to be performed by the previously mentioned economic unit. This unit should work in close cooperation with auditors from the assessing office. After the GEIs have been prepared, a review of the tax files of professionals should be conducted, so that after one or two years, all of the declarations of the professionals who are registered with the tax office will have been subjected to the requirements of the new system. It is also recommended that professionals be required to pay tax on a quarterly schedule that would be based on the previous year's payment.

NOTES

1. This conservative approach is recommended, even though a high level of presumptive tax would be more effective in encouraging the preparation of well-documented declarations.

2. The information on estimated sales which is generated in this process will also be useful in administering the sales and excise taxes; however, the estimated-income tax (as distinct from the presumptive-income tax) should not be used in lieu of the sales tax.

3. The prices used to estimate sales are net of tax, so that gross sales (including tax) are estimated by multiplying by 1.23 where the tax rate equals 23 percent.

Part Five

The Reform of Indirect Taxation

Indirect taxes on foreign trade and consumption have long been the mainstay of taxation in developing countries. Such taxes provide two-thirds or more of tax revenues in many countries, with taxes on foreign trade (especially imports) more important in the poorest countries and domestic taxes on goods and services more important in the others (see chapter 1). Few tax questions are more important in developing countries than the appropriate mix and design of indirect taxes.

Until recently, however, this obvious fact was accepted only reluctantly by most tax analysts. The dependence of developing countries on indirect taxation was of course widely recognized, but few were enthusiastic about this fact. Fiscal history suggested that the observed heavy dependence on indirect taxes in developing countries was only a passing phase in their development, with the income tax likely to take over pride of place as per capita income rose (Hinrichs, 1966; R. A. Musgrave, 1969). Moreover, indirect taxes were generally considered to be clearly inferior to direct taxes in virtually every relevant way, particularly with respect to equity. Only as regards ease of administration did indirect taxes score highly.

Recently, however, it has become increasingly recognized that the day when direct taxes on income will carry the major fiscal load is remote at best in most developing countries. The fact is that indirect taxes have not only retained their share of revenues in most countries, they have even increased it. This surprising outcome reflects both the recent widespread move to value-added taxes and, more importantly, the greater buoyancy (responsiveness to income changes) of indirect than direct taxes in most countries—a development, quite contrary to the experience of developed countries, which demonstrates clearly the importance of the administrative constraint on taxation in developing countries.

Moreover, for a number of reasons indirect taxes have come to be viewed more favorably by many analysts (Bird, 1987b). Recent economic literature has, for instance, emphasized the potential virtues of properly designed selective taxes on the consumption of particular goods and services as a means of correcting externalities (Cnossen, 1978). Renewed concern for economic growth has highlighted the traditional arguments for taxing consumption rather than saving (Chelliah, 1960). Most importantly, growing concern with the inevitable administrative inadequacies of developing countries (see Part 7) has highlighted the relatively greater administrative ease of raising required revenues through indirect taxes.

Two major topics developed in this chapter are thus the distinct but related roles of a general sales tax and selective excises in developing countries (see chapters 29 to 31). These subjects have also been extensively analyzed in two useful monographs (Due, 1988; Cnossen, 1977), as well as in numerous papers by these authors and others. Indeed, most of the discussion of indirect taxation in developing countries has focused on the taxation of domestic goods and services.

The great attention now paid to such general sales taxes as the value-added tax, however, should not be allowed to obscure the fact that, as already noted, in many developing countries taxes on foreign trade—on imports and exports—are more important in revenue terms than domestic consumption taxes. The treatment of these revenue sources has, on the whole, been less satisfactory in the tax than in the trade context. Perhaps the main impression one gains from the literature (e.g., Johnson, 1965; Gillis and McLure, 1971), with respect to import taxes, for instance, is that if they must exist they should be, on the one hand, uniform (to provide any desired protection in as nondistorting a fashion as possible) and, on the other, equal to domestic consumption taxes on the same products (essentially for the same reason). This balancing act is strictly tenable only if a uniform tax is levied on all domestic consumption of tradeable goods—but then, of course, tariffs would afford no protection at all to domestic production.

Similarly, the usual view of export taxes is that they are always and unequivocably bad. Yet many countries not only rely on such taxes to some extent but must continue to do so if they wish to tax their agricultural sectors effectively (Bird, 1974) or simply to raise enough revenue to meet the minimal needs of government (Bird, 1989). It is therefore important to include some consideration of these issues in this book, although the appropriate taxation of exports, even more than that of imports, is clearly related as much or more to trade or agricultural policy as to tax policy. Chapters 27 and 28 consider, in turn, how best to tax imports and exports in developing countries.

Finally, while most of the selections in this part consider the different possible approaches to indirect taxation—excises, general sales taxes, export duties, and import duties—quite separately, the first chapter included here takes a much broader approach to the design of tax policy in a small, open economy. Chapter 26, which focuses on the linkages between the design of direct and indirect taxes in such a setting, constitutes an appropriate bridge between the direct and indirect taxation sections of this book, as well as a useful reminder of the need to take a general equilibrium approach to tax policy design in developing countries.

26

Taxation in an Open Economy

Development taxation has been fortunate in the calibre of the analysts who have taken the subject seriously and contributed to the field. Carl Shoup, Richard Musgrave, and Richard Goode, for example, have all made outstanding contributions to the analysis of taxation in developing countries and played an important part in the development of public economics in general. The same is true of Arnold Harberger, the author of the following selection. Not only was Harberger largely responsible for the introduction of formal general equilibrium analysis into public finance but he has also long had an interest in the problems of the developing countries, particularly in Latin America. This brief selection displays well the mixture of strong simplifying assumptions, careful theoretical reasoning, awareness of practical problems, and bold policy conclusions that characterizes Harberger's work.

The chapter begins with a discussion of the incidence and design of corporate and personal income taxes in small, open economies. Although brief, this analysis deserves careful comparison to the lengthier treatment of such topics as the integration of corporate and personal taxes and the design of personal consumption taxes in Part 4. The paper then sets out briefly the arguments for using both a uniform value-added tax and selective excise taxes in developing countries, partly on the grounds that "multiple approaches" are in themselves useful and partly because, in different ways, both taxes constitute necessary complements to the limited range of direct taxes Harberger considers feasible in the face of the (assumed) perfectly open world capital market. Finally, the appropriate role and design of import and export taxes is considered: tariffs, he argues, should be uniform, although non-uniform export duties may have a role to play in many developing countries—in part as a means of taxing imports. Each of these arguments is developed further in the balance of this part. Even if one does not agree with all the assumptions or all the conclusions in the analysis in the following selection, one can, we think, learn a great deal from close study of this brief, tightly packed argument.

Tax Policy in a Small,
Open, Developing Economy

Arnold C. Harberger

Labor Bears More Than the Full Burden of the Corporation Income Tax

My definition of a small open economy is one in which the prices of tradeable goods are governed by world market prices. The presence of tariffs and excise taxes, so long as they are not prohibitive, creates no problem at all. Prohibitive tariffs, quotas, and perhaps other kinds of quantitative restrictions do unhook the internal prices of the affected commodities from the world price. In effect, such policies end up by converting tradeables into nontradeables. For the purposes of the present discussion I am prepared to admit a substantial number of goods affected by such restrictions. All that one really needs is that there still remains a significant tradeables sector, defined as above by the linkage between world market prices and the internal prices.

For simplicity assume that the tradeables sector has both corporate and noncorporate subsegments. The corporate subsegment would most naturally consist of manufacturing activities, whose outputs are nearly all, at least in principle, tradeable. The noncorporate sector would consist predominantly of agriculture. Side by side with these would be a corporate nontradeable sector, consisting of public utilities and internal transport, and in some economies also including the "overprotected" manufacturing activities that have been shunted by policy into the nontradeable category. Finally, there would be a noncorporate, nontradeable sector, consisting mainly of localized services (restaurants, electricians, plumbers, perhaps construction).

Assuming for simplicity that each of those sectors can be characterized by a production function homogeneous of the first degree, we may easily construct price formation equations, following upon imposition of a corporation income tax, here taken to be a tax $T_{Kx} = T_{Kz}$ on the earnings of capital in the corporate sector. The prices of labor and capital p_K and p_L are initially assumed to be unity; coefficients like f_L, f_K, g_L, g_K, etc. represent the initial shares of the factors in each line of activity. Competition is assumed, so that the sum of factor payments (including taxes) exhausts the price of the product. The only important factor other than capital and labor, is land (A), which enters only into the production function of agriculture.

In the presence of the tax, the following equations will hold [where dp is the change in price].

$$dp_x = f_K(dp_K + T_{Kx}) + f_L dp_L \qquad \text{Manufacturing (26.1)}$$

$$dp_y = g_K dp_K + g_L dp_L + g_A dp_A \qquad \text{Agriculture (26.2)}$$

Excerpted from Harberger (1985).

$$dp_z = h_K(dp_K + T_{Kz}) + h_L dp_L$$

Public utilities
and transport (26.3)

$$dp_s = m_K dp_K + m_L dp_L$$

Services (26.4)

Equation 26.1 provides the driving force in this system. For, since X is tradeable, $dp_x = 0$; and since capital is mobile, $dp_K = 0$. Thus

$$dp_L = -f_K T_{Kx}/f_L. \tag{26.5}$$

With initial prices equal to one, $f_K/f_L = K_x/L_x$, hence $dp_L = K T_{Kx}/L_x$. Since $T_{Kx} = T_{Kz}$, we have that the total tax revenues will be $(K_x + K_z)T_{Kx}$. Labor's loss will be $-(K_x T_{Kx}/L_x)(L_x + L_y + L_z + L_s)$. Labor's loss will exceed total tax revenues, then, so long as $[(L_x + L_y + L_z + L_s)/L_x] > [(K_x + K_z)/K_x]$. That is to say, labor loses more than the whole burden of the tax so long as the fraction of the entire labor force that is occupied in the corporate tradeables sector is less than the fraction of the *corporate* capital stock that is occupied in making corporate tradeables. I know of no country where a plausible case could be made asserting that this inequality was not fulfilled by a wide margin.

We thus conclude that labor significantly overbears, that is, bears more than the full burden of, the corporation income tax in a small open economy. The principal beneficiaries are the owners of land, whose price goes up to offset the fall in the price of labor (see Equation 26.2), and the consumers of services, whose price goes down to reflect the fall in the price of labor. (The price of public utilities and transport will remain the same if $h_K = f_K$, $h_L = f_L$, that is, if the capital intensity in the z-sector is the same as that in the x-sector.)

The mechanism by which all this works is the movement of capital out of the country, in the presence of the tax. Rewards are assumed to have been "equalized" (with due allowance for risk) before the tax was imposed; the same sort of equalization is assumed to exist in the presence of the tax. The mechanism that brings this about is capital outflow; which I assume (realistically, I think) that no small country can prevent or even seriously curtail.

Integrate the Corporation Income Tax with the Personal Income Tax

Such integration in effect eliminates the corporation income tax for local resident taxpayers. The advisable procedure is to maintain the corporation income tax "on the books," and to collect the tax from corporations. For local residents, these collections should be treated as a form of withholding. They must count as part of their personal income the corporation's gross-of-tax profit per share times the number of shares they own, and they must pay tax on their full income including this component of corporate profits. What was paid by the corporation in tax, on their shares, however, becomes a credit when the amount of personal tax due is calculated.

This scheme has the virtue of still collecting corporation income tax from foreign corporations. In most cases, the outright abolition of the corporation income tax would simply mean a gift to the treasuries of the United States, the United Kingdom, Germany, and other developed countries where international and multinational corporations are domiciled. By maintaining the facade of a corporation income tax, at something like the nominal rate prevailing in these advanced countries, an LDC can avoid simply transferring tax money to other countries' treasuries.

Convert the Personal Income Tax to a Consumption-Expenditure Tax

Like the corporation income tax, a personal income tax will have the effect of driving capital abroad. In my own opinion, few LDC taxpayers pay tax to their own governments on the interest, dividend, and capital gains income that they earn on their holdings outside the borders of their countries. Whether they pay tax to the host country doesn't matter, analytically, for such payments, if made, will presumably be made whether or not the LDC taxes personal income from capital. Capital market equilibrium in the LDC will occur when the net-of-tax return on capital invested at home bears the appropriated risk-adjusted relationship to whatever return its citizens are able to get from abroad. Thus, when capital invested at home is subject to tax, more of it will end up abroad. Once again, labor will effectively bear the burden of whatever tax is collected, and perhaps more than the full burden.

A consumption tax designed to fall on goods and services consumed in the LDC will, in effect, raise their prices above world levels. This is obvious when the tax takes the form of a value-added or excise tax (see below), but it is equally true when one is dealing with a consumption-expenditure tax administered through an income tax type of framework. In this case, people pay world prices for tradeables, and the consequent equilibrium prices for nontradeables. The surcharge over these prices they pay directly to the government in the form of the consumption-expenditure (CE) tax.

Capital Invested Abroad Should Be Nondeductible
and Treated as Consumption

The simplest and most straightforward approach to consumption taxation, particularly for countries that already have a personal income tax, is to permit the deduction, from income subject to tax, of certain specified investments. This has long been true of registered retirement plans in the United States; its scope has in recent years been amplified by Keough plans and Individual Retirement Accounts. All of these schemes allow for ample flexibility in shifting portfolios within the plan. The money that goes into such a plan is not taxable, nor are the interest, dividend, and capital gains receipts that accrue within the plan. Tax is paid only as money is withdrawn from the plan.

Characteristic of this sort of consumption tax system is a listing of eligible institutions. Banks, savings and loan institutions, and registered brokerage houses come immediately to mind. To them could easily be added real estate management firms, mutual funds, etc. The principle is to make the coverage as wide as possible without inviting invasion or creating undue enforcement difficulties.

The one area to avoid including in the eligible list is foreign investments (unless, of course, the government of the LDC can make reliable enforcement arrangements with foreign banks, brokerage firms, etc.). This means that investments abroad are treated as if they were consumption. They therefore pay tax *now*. Investments at home, in eligible entities, will pay tax *later*. Assuming the yields in both classes of investment to be the same, there is no gross discrimination involved; the present value of tax would presumably be the same in both cases. Only the timing of the tax would differ. But, and this is the important point, no evasion would be involved so far as foreign-source income from capital is concerned.[1]

A Progressive Consumption-Expenditure Tax Can Be Superimposed on a Consumption-Type Value-added Tax

The issue here concerns the ease and effectiveness of enforcement. In the first place, the value-added tax (VAT) is administered through channels that are substantially different from those of the personal income (or consumption-expenditure) tax. Separate channels are a virtue in this case, because those who may be able to evade or avoid one of the taxes are unlikely also to be in such a lucky position vis-à-vis the other. Moreover, the value-added tax has a lot of self-correction built into it. If farmers are exempted from the tax, it will still be paid by the canners, freezers, and other food processors, because they do not have a voucher indicating that tax was previously paid at the farmer stage. (Actually, the exempting of farmers is likely to lead to higher tax collections than would occur if they were full-rate members of the system. If in the system, they would be able to deduct purchases of, say, tractors, gasoline, fertilizers, seeds, etc. Out of the system they cannot deduct these items, but they are free of tax when they sell directly to the public—for example, at open-air markets. I believe that in most countries the amount of inputs for which no deduction can be claimed is higher than the amount of direct sales from farmer to public; hence, the assertion that tax revenues are actually increased by exempting farmers from the value-added tax.)

In a consumption-type value-added tax, investment outlays are treated in the same way as current expenses. Thus, they are in effect exempt from tax, and the type of problem provoked by the corporation income tax simply does not exist.

Border tax adjustments are, to my mind, an essential counterpart of a consumption-type value-added tax. While it is theoretically conceivable to have a value-added tax *without* border-tax adjustments, this particular solution requires that factor rewards be pressed down, while product prices remain at world-market levels. In turn, this creates difficulties if capital is internationally mobile. A value-added tax *with* border-tax adjustments, on the other hand, simply raises internal prices above the world price level by the amount of the tax. All consumers of products within the boundaries of the country will pay more for them. This includes visitors from abroad as well as local purveyors of the services of capital and labor. These, in turn, can escape the tax by being tourists in countries that do not have a VAT. But that is the only important way in which the VAT can be avoided—and, as mentioned, it is counterbalanced by the fact that visitors from abroad in the VAT-imposing country do indeed pay the tax.

Selective Excises on Luxury Goods Could Reduce the Progressive Consumption-Expenditure Tax Burden

I have always felt, at least outside the classroom, that in tax policy the pitchfork is better than the spear. That is to say, a multipronged approach is better than a single-pronged one, however elegant may be the arguments saying that the single-pronged approach is superior. At bottom, my argument is a moral one—different groups have different capacities and possibilities for evasion. Worse yet, this statement gets to be more true, and carries more weight, as one moves from simple excise, sales, and value-added taxes toward more delicate and sophisticated income and consumption-expenditure taxes.

One of the deepest lessons of applied welfare economics is that one should strive to equalize costs at the margin. If, then, an income or consumption expenditure tax carries with it large opportunities for selected groups to evade or avoid, it is worth paying some price in other dimensions in order to limit the extent of the resulting inequity. A general excise running from, say, 20 to 50 percent on goods of a luxury nature can assuage the (political) need for heavy progression in income or consumption taxation, and, if well designed, can do so at a relatively low cost in terms of economic efficiency. Good design entails taxing at approximately equal rates "packages" of goods that are presumptively close substitutes for each other.

Needless to say, selective excises would apply both to domestically produced goods and to imported goods in similar categories. Domestically produced goods that are exported would not be subject to such taxes. If perchance the tax were levied at the producer level, goods that were subsequently exported would receive tax remission according to the border tax adjustment formula approved by GATT.

For a Developing Country, a Moderate Import Tariff May Be Justified

Like the previous case, the arguments for tariffs are never (for small countries) "first-best." For a tariff to be justified on first-best grounds, the importing country must occupy a monopsony position vis-à-vis the world market for the imported good. Such is the case for the United States and the European Common Market with respect to products like tin, copper, manganese, coffee, bananas, and rubber, all of which have a fairly low elasticity of global supply; the excess supply curve of the "rest of the world" facing the United States or the Common Market is undoubtedly upward sloping for all the named commodities. This is not so, however, even for Brazil or Argentina. Frankly, I know of no case of a low- or middle-income country that occupies a monopsony position with respect to any commodity (loans are another matter, to be dealt with later).

But while developing countries are not monopsonists, they are monopolists in at least a limited sense. Coffee from Brazil, copper from Chile, karakul from Afghanistan—these are cases of a genuine capability of the country to influence the world price of its principal export product. But above and beyond these obvious cases, there is a sort of quasi-monopoly power present in many situations. Does anyone think, watching Argentina, Brazil, Chile, Mexico, and Venezuela try to cope with the present international debt crisis, that they can export all they want of any given tradeable (other than, say, their principal export product) at a given world price, which would be unaltered by any action they might take?

No, the fact is that even heavy real devaluations are not capable of multiplying exports by three or four. For many goods, even such a simple phenomenon as transport costs is enough to give a downward slope to the relevant demand curve for a given export product.

All of this ends up justifying export taxes. The optimum export tax for any product, from the country's own point of view and assuming no "retaliation," would be the difference between the foreign demand price and the marginal revenue to the exporting country, that is, it would be $P^d (-1/\eta_x)$, where P^d_x is the demand price (f.o.b.) and η_x is the elasticity of demand on the part of the rest of the world for exports of this good from the country in question.

Export taxes are thus *justified*, at least from the country's own point of view. But they are not *popular*. What is popular are import tariffs. George Stigler notes with wry amusement how the economists have won all the debates on free trade for the past more than two hundred years, while the protectionists have written all the tariff laws. Given the downward slope of the demand curve for most exports, and given also the political unpopularity of export taxes together with the inexplicable enthusiasm for tariffs, a sort of second or third best solution can be found by imposing an import tariff instead of export taxes. Here we rely on an old theorem of international trade, to the effect that a uniform import tax has the same effect as a uniform export tax at the same effective rate. (The intuition is clear: in international trade we pay for our imports by the sales of our exports; if trade is balanced, as on the whole it approximately is, an import tax [taxing the payment], an export tax [taxing the receipt], or a hypothetical transactions tax [simple taxing the act of trade itself] should all have the same ultimate effect.) In lieu, then, of a whole set of export taxes aimed at exploiting the monopoly or quasi-monopoly power that a country possesses, one could substitute (with some loss of economic efficiency) a general import levy.

Any Import Tariff That Is Imposed Should Be Uniform

The motivation for this recommendation stems from the theory of effective protection. This theory, developed largely in the 1960s, showed conclusively how the actual degree to which domestic value added is protected can vary greatly, depending on the tariff rates applying to different outputs and their respective inputs, as well as on the world prices of these outputs and inputs. The standard formula for the rate of effective protection on the value added in making product j is

$$t_{ej} = \frac{t_{nj} - \sum_i \alpha_{ij} t_{ni}}{1 - \sum_i \alpha_{ij}} . \tag{26.6}$$

Here t_{ej} = the effective rate of protection on value added in producing product j, t_{nj} = the nominal rate of protection on the final product j, t_{ni} = the nominal rate of protection on the imported (or tradeable) input i, and α = the fraction of the total cost (at international prices) of product j that is accounted for by imported input i.

A numerical example will show the sort of absurdity to which non-uniform tariffs can lead. If there is a 30 percent tariff on men's shirts, and the country in question produces its own cotton, t_{ej} will be 30 percent for cotton shirts. However, the country may also produce wool shirts, where imported wool accounts for 50 percent of the cost at international prices. If imported wool enters free of duty, the effective protection rate for wool shirts is 60 percent. If silk shirts are also made, using imported silk accounting for 75 percent of the cost (at international prices), and if imported silk also enters free of duty, the effective rate of protection of value added in producing silk shirts becomes 120 percent. As mentioned, these rates of effective protection will vary not only with the tariff rates on men's shirts, on wool, and on silk, but also with movements in the international prices of these goods.

The sensible way out of the absurdity just described is to have a uniform tariff. If a 30 percent tariff applies on all outputs and inputs, the rate of effective protection is 30 percent for everything. Recalling that our justification for tariff protection was second or third best in any event, the wisdom of applying a uniform rate (as a protection against the arbitrary and capricious possibilities that arise when tariffs at different rates are imposed) appears obvious.

Regulate the Inflow of Foreign Debt Capital

In Harberger (1980) I developed a case for a quasi-monopsony position of most debtors vis-à-vis the capital market. We all—individuals, firms, and countries alike—face upward rising supply curves of borrowable funds. Taking the rise in the supply curve at face value, borrowers face marginal costs of funds that exceed average costs. If the borrower is you or me or General Motors, the rising average cost is perceived by us, and we presumably will act in full recognition of what the marginal cost of funds really is.

But if a part of the cost of credit is a premium for "country risk," and if this premium increases as a function, say, of the country's international debt (public plus private), then the country will find itself in what I call a quasi-monopsony position with respect to its international indebtedness. Under such circumstances, a tax on international borrowing would be justified.

Many subtleties can be brought into play here, such as the distinction between lenders' and borrowers' perceptions of risk, but I do not think that this is the appropriate place to enter into detail on them. Rather, I shall take a rather pragmatic position and note that not only do countries face upward rising supply curves of funds; they also face supply curves that shift around a great deal, largely at the whim of the international banking community.

The most reasonable response of a small open economy to this combination of both upward rising and rather volatile supply curves of funds is, in my view, a set of incentives that discourage short-term borrowing. The tried and tested formula is a requirement that national borrowers from foreign sources place a fraction of their borrowings in deposit at the central bank (usually at zero interest), the fraction being quite high (perhaps one-half) for loans of less than a year's duration, somewhat lower (perhaps one-third) for loans with a term between one and two years, and finally tapering off to zero on loans with terms of five years or more.

Though not nominally a tax, such a scheme is one in effect, for the central bank can gain interest on the funds deposited with it, while the borrower forgoes interest on these sums.

This device has the virtue of giving some recognition to the quasi-monopsony element that is present in international borrowing and at the same time addressing the problem of protecting a country against abrupt shifts in the supply of funds facing it.

NOTE

1. This must be qualified. If one started with such a consumption tax system today, wealth that was already held abroad would escape the net; no LDC tax would be paid as the income from that wealth, or the wealth itself, was consumed. But, of course, under my assumptions about how the world really works, such wealth would not pay tax to the LDC government under an income tax either. "Old capital abroad," if you like, would escape tax under both regimes. "New capital going abroad" would pay approximately the same present value of tax under a consumption tax. New capital going abroad would pay less under an income tax, paying tax, presumably, on the income out of which the savings were made but not on the interest and dividends generated.

27

Taxing Imports

In many developing countries, particularly those at lower income levels, taxes on imports remain the most important single source of government revenue. The main reason for this predominance is simply, as Richard Musgrave (1969) has put it, that imports constitute one of the main "tax handles"—or easily administrable sources of revenue—available to such countries. As chapter 1 noted, import taxes are less dominant in more advanced developing countries, but even there this source of revenues remains much more important than in industrial countries (Greenaway, 1981, 1984). It is thus somewhat surprising that so little attention has been paid to import taxation by tax specialists. For the most part, the analytical running in this area has been left to trade specialists, with the result that the important revenue aspects of customs duties have too often been neglected (De Wulf, 1980). The important revenue role of tariffs in most developing countries means that the liberalization of trade policy must usually be gradual, to avoid creating serious budgetary problems.

The following selection sets out briefly a most useful check list and set of possible objectives for the reform of import tariffs viewed in the context of the tax system as a whole (see also Tanzi, 1978). As in the preceding chapter, the need for close coordination between domestic consumption taxes and import taxes in order to avoid unwarranted protection is stressed (see also Gillis and McLure, 1971; Johnson, 1965). The appropriate role of export taxes is also discussed briefly, in a somewhat different fashion than in the previous selection: this matter is discussed in more detail in chapter 28. The possible case for special export incentives is also mentioned briefly: for a fuller exposition, see De Wulf (1978). The chapter also reminds readers that any protective tariffs established should ideally have a limited life span. Unfortunately, there is all too much evidence that this advice is normally disregarded, with the result that the "infant industries" supposedly fostered by import protection are likely never to be recognized as having grown up.

Another important point mentioned briefly in this paper is the distinction between tax design and tax reform (Feldstein, 1976; Bird, 1977). In the real world, since some tax system is invariably already in place, the problem is not one of designing the best conceivable system on paper but rather how best to change what exists in the hope of improving the outcomes. Moreover, what can be done in developing countries is heavily constrained by administrative limitations. For instance, theoretical economists often assert that temporary subsidies to particular industries are preferable to protective tariffs, but there are few, if any, developing countries that can administer (or finance) such subsidies. For similar reasons, the wage subsidies that sometimes seem to be called for by theory in labor-intensive economies may have to be replaced by some decidedly inferior substitute such as capital taxes (Bird, 1982), and food subsidies that appear desirable on distributional grounds may have to be replaced by much less "targeted" exemptions from sales taxes (Bird and Miller, 1989). The world of the policy analyst in developing countries is always and inevitably a world of the second-, third-, and fourth-best.

Taxation of Imports in LDCs: Suggestions for Reform

Luc De Wulf

Customs duties in less developed countries can assist in achieving a variety of policy objectives.[1] They can (a) provide significant amounts of revenue, (b) help to keep the level of imports consistent with the other balance of payments components, (c) influence the structure of imports so as to free valuable foreign exchange for essential or developmental imports, (d) grant protection to local producers of goods that are also imported, (e) redistribute incomes, and (f) sometimes serve as bargaining tools in trade negotiations. This multitarget aspect of the use of customs duties highlights their importance, but it also indicates the special problems that they can create, as it is only by pure chance that a particular use of one policy instrument will influence all targets in the desired direction (Tinbergen, 1952).

It is more likely that one target—be it revenue raising or protection—will acquire priority and profoundly shape the import tax system to its purpose, thereby adversely affecting the other policy targets. In light of this multitarget use of customs duties, there is often an urgent need to investigate carefully whether the existing import tax system satisfies the basic efficiency and equity criteria of taxation. This note provides a guideline for such an examination. It discusses in the first part the taxation of inputs in a situation where the only restraint on the use of an optimal tax mix is that no production subsidies can be used. Such a constraint does not exist in more theoretical discussions of import taxation where there is no cost to the government for granting a subsidy. However, budgetary considerations in LDCs, where it is more difficult to raise taxes to finance production subsidies than to protect the industry with a revenue-raising tool, often strictly limit the use of producer subsidies. Hence, as a first concession to a real world situation, the use of production subsidies is ruled out. In the second part, import taxation is discussed in an economy whose production structure is influenced by past protection policies and where administrative and political factors constrain the tax policy options.

IDEAL TAXATION OF IMPORTS

A close coordination between the various policy tools and, when sufficient such tools are available, an attempt to obtain a one-to-one relation between the policy

Excerpted from De Wulf (1980a).

tools and objectives can attain consistent economic policy and improve the chances for the attainment of the various objectives. Such a policy package pertaining to the taxation of imports is now briefly sketched. It contains the judicious use of foreign exchange rate adjustments, and the coordination of domestic sales and excise taxes and customs duties.

First, the exchange rate together with monetary and fiscal policies should maintain the balance of payments equilibrium. Where traditional exports loom large in the trade accounts of a country, this equilibrium may be associated with an exchange rate that hampers the development of the import substitution and nontraditional export sectors. In such a circumstance, either the use of customs duties in combination with export incentives or (what in fact is the same thing) the use of multiple exchange rates could provide an adequate production-incentive structure to those sectors without endangering the balance of payments equilibrium. However, both methods may be complex and difficult to administer, their use may not be consistent with international obligations, and they may lead to problems with trading partners. In addition, they often tend to be used directly for balance of payments purposes, thereby distorting the production-incentive structure they were intended to implement. Consequently, in particular circumstances it might be preferable to accept an exchange rate that is adequate for the development of the import substitution and the nontraditional export sectors in conjunction with an export tax levied on traditional exports so as to drain off some of the excessive profits that would accrue to these exports.[2]

Second, a general consumption tax that does not discriminate among products according to where they are produced should provide the bulk of tax revenues raised through commodity taxes. The use of this tax would prevent the actual or potential misallocation of resources induced by taxing imports at a higher rate than domestic production.

Third, excise taxes or sales taxes applied at rates that differ according to the "luxury" content of the products should be useful in implementing the distributional objectives. Detailed consumption studies might be used to identify those products which should bear higher-than-average taxes and those to be exempted from the general consumption tax.

Fourth, tariff protection should provide protection to sectors that have a good chance of becoming successful competitors with imports or to sectors that the government wishes to promote for particular reasons. Tariff protection should be short lived. The determination of the effective protection to be granted to individual firms should rely on an analysis of the cost structure of these firms and how this cost structure compares with the price of competing imports. Hence, effective protection would differ amongst sectors. In the absence of tariffs on intermediate inputs, such an outcome implies different tariffs on the products whose local production is to be stimulated. Because such protective tariffs are to be reduced over time and because protection may be granted to new products, one should expect the tariff structure to be changing over time. This added complexity of the tariff structure would be compensated by tariff rates that would exist for only well-identified products.[3] Because tariffs raise revenue, one would also expect that the changes in these protective duties would have revenue implications. Yet, such implications must not necessarily lead to revenue losses, as the production of import substitutes raises domestic economic activity from which extra revenues could be obtained.

REFORM OF A GIVEN TARIFF

Efficiency and equity considerations of tax reform imply that tax reform cannot result in a tax system that is identical to the one that would result from a *de novo* design (Feldstein, 1976). Tax reform is further complicated because it must take into account an existing set of policies, institutions, and power bases that have brought about (or have been brought about by) the defective tax system. Hence, tariff reform requires an understanding of the forces that brought forth the present tariff structure and of the economic consequences of its application. Only then will it be possible to gradually introduce aspects of the "ideal" tariff discussed above and thus to eliminate the most serious deficiencies of the present system. The basic factors that should guide a tariff reform are now discussed.

Many countries adhere to an overvalued exchange rate for historic, political, and social reasons and use tariffs or direct controls to keep imports down to a level that can be financed by exports and net foreign capital flows. A uniform tariff rate could fulfill this function. Such a tariff would provide a uniform protection to the whole import-replacing sector[4] yet would be equivalent to an export tax.[5] While the protection to the import-replacing sector could be defended on the grounds of general infant protection to this sector, export incentives would be needed to compensate the sector of nontraditional exports for this quasi-export tax (De Wulf, 1978).

Using import duties for balance of payments purposes may yield appreciable amounts of revenue, despite the fact that some of this revenue would be needed to finance export subsidies or tax expenditures related to the export subsidy program. The net revenue obtained from the uniform import tariff and export subsidy program would depend on the degree of currency overvaluation, on the type of export incentives, and on the size of the export sector that was to be stimulated. Attempts to use custom duties to raise revenue in excess of this amount should be resisted. Instead, general sales taxes that do not discriminate according to the origin of the product should be used and should be introduced as early as possible.

The introduction of a general sales tax at a time when no local production of import substitutes exists would de facto be an additional import tax. However, its early introduction would prevent firms whose profitability depended on tariff protection from effectively blocking needed tax changes or from coming into existence. The early introduction of a sales tax would also obviate the need for raising customs duties to make up for the revenue losses due to the tax base erosion. Such erosion frequently results from the process of economic development itself, and takes the form of a structural shift in the import structure away from the highly taxed consumer goods towards the lower taxed intermediate and capital goods.

An early introduction of a sales tax may present administrative problems. However, these problems can be kept within manageable proportions by choosing the particular type of sales tax that best fits the economic characteristics and administrative capabilities of the country. In any event, small producers and distributors could be excluded from the tax or would escape its payment, thus giving them some protection against imports. While decidedly not neutral, this aspect should not overly worry the tax authorities, as some protection of the small producers and distributors may be desirable from a social point of view insofar as these activities are probably artisanal and labor intensive.

With general sales taxes in place, it is possible to achieve some redistribution of income through differentiation of the tax rates or by levying excise taxes on luxury products. Whether such excises are to be used in conjunction with the differentiated sales taxes or must bear the major thrust of the redistributional impact of commodity taxation must depend on administrative factors of the country concerned.

The industrial structure that exists in many countries is often influenced by tariffs that perform protective and redistributive functions. The result is often an uncoordinated and inefficient industrial structure. The rationalization of this situation requires that policy makers determine, first, how much protection should be given in the future to the different sectors and, second, what policy instruments should be used for this protection. Answering this question goes to the heart of the industrialization policy of a country. To address it fully is beyond the present scope. Therefore, the following comments will suffice here.

Positive protection condones inefficiencies in production or the extra remuneration of some factors of production and penalizes the consumer, who has to pay higher prices for his consumer goods. Hence, each country should state the maximum rate of effective protection it is willing to grant.[6] Given the constraints on the use of foreign exchange rate adjustments, the countries should also state what average rate of effective protection it is willing to grant the domestic producers.

The major policy implication of the above statement of policy intentions should be made clear. This would entail that indications be given that (a) the protection granted to new projects will not exceed the above stated maximum and will be reduced over an agreed upon period to reach the average level of protection granted to all domestic producers; (b) existing firms with above-average protection will have that protection gradually reduced, first to the maximum and then to the average. The time period allowed for this reduction should be sufficiently long to avoid undue hardship. While possibly varying for different industries, this period should be announced in advance and strictly adhered to; and (c) protection to firms with below-average protection will be raised.

Effective protection at levels beyond that granted by a uniform import tariff could be granted through higher-than-average nominal tariffs on outputs or through lower-than-average nominal tariffs on inputs. Granting protection through higher-than-average rates on outputs seems to be preferred because (a) the end-users of some imported inputs are hard to identify; (b) the knowledge of prevailing input-output relations required to effect a desired level of effective protection is deficient in many countries; (c) technologies change and substitution among inputs is possible so that tariff rates on inputs would constantly have to be adjusted to maintain the desired level of effective protection; and (d) lower tariffs on intermediate inputs deprive the local producer of these inputs of the necessary incentives. Some countries may not accept such a uniform tariff with exceptions for some final products, because it raises the domestic price level and, by reducing the domestic demand for these products, may prevent local industries from reaching the scale of operation necessary to benefit from economies of scale. For these or for other reasons, rates on intermediate imports may have to be lowered, requiring that nominal rates be graduated in accordance with the degree of processing. This approach to tariff protection requires an intricate knowledge of the input-output relations of the production processes that are to be protected.

SUMMARY AND CONCLUSION

The main policy recommendation that follows from this paper is that the taxation of local products and of imports should be coordinated so as to yield desired revenue and distributional objectives without undue resource misallocation. This recommendation implies that (a) commodity tax revenue be raised by taxes that differentiate between products according to their nature rather than their origin; (b) differentiated sales taxes or excise taxes rather than customs duties be used to achieve the distributional objectives; and (c) tariff protection be coordinated with other policy tools to obtain a production-incentive structure considered adequate for the various sectors of the economy.

Import taxes in LDCs provide a large share of total budgetary revenue. They stimulate local production, redistribute income, assist in securing balance of payments equilibrium, and influence the import structure. Given this multitarget aspect of the use of customs duties, an in-depth analysis of these factors is a prerequisite to any tariff reform. While such a reform will improve the allocation of domestic resources it will affect the owners of factors of production whose allocation decisions are based on the old tariff. This will cause problems of horizontal equity. Providing compensations for blatant infringement on horizontal equity may be possible, yet probably will be the exception rather than the rule. Therefore, methods should be found to minimize these inequities. One method that may work in some countries consists of advance announcements of the tariffs that will be applied in the future in order to allow factor prices to adjust to the new rate structure and to phase the reallocation of resources.

NOTES

1. The term *customs duties* is used in this paper to refer to those taxes that are levied on imports but not on similar domestic products.

2. This solution is reinforced whenever administrative difficulties make difficult the taxation of these profits through an income tax. For more on the use of export taxation in such circumstances see Goode, Lent, and Ojha (1966).

3. However, a more refined classification of imports would still be needed to enable the assessment of excises and differentiated sales taxes and for statistical purposes.

4. This conclusion is somewhat oversimplified as it ignores the fact that effective protection of the firms that use unprotected primary products as inputs would exceed somewhat the nominal protection provided by the uniform tariff rate; see Corden (1971), pp. 188–89.

5. For an early statement of the equivalence of import and export taxes, see Lerner (1936).

6. "Given the small size of domestic markets for manufactured goods in most LDCs, they are well advised to follow the example of the smaller developed nations in setting low levels of protection. Considering also the lack of evidence on external economies and the observed adverse effects of high protection, it would appear that effective protection rates on manufacturing activities in excess of 10–15 percent would involve costs that are not commensurate with the expected benefits," Balassa (1975).

28

Taxing Exports

A well-established proposition in international trade is that a uniform tax on imports is essentially the same as a uniform tax on exports (see chapter 26). The fiscal treatment of exports and that of imports are thus, in principle, two sides of the same coin. In practice, however, export and import taxes are usually designed and implemented largely in isolation from each other. In some countries, exports—usually of manufactured goods—are subsidized (De Wulf, 1978). In others, exports—usually of natural resources—are taxed, sometimes explicitly, sometimes through the operations of state marketing boards, and sometimes through multiple exchange rates (Goode, Lent, and Ojha, 1966). In still others, both export subsidies and export taxes may simultaneously exist in different sectors. Moreover, the precise significance and effects of these various arrangements may differ greatly, depending on how such other policy levers as exchange rates are set (see chapter 15). It is obviously not possible to discuss here all the considerations that may (or should) influence export policy, including export tax policy in developing countries (for more general discussions, see, for example, Corden, 1974, and Balassa, 1975). The following selection therefore undertakes only the more limited task of explaining briefly the economic rationale for taxing exports.

Traditional arguments for export taxes are that they may serve as a means of stabilization policy (McBean, 1966), as a substitute for income or other taxes on farmers (Oldman, 1964; Bird, 1974), as a means of offsetting restrictions on importers, or as a means of reaping monopoly benefits (chapter 26). Each of these arguments may have merit in particular circumstances. Nevertheless, with respect to export taxation as to most other areas of development taxation, the apparently strong and clear conclusions emerging from simple economic analysis need to be carefully considered, and often modified, before they can serve as the basis of sound policy recommendations for any particular country.

Although the full details of the rigorous empirical analysis of the effects of export taxes included in the original source (Sanchez-Ugarte and Modi, 1987) could not be included here, a point of particular interest emphasized in the conclusions reproduced in the following chapter is that many countries levy heavier implicit taxes than explicit taxes on exports (see also Levin, 1960, and Bird, 1968). "Implicit" or "quasi" taxes reduce the income accruing to exports but do not produce any revenue for the government: instead, the proceeds are generally used, one way or another, to subsidize imports. Governments thus incur the opprobrium and distortions associated with taxation without receiving the benefits conceivably associated with expenditures. Such "nontax" taxes are by no means limited to the export sector in developing countries (McLure, 1988a), nor indeed are they limited to developing countries (Prest, 1985a).

If an import tariff, for example, succeeds in discouraging all imports of a production, it effectively levies a "tax" on all consumers of the (domestically-produced) product and pays a subsidy to the factors of production engaged in the protected sector. Quantitative restrictions on trade, the pricing policy of public enterprises, price controls, financial and other regulations—all these and many other government policies may affect the pattern of production and prices and hence have an impact on income distribution and allocative efficiency in exactly the same way as taxes. These devices do not, however, yield budgetary revenue for the most part and hence are not reflected in the conventional tax ratios discussed in chapter 1. This subject is, unfortunately, too new and vast for further discussion here.

Export Taxes in Theory and Practice

Fernando Sanchez-Ugarte and Jitendra R. Modi

Export duties play an important role in the revenue structures of developing countries. For these countries, export duties are a useful tool for raising revenue, since compared with their enormous financing needs for social and economic development they generally have few tax bases at their disposal and also are hampered by their limited capacity for tax administration. Government budgets in a number of developing countries rely rather heavily on export duties, accounting for more than 1 percent of gross domestic product (GDP) and, with some minor exceptions, exceeding 10 percent of total tax revenue. In most cases, export tax receipts are derived from high rates of taxes on one or two commodities that feature prominently in the exports of these countries. Frequently, export duties in developing countries are levied in lieu of income taxes on exporters and are justified on grounds of the ease of tax administration. They are also generally made progressive with respect to export prices, and thereby incomes earned by exporters; this is justified on grounds of equity and need for macroeconomic stabilization. Furthermore, exports from developing countries are frequently subject to implicit export duties in the form of overvalued or multiple exchange rates, producer price ceilings, and quantitative restrictions on exports. These implicit export duties probably lead to a reduction in the level of exports even though they often do not yield fiscal revenue.

THE RATIONALE FOR EXPORT TAXES

Developing countries apply export taxes for many reasons, among which the most important are (1) to limit exports to take advantage of the monopoly power in a certain market or to benefit from other market imperfections, (2) to raise revenue from export commodities, and (3) to stabilize producer incomes.[1] This section describes these arguments and shows that export duties used in connection with (1) may increase the welfare of the country while reducing that of the rest of the world; export duties used in connection with (2) may distort economic efficiency in general; and export duties used in connection with (3) may improve a country's economic welfare without lowering the welfare of the rest of the world.

Excerpted from Sanchez-Ugarte and Modi (1987).

Export Duties and Market Imperfections

The literature focuses on two kinds of market imperfections: those relating to the existence of some form of monopoly power in the commodity market (the optimal tariff argument) and those arising from protectionism on the part of consuming or importing countries and from other restrictions in commodity markets.

Monopoly Power of the Exporter

The optimal export duty argument is that a given country, or a group of countries, with monopoly power in the world market of a commodity should levy an export duty to extract monopoly profits[2] and thus to obtain a net welfare gain. The export duty, however, will improve the welfare of the individual country that exerts monopoly power but not of the world as a whole. Partial equilibrium analysis shows that the level of taxation that can be considered country optimal (i.e., that will maximize the gain to an exporting country) equalizes the marginal revenue and the marginal cost of exporting the commodity as given by the inverse elasticity rule (Corden, 1974):

$$t_k^i = 1/\eta_k^i, \tag{28.1}$$

where t_k^i is the country optimal ad valorem export duty on the f.o.b. price of the export commodity k and η_k^i is the country-specific long-run elasticity of demand for exports of the taxed commodity. The country in question does not have to be a "pure" monopolist in the export market for the optimal tariff argument to apply.

Protection by Importing Countries and Other Restrictions on Trade in Commodity Markets

Importing countries often protect domestic producers of particular commodities by restricting the volume of imports through import quotas or other means.[3] Furthermore, producing countries have signed agreements, sometimes with the participation of major consumers, to stabilize and regulate commodity markets by means of restrictions on the level of exports by assigning export quotas to producing countries or by relying on international buffer stock arrangements.[4] Such trade restrictions give rise to a dual world market price structure—the commodity price in countries that have a protected market is higher than the price in the non-restricted market—and the producers in an exporting country have an incentive to overproduce, given a positive elasticity of supply, as long as they assign a positive probability to selling extra output in the protected market.[5] The authorities of exporting countries can restrict overproduction and avoid an excessive world supply of the commodity by levying an export tax, which would efficiently achieve the desired level of production.

Taxes on Exports as Income Taxes

Export taxes are commonly used simply to collect revenue from export activities. Public finance literature has tended to assimilate these taxes under income or direct taxes because insofar as export taxes cannot be shifted to consumers in the international market, they obviously affect the income of domestic producers.[6] The export tax can also have an "excise" effect to the extent that the decline in the export price of a commodity relative to its domestic price reduces the level of exports (Tanzi, 1976). Whether export duties should be treated as an income tax or an excise tax is still controversial.

It might be argued that the supply of the typical export of a developing country is highly price inelastic, either because its producers are not price responsive or because the commodity is produced with the help of a sector-specific factor of production whose supply is fixed. In this case, a tax on exports can be simply considered as an income tax on an immovable factor of production and hence nondistortionary.[7] The assumptions underlying this conclusion can be questioned. With respect to the first point, there is ample empirical evidence that the supply of export commodities is affected by the producer price.[8] With respect to the second point, it can be argued that even when an export duty is fully capitalized in the price of an immovable factor of production (say, land), it still can have undesirable "excise" or supply-side effects.[9]

In the long run, an export duty imposed on an activity that employs an immovable factor of production will tend to be fully capitalized in the price of this factor of production—a result which may seem to indicate that the tax is nondistortionary.[10] The output of the taxed commodity, however, will tend to decrease because the export duty reduces the producer price of export goods compared with other goods and thus creates a distortion. It is the contraction in the level of output of the export good that reduces the price of the immovable factor of production. Furthermore, the export tax will create a "wedge" between the international price and the price paid by domestic consumers, creating an additional distortion. Hence, notwithstanding the fact that the export tax is fully shifted back to the immovable factor of production, the tax still can have excise effects; that is, it distorts the production and the consumption decision. To this extent, the export tax in the long run is not necessarily equivalent to a tax on the income of the immovable factor of production. In the more general case, when the export sector employs factors of production that are movable across sectors, the distortionary effects of the export tax are straightforward.

It might also be argued that over the short run, unexpected increases in the international price of an export commodity can sometimes lead to temporary "windfall" gains to exporters that can be taxed through an export duty.[11] This tax is presumed to be nondistortionary and, some might argue, the windfall gains are "unnecessary" to induce the given level of exports. For the analysis here, the distinction should be made between systematic (expected) and unsystematic (unexpected) tax policy changes. A systematic export duty that applies when prices are above a certain "normal" level will discourage production and exports because if the market is, by and large, competitive, there will be no "excess" profits in the long run, as good years will balance out the bad ones.[12] In addition, any systematic, though temporary, export tax policy with respect to windfall gains will sooner or later be incorporated by producers in their expectations, distorting their economic behavior. Only the taxation of profits, resulting from unsystematic changes, will have no effect on producers' behavior concerning exports, although it might make smuggling more profitable.

Devaluation of the exchange rate can generate windfall profits for exporters, similar to the unexpected increase in the international price of a commodity described above; however, it will also raise the cost of imports and other costs to the exporter. Therefore, it should not be assumed automatically that after a devaluation exports must always be taxed additionally. In fact, the levy of an export tax after devaluation can hamper the achievement of an increase in exports needed to restore the balance of trade equilibrium, which was the primary reason for the devaluation.

Export Duties in Connection with Stabilization Schemes

Developing countries can also rationally use export taxes in connection with three kinds of stabilization schemes: (1) the stabilization of the international price of a commodity or group of commodities, especially in support of international commodity agreements; (2) the stabilization of foreign exchange export earnings derived from the exports of one commodity or group of commodities; and (3) the stabilization of the domestic consumer price of a traded or exportable commodity.[13]

The economic efficiency arguments in favor of commodity stabilization efforts are well known. It has been stated that the free market solution does not necessarily allocate resources efficiently because there are no perfect and complete futures and risk markets and there is no perfect information. Hence, market intervention is called for. The first-best solution would be to encourage the development of efficient futures and insurance markets. If this is not feasible, as a second-best solution, a commodity stabilization scheme can, under certain conditions, improve domestic economic welfare.[14] Since it is reasonable to assume that economic agents generally, and exporters in particular, are risk averse, a commodity stabilization program that reduces the variability of the permanent income of exporters without reducing the mean[15] will improve welfare.[16] Even when the administrative costs of the stabilization scheme are taken into account, exporters could be better off as long as the cost of administration does not exceed the welfare gain from reduced riskiness. Risk averse consumers can also benefit from domestic price stabilization. Finally, from a macroeconomic point of view, the stabilization of foreign exchange earnings can also lead to welfare gains for both producers and domestic consumers. Notice, however, that an efficient export tax used to attain commodity stabilization will not yield tax revenue in net present value terms.

The commodity stabilization schemes can also conceivably have an adverse effect on the economy in two main respects, namely, the size of the levy on producers and the uses to which the proceeds of the levy are put relative to what the producer would have done with it if he had not been subject to such an impost.[17] With respect to the size of the levy, the point is that a high level of export duty implicit in the stabilization levy may adversely affect the producer's incentive to produce the commodity concerned—the actual impact being dependent on the supply elasticity. Second, with respect to the use of the levy, the adverse impact may stem from the fact that the outlays undertaken by the stabilization scheme are much less productive (in terms of additional output generated) than those which the producer would most probably have undertaken in the absence of the levy.

APPRAISAL OF THE IMPACT OF EXISTING EXPORT TAXES

Most of the export tax revenue in developing countries is derived from a select group of commodities that have relatively inelastic demand and supply. Furthermore, for some of these commodities, a small number of developing countries seem to have a large share of the world market. This suggests that the country optimal export taxation of these commodities could be different from zero, at least for such countries. Developing countries generally tax the exports of those commodities that can be taxed according to the country optimal criteria. However, the levels of taxation adopted by individual countries do not correspond to the estimated country optimal tax levels. Most developing countries seem to overtax exports as a result of high "explicit" and "implicit" export taxes.

The empirical evidence, therefore, shows that the majority of developing countries examined in Sanchez-Ugarte and Modi (1987) are overtaxing exports and further that, in general, the observed level of export taxation cannot be justified on the basis of the country optimal export duty criterion. The reliability of this conclusion, of course, hinges on the reliability of the elasticity estimates used as well as the methodology used for estimating the country optimal export duty rates.

The estimated reduction in output for the generally overtaxed commodities, such as coffee, cocoa, cotton, rice, and bauxite, is quite high, especially if the low estimated values of the country optimal tax rates are used as the point of reference.[18] It would appear that for many of the individual countries, the lowering of export tax rates would significantly increase the output of the taxed commodity, if the elasticity estimates are to be trusted. For instance, coffee exports from Côte d'Ivoire, El Salvador, Ethiopia, Sierra Leone, Tanzania, and Togo; cocoa exports from Togo; rubber exports from Sri Lanka; and cotton exports from Sudan could increase more than 40 percent if these countries lowered their export duties to the country optimal level. Furthermore, exports of coffee from Honduras, Rwanda, and Uganda; exports of cocoa from Côte d'Ivoire and Ghana; and rice exports from Brazil could increase from 20 percent to 40 percent if these countries lowered their export duties. Other countries, such as Guatemala, Haiti, Jamaica, Mauritius, and Thailand, would have more modest, but still significant, increases in their volume of exports of the taxed commodities if they lowered their export taxes. Very few countries with large world market shares, such as Colombia for coffee and Malaysia for rubber, would *decrease* the volume of exports of the indicated commodity if country optimal export duties were adopted.

High export taxation also has a depressing effect on the average foreign exchange earnings by commodity. In most cases, the impact on foreign exchange earnings is similar to, though somewhat smaller than, the effect on output. Those countries that are overtaxing the export commodities could increase their foreign exchange earnings if they lowered the level of export tax rates (for example, on coffee, Côte d'Ivoire, Tanzania, and Togo; on cocoa, Togo; on rubber, Sri Lanka; and on cotton, Sudan).

To conclude, in the majority of cases analyzed, the observed levels of export taxation seem high and are detrimental to both the level of exports and foreign exchange earnings. Hence, the supply-side prescription of reducing export taxes, in most cases, would not only increase the volume and the value of exports but could also enhance welfare. Furthermore, a number of countries could lower export taxes to the country optimal level and increase tax revenue by transforming the nonrevenue-yielding implicit export taxes into revenue-yielding export taxes. The last result is particularly relevant for those countries that have a relatively large share in the world market and that are currently overtaxing exports by way of nonrevenue-yielding implicit taxes.[19]

The preceding generalizations need to be qualified. First, certain imperfections in the commodity markets could preclude some developing countries from benefiting, in the short run, from lowering export taxes. As was noted before, commodity agreements and certain import restrictions imposed by industrial countries predetermine, in the short run at least, the feasible level of exports. Any small country that wants to increase output by lowering export taxes may have to sell its output in nonquota markets at a discount. This qualification applies especially to commodities such as coffee, cocoa, tin, rubber, sugar, cotton, and tobacco.

Second, the methodology used in Sanchez-Ugarte and Modi (1987) assumes that there are no other relevant distortions in the economy. For the actual application of the above methodology as a tool for policy making, this assumption should be checked. In most developing countries, it is likely that other agricultural producer prices are also distorted. The increase (or decrease) in production of the taxed commodity would lead to a reduction (or increase) in the production of other agricultural products and could generate positive or negative external effects that should be taken into consideration.

Third, the country optimal export duty should, in general, be estimated taking into account the effect of the export duty on the price of close substitutes and complements in demand and in production. The adjustment is particularly relevant for such commodities as coffee, tea, and cocoa that are close substitutes in demand, but it should also be made in other pertinent cases. The adjustment, however, is expected to increase the value of the optimal export duty relative to the estimates.[20]

Fourth, the approach used here, static partial equilibrium, has its limitations. In a dynamic context it could be expected that a high price of export commodities would lead to technical innovation, either in the form of more efficient use of inputs or creation of substitutes; either of the two would reduce further the demand for the commodity. The dynamic demand function is thus expected to be more elastic than the static one. When general equilibrium considerations are taken into account, the increase in exports in one sector could be compensated by the decline of exports in other activities. The only way of solving this problem is by estimating optimal export duties in a general equilibrium model that takes into account all the interaction that one policy measure generates in the economy.

Fifth, the assumption of constant elasticities for demand and supply has its limitations that can lead to error, because the correct functional specification could be a variable supply function.

Sixth, it is assumed in the analysis that all countries act independently, so that there is no strategic reaction from either producers or consumers when the export duty is changed. In the real world, countries might react strategically to tax changes in forms that could invalidate the optimality of a given export duty derived under the assumption of nonstrategic behavior.

Seventh, the approach followed to estimate country optimal export duties in this paper does not incorporate any distributional considerations. Since export commodities are often produced by low-income farmers in developing countries, it is very likely that export taxes are quite regressive (Tanzi, 1976, and Booth, 1980). It should be noted, however, that government could reduce and even eliminate the regressivity of export taxes by way of income redistribution through expenditure policy. This is unlikely to happen in practice, however, because government expenditure tends to have an urban bias.

Finally, should production of the export commodity be mainly undertaken by a government enterprise, the effect of the reduction in export duty on production could be blurred.[21] For example, the taxation of oil in Mexico, where it is produced under government monopoly, and the taxation of minerals in Zaïre, where production is dominated by a public enterprise, La Générale des Carrières et des Mines (GECAMINES). In Togo, a public enterprise, Office Togolais des Phosphates (OTP), is responsible for the production and marketing of phosphates, the principal export commodity. In all such cases, the tax payment is determined in accordance with the budgetary needs of the government, the financial situation of the public enterprise, and international market conditions. A reduction in the prevailing level of export taxes, however, might have an effect in terms of attracting new private investment into these sectors, provided market entry were permitted.

CONCLUSIONS

Two major conclusions can be derived. First, most of the developing countries we have used as illustration here seem to be overtaxing exports of the selected commodities. This becomes particularly apparent when the high implicit export taxes prevalent in many of these countries are also taken into account. The overtaxation of exports is also suggested by the operation of commodity stabilization schemes that markedly reduce the present value of revenue to producers without similarly reducing riskiness. Hence, the observed levels of export taxation cannot, in general, be justified on grounds of the country optimal export duty argument or based on commodity stabilization. Second, the estimates made here show that the overtaxation of exports of certain commodities may have reduced substantially the level of exports of these commodities for the majority of the countries under study. It also seems to have reduced the level of foreign exchange earnings in most of the cases analyzed.

The main policy recommendation that emerges is that lowering the explicit and implicit levels of export taxation would be advisable not only from a supply-side perspective but also from the point of view of economic efficiency. Over the short and medium runs, however, the existence of market imperfections, introduced by both commodity agreements and protectionism imposed by industrial countries, could well preclude exporting countries from benefiting from the supply-side effects of lowering export taxes and expanding their exports,[22] at the same time government revenues would be lowered.

The ensuing loss of government revenue, in most cases, may turn out to be a major obstacle in lowering export taxes. Many of the developing countries have few alternative sources of revenue, given the difficulties that could be encountered in the administration of more sophisticated, but less distortive, tax systems. It should be mentioned that many of the countries under review could reduce effective levels of taxation and promote exports without losing revenue (and in a few cases even gaining revenue), if the implicit (nonrevenue-yielding) export duties were transformed into formal (revenue-yielding) export taxes. Furthermore, in many instances the reduction of export duties could be undertaken along with the devaluation of the exchange rate, in which case the impact of lowering the tax rates on tax revenue would be reduced and could even lead to an increase in government revenue.

NOTES

1. Export duties are also used to promote the growth of the untaxed activities by changing the producer terms of trade against traditional exports. This rationale for export duties is not pursued here since import tariffs are more commonly employed for this purpose. See Corden (1974).

2. Quotas can be used instead but in that event monopoly profits accrue to individual producers rather than to the government.

3. For instance, domestic sugar production is protected in the European Community (EC) countries and the United States; tobacco is protected in the United States; and rice is protected in Japan.

4. Of the five international commodity agreements that were in existence in the early 1980s, only those for coffee, cocoa, and rubber are fully operational at present. An arrangement for stabilizing sugar prices through export quotas and special stock provisions lapsed after 1983, following the lack of agreement among the parties concerned. The tin agreement lapsed in October 1985 when it ran out of resources required to finance buffer stock purchases. See Hart (1976) for the use of export taxation in connection with commodity agreements.

5. Given that exports to the quota market are restricted, the marginal social revenue to the exporting country is equal to the free trade nonquota price. Optimality would dictate equality between the marginal social revenue and the marginal social cost. If the expected producer price (private marginal revenue) is a weighted average of the free and protected market price, the producer will tend to produce more than what is actually optimal in the hope that he can export more to the quota market. An export tax could close the gap between the private and the social marginal revenue.

6. This is strictly true of export duties levied by a country that is a price taker in the world market and faces a perfectly elastic demand curve for its exports. Hence, a tax imposed on exports will, by necessity, be shifted back to producers. When exports are intermediated by traders, part of the tax burden can be borne by them as well. See Tanzi (1976).

7. A tax on the income of an immovable factor of production is nondistortionary because it does not alter either the level of production or the level of exports of the commodity that employs the taxed factor, since the factor of production has no alternative use.

8. The elasticities of supply of export commodities that have been estimated in the literature for developing countries are all positive, though small.

9. The land used in the production of certain cash crops is not necessarily suitable for the production of other crops.

10. See Mussa (1974), who derives the above result for an import duty.

11. For the sake of symmetry, this argument would require that producers are subsidized when a windfall loss occurs.

12. The international price of a commodity is a random variable. Even though one might attempt to forecast future values, nobody can predict with certainty the price of a commodity at every moment of time. For some commodities there are futures or forward markets which allow producers to reduce the risk involved in the production process, but these markets do not work as efficiently for all types of commodities.

13. Stabilization efforts in these areas have been attempted by a number of developing countries mostly through marketing boards, but export taxes have also been used as one of several complementary policy instruments to attain the desired goal.

14. See Newbery and Stiglitz (1981) for the economic rationale for stabilization.

15. Helleiner (1964) and (1966) examine the role of commodity marketing boards in Nigeria in stabilizing prices paid to producers and their incomes.

16. See Newbery and Stiglitz (1981) for cases where the stabilization of prices is likely to lead to the stabilization of incomes.

17. See Helleiner (1966, chapter 6) for this line of approach.

18. Other circumstantial evidence supporting the above conclusion is substantial. For instance, Ghana has overtaxed exports of cocoa to such an extent that its ranking among producer countries has slipped from first to third place (after Côte d'Ivoire and Brazil). Haiti has also suffered a decline in coffee exports from three-fourths to one-half of total output over the last twenty-five years. Production has remained stagnant, and consumption has increased substantially. The export duty was reduced to 25 percent in 1983 from a high of 40 percent, but no effect has been felt in production yet.

19. Multiple exchange rate practices, for instance, are an implicit form of export taxation that does not yield revenue. In many instances, it might be feasible to eliminate multiple currency practices and keep the explicit ad valorem level of taxation constant; this would certainly increase the yield of the export tax.

20. For instance, the increase in the price of the taxed commodity induced by an increase in the export duty will tend to increase the price of the close substitutes. These higher prices of substitutes counteract the own-price effect. As can be seen, the effect on the price of complements will also tend to counteract the own-price effect.

21. In the case of commodities handled by state-controlled marketing boards, the reduction in the tax burden implicit in their operations may hamper their role, albeit limited, in stabilizing prices paid to producers and their incomes.

22. See Golub and Finger (1979), which discusses the impact of protectionism and taxation on the world commodity market.

29

The Case for Selective Taxes

In many developing countries, particularly lower-income ones, next in importance to taxes on foreign trade are selective taxes on consumption, or "excises." Taxes on such traditional fiscal "vices" as smoking, drinking, and driving are especially important in revenue terms in many countries. Even when more revenue appears to accrue from general sales taxes than from such special commodity taxes, closer examination often shows that a large share of such "general" revenue really comes from taxes on the traditional excise goods of tobacco, alcohol, and petroleum products (see chapter 1).

The following chapter demonstrates that, quite apart from their revenue importance, a surprising number of other arguments can be made to support a continuing substantial role for selective taxes in particular instances. Whatever one may think of the individual merits of each of these arguments, it seems fair to note that not enough attention has been paid to them in most countries (Bird, 1987b). Even when there has been a significant theoretical literature—as there is, for instance, on the virtues of properly designed road charges (Walters, 1968; R. S. Smith, 1975; Prest, 1969)—the resistance of the articulate middle classes has usually ensured that practice has not gone very far down this road (see also chapter 33). Even less attention has been paid to the potential relation between commodity taxes and employment touched on in this chapter (but see Bird, 1982).

Other points of interest touched on in this selection include (as in chapter 27), the need to coordinate taxes on imports and domestic production, methods of adjusting the rates of excise taxes in inflationary circumstances (compare chapter 21), and the equity aspects of excises, both the generally progressive effects of taxes on vehicles and motor fuel and the possibly regressive effects of some other common selective taxes on the urban poor (see chapter 34).

The Case for Selective Taxes on Goods and Services in Developing Countries

Sijbren Cnossen

On the whole, selective taxes on goods and services, also called excises, have received little attention in the professional literature. The ostensible simplicity of the excise base and the forms of imposition have caused some to devote greater analytical and empirical efforts to general taxes on goods and services, also referred to as sales taxes, held to be intellectually more challenging, even if sometimes less relevant to actual policy issues. Important factors, too, in the relative neglect of excise taxation are that historically excises have been reviled for falling more heavily on the poor than on the rich, and for causing distortions or excess burdens in the allocation of economic resources that were thought to be largely absent in the case of sales taxes.

The almost automatic association of excises with a regressive distribution of the tax burden may have prematurely encouraged forms of taxation in developing countries that are more equitable in intent but not necessarily in effect, and also obscured the potential for progressivity in excise design. In recent years, too, there has been a growing recognition that the excess burden argument has less validity than seemed to be the case. In developing countries, inefficiencies in production may be less under excises than under other taxes. In fact, excises may promote economic growth precisely because they are selective. Moreover, feasibility considerations should loom large in the assessment of the effectiveness of any tax. It may be that the excise method of taxation as an intermediate form of tax technology is more capable of being implemented successfully than seemingly more advanced forms of taxation.

The sales tax is the major alternative and indeed the logical successor to an excise system. Throughout the article, therefore, comparisons are drawn with sales (and income) taxes, as well as with the situation in industrial countries. Since excises and sales taxes are twin branches of the same tree, much of what is said should also have a bearing on the latter form of commodity taxation, particularly the sales tax levied at the manufacturing and import stages. Of course, in examining the excise phenomenon the relevant comparison is with broad accounts-based sales and income taxes. The difference between excises and sales and income taxes that are narrowly defined and in effect administered on some presumptive excise basis is not fundamental, but one of name only.

The indirect effects of excise taxation on the rate of economic growth and on stability are not dealt with, because there is no conclusive evidence favoring one

Excerpted from Cnossen (1978).

form of taxation over another to promote these goals. The fine tuning required for the latter is difficult, if not impossible, to implement and monitor in industrial countries. It is perforce of doubtful relevance in developing countries where realistic choices between alternative fiscal instruments are limited. Finally, the argument is one of the relative emphasis to be placed on various forms of taxation not one for the use of excises to the exclusion of other taxes.

WHAT ARE EXCISES?

Broadly speaking, the distinguishing features of excise taxation are selectivity in coverage, discrimination in intent, and usually some form of quantitative measurement in determining the tax liability. The scope of coverage is the most useful distinction between excises and sales taxes. Under an excise system, taxable commodities are individually enumerated in the law, but under a sales tax, the base is typically defined to include all commodities for sale other than those specifically exempted. In practice, coverage may be similar, particularly between an excise system with extended coverage and a sales tax with a large number of exemptions.

Historical precedence and usage in many countries support a broad application of the excise label to include selective taxes on goods, on services, and on road use; these three groupings may be said to comprise an excise system.[1]

Some excises have been enacted solely for revenue purposes, the main consideration being that they could be administered more readily than other taxes. Large sales volume, few producers, inelastic demand, ready definability, and no close substitutes (unless these can be included in the base), are the requirements for excises on products levied for revenue. But most excises are also rationalized on other grounds, or viewed as serving a special purpose. Specific justifications for the imposition of excises may further their acceptability and serve to reduce tax tensions. This contrasts with sales taxes that have been introduced to meet general revenue needs, and are, therefore, "general" in intent, if not in effect.

Various reasons may be advanced to support the imposition of excise-type levies:

1. Excises may be justified to control the consumption of items that are considered immoral or unhealthy, prime examples being sumptuary goods such as tobacco products and alcoholic beverages. At one time or another similar reasons have been given for the excise taxation of sugar, soft drinks, playing cards, fireworks, cabaret admissions, and betting and gaming activities. In the case of sumptuary goods the objective is difficult to attain, since the demand for them is relatively inelastic. Sometimes excises on these goods are alleged to charge consumers for external diseconomies associated with the consumption of cigarettes and liquor.

2. Excises may also be imposed on nonessential or luxury items considered proxies for taxpaying capacity. The most obvious examples are excises on cosmetics, perfumes, jewelry, and furs, but in developing countries selective taxes on electrical appliances, various entertainment-related goods, and motoring fulfill a similar role. In addition, excises on services such as those related to foreign travel, restaurants, hotels, admissions, and club dues, would fall within this category.

3. A special purpose is served by the use of selective taxes to promote employment. It is hypothesized that aggregate employment can be increased directly through alterations in the factor mix, or indirectly by changing the product mix. For instance, excises might be imposed on capital equipment that has strong labor-displacing effects, or more generally, higher taxes might be levied on goods that are produced with capital-intensive technology to induce a shift of consumer demand toward more labor-intensive products. In view of the high rates of unemployment in developing countries, these approaches deserve attention.

4. Fuel taxes and motor vehicle duties may be designed and rationalized as charges for the use of road services provided by governments, although benefits are only partly discernible and charges only an imperfect approximation of price. . Transportation taxes, for example on air fares and freight, may be similarly justified.

5. Related to the sumptuary excises are regulatory type levies, designed to improve efficiency in the use of resources. Examples are the pollution taxes that have recently received so much attention. Like excises on tobacco products and alcoholic beverages, these levies are also designed to internalize external diseconomies generated by the producer or consumer, but unlike the former generally no moral or ethical reasons underlie the objective of a reduction in consumption. A difference, too, is that here the main aim is regulation, whereas revenue is an important objective of sumptuary excises.

The pricing function of road user charges is not discussed further in this article, primarily because it is overshadowed by revenue and equity considerations in developing countries. Pollution is also not a great concern of low-income countries. A clean environment is typically a problem that comes with affluence; it is a "luxury good" with a high income elasticity of demand. Effluent taxes, therefore, are not dealt with either.[2]

The sumptuary or regulatory aspects of excise taxation generally involve some form of physical measurement or control by the excise authorities to determine the tax liability and to ensure compliance with the law. The premises of cigarette producers and alcoholic beverage manufacturers are almost always closely guarded by excise staff, but this form of excise control is often also an integral part of the administrative enforcement mechanism of excises on other goods, including the extended excise systems that are operated on the Indian subcontinent and in the Far East. In some instances, excise staff are replaced by metering devices that record the quantities produced.

The outward sign of physical control is often the stamp or banderol on cigarette packages, liquor bottles, sugar bags, or containers for other excisable goods, the officially numbered ticket to entertainment events, or the license plate or window sticker on motor vehicles. The excise form of control contrasts with compliance procedures for sales taxes, under which liabilities are almost always verified through checks upon written records. Recently, the trend in industrial countries has been to shift excise control to books of account, but even then, statutory provisions for quantitative checks are retained in full force, as exemplified by the updating of excise legislation in the Netherlands in the 1960s.

CULTURAL AND INSTITUTIONAL FACTORS

There is a close interaction between a country's tax system, on the one hand, and the economic, social, and political environment in which it operates, on the other. The importance of cultural and institutional factors is often underestimated by governments and their experts when contemplating the introduction of new taxes or the modification of existing ones. The environment that favors the use of excise taxation in developing countries is broadly the opposite to that described by Richard Goode (1952) as conducive to the successful use of income taxation as a major source of revenue.

1. In a predominantly subsistence economy with little commercial integration, most consumption items are home-produced, or local artisans provide whatever is needed in the form of furniture, clothes, and utensils; generally, even these products are made to order and sold directly to the consumer. Large segments of the population purchase only a limited number of regionally or nationally traded products that can be taxed: cigarettes, matches, sugar, tea, coffee, trinkets, and a few others. Production units of any significance are island-like enterprises with few established forward linkages. In this situation, a broad-based sales tax is not necessary and an income tax not feasible, but selective taxes should suffice for revenue purposes.

2. In a subsistence economy, where a majority of the population is illiterate, the excise method of assessment is better understood and therefore probably regarded as fairer. There are no complicated forms to fill in, nor the temptation or opportunity to make a false return. Broad-based sales and income taxes require a level of literacy that is usually not found among craftsmen and cottage-type industries. Income or turnover concepts, even when they are explained in instructions that accompany tax returns, cannot be comprehended easily. That may also be true in the case of larger establishments that have grown out of cottage industries.

3. In such economies, quantitative measurement of the tax liability and physical forms of control should be easier to apply and more effective than checks upon written records, because books of account are hardly kept at all or are not reliably and honestly maintained. The notion that ledgers might have to be kept to serve some other interest than that of the taxpayer is absent in the small family-type establishment. Usually transactions are settled against cash and not recorded. That situation is difficult to change if the tax administration has no allies in the form of stockholders, parent companies, insurance agents, or other third parties.

4. In most developing countries, the tradition of voluntary compliance that is a basic ingredient for the successful application of income and sales taxes does not exist. Most people define their interests narrowly and do not include among them paying taxes to a remote authority. They regard taxes as confiscatory in nature and will only pay those which are inescapable. Excises are at an advantage here, because they are less easy to evade than paper-controlled levies. Perhaps paradoxically, the successful administration of excises is more likely to improve taxpayer morale than more sophisticated levies that break down in implementation.

5. Selective taxes do not require broad-based political support, but merely an

excise-type of control of designated segments of industrial activity. Returns do not have to be filed by the majority of the population and in contrast with sales and income taxes most people are therefore little aware of the taxes that are being paid. This should be in the interest of the authorities and accord with the desire of the populace to see the tax gatherer as little as possible.

6. Finally, an honest and efficient administration is easier to obtain in the excise field than under sales and income taxes, because the tax base is simpler, enforcement less complicated and internal control of the tax administration easier to accomplish. Comprehensive auditing of taxpayers' accounts is not necessary and there are no collection arrears. Counting goods or establishing their weight, strength, or other physical characteristics requires fewer skills (although more hands) and is less subject to differing interpretations than intricate valuation principles or the handling of non-arm's-length transactions. For lack of adequate records, the determination of sales and income tax liabilities involves judgmental factors which increase the margin for a personal rather than a professional decision and are more likely to lead to dishonest practices.

THE EQUITY OF EXCISE TAXATION

Excises have often been faulted for their lack of progressivity. It is alleged that excise payments as a percentage of an individual's income decline as income rises. Therefore, it is argued, excises do not contribute to a fair distribution of the tax burden. This image, strongly rooted in history, contrasts with that of income taxes that are held to be more capable of imparting progressivity and more adaptable to the individual circumstances of taxpayers. This view is largely correct with respect to industrial countries where there are no major contraints on administrative capacity. In developing countries, however, many people who should be taxed are self-employed and income accrues mainly in kind or from capital sources, forms that are difficult to tax satisfactorily even in industrial countries.

Moreover, the results of recent tax incidence studies for developing countries indicate that their excise systems may exhibit progressivity on account of the dualistic nature of the economies, class-differentiated consumption patterns, excise structures that discriminate against nonessentials, and the generally more adequate administration of excises and related taxes compared to income taxes (Bird and De Wulf, 1973; De Wulf, 1975). There is a presumption that patterns of expenditures on excisable goods, and by extension their excise content, are likely to differ substantially between highly monetized rich urban areas and essentially poor rural subsistence sectors of a developing economy. Rural families purchase most of their goods from local small-scale producers whose output is either exempted or escapes taxation, while urban families are likely to buy more factory made or imported goods that tend to be taxed more effectively. The urban poor probably form an exception to this hypothesis, because they are much less in a position to escape excise burdens than low-income rural families.

An important, if qualified, conclusion of the tax incidence studies is, therefore, that although not ideal, excises may be a better index of taxpaying capacity than is generally believed. In many developing countries almost certainly some progressivity can be imparted through the heavy taxation of expensive cigarettes, liquors, refined sugar, soft drinks, expensive clothing, cosmetics, perfumery, electrical household appliances, air-conditioning units, radios, television sets, musical instruments, photographic equipment, gasoline, passenger cars, foreign travel, hotel rooms, restaurant meals, admissions, and club dues. On equity grounds, much can be said for excise systems with a broad coverage of luxury and semiluxury goods, whether domestically produced or imported. Overall, this should also improve the horizontal equity of excise systems as individuals within higher-income groups may have different tastes for luxury goods, but may spend similar amounts, for example on either cars or pleasure boats. Interestingly, in developing countries income is often assessed on the basis of the most readily available external indices of wealth, including housing, cars, servants, television sets, or other manifestations of spending power that are used as proxies in estimating income. The income tax liability may then be viewed as the sum total of a number of separate excises.

The distinction that would have to be made for progressive excise taxation of goods and services into essentials and nonessentials, or necessities and luxuries, has often been the subject of controversy. Much of the misunderstanding arises from the belief that any definition inevitably involves highly subjective social and moral considerations. In a somewhat cynical view, luxuries are goods and services that only the other person can afford. In another, necessities are defined as goods and services required for maintaining a reasonable standard of living. Generally, these definitions substitute one ambiguity for another. Subjective notions on what people "need" or "do not need" should be avoided.

The following lists more precisely the requirements for progressivity in excise taxation.

1. The cross-section income elasticity of demand for goods and services subject to excise taxation should exceed unity. Under this definition, luxuries are commodities for which expenditure rises proportionately faster than income. An ad valorem excise would then be progressive, that is, excise payments would be an increasing percentage of income when moving up the scale. However, if the good in question is highly sensitive to price changes (which will happen when it is narrowly defined so that substitutes are available), an excise would restrict consumption and hence the effect of the progression would be limited. A subsidiary requirement, therefore, is that excisable commodities should have low price elasticities of demand (after the income effect of changes in price has been accounted for).

2. For the progression to be appreciable, consumption by the higher-income classes must be significant. Excisable commodities should account for a large fraction of the income in the middle and upper parts of the income scale, but they should be minor items in the budgets of low-income groups. Among individual goods fountain pens do not satisfy this criterion, but motor vehicles do.

3. However, even if the second requirement is satisfied, it may well be necessary for revenue purposes to extend excise taxation fairly far into the lower-income

ranges. This would not necessarily be incompatible with the first requirement on income elasticity, but to increase the progressive impact of the excise system, it should then be possible to break excisable commodities down into subgroups. Easy specification is therefore required. It would permit the application of graduated rates that differ on the basis of the nature, quality, or price of excisable commodities, on the assumption that consumption patterns vary accordingly.

4. The key to the whole issue of progressive excise taxation is simplicity in administration, which may involve a trade-off against the third requirement on easy specification. Administrative feasibility requires precise definitions of excisable goods in order to minimize the number of disputes and arbitrary assessments by tax officials, as well as the possibility of imposing enforceable controls or accounting checks on production. Excises on silver, gold, or jewelry and handicrafts often do not satisfy this criterion.

5. The support that taxation derives from prevailing social and moral views on what goods and services should be considered luxuries, should not be lost on policy makers. Therefore, to increase the acceptability of progressive excises, a requirement might be that the commodities in question should be widely regarded as signs of affluence; by implication their taxation would be viewed as an indication of governments' determination to strengthen economic equality.

As an example, the motoring field is probably the single most important vehicle for increasing the progressivity of excise systems in developing countries. The demand for passenger cars and gasoline is usually highly income elastic, expenditures comprise a sizable part of household budgets, related levies are easy to administer, and meet socially with a high degree of acceptance.

EFFICIENCY ASPECTS OF EXCISE TAXATION

During the past thirty-five years, the excise has been singled out in the professional literature as especially inefficient because the price distortion it causes induces a consumer to purchase some good that has an inferior ranking on his preference scale. An excise, the conclusion was, creates an excess burden that could be avoided if instead a general tax on consumption or income were levied that would not interfere with consumer preferences. Recently, though, there has been a growing recognition that the excess burden argument has less validity than seemed to be the case. Thus, it has been demonstrated that in a multiperiod setting in which anticipated spending patterns fluctuate more than anticipated income receipts, an individual who has to meet a fixed tax obligation would prefer to pay a single excise on a residual and postponable item of consumption rather than any other tax—whether levied as a lump sum, on income, or on general consumption expenditures (Buchanan and Forte, 1964).[3]

This institutional approach to taxation, which has not been fully developed, reflects an older philosophy that selective taxes on goods and services are largely "self-imposed," that taxpayers may be aware of the wider range of options available under excise taxation, and that they may well agree with the sumptuary purpose of high excises on tobacco products and alcoholic beverages, or the equity objective of the heavy taxation of luxury goods. Generally, these considerations are not applicable in the case of producer burdens, however, and there is therefore some basis for requiring policy makers to be primarily concerned with divergencies among rates of substitution in production. Thus, the imposition of an excise or a sales tax may exert pressure on producers to reconsider the size of manufacturing establishments, or to adopt alternative production techniques, or yet to change the location of production. These issues are discussed in some detail below.

It is often argued that sales taxes may induce the vertical integration of business firms, owing to the taxation of successive stages of production and distribution. These tax-induced arrangements would be inefficient if they reduced specialization. In developing countries, it is difficult to exclude inputs from the tax, and cumulative effects may occur even under sales taxes that ostensibly avoid these effects in design, because experience indicates that credits or exemptions are not extended in practice. In this setting, excises may be more efficient, precisely because they are selective. By concentrating on a few important commodities, excises involve less interference with business and trade, a criterion that was at one time one of the established principles of a good tax. Also, care can be taken that no tax is levied on goods destined for export, a factor that is especially relevant in an economy with many smallholders and processors of agricultural export products.

Sometimes, excises are intended to bring about changes in forms of economic organization so as to increase aggregate employment or promote other social and economic goals. This could be important for developing countries where capital is relatively scarce and labor is abundant, for it has become clear that expansion of the manufacturing sector alone cannot absorb the increase in the labor force (Morawetz, 1974). Thus, excises may influence the output mix by favoring labor-intensive goods over capital-intensive goods (relying upon the consumer to substitute the former for the latter), or the factor mix by inducing changes in the techniques of production.

Excises may also influence the choice of technology, either directly by taxing capital goods, or indirectly by promoting the use of labor-intensive business forms or methods. Thus, it has been pointed out that factor proportions should be changed in favor of labor for handling, packaging, and storing activities. Here the selective taxation of certain capital goods with a strong labor-displacing effect such as conveyor belts, fork lifts, tractors, and certain types of construction equipment, may be called for. Another possible way the excise system could increase employment would be to use it to discriminate in favor of small-scale industries. These industries, defined to include all firms with twenty to fifty workers each, employ well over half the labor force in most developing countries, and there is evidence that they use more labor-intensive production methods than large-scale manufacturing establishments.

To be sure, a more labor-intensive production technique is not necessarily capital-saving; in other words, it need not have a low capital-output ratio. Hand-pounding rice, for instance, uses only one-hundredth as much capital per man as machine milling, yet it yields only half as much output per unit of capital. For most goods, it would not be feasible to use discriminatory excises either because the rate differential is not large enough to have an appreciable effect, the production process cannot be clearly separated in labor- and capital-intensive parts, or because the method is so complex and introduces so much administrative discretion that any beneficial effect is lost in red tape or collusive practices.

Moreover, there is a presumption that small-scale industries are more labor-intensive than large, not because of the characteristics of the production function, but because their cost structures reflect scarcity prices more closely than those of large firms that are able to import capital goods and raw materials below shadow prices and have easier access to credit facilities and government subsidies. Equally important, wage legislation may be less effective in the small-industry sector and wages therefore lower. If, as appears to be the case, most of the rigidities in the structure of production lie in the factor rather than the product market, then differential excise taxation may be of little help, but more general pricing policies affecting capital goods, wages, and the exchange rate are called for.

Finally, attention should be drawn to the need for coordinating excises on domestically produced commodities and duties on imported goods. In most industrial countries compensating import duties are equivalent to the domestic excise, but in developing countries the duties are generally higher. As a result, the domestic industry might be unduly protected. Resources would be drawn into the production of goods that could be produced less expensively elsewhere, and away from goods for which the country might have a comparative advantage, such as labor-intensive exportables. This protective differential could unintentionally lead to the establishment of uneconomic forms of import substitution.

Coordination is readily achieved by including imported goods that are subject to excises when produced domestically, in the domestic excise base. In addition, a protective import duty, if desired, could be levied to ensure that domestic industries have a chance to build up a competitive position. Distinct treatment focuses the attention of policy makers on the different role that each duty fulfills; possible confusion between ends and means may thus be prevented.

CONFLICTS AND TRADE-OFFS

There are important areas in which excises may both further a less unequal distribution of income and a more efficient allocation of resources although their effects are probably marginal. High excises on capital-intensive luxury goods, for instance, could affect the after-tax distribution of income favorably and also redirect resources into more labor-intensive modes of production. If properly coordinated with import duties, they should also result in foreign exchange savings and prevent undesirable forms of import-substitution. An increase in employment through the differential taxation of output or technological processes may also be expected to improve the income position of the poor. As their demand for labor-intensive agricultural and other products is generally higher than that of the well-to-do, further employment linkages may ensue.

But a conflict between equity and employment arises when a more even income distribution reduces the demand for labor-intensive services such as construction and domestic help. Neither is the case for high excises on luxury goods always as simple as it seems to be. For a large number of people in the middle-income ranges in developing countries—people who play a crucial role in economic development—the opportunity to purchase semiluxury or luxury products may act as a powerful incentive to work harder and save more. Meat, bicycles, toilet preparations, transistor radios, and musical instruments have been cited as incentive goods. If high excises on these goods have a substitution effect in favor of leisure that would outweigh the income effect, the potentially favorable influence on productive effort would reverse direction. On the other hand, it could be argued that this effect is less important than the strong income effect of heavy excises on tobacco products and alcoholic beverages. If these goods were not subject to excise, families at the lower end of the income distribution might have more to spend on high-protein foods and consequently be able to work harder.

Thus, it appears to be difficult sailing between the equity and the efficiency roles of excise taxation. Intuitively, the choice might be made in favor of progressive excises—and the case for them remains strong—but efficiency trade-offs and revenue and feasibility considerations should not be ignored. Ultimately, the weight attached to each goal and the use that is made of each excise instrument depends on each country's social and economic policies. Often there may be more goals than instruments available, the effect of an instrument may not be fully predictable, or it may be used so intensively that it reverses disrection. But if the various goals and excise instruments are viewed together, broadly the prescription should be followed that internally the highest excises should be applied on luxury goods produced with capital-intensive technology, and the lowest on necessities or sumptuary goods made with labor-intensive production techniques. On the external side, the highest excise-cum-import duty should be levied on luxury goods that can also be produced domestically, and the lowest on necessities that cannot be produced domestically.

ADMINISTRATION AND COMPLIANCE

Basically, the administration of excises is similar to customs operations, with the difference that instead of crossing international boundaries, goods enter the domestic market from premises closely guarded by excise staff. In a sense then, factories in which excisable goods are being produced may be considered "extraterritorial," because nothing is admitted into the rest of the country without the permission of the excise staff. The role of excise and customs staff is to canalize the flow of goods, verify and examine contents, classify, appraise values, undertake laboratory tests if necessary, and check quantities and values against accompanying records. The problems of the custom house—misclassification, improper valuation, underreporting of magnitudes—are frequently also those of an excise administration.

In this capacity, excise and customs personnel resemble policemen, appraisers, and chemists, but not accountants or auditors. They may be familiar with the records of a warehousekeeper, but they would not feel at home with balance sheets, and profit and loss statements. This is in sharp contrast with sales taxes that rely on examinations of books of account and other documentary evidence to verify compliance with the law. To ascertain taxable turnover, sales tax auditors are concerned with financial flows and transactions, with debtors (sales) and creditors (purchases), and with cash and bank statements, but not with physical properties and quantities. A sales tax auditor is an expert in analyzing the flow of funds, in detecting the underreporting of sales, and in making net worth statements, but he is not acquainted with the technicalities of production processes and warehousing. In terms of ensuring compliance, therefore, a sales tax is much more akin to a business income tax, where the proper computation of turnover is also the key to the examination of a taxpayer's return.

The fundamental differences between tax systems (such as excises and customs duties) that rely on quantitative checks, and those (such as sales and income taxes) that depend on accounting controls for enforcement purposes should be emphasized. In implementing the law, sales and income taxes rely on voluntary filing of self-assessed returns by taxpayers. For these taxes to be effective, taxpayers must be willing and able to maintain proper accounts, while the tax administration must have enough trained and experienced auditors to examine the records proficiently. Excises and customs duties, on the other hand, do not need taxpayer cooperation for assessment, and there are almost no collection problems. The reverse of the coin is, of course, that these taxes offer a greater opportunity for exercising leverage, and this may in fact lead to undue interference with taxpayers' activities.

On the whole, excises are an especially certain form of taxation. There is little room for arbitrary decisions and interpretations by the tax authorities. This contrasts with sales taxes under which provisions on valuation and arm's-length transactions (important in developing countries) have to be applied that may put the taxpayer at the mercy of the tax assessor. Income taxes, too, have underlying concepts that are difficult to define and apply in developing countries. The various discontinuities in definitions and classifications that may occur in the excise field are almost always factual as opposed to the more conceptual nature of the tax base under sales and especially income taxes that often create high levels of dispute between tax administration and the taxpaying community. If properly designed, excise laws can offer both taxpayers and tax officials a better understanding and appreciation of their respective obligations.

CONCLUDING REMARKS

Excise forms of taxation emerge rather well from a comparison with broad-based sales and income taxes, particularly when various institutional constraints in developing countries are taken into account. Excises are certainly an important source of revenue; they are not necessarily inelastic in response to changes in income as has often been contended. In fact, in some countries excise forms of control may better ensure the real value of government receipts under inflationary conditions than procedures for sales taxes. In general, more use might be made of ad valorem rates applied to constructive values (appraised retail prices, for instance) so as to retain the administrative simplicity of the excise method of control and to steer clear of any discrimination against forward-integrated producers.

The widely held belief that most excises are regressive is, except for tobacco products, not supported by the incidence surveys that have been made. In countries that lack a substantial degree of commercial integration and in which consumption patterns differ between the poor and the rich, excise incidence may even exhibit progressivity. Regressive excises are acceptable if revenues cannot be raised by other means and if they finance badly needed public services for the poor. More can be done in excise design to increase the progressivity of excise systems. In developing countries progressive commodity taxation is called for because income taxes do not always seem to fulfill the equity function satisfactorily.

On the whole, the use of excise systems for nonfiscal purposes, unless broadly stated, greatly complicates administration. It is likely that the benefit, if any, of intricate schemes of exemptions and concessions, for instance to encourage the production or use of labor-intensive commodities or processes, is out of proportion to its cost and jeopardizes the revenue role of the excise system. Generally, excises are not finely calibrated instruments capable of achieving social and economic policy objectives.

In developing countries, excise systems may contribute substantially to certainty in taxation. By focusing on single commodities and prescribing in detail control and collection procedures that are attuned to the peculiarities of each production process or the way in which a service is rendered, the policy maker leaves no doubt who should be taxed and to what extent. No room is left for an arbitrary determination of the tax liability, a factor of which the social and economic importance can scarcely be overemphasized. Compared to other taxes, excises may appear rudimentary in design and cumbersome in operation, but in practice they may be administered more effectively with ultimately more equitable and efficient results.

NOTES

1. For a more elaborate treatment of definitional aspects of excises and sales taxes, see Cnossen (1977).

2. But see Cnossen (1977), chapter 5, and the literature cited therein. In addition to the justifications mentioned above, excises on raw materials have been thought to prevent waste or induce the growing of high-yielding plants. An example is the old sugar excise in Germany. Mention should also be made of a presumptive form of excise taxation operated on the Indian subcontinent that has been viewed as a stimulus to production. For a treatment of the theoretical aspects of and practical experience with this levy, see Cnossen (1977), chapter 6.

3. Of course, there is also the well-known argument that in the real world an excise system that disturbs more optimum conditions is not necessarily inferior to an income or sales tax that disturbs fewer, because if one of the Paretian optimum conditions cannot be fulfilled, a second-best optimum situation is achieved only by departing from all other optimum conditions.

30

Improving General Sales Taxes

Despite the eloquent plea made in the preceding selection for closer attention to the merits and design of selective taxes, there is no question that general sales taxes are the wave not only of the future but of the present in most developing countries. In 1977, for example, 16 out of the 26 countries in the Caribbean and Latin America included in Cnossen (1977) had sales taxes of some description; by 1983, 26 of 29 developing countries in the western hemisphere had such taxes in place (Bird, 1987b). In particular, the value-added tax is clearly on the rise. In 1976, for instance, Due (1976) identified 5 countries in Latin America with such a tax; by 1984 Goode (1984) listed 11 such countries. Since 1984, some form of value-added tax has been introduced in Turkey and Indonesia, and similar taxes are under consideration in many more developing countries.

Despite this impressive trend, there are still many developing countries, especially including such less-developed countries as those of sub-Saharan Africa, that have at best a limited basis on which to establish a general sales tax, let alone a full-fledged value-added tax. (For useful earlier discussions of sales taxes in Africa, see Due, 1963, and Hill, 1977). The central argument in the following chapter is that such countries as a rule would be better advised to build on the variety of indirect consumption taxes they already have in place rather than leaping at once to a value-added tax on, say, the Korean model discussed in chapter 31 below. (Other discussions of the relative merits of alternative types of sales taxes may be found in Due, 1972, and Bird, 1985.)

Several points in this discussion deserve emphasis. In the first place, even if a full-fledged value-added tax is not feasible it is indeed important to limit "cascading," or the cumulation of taxes in the prices of final products as a result of the taxation of inputs. Studies in various countries have shown that pre-retail stage sales taxes may sometimes produce very large "cascaded" taxes on nominally exempt goods and services, often with undesirable allocative and distributive results (Ahmad and Stern, 1983; Bird and Miller, 1989a). The only way this problem can be fully resolved is to go to a tax, either single-stage or value-added, that goes through to the retail stage.

Secondly, this paper is a good example of how the rather abstract optimal tax arguments presented earlier in chapter 4 may be used in combination with practical considerations to design a sensible tax structure. For example, uniform rates are not, according to the authors, particularly desirable in a general sales tax, largely on "optimal tax" grounds. Unfortunately, the authors do not consider the possible virtues of an alternative "luxury excise" approach (chapter 29) in achieving their desired progressive end (see also Bird, 1970a). Nor, more importantly, do they pay adequate attention to the administrative problems to which rate differentiation inevitably gives rise (Cnossen, 1982).

Finally, picking up a theme already noted in the introduction to chapter 27, this chapter notes how sales tax structures in various countries have adapted both to the need for revenues and to trade policy liberalization and emphasizes the importance of considering such changes in a broad public finance framework in view of the revenue importance of trade taxes.

Consumption Taxes in Sub-Saharan Africa

Zmarak Shalizi and Lyn Squire

The theme of this paper can be summarized in the form of three propositions: First, a tax on consumption expenditure should be a feature of a well-designed tax structure in the long run. Second, while recognizing the limitations imposed by the administrative capacity of tax departments in developing countries, tax reforms should, nevertheless, be consistent with the desired long-run structure of taxation. And third, to the extent possible, tax reforms should build on existing tax instruments.

The three propositions, however, are treated in different ways in the paper. The first proposition, the desirability of taxes on consumption, is accepted with little elaboration on the grounds that consumption expenditure is an important base for taxation and that it is preferable for commodity taxation to avoid interfering with the efficiency of domestic production or the opportunities provided by international trade.

The core of the paper is concerned with a discussion of the second and third propositions, that is, that incremental changes be consistent with the long-term desired tax structure and that the incremental changes build on existing tax instruments. Note first, that these two propositions are potentially incompatible. There is nothing to guarantee that the existing tax structure will possess the rudiments of the tax structure that is desired in the long run. One purpose of this paper, therefore, is to identify situations where these propositions are compatible and where they are not. And second, note that there is no established theoretical justification for either of these latter two propositions, although they accord well with common sense. The second purpose of the paper, therefore, is to identify issues of practical importance which merit further theoretical analysis.

Before proceeding to the main discussion in the paper, those features of commodity taxes which qualify a tax instrument as a consumption tax are restated. We reserve the term "full-fledged" consumption tax for a tax which

1. avoids taxation of transactions between producers (i.e., does not tax inputs used in production) and does not cascade through interindustry links in the production process;
2. is based on the "country of destination rule" and does not differentiate between different sources supplying the domestic market—imports or domestic production—and does not include in its base domestic production destined for external markets—exports;

Excerpted from Shalizi and Squire (1986).

3. goes through the retail stage of the production-distribution chain; and
4. is broad-based and includes in addition to manufacturing activities, non-manufacturing activities such as construction, utilities, and some services.

Note that the list of characteristics of our "full-fledged" consumption tax does not include uniform tax rates across products. The latter can be justified on the basis of administrative convenience. However, in general, some degrees of differentiation will be necessary and appropriate either on grounds of equity or, where adequate information is available, on grounds of equity and efficiency.

Taxes which exhibit characteristics (1) and (2), or can readily be converted to have these characteristics, are referred to as "embryonic" consumption taxes in this paper. Characteristic (3), that the tax go through the retail stage, is a necessary but insufficient condition for a sales-type tax to avoid taxing transactions between producers, whereas a VAT-type tax through the manufacturer/importer stage can exhibit the first two characteristics without going through the retail stage. It is, for this reason, that the most likely type of tax to be referred to in this paper as an "embryonic" consumption tax is a commodity tax with VAT-like characteristics.

THE PROCESS OF REFORM

As noted above, there is no well-established theoretical justification for presuming that tax reforms made today need necessarily be consistent with long-run objectives for the tax system. Two practical arguments can be suggested, however, in support of this position. The first is that, other things being equal, investors are more willing to invest when the fiscal environment is relatively stable than when many tax changes are being made and then reversed. It pays, therefore, to minimize the number of tax changes in order not to reduce business uncertainty. The second reflects the fixed set-up costs of changing administrative practice and learning to apply new measures well. It is desirable, therefore, to minimize the frequency of tax reforms which involve the introduction of new instruments and/or administrative procedures.

In the past, departures from the path consistent with long-run objectives have been justified for administrative reasons or in response to other short-term pressures. The administrative constraint is presented in the form of a lack of familiarity with the implementation of suitable instruments. This rationale has been used to justify the heavy reliance on production and trade taxes in sub-Saharan Africa. A substantial number of countries in sub-Saharan Africa are capable of administering "embryonic" consumption-type taxes which do not interfere with production efficiency, and the revenue role of these taxes has been increasing steadily. How to build on these "embryonic" consumption taxes, or convert existing taxes on production and trade into "embryonic" consumption taxes, is addressed at the end of this section. Before, that, however, it is necessary to discuss some of the short-run pressures that may cause the tax structure to depart from a desired long-run path.

Two categories of pressure are identified. The first includes pressures arising from the expenditure side of budget. These in turn are of two types, those arising from shocks to the economy, such as changes in the price of oil, global interest rates, etc., and those arising from poor planning of revenue needs associated with growing capital and recurrent expenditures. Both types of expenditure pressures have resulted in "urgent" demands for additional revenue which have been accommodated by hasty, ad hoc responses that have either not recognized the possible consequences for dynamic and static efficiency or have placed a lower weight on these consequences. The second arises from trade liberalization reforms which result in the restructuring of trade tariffs based on a specific interpretation of efficiency, whose intellectual antecedents are found in the literature on effective protection. Examples of trade policy recommendations that reduce effective protection but move the tax system away from its long-run, preferred position are used to illustrate this point.

Revenue Pressures: The Case of Malawi

In principle, there is no reason why a rapid increase in tax effort should involve a departure from an appropriate system of taxation. In many countries, however, the urgency of revenue requirements has precluded the careful assessment of alternatives that might otherwise have been used. While the particular method of revenue generation varied among countries, the particular case of Malawi illustrates one mode of fiscal adjustment that clearly increased the distortionary costs of taxation and moved the tax system away from a preferred long-run tax structure.

Much of Malawi's revenue-generating effort, in the last decade or so, involved increased taxation of imports. The implicit effective rate of taxation on imports—revenue from imports divided by the c.i.f. value of imports—increased from 11.7 percent in 1976 to 32.1 percent in 1982. Between 1976 and 1982, nominal protection increased for consumer goods and intermediates. Second, the taxation of inputs—for both intermediate and capital goods—increased. In other words, Malawi generated additional revenue but, in doing so, increased protection[1] for import substitutes, reduced the competitiveness of export-oriented production in the absence of a well-functioning duty drawback scheme, and introduced distortions in the choice among inputs used in production.

Given the constraints on the level of public expenditures in Malawi and the rate at which it could be reduced, the relevant question is whether the same revenue could have been generated in a more efficient manner. The government's revenue requirements could have been met by increasing the surtax [a tax on imports and domestic manufacturing, with goods sold to other surtax payers being tax free] rate from 25 to 33 percent rather than by relying on increases in less desirable import tariffs, and the eventual introduction of an explicit export tax. This strategy would have yielded the required amount of revenue, avoided the taxation of inputs used in production, avoided an increase in nominal and effective protection rates, and avoided the disincentives resulting from the taxation of exports. Within the large-scale manufacturing sector and the export sector, therefore, production would have been more efficient as it would have responded to a different pattern of price signals. Moreover, the use of the surtax would not have required any new administrative mechanism. Thus, the required revenue could have been generated in the short run within the existing administrative framework without compounding existing distortions. At the same time, the resulting high surtax rate focused attention on the narrowness of the existing commodity tax base and the need to improve administrative capacity over the medium term to expand the base subject to the surtax.

The point remains, however, that, under the pressure of urgent demands for extra revenue, countries adopt tax measures that are inconsistent with long-run objectives and which subsequently have to be changed. Such an approach to generating revenue reduces production efficiency and increases business uncertainty, both of which are avoidable.

Tariff Reforms: The Case of World Bank Recommendations

A second source of pressure that causes countries to diverge from a steady approach to a more desired tax structure arises from tariff reform recommendations frequently made by the World Bank as part of policies to liberalize international trade. Much of this advice derives from trade theory in general and the concept of effective protection in particular. While the normative content of effective protection rate analysis is limited,[2] in practice rates of effective protection are often so high and uneven that some effort to reduce the average rate and its variance are probably desirable. The important question, however, concerns the manner in which this should be done.

Trade policy recommendations often contain the following three steps: (1) quantitative restrictions should be replaced by tariffs; (2) nominal protection, mainly for consumer goods, should be reduced by lowering nominal tariffs; and (3) in order to reduce effective protection below that implied by the second step, tariffs on intermediate goods should be increased until eventually a single tariff rate applies to all imports with no exceptions.[3]

The first two recommendations are consistent with a move towards an increased reliance on consumption taxes. The third recommendation, however, is more problematic. While country circumstances may occasionally justify this particular set of policy recommendations, its use as a general policy prescription raises a number of issues. First, taxes on inputs are not a feature of the long-run, preferred tax structure, both because they distort production choices where there are substitution possibilities between inputs and because they cascade as a result of interindustry transactions. At some point, therefore, they will have to be eliminated. Their imposition and subsequent withdrawal may harm business confidence and strain local tax administration capability as noted above. Whatever their merits in the short-run, these longer-run consequences should be borne in mind.

Second, even in the short run, taxes on inputs are not always the preferred method of reducing protection. As far as consumer goods are concerned, a reduction in nominal protection coupled with an increase in tariffs on imported inputs will obviously reduce effective protection. It will also provide protection to the domestic production of intermediate goods even if there is no basis for such protection (e.g., on infant industry grounds). There is no argument in theory or general empirical principle to suggest that this "compensatory" protection is superior to accepting the level and variance of effective protection for consumer goods arising from the reduced level of nominal protection (step two of the trade policy recommendations alluded to above).

The earlier discussion of consumption taxes, however, offers an alternative approach to reducing protection for consumer goods which avoids increasing nominal tariffs on imported inputs. Recall that many countries already have broad-based taxes that are levied ex factory on the domestic production of consumer goods. Nominal protection, and therefore effective protection, can be reduced without loss of revenue by increasing the taxes on domestic production of consumer goods relative to the nominal tariffs on competing imports. Where an "embryonic" consumption tax is available, this recommendation requires a temporary supplemental tax on domestically-produced goods until the nominal tariff on consumer goods can be reduced further. Where "embryonic" consumption taxes are not yet available and taxes on domestic production are separate from tariffs on competing imports, implementation is straightforward. The commodity tax on domestic production can be increased up to the point where it equates the tariff on competing imports.

This use of taxes on the domestic production of consumer goods to reduce nominal and effective protection beyond that possible through a direct lowering of nominal tariffs on consumer goods, has not always been recognized in the context of trade reform, mainly because the focus of such exercises is usually confined to quotas, duties, and exchange rates. A broader, public finance perspective that integrates duties and domestic taxes provides a better framework for the analysis of policies to reduce protection even in the short run.

Even if the limitations of the "compensatory" protection arguments are conceded, it is argued that tariffs on inputs be increased for *revenue* reasons. In fact, World Bank advice on trade reforms has sometimes resulted in a failure to consider the implications of tariff reform for the budget. Since taxes on international trade form an important part of total revenue (around 43 percent in 1981 in sub-Saharan Africa), the effect of a major tariff reform could have significant—positive or negative—effects on the budget. A reform that leads to a major loss of revenue runs the risk that ad hoc revenue-generating measures will be introduced that not only negate the beneficial effects of reform but also jeopardize future efforts to restructure taxation. The revenue argument to increase tariffs on inputs used in production can only be justified if the revenue-generating capabilities of less distortionary taxes, such as consumption-type taxes, have been exhausted. In light of our previous discussion regarding the growing share of revenue generated by consumption taxes, constraints in adequately offsetting tariff reductions through higher consumption-type taxes must be demonstrated, not assumed.

Implications for the Process of Tax Reform

The basic point of the present section is that consumption taxes should play a more important role in tax reform. As the above examples suggest, changes in the tax system often occur during crises. Countries will take new tax measures in order to generate urgently needed revenue. Often this will be accompanied or followed by changes in the system of tariffs when it becomes overwhelmingly clear that the efficiency of domestic production is seriously impaired. In both sets of circumstances, an expansion in the role of consumption taxes should be given serious consideration primarily to avoid ad hoc or short-run measures that will ultimately have to be reversed.

Where "embryonic" consumption taxes are already in place, their role as a source of revenue should be increased at the expense of tariffs. In the short run, this can be achieved by means of an increase in the consumption tax rate with a compensating reduction in tariff rates. In the long run, expansion in the base will allow further reductions in rates and cause an increasing amount of revenue to be generated from the taxation of domestic activities. The development of the value-added tax in the Ivory Coast illustrates this process. In 1960, the tax accounted for 15 percent of total revenue with 70 percent of its contribution coming from the taxation of imports. By 1982, the corresponding figures were 30 percent and 40 percent. Thus, the tax has increased in importance and an increasing share of its total revenue is coming from the taxation of domestic activities. Similar though slightly less dramatic changes occurred with the Malawian surtax. Tax reforms in countries with "embryonic" consumption taxes should concentrate on administrative improvements that will enable an expansion of the base of these taxes by gradually incorporating more nonmanufacturing sectors into the tax net and moving the collection points further along the production-distribution chain from the import/ex factory level towards the retail level.

While many countries in sub-Saharan Africa have "embryonic" VAT-like consumption taxes whose expansion is administratively feasible, many others do not. In some cases existing tax instruments can readily be transformed into "embryonic" consumption taxes. Consider Ghana's sales tax. Unlike a genuine consumption tax, this tax discriminates between imported and domestic goods. Nevertheless, the administrative structure is already in place for conversion to a consumption tax through the import/manufacturing stage. That is, establishing a common rate for the two bases subject to tax (imports and domestic production) will transform this tax into a more fully developed consumption-type tax.

There are other cases, such as Zambia, where the base of the sales tax is domestic production only and competing imports are subject to tariffs. In this case, extending the sales tax to include imports and eliminating tariffs by an equivalent amount will result in an "embryonic" consumption tax. Since importers are already being taxed, and since the domestic production of consumer goods is also subject to tax, the development of this "embryonic" consumption tax requires coordination/restructuring of existing tax instruments rather than the introduction of an entirely new one. It should, therefore, be administratively feasible. Thus, restructuring trade tariffs and domestic taxes to produce a broad-based consumption tax that is, or becomes, a major source of revenue should be the primary objective of tax reform in countries which do not already have an "embryonic" consumption tax.

In still other countries—for example, Ethiopia, Tanzania, Cameroon—the only broad-based domestic tax may be a turnover tax. This type of tax implies the taxation of inputs which cascades through the production process and encourages vertical integration. In this case, movement to a consumption tax requires elimination of taxes on inputs and integration with the taxation of imports. Once again, however, the presence of a turnover tax provides the administrative structure for a relatively simple transition to a consumption tax.

Taxation of inputs can be eliminated in several ways. Malawi's surtax, for example, is based on the exemption principle. "Registered" producers—those paying surtax on their output—are exempt from the payment of tax on their inputs. This scheme, generally described as a "ring" system is probably the simplest to administer where the tax base is relatively small. In Malawi, for example, 85 percent of total revenue from surtax is generated from imports and eleven large firms. As the tax base extends beyond the manufacturing sector, however, the crediting system associated with the value-added tax may be more appropriate. This is the approach adopted in the Ivory Coast, for example. An intermediate approach—part exemption, part crediting—has been introduced in Kenya. In this scheme, goods that are clearly intended for production, such as major capital goods, are exempt while other goods, such as sewing machines or textiles, which could be for final consumption or intermediate use, are subject to the crediting system. This hybrid approach may be a convenient intermediate step in the move towards a genuine value-added tax with full crediting.

Given existing administrative capacity, it is unlikely that these "embryonic" consumption taxes can be extended to agriculture, small-scale enterprises and services (including trade and transportation) in the short run, given valuation and enforcement problems. As a result, the "embryonic" consumption taxes achieve production efficiency within the large-scale, import-substituting and exporting sectors but not necessarily between these sectors and the rest of the economy. Thus, the system confers a competitive advantage on sectors whose output is not subject to tax ex factory but which compete with large-scale, taxpaying manufacturers or with imports. As noted above, however, "embryonic" consumption taxes are usually designed such that those who escape taxation of their output are obliged to pay taxes on their inputs. This reduces, but probably does not offset, the competitive advantage in the domestic market that the tax system would otherwise confer on those sectors whose output escapes taxation. In addition, the taxation of inputs distorts production decisions, thereby impairing the efficiency of production in these latter sectors. Moreover, it reduces their competitiveness in export markets. As the tax system develops, however, it will be possible to extend the consumption tax along the production-distribution chain to the retail level and to include more and more enterprises and sectors. As this happens, the proportion of inputs subject to taxation will decline. In this way, the existing rudimentary consumption taxes are transformed into genuine consumption taxes and the taxation of inputs is phased out naturally without any change in the structure of tax instruments.

While reform during crisis may be the norm, there are exceptions. Countries, such as the Cameroon, with adequate flows of revenue from nonrenewable resources are well advised to plan for the future. Thus, the Cameroon has recognized that the current source of revenue—oil—will be gone in about ten years' time and that new sources of revenue will be required. Introducing a sound tax system at this time would ease the transition from oil to other sources of taxation. In this process, consumption taxes should play an important role. The Cameroon is currently experimenting with a standard value-added tax (VAT) in the construction sector. If the experiment proves successful, its extension to other sectors will presumably follow shortly. Cameroon is probably one of the few countries in sub-Saharan Africa which has the time to experiment with new forms of tax administration. It is less dependent, therefore, on the current existence of rudimentary consumption taxes which can serve as the administrative base for a more extensive reliance on such taxes. For other countries, where the need for reform may be more pressing, the existence of "embryonic" consumption taxes is a critical factor in the design of an appropriate reform strategy.

CONCLUSION

This paper has argued that "embryonic" consumer taxes are already in existence in many sub-Saharan African countries and that, in designing tax reform, every effort should be made to build upon these existing bases. It was noted, however, that these taxes are incomplete and partial and will remain so for some time. Their extension and development depend on improvements in tax administration and the general expansion of the formal sectors of the economy.

This observation highlights an important link between the structure of the tax system and its administration. If consumption taxes are part of the present system but are still underdeveloped, and if consumption taxes are seen as a desirable component of the tax system in the long run, then selected improvements in administration can easily be identified. That is, ways need to be found (1) to improve the exclusion of interindustry transactions from the tax base, (2) to "widen" the tax base by including more and more enterprises from the informal sector, and (3) to "lengthen" it by moving further down the production-distribution chain. Appropriate administrative reform, therefore, should accompany reforms in the structure of taxation involving greater reliance on consumption-type taxes.

NOTES

1. In spite of the more rapid rate of increase in the implicit tax rate on imported inputs relative to those on imported consumer goods, it cannot be concluded that "effective protection" of domestic value added decreased across the board because the level of aggregation obscures the fact that some industries had negative effective protection and others obtained inputs which were not taxed.

2. See, for example, Newbery and Stern (1987).

3. We are here abstracting from other elements of stabilization and adjustment policies such as changes in exchange rate, interest rate policies, price controls, etc., not because they are in any way less important but because the focus of this paper is on the incentive and revenue implications of different types of explicit commodity taxes including tariffs.

31

The Value-added Tax

As already mentioned, the value-added tax is clearly the tax of choice in many developing countries. Indeed, the only phenomenon comparable to the rapidity of its spread in recent years was probably the implantation of the income tax earlier in this century, largely under colonial aegis. It is therefore important to understand just what a value-added tax is and how it works.

The following chapter describes in some detail one of the more striking cases in recent years of the introduction of a value-added tax in a developing country, Korea (see also Han, 1987). As noted earlier with respect to chapter 7, some features of the Korean experience are undoubtedly unique, such as its cultural and political setting. Some developing countries have not done nearly so well with implementing a value-added tax, for example, Guatemala (Bird, 1985a). Moreover, not even the countries of the European Community have gone as far as Korea in computerizing some aspects of the value-added tax. Despite these facts and despite its length, this chapter repays close attention, owing to the thoroughness with which it reviews the relevant issues. (For further discussion, see Gillis, Sicat, and Shoup, forthcoming; Tait, 1988).

Only a few points from this detailed account are singled out for brief comment here. In the first place, it should be emphasized that, as Choi notes, some of the economic advantages cited for the value-added tax in Korea seem to be specious or at least overdone, notably the alleged promotion of exports (Krauss and Bird, 1971). On the other hand, there is no question that the outstanding advantage of a value-added tax—even in comparison to a retail sales tax—is that it permits the complete elimination of cascading.

Secondly, the administrative advantages of the value-added form of collecting sales taxes can also easily be overemphasized. Outside of the unusual case of Korea in the first years of the tax, individual invoices are not usually cross-checked except on audit, and even in Korea this practice has since been de-emphasized as it proved to be exceedingly costly in terms of revenue produced. Ultimately, the effectiveness of a value-added tax, like that of an income tax, depends upon efficient administrative audit to ensure taxpayer honesty, not on gimmicky "self-enforcing" structural features. Moreover, the value-added tax not only imposes a selectively heavier compliance cost on smaller firms (Sandford et al., 1981), but it is also subject to some special frauds of its own concerning false invoices used to claim refunds. As Korean experience shows, to introduce a value-added tax successfully requires a considerable amount of planning and preparation.

To administer a full-fledged value-added tax properly is also not an easy task. Even a poorly-administered broad-based sales tax, however, can produce a lot of revenue with relatively few complaints from taxpayers. The revenue productivity of value-added taxes, even when relatively poorly administered, is undoubtedly one of their most attractive features to governments all over the world, in developing and developed countries alike (Aaron, 1981). While, as Tanzi (1987) has shown, in this respect one broad-based sales tax may be largely substitutable for another, there is no doubt that the value-added tax is, so to speak, the fashionable way these days to tap the revenue potential, even in poor countries, of mass consumption taxation. For an interesting early argument on the desirability of such taxation, see Chelliah (1960).

Value-added Taxation:
Experiences and Lessons of Korea

Kwang Choi

The value-added tax (VAT) is a tax system whereby enterprises are taxed on the value that they add to the goods and services that they purchase from other enterprises. Unlike a retail sales tax, VAT is collected at each stage in the production and distribution process.

REASONS FOR AND OBJECTIVES OF
THE INTRODUCTION OF VAT

The introduction of VAT in Korea was a response to a complex network of political, economic, administrative, budgetary, and tax goals. The reasons for the introduction of VAT in Korea, as announced by the government, include the simplification of the indirect tax system and its administration, the promotion of exports and capital formation, and the preservation of the neutrality of indirect taxes.

VAT was introduced to simplify the previous indirect tax system and its administration. Each of the previous indirect taxes replaced by VAT had its own rate structure as well as a different tax base and administrative procedure. The consolidation and incorporation of numerous indirect taxes into the VAT would simplify the rate structure, tax base, and administration of the indirect tax system, thereby eliminating the overlapping auditing practices that had plagued the previous system. VAT also represents an important instrument against tax evasion by means of the reciprocal controls exercised by taxpayers themselves.

VAT was implemented to promote exports and capital formation. With the introduction of VAT, exports are zero rated at the final stage of production and rebates are available on taxes paid at earlier stages of production, while the cumulative taxes paid at earlier stages of transactions in exported goods were either not rebatable or only partly refundable under the previous system. Therefore, it was believed that the introduction of VAT would have a favorable effect on exports, which have been the driving force behind the rapid growth of the Korean economy. While the previous indirect tax system did not provide credit for the taxes paid on investment goods, taxes were not to be imposed on capital investment under the new regime of consumption-type VAT. Accordingly, the substitu-

Excerpted from Choi (1984).

tion of VAT for previous indirect taxes was thought to encourage capital formation.

The introduction of VAT was strongly recommended because the previous cascade turnover tax system was believed to have the following disadvantages resulting in resource misallocation and inefficiency: first, the turnover tax encouraged vertical integration because the reduction of interfirm sales reduced total tax liabilities; second, it penalized specialization for the same reason; and third, estimates of the tax content of a price at any particular stage of production were perforce arbitrary, which in turn made indirect tax adjustment at country borders arbitrary. All in all, the adoption of a VAT was regarded as a reform of an unwieldy and distortionary indirect tax system.

Although the government emphasized that the VAT was designed not to increase tax revenue but to remove the baneful effects of the previous gross turnover taxes, it must be stated that the government expected the VAT to yield the substantial revenue necessary to meet the fiscal demands required for the successful implementation of the Fourth Five-Year Economic Development Plan. The influence of budgetary needs was, if not the only cause, at least an important reason for the decision to establish VAT in Korea.

The VAT is superior to a business tax or a sales tax from the point of view of revenue security for two reasons. In the first place, under VAT it is only buyers at the final stage that have an interest in undervaluing their purchases, since the deduction system ensures that buyers at earlier stages will be refunded the taxes on their purchases. Therefore, tax losses due to undervaluation should be limited to the value added at the last stage. Under a retail sales tax, on the other hand, retailer and consumer have a mutual interest in underdeclaring the actual purchase price.

Secondly, under VAT, if payment of tax is successfully avoided at one stage nothing will be lost if it is picked up at a later stage; and even if it is not picked up subsequently, the government will at least have collected the VAT paid at stages previous to that at which the tax was avoided, while if evasion takes place at the final stage the state will lose only the tax on the value added at that point. If evasion takes place under a sales tax, on the other hand, all the taxes due on the product are lost to the government.

There is a big difference between the theoretical advantages of a hypothetical tax and the actual advantages of a particular form of tax. However simple the VAT may be in theory, the Korean experience with the VAT in the past seven years makes it clear that it is not simple in practice. It creates a host of problems that give rise to voluminous paperwork, more or less arbitrary distortions in trade and consumption, and inequities in the tax burden.

VAT AS A MAJOR SOURCE OF REVENUE

Since its introduction, VAT has become a major source of revenue in Korea, fulfilling the chief, if tacit, goal of the government. In 1982, VAT yielded 22.0 percent of total tax revenue of the Korean government, national and local, making it by far the single largest tax in Korea. The VAT represents more than 36 percent of the national taxes on goods and services and accounts for approximately 6.5 percent of private consumption. However, the VAT, as a percentage of GNP, was only 4.4 percent in 1982, low compared with that in major European industrial countries.

The central government of Korea relies heavily on taxes on goods and services, which account for more than 68 percent of total national tax revenue. Though the relative importance of indirect taxes in the Korean tax system has been high, there was no significant change in their importance before and after the introduction of VAT. National taxes on goods and services as a percentage of GNP were 10.2 percent in 1976 and 11.0 percent in 1978.

IMPLEMENTATION OF VAT

Careful examination and long preparation preceded the introduction of VAT in Korea. Much of the interest in the introduction of VAT was undoubtedly stimulated by widespread acceptance of the VAT in Europe. Although the law was enacted on 22 December 1976 and took effect on 1 July 1977, the decision to introduce VAT was made in 1971. However, it is not clear whether the intensive preparations of the last two years or so before the adoption of VAT were sufficient for its successful implementation.

In order to benefit from the European experience, the government sent a small delegation to visit the EEC countries where VAT already existed and talk to tax officials who were running it in those countries. Extensive studies on the VAT system were conducted before the government's formal VAT announcement on 19 January 1976.

Educating the taxpayers and the general public about the characteristics of the new tax, as well as about the new requirements with which taxpayers would have to comply was important for the successful implementation of the VAT. Starting in September 1976, less than one year before the tax became effective, the Korean government inaugurated elaborate information and education programs aimed at both taxpayers and the general public.

The programs, which described the operation and effects of the new tax, relied heavily on newspapers, television, radio, and the dissemination of information by trade associations. The VAT guidebooks were published and distributed through trade associations and to businessmen registered for the business tax. The Ministry of Finance prepared four kinds of handbooks of which 7.8 million copies were distributed; 16.57 million copies of twenty-eight different kinds of guidebooks and brochures were published by the Office of National Tax Administration (ONTA). The Ministry of Finance prepared and distributed eighty films explaining the VAT, and these were shown in all cinemas during the months prior to the introduction of VAT. Officials from the ONTA attended public meetings throughout the country to explain the new tax.

In addition to guidebooks on VAT for general distribution, the government prepared a staff handbook for the officials who would be dealing with VAT. The staff handbook set out all the tax procedures in some detail and provided answers in advance to all important questions which were likely to be asked either by the staff themselves or by the traders.

The success of the tax depends to a large extent on the degree of voluntary cooperation forthcoming from the business community. To secure the cooperation of the business community, the government set up a special committee, composed of government officials and representatives of the Chamber of Commerce, the Korean Federations of Industries, the Korean Traders' Association, the Korea Tax Accountants Association and Korea Institute of Certified Public Accountants, and the Customs Brokers Association. Despite this effort, insufficient communication between the government and organizations of taxpayers and consumer groups damaged the prospects for close cooperation. Unhappiness with the VAT on the part of the business community was demonstrated by its call to postpone the implementation of VAT right before the VAT became effective.

Nationwide trial exercises of filing tax returns were carried out on three separate occasions (in March, May, and July 1977) before the changeover to the VAT. On the average, more than 98 percent of the taxpayers in the groups concerned participated in these trial runs. Important steps taken prior to the introduction of the VAT included the introduction of new invoices for business tax withholding at the beginning of 1975. This was a good provision for the transition to the invoicing system needed for the VAT. The withholding system under the business tax was successfully adapted to the transitional needs of the administrative structure needed for the VAT.

Concurrent with the consultation and information program, the Korean government expanded and retrained the tax administration staff. The fact that there already was a substantial reservoir of trained personnel with experience in administering the very complicated business tax and other indirect taxes made this task easier. The government provided additional training for 32,444 public officials under the auspices of the Ministry of Finance, the Office of National Tax Administration, and the Office of Customs. The number of staff at the ONTA increased by 1,999, from 9,443 in 1976 to 11,442 in 1977. Most of this increased recruitment was for the VAT. However, the new recruits did not go directly on to VAT work but were put into other sections in order to release more experienced officers for the VAT. Since the VAT replaced another kind of consumption tax, there were no structural changes in the organization of tax administration.

Passive and active opposition to the introduction of VAT came from many sources. Each interest group had its own reasons for opposing the new tax and each had different reasons. The VAT was opposed by labor as regressive. Business in general and small business in particular opposed the tax on the ground that compliance costs would be too high. Even some tax administrators did not support the tax, pointing out the administrative problems of collecting the tax from retailers and the higher cost of collecting the VAT than of collecting the taxes it would replace.

The VAT has gone through a number of changes since its introduction, although these have not been extensive. By 1 January 1984, the VAT Law had been amended three times, the VAT Presidential Decree fifteen times, and the VAT Ministerial Ordinance twelve times. From the very fact that the government has not tried to alter the basic structure of the tax, as can be seen from the above list of legislative changes, it can be concluded that the designers of the tax did their work well. It should not be denied that a lot of difficulties remain to be overcome. However, it can also be stated that those difficulties are within the bounds of what can be expected on the occasion of any major tax reform.

OUTLINE AND CHARACTERISTICS OF THE KOREAN VAT

The structure of VAT and its administration in Korea are basically similar to those of the EEC countries. Businesses under the Korean VAT are permitted to treat investments exactly as they treat purchases of current inputs and to deduct immediately from sales the full value of investments made during the taxable period. So the Korean VAT is of the consumption type, the variety in use throughout Europe.

The method of collecting the VAT adopted in Korea is the invoice method, under which each firm must collect the VAT on all of its sales, unless they are exempt, and it is entitled to a credit against its ability for taxes invoiced by its suppliers. Credit is allowed only if it is supported by invoices provided by suppliers. This method of administration is alleged to facilitate audits because each firm is required to supply evidence regarding taxes that should have been paid by all of its suppliers.

Scope and Tax Base of VAT

The scope of the VAT is usually defined with reference to both taxable transactions and taxable persons. The Korean VAT code defines taxable transactions as the supply of goods or services and importation of goods. Supply of goods is the delivery or transfer of goods based on contractual or legal actions. This includes the sale of goods on an installment basis as well as inventory goods at the closing of a business. This definition also includes the personal use of business assets. The supply of services includes the rendering of services or having a person use or utilize goods, facilities, or rights on any legal or contractual basis. The importation of goods is simply the entry of goods into Korea from abroad.

A taxable person is anyone who independently engages in the supply of goods or services. Taxpayers include individuals, corporations, any organization of persons, foundations, or the state and local authorities, regardless of whether or not the taxable transactions generate profits. The requirement that a taxable person act in an independent capacity excludes employees from an obligation to charge VAT on services provided to their employers.

The taxable amount or tax base is the full consideration received for the supply of goods or services. It includes taxes (other than the VAT and the defense surtax), duties, and incidental expenses such as packing, transportation, and insurance costs charged to the purchase. In the case of sales on installment or credit, the tax base is the total amount of supplied goods. The taxable amount does not include discounts or rebates and the value of returned goods or goods broken, lost, or damaged before they are delivered to their purchaser.

Tax Rates

Before the introduction of VAT, Korea suffered from a complicated rate structure of indirect taxes. The business tax, which was a major target of the tax reform, had six differentiated rates ranging from 0.5 percent to 3.5 percent of turnover, depending on the categories of business. The previous indirect tax system had more than fifty rates ranging from 0.5 percent to 300 percent. This background led to a strong desire to simplify the structure of the indirect tax system, and consequently, to adopt a single VAT rate.

Even though Korea has a single rate VAT system, as do Denmark and Sweden, an allowance is made to vary the rate, using it as an economic stimulant or brake. The VAT code allows the government to adjust the normal rate (13 percent) up to 3 points lower or higher when deemed necessary due to the general state of the economy. The more urgent reason for granting the Minister of Finance discretion to increase or decrease tax rates was to give the authorities the flexibility to cover themselves against a tax shortfall and at the same time to allow them to react quickly if VAT revenue was larger than expected. The VAT has been implemented so far at the minimum level of 10 percent.

Although Korea adopted a single 10 percent VAT rate, small businesses receive special treatment. Small businesses whose sales are less than 24 million won a year are taxed at a rate of 2 percent of turnover. Furthermore, those individuals who are engaged in brokerage and intermediary services are subject to a 3.5 percent tax on their turnover unless their annual turnover is more than 6 million won.

A comparison of the tax system of Korea with that of other VAT adopting countries reveals that many items subject to the special consumption tax in Korea are included in the VAT in other countries, where an increased tax rate is applied to them. Items to which a reduced or zero rate applies in many other countries are goods and services which are exempt from the tax in Korea. These differences point out one important fact: the Korean VAT system cannot be directly compared to the VAT systems of other countries. We should look at the indirect tax system as a whole to make a valid comparison of one country with another. It should also be pointed out that even though Korea does not have a multiple rate VAT system, the addition of other taxes (such as the special consumption tax and the liquor tax) on top of the VAT for many items produces the same effects as having a multiple rate VAT system.

Zero Rating and Exemption

A sharp distinction can be drawn between the two reasons why a particular supply of goods or services is not taxable: zero rating and exemption. Zero rated supplies are technically taxable but at a low (zero) rate; the implication is that VAT charged on inputs relating to them can be reclaimed just as were inputs relating to taxable supplies. Exempt supplies are outside the scope of VAT altogether so there is no question of reclaiming the relevant input tax.

In Korea the zero rate applies to goods for exportation, services rendered outside Korea, international transportation by ship and aircraft, and other goods or services supplied to earn foreign exchange. Zero rating is applied only on traders who are residents or domestic corporations. However, in the case of international shipping and aerial navigation, traders who are nonresidents or foreign corporations are subject to zero-rating on a reciprocity basis.

If a good or service is exempt, no tax is charged on its supply, but unlike zero rated items, no deduction is allowed for taxes on purchases. In contrast to the zero rate, exempt transactions bear some VAT. Tax is charged on purchases from the exempt supplier, but not on the value added by the exempt organization. If the exempt firm sells to households and has positive value added, exemption reduces net liabilities. If the exempt firm sells to other firms, then exemption increases tax burdens, because businesses that purchase exempt inputs have no credits to apply against their own tax liability.

The Korean VAT allows a variety of exemptions for social, political, and administrative reasons. Exemptions are awarded to basic life necessities such as unprocessed food stuffs and piped water; to certain classes of commodities that would be hard to tax, such as banking and insurance services and owner-occupied housing; and to certain commodities classified as social and cultural goods, such as medical and health services, education, books, newspapers, and artistics works. Goods and services supplied by public enterprises, independent professional services, and duty exempt goods are exempt from VAT. Monopoly goods, telephone services, postage stamps, and so forth are exempt from VAT because supplementary separate taxes are imposed.

It seems indispensable that the very small taxpayer be exempt from the VAT. By excluding those taxpayers with small turnovers, the government can reduce administrative and compliance problems. Of course, this advantage should be weighed against other considerations like the revenue potential of those small businesses and the neutrality of a VAT. In Korea, small taxpayers whose biannual tax liability is less than 10,000 won are not subject to the VAT.

All in all, the exemptions allowed under the VAT are more extensive than those of the old business tax.

Administrative Aspects

Registration with the value-added tax authorities is the initial step in the administrative process. A trader must register at the VAT office in the district in which he resides within twenty days after he commences taxable activities. A record of all registered taxpayers is maintained on a computer file. The information includes VAT registered number, taxpayers' name and residence number, firms' name and address, telephone number, business code, trade classification, date of registration, and date of commencement of business.

The Korean VAT law requires an enterprise to register separately each place of business which it carries on and to furnish a separate return for each place. These requirements for registration of each place of business and the rendering of separate VAT returns for each are a carryover from the previous business tax law and deter efficient business administration without increasing the tax yield.

When a registered trader supplies goods or services, he should issue an invoice to the other party. The Korean VAT requires an invoice to show the date of supply, the seller's name, address, and VAT registration number, customer's name and registration number, the value and identity of goods or services supplied, and the amount of the VAT.

There are two types of tax invoices, the general and the simplified form. Simplified tax invoices are for use by special taxpayers. General tax invoices are presented by the taxpayers to the district office and numbered serially. There is no requirement for a special taxpayer to submit any invoices to the tax authority.

Each general taxpayer has to complete four invoices for each sale at the time of the supply of good and services. One copy is kept by the person or business making the sale, another copy is sent by that person to the district tax office, the third copy is kept by the purchaser, and the fourth copy is sent by the purchaser to his district tax office. The two copies of the invoice held by the appropriate tax offices are then sent to the computer data processing unit which carries out a cross-check of sales against purchases. Tax invoices issued or received should be kept for five years. Tax invoices in which the value of a transaction exceeds 300,000 won are computerized to audit.

In the last half of 1977, 7.2 percent of all invoices did not match. In 1982, the proportion of mismatches decreased to 1.4 percent. Interestingly, output invoices caused less difficulties than input invoices. The mismatching ratio for output invoices for each year was about half of that for input invoices. This result is consistent with expectations since the VAT tax liability can be minimized by maximizing input claims. The percentage of mismatched input invoices fell from 12.1 percent in 1977 to 2.4 percent in 1982. Erroneous data, which means that sales and purchase invoices match but the details of the invoices do not, decreased from 5.9 percent in 1977 to 0.3 percent in 1982.

There are two steps in the tax payment and return procedure. First, taxpayers are required to furnish the tax authorities with preliminary returns stating their tax base and the tax amount payable or refundable within twenty-five days (fifty days in the case of foreign corporations) from the date of termination of each preliminary return period: from January to March and from July through September. Second, taxpayers must file with the tax authorities the tax base and tax amount payable or refundable for each taxable period within twenty-five days (fifty days in the case of foreign corporations) after its expiration: the first tax period is from January to June and the second tax period from July to December. Taxpayers are required to submit tax invoices at the time of the preliminary or final return concerned. This quarterly payment of the VAT has proved easier to work with than the more frequent two-month tax period used under the old business tax system.

The Korean VAT law requires each trader to record all transactions and to keep the files at his place of business. A trader is obliged to keep the recorded books and tax invoices, general or simplified, for a period of five years from the date of final return.

Traders who are engaged in retail business or run ordinary eating houses and hotels, and so forth, must install a cash register and issue tax invoices which show the value of supply. When a trader who installs a cash register issues tax invoices and keep audit tapes, he is deemed to have fulfilled his obligations of bookkeeping and of issuance of simplified tax invoices. In return the trader gets a tax deduction equivalent to 0.5 percent of total sales.

Penalties sufficiently high to deter offenses, minor or serious, are imposed on failure to register or to apply for inspection, nonissuance of tax invoices, and default on tax returns and payments. Penalties equivalent to 1 percent and 2 percent of total sales in the cases of individuals and corporations, respectively, apply for the biannual inspection. For failure to issue a tax invoice in transactions between taxable persons or failure to keep proper records, the penalty is 1 percent of the sales amount in the case of individuals and 2 percent in the case of corporations. Where a trader fails to file a return, or does not pay the tax amount due, or files a tax return underreporting his obligations, he is liable to a penalty equivalent to 10 percent of his tax liability. Penalties have been imposed mostly on general taxpayers. General taxpayers are liable to penalties because they do not issue tax invoices or delay the submission of invoices to government or because they file incorrect returns.

Transitional measures were necessary to eliminate certain problems of double taxation that otherwise would have arisen when the VAT was introduced in Korea. Special transitional provisions dealt with investment goods and inventories because these had borne some taxes imposed before the introduction of the VAT. Taxpayers were allowed to take credit for previous taxes that had already been paid on inventories on the date of the changeover. Since the taxes replaced were of a multistage turnover variety, a difficult problem arose in determining the effective tax rate on the many types of goods in inventory. The government imposed the average rate on each inventory item.

Treatment of Small Businesses

Under any form of sales taxation, small businesses have to be granted special treatment because of their inability to cope with the requirements of keeping adequate records which larger enterprises can handle at a reasonable cost. The intent of the special treatment is to reduce the administrative burden on small enterprises, but not the taxes that normally would be charged on the goods and services they supply.

Small businesses, called special taxpayers under the Korean VAT, are those whose total sales are less than 24 million won a year. In the case of businesses engaging in transactions through a proxy, agent, intermediary, consignee, or contractor, any trader whose annual sales are less than 6 million won is treated as a special taxpayer. Unlike general taxpayers whose tax base is value added, a 2 percent tax rate applies to calculate the amount of tax payable to the government. Small businesses engaged in transactions through a proxy, agent, intermediary, consignee, or contractor face a tax of 3.5 percent on their annual sales.

When a business eligible for special taxation has submitted tax invoices received to the government, an amount equivalent to 5 percent of the input tax amount is deducted from the tax amount payable. Special taxpayers issue simplified tax invoices and file their tax returns every six months while general taxpayers issue standard tax invoices and file returns and pay taxes every three months. Special taxpayers do not have to file a preliminary tax return but do have to pay half of their taxes paid to the government during the immediately preceding tax period.

In Korea special taxpayers file about 76–78 percent of all VAT tax returns. Although general taxpayers are in the minority, they are the more important source of revenue. General taxpayers pay approximately 94–95 percent of the total VAT while the tax amount contributed by special taxpayers comprises only about 5–6 percent of the VAT collected.

ECONOMIC EFFECTS OF VAT

With regard to the economic effects of VAT, we are concerned with four major issues: VAT's effects on price level, exports, investment, and income distribution. It seems that VAT has had less and fewer economic effects than its supporters claimed or its opponents feared.

Price Level

In assessing the impact of VAT on the general price level, a conceptual distinction must be made between the VAT as an additional tax and as a substitute revenue source. As a new or additional tax, a VAT is likely to increase prices, provided that there is an accommodating monetary policy. It should be pointed out that even though the VAT would be reflected in higher prices, the result would be a one-shot increase, not a recurrent increase in the price level unless mismanagement of aggregate demand led to a wage-price spiral.

In the strictly logical sphere, assuming parity in the yield of suppressed taxes and of the new VAT and a perfect market, it may be stated that the substitution of the VAT for existing indirect taxes should not have increased the overall price index since the level of public expenditure was not changed nor was the economic nature of taxation which, in all of these hypotheses, presents the same forward shifting characteristics.

Since the VAT in Korea was expected to yield the same amount of revenue as the replaced indirect taxes, direct effects on the general price level were expected to be small, if present at all.

Although the average effect on prices of replacing the previous taxes with the VAT was expected to be small, the effective tax rates on different goods and services were expected to change significantly because the distribution of the replacing and replaced taxes was not identical. There were some fears that the prices of goods on which the tax burdens were reduced would not fall or would fall by less than the prices of goods on which the tax liability rose. To the extent that increases in the prices of commodities on which the tax burden increased were more certain than decreases in the prices of commodities on which the tax burden decreased, some stimulus to inflation would have occurred.

It was predicted that the introduction of a 10 percent VAT rate would lead to an increase in the wholesale price level by 0.155 percent and to a decrease in the consumer price level by 0.537 percent. In the two months after the introduction of VAT, the wholesale price level went up 3.4 percent, of which the implementation of VAT is estimated to have contributed 0.061 percent points.

At the time the VAT was introduced, the government estimated that a 13 percent

VAT tax rate would boost consumer prices by 3.4 percent and a 10 percent VAT rate would have no effect on the consumer price index (CPI). During the six-month and twelve-month periods before the introduction of VAT, the CPI rose by 6.7 percent and 10.1 percent, respectively, while consumer prices rose 3.9 percent and 14.0 percent in the first six and twelve months, respectively, following the introduction of VAT.

How much of the increase in prices should be attributed to the introduction of VAT is far from clear. However, it can be safely concluded that, while due to the tight price controls by the government the introduction of VAT does not seem to have had a strong impact on prices, most of the increase in prices was attributable to the general inflationary situation in the economy.

In an attempt to meet widespread uncertainty about the price effects of the VAT, the Korean government took two steps. First, the government decided to reduce the initially proposed single tax rate from 13 percent to 10 percent just before the introduction of VAT. Second, to prevent use of the new tax as an excuse for firms to raise their prices to consumers, the government imposed strong price controls. The last minute decision to reduce the rate from 13 percent to 10 percent was made to avoid many unnecessary problems resulting from the application of the 13 percent rate. However, this last minute change found taxpayers already prepared to increase prices in response to the 13 percent rate.

The government had control over the prices charged by monopolies and oligopolies and set ceilings on factory and wholesale prices for 251 goods. A list of pre-July 1977 prices was prepared in order to hold prices to that level immediately before the tax change. The government launched a large scale campaign to publicise recommended retail prices for a variety of consumer goods. This campaign and the existence of widespread price controls curbed any price increases that could have occurred through uncertainty, increased business margins, and profiteering.

Despite the inflationary condition of the economy, price controls appear to have been successful in dampening the wage-price nexus for inflation. It is also noteworthy that increases in the general price level were mainly due to a price increase in food products, which are exempt from the VAT.

Broadly speaking, the introduction of VAT does not seem to have had a major impact on the rate of price increases in Korea. The full effects on prices of the increase in the VAT depend not only on the initial impact but also on market interactions, the stage of the business cycle, and other policy measures. The experiences of other VAT adopting countries confirm the same result (Tait, 1988).

Investment and Savings

Unlike most of the taxes it replaced, the VAT does not burden capital goods because the consumption-type VAT provides a full credit for the tax included in purchases of capital goods. The credit does not subsidize the purchase of capital goods; it simply eliminates the tax that has been imposed on them.

Because investment was taxed under the previous indirect tax system but was to be exempt under VAT, investment costs fell accordingly. The switch to the VAT provided industries such as manufacturing and electricity and gas with substantial benefits. Tax refunds for investment amounted to 18,336 million won for the second half of 1977 and 64,655 million won for all of 1982.

Comparison of the rates of savings and investment in years before the introduction of the VAT with those in years since its adoption is not instructive enough to produce any conclusion regarding the effects of VAT on savings or investment. Though there is no evidence that investment or savings increased, a questionnaire survey by the government shortly after the adoption of VAT shows that the VAT was more conducive to investment than the old indirect tax regime.

International Trade

It is commonly agreed that the introduction of VAT with zero rating on exports has a very favorable influence on exports. Zero rating removes any tax paid on a good at any stage because zero rated goods are fully exempt from any tax when sold, and producers of such goods are entitled to a refund of any tax paid on purchases to produce such goods.

In abstract terms, VAT is neutral in what concerns international trade if exports are exempt from payment of tax and imports are subject to the tax. The exported commodity is totally exempt from any taxes while the imported commodity pays a tax equal to that levied on the commodity sold in the domestic market. In actual fact, these neutral characteristics of the VAT are under two limitations. The first is the difficulty of verifying the forward shift in the incidence of tax burdens; the second is that the technical regulations needed to enforce the tax limit its neutral characteristics.

Giving greater tax benefits to exporters was one of the stated goals of introducing the VAT into Korea. Much of that claim is incorrect, but it is politically appealing, and a lot has been said and written about the effects that the adoption of VAT would have on the competitiveness of Korean industry, and therefore on Korean exports and the balance of payments.

In order to examine the effects of VAT on exports, we have to distinguish between two cases: substitution of VAT for direct taxes and replacement of indirect taxes by VAT. When a country adopts a VAT as a replacement for direct taxes or with a reduction in direct taxes, it gains a trade advantage because the government can rebate a larger proportion of the tax content of exports and collect VAT on imports. When a country substitutes a VAT for indirect taxes, as in Korea, the trade advantage of the VAT substitution is negligible because the refund system on export goods is a part of the replaced indirect tax system.

Regardless of which tax the VAT replaces, many believe that a VAT rebate, in itself, will expand exports and that a VAT levy will retard imports. This belief might have a positive effect on trade if it encourages businesses to compete more rigorously in international markets. This result would depend on the importance of nonprice considerations in explaining export activity. In a questionnaire survey conducted by the government, a large number of Korean businessmen expressed the view that the new VAT was more favorable to exports than the old indirect taxes.

The effect of the VAT on exports can be indirectly investigated by comparing the general characteristics of the new VAT system with those of the previous tax system and by looking at the trend of the indirect tax rebates in supporting exports.

The exact determination of taxes paid under the turnover tax scheme was generally difficult and frequently impossible to calculate. Since the business tax and other indirect taxes were hidden in the price of export goods, they could not be readily rebated even though rebates of all indirect taxes were permissible under the law. Because of the cumulative nature of the turnover type business tax, export goods were exempt only at the final sales stage, and the government had to estimate the border tax adjustment for export rebates on the taxes previously paid in the production and distribution process. The awareness of the problem that it is impossible to calculate the tax content of prices was one of the factors behind the reform of the indirect tax system in Korea.

Since it was difficult to determine the amount of taxes included in the price of export goods under the previous indirect tax system, the government had to issue rules prescribing how much tax was buried in the price of each type of export good. The average rate on the credit for export goods was imposed by the government. Therefore, the prescribed average rate was normally lower than the actual payment in some cases and higher in others. As a result, export prices usually included either a hidden penalty or a hidden subsidy.

The substitution of VAT for the previous indirect tax system has made the determination of taxes paid on exporters much easier because the characteristics of a typical VAT can overcome the problem of calculating the taxes paid. This so-called border tax adjustment merely guarantees that both imports and domestically produced goods consumed in Korea bear the same tax and allow Korean exports to enter the world markets free of tax. However, it should be noted that this border adjustment does not stimulate exports and inhibit imports more than would a comparable turnover tax imposed on sales to Korean consumers.

By examining the trend in the average indirect tax rebate per dollar of exports, one can indirectly estimate the impact on exports of the change in the Korean indirect tax system. Though the actual effect may have differed from product to product, there was a sharp increase in the average tax rebate per dollar of exports, from 33.56 won per dollar in 1976 to 53.56 in 1978, and in the average rebate as a percentage of export value, from 0.06 percent in 1976 to 0.09 percent in 1978. This result shows that the government underestimated the border tax adjustment under the previous tax system. In this sense, the adoption of the VAT benefited the export industry.

Though we may conclude that a switch to the VAT with zero rating on exports may have made a modest contribution to the improvement of balance of payments in Korea, particularly due to its ease and precision in calculating tax rebates, this conclusion should not be overemphasized. Because exchange rates or domestic inflation would soon adjust in response to any initial improvement in the balance of payments, any competitive edge induced by tax substitution would soon be dissipated.

Distribution of the Tax Burden

Like other taxes, the VAT has distributive properties in that its burden will fall more heavily on some sections of society than on others. Perhaps the most controversial aspect of the introduction of VAT was its effect on the distribution of tax burdens when the tax was under consideration. The regressivity issue of the VAT continues to be a topic for hot debate.

A comprehensive VAT is regressive since lower-income taxpayers consume a higher proportion of their income than do middle- and upper-income taxpayers. A number of studies have been carried out to estimate the distribution of VAT burdens. Using the household income and expenditure survey, all these studies base the distribution of VAT burdens on consumption patterns and the estimated rate of taxation on each category of consumer goods. In all these studies, the VAT is more or less regressive with respect to income.

The incidence studies vary in their estimates of the distributive effect of the VAT itself and in their comparisons of the distributive effect of the VAT and previous indirect taxes. Still, all these studies indicate that, as expected, the VAT is regressive and that the replacement of the previous indirect taxes with the VAT and the special consumption tax has not improved the regressivity of overall indirect tax burdens.

Since Korea relies heavily on indirect taxes for its revenue, the regressivity of indirect tax burdens implies that the overall tax burden in Korea is regressive. Therefore, there remains a need for the government to improve the distribution of income by moderating the regessivity of the VAT and the indirect tax system in general and by moving toward greater reliance on direct taxes.

CRITICISM, CURRENT ISSUES, AND LESSONS

Since about seven years have elapsed since the implementation of the VAT in Korea, an interim, although still tentative, assessment is possible. The VAT in Korea has been working relatively well, in some cases much better than its designers and taxpayers had anticipated. The number of complaints has been small, though some have been loud. Complaints have been made and will continue to be made about various aspects of the tax structure and the details of its operation. However, many of these protests are much more in the nature of special interest pleading or general grumbling than attacks on the concept of the tax.

On almost all counts, the VAT in Korea should be considered an improvement over the indirect taxes it replaced. The base of the VAT is broader. It permits more precise border adjustment. Taxpayers have by now familiarized themselves with VAT. There is no evidence of large-scale tax evasion. Revenue from VAT is large and in line with the calculations based on the volume of private consumption.

Even though the VAT can and does work in Korea, it is not free from arbitrary elements and controversies. In order to deal with the annoying problems associated with the VAT, a distinction must be made between problems inherent in the VAT and those also true of other tax. By way of conclusion, the major issues currently facing the VAT system in Korea are reviewed to help other countries learn from the Korean experience.

Scope and Coverage of VAT

One recurrent question about the structure of VAT in Korea concerns the possibility of extending VAT to sales that are currently exempt. The widespread use of exemption is founded on the desire to reduce the regressivity of the VAT burden. Needless to say, the extensive use of exemption reduces the efficiency advantages that might have been gained from a more neutral tax structure.

Exemptions facilitate the administration of the VAT. This is true particularly of exemptions for small taxpayers and certain services. However, it should be borne in mind that excessive exemptions complicate administration because of the difficulty of distinguishing taxable from nontaxable transactions and the resulting need for more detailed records and invoices.

Current issues on the Korean VAT exemption scheme center around two major questions. The first is the very purpose of the VAT exemption and the second is the possibility of narrowing the scope of the exemption. It is generally understood that exemptions are allowed to reduce the regressivity of the VAT burden. However, it must be pointed out that the reasons for the exemption scheme in the VAT structure lie not in the reduction of regressivity but in the simplification of administration and compliance.

Moderation of the regressivity could be achieved more effectively through the zero rating scheme rather than through the exemption scheme. This simple but important point has not caught the eyes of the VAT designers in Korea and many other countries. Zero rated supplies are technically taxable but at a low (zero) rate; the implication is that the VAT charged on inputs relating to them could be reclaimed just as were inputs relating to taxable supplies. Exempt supplies are outside the scope of VAT altogether so there is no question of reclaiming the relevant input tax. Since, in contrast to the zero rating, an exempt transaction bears some VAT, the relief of the tax burden on the low-income people should be sought through the application of a zero rating scheme rather than an exemption scheme to goods and services consumed disproportionally by the poor.

Even under the present exemption scheme a review of the list of goods and services currently exempted leads one to question the appropriateness of the inclusion of some items on the list. In principle, exemptions from the VAT should be limited to basic necessities, such as unprocessed food stuffs, and to goods and services the government wishes to exempt for social or cultural reasons.

Several selections on the exemption list have been controversial, including services provided by financial institutions and insurance companies, government-provided goods and services that compete with commercial operations, and independent professional services. On the grounds of tax equity between privately and publicly supplied goods and services and the economic efficiency of preserving the capacity of private firms to compete with business by public agencies, it has been strongly suggested that some commercial activities by semigovernmental bodies not be exempted.

The exemption of rent, insurance, and financial services means that traders of these outputs have to bear input taxes but cannot reclaim them. They are expected to pass the tax on to their customers. Business users of those services thus have to bear some VAT costs, despite the philosophy of the tax. The major problem with taxing financial services is the difficulty of calculating the correct tax base. One way to tax the value added of insurance and banking services would be to rely on the direct additive method, that is, adding together their annual wage and salary payments, rental payments, and profit (direct additive method). A tax of 0.5 percent on gross receipts of banking and insurance companies has been imposed in Korea since the beginning of 1982. In order to determine whether it is desirable to bring these financial institutions within the scope of VAT, one has to consider whether to eliminate the special tax recently imposed or to accept the consequences of imposing a heavier burden on this sector than on others.

Practically all independent professional services, such as those provided by doctors, lawyers, accountants, and architects, are currently exempt. It has been suggested that all these professional services be taxed. Given the fact that these independent professionals currently pay relatively small tax under the personal income tax, it would seem advisable to make their services subject to taxes so long as they cannot fully shift their tax burdens to their customers. Furthermore, from an equity point of view, it is desirable to adopt a common policy toward all the professional services rather than to single out one particular service for exclusion from the exemption.

All in all, exemption should be kept to a minimum not only in order to keep the VAT base broad but also to minimize administrative problems and distortions in the economy. The neutrality of the tax would be improved if the coverage of services were broadened and if exemptions were replaced by zero ratings. Increased use of zero rating rather than exemptions would reduce the advantage that large firms have over small firms.

Tax Rate Structure

A single rate of 10 percent has been used in Korea since the introduction of the VAT in 1977. If the VAT were imposed at a uniform rate on all consumption, it would be regressive when measured against income, since consumption expenditures take a decreasing fraction of personal income as income levels rise. In order to reduce the tax burden on low-income taxpayers and to inject an element of progressivity into the VAT, suggestions have been made to use differentiated multiple rates rather than a single uniform rate.

Experience with rate differentiation elsewhere did not recommend its use in Korea; the EEC countries have found that such a differentiation complicates administration and compliance and destroys both neutrality and the advantages that uniformity may bring. Furthermore, using multiple rates is an inefficient way to achieve redistributive objectives.

The tax rate structure of VAT has a direct influence on its administration and compliance. Many problems rise from the use of multiple rates. First, the rate structure may not be sufficiently defined, leaving products which can fit into more than one category. Second, the categories themselves may be based on criteria for which information is not readily available. Third, multiple rates cost too much for small businesses dealing with a variety of goods because it is extremely time-consuming for them to account separately for each different category when filling out tax returns. Fourth, multiple rates provide taxpayers with the opportunity to evade the taxes through either miscalculation or manipulation.

Given the limitations of record keeping on the part of taxpayers and auditors, it is imperative that the tax be kept simple. The most important requirement for simplicity is the use of a single rate. If a higher tax burden is desired on certain classes of goods or services, this should be attained by separate levies like the special consumption tax at either the importation or manufacturing level, as is the case now in Korea.

The regressivity of the VAT can be moderated, but not eliminated, by special measures like exemptions and differentiated rates. Even if many commodities were zero rated, significant progressivity or even a decided decrease in regressivity could not be obtained. A set of distributional goals can be more easily achieved using the available alternative devices.

Administrative Problems

The administrative problems presented by the VAT have been considerable even though the administrative efficiency of the VAT was an important consideration behind the adoption of the VAT system in Korea. All taxable transactions must be fully recorded. Invoices must be issued so that the purchaser can deduct the tax charged on the sale. For some time, administration of the VAT has been subject to criticism. The administration aspects of VAT are still controversial, and recent public concern about the VAT system in Korea centers around the issues of administrative efficiency and compliance costs.

The degree of compliance and the cost of administration depends on whether businesses are accustomed to keeping good, written records, on the establishment of a modernized distribution system, and on the share of business activity carried out by small establishments. The lack of systematic record keeping in many parts of the Korean economy would make administration difficult and evasion easy even under the best of circumstances. Unless distribution channels through which commodities change hands are modernized and solidly established, there is no way of controlling the illegal transfer of tax invoices to a third party.

The VAT is said to be self-enforcing because of how it is usually administered. There is a measure of self-policing in that evasion by suppliers through the understatement of the tax collected is balanced by the purchasers' interest in ensuring that all tax payments are recorded. Similarly, evasion by purchasers who overstate the taxes they pay runs counter to the interests of suppliers.

The advantages of the invoice method have not been fully realized in practice, and are not likely to be fully realized, because of the practical impossibility of checking all invoices on the part of tax collectors and because of the efforts to evade the tax on the part of taxpayers. Much evasion occurs through the failure of some parties to report all transactions. Korean experience with the VAT, however, suggests that the so-called built-in self-enforcing aspect of the tax, which permits the matching of the tax credits of one taxpayer against the tax payments of another, is illusory or, at best, a much overrated advantage because invoices can be falsified.

It must be stressed that the VAT is not a self-enforcing tax. Although taxpayers do have an incentive to request invoices for their purchases in order to increase their input tax credit, this incentive is in many instances counterbalanced by the desire to suppress both purchases and sales in order to avoid not only the VAT but also income taxes.

The ability to administer the VAT is a function of a large number of factors. One group of factors, which are internal to the VAT system, comprises the scope of the tax, the degree of its complexity in terms of rate structure, the exemptions, the reporting techniques and procedures, the tax payment procedures, and the treatment of small businesses. Another group of factors, which are external not only to the VAT but also to any other kind of tax, includes the degree of literacy, the size of monetary economy, the adequacy of bookkeeping, the attitudes toward taxation and tax administration, and the efficiency of tax administration services. Administrative difficulties can be overcome when the intrinsic complexity of the tax law is compatible with the external factors mentioned above.

Special Taxpayers

One of the major criticisms of the VAT in Korea has been the burden on businesses, particularly on small businesses, to keep books and file returns to the tax authorities in the prescribed format. Taxpayers' records must show clearly not only total sales and the taxes payable but also all purchases and taxes paid. Large or medium sized firms can absorb the accounting and procedural requirements of the VAT with relative ease.

However, the problem lies in the size of small businesses. Even though the control and audit of special taxpayers may be kept to a minimum, their numbers alone pose problems of registration, of filing returns, and of tax collection that could impede the efficient administration of the entire tax system. The cost of managing a large number of special taxpayers must be weighed against the considerations of revenue and equity. If the administrative burden outweighs their revenue potential, such special taxpayers had better be exempt from the VAT.

From a purely administrative point of view, exemption of special taxpayers from VAT would be attractive in that both administration and compliance are made easier with no substantial loss in revenue. The temptation to move toward more lenient treatment of troublemaking small taxpayers should be resisted, because such concessions are costly in government creditability and would have a profound effect on the bookkeeping and accounting practices of all taxpayers, both general and special.

Tax Inequity between General Taxpayers and Special Taxpayers

In the public at large the most debated issue involving the Korean VAT system centers on the inequity in the tax burden between general taxpayers and special taxpayers. Taxpayers are hesitant or reluctant to become general taxpayers simply because special taxpayers are treated preferentially relative to general taxpayers. The manipulation of sales totals or disguised closing of businesses is a well-known practice. This illegal practice in large part explains the fact that despite the rapid growth of the economy there is no growth in the number of special taxpayers as a percentage of total VAT taxpayers.

An adjustment has to be made to attenuate the benefits enjoyed by special taxpayers. This can be done by increasing the tax rate applied to sales of special taxpayers, the input tax credit, or both. Another suggestion is to incorporate in the definition of special taxpayers other objective elements such as the value of total assets or the number of employees.

Coordination of VAT with Direct Taxation

A high degree of coordination between the staff in charge of VAT and those in charge of direct taxes is very important. It is an open secret that in Korea taxpayers cheat on their sales not to evade the VAT but to evade personal and corporate income taxes. Operation of a VAT resembles that of the income tax more than that of other taxes and an effective VAT greatly aids income tax administration.

Countries differ in the degree to which they combine administration of their VAT with individual and corporate income taxes. To secure a close coordination between them, institutionalization is necessary at the technical level through means such as automatic processing of data obtained through tax returns or audits, the exchange of such information, consultation as to special audit programs, and the design of forms. In any event, close cooperation with the income tax administration is of great importance for strengthening both the VAT and the income tax.

One lesson that the Korean experience holds for a country contemplating the adoption of the VAT is that the VAT that is implemented is bound to fall well short of the theoretical ideal. However simple the VAT may be in theory, Korean experience makes it clear that it is not simple in practice. It creates a host of special problems that give rise to paperwork and more or less arbitrary distinctions.

Still, there is no reason to regret the adoption of the VAT and to return to the previous indirect tax system. We had to jump into the water before we could feel how hot or cold the water was, and with a fright we realized that the water was cold, pretty cold indeed. However, nowadays the water is heated. So we can swim in it with pleasure.

Part Six

The Role of Local Taxes

An important aspect of taxation in developing countries that is too often neglected is the role of local government revenues. Not only are such revenues
already important in some countries, but their potential importance in almost all
countries is much greater than is usually recognized. As the first chapter in this part
argues, the appropriate design and administration of local revenue systems thus
constitutes an important aspect of development finance.

This is particularly true with respect to larger cities (Bahl and Linn, forthcoming). It is, to say the least, incongruous that scarce national government tax
revenues—perhaps derived from poor farmers in outlying areas or from natural
resources—are so often used to subsidize well-off urban residents through the free
(or virtually free) provision of urban public services. Since most of the (non-
natural resource) tax base of developing countries is generally in larger urban
areas, and most government expenditure also takes place in those areas, there is
clearly a strong case in many instances for more use of "benefit tax" systems to
finance urban development (Bird, 1984).

The first two chapters in this part outline the sorts of changes in local public
finance needed to rectify this situation and to put the onus for financing local
services on local residents. In contrast, the third chapter takes up the distributive
effects of taxes, both local and national, on the urban poor. In addition to comple-
menting the earlier emphasis on the revenue and allocative aspects of local taxation, this chapter is the major representative in this book of the large literature on
the distributional aspects of taxation. For a fuller survey of this subject, see De
Wulf (1975), and for a recent examination of the effects of government finance on
the poor in relation to the "structural adjustment" programs so many developing
countries are currently undergoing, see World Bank (1987) and Bird and Horton
(1989).

The final chapter included in this chapter takes up the rather different question of
agricultural taxation. This paper has been included at this point largely because of
the important potential role for local authorities in raising such inherently local
taxes as rural land taxes (Bird, 1974). Indeed, any book on taxation in developing
countries needs to include such a paper somewhere in view of both the sectorally
distinct characteristics of the agricultural sector and its sheer importance in most
developing countries (Lewis, 1967, 1973; Newbery, 1987).

One important link between urban and agricultural taxation is through migration, which responds at least in part to differences in real incomes between sectors (Todaro, 1969). Higher taxation of agriculture—levied perhaps, as noted above, to finance urban expenditure—may, for example, result in increased migration to urban slums (McLure, 1977), thus exacerbating the perceived urban problem and perhaps leading to further, and possibly perverse, policy reactions. The search for sectoral balance in this and other respects has long been a theme in the literature on agricultural taxation (see Bird, 1974, and, for a more general discussion, Eicher and Staatz, 1984). No resolution of this problem has been reached in most countries. At present, in contrast to the 1960s, when the need to tax agriculture heavily in order to finance industrialization was commonly emphasized in the literature (Kaldor, 1965), the tendency is clearly to reduce such taxation in most countries: China offers a particularly striking recent example (World Bank, 1983). Perhaps, however, the pendulum may swing again in the future. In any event, agricultural taxation will undoubtedly remain a matter of considerable controversy and difficulty in many countries. The brief selection included at the end of this part is intended simply to introduce this complex area to readers; for a more comprehensive recent treatment, see Newbery (1987).

32

Mobilizing Local Resources

The following chapter's thorough review of the general issues involved in mobilizing local resources in the context of a developing country (see also Hicks, 1961; Davey, 1983) also serves the useful role of redressing to some extent the inevitable overemphasis here on taxation as a means of mobilizing resources. It does this by making a strong case for more use of properly designed user charges (Bird, 1976a; Meier, 1983) as well as such other potential sources of revenue as voluntary labor contributions to help build local schools.

An important point that is perhaps insufficiently emphasized in this selection is the considerable extent to which local government finance in most developing countries is constrained—indeed, positively hampered—by deliberate central government policy (Bird, 1980b). Indeed, it does not seem too much to say that as a rule central governments get the local governments they deserve—and, for political reasons, often want: that is, weak, poorly run governments that can offer no rival to precarious central government authority in fragile national states.

Many of the themes touched on in this paper are of course developed at much greater length elsewhere. African personal taxes, for example, are discussed much more extensively in Hicks (1961), Davey (1974), and Arowolo (1968). Local business taxes are treated in more detail in Bahl and Miller (1983) and Bird (1984). User charges are discussed in considerable detail in Bahl and Linn (forthcoming), as well as in Bird (1976a) and Meier (1983).

The authors of this paper advise that local governments build on what is there (compare chapter 30) and create the proper incentive structure for local officials to do their jobs properly, by making the right expenditures so that the taxes can be sold to the public and by giving the right incentives to administrators (see Part 7). This advice is of course fully consistent with that offered elsewhere in this book. Indeed, the only unique feature of local finance from this perspective is that in most countries there is probably even more room for improvement than in national government finance.

Mobilizing Local Resources in Developing Countries

Roy Bahl, Jerry Miner, and Larry Schroeder

The current interest in local government resource mobilization in developing countries is hardly surprising. It stems from several sources: (*a*) the push to decentralize government decision making, (*b*) the desire to improve the relative quality of life in secondary cities and rural areas both for its own sake and to slow the rate of migration to the largest cities, and (*c*) the recognition that local governments might be in a better position than the central government to capture local taxable capacity outside major cities and to determine appropriate local service priorities. With this new concern for local government resource mobilization has come a number of difficult questions. What mechanisms are available for increasing local government revenues in developing countries? How can the substantial administrative barriers be overcome? What standards might be used to judge whether one revenue raising system is more or less suitable than another?

This paper is an attempt to address some of these issues in a context of the current practice in LDCs. Three types of revenue mobilization schemes are considered throughout this paper: taxation, voluntary contributions, and user charges. Too often the focus is exclusively on taxation, but in a sense the three are alternatives and all are important in the LDC context. User charges may take the form of direct payments by beneficiaries for such services as water, sewers, or transportation, or may be seen by the local government as fees raised from locally managed public enterprises such as markets or slaughterhouses. The use of voluntary labor to build a road, construct a school building, or repair an irrigation canal is not an uncommon practice in rural areas in developing countries.[1]

OBJECTIVES OF REVENUE REFORMS

There are several general objectives against which any local revenue scheme might be judged. These include the ability to raise revenues, effects on economic efficiency or neutrality, equity implications, and administrative feasibility.

Mobilizing Resources

Foremost among the criteria for evaluation is the ability to raise revenues. We are interested here in both the potential for mobilizing sufficient resources at any

Excerpted from Bahl, Miner, and Schroeder (1984).

given point in time and the potential for stable growth with an increasing demand for public services.

The first of these concerns, revenue adequacy, depends on the levels of the rate and base. An overriding difficulty facing most localities in developing countries is the small size of the available revenue base. For example, local governments in rural areas may be able to devise any number of methods of collecting revenue—for example, charging for a sheep dip, levying a wheel tax on vehicles, charging vendors an entrance fee to the market, charging a berthing fee for boats. Unfortunately, none of these is likely to have a large enough base to produce substantial revenues at low rates of tax. The question, then, is whether high enough rates can be imposed.

The answer, of course, is that the rates applied to a small base cannot be increased without limit. One constraint is legal, that is, the central government often imposes a strict rate limit on all local government taxes. Moreover, high rates will be more likely to produce excess burdens through reactions in behavior by taxpayers attempting to avoid the levy (discussed below) and possibly will increase evasion of the tax. Furthermore, any inequities inherent in the levy will be exacerbated by higher rates. This, then, suggests a need for policies designed to broaden the base for resource mobilization—through either redefinition of the base or identification of new revenue sources.

The second criterion, sufficient growth, has to do with the elasticity of the revenue source.[2] That is, as the resource needs of local governments increase due to population growth, increased service demands, or inflation, a "good" revenue source will respond in like manner. For example, if prices for the inputs used by a local government increased, one would want revenues to expand without the need for discretionary or administrative changes in the tax base or rate. The principle here is that the revenue base should be as responsive to inflation or real economic expansion as are spending needs.

Certainty or stability of revenue growth, too, cannot be ignored when evaluating resource-raising instruments. Erratic growth not systematically related to changes in income, population, or prices creates considerable uncertainty in budgeting and hinders longer term planning. Although this aspect of revenue growth and adequacy is often ignored, it constitutes a major problem for many local bodies and is often traceable to administrative practices which either fail to capture increases in the revenue base or are inconsistent over time, thereby leading to revenue instability.

Tax revenue sources based on the gross receipts of businesses, sales, or income are likely to be responsive to inflation or to increases in local economic activity. Property taxes, on the other hand, may not be so elastic, since they depend greatly upon the administrative structure by which the tax base is determined. Much research on the subject indicates a low income elasticity to the property tax (Bahl, 1979).

Still less responsive are the personal taxes used in rural sectors where land tenure considerations preclude taxes on agricultural land. Head taxes, taxes on occupations, and licenses do not respond to changing conditions or expenditure needs. For example, personal taxes (including poll and graduated personal taxes) have, since 1970, become much less important revenue sources for central governments in most African states (Wozny, 1983).

Contributions, both monetary and in-kind, rarely account for substantial amounts of revenue, and their growth potential is limited. Even in societies where tribal customs favor voluntary communal services, they are not responsive to current circumstances. One might even expect voluntary contributions to fall off as income rises. For example, as wages increase, especially in real terms, fewer and fewer local laborers are willing to donate their services to the local governments because of their higher opportunity costs. This suggests that the income elasticity of this revenue source will be low. In a similar manner, the responsiveness of these revenues to inflation may be low if laborers suffer from a "monetary illusion" and do not recognize that increased money wages in the face of inflation do not constitute increases in real wages.

User charges and fees offer an opportunity to raise significant amounts of revenue, but generally offer a low potential for growth. Most charges are tied to the number of units of a service consumed—for example, a gallon of water or a bus ride—and do not respond to income or inflation. Legal rate changes, which are politically unpopular, are required to increase revenues. On the other hand, increased populations may yield greater usage of these services, thereby raising revenues.

Economic Efficiency

Resource raising techniques nearly always affect some economic choice. Given the revenue bases available to rural local governments in developing countries, the choices in question may include whether to live in a high-taxing or low-taxing jurisdiction, whether to improve a building at the risk of property tax increase, whether to support a proposal for a local capital improvement at the risk of paying a benefit charge or whether to volunteer labor to the public sector in return for a public sector benefit. To the extent that local taxes and charges alter choices that otherwise would have been made, they are economically inefficient.

Such inefficiencies may or may not be detrimental in terms of local and national objectives. For example, a business license may raise the cost of doing business in a community but can be a justifiable charge for the proximity to public services which the business enjoys. On the other hand, some revenue sources may have built-in non-neutralities that are undesirable. The local property tax is an often-cited culprit. Placing a heavier tax burden on the value of improvements (buildings and equipment) than on the value of land discourages investment in improvements. To the extent that investments in these improvements contribute to economic growth, such inefficiencies are undesirable. However, in many LDCs, the problem is mitigated because rates are so low. Furthermore, differential rates on used versus idle land (with the latter taxed more heavily) are also used in some developing countries where land speculation and nondevelopment is a problem.

User charges and fees raise other important efficiency issues. One problem arises when local authorities attempt to recoup full costs with charges for activities which generate benefits to non-users as well as users. For example, a health clinic provides benefits even to those not innoculated against contagious diseases. Efficiency requires charging users only for that portion of the marginal costs of the service that benefits them and covering the remainder of the costs from general revenues. If charges and fees are set too high, under-use of the service will result. On the other hand, too low a price will produce over-use and either lower the effectiveness of the service or fail to provide adequate revenues for maintenance of the activity. Still, user fees provide the opportunity to mobilize resources in a manner that is both reasonably equitable and reasonably efficient, for example when motor license fees are imposed on users of roads built and maintained from public funds.[3]

The efficiency of a voluntary contribution of labor or materials depends on the opportunity costs of the labor or material and the benefits it produces. At certain times of the year in developing countries the opportunity cost of labor is extremely low. During such times use of labor for public projects has little or no opportunity cost other than the value of leisure forgone and perhaps extra food consumption required. Efficiency requires, however, that the individuals who donate labor derive benefits from the project at least equal to the low opportunity costs.

Equity

Equity is an overriding concern, especially in developing countries where inequality in the distribution of income and wealth is pronounced. The problem is that equity means different things to different people. One interpretation is that those better able to bear the burden of resource mobilization ought to pay more than those in less fortunate circumstances. In practice, this is sometimes translated into tax policies where those with relatively small property holdings are exempt from the property tax or where progressively higher rates are applied to higher valued properties.[4]

Although such provisions for vertical equity are desirable in that they seem "fair," they may give rise to other, undesirable effects. For example, the granting of exemptions for lower income taxpayers may erode the tax base, whereas the use of a progressive rate structure may encourage uneconomic splitting of holdings to avoid the tax. Both actions might encourage the payment of bribes to the property tax administrators to place the property into a lower-valued property classification.

The equity criterion can also be interpreted to mean that those who benefit from particular services should contribute proportionately to the financing of these services. The benefits-received version of equity in taxation is usually associated with special assessments and user charges rather than with general taxation. Betterment levies and special assessments on properties which benefit most from a particular capital investment, for example, a new water project or an improved road, reflect an attempt to distribute financing according to benefits received (Macon and Manon, 1977; Doebele, Grimes, and Linn, 1979).

In a similar manner, user charges based on the cost of providing services can conform to the benefit criterion of equity. In the context of developing countries, however, these methods of resource mobilization are likely to be at variance with ability-to-pay criteria. Yet, in the absence of user charges, highly beneficial services such as water supply and ferry service may not be provided at all, and others, such as wells and irrigation ditches, may deteriorate owing to lack of funds for maintenance and operating expenditures. Thus, the ability-to-pay criterion of equity needs to be applied with appropriate concern that it not totally curtail service provision.

In-kind services raise serious equity questions. Voluntary arrangements may specify equitable labor contributions for projects, and local customs and the influence of local leaders may ensure compliance with these provisions. On the other hand, inequitable distribution of the burdens of in-kind services inevitably leads to the withdrawal of voluntary services. The use of compulsory labor services for local projects in the colonial periods of most developing countries has left a legacy of negative attitudes toward this policy; consequently, relatively little serious consideration is given to proposals for compulsory, in-kind contributions of services in developing countries (outside of China). Still, local responsibility for the construction of buildings with voluntary labor for centrally provided administrative or educational staff is characteristic of many parts of Francophone Africa.

Administrative Feasibility

It is one thing to set down on paper an ideal revenue system, but quite another to implement it successfully. Although the constraints discussed below play a crucial role in determining the administrative feasibility of any revenue source, the general question that must be asked is whether or not, given these constraints, the resource mobilization system can be carried out in a just manner. For example, if few local businesses keep written records of transactions, a general retail sales tax that exempts "necessities" (which may look fine on paper in terms of its elasticity, economic efficiency, and equity) will in fact be impossible to administer. Likewise, in a village where nearly all of the transactions are made in-kind and most residents are illiterate, there is little likelihood that an equitable income tax can be collected. Even when simpler head or asset taxes are used, the task of maintaining an up-to-date census of population, land, or livestock may exceed local administrative capacity. Recommendations for improved tax procedures thus require investigation of such factors as whether or not tax maps have been drawn, the capabilities of the local revenue administration personnel and, whether or not most local properties are privately owned rather than owned by tribes, classes, or extended families. This suggests the need for a thorough understanding of the economic, administrative, and institutional and cultural constraints associated with the area.

CONSTRAINTS

Any resource mobilization effort will be made within an institutional frame. An understanding of these institutions and the contraints that they pose is a necessary first step in any reform effort aimed at increased mobilization. Here we note legal/political contraints, constraints imposed by the administrative structure, economic contraints, and technological or cultural constraints. The lesson is that, although one should search for an optimal resource mobilization package, no more than an acceptable second or third best solution may be possible.

Legal and Political Constraints

Although some alteration of the statutory basis of particular revenue sources is usually necessary to improve the revenue structure, a complete overhaul of the existing legal framework is unrealistic and probably even undesirable. Such changes are less likely to be carried out than are improvements in administration or in provisions of existing revenue sources.

The trick is in recognizing which constraints can be bent and which cannot and in knowing whether institutional reforms are necessary or whether roughly comparable results might be had from less drastic changes. Two common issues come quickly to mind. The first has to do with the assignment of functions—the division of taxing powers and expenditure responsibility among levels of government. Some taxes are specifically reserved for higher levels of government whereas others are made available for local government financing. Whether this division is by constitution or long-standing custom, it presents a very rigid constraint in most countries. To be sure, there have been gradual changes in the assignment of financing and spending responsibilities, but these are "harder" reforms than modifications of presently available tax bases.

The revenue assignment issue is a particularly troublesome one. As Davey (1983) notes, central governments tend to reserve for themselves the most elastic and productive revenue instruments. Although this can be justified in some instances—for example, on grounds of administrative convenience or due to inefficiencies or inequities which would result if each locality imposed its own levy—in other cases it can be done primarily to gain political favor. For example, the abolition of the community tax in Nigerian states in 1980 may have been as much a political ploy as a legitimate policy to improve the local revenue structure.[5] It certainly did little to support the 1976 local government reform's goal of community autonomy.

The political system and the degree of patronage embedded within that system constitutes another serious constraint. Altering these political arrangements is unlikely. Thus, if the ministry of local government has statutory responsibility over all local financial affairs, it is unrealistic to expect that a program carried out by a rival ministry will be gracefully endorsed by both ministries, even if the program has potentially large local revenue implications. The ministry in charge of the program, unless it is likely to gain additional power or political "points" through a successful administration of this program, is likely to approach it enthusiastically whereas the ministry of local government may see it as an infringement upon its own authority and may even impede its successful completion. For example, a property tax administration reform program initiated through the Ministry of Local Government in the Philippines was constrained from the outset because local assessors and treasurers were in fact employees of the Ministry of

Finance (Holland, Wasylenko, and Bahl, 1980). Another example of this problem is the use of food-for-work programs in Bangladesh as a grant for rural works activities. The explicit relief objectives of the ministry of food, where food-for-work programs are administered, may run contrary to the development objectives of the rural works program which is administered by the ministry of local government.

Administrative Structure

Closely related to the above is the structural organization of administration within the developing country. If, for example, local revenue officials are directly tied to the higher levels of government, programs that are primarily initiated and carried out at the local level may be unsuccessful. This lack of success may not be due to any inherent weakness in the program but because it is not in the best long-term interest of the local revenue officer to conform to the proposed local reform. In the same manner, if different departments within a local government must cooperate in order for a local revenue source to be successfully administered, joint inputs of higher officials are required. Yet such cooperation is much more difficult to achieve than in the case where their own success is directly tied to such cooperation.

There are formal administrative arrangements for handling potential conflicts among field offices of central ministries through designation of the representative of one ministry, usually the ministry of the interior, to supervise and coordinate the regional activities of other ministries. As the above illustrations demonstrate, such arrangements are often insufficient to reconcile the varying goals, motives, and incentives of representatives of different central agencies.

Although one should not rule out any attempt to alter the administrative structure, the severity of administrative constraints must be recognized. It is essential to recognize these constraints and to work within them rather than to propose a total reorganization of the structure when focusing on improved resource mobilization techniques.

Economic Constraints

Local governments are not isolated entities. They exist within a larger economy and, whereas their own resource constraints may preclude particular "solutions" to resource mobilization problems, it also must be recognized that broader macroeconomic considerations may also arise (especially where the governmental structure is a unitary one). Currently, many developing countries are experiencing foreign exchange and inflationary difficulties. To ignore entirely these constraints may lead to a set of recommendations that, within the broader context, are entirely unrealistic. For example, although a significant increase in grants to localities may seem justified, it may be an impossible short-term objective if the central government is already facing budgetary deficits. Also, programs aimed at services relevant to increased local agricultural production for export require exchange rate policies which do not so overvalue local currencies as to price such exports out of world markets.

Technological, Cultural, and Institutional Constraints

Efforts to improve local revenue mobilization must also recognize the current environment in which the local government operates. To advise computerized annual reassessment of property values in an environment in which computers are nearly nonexistent is, of course, totally unrealistic. Likewise, if many transactions are carried out on a barter or in-kind basis, the use of monetary resource mobilization tools is inappropriate.

When devising a new set of practices or policies, one must keep in mind the institutions that exist currently and their limited capacity. To recommend increased use of credit financing for development projects when the national credit market is almost totally undeveloped is as unrealistic as recommending the imposition of a sales tax where transactions are nearly all of the barter variety.

Cultural considerations also play a role in the determination of feasible policy options. For example, within the context of an Islamic society, certain taxes and debt financing may be limited by religious doctrine (Shemesh, 1969). Similarly, resource mobilization techniques that are carry-overs from colonial times may be viewed with sufficient suspicion to preclude their inclusion in a menu of taxes, fees, or voluntary contributions.

INCENTIVES AS THE KEY TO RESOURCE MOBILIZATION

Given these objectives and constraints, we would argue that the provision of incentives and disincentives is a key to improving local government resource mobilization. These incentives may be focused on different actors—taxpayers, administrators, and local government decision makers.

Compliance Incentives

The incentives associated with taxpayer behavior can be tied to penalties for not paying, the benefits of complying, and the cost of compliance. These incentives may be instituted in a variety of ways including revenue structure revisions, changes in collection procedures, and moral suasion applied by community leaders.

Benefits of Paying

Increased revenue mobilization in developing countries may be as much a job of "selling" as it is of direct administration; the taxpayer may be more willing to pay if he believes the taxes will be spent on something useful to him.[6] The potential purchaser of a glass of beer does so because he sees it as yielding personal benefits. In the same manner, the potentially complying taxpayer may be much more likely to cooperate if there are perceived benefits associated with such action. The transfer of tax receipts to the central government treasury is generally perceived as yielding no benefits to local residents, but rather as supporting the salaries of government bureaucrats, including the military, and to some extent those who have left the countryside for the capital. Thus, to enhance voluntary tax compliance, taxpayers must be convinced that a significant portion of their taxes will be retained locally and that these revenues will be used for projects and services which they value.

Where there is not a high degree of tax compliance, campaigns designed to illustrate the benefits to the potential taxpayer may be a necessary first step in the process. This may be done in a number of ways. One of these is a simple passing of information, that is, holding village meetings to tell taxpayers what their tax money will buy. A second possibility is to permit the village area to retain a percentage of the amount collected: for example, *barangay* (neighborhood) units in the Philippines receive a 10 percent share of property taxes collected in the *barangay*. A third possibility, where traditional leaders still have a role in tax collection, is to compensate the village chief with a percentage of taxes collected from residents of his village. This is, for example, the case in Senegal where the village chiefs receive 7 percent of the "rural tax" (Wozny, 1983).

The previous arguments are also applicable in the case of voluntary contributions. Moral suasion by community leaders is probably necessary to evoke response in this revenue source. Taxpayer compliance and contributions may even be linked, for example, when a community leader donates a parcel of land to the local government but completion of the facility requires the generation of sufficient local revenues.

Penalties

Although the "carrot" may work in some situations, the "stick" can also be an effective means of stimulating taxpayer compliance. Necessary conditions for imposing a cost on noncompliers are the existence of legal remedies and an effective enforcement program. By their very nature, voluntary contributions lack this feature and thus are not amenable to this compliance technique.

The penalties themselves must be severe enough to be binding. One thinks immediately of cash penalties equivalent to interest charges on unpaid amounts, but often these charges are too low: the rate of return to owners of capital in LDCs may be so high that it would be profitable to be delinquent in paying taxes. Other penalties can be more severe—the legal system may provide that the property be sold at auction to recover back taxes, or that personal property be confiscated.

There is a direct relationship between the severity of the penalty and the hesitance of the government to enforce the penalty. The sanctions are especially difficult to enforce in rural areas where the "neighborhood" includes the administrators. For example, where a legal system provides that the tax-delinquent property be sold at auction, a potential response is for no one to be willing to bid on the parcel. Moreover, the taking of property is so drastic a step that it is opposed (perhaps feared) by local politicians and administrators—to a point where very little use is made of this penalty. On the other hand, there may be an advantage of the area being small in size and population. If compliers recognize the "free rider" problem associated with noncompliers, they may put pressure on their non-taxpaying neighbors. In such cases, techniques such as publishing or making public the list of noncompliers may provide sufficient "cost" to pressure the nonpayer into action.

Other extralegal incentives involve the tying of particular privileges to payment of taxes. In some countries, properties on which there are taxes delinquent cannot be sold until such delinquencies are cleared. This approach could be extended to require that any transaction with the local government (or possibly even higher levels of government) would not be possible until proof of payment on past-due taxes is shown. For example, a local permit to transact retail or wholesale business may be made contingent upon proof of payment of all local taxes. Few rural local governments have carried the incentive approach this far.

In Upper Volta and other West African countries it is not uncommon for the names of delinquent village taxpayers to be required to remain on display at the local administrative center until taxes are paid. Relatives, shamed by this display, generally pay the amounts owing in a short time. Another example is the requirement that tax receipts be shown in order to obtain travel permits, register a birth or marriage, or enroll a child in primary school (Syracuse University, 1983, pp. 138–53).

But to carry out these policies successfully will require a degree of interagency and even intergovernmental cooperation not always found in governmental institutions.

Compliance Costs

The technology, institutions, and possibly even culture in developing countries often require that financial transactions be carried out on a face-to-face basis. With no checking accounts or comparable financial instruments, and relatively little self-assessment, taxpayers are faced with the time and travel cost of paying taxes. If these costs can be lowered without greatly burdening the local government, overall rates of tax collection may improve.

A number of remedies have been applied. Programs that take tax collectors "to the people" rather than requiring the people to come to the tax collector, are especially effective in rural areas. The allowance of discounts for those who pay taxes on time is also a potentially powerful incentive.

Structural Reforms

One major impediment to improved collection may lie with the structure of the tax. People are more willing to pay taxes when they feel that they are being taxed fairly (relative to their neighbors), when they understand how the tax is levied and when the tax rate structure does not provide especially attractive gains from underreporting. Any number of reforms have been instituted to deal with such structural problems. The following are examples of the kinds of specific issues which arise:

1. Assessment biases in favor of higher income property taxpayers may discourage other taxpayers from complying. Inconsistent assessments among similarly situated taxpayers may produce the same result.
2. High property transfer tax rates will induce sellers of property to understate transaction values.
3. Progressive business tax rates will provide an inducement for owners to understate the base (e.g., gross sales) in order to reduce tax liability.

4. Property taxes levied on the total value of all holdings may induce property
owners to split or subdivide their property or undertake other subterfuge to
reduce tax liabilities.

These kinds of problems have led to many reforms of local tax systems. The
general direction of this reform is towards simplification, flat rate structures, and
more standardization in assessment practices.

Administrative Incentives

The role of the administrator in local taxation is crucial. Administrators as well
as taxpayers respond to incentives or disincentives in the system. It follows that
successful administration also requires the construction of a "proper" set of
incentives.

Pecuniary Incentives

Where there is little likelihood of pecuniary gain from "successful" administrative performance, effectiveness is likely to suffer. Yet, there may be few built-
in pecuniary incentives for doing a good job. Under a unitary governmental
structure, salary structures are generally determined by central civil service regulations with the successful local financial manager compensated no differently from
the less successful manager. Although the negative incentive of dismissal potentially exists, it may not be used often enough to be an effective management tool.

Where local government managers and administrators are employees of local
authorities, compensation is likely to be low in comparison with similar positions
in the private sector and in the central government. This explains the shortage of
qualified personnel for such local staff as assessors, collectors, treasurers, and
accountants in the local government sector and suggests that the training of local
staffs may be deficient. This raises another reason for poor revenue administration
performance and, although it suggests the need for training local government
workers, it must also be recognized that newly-trained employees may still be
attracted by higher paying jobs in other sectors. In fact, the creation of autonomous
bodies for transport and water supply, partly to get around salary limitations, is a
response to this constraint.

Power and Advancement

Closely related to pecuniary incentives is simply power or advancement to more
influential positions. If these moves can somehow be related to performance, they
can also encourage improved performance.

Where a local financial manager feels that there is no likelihood that improved
performance will result in a "better" position, or if poor performance is unlikely to
result in demotion, there is little reason to expect improvements in performance.
For example, if a tax collector feels that employment will continue whether or not
delinquent taxes are actually collected, there is little reason to expect this individual to put forth much effort in carrying out the assigned duties. On the other
hand, if there is a likelihood that the successful collector will become a strong
candidate for a supervisory position, he may be more willing to carry out assigned
duties enthusiastically.

Governmental Incentives

There are particular incentives associated with public sector decision making that are not necessarily in the best long-term interest of development efforts nor of effective use of locally mobilized resources. These incentives tend to favor more visible, shorter-term projects over projects which can have longer-term returns as regards both growth and additional resource mobilization. Intergovernmental aid provides an especially effective method of inserting incentives for greater resource mobilization into the system and can be carried out in a sufficiently selective manner to alter the previously mentioned expenditure biases.

Expenditure Incentives

In democratic political systems, elections occur frequently.[7] As a result, political and administrative decision makers may prefer to undertake short-term projects with immediate returns rather than long-term projects that may not be completed during the present elected or appointed term. Such myopia is difficult to overcome; nevertheless, techniques used by politicians everywhere such as erecting signs reminding passers-by of the mayor's name or the construction of prominently observable cornerstones may partially overcome the short-term bias. Closely related to the preference of short-term payoff projects is the incentive to support "visible" projects, such as new municipal buildings, rather than infrastructure development projects such as road repairs or water main improvements. Again, this bias is difficult to overcome, although skillful politicians and officials may be able to devise schemes to remind constituents that their "tax money is at work here." These constraints are important and development is unlikely to proceed unless they can be overcome.

These biases may be even more difficult to overcome when the project is aimed primarily at improving resource mobilization efforts in the long-run. For example, tax mapping for property tax purposes is seen as a desirable project but its payoffs will be in the future. Convincing citizens of the desirability of tax mapping may require a broad educational program focusing on the fact that tax mapping may increase the taxable base thereby reducing the relative burden on already-taxed parcels. To encourage local policy makers to enter into such a project may require that low interest loans or categorical matching grants be provided. Here the expectation is that the locality will be better off over the longer term but that the payoffs will be rapid enough so that currently elected officials can use these benefits in their own reelection pursuits. Finally, local administrators of the property tax system may have to be convinced that the existence of tax maps will make their jobs easier to carry out, and that such efforts can indicate that they are "successful" tax administrators and lead to advancement through a hierarchical personnel system.

Intergovernmental Aid

It is well recognized that intergovernmental aid arrangements may alter local governmental behavior of authorities with some degree of fiscal autonomy. The local government's response to transfers is likely to depend upon the form of such aid and, as well, may depend upon local preferences. Still it can provide a powerful weapon in achieving greater resource mobilization.

Grants may elicit several responses from local governments. They may continue to spend as much or more than would have been spent in the absence of such aid. When local resource mobilization expands in response to the transfer, the aid is termed *stimulative*. On the other hand, local governments may cut back on locally-raised revenues and *substitute* the intergovernmental aid. Which response is more likely is an especially crucial question when the stated objective of a higher level of government is to stimulate local government activity. When the aid is substitutive the system is actually acting contrary to its stated goals. Thus, to the extent that a local government decreases its local tax raising efforts, for example by being less concerned with tax delinquency or lowering its tax rates, it has responded perversely to the intergovernmental aid system. One method by which such reactions can be discouraged is by specifically including tax effort or matching requirements in the aid distribution formula. In such cases those localities putting forth a greater effort (relative to their own taxable capacity, however measured) are rewarded directly for their efforts.

CONCLUSION

Achieving increased revenue raising goals through a system that simultaneously pursues revenue sufficiency and elasticity, economic efficiency, equity, and administrability is difficult. First, these goals often conflict such that there will be trade-offs encountered in the active pursuit of each. As important, however, are the numerous constraints that are encountered in evaluating or building a revenue structure. Still, it seems that the principal question to be asked when attempting such evaluation is the extent to which incentives or disincentives are inherent in that structure and how these influence the attainment of the objects. Unless the incentives to taxpayers, administrators, and politicians are considered, it is unlikely that any set of proposed reforms or alterations in the revenue structure is likely to be successful.

NOTES

1. The recent book by Kenneth Davey (1983) addresses many of the same issues as are raised here. He does not, however, consider the role that voluntary efforts may play in resource mobilization and places less emphasis on the importance of incentives.

2. The term *elasticity* is usually taken to refer to the percentage increase in revenues associated with each 1 percent increase in local income.

3. Efficient pricing of roads in developing countries is emphasized by Walters (1968).

4. See, for example, Bahl (1979) and Harriss (1979). As Harriss (p. 195) notes, however, progressive rates based upon value of property do not necessarily translate into progressivity in terms of income.

5. This policy was, of course, less difficult to implement given the large increase in Nigeria's oil revenues during that same period.

6. This is why compliance incentives are less important in the case of user charges. With fees attached to a publicly provided service the payer is getting a direct benefit in return for his payment.

7. In fact, even where nondemocratic regimes are in power, an often necessary condition to maintenance of that power is a reasonably satisfied citizenry.

33

Taxation in Urban Areas

The dominant feature on the local fiscal scene in virtually all developing countries in recent years has been the rapid growth of large cities. Much of the population increase in developing countries has been and will be absorbed in urban areas (Linn, 1983). The obviously associated problems of poverty, migration, congestion, pollution, and sheer city size require huge increases in public spending to accommodate this growth without serious deterioration in the quality of life. The other side of this proposition, however, is that to at least some extent the same growth may contribute to the fiscal resources available to resolve these problems (Smith, 1974). For example, increasing land values increase the potential property tax base, increased "motorization" means more (easily taxable) automobiles, and increased economic activity increases the business tax base.

In practice, of course, it is not always easy—and sometimes not even possible—for cities to capture these potential revenue increases, owing to political resistance and to constraints imposed by higher levels of government. Nonetheless, as suggested in the following survey of urban tax practices and problems, much more can be done in most countries than has been to date. What seems required is not so much radical reform as intelligent incremental changes in existing taxes. As one example, in light of the report of an official commission in 1981 (Bird, 1984), Colombia has recently introduced substantial reforms in its local finance system, including the indexation of the property tax base and the introduction of a new, simpler form of local business tax (Bird, forthcoming).

Automobile-related taxes, as emphasized here (see also R. S. Smith, 1975, 1984; Churchill, 1972; Linn, 1979), offer one of the very few instances in which one can have one's cake and eat it too—that is, obtain revenue in an allocatively efficient and distributionally progressive way. The failure of most countries to make full use of this important potential tax base may perhaps be explained only in political terms, similar to those the authors of the following chapter employ to explain the relative neglect of property taxes.

A particular problem with the property taxes imposed in many cities in developing countries is that they are frequently cluttered with special provisions intended to affect the allocation of urban land use—for instance, to encourage low-cost housing or to discourage the holding of vacant land. The authors of the following selection are clearly skeptical about the efficacy of such measures, a view shared by many others (Oldman et al., 1967).

On the other hand, there are some important local policies in certain countries that appear to have more significant, and generally beneficial, effects on the development of urban areas (Grimes, 1975). Examples are the land value increment tax of Taiwan (Riew, 1987) and the land readjustment scheme of Korea

(Doebele, 1979). Another impórtant example is the valorization tax of Colombia (Rhoads and Bird, 1967; Doebele, Grimes, and Linn, 1979). In all these cases, the key to the successful use of such devices lies in their careful integration with expenditure planning and their careful implementation.

Given the poor state of administration, and especially local administration, in most developing countries, it may seem to be expecting too much for most countries to proceed very far along this path. A careful analysis of the postwar British "development charge" scheme, for example, suggested that this scheme failed not just for the reasons mentioned in this chapter but more fundamentally because of the impossible demands it imposed on even the well-trained and highly capable administrative structure in Britain (Hood, 1976). As suggested in chapter 32, most developing countries would seem better advised to keep their urban property tax simple and enforceable rather than trying to turn it into a tax serving mainly nonfiscal purposes—a judgment echoed for rural property taxes in Bird (1974).

Nonetheless, it is too easy to become discouraged about the prospects for rational and successful tax policy in developing countries. Here and there throughout the world, encouraging instances of excellently-conceived and well-executed policies, often carried out in extremely difficult circumstances, may be found. It is only through discovering and exploiting such small successes as valorization in Colombia or land adjustment in Korea that developing countries may perhaps be able to cope with such overwhelming problems as the need to accommodate over a billion additional people in their cities in the last quarter of the twentieth century. The problems of financing and guiding urban growth in developing countries are by no means simple; but they may, with some ingenuity, some luck, and a great deal of persistence, nonetheless be potentially soluble.

Urban Taxes: Practice and Problems

Roy Bahl, Daniel Holland, and Johannes Linn

PROPERTY TAXATION

The Theory

Increasing urbanization should increase revenues from the local property tax. As land runs short, the housing stock is expanded, and as commercial and industrial activities grow, property values also grow. Indeed, urban property values may well have grown as fast as urban public expenditure requirements, but property tax revenues clearly have not. The evidence suggests that urban property tax revenues have not kept pace with the growth of the base, largely because of the way the tax is administered in most developing countries. Assessment practices are inadequate, there is a great shortage of professional expertise in the valuation area, collection problems are severe, and taxpayer resistance to higher taxes on property is to be counted on. To understand better the failings of the property tax in capturing the revenue benefits of urban growth, it is necessary to turn to a brief statement of the existing practice in developing countries.

The Practice

In principle we can describe three basic forms of property taxation: annual or rental value systems, capital value systems, and site or land value systems (for a more detailed comparison of practices, see Bahl, 1979). All are used in developing countries. In the first, the property tax rate is assessed against annual rental value; capital value systems use some proportion of the market value of property (both land and improvements) as the tax base; and site value systems are based on the market value of land, excluding improvements.

While this trichotomy in the property tax base is a useful point of departure, a classification formulated in the legal tax base greatly oversimplifies and does not necessarily identify "similar" systems. In practice, there are many more than three systems, and these are differentiated by varying inclusions in the base, different rate structures, and perhaps most important of all, different assessment practices. In a sense, each country/city implants its own style—its cultural values and a unique set of political considerations—on its property tax system. As a result, it is not possible to point to any one of these basic systems as clearly superior, though it is possible to identify specific practices that have favorable or unfavorable effects.

Excerpted from Bahl, Holland, and Linn (1983).

Annual value property tax systems, more or less resembling the British rates, are still used in most countries colonized by the United Kingdom. However, there are assessment problems (particularly with respect to industrial and owner-occupied residential property) that have prompted a switch to something resembling a capital value system. Indeed, perhaps the most significant feature of existing annual value systems is that all resort to some use of capital value assessment. There is little evidence of a trend toward annual value and away from capital value systems, and the capital value base does not resort heavily to assessment on a net rent basis.

There appears to be much more diversity among cities using capital value systems than among cities using annual value systems, with respect both to tax structure and the effectiveness of the practice. At least in intent, there are many common features in the use of capital value systems. The more important of these features, which also distinguish the capital from the annual value system, are (a) a differential tax treatment of land and improvements; (b) an objective assessment practice for residential properties; and (c) a uniform assessment procedure for various types of land. Though there is much diversity in specific practices, there is a tendency for capital value systems to involve central and state government more heavily, especially in the assessment function.

In the last analysis, the capital value system is probably gaining in popularity because the concept of the sales value of property is more easily understandable and would appear to be more measurable. There lies the rub. Property value assessment and reassessment are highly technical matters and require a staff of substantial size and skill. The shortage of valuers in developing countries is acute, and governments have to make do with inadequately trained personnel, contract out, or simply not reassess.

Site value property tax systems are attractive in theory since, unlike either annual value or capital value taxes, the site value levy would have an income effect but no allocation effect. With the amount of tax invariant with respect to the degree of development on the land, the tax would raise revenue and not alter the pattern of development that would otherwise have occurred. Capital value taxes, however, levied on both land and the development thereon, tend to deter the degree of development.

Thus, site value taxation (SVT) has also been supported because it leads to more dense development than does capital value taxation (CVT) and therefore means lower government expenditures on certain urban infrastructure—streets, sewer and water lines, electric wiring, etc. An additional reason for preferring site value taxation has been the belief that, as compared with capital value taxation, the site value base will be more effective in energizing "sleepy" holders of vacant land, inducing them to develop or sell to others who will.[1]

Can We Expect More from the Property Tax?

In a reflective essay, Carl Shoup has raised the question: "Why so modest is the use made of the urban real estate tax in less developed countries . . . ?" (Shoup, 1979, p. 272). There are, as we have already noted, formidable administrative obstacles to property taxation. But Shoup does not emphasize them in answering his own question.

In particular, Shoup finds a primary reason for the unsalutary neglect of the property tax base to lie "in the pattern of ownership of urban real estate in most developing countries" (Shoup, 1979, p. 273). Not much commercial real estate is owned by the large domestic and foreign corporations that can be taxed at relatively little political cost. A heavy proportion is owned by important government officials and their families, and the substantial urban residential properties tend to have similarly influential owners. Lacking is a substantial proportion of middle-class housing. Thus, Shoup sees the tax base divided between "the politically nontaxable mansions and luxury apartments in high-rise structures, on the one hand, and the shanties of the poor that are not worth trying to tax, on the other."

Another reason for the "underdeveloped" property taxation in developing countries is the heavy reliance on the central government for the provision of public services such as education, police and fire protection, and roads. Shoup notes that the rich can afford to buy these services in the private market, and the relatively large middle-class demand that would be more effectively met by their finance in the public sector has not yet developed. If and when it does, real property taxation may be more heavily availed of.

Another factor noted by Shoup is the imperfect land-tenure and leasing arrangement, which makes valuation more difficult. And, finally, he points out the obstacles posed for property taxation by high and endemic rates of inflation. Property values are perpetually out of date, the dispersion of assessed around true values becomes more pronounced, and taxation, in effect, of unrealized gains poses still further difficulties to successful property taxation.

In the face of this formidable list of difficulties, is there any real prospect that property taxation will have a more appropriate role in urban finance in developing countries? Clearly this listing of obstacles suggests that it would be fruitless to look for a sharp improvement from a major reform or a particular device.

Some have urged, for example, that the formidable administrative obstacles and costs of property taxation could be circumvented by a scheme of self-assessment under which the taxpayer would set the taxable value for his property with the obligation to sell it for that price (or that price plus a premium) or pay a penalty based on that value if it should turn out to be too far below some minimum. But the success of such a scheme rests on a credible threat, and the factors cited from Shoup suggest the difficulty of mounting such a threat.

If there are no panaceas, what are the prospects, what can we reasonably expect and seek to accomplish? For one thing, we can be more realistic. We should not exhort, encourage, or expect "substantial real estate tax in a country where tradition, custom, mores, political and power structures, and similar influences stand opposed to such a levy. What is badly needed is to know how to improve and evaluate the tax in those urban areas where it has taken firm root and could be, perhaps, transformed into a powerful engine of urban development" (Shoup, 1979, p. 282).

For another, we should remind ourselves that change in urban public finance, as in so much else of human affairs, consists of slow, small, and uneven adjustments "such as the creation of special districts for capital cities with special expenditure responsibilities and revenue authority (Bogotá and Seoul); enlargement of metropolitan jurisdictions by annexation of adjacent municipalities (Bogotá); gradual development of new revenue sources (betterment levies in Colombian cities, land readjustment schemes in the Republic of Korea, and vehicle taxation in Jakarta); minor reassignments of expenditure functions (Kenya and Zambia) . . ." (Linn, 1981).

Finally, we should encourage simplification of property tax design and objectives. Casual observation of the structure of property taxes in developing countries suggests a major difference from the practice in the United States. The cities in developing countries tend to use property taxation to induce allocative effects, that is, to discourage land speculation, promote the decentralization of metropolitan population, encourage housing maintenance and urban renewal, encourage higher buildings, and encourage home ownership. These features have been built into property tax systems in a variety of ways, including marginal adjustments in the property tax rate structure and assessment practices and through the institution of specific property tax coercive measures.

But these are triumphs in principle that do not get translated into practice. The special features are rarely implemented. They stand as a statement of intention, not accomplishment. And they may well do more harm than good because they suggest "we are doing something" and therefore tend to forestall more constructive efforts.

There simply is no hard evidence to suggest that these efforts to induce allocative effects actually work. Yet the practice in LDCs suggests that decision makers in many developing countries believe that such an effect can be induced. In any case, there is need to evaluate these benefits against revenue and equity costs and to rethink the use of such adjustments in terms of whether offsetting or reinforcing effects exist elsewhere in the property tax structure. One cannot achieve too many objectives with the same tax treatment; and one can hamper the achievement of a single primary objective by surrounding it with gingerbread.

We turn next to a promising new local government tax base that illustrates the strong relationship between revenue and allocation effects.

AUTOMOTIVE TAXATION

Motor vehicle ownership and use represent an excellent, but neglected, tax base for urban governments in LDCs (see also Linn, 1979). The automobile population growth is more rapid than the city population growth in many cities, automobile ownership and use are easily taxable, and such taxes are likely to fall on persons with higher incomes. On the negative side, the growing automobile population increases urban government revenue needs by increasing expenditure requirements associated with road use and imposing considerable external costs of congestion and pollution on the urban environment. Much more attention has been focused on these costs than on the fiscal instruments that urban governments might develop to utilize this important revenue base and to control the high costs of urban congestion. A major difference between automotive taxes and all other local government taxes should be noted at the outset. This is the one case where efficiency objectives are as important as revenue-raising objectives, a factor that leads policy analysts to worry at some length about tax policy effects on road use and automobile ownership. Fortunately, automotive taxation in urban areas provides one of the rare examples where the benefit and ability-to-pay principles of tax policy converge. Comparing automobiles and populations in urban areas with national totals shows that car ownership is heavily concentrated in the largest cities of developing countries (see also Smith, 1974). For example, in 1970, Bangkok had 8 percent of the national population and 83 percent of the nation's cars. Comparable figures are 7 and 57 percent for Seoul, 15 and 65 percent for Tunis, but 17 and 16 percent for Paris. These trends of growth and concentration are likely to persist with continued expansion of urban populations and income increases. This pretty much makes the case for automobiles or automobile use as a viable tax base.

Associated with the rise in the urban motor vehicle fleet is the increase in investment and maintenance requirements for street infrastructure and traffic management. That more cars will increase the pressure for more road and street expenditures is only half the story. The unit costs of these services are also likely to rise with increasing congestion and land prices in central urban areas and with increases in the relative price of materials (e.g., asphalt, concrete).

Besides these two reasons for taxing motor vehicles—the base is there and increased numbers of cars generate revenue needs—there are the strong efficiency arguments for controlling the use of motor vehicles in urban areas. Traffic congestion and air and noise pollution are as bad, or worse, in many of the cities of developing countries as in the industrialized nations. And while it may be argued that higher congestion and pollution levels are likely to be more acceptable in the LDC cities than in the cities of developed countries, there can be little doubt but that the actual levels of congestion and pollution observed in most of the large LDC cities are far beyond optimal levels. Perhaps more important, things are likely to get worse in the years ahead.

This presents a quandary. If local governments are successful in using automotive taxes to reduce congestion and pollution, they will dampen the revenue productivity and elasticity of the tax base. On the other hand, there are considerable benefits to reducing congestion and pollution. Some of these benefits, reduced street and traffic related expenditures, accrue to the local governments. Other benefits, time savings and healthier air, accrue to the private sector rather than to the local government. Therefore, the decision to tax so as to selectively discourage road use rather than to maximize revenue yield from the automotive base may reflect the local government's view that controlling congestion and pollution is a higher goal. The choice to tax so as to discourage congestion implies a different automotive tax schedule than would taxation to maximize revenue.

Local Automotive Tax Practices in LDC *Cities*

Despite this seemingly excellent case for local taxation of urban motor vehicle ownership and use, urban governments in LDCs are not universally authorized to levy such charges. For instance, in Manila local authorities are expressly enjoined from levying any taxes or fees on motor vehicle registration. Where governments can impose taxes on motor vehicles or fuel consumption, they generally have not made a major effort to tap this revenue source at anything like its full potential. Comparative studies have shown that it is rare for automotive taxes to contribute more than 10 percent of total local revenue, or even more than 10 percent of total local tax revenue.

However, the example of Jakarta underlines that automotive taxation, if turned over to local authorities and if given sufficient attention, can make a major contribution to local revenues even in an environment not otherwise outstanding in fiscal or administrative achievement (Linn, Smith, and Wignjowijoto, 1976). Thus, while in all cities for which detailed revenue and expenditure data could be assembled, the expenditures on urban roadways by far exceeded revenues from automotive taxes, in Jakarta the reverse held true, with motor vehicle tax revenues exceeding road-related expenditures by 120 percent. Although there is no presumption that on economic grounds total municipal expenditures on the urban road network should equal the revenues collected from road users through automotive taxes, the general revenue shortages of local urban authorities in LDCs, which in part are due to an insufficient use of local automotive taxes, lead to a generally poor record on urban road investment and maintenance.

The practices in selected developing countries and cities—as reported in Bahl and Linn (forthcoming)—reveal that local automotive taxation consists of a very heterogeneous set of levies. In most cities where local authorities are permitted to levy automotive taxes at all, this takes the form of annual license taxes levied on all motor vehicles whose owners reside in the particular taxing jurisdiction. In some cities, a one-time tax is levied at the registration of a motor vehicle. In two cities, a local fuel tax was imposed by local governments. Finally, only in Singapore has an effort been made to apply restrictive licenses according to time and area of road usage within the city. Singapore also appears to be the only city in this sample where parking fees have been introduced and collected at more than a nominal level. Tolls on urban roads are not widely used.

The unrestricted local license taxes fall into three major categories: In Guatemala City, Ahmedabad, and Honduran municipalities, flat annual taxes are levied, differentiating only by type of vehicle. In Colombian and Korean cities and in Bombay, the tax varies not only with type of vehicle, but also according to weight. In Jakarta and in the South Korean cities, the tax varies according to type of vehicle and cylinder size. In addition to these three basic types of annual license taxes, there are special features in a number of cities: In the Republic of Korea, the local license tax is lower for business than for nonbusiness use, and for large cars the tax varies with axle length. In Bombay, higher taxes apply to vehicles not equipped with pneumatic tires. In Bogotá, the license tax declines with the age of the vehicle. Finally, in Colombian and South Korean municipalities, buses are charged according to the number of seats.

In contrast to annual license taxes, registration fees and transfer taxes are levied whenever the title to the motor vehicle changes hands (Bogotá, Cartagena, Jakarta), or only once at the time of initial registration (Tehran). In the Colombian cities, the registration fee appears to be nominal (less than US$1) and is presumably intended only to reflect the administrative cost of registration. (The illustrative data reported here and below are for the mid-1970s and taken from Linn, 1979). In Jakarta and Tehran, however, the registration "fees" are clearly in the nature of taxes, since they amount to a sizable proportion of vehicle value in Jakarta (10 percent for initial title transfer and 5 percent for any subsequent transfer) and to a flat charge of approximately US$44 for the initial registration of cars, taxis, and buses in Tehran (half that amount for trucks).

In those cities where local fuel taxes apply, they are usually levied on a specific basis—US$0.42 in Singapore, US$0.02 in Guatemala city, and a nominal US$0.0016 in Bogotá—and generally apply only to gasoline. The case of Singapore is exceptional since the fuel tax is a combination of a local and national tax, but it is of interest that Singapore had one of the highest national gasoline tax rates in a sample of forty-eight LDCs surveyed by Smith (1974). In the Philippines, cities and municipalities could impose a tax on gasoline up to 25 percent of the national gasoline tax up till 1974. In the Manila metropolitan area, different percentage rates applied in the various local jurisdictions, varying from 0 to 25 percent of the national tax.

The case of Singapore is, however, even more exceptional since it is the first city in the world (that we know of) that has made a significant effort to restrain central city congestion by the application of area- and time-specific licenses and parking charges. The scheme was initiated in June 1975 and was monitored extensively by local officials and World Bank staff (Watson and Holland, 1978). In essence it consists of prescribing a restricted zone in the city which is defined to include the most congested central business districts, covering sixty-two hectares and having twenty-two entry points. Between 7:30 A.M. and 10:15 A.M., entry into this restricted zone by private automobile is permitted only if the vehicle exhibits a license which is sold at US$26 a month or US$1.30 a day. Buses, commercial vehicles, motorcycles, and car pools (i.e., cars carrying four persons or more) are exempt. This scheme was supplemented by a drastic increase in public and commercial parking fees. In addition, fringe parking lots were opened up with park-and-ride schemes to offer motorists an alternative form of transportation.

Objectives and Yield Potential

Automotive taxes may serve multiple objectives, and there are several tax instruments that might be used to emphasize one objective over another. The simple cross-tabulation in table 33.1 is suggestive of the possibilities and underlines the need for a coordinated approach to developing an integrated automotive tax structure. First, efficiency and revenue-raising goals may overlap; for example, if the price elasticity is known to be quite low, the primary objective of fuel

Table 33.1 Objectives of Automotive Taxation

| | Types of Taxation | | | | | | | |
| | Direct Taxes on Ownership | | | | Indirect Taxes on Use | | | |
Objective of Taxation	Import duties[a]	Sales tax[a,b]	Registration fee	Transfer tax	Fuel	Toll, area license	Sales tax on tires, part	Parking fees
Reduce road use, congestion, pollution; or charge road user for social costs					X	X		X
General revenue instrument	X	X	X	X				
Instrument of energy policy			X		X			
Income redistribution	X	X						
Restrict automobile ownership	X	X	X				X	

[a]Central government.
[b]Including excise on domestic production.

taxes will be to increase revenues. Second, the central government may have yet other objectives in taxing automobiles, for example, to channel private savings into more socially productive investments, to reduce imports in order to address balance-of-payments problems, etc. Third, each of these instruments can and has taken on many forms; for example, fuel taxes may vary by location or vehicle type depending on the efficiency versus the revenue objective of the local government.

One view is that the efficiency goal is the primary criterion for evaluating the success of automotive taxation. The efficiency effect of automotive taxes depends on how far they are able to approximate the marginal costs imposed by the use of the motor vehicle. This marginal cost includes the variable maintenance and pollution costs and the marginal social costs of congestion, that is, the increased operating cost, time losses, noise, foul air, etc., imposed on society by the additional vehicle on the road. If automotive taxes are imposed to exactly equal these marginal costs of vehicle operation, then they will produce an optimal efficiency of road use. If, on the other hand, these taxes exceed or fall short of marginal social cost, then road use will be inefficiently restricted or expanded, provided only that the price elasticity of demand for road space is greater than zero. Obviously these marginal costs cannot be exactly measured, but they can be closely enough approximated to generate a set of tax rules or guidelines.

Even so, few would believe that automotive taxes are perfect benefit charges, and one might be left to consider pure fiscal impacts. Increased automobile use will increase expenditure and will raise the size of the public service deficit. Our question is: What is its potential for also increasing revenues and thereby offsetting this deficit?

The revenue performance of various types of automotive taxes has been mixed.

Local government taxes on motor fuels have excellent revenue potential, though they are usually levied at inordinately low rates. The revenue elasticity of this tax depends crucially on whether it is levied at a specific rate or ad valorem. In the former case, tax revenues are likely to be quite inelastic, especially where inflation rapidly erodes the real value of the specific tax[2] and when gasoline consumption is not growing. In the latter case, however, tax revenues are likely to be quite buoyant, given the rising price of fuel. What is more, fuel tax revenues are likely to be quite stable, since motor vehicle use is not likely to vary much with short-term fluctuations in economic activity.

Besides the excellent revenue potential, fuel taxes have the great advantage of being relatively easy to administer, especially where the production and wholesale distribution of fuel is in the hands of a government-owned enterprise, as is the case in many developing countries. Ad valorem taxes are more difficult to administer and police than specific levies because of the possibility of evasion, especially at the retail level. This explains the general preference for specific fuel taxes in LDCs at the national and local level. There is finally the issue of whether higher-level governments are likely to be willing to let local authorities share in such an important revenue source. The fact that few local governments actually levy a fuel tax may lead to some skepticism on this score. The example of Jakarta confirms this: In 1969, the local authorities imposed a local fuel tax at a rate of approximately one US cent per gallon. Other local governments in Indonesia followed suit, but within a year the national government had taken over the tax.

Local government sales and transfer taxes on motor vehicles would increase the price of the vehicle and the cost to the purchaser. This would have three effects. First, it may restrict ownership to the extent the demand for automobiles is price elastic. In this way, road use might be indirectly limited. Second, the higher price of the car would increase its annual cost to the purchaser and its use to the extent depreciation is linked to use. Third, it would generate increased local government revenues. The uncertainty is the magnitude of these effects.

On the revenue side, an important consideration is that it is likely to be quite difficult to administer higher local sales taxes on automobiles in urban areas, since the potential for evasion is considerable. Automobiles may be purchased in jurisdictions with lower tax rates, or out-of-town addresses may be given if the tax is linked to the residence of the purchaser. The incentive for evasion is likely to pose a much greater problem in the case of sales taxes than for annual license taxes. This may explain why local governments have generally been given access to license taxes, but only in rare cases to sales taxes on automobiles. An exception is Jakarta (Linn, Smith, and Wignjowijoto, 1976).

In general, motor vehicle sales taxes are not on a par with fuel taxes or annual license taxes as a local government revenue source. Both of the latter have the advantage of being more easily administered, permitting a greater degree of regional differentiation, and neither results in unfair windfall gains to current motor vehicle users.

Unrestricted annual license taxes are levied according to residence in the area, rather than according to use of the motor vehicle. This tax, therefore, does not affect the use of a vehicle once it has been purchased; however, the decision on whether or not to own a motor vehicle is affected by the license tax, since the annual cost of ownership will increase. This means that unrestricted license taxes may reduce automobile expenditure requirements in the public sector, but the more important fiscal effects are likely to come on the revenue side.

The revenue success with license taxes depends largely on how the tax is structured. As with the local fuel tax and the motor vehicle sales tax, the problem of evasion arises. In the case of the annual license tax, vehicle owners may escape the tax by registering these vehicles in low-tax jurisdictions. This limits the degree to which license taxes can differ, especially between adjoining jurisdictions. However, there is reason to believe that with vigorous enforcement and sizable penalties, some differentiation without major evasion is feasible.

The capacity of the motor vehicle license tax as a major revenue source for urban governments depends very much on how it is structured and how aggressively it is administered. The rapid growth in the base will ensure a certain amount of revenue growth, but evasion and inflation are likely to cut heavily into this growth potential where administration is poor and specific tax rates are not increased to keep pace with changing prices.

The taxes discussed above might all be viewed as potentially important revenue-raising instruments. The efficiency impact of these taxes is uncertain, and for relatively low tax rates, probably not of much importance. This is less true for the more pure congestion charges: area- and time-specific vehicle licenses, parking charges, and tolls. All of these are suited for local government administration.

Singapore is one, perhaps the only, example of a large city making use of unrestricted motor vehicle licensing. The costs of introducing the scheme were minimal. To quote Watson and Holland (1978, p. 37): "Overall, the total cost was less than it would have cost to build two kilometers of four-lane urban expressway." The revenue implications of the scheme, while not of great scope, are on balance favorable. Annual revenues net of operating costs amount to approximately US$2.4 million. Compared with revenues collected from other taxes on motor vehicles or from property taxation, these revenues are not substantial (approximately 1 percent of property taxes), but in any case the system does not constitute a net drain on the public purse and compared with other tax measures has a low ratio of administrative costs to revenues.

Parking fees and taxes have been suggested as the major alternative to charging motor vehicle operators directly for the use of congested urban streets, but they are rarely used to any significant degree. The parking tax would have two major components: taxing commercial and private parking facilities in congested central city areas (e.g., as is done in Singapore) and levying fees for on-street parking either through attendants (as in Jakarta) or through parking meters (as in Central American cities). The study by Bahl and Linn (forthcoming) showed no case where these taxes yielded significant revenues.

One is hard-pressed to find examples of LDC cities where *tolls* are used as a means to control congestion or raise significant amounts of revenue. To the extent that tolls are levied at all in urban areas they affect the more uncongested, special-purpose expressways, such as the expressway to the airport in San Jose, Costa Rica, where the main goal of the charge is presumably to recover the capital costs from the users. Indeed, the dilemma with toll roads is that they are always inefficient: in uncongested traffic, because they restrict traffic below the optimal use of the road; and in congested traffic, because they tend to worsen, rather than alleviate, congestion and are furthermore costly to administer.

OTHER URBAN TAXES

Apart from property and automobile taxes, local governments can and do use a large number of other taxes and licenses. While these alternative sources of revenue are not always easily administered or free from unwanted efficiency or equity effects, and while they tend not to be the more comprehensive income and consumption bases that local governments would prefer, they have the advantage of being available. They also offer local governments the advantage of capturing some of the income and consumption growth that is characteristic of urbanization.

Local governments in developing countries typically have one major nonproperty tax revenue source, usually some form of indirect tax on local trade or business activity; some form of automotive taxation; and a large number of "smaller" local taxes. Often the latter are quite large in number but add relatively little to total revenues.

Income Taxes

There is more use of local income taxation in developing countries than one might expect. Local income taxes may not capture the benefits of urban growth as fully as one might expect, for three reasons.

First, the law usually does not permit a pure income tax, that is, one that covers nonwage incomes. More commonly, local governments must rely on some combination of a poll (head) tax, a wage tax, and limited income tax sharing with higher authorities. The poll tax element is important in Guatemala City, where a specific tax is levied on all men (and women in public-sector employment), distinguishing only between three income groups. In Zambia, a similar system applies, except that there are seven income groups taxed at different rates. In Zaïre, local authorities are permitted to levy what amounts to a local wage tax at approximately proportional rates and a specific tax on traders and professionals, but only for those income earners who are exempt from the national income tax. The South Korean cities combine a head tax on heads of households (and on corporations) with a surtax on all tax liabilities of the national personal income tax, the corporate income tax, and the farmland tax. Nigerian cities, including Ibadan, have levied a local income tax on all taxpayers exempt from state income taxes, and the cities share in the state income tax. State law permits the local government in Calcutta to tax all professions, trades, and salaried persons. The point is that many of the fruits of urban growth are simply not included in the tax base.

Second, even where property and proprietorship income is taxable, the evidence shows that it is not taxed because of the difficulty of controlling evasion and underreporting. Presumably, this problem has moved at least the Zaïre government to tax nonwage earnings at flat rates irrespective of the amount of income earned.

The third, and perhaps most important, limitation on the coverage of local income taxes in LDCs is simply the unwillingness of most central governments to give up any share of the income tax base.

To the extent that any generalizations are possible regarding this varied experience with local income taxes, one might conclude that all local income tax in LDCs can hope to achieve is to tax wage earnings in the modern sector of the urban economy.

General Sales Taxes

Few local governments in LDCs are permitted to levy broad-based sales taxes. Typically, this potentially important source of revenue is reserved for higher-level governments. Bahl and Linn's [forthcoming] survey could turn up only Bogotá, Managua, and Rio de Janiero as deriving (at one time or another) significant amounts of revenue from broad-based local sales taxes. However, the sizable revenue yield in these three cities (69 percent of total tax revenues in Managua and 89 percent in Rio) attests to the considerable potential of local sales taxes.

Local Taxes on Industry, Commerce, and Professions

Taxes on industry, commerce, and professions are a common source of local government revenue. In many Latin American cities, this form of taxation contributes sizable proportions of total local tax revenue. For example, the local taxes on industry, commerce, and services (in the mid-1970s) accounted for 84 percent of local taxes in San Salvador, 67 percent in Valencia, and for as much as 73 percent in La Paz. In the Philippines, about 40 percent of locally raised revenues are from the local business tax.

The nature of this local tax varies widely among countries and even among cities within a country. In Colombia, for instance, five types of local taxes carry the title of "industry and commerce tax." A turnover tax is used in Bogotá, Medellin, Armenia, and Monteria. A tax on the value of gross business assets is levied in Cali, Barranquilla, and Cartagena, among others. Some Colombian cities levy a tax on the value of fixed assets of the firm located in the taxing jurisdiction (e.g., Popayán, Neiva), others on the rental value of the business establishment (e.g., Cúcuta). Finally, most smaller municipalities in Colombia levy the tax in the form of specific levies by type of enterprise. Thus, while in all municipalities this tax carries the same name, it actually represents a sales tax in some cities, a tax on business capital in others, an annual value tax on business real estate in yet others, and in most small municipalities simply a business license tax.

The revenue yield potential of business taxes can be substantial. With urbanization, the number and size of business establishments increase and the taxable base grows. Even though the base may be inadequately assessed, the tax yield can grow rapidly. An analysis of the Philippine business license tax shows that even under quite poor assessment and collection practices, the income elasticity of the tax yield often has been greater than unity (Bahl and Miller, 1983).

Octroi

In many cities in India and Pakistan, octroi is a dominant revenue source. The base of the octroi is the value, the weight, or the number of items entering a local jurisdiction by road, railway, sea, or air. Obviously the base will expand rapidly with local economic growth; hence despite its many flaws, the octroi is a productive revenue source. In fact, in many Indian and Pakistani cities, octroi dominates the revenue structure. Elsewhere, to the extent that they ever existed, taxes on intercity trade have become virtually extinct.

Local Sumptuary and Entertainment Taxes

If "bright lights" are a cause of rural-to-urban migration, they also offer some potential for urban government taxation. Taxes on beer, liquor, and tobacco—usually referred to as sumptuary taxes—are widely in use in LDCs, and in some countries local authorities are entitled to levy such taxes or to share in the proceeds of sumptuary taxes imposed by higher-level government. For example, in Zambian cities, the local tax on beer consumption is by far the most important source of local tax revenues. In the long run, the income elasticity of sumptuary taxes is likely to be quite low unless real tax rates are continuously increased because of the low income elasticity of liquor and cigarette consumption.

It is common in many LDCs for local government, particularly in the larger cities, to levy taxes on various forms of entertainment. Among these are taxes on restaurants and hotels; on theaters, movies, and other types of public entertainment events; and on gambling. Revenues derived from lotteries operated by local governments also may be counted as an entertainment tax. Bahl and Linn's survey has shown that most cities in LDCs derive some revenues from entertainment taxes.

There are problems with respect to the revenue performance and administration of entertainment taxes. Assessment and collection can be difficult, as observed for instance in the case of Seoul or Jakarta. Revenues are generally not substantial, although their buoyancy can be considerable. For instance, entertainment tax revenues in Seoul and Jakarta had a buoyancy greater than unity, and in many of the other cities revenues from these taxes were among the most rapidly growing of all local taxes.

CONCLUSION

Three tax bases are particularly appropriate for financing urban growth in developing countries: real property, automobiles, and consumption. All tend to grow at least as rapidly as population or income and could, therefore, support the increased urban expenditures that support economic growth. In all cases, appropriate tax design could minimize allocative inefficiencies and set the stage for effective administration. For the property tax, this need not necessarily be at the expense of revenue. With respect to automobile taxation, there is clearly a revenue-allocation effect tradeoff.

NOTES

1. Designating the value of land in the taxing jurisdiction as L and the value of improvements as I, and required revenue (the same under either tax) R, the rate of site value tax λ, and of capital value tax α, then:

(1) Under the capital value tax: $R = \alpha(I + L)$
(2) Under the capital value tax: $R + \lambda(L)$, and

$$\lambda = \frac{\alpha(I + L)}{L} .$$

Therefore, the site value tax will always be levied at a higher rate than the capital value tax, the difference between them being determined by the ratio of improvements plus land to land.

If, for example, L is one-fourth of total value and I is three-fourths, then $\alpha = 1$ and $\lambda = 4$ would raise the same revenue from their respective bases. On a vacant plot, however, the tax liability would be four times as large under SVT as under CVT. On an "average" property, i.e., one with L equal to one-fourth and I equal to three-fourths of total value, the tax liability would be the same under both bases, and for a property developed to a greater extent than average, the tax liability would be less under SVT than CVT.

2. In Bogotá, per capita gasoline tax collections in constant prices declined between 1961 and 1972.

34

Taxation and the Urban Poor

Most poor people in developing countries, and especially the poorest people, are invariably found in rural areas. Nevertheless, the conditions of rural poverty, to those who do not have to endure them, often appear rather picturesque. Moreover, the very nature of the rural economy and rural life means that the rural poor are seldom politically visible—except very occasionally when driven to outright rebellion. In contrast, the problems of urban poverty are both much higher on the political Richter scale and also much more visible to visitors from abroad. For both these reasons, there has been considerable concern in recent years with urban poverty.

The following chapter surveys some of the major issues with respect to the impact of taxation and the most important alternative to taxation in the urban setting, user charges, on the urban poor. (To a lesser extent, reflecting their lesser involvement in the market economy in most developing countries, similar arguments may be made with respect to the rural poor.) Apart from the importance of this question in its own right, this chapter also serves to redress somewhat the relative neglect of distributive issues in this book, since it also contains a brief review of some of the many fiscal incidence studies that have been carried out in developing countries. Although we are not particularly sanguine about the results to be expected from such studies (Bird and De Wulf, 1973; Bird, 1980), there appears to be, as indicated in this paper, some hope that more useful results may emerge from future incidence studies.

Taxes, User Charges, and the Urban Poor

Richard M. Bird and Barbara D. Miller

A decade ago, a comprehensive review of fiscal incidence studies concluded that in only two of the forty-four studies examined (covering twenty-two developing countries) was the tax system regressive in the sense that the poor—broadly defined—appeared to pay a larger proportion of their incomes in taxes than did the rich (De Wulf, 1975). In a number of other cases, however, there was evidence of some regressivity toward the bottom of the income scale. The same review found that most of the incidence studies that distinguished between urban and rural sectors found that taxes represented a relatively smaller share of (usually lower) incomes in the agricultural than in the nonagricultural sector. Almost no attention was paid in any of these incidence studies to the dispersion around the average of the effective tax rate within each income class. The focus of tax-incidence studies has invariably been on the *vertical* equity of taxes (do the rich pay a larger share of their income in taxes than the poor?), to the virtual neglect of the equally interesting *horizontal* equity question (do two equally poor people pay the same taxes?).

McLure (1977) subsequently examined the results of some of the same incidence studies—three in India and one each in Colombia, Brazil, Pakistan, Lebanon, and Jamaica—with particular attention to the poor. Although none of these studies provided sufficient data to analyze the tax burden on the poor in detail, on average it appeared that taxes took around 10 percent of the incomes of the urban poor and a bit less of the incomes of the rural poor. Jamaica was found to be an exception in both respects, however, with taxes on the poor being close to 20 percent of income throughout the island.

A comprehensive recent review of urban finance in developing countries by Bahl and Linn (forthcoming) turned up nineteen studies of the incidence of property taxes in thirteen different countries, most of which found the property tax to be generally progressive, or even very progressive. This diverse group of incidence studies employs so many different and sometimes inconsistent assumptions that it is difficult to know what to make of these results. On the whole, however, the conventional view that the property tax is regressive seems less likely to be correct in developing than in developed countries, largely because the income elasticity of housing is likely to be unity or greater in developing countries.

Bahl and Linn (forthcoming) have also reviewed carefully the scanty evidence on the incidence of the user charges levied to finance various urban services in some developing countries. In the case of water, perhaps the most important such

Excerpted from Bird and Miller (1989).

service, both the precise nature of the rate structure employed and the physical nature of the city in question were found to affect the distributive impact of user charge systems. In Nairobi, for example, low-income areas can be supplied at lower cost, so efficient water charges would have a generally progressive incidence. The opposite, however, is true in Cali (and probably many other cities), because it is the poor who tend to live in the areas where land values are low owing to difficult access and unfavorable physical factors. On the whole, property taxes probably constitute a more progressive way to finance the expansion of basic urban services than even progressively structured service prices, essentially because housing consumption is more income-elastic than water consumption.

Most studies of the distributive effects of various tax and pricing systems in different developing countries suggest that the tax systems existing in developing countries are *not* very regressive. Few of these studies focus explicitly or in much detail on the poor. It cannot be said, however, that the taxes—mostly indirect taxes—now levied on the poor in most countries are regressive, contrary to an impression that is still widespread (e.g., Chenery et al., 1974, p. 84). Almost no study pays attention to the important question of the horizontal equity of the tax system within the heterogeneous group called "the poor," however. The results for any country often depend on a very detailed understanding of the precise structure and working of the fiscal instruments in question.[1] And, finally, almost all these studies rest on questionable logical and statistical bases in the first place (Bird and De Wulf, 1973).

Nevertheless, the evidence is clearly that taxes *do* take a relatively substantial fraction of even very low incomes in most developing countries. Moreover, governments are clearly concerned with the distributional effects of taxes. There appears to be considerable interest in the scope for improving the well-being of the poorer half of the populace through appropriate redesign of taxes.

Focusing on redistributing income through the fiscal system after it has initially been distributed by the economic system may, indeed, give a misleadingly small impression of the potential of the tax system to redistribute income. The tax system may also affect the initial distribution of income through its effects on, for example, the structure of industry and the demand for unskilled labor as well, in a more long-run framework, through its effects on saving, capital formation, and real wage levels. For example, the potential scope for tax policy to influence employment, the major source of income for most people, is enormous: "Apart from the effects of taxation on capital formation itself, the proportions in which capital is combined with labour may be influenced (1) by operating on the 'big' relative prices through altering the intersectoral terms of trade, the effective exchange rate, or the wage-rental ratio itself; (2) by altering the distribution of income, and hence the composition of demand; (3) by altering relative product prices; (4) by influencing the rate and nature of technological innovation; and (5) by bringing about a more unified (and price-sensitive) factor market" (Bird, 1982, p. 214). Payroll taxes and tax incentives for investment almost by definition do not impinge directly on the incomes of the poorest 40 percent (or 60 percent) of the population in most developing countries. Nevertheless, by tending to reduce employment in the modern sector, such fiscal measures probably mean that the poor will stay poorer longer than they would otherwise.

Similarly, as Kuznets (1966) has argued, the principal long-run redistributor of income in developing countries is almost certainly the move out of agriculture. Tax factors affecting this move may, therefore, have a much greater long-run impact on the poor than the current regressivity of tobacco taxes or whatever. Similarly, within the agricultural sector, Bird (1974) has argued for more use of properly structured land taxes. Even though such taxes might seem at first to penalize poor peasants, they may well in the long run improve the well-being of both the rural and the urban poor through encouraging more efficient utilization of land and rural labor (particularly if coupled with appropriate land reform).

In short, tax policies that in effect encourage resources to be allocated to their "highest and best uses" will, as a rule, tend to make the poor better off—perhaps not as obviously or immediately as would the elimination of the tax on tobacco, for example, but probably in the end more significantly.

PROPERTY TAXES

Linn (1983) suggests three rules for those who want to alleviate urban poverty through local fiscal policy: (1) reduce regressive taxes; (2) increase progressive taxes; and (3) use benefit charges appropriately to finance urban services. The first rule relates primarily to the indirect commodity taxes levied by some local governments—the octroi in India and beer taxes in Zaïre, for example (Linn, 1981)—and is further discussed in the next section in the context of indirect tax policy as a whole. The other two "rules" are taken up below.

Apart from the strong case that can be made for more local use of generally progressive taxes on automobile use and ownership (R. S. Smith, 1975; Linn, 1979), the main progressive revenue source available to local governments in most countries is the property tax. There is increasing evidence that the property tax is, or can be, a fairly progressive way to finance urban services. As Linn (1983, p. 77) notes, however, the precise distributive effect of property taxes depends very much on the details of their structure and administration. The relative legal and administrative treatment of a rental versus owner-occupied properties, of land versus improvements, of low-value versus high-value properties, and so on, may have a profound effect upon the progressivity or otherwise of a property tax.

Higher taxes on land than on buildings, for example, would likely increase both the progressivity and the efficiency of the property tax (Holland and Follain, 1985). Because the value of landholdings generally rises with income class, a tax levied solely on land—the burden of which falls on landowners—is obviously more progressive than a tax on all real property, which in an open economy will inevitably bear more heavily on labor and on the consumption of locally produced goods than on capital. In addition, a tax on land is more neutral—less likely to deter development—than an equal-revenue tax on land and improvements (Follain and Miyake, 1984).

While there is no good distributive case for progressive rates of property taxation (Bird, 1974, p. 211), there may often be substantial distributional (and administrative) benefits from combining an exemption with a flat rate. In Jamaica, the property tax is at present levied on the basis of the unimproved value of land at rates varying from 1 percent to 4.5 percent. Parcels valued at less than $J2000, however, pay only a flat tax of $J5. Approximately the same distributional effect could be attained with much less administrative and efficiency cost by levying a flat rate of 1.5 percent and exempting the first $J6000 in value (Holland and Follain, 1985).

In particular circumstances, such features as the exemption of improvements (Holland and Follain, 1985) or the imposition of different tax rates in different locations (Holland, 1979) may provide sufficient gains in terms of both equity and efficiency to seem worthwhile. As always, however, it is a rather dangerous game to advocate undue complexity in tax design in countries in which the limits of administrative feasibility are very real (Bird, 1977).

USER CHARGES AND PUBLIC SERVICES

Complexity introduced for distributional reasons may also produce perverse results. Nominally progressive public utility rates proved to be an inefficient technique of income distribution in Malaysia because many poor families consume more water than do rich families (Katzman, 1978). That portion of the poor population receiving services was in effect penalized by a supposedly 'pro-poor' rate structure. Similarly, in Colombia, where the subsidization of urban public services through progressive rate structures is relatively important, the benefits of this subsidy are generally *regressively* distributed within the poor population (Bahl and Linn, forthcoming). At the same time, the large group of the poor who receive no services have also often been burdened, through either taxes or inflation, in order to make up the deficits of public utility enterprises.

Once again, it is very important to be clear about the details before generalizing. In some instances, for example, "life-line" tariffs (a low tariff for an initial small block of consumption) may well provide both an efficient and an equitable way of pricing water, provided that the low rate is not below the amount appropriate to reflect the presumed external benefits from such consumption and that it is not financed by charging larger consumers at prices higher than marginal cost (Bahl and Linn, forthcoming). Since the income elasticity of demand for water is relatively low even in poor countries, however, and since to some extent at least household size and income may be negatively correlated, in other instances this policy may produce perverse distributional results, especially to the extent that multiple-household connections are more prevalent among low-income households.

Other water-pricing schemes besides rising block prices (progressive tariffs) are found in many countries. In Colombia, water charges are frequently related to property values in a progressive fashion. Again, however, the distributional effect of such charges depends on a wide variety of factors. In Cali, it was found that although the average price of an initial block of water rose steadily with assessed property values, the final impact of these charges was in fact regressive in terms of income (Bahl and Linn, forthcoming). A broader study of the incidence of the public-service charges levied in Colombian cities for residential water supply and sewerage, electricity, garbage collection, and local telephone service found, using some strong assumptions, that the incidence of these subsidies was generally progressive. But relatively few of these benefits flowed to the lowest 20 to 30 percent of the population, largely because of their lack of access to services (Linn, 1980).

It may be seriously misleading to concentrate on redistribution only within the select group of consumers receiving such services because the most important consideration may be whether the poor have *access* to services at all, not how much they have to pay for them (Selowsky, 1979; Meerman, 1979). The poor can benefit from subsidized services only when they have access to them.

In Colombia, the proportion of the urban population with access to public water supply in 1977 ranged from a high of 93 percent in the Department of Quindio to a low of 37 percent in the national territories (Bird, 1984, pp. 137–8). Even in the largest cities, about 25 percent of the population had no access to services in 1974, the poorest being those most likely to do without (Linn, 1980, p. 101). One reason for this outcome is that the poor are less able to afford the high connection and installation costs charged by the largely self-financing public enterprises responsible for providing urban services in Colombia. Because the extent of access is often related to the financial and other incentives under which service is provided, it makes little sense to discuss the distributive effects of user-charge financing of urban services without considering explicitly the precise institutional links between financing and service provision.

Another reason for lack of access may be simple political bias in favor of the better-off, the traditional and expected recipients of such services. Yet another reason may be, in contrast, that the relative insulation of the public enterprises from day-to-day political pressures may result in *reduced* access to services by the poor. The more technocratically determined investment decisions of bureaucrats, for example, may result in favored (and usually relatively high-income) consumers receiving better services (Bird, 1980b, p. 32). The poor may thus lose out in many ways: through having to bear through taxes or inflation some of the cost of providing subsidized services to the rich, through being faced with high "benefit" charges for a self-financing system, and through the bureaucratic and political machinations determining who gets what service in either case.

INDIRECT TAXES AND THE POOR

Indirect consumption taxes, particularly those on the traditional "excisables," account for most of the existing direct impact of taxes on the poor. In addition, such taxes as those on fuel may also have a substantial indirect impact on the poor through increasing transport costs.

A recent review of the incidence of different excise taxes in developing countries found the tobacco tax to be the most regressive tax in the Philippines, Guatemala,

Colombia, Argentina, and Greece, among other countries (Cnossen, 1977). In Lebanon, however, the tobacco tax was actually progressive, largely because of the higher tax content of the imported cigarettes consumed by the rich (De Wulf, 1974). A similar result has also been noted in the Philippines (Asher and Booth, 1983, p. 142).

The incidence of taxes on the other important "traditional" excise products—alcoholic beverages and hydrocarbon oils—is similarly important to the poor in many countries. As in the case of tobacco, the incidence of these levies appears to vary sharply from country to country, depending on the specifics of local consumption patterns and tax structures. Generalizations about incidence based on predetermined value judgments concerning the "inherent" progressivity or regressivity of particular levies can be misleading. As Cnossen (1977, p. 47) notes, the income-distribution approach used in most incidence studies suppresses the potentially much more important differences between families in the same income class. Tanzi (1974) has suggested that the dispersion around the average increases as income rises, so that estimates of average tax rates by income classes have little significance. Equally important, however, it may be argued that a given degree of dispersion has more significant equity implications at lower than at higher income levels. One early study of Guatemala, for example, suggested that heavy smokers and drinkers probably paid 3 percent of their income taxes while moderate consumers paid only 1 percent (Adler, Schlesinger, and Olsen, 1952). Differences of this magnitude at low income levels obviously raise important equity questions, particularly because the low price elasticity of demand for these products implies that it is mainly the consumption of other goods ("basic needs"?) that is necessarily reduced as a result (McLure and Thirsk, 1978).

Recent analysis also indicates that the efficiency effects of commodity taxes need to be taken much more explicitly into account in designing and reforming indirect tax systems (Stern, 1984). In particular, this analysis casts doubt on the traditional view that a uniform commodity tax such as a general sales tax is in principle better than a more differentiated set of taxes on goods and services (Due, 1970a).

Rate differentiation of varying types has been urged on efficiency grounds, on distributional grounds, and even on stabilization grounds (Asher and Booth, 1983, p. 132). Many countries have listened to this advice, at least to the extent of having a system of progressive sales and excise tax rates intended to make the incidence of their indirect taxes progressive. However, a strong case may be made against using rate differentials in a general sales tax in order to achieve distributive ends, essentially because any equity gains from differentiation may be more than outweighed by administrative costs (Cnossen, 1982, 1984). In most developing countries, however, there are substantial differences in consumption patterns between income groups that can be differentially taxed through sales. It is not enough in such countries to say "whatever meagre progressivity that may be achieved by a differentiated sales tax rate structure can be attained far better through a small change in the income tax" (Cnossen, 1982, p. 213). With respect to the poor, who are largely outside the income tax, this statement is not true, while with respect to the rich it assumes that the income tax is in fact an effective instrument of re-distribution. This assumption is erroneous for most developing countries particularly with regard to nonwage income.

The appropriate distributional role of indirect taxes in any developing country cannot easily be decided on a priori grounds. What matters is the relative *quantitative* importance of different tax and income characteristics. Textbook advice, such as that in Chenery et al. (1974, p. 84), to discriminate between income groups through higher taxes on goods with high income elasticities and low price elasticities is as uselessly simplistic as the judgment on the same page that "in most cases the [existing] structure of indirect taxation is markedly regressive."

Similarly, the sweeping condemnation of sumptuary taxation of alcohol and tobacco in McLure and Thirsk (1978) offers as little guidance to what should be done in any particular developing country as does the recent evidence suggesting on grounds of efficiency that such taxes should be retained and perhaps even strengthened, at least in industrial countries (Shoup, 1983). Although, presumably, "being poor should not entitle one to an unlimited license to create negative externalities" (Shoup, 1983, p. 262), little, if any, attention appears to have been paid to these questions in developing countries.

The sumptuary rationale appears to be important in most Asian indirect tax systems, but Asher and Booth (1983, p. 135) express substantial scepticism about the realism of this rationale given the low price elasticity of demand for such goods. They quote with approval the dictum of Due (1970a, p. 63) that "the primary argument for excises on alcoholic beverages and tobacco products is their revenue productivity." As Shoup (1983) has noted, however, what an observed low price elasticity really shows is that the tax rate is still some distance below the maximum-revenue rate. Moreover, the observed reluctance in many countries to maintain the real level of sumptuary taxes in the face of inflation casts further doubt on the view that these levies are just a simple way to gouge the poor. Those who advocate much higher taxes on alcohol on social grounds in developing countries (Marshall, 1982) are not necessarily talking hypocritical nonsense, as McLure and Thirsk (1978) appear to suggest, especially when higher alcohol taxes would often not be regressive.[2] Once again, detailed, quantitative study, not sweeping generalization, is what is needed to advance knowledge and formulate good tax policy in this area.

The most useful data sets for the analysis of indirect taxes will include several features: longitudinal data on expenditures so that changes over time can be analyzed; expenditure categories that are sufficiently fine-tuned that the details of the tax ratio can be examined; actual price data rather than imputed prices; and demographic information on the population surveyed. Such features are basic to the endeavor, yet are rarely found in any study in the literature on indirect tax incidence.

For an even better understanding of fiscal impacts, still other information is needed. For example, beyond the bare facts of household composition such as number of household members and their age and sex, it is important to try to find out both who is the "household head" (not always an easy question) and the number of income earners in the household. Such factors may affect substantially the pattern of expenditures and consequently the effects of tax changes. Household characteristics greatly influence the nature of consumption patterns. An obvious example is one cited by Brown and Deaton (1972) in which a household with beer-consuming adults but no children will have a higher per capita consumption rate than a household with beer-consuming adults and children. We must be able to separate adults from children in order to see clearly the incidence of a tax on beer in this case.

The conventional analysis of tax incidence in effect assumes that the family is a sort of "black box." If one tax on a family is reduced and another increased by the same amount, it is assumed that there will be no net effect on the family. But what if the tax reduced is on beer consumed by the husband and the tax increased is on condensed milk consumed by the children? Would the effects be different if the increases and reductions were reversed? Households organize their finances in many ways, and there is no certainty that the effect on expenditure patterns will be the same in all cases.

Even more ideally, and to our knowledge nonexistent in the fiscal-incidence literature, would be a data set that would combine the features on the "whole consumption/production vector" (Behrman and Deolalikar, 1985) and so allow us to learn how consumption would be altered, within the household and among households, by changing prices, how such changes would affect nutrient intake, and how changes in nutrient intake would affect productivity.[3] Studies that could incorporate such data would greatly advance our knowledge of current tax incidence, changes in incidence over time, and how such changes alter consumption, nutritional status, and productivity. All these processes must eventually be taken into account if we are to place taxation in the wider context of how the poor will fare in the course of development.

CONCLUSION

The first, and perhaps the most important, conclusion of this chapter is simply that the issue of fiscal incidence and the poor matters. The tax system in most developing countries impinges on the lives of many poor people in potentially important ways. The poor, especially the urban poor, *do* pay substantial taxes. The extent, nature, and perhaps duration of their poverty *are* affected in many ways by the characteristics and operation of the tax system. Both governments and researchers concerned with poverty in developing countries should, therefore, be aware of these effects. The interaction of taxation and poverty is thus an important subject for research.

A second conclusion is that unfortunately this interaction is a very difficult subject to study. Not only are the underlying theoretical issues inherently complex and the needed facts hard to find, but it is essential to understand the detailed reality of the fiscal instruments under examination and to ground that understanding firmly in the relevant broad policy context. Such generalizations as "income taxes are better than sales taxes" or "beer taxes are always regressive" are useless guides to designing or reforming tax policy in any particular country.

New data and techniques may make it possible in the future to refine answers to meaningful old questions (will the substitution of a general sales tax for a set of excise taxes be progressive or regressive?) and to answer important new questions (will an increase in tobacco taxes impact differently on children in female-headed households?). There is still a long way to go in the analysis of the distributional effects of taxes.[4] But it is gradually becoming possible to carry out serious studies in a field that has far too long been dominated by misleadingly overly simplistic quantifications of untested, and too often ad hoc, hypotheses.

The set of those who can simultaneously deal with complex theoretical issues, primary data-grubbing, institutional realities, and broad economic policy concerns is probably almost an empty one. Nonetheless, a final conclusion suggested by this chapter is that much more attention should be paid to collecting and analyzing data bearing on these matters, with particular emphasis on trying to obtain a better understanding of the extent and nature of the variations among the poor. It may be useful for many purposes to seize upon the simple lack of command over economic resources of the poor as their dominant and most important characteristic. What has been too often neglected, however, are the very great differences *within* those classed as "the poor": between urban and rural, between employed and unemployed, between those in male-headed and female-headed families, between those with and without children, between smokers and drinkers and the abstemious, and so on.

Yet if we know anything about the effects of taxation on the poor in developing countries, we know that these effects often vary more with such characteristics than they do with any measure of total income or expenditure. Beyond gathering more detailed data in order to be able to depict more accurately the impact of taxation on the poor, we also need a much clearer idea of the normative and positive relevance of the observed deviations among different groups of poor people. Do the non-smoking poor care that their addicted colleagues pay heavy taxes? Should they? Do their colleagues care? Should anyone care?[5]

We do not, as yet, *know* much about either the short-run or the long-run impact of taxes on the poor in developing countries. But we are perhaps approaching a point where the economist's increasing understanding of the implicit models underlying incidence analysis and the increasing availability of relevant data are, despite a continued lag on the data side, better matched than ever before. We are able, at last, to begin to respond to the oft-expressed concerns of policy makers with respect to the distributional impact of revenue measures with something other than qualitative bromides or quantitative exercises in sleight of hand.

NOTES

1. See, e.g., Bahl and Linn (forthcoming), on the effects on property tax incidence of different administrative systems.

2. See, for example, the case of Papua New Guinea discussed in Bird (1983a).

3. Behrman and Deolalikar (1985) do an excellent job of bringing the consumption/production function together in an analysis of data from rural southern India. Taxation, however, is not a concern of their study.

4. Many common layman's questions on incidence ("is the tax system as a whole progressive?") can probably never be answered satisfactorily (Bird, 1980). But increasing familiarity with general equilibrium and other modeling techniques has made clearer how dependent the results of incidence studies are not only on data but also on our implicit models; for example, assuming the forward shifting of excise taxes in the face of trade restrictions, as has been done in all studies cited here, requires some strong, and rather strange, assumptions.

5. Some arguments suggest no one cares—or should (Buchanan, 1969).

35

Taxing the Agricultural Sector

The final chapter in this part takes up a different, and important, question: the taxation of agriculture. The appropriate taxation of agriculture has long been seen as a crucial development finance issue. Early writers (Kaldor, 1965; Nurkse, 1957; Lewis, 1955) basically advocated heavy taxes on agriculture for three reasons: to generate food for the urban (modern) sector, to supply labor for that sector, and to supply capital for the modernization of the country (for excellent surveys, see Lewis, 1967, 1973). The agricultural sector was thus seen as, in effect, little more than a milch cow for the rest of the economy. Taxes on agricultural land in particular were considered to have an especially important role as a means not only of mobilizing resources but of encouraging increased productivity within the agricultural sector itself by bringing into use the so-called "slack" resources thought to be prevalent there (Gandhi, 1966).

Subsequently, however, revisionist writers (surveyed in Bird, 1974) recognized both the need to build up the agricultural sector in many developing countries and the deleterious effects of heavy agricultural taxation (especially on exports, always the easiest base to tap). Although these writers also agreed that the land tax was the best way to secure revenue from the agricultural sector (Wald, 1959, Bird, 1974), they placed much less stress on the "need" to levy heavy agricultural taxes. Most recently, more emphasis has been put on such matters as the effects of taxes on risk taking in the agricultural sector (Newbery, 1987). It is still obvious, however, that almost all writers on the subject of agricultural taxes have a soft spot in their hearts for land taxes. Unfortunately, it is even more obvious that no country makes much use of such taxes.

Export taxes were discussed in chapter 28, where it was noted that such levies could produce a good deal of revenue in some instances, albeit at high economic costs. In contrast, theory tells us that land taxes can produce revenue at little or no cost. In practice, however, as the following excerpt from a recent survey paper makes plain, the agricultural land tax has never lived up to either its promise or its publicity. Although this paper sets out the conditions needed to make the land tax an effective instrument of development policy, the concluding discussion of the political and other obstacles to this actually occurring make it seem unlikely that matters will soon change.

As in the case of urban land taxes, agricultural land taxes in principle may play an important role in implementing development objectives—but only as part of a well-planned and well-implemented system, and in a supportive rather than a leading context. In a sense, telling a developing country to make heavy use of such taxes is equivalent to telling them what they could do if they were not poor: it may be interesting, but it is not very useful. It may sometimes be worthwhile to set out what should be done, if it could be done, as a long-run aspiration, but perhaps the most important message about land taxation in the agricultural sector is that it is more important to keep it simple—and especially to keep the tax base up to date—than to incorporate fancy gadgets intended to short-circuit administrative deficiencies, such as self-assessment (see chapter 38) or to substitute for land reform (Bird, 1974). In the circumstances of most developing countries, not only will most such attempts to use taxation for nonfiscal purposes fail, but they will also all too often damage the extent to which the tax system is able to achieve its fundamental economic objective, namely, to raise revenue in a non-inflationary manner.

Agricultural Taxation in Theory and Practice

John Strasma and others

In spite of the apparent theoretical attractiveness of taxes on agricultural land, the empirical literature, though mostly ten to twenty years old, is highly critical. The criticism boils down to four main points:

1. Land taxes produce relatively little revenue.
2. Land taxes seldom achieve their nonfiscal goals.
3. Land taxes sometimes are counterproductive, discouraging production.
4. Land taxes are unpopular, costly to administer, and plagued with corruption.

In short, taxes on agricultural land have often been described as being neither fair to farm people nor useful to governments.

It is sobering to begin by examining the actual results of agricultural taxation in developing countries. For over thirty years, there has been widespread agreement that there is substantial potential for taxation of agriculture in developing countries.[1] In many developing countries agriculture is a large sector of the economy, and in some it is the dominant sector. In these cases, revenues cannot be adequate unless government taxes this sector. In addition, agricultural taxation can be used to pursue various allocative and distributional goals, and even to accelerate the transformation from an agricultural to an industrial, developed nation. Even those who argue that development policies should encourage an expansion in the size of the agricultural sector—and this view is becoming the dominant perspective in development thought—acknowledge that some taxation of agriculture is necessary.[2]

It is perhaps surprising, therefore, that there are few countries in which this advice has been followed. Statistics on the magnitude of taxation, agricultural and otherwise, in developing countries are notoriously incomplete and inaccurate. Still, the available evidence from international agencies and country studies almost all indicates that agriculture is lightly taxed, and that the trend is, if anything, to lower taxes further.[3]

Very few countries collect as much as 10 percent of total government tax receipts from direct taxes on agricultural land. There are no countries in which land taxes account for more than 20 percent of revenues. In most, all kinds of taxes on property bring less than 5 percent of central government revenues.

For the most part the major tool by which agriculture is taxed in developing countries is the taxation of food exports. According to Goode, Lent, and Ojha (1966), export taxes accounted for over 20 percent of government revenues in four

Excerpted from Strasma et al. (1987).

countries and over 10 percent in twelve countries. Bird (1974) indicated that export taxes then generated over 10 percent of government revenues in eighteen of fifty-eight countries. Export taxes are still quite significant as revenue sources. Countries in which there are significant amounts of cash crops tend to rely more heavily upon export taxes.

METHODS FOR MODERNIZING AGRICULTURAL LAND TAXES

To turn the agricultural land tax into a development instrument that is both fair and useful, one must find solutions for problems in the structure and the administration of this tax. In particular, government must find equitable and low-cost methods for assessing farm land. Government must achieve rate structures and levels that produce substantial revenues and are heavy enough to create the other effects of land taxes predicted by economic theory. And, as with other taxes, government should administer the tax fairly and efficiently, and use the revenues in ways which the taxpayers consider acceptable, hence offsetting in part the burden they feel in complying with the tax. While this is an ideal, experience shows that countries that come relatively closer to the ideal seem more likely to succeed in the efforts to use land tax as a development instrument.

The existing literature suggests above all certain conditions, some inherent and others extraneous to the tax itself, under which a positive efficiency impact of land taxes might be expected:
1. The tax must not penalize new investment or good management.
2. Its impact on economic rent must be significant.
3. Other taxes must not nullify the effect of the land tax.
4. Productive and potentially productive land must be scarce (that is, there is no frontier open to settlement at minimum cost).
5. There must be an unexploited economic slack—market incentives must be effective, and appropriate technology, capital, and physical inputs must be readily available.

The creation or modernization of a tax on agricultural land involves at least seven major stages:
1. Design and planning of the project: definition of the tax base, decision as to the rate structure, and creation of a means of automatic future updating
2. Legislation, organization, staffing, and training for the project
3. Identification and description of the lands to be taxed (ideally, a full-blown cadastral survey)
4. Determination of the value of each land unit
5. Notification to taxpayers
6. Resolution of appeals
7. Billing and collection, including dealing with nonpayers

None of these stages is so easy that it requires no major effort, though the fourth stage, valuation, is usually considered the hardest. In practice, the inadequacy of most existing land taxes is precisely the result of values that were set (or have drifted during inflation) to levels far below market values of the land, or actual going rentals, the usual stated standards. The relatively few instances of successful land valuation for tax purposes do demonstrate that effective design, planning, and implementation are possible.

Design and Planning

The first step, naturally, should be to determine the objectives for which the land tax is to be created or modernized. Is it primarily for revenue, and, if so, how will that revenue be used? (For instance, will it finance local schools, roads, and other productive investments, or will the taxes collected disappear into the general revenue of the central government?) Is the tax also supposed to encourage more intensive land use, or the subdivision of large estates? Is it to encourage investment in irrigation and other capital outlays, to increase production, employment, and exports?

The second step is to design the creation or modernization of the land tax to achieve the stated purposes; in some cases a closer look at what would be needed to achieve them will lead to a redefinition to a more feasible set of objectives. The decisions made at each stage may determine key impacts, such as who bears the tax burden, possible changes in food supplies and prices, changes in the market values of land, changes in land tenure, and the distribution of landholdings by size. Tax design may even affect urban sprawl and other land use variables.

Most countries that tax agricultural land assign a capital value to each farm, as the tax base. However, some countries assign instead an annual rental value or an estimated potential income-generating ability. This is particularly likely to be used when the tax is collected as a presumptive income tax rather than as a tax on the land as a form of wealth. (Note that we are not concerned here with efforts to apply income taxes to *actual* farm income nor to gross sales of farm products; taxes on actual net farm incomes are difficult to enforce, and both net income and gross sales or export taxes may have serious disincentive effects.)

Taxes on agricultural land are usually at a flat rate, except that the very small holdings are often exempt. However, farms large enough to be taxed are subject to the tax on their entire value, rather than on the amount by which the value exceeds an initial amount that is exempt (as in an income tax).

Nonetheless, some countries have land taxes with rates that are highly progressive according to the size of holdings. This structure could reflect a belief that large holdings are more profitable, and hence that the owners of larger landholdings have a relatively greater ability to pay taxes. It could be intended to encourage the owners of large estates to divide them. It could even be designed to offset the well-documented fact that assessors tend to value larger properties at lower amounts per hectare than smaller properties. Actual market values may show a similar difference; there are many more potential buyers for small parcels than for large estates, so the price per hectare of small parcels is often higher in fact than it is for large estates. (Division into smaller parcels requires some effort and investment, so market forces alone do not keep prices per hectare uniform for different farm sizes, even for similar soil, water, and locations.)

Argentina, for instance, has progressive taxes in many provinces. However, current values are so far below market values that the steep tax rates do not appear to have induced subdivision, real or fictitious, nor to have led to more intensive land use.

Those who oppose land reforms often assert (erroneously) that large estates are more productive than smallholdings. As a rule, this is true in terms of output per employee or per dollar invested, but not in terms of output per unit of land. The reason is that large estates tend to use much less labor per hectare, because of the diseconomies of large-scale operations, such as the extra layers of supervisors required. The fear of future land reform, or of populist labor laws, also motivates mechanization on large estates.

For most situations, a flat rate seems more appropriate than graduated rates. The land tax is usually an in rem tax, levied in theory on the land and due from whoever controls the use and products of the land, rather than a tax on the owners as persons. It is much easier to administer a flat-rate tax, parcel by parcel, than one that requires identifying all the landholdings of each owner, in order to apply a progressive rate scale. It is also not obvious that equity or ability-to-pay concepts require taxing progressively by size of holdings, regardless of soil quality, if the tax base does not include other types of property such as factories, movie theaters, apartment buildings, or shopping centers.

On the other hand, the use of computers to handle land records has now made it relatively easy to sort records and compile such lists—thus land taxes that are progressive with respect to total holdings of farm land are more feasible than they were when land and tax records were all compiled by hand.

Updating Land Taxes

There is little point to making the effort involved in creating or modernizing a tax on agricultural land, if no provision is made to update it and prevent a recurrence of the problems that plague many existing land taxes. Many countries rely mainly on adjusting tax values to reflect declared sales prices when land is transferred. However, most such countries also tax the transfers at steep rates—and buyers and sellers respond by routinely reporting false prices that greatly understate the actual transfer prices.

This method is seldom effective for updating land values when land is sold, much less in updating the tax values of land that does not change hands. If one purpose of land taxation is to encourage the division of large estates, heavy transfer taxes work in the opposite direction. If reported sales prices are then used to raise assessed values, there is even more incentive for false reporting of sales prices.

The only cost-effective method of updating tax values is the use of a price index. A specialized index of farm land prices could be developed on the basis of auction and other transfer prices thought to be accurate, but it would require a substantial effort and most developing countries probably have more urgent uses for the staff who could create and maintain such an index. An index of prices received by farmers, adjusted for an index of farm costs, may be easier to develop in countries already gathering these data for other purposes.

The only reliable method of automatic updating for most countries is also the simplest method: let the land tax law specify automatic updating. Apply a general price index to land tax values each year. A suitable figure readily understood in many countries would be the same index used to adjust legal minimum wages for inflation. If there is reason to believe that land values lead or lag the general price index, government may want to adjust the index for this purpose—but this runs the risk that it will be abused and instead serve to reduce real land taxes under the guise of a technical adjustment.

Determining the Value of Each Land Unit

The tax value of each parcel, or piece of agricultural land, may be set by the government, with a formal evaluation of each parcel; it may be determined by the owner, and reported in a declaration that is also a self-assessment; or it may be calculated on the basis of physical features of each property and unit values used by the government to value all properties of that type in the region, valley, or province.

Individual Assessment at Market Value

In many countries, the law establishing a tax on agricultural land (and usually on urban property as well) requires the government to send a valuer to assess each parcel of real estate individually. In theory, the assessed value is usually supposed to be about the same as the figure that would be given by an appraiser, as the estimated "market value" of a parcel being sold by a willing seller to a willing buyer, neither under any special pressure.

When a landowner objects that the tax assessment figure is too high, the legislation in these countries usually allows the taxpayer to appeal the value. In most cases, the first appeal is to the tax assessment body, and if the taxpayer is not satisfied by the result of this administrative appeal, he may then go to the courts. The owner hires an expert, the state provides a valuer, and in many cases the first two experts then jointly choose a third expert, who becomes the tiebreaker.

The traditional appeals process is slow and quite expensive. It is thus available mainly to the wealthy, although if many appeals are presented even merely at the administrative level, the tax becomes ineffective because the government cannot deal with a relatively large number of appeals. (More than five percent is probably enough to lead most governments to cancel a tax reassessment rather than fight through all the appeals.)

Individual Self-assessment by Owner Declaration

Some governments, realizing the physical impossibility of professional valuations at market prices on a parcel-by-parcel basis, rely instead on declarations by the landowners that include a physical description of the property, and the owner's declared estimate of its market value. Tax officials and scholars alike agree that owners tend to declare values well below market prices in most cases (Bird, 1974).

Economists have long tried to devise effective incentives or sanctions to induce owners to declare the true values of their properties. For instance, Harberger (1965) and others have proposed allowing anyone to buy any property at the value declared by its owner for tax purposes, whether or not the owner wishes to sell. A subsequent proposal modified the Harberger scheme to make it administratively feasible and politically more palatable. For instance, owners not wishing to sell at any price could reimburse the government for the cost of a professional appraisal of their property, and that value would then not be subject to bids from would-be buyers (Strasma, 1965).

The new proposal, called "market-enforced self-assessment," also allowed owners to decline offers, but only upon accepting an increased assessment at the amount rejected, plus the payment of several years' tax differences. As an incentive to induce bids even if owners could refuse to sell, this payment would be split between the government and the frustrated offeror (Strasma, 1965). Even with such provisions, the market-enforced self-assessed proposal has been criticized by many scholars, such as Holland and Vaughan (1969).

Market-enforced self-assessment has not been tested anywhere, so far as we have been able to determine. However, it has found a simpler, feasible role as a low-cost appeals procedure. Owners who want to appeal, but do not want to face the cost and delays of the traditional method, may submit a statement that the property is only worth a certain amount, lower than the assessment. The tax office then advertises the property for sale at auction, with the owner's price as the lowest acceptable bid. If there are no takers, then the assessment is changed to the lower figure. (If someone does buy the property, that establishes a market price, and the assessment changes to that amount.) This appeals method has actually been applied in Ocean County, Florida, and perhaps elsewhere.

Mass Valuation Methods

For the creation of a new land tax, or the updating of an existing one, individual assessments parcel-by-parcel are often impossible. They cannot be carried out in a reasonable time with the staff who are likely to be available. In many developing countries, by the time the parcels in one valley are assessed, inflation tends to make hopelessly obsolete the assessments set the previous year one valley over.

The alternative method, which may be called "mass valuation," makes no pretense of determining the precise market value of each property. Rather, it starts with objective data that describe the agricultural potential of each parcel, and then applies average or unit values per hectare to each parcel, with an adjustment for access to markets. The generation of those unit values is, of course, the critical factor in determining how closely the result will approach average actual market values.

This process was used in the successful reassessment in Chile (1963–65), and similar methods have been used more recently in the Philippines.

The most important single factor in the success of mass valuation methods is undoubtedly elimination of the visit by an assessor to every property, and the costly and largely subjective appeals based on alleged market value of a given property at a given time. The key to success lies precisely in the use of unit values and in developing a sense that these values fairly reflect relative values of different kinds of land and location. As Bird observed, the success achieved in Chile and Jamaica is owed in part to a willingness to proceed with a "second best" method if the theoretically best method was stymied. Dreams of the unattainable perfect must not be allowed to prevent doing something that is good (Bird, 1974, p. 110).

POLITICAL OBSTACLES AND CONSTRAINTS

Policy makers have generally been hard-pressed to find the political constituency to support implementation of agricultural land revenue systems for nonfiscal purposes. Dorner and Saliba (1981, p. 6) maintain that "the initial and most difficult hurdle which all taxation proposals must overcome is political opposition from those likely to be taxed most heavily." Ironically, they may be understating the implacability of the political opposition by identifying it merely as "those likely to be taxed most heavily."

There is no question but that large landowners have a political interest in opposing land revenue systems and, in practice, they do. Davis (1967, p. 10) attributes problems in application of the land revenue system in Colombia to opposition from large landowners. Schwab (1972) shows how enactment and application of Ethiopia's agricultural land revenue system in 1966 got caught up in the national and regional political process and was ultimately frustrated by the landed aristocracy. "The law, which was initially seen as an instrument of land reform, through existing political pressures became merely an additional tax poorly implemented" (Schwab, 1972, p. 183).

Much the same happened in Turkey. An annual land tax at one percent was based on sales values declared in a 1936 self-assessment, vetted mainly and casually by local officials. However, there was little adjustment for inflation and economic growth over time. Thus by 1960, actual land values were up about 50 times, but revenues rose only 2.7 times and the tax had become insignificant in total revenues. Nicholas Kaldor (1962) advised replacing the tax with a substitute tax based on the average net product per hectare for major land types. It would have been fairly simple to implement this approach, because such estimates were already prepared each year for the national economic accounts. However, the landowner lobby in the legislature called his plan "too complicated," and they and the military compromised by merely tripling the existing assessments, leaving the tax still about one-fifth of what it was in 1936 in real revenue terms (Bulutoglu, 1968).

Most writers on the problem would agree with Hirschman that, "the weakness of land taxation is that while it arouses the opposition of the landed interests, it does not hold out an obvious appeal to any other important social groups" (1963, p. 433).

Experience has shown that active political opposition to taxes aimed at subdivision of large estates is not restricted to the large landowners. Why is it that small and medium landholders make common cause with large landholders in opposition to agricultural land revenue systems? In what ways do all their interests converge? Or are the large landowners simply hoodwinking or intimidating the small and medium landowners?

The key to the paradox is that agricultural land revenue systems generally propose levies on small and medium landholders to some extent yet make no credible promises of benefits. The impact of a given revenue rate is often heavier on the smallholder, living close to subsistence, than on the larger landowner. As Mathew (1968) points out, the levy will represent a much greater share of the smallholder's annual cash income than it will of the larger landholder's. That is one reason for smallholder opposition to agricultural land taxes.

People do not support new tax levies unless they are convinced that they will somehow benefit from them. Agricultural smallholders are skeptical of agricultural land taxes because they do not believe they will get any benefits from them. Domike and Shearer (1973, p. 77) blame this belief for the failure of a Bolivian effort to create a modern land tax in 1968. A coalition of peasant organizations originally supported the idea, but opposed it when the finance minister insisted that the revenue go into the general revenues of the central government. The earlier proposal allowed the peasant leaders to decide and direct the use of the revenues for local projects.

The problem is to detach smallholders' political interest from that of the large landholders. Political support from smallholders for an agricultural land revenue system cannot be mobilized without convincing them that returns from their cash payments will benefit them. Smallholders are more interested in how they will benefit from paying the levies than in the macro-policy ends of the land revenue system.

Overcoming the political obstacle is absolutely crucial to creating an effective agricultural land tax. To recruit smallholder political support, planners must build two types of consideration for the smallholder into an agricultural land revenue proposal. The first is in the realm of exemptions. Smallholders will mistrust any new tax measure. A high exemption level which, in effect, excuses a large number of property owners from liability, leaves the large landholders politically isolated in opposition. The second is in the area of benefits. While smallholders will seek to avoid new taxes, they will welcome certain benefits which only money can buy. Agricultural land revenue system planners will have to determine what those benefits are and make their provision an integral part of the revenue system package. To the degree that planners can convince smallholders that they will receive valuable benefits from the proposed system, the planners will not simply be avoiding opposition, they will be building political support.

ADMINISTRATIVE OBSTACLES AND CONSTRAINTS

Once an agricultural land revenue system has been legislated through the political process, the administration is responsible for its application. Effective operation of a land revenue system often simply adds new strains on an already overburdened administrative management system. At the same time, adding implementation of land revenue legislation to the responsibilities of the bureaucracy further challenges its administrative capacity.

There is general agreement (see Dorner and Saliba, 1981, p. 6; Schwab, 1972) that a general lack of funds and lack of trained personnel have hampered implementation of agricultural land revenue systems. The civil services of aid-recipient countries simply do not have trained staff in place in sufficient number to take on the burdens of administering an agricultural land revenue system. Nor do they have access to the funds needed to implement the system effectively.

As a general rule, the more decisions the agricultural land revenue system requires the administrative staff to make to arrive at the tax for a particular plot, the more costly the implementation of the system in terms of personnel time and expertise. The chief attraction of market-enforced self-assessment, for example, is the theoretically low cost to the administration of assessing the value of the property. Systems in which holdings are divided into several land categories, to be taxed differentially, for assessment purposes, such as the Ethiopian system, are more difficult to administer than systems which recognize only absolute land areas as the basis of assessment. Similarly, progressive systems, in which larger land-owners have heavier taxes per unit area than smallholders, are difficult for the bureaucracy to administer and invite abuse by the large landowners.

The most serious administrative constraint to an agricultural land revenue system implemented with agricultural production objectives is intertwined with political constraints. Application of levies high enough to have an impact on the landowner's pocketbook has often been an insurmountable political problem. Carrying out the cadastral survey on which the assessment system is based likewise creates political tensions. Finally, assessing the value of the land is fraught with political controversy. Carrying out the cadastral survey, assessing the value of the land, and levying the revenue charge are, however, the three fundamental administrative actions upon which a successful agricultural land revenue system is built.

The more tractable administrative problems fall under the general rubric of institution-building. With adequate time, money and technical assistance, people can be trained. They can acquire new skills. The general level of administrative performance of a bureaucracy can be raised. Improved record keeping would, for example, resolve most of the titling and collection problems in the administration of agricultural land revenue systems.

The political problems associated with the administration of these systems would have to be tackled at the outset, at the same time as the political problems associated with creating the systems in the first place.

CONCLUSION

Finally, perhaps the most important reservation about application of an agricultural land tax concerns using a fiscal instrument to achieve nonfiscal objectives. First of all, as a rule of thumb, landowners, including low-income landowners, will resist payment of any levy for any purpose. The resistance hardens if authorities cannot show the landowners a material benefit in the form of goods or services in exchange for their payments. Furthermore: "many countries have learned that failure to employ discretion and restraint in nonfiscal applications of taxes can be a costly fiscal experience. Above all, governments should be alert to two insidious dangers: first, the usefulness of the taxes as fiscal instruments might be impaired, and, second, the equitableness of the taxes might be undermined" (Wald, 1959, pp. 210–11).

Agricultural land tax systems are not implemented in a vacuum. They are necessarily applied in a particular context of institutional support, administrative capability, political and economic conditions. This context exhibits its particular profile of obstacles and constraints to successful implementation of the revenue system.

The conclusion is, then, that the agricultural land tax, in the context of obstacles and constraints to its effective implementation, is an instrument of limited effect at best. It will probably perform best as one of a group of mutually supporting instruments, measures, institutions, etc., all conspiring toward the end of a more productive use of resources.

NOTES

1. See, for example, Wald (1959), Lewis (1967), and Bird (1974). Bird, however, is less optimistic than the earlier writers—and so are the authors of this study.

2. See, for example, Mellor and Johnston (1984).

3. See Bird (1974, chapter 3) and the references cited there for a discussion of the quantitative importance of the taxation of agriculture.

Part Seven

Tax Administration and Tax Policy

A theme running throughout this book is, to vary the title of this part slightly, that "tax administration *is* tax policy" (Casanegra de Jantscher, 1987). The papers included in this final section take up several different aspects of the all-important administrative dimension of taxation in developing countries. For a recent survey of this important area, see Bird (1989a). The importance of good administration has long been as obvious to those concerned with taxation in developing countries as has its absence. As Stanley Surrey (1958) noted over thirty years ago, "the concentration on tax policy—on the choice of taxes—may lead to insufficient consideration of the aspect of tax administration. In short, there may well be too much preoccupation with 'what to do' and too little attention to 'how to do it.' "

One reason for the importance of administration is simply that poor administration is so obviously widespread, as documented by the recent survey of evasion in Richupan (1984, 1984a). Moreover, even when there is not outright evasion, the tax structure in developing countries is often designed, administered, and judicially interpreted in such a way as to ensure the emergence of a huge gap between the tax base in law and in practice. Sometimes this result is achieved crudely, as through the continued use after a major devaluation in Guatemala of values converted at the old exchange rate for purposes of customs duties (Bird, 1985a). Sometimes it is achieved through more subtle (and usually peripherally legal) exploitation of the peculiarities of banking and tax laws, perhaps particularly with respect to the widespread availability of tax "incentives." And sometimes this result is achieved by the functioning—or nonfunctioning—of the appeals system. However it is accomplished, whether at the legislative, administrative, or judicial levels, the result in most developing countries is that there is a great discrepancy between what the tax system appears to be on the surface and how it actually works in practice (Radian, 1980; Gray, 1987).

The effects of this discrepancy are more important and pervasive than seems generally to be recognized. Not only is revenue "lost" but the elasticity of the tax system is also reduced—particularly, of course, in inflation when administrative lags alone will usually suffice to yield this result (Tanzi, 1977). The result is that additional revenue must continually be secured through a series of discretionary ad hoc rate increases and new taxes. The "patchwork" character of the tax system of many developing countries arises in large part from their inability to administer the taxes they legislate, which leads to a continual need to legislate further tax changes.

The incidence and effects of the tax system are as sensitive to how it is administered as is its yield. Tax evasion inevitably undermines both the vertical and the horizontal equity of the tax system. For similar reasons, the real incentive effects of the tax system are often quite different from those that may be surmised from reading the statute. This catalog of woes is not easily remediable even in principle, let alone in practice. In many developing countries, the honesty of both taxpayers and tax officials is suspect (Virmani, 1987). Governments have little control over officials, little information as to what is going on, and no easy way to get it (Gray, 1987). Even if the information were available, the problem is inherently complex: market structures (and hence adjustment costs) vary widely, as do risk and time preferences, so that the costs, probabilities, and benefits of detecting evasion and corruption vary widely (Virmani, 1987). Administrative cost functions are discontinuous and hard to interpret (Bird, 1982a). Tax schedules, the interpretation of the law, the penalty schedule, and the appeals process all vary over time, as do enforcement efforts—and the reaction of taxpayers to such efforts.

One approach to relieving the constraints imposed on tax reform by administrative limitations is to tackle those limitations directly. Too often, as was recently noted in India—sometimes thought to be among the best of all developing countries in this respect—the tax administration is "neglected" and "archaic," characterized by poor training, low status, poor salaries, and poor equipment (Acharya and Associates, 1986). An obvious remedy is to tackle these and other organizational and procedural problems head on: to see that the law is properly drafted and codified; that the administration is properly organized, staffed, and trained; that taxpayers are located, placed on the rolls, and their returns adequately examined and audited; that relevant information is obtained from other governmental departments and elsewhere and properly utilized; that controversies between taxpayers and the administration are satisfactorily resolved; that taxes due are collected; and that penalties are properly applied. This is the approach taken by Surrey (1958) in his seminal paper on tax administration in developing countries.

On the whole, however, necessary as such measures are, a better way to cope with the administrative problem is probably to design tax reforms for developing countries in full recognition of the severe limitations imposed by administrative realities. The administrative dimension is central, not peripheral, to tax reform. Without significant administrative changes, the alleged benefits of many proposed tax reforms will simply not be achieved, and, as a rule, it is unrealistic to expect such changes. Too many tax reform efforts have regarded tax policy and tax administration as quite separate matters. The world is not like that. No policy exists until it is implemented, and it is the manner of its implementation which determines its impact (Pressman and Wildavsky, 1973). Those who would alter the outcomes of a tax system must therefore understand in detail how it is administered and adjust their recommendations accordingly if they want to do good rather than ill (Bird, 1989a).

The best solution to the administrative problem in developing countries is thus to design a tax reform that will work, that is, produce better results than the existing system with an administration similar to that now in place. Complex schemes simply will not work in the conditions of most developing countries. Too often would-be tax "reform-mongers" have been led astray in the futile search for the perfect fiscal instrument in theoretical terms. The perfect in this sense, however, is too often the enemy of the good in the sense of a roughly acceptable tax system, that is, one which can be administered roughly and still produce acceptable results. The chapters in this final part offer some guidance as to how to go about this difficult, but essential, task.

36

Improving Tax Compliance

Tax evasion is by no means a problem limited only to a few very backward developing countries. A recent survey by Richupan (1984a), for example, cites studies of tax evasion in a number of different developing countries indicating that it is not uncommon for half or more of potential income tax to be uncollected. (For additional evidence, see Richupan, 1984; Acharya and Associates, 1986; Bahl and Murray, 1986; Virmani, 1987. An earlier survey may be found in Herschel, 1978.) Matters are not much better with respect to indirect taxes (Rao and Pradahan, 1985; National Institute of Public Finance and Policy, 1986; Bird, 1985) or property taxes (Bahl and Linn, forthcoming). Wherever there are taxes, there is tax evasion.

What can be done about this problem? As the following chapter shows with respect to the income tax, in principle at least, there is quite a lot that can be done. In the first place, taxpayers have to be located, or registered. In many countries, one hears a great deal about the countless prosperous people—traders, professionals, and so on—who are completely outside the scope of the tax net. That such people exist is clearly true, as surveys in some countries have shown (e.g., Bahl and Murray, 1986). Campaigns to expand the tax roll are thus frequently advocated, as in the following chapter. On the other hand, other studies suggest that the major evasion problem is less with those who are completely unknown to the tax system than with those who are in the system but declare derisory amounts of income (Musgrave, 1981). In this case, the remedy is not to add still more names to the list but rather to attempt to improve the compliance of those who are already nominal taxpayers.

Secondly, adequate withholding structures must be developed and implemented (Bird, 1983; DeGraw and Oldman, 1985). Thirdly, an appropriate penalty structure (see Oldman, 1965) must be designed, and enforced. Fourthly, the law should be designed in the first place so that it can be satisfactorily applied and enforced (Bird, 1989a). And finally, adequate audit procedures must be established and, again, utilized.

Much the same can be said about any accounts-based tax, including the value-added tax. The only differences of any substance in this respect between the value-added tax and the income tax are, first, that the former is basically collected entirely by withholding and, second, that most payers of value-added tax think someone else is ultimately paying the tax.

There is no shortcut to good tax administration. Tax "gadgets," such as amnesties, have little to offer developing countries, frequent and widespread as their use may be. Recently there has been a revival of interest in this shopworn device as a result of some apparent success in, of all places, the United States (Jackson,

1986; Lerman, 1986). On the whole, however, there seems no reason to change the traditional view that this approach is a loser—unless, of course, the new day really has dawned and henceforth the tax in question will be fiercely and strictly administered. Leonard and Zeckhauser (1987), for example, suggest that an amnesty may be needed to facilitate tougher enforcement. As Zweifel and Pommerehne (1985) have shown, however, many of those who support amnesties are willing to do so only if there is no subsequent tightening of administration. More importantly, history suggests that such tightening seldom follows in any case and that those who miss out on one amnesty can likely count on another one in the future. For these reasons, tax amnesties and similar gadgets will doubtless continue to be more popular with politicians than with tax analysts. The only way to administer a tax properly is to do so.

Income Tax Compliance and Sanctions in Developing Countries

Richard K. Gordon, Jnr.

Before examining the issue of income tax compliance in poor countries, one should know the revenue importance of the income tax relative to other forms of taxation in those countries. While developed countries rely heavily on income taxes, most developing countries tend to rely far more on indirect forms of taxation, particularly in rem taxation.[1] A survey of sixty-two developing countries showed that less than one-quarter of all government revenues were raised by income and profits taxes (Tait, Grätz, and Eichengreen, 1979). It might be that the best way of combatting income tax evasion is to further reduce reliance on income taxes.

In 1951, Richard Goode (1952) enumerated those qualities he saw as essential if an income tax is to be useful and effective: (1) a predominantly monetary economy; (2) a high standard of literacy; (3) the prevalence of honest and reliable accounting; (4) a large degree of voluntary compliance on the part of taxpayers; (5) a political system not dominated by wealthy groups acting in their self-interest; (6) an honest, reasonably efficient administration. While some of these qualities might be directly related to the existence of tax compliance mechanisms, most are intimately tied to the country's stage of social and political, as well as economic, development. Countries in earlier stages of development might do well to avoid general income taxes and concentrate on the easier to administer in rem taxes, such as excise, sales, import and export, and property taxes. Redistributive and other equity goals could then be achieved by nontax fiscal measures.[2]

Another way would be to rely on those in personam taxes, such as the forfait system in France, which only approximate the income of an individual or entity but do not measure actual income. The exact boundary between estimation of income and determination of actual income is not easily defined. This becomes increasingly true as estimation systems become more refined, and as the actual fixing of tax due becomes rebuttable.[3] It may be beneficial for developing countries to depend more on estimates and less on actual income as a tax base.[4]

Even if it is decided that an income tax is necessary, enforceable statutes need to be designed. Complex laws which permit the manipulation of tax liability through avoidance, or which tax transactions which are particularly difficult for the income tax service to discover or verify, will make enforcement of compliance difficult. It

Excerpted from Gordon (1988).

is careful consideration of these issues which may be the most important factor in fashioning sanctions for those laws eventually adopted (Radian, 1980; Oldman, 1965).

AVOIDANCE VERSUS EVASION

The line between tax avoidance, or the using of laws so as to minimize payment of taxes, and tax evasion, the breaking of laws, is difficult to define clearly. In addition, it is often difficult to decide where along the continuum of avoidance and evasion sanctions should be applied. For example, taxpayers may seek to take the most favorable interpretation of existing law so as to take advantage of the use of money temporarily saved on taxes. Sometimes the taxpayer will win, sometimes not. Because not every return will be audited, the taxpayer will benefit not only from the time-value of money, but from those instances in which he or she is wrong but not found out. As the taxpayer's interpretations become increasingly far-fetched, and as the taxpayer relies more and more on the "audit lottery" to escape tax, the avoidance of tax comes closer to the evasion of tax. But before this point is reached, the tax administration may wish to penalize the taxpayer so as to encourage closer adherence to a "reasonable" interpretation of the tax law.

The issue of the time-value of money can in theory be dealt with by ensuring that market interest rates are charged. But this solution generates a number of difficulties. Even in developed countries there is no single "market rate" of interest; for the poor person without credit, a chosen "market rate" of interest will be too low, while it will be too high for a large corporation.[5] But it is the second issue, the interpreting of laws as loosely as possible so as to play the audit lottery, that causes the most difficulty, especially where audits are scarce. It may be impossible to draw the line exactly between reasonable and unreasonable interpretations, and perhaps even between avoidance and evasion.

Perhaps the most effective way of dealing with tax avoidance, and thereby reducing the need to draw lines between reasonable and unreasonable avoidance, or between avoidance and evasion, is to design laws which leave relatively less room for interpretation, although not all problems in tax avoidance or evasion can be solved by changing the underlying law. Because no detailed studies exist in developing countries concerning the extent to which unjustifiable avoidance occurs, it might make sense simply to experiment with different penalty levels. It would at all times be necessary not to raise the levels too high if the number of audits gets too low; otherwise taxpayers will feel that the system is arbitrarily singling out individuals for punishment.[6]

NONCOMPLIANCE VERSUS EVASION

In addition to the audit lottery in cases where the taxpayer's position is essentially untenable, Boidman (1983) defines three different types of noncompliance: (1) failure to file a tax return of any kind; (2) failure to declare earned income on the tax return; and (3) reducing taxable income by incorrectly reporting tax deductions, exclusions, or credits.

First, each of the above failures could be due not to an intention to avoid, but to an error on the part of the taxpayer. If the error is unreasonable or due to negligence, it once again begins to approach fraud, and should subject the taxpayer to a special penalty in addition to interest. Somewhere between negligence and unavoidable delays lies a middle ground, where the taxpayer is not playing some kind of audit lottery, but is simply making a mistake. A penalty needs to be applied here to encourage the taxpayer to take greater care.

In both of these instances, even assuming that the taxpayer has no ulterior motive, the effect of the penalties will be felt only if they are applied. As is the case with the audit lottery, it is the actual audit and the application of sanctions which determine their effectiveness.

THE COMPONENTS OF TAX EVASION

It is in the area of willfully evading tax laws that the issue of sanctions normally receives the most discussion. Before understanding tax evasion, it is necessary to know something about how much evasion there is and how it is executed. Unfortunately, even in the United States, which has a large, relatively efficient revenue administration, estimates concerning noncompliance are not very reliable. The problem is even greater for developing countries, where resources to study the problem are far more scarce.

While accurate studies are lacking, some general observations can be made. Looking back to Boidman's definition, it is clear that all tax avoidance can start with failure to file a return. Simply getting income earners registered as taxpayers is the first step in effective tax administration; therefore, using all possible sources to establish a taxpayer master list has to be the most important task of a developing country's tax administration. Obtaining relevant information (particularly business and professional licenses, land records, and tax records from other jurisdictions) from regional and local governments, as well as the more traditional information from national departments, can be very helpful in finding missing taxpayers. This technique has been of particular help to tax administrators in Tanzania and Zimbabwe.

In the United States, almost half of lost revenue is estimated to come from illegal activities, though most taxpayers with illegal income file some kind of return. In some developing countries, that portion of tax evasion due to unreported illegal activity is probably smaller, as so much perfectly legal activity goes unreported (Richupan, 1984). In some countries with relatively greater amounts of economic regulation, however, this problem would still be substantial. This is often true in those developing countries which have elaborate laws concerning price controls, resource allocations, foreign investment, and currency convertibility. Briefly, the fewer the activities deemed illegal, the less the incentive for individuals not to report; the greater the confidentiality of returns, the less the incentive not to report.

Besides the obvious motive of saving money, there are other, fundamental questions regarding why some people do not pay their taxes. At first lies the issue of whether a particular culture, or a group within that culture, feels compelled to obey the law. Upandra Baxi (1982), writing on the increased acceptance of law-lessness in India, attributes much of the problem to overregulation (too much law) and a separation between those who need not follow the law because of special status, and the rest of the population, which is expected to follow the law (law applied unequally). As laws get more complex and far-reaching, people know that they cannot effectively be followed, and respect for all law fails. As the general population sees some individuals (whether members of a governing or economic elite) disobey the law, lawlessness increases; if elites can disobey, why can't we? Second, and almost as important, is the issue of relative compliance; in some cases, only certain laws might be ignored if the proscribed activity does not fall afoul of social norms.[7] Each of these hypotheses may apply to revenue laws, depending on the general legal climate, the type of example set by elites, and the degree of seriousness with which society views paying taxes. In at least the second two cases, the seriousness with which the government enforces the revenue laws will have a profound effect on public attitudes. In the first instance, the extent to which the government overreaches in trying to tax income may effect overall compliance. In short, saying that you are trying to collect relatively less, and then trying relatively harder to collect that reduced amount, may foster better overall compliance.

There is some evidence which indicates that decreasing levels of compliance in the United States may be due in part to a growth in the perception that large numbers of individuals do not comply with the tax laws and a growth in the belief that the tax system does not treat all individuals in comparable ways. This was a constant refrain among taxpayers in India, and was a motivating force behind Indonesia's recent tax reform. Related to these issues is whether the public believes that the laws themselves are substantially unfair on their face—either by favoring certain groups over others or by taxing everyone too much. Opinion polls indicate that the U.S. electorate views the tax code as being fraught with unfair special-interest provisions, while many believe that taxes simply are too high.[8] To the extent that evasion is due to these factors, sanctions should have relatively less effect.

According to the Senate Finance Committee Report to the Tax Reform Act of 1986, an important motivation for tax reform was the perception by the average taxpayer that the proliferation of loopholes meant that only the naive and un-sophisticated paid any taxes. If that were so, why should the taxpayer be honest? No one else was paying taxes. The same report also concluded that high marginal rates of taxation were causing an increasing loss of confidence in the tax system by the average taxpayer. It is too soon to tell if the reduction in loopholes and in individual rates wrought by the Tax Reform Act of 1986 will have any real effect on taxpayer compliance. Revenue officials in India, however, have claimed that a major reduction in individual tax rates, coupled with increased enforcement, was responsible for an increase in direct tax revenue of over 25 percent.[9]

High absolute levels of taxation, besides having an effect on the perceived fairness of the taxation system, might have additional effects due to the increased monetary value of evasion. One would expect that the higher the marginal rate, the more gain to be received by understating income or overstating deductions, and hence the greater the amount of evasion. If one were to compare two countries of equal wealth, one would expect the lower marginal rates (other things being equal) to experience less evasion. Within a single country, one would expect those taxpayers with higher marginal rates to cheat more.

Working against these assumptions, however, is another tendency. One might also expect lower income taxpayers to cheat more, as each tax dollar would for them have greater utility. Which of these two conflicting forces is dominant is not clear.[10] Nonetheless, it may be less troublesome to tax administrations if poorer people are cheating because of a relatively higher marginal utility for each dollar collected. In addition, one would expect "bracket-creep," an increase in taxes due to inflation, to result in diminished compliance, as there would be no offsetting decrease in marginal utility. Sanctions may affect the wealthier if their tax brackets are sufficiently high that the benefits from evasion are simply too good to miss. Once again, substantial sanctions enforced only rarely will be seen as arbitrary.

Not entirely separate from the issue of respect for law is the fear of getting caught. Not surprisingly, studies tend to indicate that this is one of the most important determinants. Witte and Woodbury (1983) found that the perceived probability that noncompliance would not be detected was the most important factor in increasing noncompliance.[11] In the case of monetary fines, one paradigm would consider the taxpayer as a rational, economic actor maximizing his or her utility by multiplying the perceived chances of detection and successful prosecution by the amount of money to be saved by evasion, and comparing that to the amount of potential fines. In fact, there is some empirical evidence of this happening. However, there is also some indication that the fear of fines may be greater than the statistical likelihood of being caught might indicate (Friedland, Maital, and Rutenberg, 1978).

PENALTIES

While almost every developing country has enacted penalties for both negligent and intentional failure to comply with revenue laws, few civil, and virtually no criminal, penalties are ever assessed and collected.

The reasons given by different developing country tax administrations are usually the same: the penalties have no clear rationale and are therefore too severe (and seem unfair); they are hard to assess because underreporting itself is difficult to discover; and, given the fact that it is the underlying tax liability which is more important, penalties can be bargained away in the process of securing the tax deficiency. The last point is an interesting one—even if penalties are never collected, they could be an important compliance tool.

The first point, the rationale regarding penalty amounts, is also a good one, and leads to the basic questions, how large should penalties be and under what circumstances can tax administrators hope to discover (and prove) underpayment so that penalties can successfully be assessed? Even in the United States there seems to be little attempt to correlate penalties with a probability formula; an amount is picked which *seems* right.[12]

Of course, only if the people believe that they will be caught and that fines will be imposed will there be any deterrent (or what psychologists call "Pavlovian") effect. There are a number of issues involved here. First is the ability of the administration to discover underpayment, second is the will and ability to see to it that fines are imposed, and third is the public's perception that this is in fact happening. The most important of these is probably the first.

Once again, the first and most important task is to get a complete taxpayer master list, and then to fine heavily those who do not file returns. This is effective for three reasons. First, once a master list is completed, it is relatively easy to cross-check and see if each taxpayer has filed a declaration. If the taxpayer has not, it would be a relatively simple task to levy the fine. The second reason is that, by implementing this easily enforced sanction, the tax administration helps instill in the public a healthy respect for all sanctions. Third, such a sanction helps coax recalcitrant would-be taxpayers onto the rolls.

Income subject to withholding and subject to reporting is relatively more impervious to evasion than other types of income.[13] All major studies carried out in the United States confirm this fact. Wages and salaries (on which there is withholding as well as easily matched information returns) show by far the lowest percentage of unreported to reported income, with self-employed income and rents and royalties having the highest (Holland and Oldman, 1981). Over the past thirty-five years, the income actually reported as a total percentage of income in a particular category has improved steadily for wages, interest, and dividends, while there has been little or no improvement for business and professional income or for rental income. This makes intuitive sense, as withholding, information reporting and matching have been extended and improved for the former, but not for the latter.

Withholding means either that the tax administration gets at minimum the amount withheld, or requires the taxpayer to explain why some money should be returned. Wage withholding is clearly the most important. Information returns can only be effective if matching is done and if the money is then collected. While in a wealthy country like the United States there may be little difference between withholding and information reporting, in poorer countries matching paper and then trying to collect taxes due could be prohibitively expensive where there is information reporting but no withholding. Penalties should be increased to the point where going through each report and collecting on each discrepancy would be financially rewarding. Unless this were feasible, both politically and administratively, it would make more sense for poorer countries to enact withholding on those payments most easily made amenable, namely wages, dividends, interest, and government contracts (Griffith, 1973). Stiff sanctions then could be used to concentrate on those third parties who fail to remit withholdings or who misstate them. The numbers of taxpayers and information remittors would be far smaller, and the earnings potential for each investigation far greater than they would be for audits of individuals without withholding.[14]

Information reports are also less likely to be subject to understatement, as companies benefit from deducting wages paid from their company returns. Pakistan, for example, has reported success by disallowing deductions for unreported wages. Simple checking of wage information returns and wages deducted for income tax purposes can help keep wage reporting honest. With relatively fewer companies to audit, and with an economic reason for accurately preparing some information returns, it is likely that the number of violations will be relatively less, and subject to relatively simple discovery. For this reason (the likelihood of being caught) and because of the importance of reporting as a tax enforcement tool, relatively high penalties can be used further to encourage compliance without subjecting the tax administrators to charges of arbitrary enforcement.

Income not subject to withholding can be given the lion's share of audit attention. Without a large number of audits, there will never be a credible threat, and without such a threat, the imposition of sanctions is not only a paper tiger but undermines the entire legitimacy of the system. The decline in audit coverage in the United States is credited with much of the decline in (or failure to improve) compliance. If the audit level were not brought up to a reasonable amount, the fines would have to be raised to levels unacceptable to those rare individuals unlucky enough to be caught, if the value of cheating were to be kept below the potential fines multiplied by the chances of being caught. Once again, too few audits would delegitimize the entire system. But audits are the most important component of tax compliance work, if often insufficiently supported by governments. In the United States, a computer selection system assists auditing by selecting returns statistically likely to be incorrect. While it might be far too difficult to replicate such a system in a poor country, a very limited use of automatic data processing, along with the correlation of a very limited number of factors, may assist auditors. The main effort must nevertheless be fieldwork.

Auditing deductions is undoubtedly one of the more difficult and time-consuming administrative activities. Preferably, the number of deductions should be limited as much as possible; and deductions should, when related to business, be subjected to some kind of reporting requirements. Standard deductions should be used whenever possible for individuals, and the auditing of deductions should be left primarily to the larger business establishments.

While audits may point out discrepancies, little overall deterrent effect will be accomplished if only interest or nominal fines are collected. The public must witness the serious attempts of the administration to punish tax evasion. In general, it is important that the tax administrators present the image, to the greatest extent possible without losing credibility, that compliance is substantial. Recent, well-publicized cases of tax levying in Massachusetts have played an important role in improving general compliance. This also appears to be the case in India, where a major new enforcement effort was begun in 1985, resulting in seizures of property in lieu of back taxes, as well as in arrests.[15] In the cases of both Massachusetts and India, arrests of tax cheaters and the vigorous enforcement of revenue laws have been very popular with the public, if not always with the special interests.[16] But, as suggested earlier, serious fines provided for in the statutes but not levied can have a reverse effect on compliance, by making the statutes appear substanceless. Serious fines for noncompliance actually levied in those areas where the noncompliance is more likely to be discovered may have a powerful deterrent effect.

Sanctions which result in jail sentences seem to have some deterrent effect, although it is very difficult to measure. Impressive jail sentences make the newspapers, and no doubt can have an effect on the average taxpayer. Once again, if sanctions are too severe, or if they are enforced too rarely, they might actually reduce compliance.

Practically speaking, very few developing countries ever use the criminal law to enforce income tax sanctions. The reasons are myriad. First, criminal penalties require, or should require, a higher standard of proof than civil penalties. Second, and perhaps more importantly, criminal sanctions can appear grossly unfair. If income tax evasion is rampant, as is the case in many developing countries, singling out individuals for criminal sanctions can appear persecutory. While civil fines may seem a slap on the wrist, jail terms may seem too harsh. Also, if almost everyone is evading tax, tax prosecutions can be used as a way of punishing political enemies while leaving friends untouched. Third, criminal sanctions are sometimes too unpopular politically to enforce, although both the Massachusetts and Indian experiences suggest otherwise. For some combination of these reasons, developing countries, and even many developed countries, very rarely enforce criminal sanctions against tax evaders.

Depending on the level of mass evasion, and on the degree of severity, civil sanctions may become subject to the same criticisms leveled against criminal sanctions.

Recently, some have suggested that the existence of criminal sanctions or punitive civil sanctions on the statute books of developing countries is actually pernicious. Rather than make serious efforts to improve compliance through tax reform and better tax administration, governments simply pass increasingly stringent criminal penalties, which themselves are rarely used.

If criminal penalties are to be enacted, they should be reserved only for the most egregious types of tax evasion, evasion of an extent far greater than the typical, evasion which would shock even the most cynical taxpayer. Once a statute exempts most typical evaders, it must be enforced.

TAX AMNESTIES

Tax amnesties, or the forgiveness of sanctions, have been used, and probably overused, in the past. The 1967 tax amnesty in Israel, for example, may have had a deleterious effect on the public's perception of the serious, criminal nature of tax evasion.[17] When followed by a major improvement in the administration and prosecution of tax evasion, a single amnesty might work. This has been the experience in Massachusetts, where not only a genuine improvement followed a tax amnesty but, during the promulgation of the amnesty, political events convinced the public that a real improvement *would* follow. While successes have been reported in other American states, the experience in developing countries has been less successful than was hoped for. Often, the only time that criminal tax evasion penalties are taken notice of is when they are suspended for a tax amnesty.

CONCLUSION

Too much attention has been paid to the type and size of penalties, while not enough attention has been paid to the likelihood of the taxpayer being caught and being forced to pay the penalties. If there exists a reasonable chance of being caught, then sanctions can become effective. As compliance increases, so can the threat of sanctions.

In some limited areas, where compliance is already sufficiently high, major sanctions can be of great use, such as against companies which fail to withhold or report wages, or against individuals who evade taxes to exceptional extremes. High interest rates and penalties on amounts assessed but not yet paid can make the collection process more profitable. Penalties high enough to militate against the audit lottery can be useful, but only when the chance of audit is reasonable. The severity of sanctions should match not only the extent of the avoidance or evasion but also its degree of uncommonness and its chance of being discovered.

In each of these areas, the statutes should reflect the practice. It is far better to restrict the scope of the statute and then enforce the more limited law than it is to have a broad, but unenforced, law.

Briefly, then,

1. in rem taxes or best-estimate taxes should be used to reduce the scope of income taxes and hence of evasion, thereby freeing up resources for policing an income tax more limited in scope;

2. the tax code should be made simpler or easier to understand and administer, and should be made to appear fairer;

3. a complete taxpayer master list should be established, and stiff penalties for failure to file should be enacted and enforced;

4. withholding and reporting of wages, interest, and dividends should be strengthened;

5. audits should be restricted to those limited areas where evasion is likely to be caught, for example, to check on withholding and information reporting;

6. special audits should be made of the most egregious and obvious cases of individual tax fraud;

7. by statute, simple penalties like interest plus an additional percentage should be left to those areas where the law is nebulous and the line between evasion and avoidance is not clear;

8. by statute, more substantial penalties should be made for failure to remit tax owed;

9. by statute, heavy civil penalties should be concentrated on those areas where fraud is clear, where discovery is possible, and where enforcement is likely, such as against companies and individuals subject to withholding and reporting; and

10. by statute, criminal penalties should be reserved only for the most heinous and obvious cases of evasion; even in those instances, the statutes should be enacted only if they will actually be enforced.

NOTES

1. Economists often divide taxes in two different ways. The first division is between personal taxes (paid at the individual or household level and adjusted to the taxpayer's personal ability to pay) and in rem taxes (paid on activities or objects, independently of the characteristics of the owner or transactor). The second division is between income taxes (paid on total accretion to wealth plus consumption) and consumption taxes (paid only on actual consumption). In rem taxes, because they tax transactions and not individuals, are usually seen as easier to collect.

2. This might include a greater reliance on expenditures in effecting a policy of income redistribution, or adopting more easily collected indirect taxes in a way which would bear more lightly on the poor.

3. Carl Shoup (1969) defines six types of tax administration related both to the degree of taxpayer participation and to the nature of the tax.

4. Personal taxes may be the least progressive, but can be modified to exclude the poorest. See Arowolo (1968). Taxes approximating expected revenue can be used either as an actual tax assessment, an irrebuttable presumption (essentially the same thing), or a rebuttable presumption or "best guess." See, e.g., Goode (1981), Lapidoth (1977), and Malik (1979), and references cited.

5. It should bother a government less if those with relatively fewer resources were able better to take advantage of imperfections in the administration of a tax system. Hence, it is recommended here that interest be charged at a (compounded) rate appropriate for the wealthier taxpayers.

6. Proposed initial levels of monetary fines can be found in Oldman (1965).

7. In some developing countries, the general level of noncompliance is so great that, if the laws were ever enforced, one would have to put nearly the entire country in jail. In such instances, the public would think of the laws as having no seriousness and little moral power and would view instances of isolated enforcement as unfair or arbitrary. See Oldman (1965).

8. See Spicer and Becker (1980). The increasing prevalence of tax protesting (refusing to pay any tax) may also be related to this phenomenon. But see Hansson, "The Underground Economy in a High Tax Country: The Case of Sweden," in V. Tanzi (1982). Though Sweden is a high-tax country, there is considerable tax compliance.

9. This claim has been made by numerous Finance Ministry officials, including the former minister, Mr. V. P. Singh. Though this author is unaware of any convincing studies supporting this claim, a completely unscientific survey of a number of advocates (lawyers) in New Delhi conducted by this author shows a remarkable 100 percent agreement that lower rates have encouraged "a greater feeling of fairness" (to quote one respondent) and a much higher level of tax compliance.

10. One of the reasons that empirical regression studies of each of these factors are difficult to perform is that, on average, lower- and middle-income taxpayers often have less opportunity to cheat. This is particularly true in developed countries, where the vast majority of lower- and middle-class income comes from wages subject to withholding. It is therefore difficult for these taxpayers to understate income or to overstate deductions or exclusions. This is, of course, full of exceptions. Domestic workers in the United States are not subject to wage withholding, and, until recently, waiters and waitresses were not subject to withholding on tips. Lower- and middle-income small business proprietors have myriad opportunities for manipulating income and expenses.

11. Other factors included increases in marginal tax rate due to bracket-creep, growth in perception that others no longer comply, growth in perception that the laws treat different

people differently and are therefore unfair, increased levels of education, and increases in unemployment and decreases in real income associated with periodic recessions.

12. A good general outline of suggested penalties and methods of application based on a general sense of fairness can be found in Oldman (1965). Given the lack of useful empirical studies in most poor countries, Oldman's numbers can serve as a useful starting-off point. Increases or decreases in these figures could be made with regard to other relevant issues discussed as well as with the success of compliance.

13. In the United States, over 90 percent of all personal income tax liability is collected through withholding via a third party.

14. Richard Bird (1983) recommends that a special withholding enforcement section be created within the tax administration, that compliance be made as easy as possible, and that serious financial penalties be enacted for failure to collect or turn over withholding or PAYE amounts.

15. See, e.g., "Business in the Dock," *India Today*, 30 November 1985, pp. 38–51. Most of the crackdown has dealt with excise and customs violations, not with direct tax violations.

16. While the revenue enhancement program in Massachusetts has been so popular that it has helped Governor Michael Dukakis in his bid for the United States presidency, some have alleged that arrests of powerful business figures in Indian tax evasion cases have (along with other causes) led to the dismissal of the instigator of the crackdowns, former Finance Minister V. P. Singh. There is little doubt, however, that Singh has benefited from enormous popularity due to his role in prosecuting tax offenders.

17. See Wilkenfeld (1973). Pakistan, however, has reported varying success with its tax amnesties, though a noted lack of success in the fifth and latest one.

37

Computerizing Tax Administration

A popular way of dealing with the administrative difficulties of taxation in developing countries is to pretend they can all be handled by a small staff equipped with appropriately up-to-date computers. There is no doubt that in certain areas of tax administration, good use can be made of computers and that, indeed, they may in some instances obviate the need to acquire the skills of many highly-trained specialists (Lane and Hutabarat, 1986).

On the other hand, as experience has shown in all too many countries, the computerization of tax administration is a complex task that has, as yet, been successfully accomplished by few. Computers must be programmed and operated by people; they must rely on information obtained and entered by other people; and their output must be acted upon by still other people. Since the motivations and incentives of all these people are unlikely to be altered by the introduction of new equipment alone, it is by no means obvious that the dawning of the computer age has significantly reduced the importance of the administrative constraint on tax reform in developing countries. Indeed, it is not hard to find instances in which the inappropriate introduction and use of computer systems has in some ways made matters worse. On the whole, as the following chapter argues, computerization seems likely to be most useful where the tax administration is already well-organized—that is, so to speak, where it is in a sense least needed! As always, shortcuts to good administration in developing countries are few and far between.

Where feasible, an important benefit of computerizing tax administration, not discussed in this chapter, is the increased availability of statistical data on taxation. Good statistics on taxation are essential in any country, for two quite distinct purposes. In the first place, such information is needed for the efficient management of the tax administration. Secondly, tax statistics are required to formulate sound tax policy and in particular to design tax reforms in full knowledge of their probable effects.

In the absence of a clear quantitative understanding of the characteristics of the taxpaying population, for example, it is not possible to allocate scarce administrative resources efficiently. A simple example of the application of this principle is the predominant role in most countries of a relatively small number of large enterprises as taxpayers—whether of company income tax, sales tax, or taxes on wages. If revenue is the main concern of tax policy, as is usually the case in developing countries, it would appear to follow that the scarce administrative skills available in the tax administration should, in the first instance, be concentrated primarily on these large firms, where even a small infraction might prove extremely costly to the revenue, rather than dissipated across the vast sea of largely noncompliant small and medium traders, where even large individual infractions may not amount to much in revenue terms. Thus concentrating on those taxpayers who are not only already in the tax system but also constitute its mainstay is of course not "fair," but it does reflect the reality of where the revenue comes from. At the very least, such information reveals the policy choices implicitly being made when administrative resources are allocated to one task rather than another.

Quite apart from their potential usefulness in allocating administrative resources efficiently, good tax statistics are of course also essential in formulating good tax policy. Indeed, it is hardly possible to prescribe changes in tax structure that will improve policy outcomes if one does not understand in detail how the present system really works—where the revenue comes from, who pays the taxes, and what changes are most likely to produce (or lose) additional revenue or to alter the distribution of the tax burden. Data alone will of course provide no answers; but in the absence of reliable quantitative information on the characteristics of the actual and potential tax base and taxpaying population, those responsible for tax policy decisions have little to go on but their intuition, based inevitably on their own perception (partial, and often biased) of the reality of the situation.

Data problems have frequently been mentioned in this book—the need for data in designing, implementing, and evaluating tax policies. In almost all cases, however, useful as such information would be, it is obviously not essential to the functioning of the tax system. The proof of this proposition is simply that most developing countries do not have such information.

In one important respect, however, every country *must* have data, namely, forecasts of tax revenue on which to base expenditure plans. In some cases, such forecasts may be so poor—or perhaps the prospects of revenue are so bad—that developing countries have to live in effect from hand to mouth, spending on Tuesday the money they manage to collect on Monday (Caiden and Wildavsky, 1980). As a rule, matters are not quite so desperate as this, and tax revenue forecasting therefore constitutes an important component of budgetary and development planning (Premchand, 1983). Simple forecasting techniques are available (see Bahl, 1972a; Chand, 1975) that, while not ideal, are almost certainly better than the simple extrapolation of past results that is often the only alternative.

An important related problem is that of determining the appropriate rate structure when a major tax is to be changed, for example, an income tax moved from a progressive to a proportional rate (Bahl and Murray, 1986) or a collection of excise taxes altered to a value-added tax (Bird, 1985). In these cases, as the sources cited indicate, a good deal of guessing is usually required. Recently, some small simulation models suitable for use on personal computers have been developed to help ensure that these guesses are as systematic and consistent as possible, but the onus is still very much on the experience of the operator. The basic rule in such exercises is probably to be as conservative as possible: if a tax change produces more revenue than estimated, that would be considered good news in most developing countries; if it produced less, it might be a disaster.

Computerizing Revenue Administrations in LDCs

François Corfmat

Developing countries increasingly face decisions on whether or when to introduce computer technology. With efficiency, capabilities, and adaptability increasing, and costs declining, computers seem to offer tempting, quick solutions to an array of problems. This article examines the potential advantages of computers in one area of government administration: revenue collection. More precisely, it provides an overview of the applications of automated data processing (ADP) systems in customs and tax administrations, examines some of the problems associated with implementation of and adjustment to the new technology, and looks at a number of ways in which these problems can be minimized or avoided.

Over the past decade computer technology has become an integral part of the customs and tax administration operations in many developed countries and has significantly increased their capacity to process forms, streamline tax procedures, compile statistics, and use data to improve forecasting of fiscal revenues. Revenue administrations in developing countries also face expanding workloads: the number of taxpayers has grown rapidly, procedures and regulations have become more complex, international trade has increased, and the need to assemble greater quantities of data for economic and fiscal policy making has intensified. Can computer technology play a role in meeting these needs as well?

The answer seems to be a qualified yes. Experience suggests that ADP can increase the efficiency of well run operations, but could prove useless, and will probably exacerbate existing problems, if it is superimposed on badly organized or inadequately rationalized revenue administrations.

APPLICATIONS

Customs Administration

In customs, ADP systems can be used principally to identify importers, clear goods, manage tariff files, control inventories of warehoused goods, and compile external trade statistics. These functions are usually divided into two categories: central processing and customs office functions.

At the central processing site, maintenance and compilation of the "integrated tariff," and data centralization and information services are the main functions.

Excerpted from Corfmat (1985).

Automated clearance requires the creation of a set of files (the integrated tariff) that would contain, for each customs tariff heading, all the data needed to verify that goods meet requirements (quotas, licenses, health regulations, etc.) and to calculate the duties and taxes payable. The data centralization and information services of an ADP system are designed to produce external trade statistics, special summaries and studies, such as analyses of import and export prices, and insurance and freight studies. Useful information, such as general accounting, estimation of cost of duty-free and privileged clearances, fraud analyses, and changes in workloads, can also be generated for customs management.

In customs offices, automated clearance of imported and exported goods is the main application of ADP systems. Principal operations include entering, checking, and storing data; printing out of declarations; application of regulations on external trade (e.g., licenses, quotas, prohibitions, and health controls); calculation of duties and other levies; and identifying where document checks and physical examination of goods might be needed. These are normally processed instantaneously (in "real time"). Less time-sensitive management tasks are often handled through batch processing; this method allows a computer to collect data and process it at a later date (e.g., overnight or at the end of the month) and can be used to maintain official records, produce daily and periodic accounting statements, and compile official activity reports and tables.

Internal Tax Administration

Tax collection procedures vary from country to country but ADP systems have commonly been used to process returns and payments, assist in enforcement operations, and compile statistics. In processing tax returns and payments, computers can preaddress forms and payment vouchers, check the accuracy and consistency of data reported, calculate taxes, identify computation errors, maintain taxpayers' records and general accounting controls and records, and prepare refund, assessment, and penalty notices. In enforcement, computerized systems can identify defaulters, prepare notices, develop mathematical formulas and statistical programs to select returns for audit, and verify data and identify tax evaders through cross-checking with external sources or other computer files. At minimal cost, ADP programs can also produce operating and statistical reports designed to assist tax managers and policy makers in management and planning, formulation of tax policy, and economic analysis and research.

Internal tax ADP systems that perform these operations require the comprehensive design of an integrated master file system. The master file system becomes the heart of the tax department's ADP program. It maintains a record of all taxpayers and all accounting, auditing, and collection transactions. Most countries use at least two master files: one for individuals (employed and self-employed) and the other for legal entities, such as corporations. Some countries also use a separate file for tax-exempt organizations. The usefulness of these master files depends mainly on the establishment of a reliable and up-to-date tax identification numbering system that can distinguish one taxpayer's document or record from another's. As a general rule, the master file system should be flexible so that, after a simple start, the system can accept new data from various sources and perform progressively more complex work.

An important function in tax administration is the selection of returns for audit so that limited resources are focused on particular areas to maximize gains in revenue and elicit compliance. In identifying likely candidates for auditing, ADP programs use selection criteria and classification techniques to assign weights to various characteristics involving the high probability of error, change, and evasion. The formulas used in this process are kept secret not only to avoid manipulation of returns by taxpayers but also to ensure impartiality in the selection of returns.

INTRODUCTION OF ADP SYSTEMS

In deciding whether or to what extent ADP systems should be used, an important first step is a feasibility study. This would describe current operations, enumerate possible constraints, and determine the performance criteria by which an ADP system would be evaluated. The study's conclusions would provide estimates of costs and benefits in terms of manpower, equipment, and time; compare costs of the various systems; define both personnel and training needs; and provide a statement of objectives.

Potential advantages then must be carefully weighed against possible problems. An ADP system can increase administrative efficiency, reduce costs, improve service, and expand statistical capabilities. But its implementation may displace workers doing routine work, elicit negative reactions from officials ill at ease with the new technology, and create a dependence upon foreign suppliers, who are needed to design and develop the system and to maintain the hardware and software. Many of these difficulties, however, can be offset by increases in capacity and efficiency and by giving staff more interesting and rewarding work.

More serious are the problems related to hiring and training officials and technical staff to implement and operate the new systems. In developed countries, training is often provided for current staff through in-house training courses arranged by computer manufacturers, software designers, and other private companies. In developing countries, training and staffing needs must often be met by hiring new personnel who have been trained outside government service or abroad. Nigeria, for example, has drawn planners and programmers from the training facilities offered by local universities and foreign institutions; Ecuador and Honduras have recruited from a training center for tax administrators that emphasizes ADP. Hiring outside people, however, may create conflicts between new technical staff and the present operational staff. For some countries the use of foreign experts for technical work and for training current staff may offer a more acceptable alternative.

Retaining qualified staff may also present problems. A separate salary scale may be one alternative, though experience suggests it may not be a viable solution in every case. Public service contracts may offer another option. Though problems of confidentiality can arise, contracting has been used successfully in a number of countries. The data processing of the Brazilian Federal Tax Department, for example, is contracted to SERPRO (Serviço Federal de Processamento de Dados), a data processing organization that has the status of a public enterprise and can offer salaries more competitive with the private sector.

DESIGN AND IMPLEMENTATION

Developing countries introducing an ADP system for revenue administration face a number of important decisions regarding design and implementation. One concerns the structure of the computer system: both centralized and decentralized systems can produce satisfactory results. In a centralized approach, the design, development, and operation of the system are provided by an organization that is independent of any of the tax collecting departments and that is responsible for providing all public entities with the information needed for their operations and decisions. In Zaïre, the Data Processing Service of the Finance Department performs the data processing activities for the department's various directorates (customs, taxation, budget, treasury, and accounting). In a decentralized approach, the finance ministry may require operating departments to be responsible for the supervision and control of their own computer systems. The U.S. Internal Revenue Service, for example, organizes its operations in the latter manner, as do most of the tax departments of the member countries of the Inter-American Center of Tax Administrators.

While the initial choice may depend upon several factors, including the scale of operations to be performed, capital expenditures, and efficient utilization of computer hardware, one major consideration is the availability of adequate numbers of skilled computer technicians. Because computer costs are falling and the number of available technicians is increasing, and because services provided by the central computer organization might prove unresponsive in terms of either seasonal fluctuations of work or unplanned events (tax legislation changes, for instance), a mixed approach may be preferable and is often applied. Under such a scheme, the central computer of the ministry of finance usually provides services for policy activities and for the ministry's own statistical and national reporting needs, and may, when necessary, provide services on a time-sharing basis for some collection work of the revenue departments. On the other hand, the data processing units of revenue departments operate their own computer systems and perform time-sensitive activities, such as issuing customs clearances, tax refund checks, assessment notices, tax receipts, and answering inquiries.

Data security presents another element in the design of a computer system; control measures must be taken against the unauthorized disclosure of information from customs declarations or tax returns, the fraudulent manipulation of data, and the misuse of terminals by unauthorized persons. A security system is necessary to ensure the integrity of the system, to restrict access to computerized data, and to protect the computer facility against fraudulent intrusion or destruction by natural disasters.

Developing countries will also need to scrutinize foreign-designed ADP projects and related services carefully. Some programs may be inappropriate for local needs or unnecessarily complicated and expensive; excessive enthusiasm by outside experts and hardware salesmen might also encourage administrations to become overambitious. Current ADP systems are sufficiently diversified to allow step-by-step progress. Increasingly, small computers are being used because they use less space, offer better service, and are more flexible than large central computers; and they do so at lower initial and operating costs. The inevitable shift toward more comprehensive and integrated software systems requires the standardization of equipment and, consequently, an appropriate administrative policy to coordinate the needs of the departments that use it. It is important to provide a link between the various computers, both large and small, to enable information to circulate among the different departments of the ministry, to allow user access to more information, or simply to share costly hardware, such as high speed printers and disc drives for storing information. There are internationally accepted standards for much of the coding and other computer-related processes, and it is preferable to ensure that these are adopted whenever possible.

TECHNICAL ASSISTANCE

A great deal of information and technical assistance is currently available to developing countries that want to automate their revenue administrations. Technical assistance, which includes both personnel and financial assistance, has traditionally been provided through bilateral cooperation agreements, sometimes in the context of a joint commission established to promote cooperation between the two countries. Agreements often involve the participation of customs or tax authorities and private contractors of each country, and sometimes entail the assistance of independent technical consultants and academic institutes. (The U.S.–Saudi Arabian Customs Program, for instance, involved the participation of Arkansas State University, while the French-Egyptian Customs Project was completed with the participation of Grenoble University.)

International organizations have recently begun to offer advice on the design and installation of ADP systems, while independent consultants and specialized institutions are additional sources of assistance. Courses on customs and tax applications of computers are, for example, regularly presented by the Institute for Tax Administration at the University of Southern California, with the assistance of the U.S. Customs Service and the Internal Revenue Service.

A country seeking technical assistance may wish to consider two types. The first would consist of the short-term assignment of customs or tax advisors to conduct feasibility studies, produce cost/benefit analyses of alternative systems, evaluate new programs designed to extend the capabilities of the existing systems, and identify personnel training needs. The second type would consist of long-term assistance, possibly spread over several years, by data processing specialists experienced in the application and implementation of all facets of computer utilization for mass processing techniques and operations and familiar with government operations in customs, tax, and budget administration.

CONCLUSION

Clearly there are potential advantages to properly applied systems of data processing. In customs work, the growing volume of international trade, new methods of transport, increasingly complex regulations, and expanded information requirements may make automation a necessity if developing countries wish to prevent undue delays at their borders and to increase, or even just maintain, their share of world trade. In tax administration, because of additional budgetary needs for revenue, increased compliance with tax obligations and more efficient collection are becoming priorities for developing countries. Automation may eventually offer the most effective means of meeting these needs.

The note of caution remains, however. For many reasons, both administrative and political, the introduction of ADP systems may not always bring about the intended result. Many of the difficulties associated with automation, however, can be avoided or minimized with appropriate planning and a careful assessment of current needs and specific goals. The experience of many developed and a growing number of developing countries, as well as the availability of technical assistance, can help a country make the transition from manual to computerized systems a successful one.

38

The Economics of Tax Administration

In recent decades, the scope of economics has been extended much beyond its traditional focus on economic markets to encompass such alien domains as the family and the political process. It is therefore not surprising that economists have also from time to time attempted to apply the tools of their trade to administration, and particularly tax administration (Shoup, 1969, chap. 17).

The following selection systematically reviews a number of important areas of tax administration in which economic analysis may help provide some useful guidelines for policy makers and administrators. Among the problems on which this discussion touches are the measurement of costs (see also Shaw, 1981; Bird, 1982a) and in particular the apparent paradox, found in most countries, of substantial underspending on such obviously revenue-producing activities as tax collection. Incidentally, in the face of the overwhelming evidence that no country comes anywhere near spending enough on tax administration to maximize revenue collections, the apparent popularity of the view of the "revenue-maximizing" state—see, for example, Brennan and Buchanan (1980)—is a little hard to understand. In the developing countries, as Goode's review suggests, revenue collections are most unlikely to be "maximized"!

A final point worth noting in this chapter is the relatively brusque dismissal of the large, and growing, academic literature on tax evasion (for a recent summary, see Mansfield, 1988). Unfortunately, most of this literature offers little of use to developing countries, in part because the solutions offered—usually gimmicky penalty structures—tend to ignore the main relevant lesson of the literature, namely, that in the absence of constraints there will be a lot of evasion when the probability of detection is as low as it invariably is in developing countries. The key to improving tax compliance in such circumstances lies more in devising and implementing more and better withholding than in revised penalty structures (Bird, 1983; DeGraw and Oldman, 1985). Those who have their taxes taken away before they get their hands on the money are more likely to pay their taxes than those whom the government has to search out and compel to pay.

Some Economic Aspects
of Tax Administration

Richard Goode

Discussions of tax administration are properly dominated by considerations derived from the theory and practice of administration and management, modified by special legal and political considerations appropriate for this branch of public administration. Tradition and expediency are also influential factors. The purpose of this paper is to examine the relevance of economic analysis for tax administration. It deals with the possible application of economic analysis to certain elements of tax legislation that bear on administration and with strategic factors in planning and programming administrative efforts rather than with the details of organization and procedures.

COSTS OF ADMINISTRATION AND COMPLIANCE

The application of tax laws requires the use of real economic resources by the government in tax administration and by taxpayers in compliance. In order to obtain usable summary measures of costs, they must be stated in money terms. That is ordinarily easy in regard to tax administration; but in connection with tax compliance, it is often necessary to impute money values to items such as the time that taxpayers spend in assembling and submitting information to the tax department.

Total Administrative Expenditures

An important issue on which economics might be expected to shed light is how much a government should spend for tax administration. By analogy with the economic theory of the firm, it may seem that the general principle governing the decision should be that expenditures should be carried to the point at which the last increment in costs just equals the additional revenue obtained—that is, to the point at which marginal cost equals marginal revenue. At that point, the excess of total revenue obtained over total administrative costs incurred will be at a maximum. That is true because expenditures will be incurred for all administrative activities that would yield revenue in excess of their cost, and no expenditures will be incurred for activities that would yield less than their cost.

Objections can be advanced against the analogy with the operations of a busi-

Excerpted from Goode (1981).

ness firm. The tax department is not a profit-seeking enterprise, and taxpayers are not customers. Tax collection is a compulsory transfer of income rather than a voluntary payment for individually consumed goods and services. Equality of the value of resources devoted to the process and the revenue obtained at the margin does not have the same significance in regard to tax administration as it does in regard to the production and sale of marketable output. For marketable output, it may be assumed—subject to important, but not overwhelming, qualifications— that the use of resources is responsive to consumers' desires and that a smaller or greater volume would satisfy them less well. For tax administration, no comparable assumption is warranted; citizens may value additional public services at more or less than the amount of revenue obtained from increased activities (Shoup, 1969, p. 433). But that in itself does not justify dismissal of the marginal principle. If vigorous administration should push total revenue beyond a politically acceptable level, tax rates could be reduced. With lower tax rates, some curtailment of administrative expenditures might be indicated. The maximization of the excess of revenue over administrative costs, at the new tax rates, might still be regarded as proof that the real resources devoted to tax administration had been used effectively.

Difficulties would be encountered in applying the marginal principle, because information is not readily available on the relation between incremental cost and incremental revenue. In addition, arguments can be made for spending more or less than the principle indicates.

It could be argued that expenditures on tax enforcement should be pressed beyond the point of equality between marginal cost and marginal revenue, on the grounds that equal application of tax laws is an important goal of public policy that should not be evaluated on narrow commercial terms (Simons, 1950, pp. 31–32). Law enforcement efforts in general are not governed by the objective of maximizing revenue from fines. It could also be argued that in the long run, additional costs incurred in rigorous tax administration will be economically justified by virtue of improved voluntary compliance. Although that contention appears plausible, it is difficult to produce reliable quantitative evidence on the relation between administrative costs and voluntary compliance.

In practice, most governments appear to spend less, perhaps substantially less, than the marginal principle would indicate. This impression is also hard to verify, because in only a few countries has information on marginal cost and marginal revenue been made public. When statistical comparisons are made, they usually relate total administrative expenditures to total revenue for all taxes combined or for all the taxes assigned to a particular administrative organization. Such data tell nothing about the relation between costs and revenue at the margin and are of limited value in appraising efficiency.

There are several reasons why governments might not wish to carry tax administrative expenditures as far as the marginal principle would indicate, even if the necessary information on marginal cost and marginal revenue were easily obtainable. First, legislators and officials may feel that the indicated level of administrative activity would antagonize taxpayers and provoke a withdrawal of cooperation and political support. This belief is the opposite of the attitude mentioned previously that would favor expenditures greater than those which would equalize marginal cost and marginal revenue in the short run and, like its opposite, is hard to evaluate. Second, it is politically difficult for governments to apply different budgetary standards to the tax department and to other departments or ministries that do not generate revenue (Farioletti, 1973). When budgetary stringency is the order of the day, as it frequently is, the tax department is likely to have its requests for funds cut back, more or less in line with other requests, even in those rare cases in which reliable estimates are available to show that the loss of revenue will exceed the saving in administrative costs. Salaries of tax officers are usually at the same level as the pay of other civil servants whose diligence and probity do not directly affect revenue. Third, taxpayers incur private costs of compliance that may substantially exceed the costs of administration. For example, a careful study found that, in England and Wales in 1970, the costs of compliance with direct personal taxes (including out-of-pocket costs and imputed costs) ranged between 1.8 and 6.0 times the administrative costs (Sandford, 1973, p. 44). Administrative and compliance costs are partly substitutes; but at the margin, increased administrative activities may well entail increased compliance costs. Fourth, political decision makers may consider it prudent to avoid even a temporary rise of revenue above the expected level because they believe that citizens will react more adversely against a budget that is larger than they desire than against one that is smaller than they wish.

Allocation of a Fixed Appropriation

The marginal principle, in my opinion, has greater value as a guide for the use of a fixed budgetary appropriation than as a standard for setting the amount of the total appropriation. Most tax departments receive such an appropriation as the outcome of a budgetary process that is influenced by a variety of factors. In deciding how the money shall be divided among the administration of various taxes or administrative processes, the relation between marginal costs and marginal revenue is a highly useful index. The maximum amount of revenue in relation to total administrative costs, and hence the most effective use of the appropriation, will be obtained by carrying each of the various activities to the point at which the difference between the marginal unit of revenue and the marginal unit of cost is equal to that of all the other activities. In this situation, no net gain in revenue could be secured by making a small reallocation of administrative resources.

It must be emphasized that data on the total costs of administering various taxes and of carrying out separate activities, such as auditing or data processing, are useful for planning the allocation of resources only to the extent that it is realistic to contemplate the elimination of a tax or an activity. In that case, the total costs, if ascertainable, are indeed the marginal costs. In the more usual situation, however, the pertinent question is whether a little more or a little less expenditure shall be incurred in applying a particular tax or carrying out a particular process. Often these marginal variations will relate to the deployment of staff. A considerable part of total costs consists of overhead expenditures, which cannot be precisely allocated. The application of the marginal principle depends on the availability of information that may be difficult to obtain. Sample studies can provide a basis for estimating various points on the curves of marginal costs and marginal revenues (Welch, 1954, pp. 216–17) but may be expensive. Even when good statistics are available, the application of the marginal principle may, in some cases, involve intricate calculations, the outcome of which is not intuitively obvious (Balachandran and Schaefer, 1980). There may be differences between short-run, medium-run, and long-run marginal costs, as staff and equipment cannot be instantaneously redeployed. It is easier to attain a uniform relation between marginal cost and marginal revenue for all taxes and all administrative processes if they are all assigned to one administrative organization than if they are distributed between two or more organizations. However, other considerations may outweigh this advantage of a unified revenue service.

Concentration of administrative resources on activities that will yield the most revenue may well result in the neglect of unremunerative taxes and of poor and remote regions. The requirements of administrative efficiency may thus conflict with the ideal of equal application of all tax laws. If so, compromises will have to be made. Similar compromises or trade-offs are common in the enforcement of other provisions of civil and criminal law. In regard to taxation, general considerations of administrative efficiency and equity may be qualified by awareness of special political sensitivities and by recognition of taxpayers' costs of compliance and the nonfiscal purposes of certain taxes. On these matters, the director of taxation will be well advised to consult the minister of finance or other responsible political leaders, informing them of any intention not to enforce certain tax provisions because of inadequate resources, and they may decide to seek legislative changes to lessen conflicts between administrative efficiency and other desiderata. Despite difficulties and qualifications, the marginal principle remains highly informative as a guide to the allocation of administrative expenditures. Any important departure from the objective of equalizing the difference between marginal revenue and marginal cost in various activities should be accepted, in my opinion, only if there is explicit and persuasive justification for it.

Views of Tax Administrators

Many tax administrators appear to disagree with the emphasis on marginal revenue as a measure of the "output" or "product" of a particular administrative activity. For example, a speaker at the 1977 general assembly of the Inter-American Center of Tax Administrators (Casanegra de Jantscher, 1977, pp. 3–4) said: "There appears to be increasing agreement among tax administrators on the fundamental objective of tax audit. Stated simply, the objective is to promote a higher level of voluntary compliance among all taxpayers. . . . Obtaining additional revenue from audit assessments should be considered only a secondary objective of audit activities."

The stimulation of voluntary compliance does not necessarily conflict with the revenue objective. Improved voluntary compliance will be reflected in greater revenue over a period of years, if not immediately. Nevertheless, two important points are at issue. One is whether marginal revenue shall be defined restrictively as only the collections directly attributable to an activity or shall include an allowance for indirect effects. The other issue is whether only the current year's revenue shall be counted or whether the estimated effects on future yields shall be included. The wide view and the long one have appeal. Common sense tells us that neither indirect effects nor future effects of administrative activities should be ignored. On the other hand, it is very difficult to obtain quantitative estimates of indirect effects or to find a basis for forecasting future effects. It is not unreasonable to suppose that direct, short-run revenue results may be correlated with indirect, long-run results. While it would be wrong-headed to rely solely on the data on costs and returns at the margin that can be quantified, it would be injudicious to apportion resources only on the basis of intuition or tradition.

Some administrators accept the marginal framework of analysis but believe that the function of tax administration is not just to prevent underpayments but also to avert overpayments. In an interesting paper on tax auditing by the State of California that was published in 1954, a senior tax official argued that the correction of overassessments was as important as the detection of underassessments. Hence, he suggested that audit performance be measured by adding together additional assessments and refunds, without regard to sign, and showed that this approach called for relating marginal cost to marginal return, defined as the marginal amount of "misplaced tax" (Welch, 1954). While I agree that both ethics and an expedient regard for public relations dictate that a tax department should not confine itself to discovering underpayments and should make prompt refunds when overpayments are found, I doubt that it is realistic to give equal weight to the correction of both kinds of error. Special attention to underpayments may be justified on the grounds that taxpayers are likely to be more prone to understatements. A director of a tax department who is especially attracted to quantitative evaluation of performance might develop an activity measure that combines positive and negative adjustments of assessments with a greater numerical weight for the former. Conceivably, an imaginative official could go even further and differentiate among additional assessments by assigning greater weight to the discovery of understatements of tax liability associated with behavior that is regarded as especially harmful on economic grounds than to understatements associated with other behavior. For example, greater weight might be given to an additional assessment obtained by preventing the successful manipulation of international transfer prices, which would result in the evasion of both taxation and foreign exchange regulations, than to an assessment of unreported income that had been hoarded in the form of national currency (Morag, 1957). The marginal principle is versatile enough to cover various quantifiable objectives (Wertz, 1979). But it is advisable to refrain from developing overly elaborate schemes that may prove to be impractical and tend to discredit the quantitative approach.

Staff Training

In many countries, the expenditures of the tax department include outlays for formal programs of staff training. Experts' reports often recommend that such programs be strengthened and expanded. Economic theory corroborates the productivity of training but points to a caution about the allocation of its costs. To an increasing extent in recent years, economists have recognized the contribution of training to productivity and have employed the concept of human capital as an aid to thinking on the subject. Human capital represents the present value of the increased productive capacity resulting from education, training, and experience. Human capital, however, differs from physical capital in one important respect. Human capital belongs to the individual worker and is taken with him when he changes jobs, whereas physical capital usually belongs to the organization that purchased it. For that reason and because of inadequate appreciation of the importance of training, there is a risk that economic incentives will be too weak to elicit the socially optimal amount of training. Although a tax department should not take an overly narrow view of the subject, it could justifiably draw an important distinction between general training to impart a skill such as bookkeeping, which is useful in a variety of jobs, and specialized training, such as instruction in departmental procedures, which is useful mainly for the purposes of tax administration. On the one hand, staff members engaged in general training could justifiably be paid at reduced rates during this period in recognition that their future earning capacity will be enhanced and that there is no assurance that they will remain with the tax administration organization. Alternatively, some general training might be scheduled after regular working hours or might be subsidized by the ministry of education. On the other hand, staff members undergoing highly specialized training should be paid at the regular rate, as it may be assumed that the tax department will obtain the benefit of the increased productivity due to the specialized training. Admittedly, it is not always possible to distinguish clearly between general training and specialized training, and some forms of specialized training may enhance a tax officer's earning opportunities in the private sector.

Tax Burdens and Administration

In discussions of tax administration, it is often asserted that additional administrative expenditures are justified because they will produce additional revenue in a manner that will be less burdensome to taxpayers than raising tax rates or imposing new taxes. There is some truth in this; well-administered taxes, being more uniformly applied than poorly administered ones, are more equitable and cause smaller economic distortions. But the argument should not be pushed too far. Revenue obtained by better tax administration, like other revenue, represents a diversion of resources from private consumption and investment to utilization in the public sector or a transfer of income from taxpayers to recipients of government payments. This is not the place to discuss the factors that bear on the real costs of taxation, and which establish economic limits to taxation, but in general it would seem that these factors relate to revenue obtained by better administration as well as to other revenue (Goode, 1980). Incomplete tax enforcement may be a safeguard against the harmful effects of excessive tax rates or poorly designed taxes.

USE OF ECONOMIC ANALYSIS AND STATISTICS
IN TAX ASSESSMENT

Audit Criteria, Best-Judgment Assessments, and Forfaits

Tax assessments rely primarily on accounting data, but economic analysis and statistics can serve as useful supplements. Economic studies can be undertaken to elaborate and update procedures used in assessing the income tax and the value-added tax. Three applications of such studies may be distinguished: (1) to establish criteria for identifying cases for detailed examination or field audit; (2) to help officials to make best-judgment or administrative assessments when the information supplied by taxpayers is believed to be incorrect or incomplete; and (3) to provide, as an alternative to conventional assessments, methods for determining estimated income or value added of certain classes of taxpayers who are not expected to maintain full accounts. The first application is a strictly administrative matter; it is an elaboration of the rules of thumb used by all experienced tax officers and the judgmental guidelines that have been developed by many tax departments as aids in checking on the plausibility of information submitted by taxpayers. The second application may also be possible without specific statutory authorization, but the third application depends on legislation that allows it. Despite fundamental legal differences, the second and third applications can be similar in practice (Lapidoth, 1977).

The discriminant function system of the U.S. Internal Revenue Service is an example of a formal set of standards for selecting income tax returns for audit. However, it is derived from statistical studies of the results of special audits of randomly selected tax returns and does not appear to draw on economic analysis or statistics from outside sources.

The Israeli *tachshiv* (plural *tachshivim*) is an example of the use of economic analysis and data to assist officials in making best-judgment assessments in cases where comprehensive and reliable information is not available from books of account. *Tachshivim* are standard assessment guides that are prepared for various trades and professions by economists of the tax department and constantly brought up to date. In 1977, they were said to cover about one hundred economic sectors (Lapidoth, 1977, pp. 124–47; Wilkenfeld, 1973, pp. 144–50).

France, in its forfait system, appears to have gone the furthest in legally establishing alternative bases of assessment, using indicators to determine estimated income and value added rather than as a check on assessments ostensibly based on conventional records. Forfaits are used in France for assessing the income tax of farmers, unincorporated business enterprises, and professional persons whose gross receipts fall below stipulated levels and also for assessing the value-added tax of small enterprises. For agriculture, forfaits reflect average rates of return per hectare for different types of farming and different regions, as estimated by the agriculture department. For other forfaits, French tax inspectors have at their disposal a monograph for each important trade or economic activity that includes descriptive material and information on gross profit margins for various activities or products. The monographs are prepared on a regional or national basis by the research division of the tax department, and representatives of business or professional organizations are invited to comment on them. In addition, the French tax administration has statutory power to assess income tax by reference to certain external indicators of the taxpayer's style of life, each of which is assigned a specific value. The external indicators are derived primarily from household consumption surveys of the national statistical institute. They include the rental value of the person's principal and secondary residences; ownership of cars, motorcycles, boats, aircraft, racehorses, saddle horses; and employment of servants.

Whether a forfait system is needed and is politically acceptable, or even constitutionally permissible, in a country depends on a number of factors that will not be discussed here. However, my impression is that there is considerable scope in many countries for productive research to extend and improve indirect or external indicators of net income and value added, regardless of whether the results are used merely as internal guidelines for the tax department or serve as alternative bases of assessment. Where possible, the studies should use samples of firms or individuals for whom trustworthy conventional accounts showing net income and value added, and also information on suitable indirect indicators, are available. For business enterprises, farmers, and professional persons, the method is to correlate the indirect indicators with gross receipts and the deductions that are appropriate for arriving at net income or value added. The indicators may include input factors such as purchases, number of workers, amount and quality of equipment, size and location of premises, imports, use of raw materials or components, and consumption of fuel and electricity. They may also include output factors, particularly gross sales or receipts but also physical units in some cases. Separate indicators are likely to be needed for various trades or industries and for different geographic areas.

The other class of indicator, comprising identifiable consumption items, is intended as an aid in approximating total personal income on the basis of the taxpayer's living style. Although this expedient has a long history, in most cases its economic basis appears tenuous. A tax department cannot be expected to undertake the extensive and costly survey that would be required to furnish better economic support for the presumptive indicators. It may be possible, however, to follow the French example and improve conventional indicators by referring to family budget data that have been compiled by the central statistical office or another agency for the preparation of a consumer price index or other purposes.

Of course, reliance on indirect indicators is less satisfactory than assessment of the income tax or value-added tax by reference to reliable accounting statements or other direct information. A forfait system or a rigidly applied set of guidelines tends to convert the levy into a tax on the indicators rather than a tax on the nominal base, and the de facto tax may have economic effects quite different from those normally attributed to an income tax or a value-added tax. But there may be no good alternative during the lengthy period required to promote reliable bookkeeping and voluntary compliance with sophisticated tax laws. Exemption of the smallest enterprises is a common feature of value-added taxes, but large exemptions are unfair and offer encouragement to forms of enterprise that are often inefficient and slow to adopt modern methods. A formal forfait system is likely to appear more equitable and to be politically more acceptable than the outright applications of different forms of taxation to small and large enterprises. Forfait systems usually allow taxpayers to "graduate" to the normal regime by establishing satisfactory accounts. There is, of course, a risk that firms whose assessments would be higher under the normal regime will be deterred from improving their accounts. As a safeguard, it may be advisable gradually to restrict eligibility for the forfait system and to keep forfaits rather high.

Depreciation Allowances

Even in the assessment of the income of firms that maintain accounts meeting established standards, some recourse to economic analysis and statistics may be needed. An important element in the measurement of business income is depreciation allowances, or capital consumption allowances. Accountants have tended to view these allowances as a conventional and systematic method of spreading the cost of capital assets over their useful life. Economists tend to regard true depreciation or economic depreciation as the decrease in the market value of a capital asset during any time period owing to wear and tear and obsolescence and to think that tax assessments ought to reflect economic depreciation. The economic concept, however, is difficult to apply owing to the absence of active markets for secondhand equipment, particularly equipment of a specialized nature.

The measurement of either accounting depreciation or economic depreciation is greatly complicated by inflation, and in recent years this aspect of the problem has overshadowed other issues. With rapidly rising prices of capital goods, conventional depreciation allowances based on the original cost of assets lose their validity as measures of capital consumption and as elements in the computation of net income. Businessmen complain that the allowances are inadequate to finance the replacement of plant and equipment—a different point but also an important one. Many countries have permitted or required one-time revaluations of depreciable assets after periods of inflation, and a few countries have introduced continuing arrangements for revaluation (Lent, 1975). The advisability of such adjustments and the merits of different techniques are being actively discussed in other countries.

The two principal techniques may be called current purchasing power (CPP), accounting for depreciation, and current cost accounting (CCA). The CPP approach adjusts depreciation allowances for changes in the purchasing power of money as measured by a broad index, whereas the CCA approach adjusts the allowances for changes in the prices of the particular assets owned by the firm. Clearly, the CPP approach is administratively much simpler and, in my judgment, should be preferred for this reason. On this point, my judgment may be influenced by my opinion that CPP is also fairer than CCA, because the latter omits from taxable income the real gains enjoyed by owners of assets whose value rises faster than other prices.

An alternative proposal, advanced by Nicholas Kaldor in another context in his well-known report *Indian Tax Reform* (1956, pp. 72–79), merits further consideration as a simple means of dealing with depreciation allowances. Kaldor's proposal was that instead of taking annual allowances over the useful life of the asset, the taxpayer be permitted to take a lump-sum allowance, when the asset is put in service, equal to the *discounted* value of all the annual allowances that would be available under normal accounting. The immediate lump-sum allowance, unlike normal allowances, would not be subject to erosion in real value because of increases in the price level occurring after the investment was made. A lump-sum, first-year allowance has recently been proposed in the United States to obviate the need for inflation adjustments and to simplify depreciation accounting (Auerbach and Jorgenson, 1980). Discounting to compute the present value of future allowances under normal depreciation would recognize the economic advantage of obtaining the tax benefit of depreciation allowances earlier than under the normal method. This is an essential feature of the proposal that distinguishes it from the practice of allowing immediate write-off of the full cost of capital investments that exists in some countries. The latter practice is very generous and, on certain plausible assumptions, is virtually equivalent to full tax exemption for the profits from the investments (Shoup, 1969, pp. 301–02).

Two critically important features of the proposal for lump-sum allowances would be the determination of the normal useful life of assets and the choice of the appropriate discount rate. The length of life and the depreciation profile (straight line, declining balance, sum of the years' digits, or other) would be set as under normal depreciation. The choice of the discount rate is debatable. With stable prices, it might appropriately be set equal to the interest rate on loans to creditworthy business borrowers. Under inflationary conditions, however, interest rates reflect both pure time discount and an allowance for the expected loss in the purchasing power of money. Use of the market interest rate under these conditions would mean that the discounted lump-sum allowance would not serve as a method of neutralizing the effect of inflation on depreciation allowances. If, however, the lump-sum allowances reflected discounting only for "pure" time discount, granting them would be an administratively simple method of alleviating the effects of inflation. To illustrate, if pure time discount (that is, the interest rate that would prevail if the price level were expected to be stable) is 4 percent and prices are expected to rise by 10 percent a year, the market interest rate should be approximately 14 percent, consisting of 4 percent for pure time discount and 10 percent for the expected decrease in the purchasing power of money. The discounted lump-sum allowance for an asset that would be eligible for five-year, straight-line depreciation under normal accounting (and would have no salvage value) would be 89.0 percent of its cost with a 4 percent discount rate, but only 68.7 percent of cost with a 14 percent discount rate. For assets with longer lives, the difference would be more dramatic; for a 20-year asset, the lump-sum equivalents would be 68.0 percent at a 4 percent discount rate and 33.1 percent at a 14 percent discount rate.

Enterprises that were able to make full use of the lump-sum allowances would be protected from the effect of inflation on the adequacy of depreciation allowances, regardless of the actual rate of inflation over the useful life of their assets. In practice, it is impossible to ascertain exactly what the pure time discount rate should be. Economists have devised methods for estimating the expected rate of inflation—and of deriving the pure time discount rate from market interest rates—but these may have more appeal to econometricians than to legislators or tax administrators. In past periods of price stability, long-term interest rates in the range of about 3 percent to 5 percent prevailed in countries with developed financial structures, and a figure in that range might be an acceptable rate of discount for use in a lump-sum depreciation system. An objection to such a system is that it would tend to favor established firms, with large incomes against which the discounted lump-sum allowances could be immediately written off, as against new or less profitable firms, which might lack sufficient income to absorb the full allowance. That discrimination could be mitigated by carrying forward unused allowances and increasing them by an interest adjustment (which should approximate the market interest rate rather than a pure time discount rate, in order to provide some protection against erosion, caused by inflation, of the real value of amounts carried forward).

Inventory Valuation

The valuation of inventories (stocks) is another item affecting the assessment of taxable profits that is distorted by inflation. The effect of inflation can be reduced by reversing the traditional assumption that goods are sold in the order of acquisition (the first-in-first-out, or FIFO, method) and assuming that those most recently acquired are sold first (the last-in-first-out, or LIFO, method). The LIFO method is fairly simple when a few homogeneous items are involved, but it becomes complex when a variety of goods are held in the inventory. In the latter cases, adjustment of the inventory value by reference to one or more price indices is feasible (Rottenberg, 1980). As is true of depreciation allowances, the use of a single broad index measuring change in the purchasing power of money is simpler than using indices of the prices of the particular kinds of goods held in the inventory, and in my judgment the simpler method would also be more equitable. Both methods use economic statistics to supplement accounting data. The tax department should inform itself about the coverage and reliability of the price index or indices.

Comprehensive Adjustments for Inflation

Adjustment of depreciation allowances and inventory values would be, at best, an incomplete correction for inflation. A comprehensive system would have to take account of gains and losses on liabilities and assets fixed in money terms and of some other items (Aaron, 1976). It would have important administrative implications, but I shall not discuss them, as I see little inclination to adopt such a system outside countries that experience extremely high and prolonged inflations.

TAX COLLECTION AND ENFORCEMENT

Time Discount

The time discount and interest rate factors, to which reference has been made in the comments on depreciation allowances, are economic concepts that merit close attention in tax administration. Even with a stable price level, it is always advantageous to a taxpayer to postpone payment because he can use the money meanwhile to gain interest or profit income by lending or investing, to avoid paying interest on amounts that he would otherwise borrow, or just to remain more liquid and thus to be in a position to meet unforeseen needs or to take advantage of attractive opportunities. Time discount may seem less relevant for a government than for an individual or private enterprise; but as most governments are debtors, early receipt of revenue usually allows savings on interest payments. When revenue is to be used to finance productive investments in the public sector, the advantage of early receipt is similar for the state and for a profitable private enterprise. Under inflationary conditions, the time of payment of taxes becomes much more significant, because postponement of payment reduces its real value (Hirao and Aguirre, 1970; Tanzi, 1977 and 1980a). As most countries are currently experiencing inflation, it is especially important for tax departments to be conscious of the costs of delay in tax collection and to take all reasonable and feasible steps to reduce the lag between accrual of tax liability and collection. It may be worthwhile to give up some refinements of assessment in order to speed up collection. Delinquent accounts should be subject to realistic interest rates or should be indexed by reference to a suitable broad price index. Collection at source and other current payment arrangements for direct taxes should be strengthened and extended. Frequent remittances of withheld taxes and excises and sales taxes should be required.

Interlocking Systems

Economists have been intrigued by the possibility of devising interlocking systems that would rely on the self-interest of taxpayers to induce them to divulge information to the tax department. Usually their suggestions go no further than the familiar idea of matching invoices with value-added tax or sales tax declarations and cross-checking between these declarations and income tax returns, and economists are rarely cognizant of the practical difficulties of these operations. Kaldor, in his report on India (1956, p. 2), advanced a more elaborate proposal that he described as follows: "The five taxes—income tax, capital gains tax, annual wealth tax, personal expenditure tax and the general gift tax—would all be assessed simultaneously, on the basis of a single comprehensive return; and they are "self checking" in character, both in the sense that concealment or understatement of items in order to minimise liability to some of the taxes may involve an added liability with regard to others, and in the sense that the information furnished by a tax-payer in the interest of preventing over-assessment with regard to his own liabilities automatically brings to light the receipts and gains made by other tax-payers." Kaldor conceded that the system would not prevent evasion in cases where both the seller and buyer of goods or investment property had an interest in understatement.

Higgins (1959, chapter 23, pp. 524–44) carried Kaldor's idea to its logical conclusion and proposed a fully integrated "self-enforcing incentive tax system for underdeveloped countries." It would include: (1) a personal income tax applying to capital gains as well as ordinary income; (2) a corporation income tax; (3) a general sales or turnover tax; (4) a wealth tax with graduated rates; (5) a tax on excess inventories defined as inventories in excess of those "normal" in relation to sales in the trade or industry; and (6) a personal expenditure tax. Liability for all these taxes would be computed by the statistical office, leaving the tax department "only the simpler task of collecting the tax after each taxpayer's liability had been clearly established."

In addition to the usual collation and cross-checking in respect of income tax and sales tax or value-added tax, the Kaldor-Higgins schemes would take advantage of the interrelations between expenditure tax, wealth tax, and capital gains tax. Personal expenditure would be defined as the excess of income over saving, and saving would equal the increase in net wealth. Hence, a person who understated his personal expenditure by overstating his saving would incur additional liability for wealth tax. A seller of investment property who understated his capital gain by either omission or underreporting would deprive the buyer of evidence of an investment made and could thus expose him to an overstatement of his expenditure tax liability (provided the buyer fully reported his own income). The excess inventory tax would be intended to discourage underreporting of sales and thus to aid in enforcing the sales or value-added tax and the income tax of the seller.

These proposals appear so unrealistic that a detailed critique is not worthwhile. In my opinion, their authors exaggerated the proclivity of taxpayers to refined calculations, the capacity of tax departments to use the great mass of data that would be generated, and the receptivity of governments to fiscal innovations. I suspect that most tax administrators will regard the idea of a self-enforcing tax system as fantastical. Even if put into operation, the proposed systems would not prevent evasion in cases in which both parties to a transaction omit it from their records or understate its amount. Both parties could evade the related taxes, and as no conflict of interest would arise between them, neither would have an economic incentive to report correctly. For example, a merchant who failed to report part of his purchases and sales could evade income tax, sales or value-added tax, wealth tax, excess inventories tax, and personal expenditure tax. His trading partners could do likewise. More subtly, the classification of consumption expenditures as business costs, or the consumption by a merchant of part of his stock in trade, could allow evasion of income tax, sales or value-added tax, and personal expenditure tax.

Shoup's conclusion (1969, p. 436) on the self-checking proposals is judicious; the separate taxes would reinforce each other in the sense that the incremental cost of adding, for example, either a personal expenditure tax or a wealth tax to a revenue system that included the other tax would be smaller than the cost of administering either tax alone. But a more efficient use of administrative resources in relation to revenue might be obtained by concentrating on the income tax and the sales tax or the value-added tax.

Incentives for Supplying Information

A less ambitious method of using economic incentives to ensure accurate reporting of taxable transactions is to offer a reward to the nontaxable party for insisting on proper documentation. That method has been used in some jurisdictions in connection with retail sales taxes or value-added taxes at the retail level. Retailers may be required to prepay the tax by buying coupons or stamps to be given to customers (who usually are not legally taxable parties, though they may bear the economic burden of the tax). Alternatively, retailers may be required to give customers copies of prenumbered invoices supplied by the tax department. Customers are offered an inducement to demand the coupons, stamps, or invoices by the government's willingness to redeem them for a small fraction of their face value or to enter them in a lottery drawing (Hart, 1967). As the redemption value or lottery prizes must be small in relation to the tax for the scheme to be attractive to the government, they will not be strong incentives to forgo collusive understatement of large sales and division of the evaded tax between seller and buyer. This kind of collusion is less feasible in small transactions; but for these, the reward to consumers may be too small to motivate many of them. On the whole, the device seems likely to be weak and capricious in operation.

By direct extension of the incentive argument, advantages could be attributed to pecuniary rewards for informers who bring evasion to the attention of the tax department and to bonuses for tax officers who uncover additional tax liabilities. The former practice is widespread but can be socially divisive if too freely used. The risk that incentive compensation payments to tax officers may stimulate excessive zeal and misdirected efforts and the difficulty of identifying the contributions of individual officers are generally recognized and have inhibited the use of such payments. Incentive compensation functions best where the output of individuals can be clearly identified, measured, and subjected to quality controls, which is rarely possible in tax administration.

Market-enforced Self-assessment of Property

Another proposal for inducing private citizens to do some of the work of tax administration calls for a market-enforced system of self-assessment of taxable real estate. It would be an extension of a provision found in several countries according to which taxpayers are required to declare the value of their property for taxation, subject to the threat of being compelled to sell it to the state at the declared value, usually increased by a margin of tolerance. That provision has not been very effective in ensuring full valuations because the state is generally not interested in acquiring property and lacks knowledge of the values of particular pieces of property. The suggested modification would rely on private citizens who are informed about market conditions to act as the enforcing agents. Self-assessed values would be made public, and an owner would be compelled to sell his property to anyone for the declared value plus a premium of, say, 10 percent to 20 percent (Harberger, 1965; Strasma, 1965). Knowledgeable speculators motivated by a lively sense of acquisitiveness would be counted on to prevent undervaluations. Harberger (1965, pp. 119–20) characterized the scheme as "simple and essentially foolproof" allowing "no scope for corruption" and having "negligible costs of administration." He conceded, however, that "the beauty of this scheme, so evident to economists, is not . . . appreciated by lawyers. . . ." Lawyers and other skeptics have less confidence in the impersonal operation of market forces and more sympathy for property owners who might ignorantly misvalue their property or cautiously overvalue it in order to ensure themselves undisturbed possession. Possibilities would exist for abuse by purchasers acting on inside information about developments that would increase property values. Another version of the proposal would dispense with the forced-sale provision and would impose a penalty on the owner who declined to sell for the declared value plus the stipulated margin, with the penalty to be shared by the frustrated bidder. This would meet some of the objections to the proposal by converting it into a suggestion for a special form of reward for informers but could expose property owners to blackmail. Both versions of the proposal would be less threatening to owners who are well informed, ready to take risks, mobile, and not sentimentally attached to their property than to other owners and would offer opportunities to alert and well-financed bidders. The real costs of valuing property would not be avoided (though they might be reduced), as bidders would need either to make expert appraisals or to engage others to do them (Holland and Vaughn, 1969; Bird, 1974).

Penalties

By application of reasoning that is used for the valuation of investment risk, economists have attempted to evaluate the efficiency of penalties for tax evasion. The probable money value of a penalty is the product of the probability of its application and its amount—pA, where p is the probability and A is the amount. For example, a $1,000 penalty that is expected to be applied in only 1 percent of the cases in which it might legally be assessed is actuarially equivalent to a $100 penalty applicable with a 10 percent probability of a $10 penalty that is regarded as certain to be applied. Some theorists have suggested that enforcement efforts be guided by this principle. They assume that administrative costs and the probability of detecting evasion are directly related and infer that economies in costs can be obtained without sacrifice of revenue if the amount of penalties is increased so that pA is held constant (Allingham and Sandmo, 1972).

A theoretical objection to this suggestion is that it assumes that taxpayers are risk neutral—that is, that they are equally deterred by, or equally indifferent to, actuarially equivalent penalties. Observation indicates, however, that some people are risk averters and are concerned to avoid risks that are actuarially small. They would be likely to be more deterred by large penalties than the formula indicates and would suffer a burden of risk-bearing that, in principle, should be recognized as a social cost and deducted from the savings of administrative costs obtained by reducing p while increasing A (Polinsky and Shavell, 1979). Other people appear to be risk seekers and are ready to gamble against highly adverse odds if the possible prize is large; buyers of lottery tickets come to mind. They might well pay little attention to penalties that were uncertain. There is no way of knowing how taxpayers are distributed among the risk neutral, the risk averters, and the risk seekers. Hence a tax department could not confidently select values of p and A that would allow it to reach its revenue objective at minimum cost, even if it had finely calibrated estimates of the cost of attaining various levels of p. Taxpayers, for their part, would not have reliable information about p and might behave erratically.

Most important, the purely economic approach is inconsistent with widely accepted beliefs about justice and equitable taxation. A system that substitutes seldom applied but severe penalties for active tax enforcement is liable to abuse and is likely to be regarded as arbitrary and unjust and to result in the progressive deterioration of voluntary compliance. Penalties have not only the function of deterring evasion but also, as a legal writer has pointed out, the objective of "keeping complying taxpayers satisfied with their compliance." And "this satisfaction may at least to some extent be a matter of retribution, a familiar aspect of criminal law" (Oldman, 1965, pp. 317–18).

References

Aaron, H. J., ed. (1976). *Inflation and the Income Tax.* Washington, D.C.: Brookings Institution.

Aaron, H. J., ed. (1981). *The Value-Added Tax: Lessons from Europe.* Washington, D.C.: Brookings Institution.

Aaron, H. J., and H. Galper (1985). *Assessing Tax Reform.* Washington, D.C.: Brookings Institution.

Acharya, S. N., and Associates (1986). *Aspects of the Black Economy in India.* New Delhi: National Institute of Public Finance and Policy.

Adler, J. H., E. R. Schlesinger, and E. C. Olson (1952). *Public Finance and Economic Development in Guatemala.* Stanford: Stanford University Press.

Agell, J. N. (1986). "Subsidy to Capital through Tax Incentives." In *Fiscal Issues in Southeast Asia: Comparative Studies of Selected Economies,* ed. P. Shome, 48–79. Singapore: Oxford University Press.

Ahluwalia, I. J. (1979). *Behaviour of Prices and Outputs in India: A Macro-Econometric Approach.* New Delhi: Macmillan.

Ahluwalia, M. S. (1973). "Taxes, Subsidies, and Employment." *Quarterly Journal of Economics* 87: 393–409.

Ahmad, E., and N. Stern (1983). "Effective Taxes and Tax Reform in India." University of Warwick, Department of Economics, Discussion Paper no. 25. Coventry.

Ahmad, E., and N. Stern (1984). "The Theory of Reform and Indian Indirect Taxes." *Journal of Public Economics* 25: 259–98.

Ahmad, E., and N. Stern (1986). "Taxation For Developing Countries." London School of Economics, Development Research Programme, Discussion Paper no. 1. London. (Also in *Handbook of Development Economics,* ed. H. Chenery and T. N. Srinivasan, vol. 2, chap. 21. Amsterdam: North-Holland, 1989.)

Ahmad, E., and N. Stern (1986a). "The Analysis of Tax Reform for Developing Countries: Lessons from Research on Pakistan and India." London School of Economics, Development Research Programme Discussion Paper no. 2. (Excerpted in chapter 4.)

Ahmad, E., and N. Stern (1986b). "Tax Reform for Pakistan: Overview and Effective Taxes for 1975–76." *Pakistan Development Review* 25: 43–72.

Ahmad, E., and N. Stern (1987). "Alternative Sources of Government Revenue: Examples from India, 1979–80." In Newbery and Stern (1987), pp. 281–332.

Allingham, M. G., and A. Sandmo (1972). "Income Tax Evasion: A Theoretical Analysis." *Journal of Public Economics* 1: 323–28.

Alm, J., and R. W. Bahl (1985). "Evaluation of the Structure of the Jamaican Individual Income Tax." Staff Paper No. 15, Jamaica Tax Structure Examination Project, Metropolitan Studies Program, Syracuse University, Syracuse.

American Chamber of Commerce of Bolivia (1986). *Tax Reform Law: An Explanation of Its Contents.* La Paz.

Andic, S., and A. Peacock (1966). "Fiscal Surveys and Economic Development." *Kyklos* 19:620–39. (Excerpted in Bird and Oldman, 1975, pp. 89–104).

Ando, A., and F. Modigliani (1963). "The 'Life-Cycle' Hypothesis of Saving: Aggregate Implications and Tests." *American Economic Review* 53: 55–84.

Andrews, W. D. (1974). "A Consumption-type or Cash Flow Personal Income Tax." *Harvard Law Review* 87: 1113–88.

Arowolo, E. A. (1968). "The Taxation of Low Incomes in African Countries." *International Monetary Fund Staff Papers* 15: 322–41.

Asher, M. G. (1988). "The Challenges Facing the Singapore Economy: What Role for Tax Reform." Paper presented to the American Economic Association, December, New York.

Asher, M. G., and A. Booth (1983). *Indirect Taxation in ASEAN*. Singapore: Singapore University Press.

Asher, M. G., and S. Osborne, eds. (1980). *Issues in Public Finance in Singapore*. Singapore: Singapore University Press.

Atkinson, A. B. (1977). "Optimal Taxation and the Direct versus Indirect Tax Controversy." *Canadian Journal of Economics* 10: 590–606.

Atkinson, A. B., and J. E. Stiglitz (1980). *Lectures on Public Economics*. New York: McGraw-Hill.

Auerbach, A. J., and M. Feldstein, eds. (1985, 1987). *Handbook of Public Economics*. 2 vols. Amsterdam: North-Holland.

Auerbach, A. J., and D. W. Jorgenson (1980). "Inflation-proof Depreciation of Assets." *Harvard Business Review* 58 (Sept.–Oct.): 113–18.

Ayub, M. A. (1981). *Made in Jamaica: The Development of the Manufacturing Sector*. Baltimore: Johns Hopkins University Press for the World Bank.

Azhar, B. A., and S. M. Sharif (1974). "The Effects of Tax Holiday on Investment Decisions: An Empirical Analysis." *Pakistan Development Review* 13: 409–32.

Bahl, R. W. (1971). "A Regression Approach to Tax Effort and Tax Ratio Analysis." *International Monetary Fund Staff Papers* 18: 570–608.

Bahl, R. W. (1972). "A Representative Tax System Approach to Measuring Tax Effort in Developing Countries." *International Monetary Fund Staff Papers* 19: 87–122.

Bahl, R. W. (1972a). "Tax Revenue Forecasting in Developing Countries: A Conceptual Analysis." Fiscal Affairs Department, International Monetary Fund, Washington, D.C. Unpublished paper.

Bahl, R. W. (1979). "The Practice of Urban Property Taxation in Less Developed Countries." In Bahl (1979a), pp. 9–47.

Bahl, R. W., ed. (1979a). *The Taxation of Urban Property in Less Developed Countries*. Madison: University of Wisconsin Press.

Bahl, R. W., ed. (forthcoming). *The Jamaican Tax Reform*. Cambridge, Mass.: Oelgeschlager, Gunn, & Hain.

Bahl, R. W., D. Holland, and J. Linn (1983). *Urban Growth and Local Taxes in Less Developed Countries*. Honolulu: East-West Center. (Excerpted in chapter 33.)

Bahl, R. W., C. K. Kim, and C. K. Park (1986). *Public Finances during the Korean Modernization Process*. Cambridge: Harvard University Press. (Excerpted in chapter 7.)

Bahl, R. W., and J. F. Linn (forthcoming). *Urban Public Finance in Developing Countries*. New York: Oxford University Press for the World Bank.

Bahl, R. W., and B. D. Miller, eds. (1983). *Local Government Finance in the Third World: A Case Study of the Philippines*. New York: Praeger.

Bahl, R. W., J. Miner, and L. Schroeder (1984). "Mobilizing Local Resources in Developing Countries," *Public Administration and Development* 4: 215–30. (Excerpted in chapter 32.)

Bahl, R. W., and M. N. Murray (1986). "Income Tax Evasion in Jamaica." Syracuse University, Metropolitan Studies Program Staff Paper no. 31. Syracuse.

Balachandran, K. R., and M. E. Schaefer (1980). "Optimal Diversification among Classes for Auditing Income Tax Returns." *Public Finance* 35: 250–58.

Balassa, B. (1975). "Reforming the System of Incentives in Developing Countries." *World Development* 3: 365–82.

Bauer, P. T. (1957). *Economic Analysis and Policy in Underdeveloped Countries.* Durham: Duke University Press.

Bauer, P. T. (1972). *Dissent on Development: Studies and Debates in Development Economics.* Cambridge: Harvard University Press.

Bauer, P. T. (1981). *Equality, the Third World, and Economic Delusion.* Cambridge: Harvard University Press.

Bauer, P. T., and B. S. Yamey (1957). *The Economics of Under-Developed Countries.* Chicago: University of Chicago Press.

Baxi, U. (1982). *The Crisis of the Indian Legal System.* New Delhi: Vikas.

Becker, G. S. (1983). "A Theory of Competition among Pressure Groups for Political Influence." *Quarterly Journal of Economics* 98: 371–400.

Behrman, J. R., and A. D. Deolalikar (1985). "How Do Food and Product Prices Affect Nutrient Intakes, Health, and Labor Force Behavior for Different Family Members in Rural India?" Paper presented to the Population Association of America, March, Boston.

Ben-Porath, Y., and M. Bruno (1977). "The Political Economy of a Tax Reform: Israel 1975." *Journal of Public Economics* 7: 285–307.

Ben-Porath, Y., and M. Bruno (1979). "Reply to Dr. Radian." *Journal of Public Economics* 11: 395–96.

Berg, E., ed. (1988). *Policy Reform and Equity.* San Francisco: ICS Press.

Best, M. H. (1976). "Political Power and Tax Revenues in Central America." *Journal of Development Economics* 3: 49–82.

Bhagwati, J. N. (1978). *Anatomy and Consequences of Exchange Control Regimes.* Cambridge, Mass.: Ballinger Publishing Co. for the National Bureau of Economic Research.

Bhatia, R. J. (1967). "A Note on Consumption, Income, and Taxes." International Monetary Fund, African Department, Departmental Memorandum no. DM/67/70. Washington, D.C.

Bilsborrow, R. E. (1977). "The Determinants of Fixed Investment by Manufacturing Firms in a Developing Country." *International Economic Review* 18: 697–717.

Bilsborrow, R. E., and R. C. Porter (1972). "The Effects of Tax Exemption on Investment by Industrial Firms in Colombia." *Weltwirtschaftliches Archiv* 108: 396–425.

Bird, R. M. (1968). "Coffee Tax Policy in Colombia." *Inter-American Economic Affairs* 22: 75–86.

Bird, R. M. (1970). "Optimal Tax Policy for a Developing Country: The Case of Colombia." *Finanzarchiv* 29: 30–53.

Bird, R. M. (1970a). *Taxation and Development: Lessons from Colombian Experience.* Cambridge: Harvard University Press.

Bird, R. M. (1974). *Taxing Agricultural Land in Developing Countries.* Cambridge: Harvard University Press.

Bird, R. M. (1976). "Assessing Tax Performance in Developing Countries: A Critical Review of the Literature." *Finanzarchiv* 34: 244–65: (Reprinted in Toye, 1978, pp. 33–61.)

Bird, R. M. (1976a). *Charging for Public Services: A New Look at an Old Idea.* Toronto: Canadian Tax Foundation.

Bird, R. M. (1977). "Tax Reform and Tax Design in Developing Countries." *Rivista di Diritto Finanziario e Scienza delle Finanze* 36: 297–306.

Bird, R. M. (1978). "Perspectives on Wealth Taxation." *Bulletin for International Fiscal Documentation* 32: 479–88.

Bird, R. M. (1980). "Income Redistribution through the Fiscal System: The Limits of Knowledge." *American Economic Review, Papers and Proceedings* 70: 77–81.

Bird, R. M. (1980a). *Tax Incentives for Investment: The State of the Art.* Toronto: Canadian Tax Foundation.

Bird, R. M. (1980b). *Central-Local Fiscal Relations and the Provision of Urban Public Services.* Canberra: Australian National University Press, Centre for Research on Federal Financial Relations. Research Monograph no. 30.

Bird, R. M. (1982). "Taxation and Employment in Developing Countries." *Finanzarchiv* 40: 211–39.

Bird, R. M. (1982a). "The Costs of Collecting Taxes: Preliminary Reflections on the Uses and Limits of Cost Studies." *Canadian Tax Journal* 30: 860–65.

Bird, R. M. (1983). "Income Tax Reform in Developing Countries: The Administrative Dimension." *Bulletin for International Fiscal Documentation* 37: 3–14.

Bird, R. M. (1983a). *The Allocation of Taxing Powers in Papua New Guinea.* Port Moresby, Papua New Guinea: Institute of National Affairs Discussion Paper no. 15.

Bird, R. M. (1984). *Intergovernmental Finance in Colombia.* Cambridge: Harvard Law School International Tax Program.

Bird, R. M. (1985). "The Reform of Indirect Taxes in Jamaica." Syracuse University, Metropolitan Studies Program Staff Paper no. 24. Syracuse.

Bird, R. M. (1985a). "A Preliminary Report on the Guatemalan Tax System." Syracuse University, Metropolitan Studies Program, Local Revenue Assistance Project. Syracuse.

Bird, R. M. (1987). "Imputation and the Foreign Tax Credit: Some Critical Notes from an International Perspective." *Australian Tax Forum* 4: 1–34.

Bird, R. M. (1987a). *The Taxation of International Income Flows: Issues and Approaches.* Wellington, New Zealand: Victoria University Press for the Institute of Policy Studies.

Bird, R. M. (1987b). "A New Look at Indirect Taxation in Developing Countries." *World Development* 15: 1151–61.

Bird, R. M. (1988). "Shaping a New International Tax Order." *Bulletin for International Fiscal Documentation* 42: 292–99.

Bird, R. M. (1989). "Taxation in Papua New Guinea: Backwards to the Future?" *World Development*, 17: 1145–57.

Bird, R. M. (1989a). "The Administrative Dimension of Tax Reform in Developing Countries." In *Tax Reform in Developing Countries,* ed. M. Gillis, 315–46. Durham, N.C.: Duke University Press.

Bird, R. M. (forthcoming). "Fiscal Decentralization in Colombia." In *New Developments in Decentralization,* ed. R. Bennett. London: Pergamon.

Bird, R. M., and D. J. S. Brean (1986). "The Interjurisdictional Allocation of Income and the Unitary Taxation Debate." *Canadian Tax Journal* 34: 1377–1416.

Bird, R. M., and L. H. De Wulf (1973). "Taxation and Income Distribution in Latin America: A Critical Review of Empirical Studies." *International Monetary Fund Staff Paper* 20: 639–82.

Bird, R. M., and S. Horton, eds. (1989). *Government Policy and the Poor in Developing Countries.* Toronto: University of Toronto Press.

Bird, R. M., and B. D. Miller (1989). "Taxation, Pricing, and the Poor." In Bird and Horton (1989), pp. 49–80. (Excerpted in chapter 34.)

Bird, R. M., and B. D. Miller (1989a). "The Incidence of Indirect Taxation on Low-Income Households in Jamaica." *Economic Development and Cultural Change* 37: 393–409.

Bird, R. M., and O. Oldman, eds. (1964). *Readings on Taxation in Developing Countries.* Baltimore: Johns Hopkins Press.

Bird, R. M., and O. Oldman, eds. (1967). *Readings on Taxation in Developing Countries.* rev. ed. Baltimore: Johns Hopkins Press.

Bird, R. M., and O. Oldman, eds. (1975). *Readings on Taxation in Developing Countries.* 3rd ed. Baltimore: Johns Hopkins University Press.

Boadway, R. W. (1987). "The Theory and Measurement of Effective Tax Rates." In Mintz and Purvis (1987), pp. 60–98.

Boidman, N. (1983). "Tax Evasion: The Present State of Non-Compliance." *Bulletin for International Fiscal Documentation* 37: 451-79.

Bolnick, B. R. (1978). "Tax Effort in Developing Countries: What Do Regression Measures Really Measure?" In Toye (1978), pp. 62–80.

Bond, E. (1981). "Tax Holidays and Industry Behavior." *Review of Economics and Statistics* 63: 88–95.

Bond, E., and S. Guisinger (1983). "The Measurement of Investment Incentives Using the Rental Cost of Capital Model." University of Texas, Dallas.

Booth, A. (1980). "The Economic Impact of Export Taxes in ASEAN." *Malayan Economic Review* 25: 36–61.

Boskin, M. J. (1978). "Taxation, Saving, and the Rate of Interest." *Journal of Political Economy* 86: S3–S27.

Bosworth, B. P. (1984). *Tax Incentives and Economic Growth.* Washington, D.C.: Brookings Institution.

Bradford, D. F. (1986). *Untangling the Income Tax.* Cambridge: Harvard University Press.

Break, G. F. (1974). "The Incidence and Economic Effects of Taxation." In *The Economics of Public Finance,* A. Blinder et al., 119–237. Washington, D.C.: Brookings Institution.

Brennan, G., and J. M. Buchanan (1980). *The Power to Tax: Analytical Foundations of a Fiscal Constitution.* Cambridge: Cambridge University Press.

Brown, A., and A. Deaton (1972). "Surveys in Applied Economics: Models of Consumer Behavior." *Economic Journal* 82: 1145–236.

Buchanan, J. M. (1969). *Cost and Choice: An Inquiry in Economic Theory.* Chicago: Markham Publishing Co. (Reprinted, 1978, by University of Chicago Press.)

Buchanan, J. M., and F. Forte (1964). "Fiscal Choice through Time: A Case for Indirect Taxation?" *National Tax Journal* 17: 144–57.

Bulutoglu, K. (1968). "Incentive and Welfare Effects of Tax Structure Change: The Case of Turkey." Paper presented at International Seminar on Fiscal Incentives to Promote Agricultural Development, Istanbul.

Bürkner, H. P. (1982). "The Portfolio Behaviour of Individual Investors in Developing Countries: An Analysis of the Philippine Case." *Oxford Bulletin of Economics and Statistics* 44: 127–44.

Byrne, W. J. (1976). "Fiscal Incentives for Household Saving." *International Monetary Fund Staff Papers* 23: 455–89.

Byrne, W. J., and M. Sato (1976). "The Domestic Consequences of Alternative Systems of Corporate Taxation." *Public Finance Quarterly* 4: 259–84.

Caiden, N., and A. Wildavsky (1980). *Planning and Budgeting in Poor Countries.* New Brunswick, N.J.: Transaction Books.

Canto, V. A., D. H. Joines, and A. B. Laffer (1983). *Foundations of Supply-Side Economics: Theory and Evidence.* New York: Academic Press.

Carson, E. (1972). *The Ancient and Rightful Customs: A History of the English Customs Service.* London: Faber and Faber.

Casanegra de Jantscher, M. (1977). "Current Developments in Tax Audit." Paper presented at the Eleventh Assembly of the Inter-American Center of Tax Administrators.

Casanegra de Jantscher, M. (1985). "Chile." In *Adjustments for Tax Purposes in Highly Inflationary Economies*. Deventer, The Netherlands: Kluwer, pp. 25–34. (Excerpted in chapter 21.)

Casanegra de Jantscher, M. (1987). "Problems in Administering a Value-Added Tax in Developing Countries: An Overview." World Bank, Development Research Department Discussion Paper no. DRD 246. Washington, D.C.

Chand, S. K. (1975). "Some Procedures for Forecasting Tax Revenue in Developing Countries." DM/75/91, International Monetary Fund, Fiscal Affairs Department, Departmental Memorandum no. DM/75/91. Washington, D.C.

Chelliah, R. J. (1960). *Fiscal Policy in Underdeveloped Countries, with Special Reference to India*. London: Allen & Unwin.

Chelliah, R. J. (1971). "Trends in Taxation in Developing Countries." *International Monetary Fund Staff Papers* 18: 254–331. (Excerpted in Bird and Oldman, 1975, pp. 105–27.)

Chelliah, R. J. (1986). *Report of the Commission of Inquiry into Taxation*. Harare, Zimbabwe: Government Printer.

Chelliah, R. J., H. J. Baas, and M. R. Kelly (1975). "Tax Ratios and Tax Effort in Developing Countries, 1969–71." *International Monetary Fund Staff Papers* 22: 187–205.

Chenery, H. B., and A. M. Strout (1966). "Foreign Assistance and Economic Development." *American Economic Review* 56: 680–733.

Chenery, H. B., et al. (1974). *Redistribution with Growth*. London: Oxford University Press.

Chen-Young, P. (1967). "A Study of Tax Incentives in Jamaica." *National Tax Journal* 20: 292–308. (Excerpted in Bird and Oldman, 1975, pp. 378–86.)

Choi, K. (1984). "Value-Added Taxation: Experiences and Lessons of Korea." *Asian-Pacific Tax and Investment Bulletin* 2: 231–47. (Excerpted in chapter 31.)

Churchill, A. (1972). *Road User Charges in Central America*. World Bank Occasional Paper no. 15. Baltimore: Johns Hopkins University Press.

Cnossen, S. (1977). *Excise Systems: A Global Study of the Selective Taxation of Goods and Services*. Baltimore: Johns Hopkins University Press.

Cnossen, S. (1978). "The Case for Selective Taxes on Goods and Services in Developing Countries." *World Development* 6: 813–25. Excerpted in chapter 29.

Cnossen, S. (1982). "What Rate Structure for a Value-Added Tax?" *National Tax Journal* 35: 205–14.

Cnossen, S. (1984). "Jamaica's Indirect Tax System: The Administration and Reform of Excise Taxes." Syracuse University, Metropolitan Studies Program Staff Paper no. 8. Syracuse.

Collier, W. L., et al. (1982). "Acceleration of Rural Development of Java." *Bulletin of Indonesian Economic Studies* 18(3): 84–101.

Collins, D. (1985). *Designing a Tax System for Papua New Guinea*. Institute of National Affairs Discussion Paper no. 18. Port Moresby, Papua New Guinea.

Corden, W. M. (1971). *The Theory of Protection*. Oxford: Clarendon.

Corden, W. M. (1974). *Trade Policy and Economic Welfare*. Oxford: Clarendon.

Corfmat, F. (1985). "Computerizing Revenue Administrations in LDCs." *Finance & Development* 22(3): 45–47 (Excerpted in chapter 37.)

Cutt, J. (1969). *Taxation and Economic Development in India*. New York: Praeger.

Davey, K. J. (1974). *Taxing a Peasant Society: The Example of Graduated Taxes in East Africa*. London: Charles Knight.

Davey, K. J. (1983). *Financing Regional Government: International Practices and Their Relevance to the Third World*. New York: John Wiley.

Davis, L. H. (1967). "Economics of the Property Tax in Rural Areas of Colombia." University of Wisconsin, Land Tenure Center Research Paper no. 25. Madison.

Deaton, A. (1987). "Econometric Issues for Tax Design in Developing Countries." In Newbery and Stern (1987), pp. 92–113.

DeGraw, S. L., and O. Oldman (1985). "The Collection of the Individual Income Tax." *Tax Administration Review*, March, 35–48.

De Wulf, L. H. (1974). "Taxation and Income Distribution in Lebanon." *Bulletin for International Fiscal Documentation* 28: 151–59.

De Wulf, L. H. (1975). "Fiscal Incidence Studies in Developing Countries: Survey and Critique." *International Monetary Fund Staff Papers* 22: 61–131.

De Wulf, L. H. (1978). "Fiscal Incentives for Industrial Exports in Developing Countries." *National Tax Journal* 31: 45–52.

De Wulf, L. H. (1980). "Determinants of the Contribution of Customs Duties to Budgetary Revenue in Less Developed Countries." *Finanzarchiv* 38: 443–68.

De Wulf, L. H. (1980a). "Taxation of Imports in LDCs: Suggestions for Reform." *Journal of World Trade Law* 14: 346–51. Excerpted in chapter 27.

Dixit, A. K., and V. Norman (1980). *Theory of International Trade: A Dual General Equilibrium Approach*. Cambridge: Cambridge University Press.

Doebele, W. A. (1979). "'Land Readjustment' As an Alternative to Taxation for the Recovery of Betterment: The Case of South Korea." In Bahl (1979a), pp. 163–90.

Doebele, W. A., O. F. Grimes, Jr., and J. F. Linn (1979). "Participation of Beneficiaries in Financing Urban Services: Valorization Charges in Bogotá, Colombia," *Land Economics* 55: 73–92.

Domike, A. L., and E. B. Shearer (1973). "Studies on Financing Agrarian Reform in Latin America." University of Wisconsin, Land Tenure Center Research Publication no. 56. Madison.

Dorner, P., and B. Saliba (1981). "Intervention in Land Markets to Benefit the Rural Poor." University of Wisconsin, Land Tenure Center Research Publication no. 74. Madison.

Drèze, J., and N. Stern (1987). "The Theory of Cost-Benefit Analysis." In Auerbach and Feldstein (1987), vol. 2, pp. 909–89.

Due, J. R. (1963). *Taxation and Economic Development in Tropical Africa*. Cambridge: MIT Press.

Due, J. F. (1970). "The Developing Economies, Tax and Royalty Payments by the Petroleum Industry, and the United States Income Tax." *Natural Resources Journal* 10: 10–26. (Excerpted in Bird and Oldman, 1975, pp. 186–200.)

Due, J. F. (1970a). *Indirect Taxation in Developing Economies*. Baltimore: Johns Hopkins Press. (Rev. ed., 1988, below.)

Due, J. F. (1972). "Alternative Forms of Sales Taxation for a Developing Country." *Journal of Development Studies* 8: 263–76. (Excerpted in Bird and Oldman, 1975, pp. 309–24.)

Due, J. F. (1976). "Value-Added Taxation in Developing Economies." In *Taxation and Development*, ed. N. T. Wang, 64–186. New York: Praeger.

Due, J. F. (1988). *Indirect Taxation in Developing Economies*. 2nd ed. Baltimore: Johns Hopkins University Press.

Eaton, A. K. (1966). *Essays in Taxation*. Toronto: Canadian Tax Foundation.

Ebrill, L. P. (1987). "Are Labor Supply, Savings, and Investment Price-Sensitive in Developing Countries? A Survey of the Empirical Literature." In Gandhi et al. (1987), pp. 60–90. Excerpted in chapter 11.

Ebrill, L. P. (1987a). "Income Taxes and Investment: Some Empirical Relations for Developing Countries." In Gandhi et al. (1987), pp. 115–39.

Edwards, C. T. (1970). *Public Finances in Malaya and Singapore.* Canberra: Australian National University Press.

Eicher, C. K., and J. M. Staatz (1984). *Agricultural Development in the Third World.* Baltimore: Johns Hopkins University Press.

Farioletti, M. (1973). "Tax Administration Funding and Fiscal Policy." *National Tax Journal* 26: 1–16.

Feldstein, M. S. (1974). "Tax Incidence in a Growing Economy with Variable Factor Supply." *Quarterly Journal of Economics* 88: 551–73.

Feldstein, M. S. (1976). "On the Theory of Tax Reform." *Journal of Public Economics* 6: 77–104.

Feldstein, M. S. (1978). "The Welfare Cost of Capital Income Taxation," *Journal of Political Economy* 86: 529–51.

Feldstein, M. S., and C. Horioka (1980). "Domestic Saving and International Capital Flows." *Economic Journal* 90: 314–29.

Follain, J. R., and T. E. Miyake (1984). "Land versus Property Taxation: A General Equilibrium Analysis." Syracuse University, Metropolitan Studies Program Staff Paper no. 13. Syracuse. (A substantially revised version appears in *National Tax Journal* 39: 451–70.)

Forte, F. (1964). "Comment on Schedular and Global Income Taxes." In Bird and Oldman (1964), pp. 185–86.

Foxley, A., E. Aninat, and J. P. Arellano (1979). *Redistributive Effects of Government Programmes: The Chilean Case.* New York: Pergamon.

Frey, B. S., and F. Schneider (1984). "International Political Economy: A Rising Field." *Economia Internazionale* 37: 308–47.

Friedland, N., S. Maital, and A. Rutenberg (1978). "A Simulation Study of Income Tax Evasion." *Journal of Public Economics* 10: 107–16.

Frisch, D. J., and D. G. Hartman (1984). "Taxation and the Location of U.S. Investment Abroad." National Bureau of Economic Research Working Paper no. 1241. Cambridge, Mass.

Fromm, G., ed. (1971). *Tax Incentives and Capital Spending.* Washington, D.C.: Brookings Institution.

Fry, M. J. (1978). "Money and Capital or Financial Deepening in Economic Development?" *Journal of Money, Credit, and Banking* 10: 464–75.

Fry, M. J. (1980). "Saving, Investment, Growth, and the Cost of Financial Repression." *World Development* 8: 317–27.

Fry, M. J. (1988). *Money, Interest, and Banking in Economic Development.* Baltimore: Johns Hopkins University Press.

Gaffney, M., ed. (1967). *Extractive Resources and Taxation.* Madison: University of Wisconsin Press.

Galbis, V. (1979). "Inflation and Interest Rate Policies in Latin America, 1967–76." *International Monetary Fund Staff Papers* 26:334–66.

Gandhi, V. P. (1966). *Tax Burden on Indian Agriculture.* Cambridge: Harvard Law School International Tax Program.

Gandhi, V. P. (1970). *Some Aspects of India's Tax Structure.* Bombay: Vora & Co.

Gandhi, V. P. (1987). "Tax Structure for Efficiency and Supply-Side Economics in Developing Countries." In Gandhi et al. (1987), pp. 225–49. (Excerpted in Chapter 10.)

Gandhi, V. P., et al. (1987). *Supply-Side Tax Policy: Its Relevance to Developing Countries*. Washington, D.C.: International Monetary Fund.

Garnaut, R., and A. Clunies-Ross (1977). "A New Tax for Natural Resource Projects." In *Mineral Leasing as an Instrument of Public Policy*, ed. M. Crommelin and A. R. Thompson, 78–900. Vancouver: University of British Columbia Press.

Garnaut, R., and A. Clunies-Ross (1983). *Taxation of Mineral Rents*. Oxford: Oxford University Press.

Gillis, M. (1982). "Evolution of Natural Resource Taxation in Developing Countries." *Natural Resource Journal* 22: 619–48.

Gillis, M. (1985). "Micro- and Macroeconomics of Tax Reform: Indonesia." *Journal of Development Economics* 19: 221–54. (Excerpted in chapter 6.)

Gillis, M., and R. E. Beals, eds. (1980). *Tax and Investment Policies for Hard Minerals: Public and Multinational Enterprises in Indonesia*. Cambridge, Mass.: Ballinger.

Gillis, M., and C. E. McLure, Jr. (1971). "The Coordination of Tariffs and Internal Indirect Taxes." In Musgrave and Gillis (1971), pp. 573–92.

Gillis, M., and C. E. McLure, Jr. (1977). *La Reforma Tributaria Colombiana de 1974*. Bogotá: Biblioteca Banco Popular.

Gillis, M., and C. E. McLure, Jr. (1978). "Taxation and Income Distribution: The Colombian Tax Reform of 1974." *Journal of Development Economics* 5: 233–58.

Gillis, M., G. Sicat, and C. S. Shoup, eds. (forthcoming). *Value-added Taxation in Developing Countries*. Washington, D.C.: World Bank.

Gillis, M., et al. (1978). *Taxation and Mining: Nonfuel Minerals in Bolivia and Other Countries*. Cambridge, Mass.: Ballinger.

Gillis, M., et al. (1987). *Economics of Development*, 2nd ed. New York: W. W. Norton.

Gittes, E. F. (1968). "Income Tax Reform: The Venezuelan Experience." *Harvard Journal on Legislation* 5: 125–73.

Goldfarb, C. F. (1965). "A Model Foreign Tax Credit Act for a Developing Nation." *Harvard International Law Club Journal* 6: 93–124.

Golub, S. S., and J. M. Finger (1979). "The Processing of Primary Commodities: Effects of Developed-Country Tariff Escalation and Developing-Country Export Taxes." *Journal of Political Economy* 87: 559–77.

Goode, R. (1952). "Reconstruction of Foreign Tax Systems." In *Proceedings of the Forty-fourth Annual Conference on Taxation*, National Tax Association. Sacramento, Calif., pp. 212–22. (Excerpted in Bird and Oldman, 1964, pp. 169–79; 1967, pp. 121–31.)

Goode, R. (1961). "Taxation of Savings and Consumption in Underdeveloped Countries." *National Tax Journal* 14: 305–21. (Excerpted in Bird and Oldman (1964), pp. 259–80; 1967, pp. 231–52; 1975, pp. 273–93.)

Goode, R. (1976). *The Individual Income Tax*, rev. ed. Washington, D.C.: Brookings Institution.

Goode, R. (1980). "Limits to Taxation." *Finance & Development* 17(1): 11–13.

Goode, R. (1981). "Some Economic Aspects of Tax Administration." *International Monetary Fund Staff Papers* 28: 249–74. (Excerpted in chapter 38.)

Goode, R. (1984). *Government Finance in Developing Countries*. Washington, D.C.: Brookings Institution.

Goode, R. (1987). "Obstacles to Tax Reform in Developing Countries." In *The Relevance of Public Finance for Policy-Making: Proceedings of the Forty-first Congress of the International Institute of Public Finance*, eds. H. M. van de Kar and B. L. Wolfe, 213–23. Detroit: Wayne State University Press. (Excerpted in chapter 9.)

Goode, R., G. E. Lent, and P. D. Ojha (1966). "Role of Export Taxes in Developing Countries." *International Monetary Fund Staff Papers* 14: 453–501. (Excerpted in Bird and Oldman, 1975, pp. 154–73.)

Goodman, D. E. (1972). "Industrial Development in the Brazilian Northeast: An Interim Assessment of the Tax Credit Scheme of Article 34/18." In *Brazil in the Sixties*, ed. R. Roett. Knoxville, Vanderbilt University Press.

Gordon, R. K., Jnr. (1988). "Income Tax Compliance and Sanctions in Developing Countries: An Outline of Issues." *Bulletin for International Fiscal Documentation* 42: 3–12. (Excerpted in chapter 36.)

Gray, C. W. (1987). "The Importance of Legal Process to Economic Development: The Case of Tax Reform in Indonesia." World Bank, Washington, D.C. Unpublished paper.

Greenaway, D. (1981). "Taxes on International Transactions and Economic Development." In Peacock and Forte (1981), pp. 131–47.

Greenaway, D. (1984). "A Statistical Analysis of Fiscal Dependence on Trade Taxes and Economic Development." *Public Finance* 39: 70–89.

Griffith, P. S. (1973). "Current Payment of Taxes on Income." In Kelley and Oldman (1973), pp. 352–68.

Grimes, O. F., Jr. (1975). "Urban Land Taxes and Land Planning." *Finance & Development* 12(1): 16–20.

Gupta, A. P. (1976). "How Fiscal Policy Can Help Employment Generation." *Economic and Political Weekly* pp. 631–36.

Gupta, K. L. (1970). "Personal Saving in Developing Nations: Further Evidence." *Economic Record* 46: 243–49.

Hall, R. E., and D. W. Jorgenson (1967). "Tax Policy and Investment Behavior." *American Economic Review* 57: 391–414.

Hall, R. E., and A. Rabushka (1983). *Low Tax, Simple Tax, Flat Tax.* New York: McGraw-Hill.

Han, S. S. (1987). "The Value-Added Tax in Korea." World Bank, Development Research Department Discussion Paper no. DRD 221. Washington, D.C.

Harberger, A. C. (1965). "Issues of Tax Reform for Latin America." In OAS (1965a), pp. 110–21.

Harberger, A. C. (1980). "Vignettes on the World Capital Market." *American Economic Review, Papers and Proceedings* 70: 331–37.

Harberger, A. C. (1981). "Proposal for an Expensing Allowance." In Musgrave (1981), pp. 583–93.

Harberger, A. C. (1985). "Tax Policy in a Small, Open, Developing Economy." In *The Economics of the Caribbean Basin* ed. M. B. Connolly and J. McDermott, 1–11. New York: Praeger. (Excerpted in chapter 26.)

Harriss, C. L. (1979). "Land Taxation in Taiwan: Selected Aspects." In Bahl (1979a), pp. 191–204.

Hart, A. G. (1967). *An Integrated System of Tax Information.* New York: Columbia University School of International Affairs.

Hart, A. G. (1976). "Taxation in the Management of Primary Commodity Markets." In *Taxation and Development* ed. N. T. Wang, 187–211. New York: Praeger.

Hartle, D. G., et al. (1983). *A Separate Personal Income Tax for Ontario: An Economic Analysis.* Toronto: Ontario Economic Council.

Hartman, D. (1981). "Tax Policy and Foreign Direct Investment." National Bureau of Economic Research Working Paper no. 689. Cambridge, Mass.

Hartman, D. (1981a). "Domestic Tax Policy and Foreign Investment: Some Evidence." National Bureau of Economic Research Working Paper no. 784. Cambridge, Mass.

Hartman, D. (1984). "Tax Policy and Foreign Direct Investment in the United States." *National Tax Journal* 37: 475–87.

Hartman, D. (1985). "The Welfare Effects of a Capital Income Tax in an Open Economy." National Bureau of Economic Research Working Paper no. 1551. Cambridge, Mass.

Head, J. G. (1968). "Welfare Methodology and the Multi-Branch Budget." *Public Finance* 23: 405–24.

Helleiner, G. K. (1964). "The Fiscal Role of the Marketing Boards in Nigerian Economic Development, 1947–61." *Economic Journal* 74: 582–610.

Helleiner, G. K. (1966). *Peasant Agriculture, Government, and Economic Growth in Nigeria.* Homewood, Ill.: Richard D. Irwin.

Heller, J., and K. M. Kauffman (1963). *Tax Incentives for Industry in Less Developed Countries.* Cambridge: Harvard Law School International Program in Taxation.

Heller, P. (1975). "A Model of Public Fiscal Behavior in Developing Countries: Aid, Investment, and Taxation." *American Economic Review* 65: 429–45.

Heller, W. W. (1954). "Fiscal Policies for Under-Developed Economies." In United Nations (1954), pp. 1–22. (Excerpted in Bird and Oldman, 1964, pp. 3–30; 1967, pp. 5–32; 1975, pp. 5–28.)

Helliwell, J. F., ed. (1976). *Aggregate Investment: Selected Readings.* Harmondsworth, England: Penguin.

Herschel, F. J. (1978). "Tax Evasion and Its Measurement in Developing Countries." *Public Finance* 33: 232–68.

Hicks, U. K. (1961). *Development from Below: Local Government and Finance in Developing Countries of the Commonwealth.* London: Oxford University Press.

Higgins, B. (1959). *Economic Development: Principles, Problems, and Policies.* New York: W. W. Norton.

Hill, J. R. (1977). "Sales Taxation in Francophone Africa." *Journal of Developing Areas* 11: 165–84.

Hinrichs, H. H. (1966). *A General Theory of Tax Structure Change during Economic Development.* Cambridge: Harvard Law School International Tax Program.

Hirao, T., and C. A. Aguirre (1970). "Maintaining the Level of Income Tax Collections under Inflationary Conditions." *International Monetary Fund Staff Papers* 17: 277–325.

Hirschman, A. O. (1963). *Journeys toward Progress: Studies of Economic Policy-Making in Latin America.* New York: Twentieth Century Fund.

Hirschman, A. O. (1968). "Industrial Development in the Brazilian Northeast and the Tax Credit Scheme of Article 34/18." *Journal of Development Studies* 5: 5–28.

Hirschman, A. O. (1981). *Essays in Trespassing: Economics to Politics and Beyond.* New York: Cambridge University Press.

Holland, D. M. (1979). "Adjusting the Property Tax for Growth, Equity, and Administrative Simplicity: A Proposal for La Paz, Bolivia." In Bahl (1979a), pp. 119–34.

Holland, D. M., and J. Follain (1985). "Property Taxation in Jamaica." Syracuse University, Metropolitan Studies Program Staff Paper no. 16. Syracuse.

Holland, D. M., and O. Oldman (1981). "Measuring and Controlling Income Tax Evasion," Fifteenth General Assembly of Inter-American Tax Administrators, Rio de Janeiro.

Holland, D. M., and W. M. Vaughn (1969). "An Evaluation of Self-Assessment under a Property Tax." In *The Property Tax and Its Administration*, ed. A. D. Lynn, Jr., 79–118. Madison: University of Wisconsin Press.

Holland, D. M., M. Wasylenko, and R. W. Bahl (1980). "The Real Property Tax Administration Project in the Philippines." Syracuse University, Metropolitan Studies Program Monograph no. 9, International Series. Syracuse.

Hood, C. (1976). *The Limits of Administration*. New York: John Wiley.

India (1955). *Report of the Taxation Enquiry Commission, 1953–54*. 3 vols. New Delhi.

India (1960). *Report of the Direct Taxes Administration Enquiry Committee, 1958–59*. New Delhi.

India (1972). *Direct Taxes Enquiry Committee, Final Report*. New Delhi.

India (1978). *Report of the Indirect Taxation Enquiry Committee*. New Delhi.

International Monetary Fund (IMF) (annual). *Government Finance Statistics Yearbook*. Washington, D.C.: IMF.

International Monetary Fund (1983). *Interest Rate Policies in Developing Countries*. International Monetary Fund, Research Department Occasional Paper no. 22. Washington, D.C.

Jackson, I. A. (1986). "Amnesty and Creative Tax Administration." *National Tax Journal* 39: 317–23.

Jao, Y. C. (1984). "The Financial Structure." In *The Business Environment in Hong Kong*, 2nd ed., ed. D. G. Lethbridge, 124–79. Hong Kong: Oxford University Press.

Jenkins, G. P. (1975). "United States Taxation and the Incentive to Develop Foreign Primary Energy Sources." In *Studies in Energy Tax Policy*, ed. G. M. Brannon, 203–50. Cambridge, Mass.: Ballinger.

Jenkins, G. P. (1977). "Comment." In *Mineral Leasing As an Instrument of Public Policy*, ed. M. Crommelin and A. R. Thompson, 91–98. Vancouver: University of British Columbia Press. (Excerpted in chapter 23.)

Jenkins, G. P., and B. D. Wright (1975). "Taxation of Income of Multinational Corporations: The Case of the United States Petroleum Industry." *Review of Economics and Statistics* 57: 1–11.

Jimenez, E. (1987). *Pricing Policy in the Social Sectors: Cost Recovery for Education and Health in Developing Countries*. Baltimore: Johns Hopkins University Press for the World Bank.

Johnson, H. G. (1965). "Fiscal Policy and the Balance of Payments." In *Government Finance and Economic Development*, ed. A. T. Peacock and G. Hauser, 157–67. Paris: Organisation for Economic Co-operation and Development. (Excerpted in Bird and Oldman, 1967, pp. 52–65; 1975, pp. 131–43.)

Johnson, H. G. (1967). "The Possibility of Income Losses from Increased Efficiency or Factor Accumulation in the Presence of Tariffs." *Economic Journal* 77: 151–54.

Jorgenson, D. W. (1963). "Capital Theory and Investment Behavior." *American Economic Review* 53: 247–59.

Kaldor, N. (1955). *An Expenditure Tax*. London: Allen & Unwin.

Kaldor, N. (1956). *Indian Tax Reform*. New Delhi: Government of India, Ministry of Finance.

Kaldor, N. (1960). *Suggestions for a Comprehensive Reform of Direct Taxation*. Colombo, Ceylon: Government Press.

Kaldor, N. (1962). "Report on the Turkish Tax System." In Kaldor (1980), pp. 272–309.

Kaldor, N. (1963). "Will Underdeveloped Countries Learn to Tax?" *Foreign Affairs* 41: 410–19. (Excerpted in Bird and Oldman, 1975, pp. 29–37.)

Kaldor, N. (1965). "The Role of Taxation in Economic Development." In OAS (1965a), pp. 70–86.

Kaldor, N. (1980). *Reports on Taxation II: Reports to Foreign Governments*. London: Duckworth.

Katz, B. S. (1972). "Mexican Fiscal and Subsidy Incentives for Industrial Development." *American Journal of Economics and Sociology* 31: 353–59.

Katzman, M. T. (1978). "Progressive Public Utility Rates As an Income Redistribution Device in Developing Countries: The Case of Municipal Water." In Toye (1978), pp. 174–92.

Kelley, P. L. (1970). "Is an Expenditure Tax Feasible?" *National Tax Journal* 23: 237–53.

Kelley, P. L., and O. Oldman, eds. (1973). *Readings on Income Tax Administration*. Mineola, N.Y.: Foundation Press.

Kemal, A. R. (1975). "The Effect of Tax Holiday on Investment Decisions: Some Comments." *Pakistan Development Review* 14: 245–48.

Killingsworth, M. R. (1983). *Labor Supply*. Cambridge: Cambridge University Press.

King, M. A. (1980). "Savings and Taxation." In *Public Policy and the Tax System*, ed. G. A. Hughes and G. M. Heal, 1–35. London: Allen & Unwin.

King, M. A., and D. Fullerton, eds. (1984). *The Taxation of Income from Capital: A Comparative Study of the United States, the United Kingdom, Sweden, and West Germany*. Chicago: University of Chicago Press.

Krauss, M. (1983). *Development without Aid: Growth, Poverty, and Government*. New York: McGraw-Hill.

Krauss, M., and R. M. Bird (1971). "The Value-Added Tax: Critique of a Review." *Journal of Economic Literature* 9: 1167–73.

Krishna, R., and G. S. Raychaudhuri (1982). "Trends in Rural Savings and Capital Formation in India, 1950–1951 to 1973–1974." *Economic Development and Cultural Change* 30: 271–98.

Krueger, A. O. (1972). "Evaluating Restrictionist Trade Regimes: Theory and Measurement." *Journal of Political Economy* 80: 48–62.

Krueger, A. O. (1978). *Liberalization Attempts and Consequences*. Cambridge, Mass.: Ballinger.

Kuznets, S. S. (1966). *Modern Economic Growth*. New Haven: Yale University Press.

Landau, L. (1971). "Savings Functions for Latin America." In *Studies in Development Planning*, ed. B. Chenery, 299–321. Cambridge, Mass.: Harvard University Press.

Lane, M. G., and H. Hutabarat (1986). "Computerization of VAT in Indonesia." World Bank, Development Research Department Discussion Paper no. DRD 194. Washington, D.C.

Lapidoth, A. (1977). *The Use of Estimation for the Assessment of Taxable Business Income*. Amsterdam: International Bureau of Fiscal Documentation.

Lent, G. E. (1967). "Tax Incentives for Investment in Developing Countries." *International Monetary Fund Staff Papers* 14: 249–323.

Lent, G. E. (1971). "Tax Incentives for the Promotion of Industrial Employment in Developing Countries." *International Monetary Fund Staff Papers* 18: 399–417.

Lent, G. E. (1973). "Taxation of Agricultural Income in Developing Countries." *Bulletin for International Fiscal Documentation* 27: 324–43.

Lent, G. E. (1974). "Tax Policy for the Utilization of Labor and Capital in Latin America." *Rivista di Diritto Finanziario e Scienza delle Finanze* 33: 3–23.

Lent, G. E. (1975). "Adjustment of Taxable Profits for Inflation." *International Monetary Fund Staff Papers* 22: 641–79.

Lent, G. E. (1977). "Corporation Income Tax Structure in Developing Countries." *International Monetary Fund Staff Papers* 24: 722–55. (Excerpted in selection 19.)

Leonard, H. B., and R. J. Zeckhauser (1987). "Amnesty, Enforcement, and Tax Policy." In *Tax Policy and the Economy*, ed. L. H. Summers, vol. 1, 55–85. Cambridge, Mass.: National Bureau of Economic Research and Massachusetts Institute of Technology.

Lerman, A. H. (1986). "Tax Amnesty: The Federal Perspective." *National Tax Journal* 39: 325–32.

Lerner, A. P. (1936). "The Symmetry between Import and Export Taxes." *Economica*, n.s. 3: 306–13.

Levin, J. V. (1960). *The Export Economies*. Cambridge: Harvard University Press.

Lewis, S. R. (1967). "Agricultural Taxation in a Developing Economy." In *Agricultural Development and Economic Growth*, ed. H. M. Southworth and B. F. Johnston, 453–92. Ithaca: Cornell University Press. (Excerpted in Bird and Oldman, 1975, pp. 389–400.)

Lewis, S. R. (1973). "Agricultural Taxation and Intersectoral Resource Transfers." *Food Research Institute Studies* 12(2): 93–114. (Excerpted in Bird and Oldman, 1975, pp. 401–9.)

Lewis, S. R. (1984). *Taxation for Development: Principles and Applications*. New York: Oxford University Press.

Lewis, W. A. (1955). *The Theory of Economic Growth*. Homewood, Ill.: Richard D. Irwin.

Lewis, W. A. (1966). *Development Planning: The Essentials of Economic Policy*. London: Allen & Unwin.

Lim, D. (1983). "Tax Incentives and Resource Utilization in Peninsular Malayasian Manufacturing." In *Further Readings on Malaysian Economic Development*, ed. D. Lim, 277–87. Kuala Lumpur: Oxford University Press.

Lindbeck, A. (1987). "Public Finance for Market-Oriented Developing Countries." World Bank, Development Research Department Discussion Paper no. DRD 212. Washington, D.C. (Excerpted in chapter 5.)

Linn, J. F. (1979). "Automotive Taxation in the Cities of Developing Countries." *Nagarlok* 11: 1–23.

Linn, J. F. (1980). "The Distributive Effects of Local Government Finances in Columbia: A Review of the Evidence." In *Economic Policy and Income Distribution in Colombia*, ed. R. A. Berry and R. Soligo. Boulder: Westview Press, pp. 69–111.

Linn, J. F. (1981). "Urban Finances in Developing Countries." In *Urban Government Finance: Emerging Trends*, ed. R. W. Bahl, 245–83. Beverly Hills, Calif.: Sage Publications.

Linn, J. F. (1983). *Cities in the Developing World*. New York: Oxford University Press for the World Bank.

Linn, J. F., R. S. Smith, and H. Wignjowijoto (1976). "Urban Public Finances in Developing Countries: A Case Study of Jakarta, Indonesia." World Bank Report no. 80-7. Washington, D.C.

Lipsey, R. G., and K. Lancaster (1956). "The General Theory of Second Best." *Review of Economic Studies* 24: 11–32.

Little, I. M. D., and J. A. Mirrlees (1969). *Social Cost Benefit Analysis*. Paris: Organisation for Economic Co-operation and Development Development Centre. (Vol. 2 of *Manual of Industrial Project Analysis in Developing Countries*.)

Lynn, L. E., Jr. (1977). "Implementation: Will the Hedgehogs Be Outfoxed?" *Policy Analysis* 3: 277–80.

Macon, J., and J. M. Manon (1977). *Financing Urban and Rural Development through Betterment Levies: The Latin American Experience*. New York: Praeger.

Maktouf, L., and S. S. Surrey (1983). "Tax Expenditure Analysis and Tax and Budgetary Reform in Less Developed Countries." *Law and Policy in International Business* 15: 739–61. (Excerpted in chapter 16.)

Malik, I. A. (1979). "Use of Presumptive Tax Assessment Techniques in Taxation of Small Traders and Professionals in Africa." *Bulletin for International Fiscal Documentation* 33: 162–78.

Mansfield, C. Y. (1988). "Tax Administration in Developing Countries: An Economic Perspective." *International Monetary Fund Staff Papers* 35: 181–97.

Marsden, K. (1983). "Taxes and Growth." *Finance & Development* 20(3): 40–43. (Excerpted in chapter 2.)

Marsden, K. (1983a). "Links between Taxes and Economic Growth: Some Empirical Evidence." World Bank, Staff Working Paper no. 605. Washington, D.C.

Marshall, M., ed. (1982). *Through a Glass Darkly: Beer and Modernization in Papua New Guinea*. Boroko, Papua New Guinea: Institute of Applied Social and Economic Research.

McBean, A. (1966). *Export Instability and Economic Development*. Cambridge: Harvard University Press.

McDaniel, P. R., and S. S. Surrey, eds. (1985). *International Aspects of Tax Expenditures: A Comparative Study*. Deventer: Kluwer Law.

McDonald, D. (1983). "The Determinants of Saving Behavior in Latin America." International Monetary Fund, Research Department, Departmental Memorandum no. DM/83/26. Washington, D.C.

McIntyre, M. J., and O. Oldman (1975). *Institutionalizing the Process of Tax Reform*. Amsterdam: International Bureau of Fiscal Documentation.

McKinnon, R. I. (1964). "Foreign Exchange Constraints in Economic Development and Efficient Aid Allocation." *Economic Journal* 74: 388–409.

McKinnon, R. I. (1973). *Money and Capital in Economic Development*. Washington, D.C.: Brookings Institution.

McLure, C. E., Jr. (1971). "The Design of Regional Tax Incentives for Colombia." In Musgrave and Gillis (1971), pp. 545–56.

McLure, C. E., Jr. (1975). "The Proper Use of Indirect Taxation in Latin America: The Practice of Economic Marksmanship." *Public Finance* 30: 20–44. Excerpted in Bird and Oldman (1975), pp. 339–49.

McLure, C. E., Jr. (1977). "Taxation and the Urban Poor in Developing Countries." *World Development* 5: 169–88.

McLure, C. E., Jr. (1979). *Must Corporate Income Be Taxed Twice?* Washington, D.C.: Brookings Institution.

McLure, C. E., Jr. (1980). "Administrative Considerations in the Design of Regional Tax Incentives." *National Tax Journal* 33: 177–88.

McLure, C. E., Jr., ed. (1984). *The State Corporation Income Tax: Issues in Worldwide Unitary Combination*. Stanford, Calif.: Hoover Institution Press.

McLure, C. E., Jr. (1987). "VAT, Income Distribution, and Tax Incidence." World Bank, Development Research Department Discussion Paper no. DRD 226. Washington, D.C.

McLure, C. E., Jr. (1988). "U.S. Tax Laws and Capital Flight from Latin America." Stanford University, Hoover Institution Working Papers in Economics no. E-88-21. Palo Alto, Calif.

McLure, C. E., Jr. (1988a). "Fiscal Policy and Equity in Developing Countries." In Berg (1988), pp. 13–42.

McLure, C. E., Jr., and W. R. Thirsk (1978). "The Inequity of Taxing Iniquity: A Plea for Reduced Sumptuary Taxes in Developing Countries." *Economic Development and Cultural Change* 26: 487–503.

McLure, C. E., Jr., et al. (1988). *The Taxation of Income from Business and Capital in Colombia*. Bogotá: Ministerio de Hacienda y Crédito Público. (Excerpted in chapters 22 and 24.) Also, an expanded version, 1989, Durham, N.C.: Duke University Press.

Mathew, E. T. (1968). *Agricultural Taxation and Economic Development in India*. London: Asia Publishing House.

Meade, J. E., et al. (1978). *The Structure and Reform of Direct Taxation*. London: Allen & Unwin.

Meerman, J. (1979). *Public Expenditure in Malaysia: Who Benefits and Why*. New York: Oxford University Press for the World Bank.

Meier, G. M., ed. (1983). *Pricing Policy for Development Management*. Baltimore: Johns Hopkins University Press for the World Bank.

Mellor, J. W., and B. F. Johnston (1984). "The World Food Equation: Interrelations among Development, Employment, and Food Consumption." *Journal of Economic Literature* 22: 531–74.

Mikesell, R. F., and J. E. Zinser (1973). "The Nature of the Savings Function in Developing Countries: A Survey of the Theoretical and Empirical Literature." *Journal of Economic Literature* 11: 1–26.

Millward, R., et al. (1983). *Public Sector Economics*. New York: Longman.

Mintz, J. M., and D. D. Purvis, eds. (1987). *The Impact of Taxation on Business Activity*. Kingston, Ont.: John Deutsch Institute for the Study of Economic Policy, Queen's University.

Modi, J. R. (1982). "Narrowing Regional Disparities by Fiscal Incentives." *Finance & Development* 19(1): 34–37.

Modi, J. R. (1987). "Major Features of Corporate Profits Taxes in Selected Developing Countries." *Bulletin for International Fiscal Documentation* 41: 65–74.

Morag, A. (1957). "Some Economic Aspects of Two Administrative Methods of Estimating Taxable Income." *National Tax Journal* 10: 176–85.

Morawetz, D. (1974). "Employment Implications of Industrialisation in Developing Countries: A Survey." *Economic Journal* 84: 491–542.

Morss, E. (1968). "Fiscal Policy, Savings, and Economic Growth in Developing Countries: An Empirical Study." International Monetary Fund, Fiscal Affairs Department, Departmental Memorandum no. DM/68/43. Washington, D.C.

Mueller, D. C. (1989). *Public Choice II*. Cambridge: Cambridge University Press.

Musgrave, P. B. (1969). *United States Taxation of Foreign Investment Income: Issues and Arguments*. Cambridge: Harvard Law School International Tax Program.

Musgrave, R. A. (1959). *The Theory of Public Finance*. New York: McGraw-Hill.

Musgrave, R. A. (1963). "Growth with Equity." *American Economic Review, Papers and Proceedings* 63: 323–33.

Musgrave, R. A. (1965). *Revenue Policy for Korea's Economic Development*. Seoul: Nathan Economic Advisory Group, USOM/Korea. (Excerpted in Bird and Oldman, 1967, pp. 45–51.)

Musgrave, R. A. (1969). *Fiscal Systems*. New Haven: Yale University Press.

Musgrave, R. A. (1981). *Fiscal Reform in Bolivia*. Cambridge: Harvard Law School International Tax Program. (Excerpted in chapter 25.)

Musgrave, R. A. (1982). "Tax Reform or Tax Deform?" In *Tax Policy Options in the 1980s*, ed. W. R. Thirsk and J. Whalley, 19–27. Toronto: Canadian Tax Foundation.

Musgrave, R. A., and M. Gillis (1971). *Fiscal Reform for Colombia*. Cambridge: Harvard Law School International Tax Program.

Musgrave, R. A., and P. B. Musgrave (1972). "Inter-Nation Equity." In *Modern Fiscal Issues*, ed. R. M. Bird and J. G. Head, 63–85. Toronto: University of Toronto.

Musgrave, R. A., and P. B. Musgrave (1984). *Public Finance in Theory and Practice*, 4th ed. New York: McGraw-Hill.

Musgrave, R. A., and A. T. Peacock, eds. (1958). *Classics in the Theory of Public Finance*. London: Macmillan.

Mussa, M. (1974). "Tariffs and the Distribution of Income: The Importance of Factor Specificity, Substitutability, and Intensity in the Short and Long Run." *Journal of Political Economy* 82: 1191–1203.

Mutén, L. (1982). "A Cascade Tax by Any Other Name." *Public Finance* 37: 263–68.

Myrdal, G. (1968). *Asian Drama: An Inquiry into the Poverty of Nations*, 3 vols. New York: Pantheon.

National Institute of Public Finance and Policy (1986). *Evasion of Excise Duties in India.* New Delhi.

Nellor, D. C. (1984). "Natural Resource Tax Policy in Developing Countries." International Monetary Fund, Fiscal Affairs Department, Departmental Memorandum no. DM/84/14. Washington, D.C.

Newbery, D. (1987). "Agricultural Taxation: The Main Issues." In Newbery and Stern (1987), pp. 366–86.

Newbery, D., and N. Stern, eds. (1987). *The Theory of Taxation for Developing Countries.* New York: Oxford University Press for the World Bank.

Newbery, D., and J. E. Stiglitz (1981). *The Theory of Commodity Price Stabilization: A Study in the Economics of Risk.* Oxford: Clarendon.

Nurkse, R. (1957). *Problems of Capital Formation in Underdeveloped Countries.* New York: Oxford University Press.

OAS (*See* Organization of American States)

OECD (*See* Organisation for Economic Co-operation and Development)

Olaloku, F. A. (1976). "Fiscal Policy Options for Employment Promotion in Nigeria's Modern Manufacturing Sector." *Bulletin for International Fiscal Documentation* 30: 318–27.

Oldman, O. (1964). "Tax Reform in El Salvador." *Inter-American Law Review* 6: 379–420.

Oldman, O. (1965). "Controlling Income Tax Evasion." In OAS (1965), pp. 296–344.

Oldman, O. (1966). "Tax Policies of Less Developed Countries with Respect to Foreign Income and Income of Foreigners." In *Taxation of Foreign Income*, 74–88. Tax Institute of America. Princeton, N.J. (Excerpted in Bird and Oldman, 1975, pp. 201–08. Revised for chapter 20.)

Oldman, O., and R. M. Bird (1977). "The Transition to a Global Income Tax: A Comparative Analysis." *Bulletin for International Fiscal Documentation* 31: 439–54. (Excerpted in chapter 17.)

Oldman, O., and J. S. Brooks (1987). "The Unitary Method and the Less Developed Countries: Preliminary Thoughts." *Revue de deroit des affaires internationales* (1987): 45–61.

Oldman, O., et al. (1967). *Financing Urban Development in Mexico City.* Cambridge: Harvard University Press.

Olson, M., Jr. (1965). *The Logic of Collective Action: Public Goods and the Theory of Groups.* Cambridge: Harvard University Press.

Organisation for Economic Co-operation and Development (OECD) (1977). *Model Double Taxation Convention on Income and Capital.* Paris: OECD.

Organisation for Economic Co-operation and Development (OECD) (1984). *Tax Expenditures: A Review of the Issues and Country Practices.* Paris: OECD.

Organisation for Economic Co-operation and Development (OECD) (1987). *Taxation in Developed Countries.* Paris: OECD.

Organisation for Economic Co-operation and Development (OECD) (1988). *Taxation of Net Wealth, Capital Transfers, and Capital Gains of Individuals.* Paris: OECD.

Organization of American States (OAS), Joint Tax Program (1965). *Problems of Tax Administration in Latin America.* Baltimore: Johns Hopkins Press.

Organization of American States (OAS), Joint Tax Program (1965a). *Fiscal Policy for Economic Growth in Latin America.* Baltimore: Johns Hopkins Press.

Palmer, K. F. (1980). "Mineral Taxation Policies in Developing Countries: An Application of Resource Rent Tax." *International Monetary Fund Staff Papers* 27: 517–42.

Papanek, G. F. (1972). "The Effect of Aid and Other Resource Transfers on Savings and Growth in Less Developed Countries." *Economic Journal* 82: 934–50.

Papua New Guinea (1971). *Committee of Inquiry on Taxation*. Port Moresby: Government Printer.

Peacock, A. T., and F. Forte, eds. (1981). *The Political Economy of Taxation*. New York: St. Martin's Press.

Peacock, A. T., and G. K. Shaw (1971). "Fiscal Measures to Improve Employment in Developing Countries: A Technical Note." *Public Finance* 26: 409–17.

Peacock, A. T., and G. K. Shaw (1972). "Fiscal Measures to Improve Employment in Developing Countries: A Reply." *Public Finance* 27: 489–90.

Peacock, A. T., and A. K. Shaw (1973). "Fiscal Measures to Create Employment: The Indonesian Case." *Bulletin for International Documentation* 27: 443–53.

Pechman, J. A., ed. (1980). *What Should Be Taxed: Income or Expenditure?* Washington, D.C.: Brookings Institution.

Pellechio, A. J. (1987). "A Model for Analysis of Taxation of Capital Investment." World Bank, Development Research Department Discussion Paper no. DRD 263. Washington, D.C.

Pellechio, A. J., G. P. Sicat, and D. G. Dunn (1987). "Effective Tax Rates under Varying Tax Incentives." World Bank, Development Research Department Discussion Paper no. DRD 262. Washington, D.C. (Excerpted in chapter 14.)

Perry, G., and M. Cardenas (1986). *Diez años de reformas tributarias en Colombia*. Bogotá: Fedesarrollo.

Petrei, A. H. (1975). "Inflation Adjustment Schemes under the Personal Income Tax." *International Monetary Fund Staff Papers* 22: 539–64.

Pigou, A. C. (1932). *The Economics of Welfare*. 4th ed. London: Macmillan.

Pigou, A. C. (1949). *A Study in Public Finance*, 3d ed. New York: St. Martin's Press.

Plasschaert, S. R. F. (1976). "First Principles about Schedular and Global Frames of Taxation." *Bulletin for International Fiscal Documentation* 30: 99–111.

Please, S. (1967). "Saving through Taxation—Reality or Mirage?" *Finance & Development* 4(1): 24–32 (Excerpted in Bird and Oldman, 1975, pp. 38–47.)

Please, S. (1970). "The 'Please Effect' Revisited." World Bank, Economics Department Working Paper no. 82. Washington, D.C.

Polinsky, A. M., and S. Shavell (1979). "The Optimal Tradeoff between the Probability and Magnitude of Fines." *American Economic Review* 69: 880–91.

Popkin, W. D. (1973). *The Deduction for Business Expenses and Losses*. Cambridge: Harvard Law School International Tax Program.

Premchand, A. (1983). *Government Budgeting and Expenditure Controls: Theory and Practice*. Washington, D.C.: International Monetary Fund.

Pressman, J. L., and A. Wildavsky (1973). *Implementation*. Berkeley: University of California Press.

Prest, A. R. (1969). *Transport Economics in Developing Countries: Pricing and Financing Aspects*. London: Weidenfeld & Nicolson.

Prest, A. R. (1971). "The Role of Labour Taxes and Subsidies in Promoting Employment in Developing Countries." *International Labour Review* 103: 315–32. (Excerpted in Bird and Oldman, 1975, pp. 350–62.)

Prest, A. R. (1978). "The Taxable Capacity of a Country," In Toye (1978), pp. 13–32.

Prest, A. R. (1985). *Public Finance in Developing Countries*. 3rd ed. New York: St. Martin's Press.

Prest, A. R. (1985a). "Implicit Taxes: Are We Taxed More Than We Think?" *Royal Bank of Scotland Review*, no. 147: 10–26.

Radian, A. (1979). "On The Differences between the Political Economy of Introducing and Implementing Tax Reforms: Israel 1975–1978." *Journal of Public Economics* 11: 261–71.

Radian, A. (1980). *Resource Mobilization in Poor Countries: Implementing Tax Policies.* New Brunswick, N.J.: Transaction Books.

Radian, A., and I. Sharkansky (1979). "Tax Reform in Israel: Partial Implementation of Ambitious Goals." *Policy Analysis* 5: 351–66. (Excerpted in chapter 8.)

Rao, M. G., and G. Pradahan (1985). "Excise Duty Evasion on Cotton Textile Fabrics." *Economic and Political Weekly* 20: 1377–89.

Rezende, F. (1976). "Income Taxation and Fiscal Equity." *Brazilian Economic Studies* 2: 105–45.

Rhoads, W. G., and R. M. Bird (1967). "Financing Urbanization in Developing Countries by Benefit Taxation: Case Study of Colombia." *Land Economics* 43: 403–12. (Excerpted in Bird and Oldman, 1975, pp. 453–63.)

Richupan, S. (1984). "Income Tax Evasion: A Review of the Measurement Techniques and Some Estimates for the Developing Countries." International Monetary Fund, Fiscal Affairs Department, Departmental Memorandum no. DM/84/46. Washington, D.C.

Richupan, S. (1984a). "Measuring Tax Evasion." *Finance & Development* 21(4): 38–40.

Riew, J. (1987). "Property Taxation in Taiwan: Merits, Issues, and Options." *Industry of Free China* 68(1): 7–28; 68(2): 17–32.

Riew, J. (1988). "Taxation and Development: The Taiwan Model." Paper presented at a meeting of the American Economic Association, New York, December.

Robbins, L. C. R. (1935). *An Essay on the Nature and Significance of Economic Science.* 2nd ed. London: Macmillan.

Root, F. R., and A. A. Ahmed (1979). "Empirical Determinants of Manufacturing Direct Foreign Investment in Developing Countries." *Economic Development and Cultural Change* 27: 751–67.

Ross, S. G., and J. B. Christensen (1959). *Tax Incentives for Industry in Mexico.* Cambridge: Harvard Law School International Program in Taxation.

Roth, G. (1987). *The Private Provision of Public Services in Developing Countries.* New York: Oxford University Press for the World Bank.

Rottenberg, I. (1980). "Modernizing the LIFO Method." *National Tax Journal* 33: 95–98.

Royal Commission on Taxation (1966). *Report.* 6 vols. Ottawa: Queen's Printer.

Russell, C. S., and N. K. Nicholson, eds. (1981). *Public Choice and Rural Development.* Baltimore: Johns Hopkins University Press for Resources for the Future.

Sanchez-Ugarte, F. (1987). "Rationality of Income Tax Incentives in Developing Countries: A Supply-Side Look." In Gandhi et al. (1987), pp. 250–78.

Sanchez-Ugarte, F., and J. R. Modi (1987). "Are Export Duties Optimal in Developing Countries? Some Supply-Side Considerations." In Gandhi et al. (1987), pp. 279–305. (Excerpted in chapter 28.)

Sandford, C. T. (1973). *Hidden Costs of Taxation.* London: Institute for Fiscal Studies.

Sandford, C. T., et al. (1981). *Costs and Benefits of VAT.* London: Heinemann Educational.

Sandmo, A. (1985). "The Effects of Taxation on Savings and Risk Taking." In Auerbach and Feldstein (1985), vol. 1, pp. 265–311.

Schumpeter, J. A. (1961). *The Theory of Economic Development.* New York: Oxford University Press.

Schwab, P. (1972). *Decision-Making in Ethiopia: A Study of the Political Process.* Rutherford, N.J.: Fairleigh Dickinson University Press.

Scott, A. (1973). *Natural Resources: The Economics of Conservation.* 2nd ed. Toronto: McClelland and Stewart.

Selowsky, M. (1979). *Who Benefits from Government Expenditure? A Case Study of Colombia.* New York: Oxford University Press for the World Bank.

Shah, S. M. S., and J. F. J. Toye (1978). "Fiscal Incentives for Firms in Some Developing Countries: Survey and Critique." In Toye (1978), pp. 269–96. (Excerpted in chapter 12.)

Shalizi, Z., and Squire (1986). "Consumption Taxes in Sub-Saharan Africa." World Bank, Country Policy Department, Resource Mobilization Division. June. (Excerpted in chapter 30.)

Shaw, E. S. (1973). *Financial Deepening in Economic Development.* New York: Oxford University Press.

Shaw, G. K. (1981). "Leading Issues of Tax Policy in Developing Countries: The Economic Problems." In Peacock and Forte (1981), pp. 148–62.

Shemesh, A. B. (1969). *Taxation in Islam.* London: Luzac.

Shoup, C. S. (1965). "Production from Consumption." *Public Finance* 20: 173–202.

Shoup, C. S. (1965a). *The Tax System of Brazil.* Rio de Janeiro: Fundação Getúlio Vargas.

Shoup, C. S. (1966). "Taxes and Economic Development." *Finanzarchiv* 25: 385–97. (Excerpted in chapter 3.)

Shoup, C. S. (1969). *Public Finance.* Chicago: Aldine.

Shoup, C. S. (1979). "The Taxation of Urban Property in Less Developed Countries: A Concluding Discussion." In Bahl (1979a), pp. 271–83.

Shoup, C. S. (1983). "Current Trends in Excise Taxation." In *Comparative Tax Studies,* ed. S. Cnossen, 257–75. Amsterdam: North-Holland.

Shoup, C. S., et al. (1949). *Report on Japanese Taxation.* 4 vols. Tokyo: General Headquarters, Supreme Commander for the Allied Powers.

Shoup, C. S., et al. (1959). *The Fiscal System of Venezuela.* Baltimore: Johns Hopkins Press.

Shoup, C. S., et al. (1970). *The Tax System of Liberia.* New York: Columbia University Press.

Sicat, G. P., and A. Virmani (1987). "Personal Income Taxes in Developing Countries: International Comparisons." World Bank Development Research Department, Report no. DRD 265. Washington, D. C.

Simons, H. C. (1938). *Personal Income Taxation.* Chicago: University of Chicago Press.

Simons, H. C. (1950). *Federal Tax Reform.* Chicago: University of Chicago Press.

Singh, S. K. (1975). *Development Economics: Some Findings.* Lexington, Mass.: Lexington Books.

Singhal, H. K. (1973). "Taxing for Development: Incentives Affecting Foreign Investment in India." *Harvard International Law Journal* 14: 50–88.

Slemrod, J. (forthcoming). "Optimal Taxation and Optimal Tax Systems." In *Journal of Economic Perspectives.*

Smith, A. H. (1975). "Income Tax Incentives for New Industries in Developing Countries." *Bulletin for International Fiscal Documentation* 29: 65–77.

Smith, R. S. (1974). "Financing Cities in Developing Countries." *International Monetary Fund Staff Papers* 21: 329–88. (Excerpted in Bird and Oldman, 1975, 439–52.)

Smith, R. S. (1975). "Highway Pricing and Motor Vehicle Taxation in Developing Countries: Theory and Practice." *Finanzarchiv* 33: 451–74.

Smith, R. S. (1984). "Motor Vehicle Taxation in Jamaica." Syracuse University, Metropolitan Studies Program Staff Paper no. 10. Syracuse.

Snodgrass, D. R. (1974). "The Fiscal System As an Income Redistributor in West Malaysia." *Public Finance* 29: 56–75.

Snyder, D. W. (1974). "Econometric Studies of Household Savings Behaviour in Developing Countries: A Survey." *Journal of Development Studies* 10: 139–53.

Spicer, M., and L. Becker (1980). "Fiscal Inequity and Tax Evasion." *National Tax Journal* 33: 171–76.

Stern, N. (1984). "Optimum Taxation and Tax Policy." *International Monetary Fund Staff Papers* 31: 339–78.

Stiglitz, J. (1974) "Alternative Theories of the Determination of Wages and Employment in LDCs: The Labor Turnover Model." *Quarterly Journal of Economics* 88:

Stolper, W. F. (1966). *Planning without Facts: Lessons in Resource Allocation from Nigeria's Development.* Cambridge: Harvard University Press.

Strasma, J. (1965). "Market-Enforced Self-Assessment for Real Estate Taxes." *Bulletin for International Fiscal Documentation* 19: 353–65, 397–414.

Strasma, J., et al. (1987). *Impact of Agricultural Land Revenue Systems on Agricultural Land Usage.* Burlington, Vt.: Associates in Rural Development. (Excerpted in chapter 35.)

Summers, L. H. (1981). "Capital Taxation and Accumulation in a Life Cycle Growth Model." *American Economic Review* 71: 533–44.

Surr, J. V. (1966). "Intertax: Intergovernmental Cooperation in Taxation." *Harvard International Law Club Journal* 7: 179–237.

Surrey, S. S. (1958). "Tax Administration in Underdeveloped Countries." *University of Miami Law Review* 12: 158–88. (Excerpted in Bird and Oldman, 1964, pp. 503–33; 1967, pp. 497–527; 1975, pp. 479–99.)

Surrey, S. S. (1973). *Pathways to Tax Reform.* Cambridge: Harvard University Press.

Surrey, S. S. (1978). "United Nations Group of Experts and the Guidelines for Tax Treaties between Developed and Developing Countries." *Harvard International Law Journal* 19: 1–65.

Surrey, S. S., and P. R. McDaniel (1985). *Tax Expenditures.* Cambridge: Harvard University Press.

Syracuse University, Local Revenue Administration Project (1983). "Local Revenue and Service Provision in Upper Volta, Phase I: Final Report." Monograph no. 13, Local Revenue Administration Project, Metropolitan Studies Program. Syracuse.

Tabellini, G. (1985). "International Tax Comparisons Reconsidered." International Monetary Fund, Fiscal Affairs Department, Departmental Memorandum no. DM/85/34. Washington, D.C.

Tahari, A. (1979). "The Impact of Taxation on Saving and Consumption in Developing Countries: A Paradox?" International Monetary Fund, Fiscal Affairs Department, Departmental Memorandum no. DM/79/21. Washington, D.C.

Tait, A. A. (1967). *The Taxation of Personal Wealth.* Urbana: University of Illinois Press.

Tait, A. A. (1988). *Value-Added Tax: International Practice and Problems.* Washington, D.C.: International Monetary Fund.

Tait, A. A., W. L. M. Grätz, and B. J. Eichengreen (1979). "International Comparisons of Taxation for Selected Developing Countries, 1972–76." *International Monetary Fund Staff Papers* 26: 123–56.

Tanabe, N. (1967). "The Taxation of Net Wealth." *International Monetary Fund Staff Papers* 16: 124–66. (Excerpted in Bird and Oldman, 1975, pp. 256–70.)

Tanabe, N. (1973). "Blue Return System in Japan." In Kelley and Oldman (1973), pp. 221–29.

Tanzi, V. (1966). "Personal Income Taxation in Latin America: Obstacles and Possibilities." *National Tax Journal* 19: 156–62. (Excerpted in Bird and Oldman, 1975, pp. 233–39.)

Tanzi, V. (1969). "Tax Incentives and Economic Development: The Ecuadorian Experience." *Finanzarchiv* 28: 226–35.

Tanzi, V. (1973). "The Theory of Tax Structure Change during Economic Development: A Critical Survey." *Rivista di Diritto Finanziario e Scienza delle Finanze* 32: 199–208.

Tanzi, V. (1974). "Redistributing Income through the Budget in Latin America." *Banca Nazionale del Lavoro Quarterly Review* 27: 65–87.

Tanzi, V. (1976). "Export Taxation in Developing Countries: Taxation of Coffee in Haiti." *Social and Economic Studies* 25: 66–76.

Tanzi, V. (1977). "Inflation, Lags in Collection, and the Real Value of Tax Revenue." *International Monetary Fund Staff Papers* 24: 154–67.

Tanzi, V. (1978). "Import Taxes and Economic Development." *Economia Internazionale* 31: 252–69.

Tanzi, V. (1980). "Potential Income As a Tax Base in Theory and Practice." International Monetary Fund, Fiscal Affairs Department, Departmental Memorandum no. DM/80/84. Washington, D.C.

Tanzi, V. (1980a). *Inflation and the Personal Income Tax: An International Perspective.* Cambridge, Cambridge University Press.

Tanzi, V., ed. (1982). *The Underground Economy in the United States and Abroad.* Lexington, Mass.: Lexington Books.

Tanzi, V. (1987). "Quantitative Characteristics of the Tax Systems of Developing Countries." In Newbery and Stern (1987), pp. 205–41. (Excerpted in chapter 1.)

Tanzi, V., and M. Casanegra de Jantscher, (1987). "Presumptive Income Taxation: Administrative, Efficiency, and Equity Aspects." International Monetary Fund, Fiscal Affairs Department, Departmental Memorandum no. DM/87/54. Washington, D.C.

Taylor, M. C. (1957). *Industrial Tax-Exemption in Puerto Rico.* Madison: University of Wisconsin Press.

Taylor, M. C. (1960). "What Happens When Exemptions End: Retrospect and Prospect in Puerto Rico." In *Taxation and Operations Abroad,* Tax Institute, 170–86. Princeton, N.J. (Excerpted in Bird and Oldman, 1964, pp. 245–56.)

Taylor, M. C. (1967). "The Relationship between Income Tax Administration and Income Tax Policy in Nigeria." *Nigerian Journal of Economic and Social Studies* 9: 203–15. (Excerpted in Bird and Oldman, 1975, pp. 528–40.)

Taylor, M. C., et al. (1965). *Fiscal Survey of Colombia.* Baltimore: Johns Hopkins Press for the Organization of American States.

Thimmaiah, G. (1977). "India: Taxation and Government Consumption." *Bulletin for International Fiscal Documentation* 31: 551–57.

Thirlwall, A. P. (1974). *Inflation, Saving, and Growth in Developing Economies.* London: Macmillan.

Thirsk, W. (1984). "Jamaican Tax Incentives." Syracuse University. Metropolitan Studies Program Staff Paper no. 9. Syracuse. (Excerpted in chapter 15.)

Tinbergen, J. (1952). *On the Theory of Economic Policy.* Amsterdam: North-Holland.

Todaro, M. P. (1969). "A Model of Labor Migration and Urban Unemployment in Less Developed Countries." *American Economic Review* 59: 138–48.

Toye, J. F. J., ed. (1978). *Taxation and Economic Development.* London: Frank Cass.

United Nations (1954). *Taxes and Fiscal Policy in Under-Developed Countries.* New York: UN.

United Nations (1979). *Manual for the Negotiation of Bilateral Tax Treaties between Developed and Developing Countries.* New York: UN.

United Nations (1980). *United Nations Model Double Taxation Convention between Developed and Developing Countries.* New York: UN.

U.S. Treasury Department (1977). *Blueprints for Basic Tax Reform*. Washington, D.C.: U.S. Government Printing Office. (Also available as D. F. Bradford and U.S. Treasury Department Staff (1984), *Blueprints for Basic Tax Reform*. Arlington, Va.: Tax Analysts.)

U.S. Treasury Department (1984). *Tax Reform for Fairness, Simplicity and Economic Growth*. Washington, D.C.: U.S. Government Printing Office.

Usher, D. (1977). "The Economics of Tax Incentives to Encourage Investment in Less Developed Countries." *Journal of Development Economics* 4: 119–48. (Excerpted in Chapter 13.)

Vasquez, J., and G. Palomeque (1976). "Reforma tributaria: Brechas entre propositos, normas y realidades." Paper presented to Annual Seminar on Colombian Economy, Bogotá.

Virmani, A. (1987). "Tax Evasion, Corruption, and Administration: Monitoring the People's Agents under Symmetric Dishonesty." World Bank, Development Research Department Discussion Paper no. DRD 271. Washington, D.C.

Wald, H. P. (1959). *Taxation of Agricultural Land in Underdeveloped Economies*. Cambridge: Harvard University Press.

Wall, P. (1981). "Fiscal Policies for the Development of Equity Markets. A Survey of Country Experiences." Washington, D.C.: International Finance Corporation, Capital Market Department.

Walters, A. A. (1968). *The Economics of Road User Charges*. Baltimore: Johns Hopkins Press for the World Bank.

Wanniski, J. (1987). *The Way the World Works: How Economies Fail—and Succeed*. New York: Basic Books.

Wasylenko, M. (1986). "The Distribution of Tax Burden in Jamaica: Pre-1985 Reform." Staff Paper no. 30, Jamaica Tax Structure Examination Project, Metropolitan Studies Program, Syracuse University. Syracuse.

Wasylenko, M. (1987). "Tax Burden in Jamaica Before and After Tax Reform." Staff Paper no. 37, Jamaica Tax Structure Examination Project, Metropolitan Studies Program, Syracuse University. Syracuse.

Watson, P. L., and E. P. Holland (1978). "Relieving Traffic Congestion: The Singapore Area License Scheme." World Bank Staff Working Paper no. 281. Washington, D.C.

Weisskopf, T. E. (1972). "The Impact of Foreign Capital Inflow on Domestic Savings in Underdeveloped Countries." *Journal of International Economics* 2: 25–38.

Welch, R. B. (1954). "Measuring the Optimum Size of a Field Audit Staff." *National Tax Journal* 7: 210–21.

Wertz, K. L. (1979). "Allocation by and Output of a Tax-Administering Agency." *National Tax Journal* 32: 143–56.

Whalley, J., and F. St.Hilaire (1982). "Recent Studies of Efficiency and Distributional Impacts of Taxes: Implications for Canada." In *Tax Policy Options in the 1980s*, ed. W. R. Thirsk and J. Whalley, 28–72. Toronto: Canadian Tax Foundation.

Wilkenfeld, H. C. (1973). *Taxes and People in Israel*. Cambridge: Harvard University Press.

Williams, R. L. (1977). "Tax Incentives and Investment Behaviour in Developing Countries." *Public Finance* 32: 97–109.

Williamson, J. G. (1968). "Personal Saving in Developing Nations: An Intertemporal Cross-Section from Asia." *Economic Record* 44: 194–210.

Witte, A. D., and D. F. Woodbury (1983). "What We Know about the Factors Affecting Compliance with the Tax Laws." In *Income Tax Compliance*, ed. P. Sawicki, 133–48. Reston, Va.: American Bar Association Section of Taxation.

Wolf, C., Jr. (1988). *Markets or Governments? Choosing between Imperfect Alternatives.* Cambridge: MIT Press.

World Bank (annual). *World Development Report.* Washington, D.C.: World Bank.

World Bank (1983). *China: Socialist Economic Development.* 3 vols. Washington, D.C.: World Bank.

World Bank and International Monetary Fund (1987). *Protecting the Poor during Periods of Adjustment.* Washington, D.C.: World Bank.

Wozny, J. (1983). "Personal Taxes in African States." Syracuse University, Metropolitan Studies Program Occasional Paper no. 81, International Series. Syracuse.

Yitzhaki, S. (1986). "On the Excess Burden of Tax Evasion." World Bank, Development Research Department Discussion Paper no. DRD 211. Washington, D.C.

Zodrow, G. R., and C. E. McLure, Jr. (1988). "Implementing Direct Consumption Taxes in Developing Countries." World Bank, Country Economics Department Working Paper no. 131. Washington, D.C. (Excerpted in chapter 18.)

Zweifel, P., and W. Pommerehne (1985). "On Preaching Water and Drinking Wine: An Analysis of Voting on Tax Amnesty and (Under)reporting of Income." University of Zurich, Zurich, Switzerland.

Index

The Johns Hopkins Studies in Development

Set in Times Roman type by The Composing Room of Michigan, Inc.
Printed by the Maple Press Company on 50-lb. Glatfelter Eggshell Cream